AMERICAN CATHOLIC

AMERICAN CATHOLIC

The Saints and Sinners Who Built
America's Most Powerful Church

Charles R. Morris

TIMES BOOKS

RANDOM HOUSE

Grateful acknowledgment is made to the following for permission to reprint
previously published and other material:
Costello Publishing Company, Inc.: Excerpts from *Vatican Council II: The Conciliar and Post
Conciliar Documents, New Revised Edition,* edited by Austin Flannery, O.P. Copyright © 1996
by Costello Publishing Company, Northport, NY. All rights reserved. No part of these excerpts
may be reproduced, stored in a retrieval system, or transmitted in any form or by any means,
electronic, mechanical, photocopying, recording or otherwise, without express permission of
Costello Publishing Co. Reprinted by permission of the publisher.
Mario Cuomo: Excerpt from a speech delivered September 13, 1984. Copyright © 1984
by Mario Cuomo. Reprinted by permission of the author.
United States Catholic Conference: Excerpt from "Responsum" from "Origins,"
November 30, 1995, pp. 403–409. Copyright © 1995 by United States Catholic Conference.
Reprinted by permission.
The Archives of the University of Notre Dame: Excerpt from a letter from John F. Cronin, SS,
to William Reuben, dated June 24, 1974, John F. Cronin, SS Papers (CCRO), Box 2/Folder 25,
University of Notre Dame Archives. Used by permission.
Naomi Wolf and The New Republic: Excerpt from "Our Bodies, Our Souls" by Naomi Wolf, *The
New Republic*, October 16, 1995. Copyright © 1995 by Naomi Wolf and The New Republic, Inc.
Reprinted by permission of the author and *The New Republic*.

Library of Congress Cataloging-in-Publication Data

Morris, Charles R.
American Catholic: the saints and sinners who built America's most powerful church /
Charles R. Morris. — 1st ed.
p.   cm.
Includes bibliographical references and index.
ISBN 0-8129-2049-x (alk. paper)
1. Catholic Church—United States—History—19th century.
2. Catholic Church—United States—History—20th century.   3. United
States—Church history—19th century.   4. United States—Church
history—20th century.   I. Title.
BX1406.2.M67   1997
282'.73—dc21   96-39191

Random House website address: http://www.randomhouse.com/
Printed in the United States of America on acid-free paper
9 8 7 6 5 4 3 2
First Edition
Book Design by Robert C. Olsson

To Simon Michael Bessie

It is a real pleasure to dedicate this book to Mike Bessie. It has consumed more years than I care to count, and throughout Mike has been an enthusiast, a sharp editorial reader, and a wise guide. I'm honored to count him as a friend.

A book of this scale requires imposing on a large number of people, friends and casual acquaintances alike. The list of everyone I am obliged to would go on for pages. Many are acknowledged in the notes, but some deserve special mention. Joe Lynaugh took an active interest in the book from the outset, introduced me to a large number of priests, and was a vigilant reader. Bob Imbelli and Joe Komonchak guided me through some daunting theological thickets. A number of friends, most of them non-Catholic, read all or most of the book in draft and supplied hundreds of helpful comments—Charles Ferguson, Claude Singer, Ellen Donovan, Dick Leone, Richard Freeland, Belle Horwitz, and Joan Hochman all took special pains. I'd also like particularly to thank the archivists and librarians in the score or more places where I worked for their unfailing courtesy and helpfulness. Patrick McNamara, who is completing his doctoral studies at Catholic University, has been an unusually conscientious and capable research assistant, and should have a shining academic career. Authors write books, but the staff at publishing companies produce them, and Nancy Inglis and Naomi Osnos are among the very best. As always, it is a pleasure to work with my agent, Tim Seldes. Last but not least my wife, Beverly, an important reader and sounding board throughout, managed to endure the gestation of yet another book with unfailing affection and good humor.

Preface

American Catholicism is the country's largest religious denomination. But it has always been as much a culture as a religion, one defined by its prickly apartness from the broader, secular American culture—*in* America, usually enthusiastically *for* America, but never quite *of* America. In its glory days, especially in the 1940s and 1950s, the Catholic Church constructed a virtual state-within-a-state so Catholics could live almost their entire lives within a thick cocoon of Catholic institutions.

The story of American Catholicism is therefore the story of the rise and triumph of a culture, and of the religious crisis that has ensued in the wake of that culture's breakdown. Most of the Church's much publicized recent problems—the financial, sexual, and other scandals that are blazoned across the front pages—can be understood as the floundering of an institution suddenly forced to make its way solely as a religion, shorn of the cultural supports that had been the source of its strength.

The fluidity, the individualism, the frankly experimental style that define the American character are in direct opposition to many of the central concepts of Catholicism—the notion of dogma, the principles of authority and hierarchy, the medievalisms. The core tension in the American Church has always been its stiff-necked resistance to the great American assimilationist engine, and the shifting terms of its accommodation with the rest of the country. Yet by the mid–twentieth century, the Church had managed to become a dominant cultural force and, with all its current problems, is arguably still the most successful national Catholic church in the world. Since the story has so many twists and turns, a very brief road map may be in order.

The roots of the modern American Catholic Church are found not in Rome, or in the early Spanish missions, but in nineteenth-century Ireland.

What most people understand today as "Irish Catholicism" was a religious reaction to the holocaust of the Great Potato Famine. The Famine, which actually lasted, with varying degrees of severity, from the mid-1830s to at least 1880, reduced the island's population by half and destroyed the Irish Catholic peasantry. A demoralized nation seized upon a strict, reformed version of Catholicism as a way to rebuild its national identity and underscore its hatred for the Protestant English. The hatred and despair was converted into a "moral mission of the Irish race"—quite explicitly adopted by the Irish Church—to save America and the rest of the English-speaking nations from heresy.

Until famine triggered a massive wave of Catholic Irish immigration to America, the American Church was a small, polyglot affair, quietly adapting to a Protestant country. Just like Protestants, Catholic lay people ran their parishes and usually hired and fired their pastors. Especially in Baltimore and Philadelphia, but even in Yankee Boston, Catholicism was gaining intellectual and social cachet, and a number of prominent ministers converted. In its 1832 session, the U.S. Congress chose a Catholic priest as its chaplain.

The Irish diaspora brought a militant and bureaucratic style of Catholicism and touched off nativist riots in most major cities. A new breed of Irish bishop—the archetype is John Hughes of New York—imposed order and discipline on fractious urban dioceses and started building the vast network of Catholic institutions that reinforced religious/ethnic identity and protected lay people from the virus of freethinking. Within a few decades, Irish bosses had taken over almost all big-city political machines using the same techniques employed by their bishops.

The Irish hegemony in the American Church was sharply challenged after the Civil War by successive waves of German, Italian, and Eastern European immigrants. The ethnic struggles and the steady progress of second-generation Irish reopened the question of how assimilated, how American, the Church could become. The "Americanist" struggles, as they came to be called, were fought out through the 1880s and the 1890s, and swept up a host of other issues, like the role of Catholic-dominated unions and the entanglements of powerful bishops in national Republican and Democratic politics. The battles were personal, mean-spirited, even sordid. Prelates told lies, money changed hands, accusations of sexual and financial corruption were tossed around freely. But when the smoke cleared, the Church had arrived at the grand American Catholic compromise that was to prevail for most of the next century.

Ethnic assimilation would be on Irish terms, and the Church was to retain a distinctively Irish rigorist style long after Irish Americans had become a minority of American Catholics. Most of the clergy and the vast majority of the hierarchy were of Irish descent well into mid–twentieth century, far out of proportion to their membership in the Church.

The old conundrum of how to adapt to American-style separation of Church and State was finessed by building a Catholic ministate. Particularly after Al Smith's presidential defeat in 1928, Catholics executed a remarkable emotional withdrawal from the rest of the country. "Parallel" Catholic organizations of every kind flourished—Catholic businessmen's clubs, medical societies, bar associations, teachers' guilds, youth organizations, historical, sociological, and economic associations, Catholic book clubs and literary guilds, and a flourishing national Catholic press. Separatism was balanced by Catholic patriotism. By the end of World War I, the loyalty of American Catholics was as unquestioned as it was unquestioning. During the Cold War, as Daniel Patrick Moynihan put it, it was Fordham men who checked the anticommunist and patriotic credentials of Harvard men.

Paradoxically, the more the Church turned in upon itself, the more powerful it became. Its public image in the 1940s and 1950s was nothing short of spectacular: if movies are to be believed, all battlefield chaplains were Catholic priests. In the booming industrial Northeast and Midwest, Catholic chaplains were fixtures at labor union meetings, and, in many cities, the majority of union officers and leaders, and sometimes even the majority of business labor negotiators, regardless of their religion, were graduates of Catholic labor schools. Bishop Fulton Sheen became the most successful public lecturer in the history of television. "Our Lady of Fatima" was a Hit Parade record. A team of alien anthropologists would have reported that 1950s America was a Catholic country.

The sudden downturn in the fortunes of the American Church after John Kennedy's election is often blamed on the Vatican Council that opened in 1962. But, by then, the breakup of the old Catholic culture was already well under way. Suburbanization was dispersing the urban Catholic village, and the social and educational advancement of Catholics was as fast as that of any other ethnic/religious group except Jews. Kennedy's victory itself signaled the end of the old system. The first Catholic president was a graduate of Choate and Harvard, an utterly secular man, a completely assimilated product of American, not Catholic, culture.

The turmoil that has gripped the Church since the mid-1960s is essentially a replay of the old Americanist struggles. The bitter disputes over papal authority, women priests, marriage rules and sexual ethics are implicitly about the limits on adapting to American culture. Can the Church assimilate and survive? Or must it assimilate *to* survive? Or will the "Americanization" of Catholicism inevitably lead to the same institutional collapse that has been the fate of mainstream Protestantism? (There are now fewer Episcopalians in America than there are Catholics in Los Angeles.) As of this writing, there is no consensus on any of these issues, and the future of the American Church, is very much in doubt.

A note on style, sources, and approach: A few decades ago, it would not have been possible to write the first section of this book, which takes the story from the Irish immigrations to the period just after World War I. A flowering of Catholic historical scholarship of a very high standard—Gerald Fogarty, James Hennesey, Robert Emmett Curran, Marvin O'Connell, and Jay Dolan are just a few of the leading figures—has been matched by a great improvement in the accessibility of Catholic archives, although some important collections, like those of New York, are still only partially open. I rely mostly on the vast amount of recently produced secondary literature, supplemented by a fair amount of archival research of my own. In addition to American sources, the Irish collections at Maynooth and especially at All Hallows, both of which became veritable American priest factories in the nineteenth century, demonstrated the close relation between the American and Irish churches.

The second part of the book, which takes the story down to John Kennedy's election, relies much more on oral history. I was delighted to find a number of people, lay and clerical alike, who were involved in some of the great events of the Church as far back as the 1930s and, in one case, to the 1920s. The archivists at Notre Dame, Catholic University, and the Philadelphia Archdiocese were also particularly helpful. For the most part, because of the great extent of the material covered, I use the more recent published literature; but in particular instances, like the chapter on Cardinal Dougherty's Philadelphia, which I take as an exemplar of the triumphal-era Catholic ministate, much of the material is based on original research.

In the last part of the book, I depart from chronological narrative in favor of a thematic exploration of the main issues facing the Church. I begin with a journalistic *tour d'horizon*. (In general, I found grassroots, parish-level Catholicism to be much healthier than I expected. The real problems are in the Church's upper reaches.) Then I move on to the theological, sexual, doctrinal, authority, and gender issues that the Church keeps grinding its teeth over. In this section, I also adopt a first-person authorial voice, not because I'm telling a personal story—I'm not—but to emphasize the journalistic character of this part of the enterprise: in effect, these are the people I talked to, this is what I heard them say, and this is what I make of it.

I don't pretend to be without biases. I am a "cradle Catholic" who feels fondly toward the Church, and whose intellectual apparatus was formed, to an extent that occasionally still surprises me, within 1950s tri-umphal-era Catholicism. I do my best, however, not to adopt a partisan "liberal Catholic" or "conservative Catholic" stance. Instead, I try to seek out the best representatives of the various positions within the Church and to report them as fairly as I can. Readers will judge whether I have been successful.

Contents

PART I

RISE

CHAPTER 1

"We Laugh to Scorn"

Gothic cathedrals are leaping prayers. The pointed arches of the triple-portaled entrances spring up into the sky. The colors of the great central window flicker with mystery, and far above, soaring steeples and spires cry hope and fear to a God more immense than the universe.

But there were no soaring steeples on the new St. Patrick's Cathedral, on the crisp and sunny Sunday morning of its dedication, in New York City, May 25, 1879. Instead, it hulked blockishly, squaring its shoulders over the tens of thousands of faithful assembling to witness the dedication ceremony. After twenty-one years of construction, and frantic round after frantic round of fund-raising, there was no money left for steeples, and the skyward sweep of the front portals was stopped flat by a brutal, straight-cut roofline. To the mind's eye of New York's Catholics, however, to the Irish hod carriers and ditch diggers, the seamstresses and chambermaids crowded onto the horse-drawn streetcars from the tenement neighborhoods in lower Manhattan; or to the bankers and lawyers, city and port officials, judges and denizens of Tammany's burgeoning Democracy rolling up Fifth Avenue in their carriages, the cathedral still soared. Indeed, contemporary pictures of the cathedral in its actual, unfinished, state are rare. Almost all the renderings, even those recounting the events of the day, show it completed, as if the spires had been willed into existence, the inadequacies of purse and physical power remedied by dreams of the spirit.

The cathedral was the dream, the lifework's culmination, of Archbishop John Hughes, already dead fifteen years by the time of the dedication. Hughes was a farmer's son, from County Tyrone in Ireland, with the square hands and thick shoulders of a former quarry laborer and field-worker. When he applied to the seminary, the rector, John Dubois, denied

Credit: Library of Congress
The anti-Catholic Harper's Weekly *was one of the few contemporary journals that showed the newly dedicated St. Patrick's Cathedral in its actual steeple-less state. Because of continuing financial difficulties, the Cathedral was not completely finished and consecrated until 1908, a full half-century after its cornerstone was laid.*

him admission for his lack of education, but Hughes stayed on the grounds and worked as a gardener until a place was found for him. Twenty years later, in 1839, he was sent by Rome to take over a chaotic New York diocese from the failing fingers of Bishop Dubois. Hughes was a prototype for a new breed of American bishop—an Irishman from the working classes, a visionary, a patriot, and a politician. Warm-tempered, but a brilliant tactician, he never lost his common touch despite a fierce self-education, and he had the demagogue's flair with a phrase and a crowd. Wonderfully open and frank, he was blunt to a fault, and his foibles, like the shameless patronizing of his relatives and the ill-fitting toupee he wore in his late years, only underscored his humanity. One priest called him "a tyrant, but with feeling." Hughes's militant, unapologetic brand of Catholicism was something new in America. He was the embodied nightmare of nativists and Know-Nothings and a hero to the Catholic masses fleeing famine in Ireland. Other prelates preached a tremulous patience when anti-Catholic arson and riots swept the country in midcentury, but Hughes armed his congregations and threatened to turn New York "into a second Moscow" if Catholics were targeted. Anti-Catholic mobs prowled and glowered, but there were no attacks.

Hughes laid the cornerstone of St. Patrick's in the summer of 1858, in an open field on upper Fifth Avenue, between 50th and 51st Streets, standing between the flags of the United States and of Ireland. An exuberant crowd of more than a hundred thousand people, the largest New York had ever seen, and almost all Irish, turned out to cheer the ceremony. Wise businessmen, their workforce gone, bowed to the carnival atmosphere and simply closed up shop. Even in the open, Hughes's high, clear voice could reach out over the huge crowd: "The spiritual descendants of St. Patrick have been outcasts from their native land and have been scattered over the earth . . . and though there may be no mark to designate the graves in which they slumber, still, the churches which they have erected . . . are the most fitting headstones to commemorate . . . the honorable history of the Irish people," a people accustomed to receiving "the largest share of justice and the smallest share of mercy" from their English overlords. Now they could "laugh to scorn," Hughes proclaimed, mocking the tsk-tsking of New York's Protestant establishment who thought cathedral building a grotesque waste of money at a time when Ireland's refugees were severely straining charitable resources and public order. Telling " 'the Irish' that they were an ill-used race," *The New York Times* sniffed the next day, was "a rude violation of the proprieties of the occasion," but just one more example "of that bad taste which, of late years, has more or less characterized everything His Grace has said or written outside the immediate sphere of his archiepiscopal duties."

Credit: Library of Congress
New York's Archbishop John Hughes, who headed the archdiocese from 1839 to
1864, was the prototype for a new breed of militant Irish working-class bishops,
who turned the American Church away from its assimilationist path and forged
a culturally and ethnically cohesive Catholic state-within-a-state.

In 1858, even many of Hughes's sympathizers thought the wastes of upper Fifth Avenue oddly remote from the main centers of the city to be the location of so important a church; and as the construction stumbled and stuttered, or simply crawled almost imperceptibly forward—"in a lazy, dreamy, sort of way," in one wondering contemporary account—the project became known as "Hughes's Folly" in the popular press. But in the decade after the Civil War, Fifth Avenue became America's grandest boulevard. The surge of industry created an enormous concentration of wealth that sucked in the world's art treasures, its silks and jewels, its Persian carpets and Boucher fans. In a frenzy of building and rebuilding, New York's "Shoddy Aristocracy" marched their palaces north toward 59th and Central Park, plundering medieval castles for staircases and tapestries, and stuffing their libraries with first editions and old master paintings.

A. T. Stewart, whose great department store draped Fifth Avenue's ladies in the most exotic satins and laces, had the "most elegant" mansion in America on 34th, until he trumped it with a massive palace of white Carrara marble just across the street. Boss Tweed, lately dead in prison, had built his own mansion at 43rd, diagonally across from the brick-walled reservoir, now the site of the New York Public Library. The top of the reservoir offered lovely strolling vistas down the length of the avenue and across the park; it was designed by James Renwick, the architect of the cathedral. Just beyond St. Patrick's, between 51st and 52d Streets, the children and grandchildren of Commodore Cornelius Vanderbilt, the old railroad buccaneer, built three mansions, two of them in the Greek Renaissance style and one aping a French château. The home of Madame Restell, née Caroline Trow, New York's leading abortionist, was on the northeast corner of 52nd and Fifth, across from the Catholic orphans' asylum; it was a gracious building featuring tesselated marble halls and frescoed ceilings. Restell had settled in matronly retirement with her grandchildren, but had been run to ground the year before the dedication by that guardian of public morals, Anthony Comstock, and cut her own throat in her bathtub rather than face the rigors of an aroused New York Protestant establishment.

Cornelius Vanderbilt Jr. was a guest at the dedication of St. Patrick's; so was A. T. Stewart's widow, although neither was Catholic. Lorenzo Delmonico, the Fifth Avenue restauranteur, was a Catholic, a patron of the cathedral from the start, and donor of a great figured window on the wall by the north entrance. The pageantry of the dedication had been sufficiently heralded in the press that the city's wealthy classes crowded the windows of the nearby avenue's mansions with their opera glasses. But the crowds that were forming behind the double line of policemen circling the cathedral almost all came from much farther downtown, mostly from the dozen or so wards squeezed between Canal Street and City Hall, just above the financial district. More than half of New York City's million-plus souls lived in those wards, the most densely populated area in the United States; more than half of them were "foreigners"; most of the foreigners were Catholic; and the greater part of the Catholics, with the most intensely felt ties to the Church, were Irish.

The fashionable "Apartment Houses" that had begun to pop up on Fifth Avenue were the wonder of New York travel guides, but they had been predated by the cruel tenements downtown. The Famine Irish, the western

Gaelic-speaking peasants who had lived by spading out their annual patch of potatoes, coped poorly with the harsh realities of a New World. Traditional strictures collapsed, and whole families sank into alcohol-dimmed degradation, a futility of violence and vice. Packs of feral children, numbering in the tens of thousands, roamed the narrow streets, stealing, begging, or running down and killing wild dogs for the bounty of a dime. Teenage girls became disease-pocked prostitutes plying the alleys and grogshops. Pigs still foraged in dark corners. In the worst of the tenements, named after their proprietors—Butcher Burke's or Sweeney's Shambles—as many as nine hundred people were crammed into six floors, five and six squeezed into ten-by-ten-foot rooms, many of them without windows, reeking of coal fumes. Running water was a luxury. A reporter visiting one of Sweeney's houses found a communal latrine in the cellar, water seeping from the nearby river, fecal matter ankle-deep on the floor. Yellow paint on floorboards raised above the muck lined out six-by-three-foot sleeping spaces that sold for 15 cents a night. Cholera, typhoid, and tuberculosis raged through the unlit halls. Thousands of carcasses—dogs, cats, horses—rotted in the streets, sidewalks were submerged in refuse and night soil, chamber pots were spilled out from tenement windows. A few days before the cathedral's dedication, the Ladies' Fruit and Flower Mission toured the noisome tenements near Five Points, passing out flowers to pipe-smoking crones, who apparently responded with gratitude: "Ah, we're plazed at the sight of a flower or a bit of laylock. It's seldom the likes of us sees flowers, Miss."

Many families managed to hold out against the degradations of the tenements, and by no means were all the tenement dwellers poor. A bricklayer earned five dollars for a ten-hour day and could afford better than the tenements. The vast public construction programs—bridges, subways, railroads—that so indelibly stamped the face of the city were just getting under way. While economic cycles were cruel and employment precarious, bridge workers, hod carriers, and teamsters could earn reasonable wages. So many were still trapped in the tenements because the island fastness of lower Manhattan had no space for affordable housing within reach of work, a problem that was solved only as bridges and rapid transit pushed out the boundaries of the city over the next two decades. Unable to spend money on housing, the decent working Irish gave generously to the Church, in sums that Protestants marveled at. If the hearts of the rough-handed men and women thronging around St. Patrick's swelled with pride, it was because they knew that the mighty building was genuinely the product of their own labors.

By nine o'clock on the morning of dedication, the police cordons had cleared the crowds from 50th and 51st Streets alongside the cathedral, pushing back the Irish flower ladies and Chinese cigar sellers, so the carriages of the city's Catholic elite could roll up to the north and south great oak transept doors. Gothic cathedrals are laid out in the form of a Latin cross, with a stubby cross-arm, or transept, just before the choir, or sanctuary. Entering by those doors, the favored few would pass along the altar rail, gaping at the splendid altar screen carved from the finest French oak and the altar canopy sculpted of Caen stone. The families disgorged by the carriages were expensively, and fashionably, dressed—the men in high silk hats and Prince Albert morning coats buttoned up to the chin, with a peek of stiff collar above and waistcoat beneath. Their wives were buried beneath layers of lace-trimmed jackets and vests, skirts blooming with live flowers, hats pouring out ostrich feathers; their young sons were in pleated wool pants to the knee, their little girls barely visible in clouds of organdy and chiffon. These men had homes in the best sections of the city—if not quite on Fifth, then on Madison, or around Washington Square; and they had summer houses on Westchester's sound, or in Newport or Nantucket.

Ushers in tails and white gloves bowed them in the doors, checked their tickets, and escorted them to a second phalanx of ushers who showed them to their seats. Only purple ticket holders—at ten dollars a ticket, two days' wages for a skilled working man—could occupy the pews this morning. Seven thousand others had bought blue tickets, at two dollars apiece, entitling them to standing room, but they were required to remain outside until it was time for Mass to free the aisles for the opening processional. *The New York Times* was scathing: "To native Americans, at least those not Roman Catholics—and very few native Americans are such—the dedication of St. Patrick's Cathedral . . . with front seats advertised at a premium . . . must have seemed like . . . some grand theologic show, and the regular sale of tickets completed the resemblance."

There is another St. Patrick's in New York, the original cathedral, a small jewel box of a church opened in 1815, the predecessor of the great edifice on Fifth Avenue. Old St. Patrick's is between Mulberry and Mott Streets, in the area now called Little Italy, just above Chinatown. It was once the most important Irish parish in the city, bequeathing no fewer than six bishops to the American Church by the turn of the century. Beneath the church, down stone stairs hollowed out with age, is a whitewashed crypt, and there, carved on the front of the tombs lining its walls are the histories of the families who were promenading into the new cathedral on that bright May morning. Beginning about the 1840s, the early French or Spanish inscriptions give way to names that, with the occasional exception like the Delmonicos, are almost exclusively Irish. For the most part, these are the men that John Hughes allied with when he arrived in New York to impose his formidable will on the fractious collection of independent, lay-controlled, churches that passed for a diocese, to expel uncontrollable foreign religious, to centralize all the diocese's considerable patronage in his own hands, and to commence the astonishing feats of public construction that culminated in the cathedral.

The men who dominated New York's Catholic elite in 1879, the friends and advisers whom Hughes had bequeathed to his successor John McCloskey, now a cardinal, were at the apex of their careers and influence. Despite the nativist sneers that still sometimes crept into the pages of the *Times,* and the comic brogues that all the city's dailies adopted when quoting working-class Irish, the city's leading Irish Catholics moved with ease and assurance in society's best circles. They or their families, typically, had emigrated well before the Famine. As often as not, they were dispossessed Irish gentry and well educated; while they often arrived in America poor, they were rarely penniless. Although there were exceptions, they tended to be loyal Democrats, members of Tammany, and among the North's most persistent opponents of the Civil War. They hated the English, and were openhanded with their wealth in supporting Irish Home Rule; but along with their Church, they were suspicious of Fenian radicalism and the militant Irish secret societies. They were deeply conservative on social issues: they saw the Church as the chosen instrument for raising up America's degraded famine-dispersed Irish underclass, but through education and discipline, not charity.

The Catholic luminaries at the dedication included Chief Justice Charles P. Daly, Judge James T. Brady (once Madame Restell's defense counsel), the bankers William and John O'Brien, the dry goods merchant Thomas O'Donoghue, Emigration Commissioner James Lynch, and, closest of all to Hughes and most deeply involved in planning the cathedral, Eugene Kelly. Kelly's background was archetypical: he had emigrated at age twenty-two, from County Tyrone, Hughes's home, in 1830. His family had been Galway nobility who lost their lands during the Elizabethan expropriations. Kelly started as a clerk in an Irish-owned dry goods house, married the owners' sister, and opened dry goods stores in St. Louis, Kentucky, and gold-rush San Francisco. In 1841, when he was only thirty-three, he was one of a small group of Irish merchants and bankers whom Hughes called together to found the Emigrant Savings Society for the immigrant Irish, eventually to become one of the city's major savings banks. Kelly went on to found banking houses in San Francisco and New York, and in 1857, widowed, and in constant touch with Hughes on the cathedral, he married the Archbishop's niece. He was known for his prudence and taciturnity, and Hughes and McCloskey seemed to have consulted him on all matters financial. Seventy-one at the time of the dedication, he was on the board of the Equitable Life Assurance Society, Lloyds', and four banks, was a trustee of the Metropolitan Museum of Art and the Geographic Society, and a member of the city's Board of Education. Kelly's longtime friend and partner, Henry Hoguet, was lay chairman of the dedication ceremony. Born in Dublin, Hoguet was also a merchant and investment banker and served for many years as the president of the Emigrant.

Charles O'Conor was seventy-five and in failing health in 1879, but he made the trip for the dedication from his vacation home in Nantucket. O'Conor was despised by the *Times* for his prosecessionist and proslavery views, but even the *Times* freely acknowledged that he was probably America's greatest lawyer and "the unquestioned head of the New York bar." His first major case had been representing Hughes in his struggle against the New York legislature to wrest control of church property from an older generation of Catholic lay trustees. O'Conor had been U.S. Attorney, and was a close adviser of Samuel J. Tilden, the former governor of New York and 1876 presidential candidate,. He had run for president himself on a third-party ticket in 1872, and had masterminded the breaking of the Tweed Ring. When Tweed jumped bail, O'Conor directed a relentless international legal pursuit until finally Tweed, broken and bewildered, more than a hundred pounds lighter, his massive suits billowing from his sagging frame, was clapped into the prison cell where he died.

Shoulder to shoulder with O'Conor, Hoguet, and Eugene Kelly at the dedication ceremony was "Honest John" Kelly (no relation to Eugene). A trustee and patron of the cathedral, Kelly had been handpicked by O'Conor and Tilden to be the first Irish boss of Tammany in the wake of the Tweed scandals. Powerfully built, with a square, flat, inscrutable face, never wasting a word when silence would serve, Kelly was America's first true machine politician; he exercised an iron but almost invisible control over the once riotous New York Democracy and created the genus of tight-lipped, string-pulling Tammany boss that dominated New York politics for the next seventy-five years. Kelly's epitaph, when he finally ceded the scepter to his protégé, Richard Croker, in 1886, was that he "found Tammany a horde; he left it a political army."

Kelly's prominence at the dedication underscored the cheek-by-jowl relation between New York's Catholic Church and Tammany Democracy*—one that was to be replicated in other big cities with Irish-dominated political machines. After the frank anti-Catholicism of earlier city administrations, a friendly local government, one willing to subsidize Catholic schools and to facilitate the Church's unflagging building drives, was a great relief. But there was much in Tammany that made, or should

---

* "God bless the two greatest organizations in the world," proclaimed the tippling Irishman of legend, "the Catholic Church and Tammany Hall!" "What's the second one?" asked his drinking companion.

have made, Catholic prelates acutely uncomfortable. John Kelly was a
deeply religious and fairly cultivated man who married McCloskey's
niece, but he was "honest" only by comparison with the Rabelaisian in-
satiety of a Tweed. A relatively brief stint as sheriff left him wealthy enough
to spend several years traveling though Europe and the Holy Land, shipping back old master paintings as gifts for the new cathedral. His travels let
him avoid being tarred by the gross excesses of Tweed's last years, making
him one of the few plausible insiders whom reform Democrats could tap to
resurrect the local party. But Kelly's Tammany still used thugs and cut-
purses to intimidate voters on Election Day, and while his personal wealth
was built from so-called honest graft, his underlings fed happily on the
sordid underbelly of the city's vice establishment—prostitution, white
slavery, opium dens, dance halls, and gin mills—or got paid for looking the
other way as the likes of tenement owner Butcher Burke preyed on the
honest poor.

    At bottom, the affinity between Tammany and the Church was mostly
one of outlook and style. In hardly more than a generation both had come
to be almost totally dominated by Irishmen, out of all proportion to their
prominence as voters or church members. Kelly's methods of bringing
Tammany to heel might have been learned at Hughes's feet—centralizing
finances; winning control over appointments and patronage; squeezing
out alien bodies, like the independent religious orders or the various dissident wings of Tammany; and constant, tireless attention to detail. The
Irish genius for bureaucratic politics was compounded of immense institutional loyalty, a flatly unsentimental, intensely fatalistic view of human
nature, and supreme disdain for theory—there were no "theories at Tammany Hall," Croker growled to a reporter, "I never went to bed on a theory
in my life." American Irish power was built from the bottom up, combining an instinct for the concrete, the practical, and the personal with an indefatigable appetite for administration and a compulsion for discipline
and order—"I will suffer no man in my diocese that I cannot control,"
Hughes bluntly put it.

At precisely ten o'clock, as the purple ticket-holders settled in their pews,
the great organ burst into a rousing voluntary, then intoned the booming
chords of the processional march. The organ, built in New York, was somewhat hyperbolically described as "the greatest in the Western Hemisphere";
if a man suspended his cane from a finger in the back of the church, the rum-
bling of the bass pipes would set it visibly vibrating. The great oak front
doors swung open, and the crowds outside caught the first glint of the gold
cross borne aloft by a surpliced altar boy enshrouded by clouds of incense

Credit: © Collection of The New-York Historical Society
Thomas Nast's portrayals of gorilla-like Irishmen and avaricious priests expressed nativist anxieties as Irish politicians, imitating Hughes, centralized and disciplined urban political machines. Here, the Irish immigrant and priest carve up the golden goose. The wall map portrays an alleged land-grab for St. Patrick's, a falsehood that has persisted even in contemporary histories of the city.

from the swinging thurible. The processants had vested in St. John the Evangelist Church, then located behind the cathedral on Madison Avenue. They entered the cathedral from the still-unfinished rear—the architect's plan hopefully called for a never-built rosette of five small chapels—emerged in two columns from either side of the altar, and proceeded down the center aisle to the great doors.

Behind the incense and cross bearers came a solemn line of altar boys in black cassocks and white surplices washed and bleached by their mothers to the brightness of snow, hair slicked down, eyes straight ahead. More than four hundred priests followed, also in black, but with surplices of lace, and scattered here and there, the brown robe of a Franciscan or the hooded figure of a Capuchin; and then a burst of color as some fifty monsignors, purple cassocks piped in scarlet, emerged in the column after the priests. The incense and cross bearers were already through the front doors before the first bishop's miter—the triangular hat of office—appeared around the altar. There were forty-three bishops and archbishops in the procession, the princes of the American Church, in full pontifical regalia, with gold crosiers, the shepherd's staff, in their right hands, attendant priests at their sides. Their miters glittered with precious stones and their vestments were uniformly reported by the press to be gold. The liturgical color of the day, in fact, was white, but the robes were so thickly embroidered with gold thread that they presented a solid field of gold to the spectator. In the column of bishops was a scattering of Germans—Heiss of Milwaukee and Dwenger of Fort Wayne, both struggling fruitlessly against the Irish dominance of the hierarchy. There were two Frenchmen, de Goesbriand of Vermont and Duhamel of Ottawa; and an Englishman, Archbishop James Wood of Philadelphia, a converted Episcopalian priest. Most of the rest were Irish— Conroy, Hannan, Healy,* Kain, Keane, Loughlin, Lynch, McCloskey (of Louisville), McMahon, McNeirney, McQuaid, Moore, Mullen, O'Hara, O'Reilly, Purcell, Quinlan, Rogers, two Ryans, Shanahan, Sweeny.

All the great figures in the controversies that would engulf the American Church for the rest of the century were there. Bishop John Ireland, the fighting chaplain of the Minnesota Fifth, and a hero of the Civil War battle at Corinth, marched proudly erect, his craggily handsome head thrown back. Presiding over a polyglot diocese scattered over Minnesota's windswept prairies, Ireland was the church's leading "Americanist," an ardent advocate of assimilation who challenged the wisdom of separatist institutions like the parochial school. Ahead of him in the procession was Michael Corrigan, bishop of Newark, soon to succeed John McCloskey in New York. Corrigan was stoopshouldered and bookish, with fleshy lips pursed in a permanent pout. He was Ireland's bitter enemy and a skillful intriguer, working behind the scenes for years until Ireland's "Americanism" was censured by the Vatican in a condemnation that, arguably, came close to branding Ireland himself a heretic.

* James A. Healy, the bishop of Portland, Maine, was that almost inconceivable of combinations—a nineteenth-century Catholic bishop who was part Irish and part black. He was born a slave from the union of an Irish slaveholder and a slave woman. His father sent him and his brothers north to be educated by Jesuits when they were boys. One brother became a Jesuit and eventually president of Georgetown University, and another was a Boston priest in line to be a bishop when he died in an epidemic. Healy was quite African in appearance, but ran one of Boston's most important Irish parishes as a young priest, and behaved like any other conservative Irish-American bishop.

Last before McCloskey was "Slippery Jim" Gibbons, the silver-haired and silver-tongued archbishop of Baltimore. In the Vatican's eyes America was still missionary country, a religious outpost on a par with Brazil or Africa, and Gibbons was the prelate who dealt directly with the missionary office, the de facto American primate. He was a consummate politician, in the mold of a skillful congressional majority leader, engaged in constant shuttle diplomacy to his skeptical Italian masters—blurring the disagreements between American liberals and conservatives; softening those Vatican demands most likely to outrage an American public hypersuspicious of foreign entanglements; and executing nimble tap dances whenever the American press inquired about the Vatican's open sympathies with Bourbon restorationists and other monarchist parties in Europe.

And finally there was McCloskey himself, sixty-nine now and frail, walking behind the huge bejeweled episcopal cross, carrying a splendid crosier, his heavy white and gold robes sparkling with rubies and sapphires, the cardinal's scarlet at his throat. With him was the entourage of priests who would assist in the dedicatory Mass, Monsignors Quinn and Preston, Fathers Donnelly, McGean, and Edward McGlynn. McGlynn was one of the great orators of his generation, able to quiet a crowd with a word or rouse them shouting to their feet. Soon, with the tacit support of liberals like Ireland, to the great alarm of Tammany Hall and Corrigan, and to the delight of secular headline writers, he would split the American church with a vision of popular social radicalism.

McCloskey's path into the clergy, like that of many young men of embarrassed means, but of the right class and spiritual disposition, had been smoothed by the wealthy Irish Catholic elite. His mother was widowed in America, and was living in genteel poverty when Cornelius Heeney appeared one day to take over the education of young John. Heeney, a bachelor who affected Quaker garb in his late years, was an original trustee of old St. Patrick's and a major force in the development of the New York church. He emigrated as a young man in 1784, became a fur trading partner of John Jacob Astor, and owned most of downtown Brooklyn when he died. Heeney steered John toward the seminary, financed his education, pulled strings to ensure that he was sent to study in Rome, paid for his transport and vacations, and oversaw his first diocesan assignments.

The Catholic prelates marching down center aisle of St. Patrick's were, in by far the greatest part, well-educated men—much more so than Hughes. They were sophisticated, well traveled, frequently multilingual, a substantial social cut above the generations of bishops who would follow them, who were much more likely to be the sons of working men. Isaac Hecker, who, along with Orestes Brownson, a fellow convert, was the leading mid-nineteenth-century American Catholic intellectual, had commented with

some surprise—perhaps betraying lingering anti-Irish bigotry—on Mc-
Closkey's breadth of reading and range of reference. John Ireland, despite
his hail-fellow heartiness, was a cosmopolitan Francophile who was lionized
by the French press when he propounded to enthusiastic audiences there, in
French, the moral and religious benefits of the American separation of
Church and State.

After the long train of processants emerged from the cathedral, and fanned
out around the cathedral steps, McCloskey intoned the psalm "Asperges
Me"—"Wash me, O Lord, with hyssop" (hyssop was a Middle Eastern
shrub used in ancient times to sprinkle sacred water)—and then the "Mi-
serere Me"—"Have mercy on me, O Lord." Both psalms were taken up an-
tiphonally by the full choir—sixty men and forty boys, with organ and
orchestra—and the priest-cantors accompanying McCloskey: Fathers Kean,
Dougherty, Rigney, Farrell, Reardon, Lammel, Barry, and O'Keeffe. Mc-
Closkey then led the procession on a stately circumnavigation of the Cathedral, sprinkling the great walls with holy water.

The architectural style of St. Patrick's is late medieval "decorative
Gothic," consciously modeled after the great Cathedral of Cologne. It is
clean and airy, marked by geometric stone traceries that convey an almost
Arabic feeling. The architect, James Renwick, an honored guest at the dedication, was a Protestant, and a friend of Henry Adams and John Hay. Besides
the Fifth Avenue reservoir, he was best known for his designs of Grace
Church in New York and of the Smithsonian Institution in Washington, and
was almost single-handedly responsible for the revival of Gothic architecture
in America. For the St. Patrick's assignment, however, Hughes, ever the
padrone, partnered Renwick with his brother-in-law, William Rodrigue.
Rodrigue came from a family of wealthy exiled Santo Domingan planters
who had befriended Hughes when he was a lonely young priest in Philadelphia. He was just beginning his career as an architect when Hughes was put
in charge of building the new Philadelphia cathedral. Naturally, Hughes
hired him, eventually stage-managing the marriage to his sister, just as he
arranged, years later, the marriage of his niece to Eugene Kelly. It was just as
natural for Rodrigue to follow Hughes to New York; among his major diocesan designs was St. John's College, now Fordham University, where he and
his wife kept a house. He was aging and ill at the time of the St. Patrick's assignment, and died shortly after the cornerstone was laid; all of the drawings
are Renwick's.

While Renwick publicly glowed with pride at the dedication, privately
he made no secret of his disappointment at McCloskey's corner-cutting.
McCloskey, an intelligent and thoroughly decent man, was in awe of

Hughes and readily accepted that his episcopacy would be spent in his predecessor's massive shadow, struggling to carry on all the multiple enterprises Hughes had set afoot. The cathedral, of course, was Hughes's crowning work, the most theatrical gesture of a highly theatrical man. It was not so much a personal monument—although Hughes was by no means free of vainglory—as it was a trumpet call to the world that Catholicism, and the Irish, had taken root on American soil, a glorious riposte to fling at the hated English. Or as Hughes put it more loftily in an 1858 letter, he would build the cathedral "for the glory of God, the exaltation of our holy Mother, the Church, the honor of the Catholic name in this country; & as a monument of which the city of New York, either in its present or prospective greatness, need never be ashamed." This was a heavy legacy for Mc-Closkey's narrow shoulders; opening the cathedral in his lifetime became almost an obsession.

The brute fact was that the Catholics of New York could not afford the cathedral that Renwick had designed. Hughes's plan was to raise $100,000 from 100 individual $1000 subscriptions by the city's wealthy Catholics—the Kellys, Hoguets, O'Conors, and their friends—followed by a second year's fund-raising aimed at $100 subscriptions from another 1000 of the Catholic upper classes. Then as he put it:

> If I should be successful for these two years, the building will have so far advanced and the people's hearts will become so interested for its completion that I have no doubt that the work will be taken up separately in the churches and by the clergy in such a manner that it need not be stopped for want of funds, until the sum of half a million shall be expended upon it. . . . And if, when completed, it should still be in debt for 2 or 300,000 dollars, I should not think much of that.

Hughes's cost estimate, unfortunately, was at least three or four times too small, and he also greatly overestimated how much money he could raise from the wealthy. The initial hundred donors signed up quickly, doubtless with the archbishop's strong arm draped around their shoulders, but only seventy-three actually paid their subscriptions. (Seventy-three is the number usually cited by historians of the diocese; the records of the cathedral, however, show only sixty-two paid-up subscribers for a total of $63,000, including one double subscription.) Nor did the hoped-for 1000 additional Catholics step to the fore the next year. The total number of recorded additional subscribers, stretching over the entire two decades up to the dedication, was only 521, for a total of $136,929.13. Hughes ran out of cash just two years after the cornerstone was laid and stopped construction in 1861, with the first-story exterior walls about three-quarters finished. Putting the best face on it, he announced he was suspending construction because of the shortages and financial uncertainties engendered by the Civil War.

When McCloskey finally managed to restart construction in 1866, albeit at a much reduced pace, there was no place to turn for the $2 million or so still required, except to working-class Catholics. The endless round of parish assessments, special fund drives, raffles, and pleas from the altars, lent substance to the Protestant charge that Catholics were "bled" by their church, and "regularly taxed beside for the building of their cathedral." The burden fell especially heavily on the Irish, who seem to have ponied up by far the bulk of the money. Beyond the subscriber lists, of course, there is no record of the cathedral's donors; but just as New York's priests were overwhelmingly Irish, so were the regular churchgoers. The only Italian name among the subscriptions is Lorenzo Delmonico's, and he was Swiss, although there was a sizable colony of Italian Catholics in New York. There was also an economically successful German Catholic population (whose tenement houses were notable for their cleanliness and order) and a sizable minority of German priests; but of the total of 583 subscribers, hardly a dozen names are clearly German. Almost all the rest are Irish.

Today, the much larger buildings on all sides of St. Patrick's obscure the skewing of proportions and the reduction of complexity imposed by McCloskey's financial exigencies. Besides the missing front steeples and the missing rosette of chapels in the rear, the most serious omission, and the most galling to Renwick, was the lack of flying buttresses. As medieval cathedrals strained ever higher, their walls became too unstable to support the great weight of their masonry ceilings, causing cataclysmic outward collapses. Gothic architects solved the problem with the system of spidery exterior braces called flying buttresses, that permitted cathedrals to leap to much greater heights and also created an intricate play of exterior light and shadow. Cologne's, although they are hard to see under centuries of industrial grime, may be the greatest example. McCloskey, however, eliminated the flying buttresses at St. Patrick's simply by specifying a much lighter and cheaper modern plaster ceiling. Switching to plaster made undeniable financial sense, but the aesthetic price was large. As the dedicatory procession marched slowly around the building, they were presented with long, bare, blank walls on both sides, and blunt, empty connections where Renwick's flying buttresses would have been.

The sharpest eyes may also have detected a color change in the marble between the first and second story of the exterior walls, and therein lurks a small scandal. The cathedral's builders were William Joyce and James Hall. They were selected in large part because Hall was part owner of a marble quarry in Eastchester, New York, which had what Renwick considered the best available exterior stone. In a letter to the cathedral trustees in the spring of 1858, Hughes actually recommended buying the quarry to secure a ready supply of marble, warning more presciently than he knew of the "caprices of quarry owners & quarry men." Before work started, however, Joyce and Hall got the contract specification changed to cheaper marble from another quarry that they owned in Pleasantville, although without lowering the price to the diocese. Then in 1869, Joyce, in clear violation of the contract, which called for hand-cut marble, switched the marble again, to much cheaper stone blasted from a quarry in Massachusetts. (Hall died shortly thereafter.)

The circumstantial evidence of skulduggery is strong. Joyce had apparently purchased the Massachusetts quarry through a shell company, so he would have made large profits by switching the marble. Although he drew only $3000 a year from the cathedral contract, and had been heavily in debt, he suddenly found the cash to buy $150,000 worth of land—in today's dollars, that is, he was a millionaire. At the same time, his assistant, Patrick Dwyer, announced that he had unexpectedly inherited $20,000 from in-laws in Ireland. A priest who dined with McCloskey about the time work was being restarted reported that McCloskey was upset because Joyce was demanding to be bought out of his contract. The problem was that Joyce was Irish Catholic, while Hall, who was willing to finish the job, was an English Protestant, and McCloskey feared that would not sit well with "the Irish." A reasonable inference is that pressure was brought on Joyce to stay on the job, and he avenged himself by cheating the diocese on the marble. In any event, the official descriptions of the cathedral in the dedication programs stress, perhaps a bit defensively, that the walls use two kinds of white marble "of equal quality." Joyce was an honored guest at the dedication and magnanimously donated a window depicting the life of the Evangelist John.

When the procession finally completed its course around the cathedral, McCloskey was joined for a brief prayer by the lay trustees and the committeemen for the dedication, wearing red-and-white rosettes, and then led the procession back to the altar. The interior of the cathedral was a spectacle of solemn beauty—the tall arches of the Gothic ceilings (no one noticed the plaster), the quiet earth tones of the stone, the soft play of light from the great stained-glass windows (manufactured in France in workshops near Chartres), the flickering of hundreds of candles, the glitter of the altar plate and the burnished gold of the vestments, the bright cascades of altar flowers against the dark carved wood of the altar screen, the muted shuffle of the long line of processants. The antiphonal chanting of the Litany of the Saints greatly heightened the effect. Gregorian chant, or plainsong, based on the hypnotic repetition of a single note ornamented with regular cadences, developed coevally with Gothic architecture. It is an extraordinarily supple and flexible musical form, able to accommodate verse lines of any length. The litany was piped in high, clear voices by a quartet of choirboys positioned on either side of the altar; the responses, by the full choir, came from the rear of the church in thrumming baritones:

> Boys: Sanc-te Pe-tre
>   DUM-da DUM-da
>
> Choir: O-ra pro no-bis
>   DUM-da da DUM-da
>   (Saint Peter, pray for us.)

Or:

> Boys: Om-nes sanc-ti A-pos-to-li et E-van-ge-lis-tae
>   DUM-da da-da da-da-da-da da da-da-da-DUM-da
>
> Choir: O-ra-te pro no-bis
>   DUM-da-da da DUM-da
>   (All ye holy Apostles and Evangelists, pray for us)

It was achingly beautiful, and great theater. *The New York Tribune* reporter, who had not been impressed with the music to that point, found the litany overwhelming.

It was eleven o'clock when the Cardinal reached the altar and the litany was completed. There was a break in the ceremony so McCloskey could vest for Mass—donning an even richer outer vestment and scarlet slippers studded with jewels. The police line by the steps opened so the standing-room ticket holders could be admitted, gawking upward at the ceiling and the stained glass of the clerestory. The doors remained open so the crowd in the streets could witness the Mass. Some began to drift off to the park or to go about their other business, but fully a third stood vigil for the entire ceremony.

The highlight of the Mass was the sermon delivered by Bishop Patrick Ryan of St. Louis, reputedly the Church's finest orator, an exemplar of the ornate, Ciceronian nineteenth-century style that was already falling out of fashion. Ryan opened, of course, with a celebration of the cathedral, pointedly including the fund-raising gymnastics:

> And what shall I say to you—the children of toil—who . . . glory in what has been said, as if in reproach, "that the great Cathedral of New York was built chiefly by the pennies of the poor." The pennies of the poor! . . . It is appropriate that the poor whom [Christ] so honored should aid to build His house which is also their home. We accept,

then, the imagined reproach as an honor, and we ask in turn where in this great city have the thousands of bondholders erected a temple like this temple, built up and adorned by the "pennies of the poor."

And of the Irish:

Today the eyes and hearts of that devoted race in every part of the world are turned to this scene. Here they behold the greatest temple in the New World dedicated to God under the invocation of their national saint, and forever more it shall be known as St. Patrick's Cathedral of New York.

Ryan then proceeded to boom on for an unmerciful one hour and forty minutes, declaiming on the role of Catholic dogma in the modern world, while the the mute thousands standing in the crowded aisles shuffled patiently, lips doubtless moving in silent prayer, beseeching the Lord that the good bishop might finally stop. When Ryan at last did sit down, Monsignor William Quinn, the diocesan vicar-general rose briefly to announce an auction of pews the following Thursday evening. (The auction drew hundreds of onlookers. The top bid, for $2100, came from José Navarro, a deliberately obscure banker and friend of the Vanderbilts, reputed to be the richest Spaniard in America. Eugene Kelly's $750 was second highest, followed by those of James J. O'Donoghue, a former parks commissioner, the bankers William and John O'Brien, John D. Crimmins, a top Tammany sachem, and William R. Grace, soon to be New York's first Irish mayor. The press turned out in large numbers to see how much John Kelly might bid, but were disappointed when he failed to appear.)

It was almost two o'clock when the sermon ended, and some in the press corps were worried about McCloskey; he was not strong, and as celebrant would have had neither food nor water since the previous evening. The choir chanted the Nicene Creed, the outline of the Catholic faith hammered out at a series of great councils more than fifteen hundred years before; then, as the hush in the cathedral deepened, came the Mass's ancient sacrifice, the Offering and the Consecration of the bread and wine, the Cardinal holding them aloft as the true Body and Blood of Christ. The choir sang the "Agnus Dei"—"Lamb of God, who takest away the sins of the world, have mercy on us"—and Communion was distributed on the altar. Finally, the Cardinal bestowed his last blessing, and shortly before three o'clock, some five hours after the processional cross-bearer first started up the center aisle, the Mass ended, the dedication was finished, and St. Patrick's had become officially the leading Catholic cathedral of the New World. The heavy Sunday clothes of the thousands of people blinking out into the afternoon sunlight were wilted and sweaty, the congregants light-headed and sore from the long hours of standing or kneeling, but they were smiling and happy, basking in the quiet pleasure of having witnessed the completion of a great endeavor.

After the Mass, a banquet dinner awaited the clergy and lay dignitaries, some four hundred in all, in the basement of St. Mary's orphanage at 52nd. The gathering, save for the nuns who prepared and served the food, was of course entirely male, and a wholly pardonable self-satisfaction, a twinkling joviality, filled the room. At the head table with the Cardinal were Charles O'Conor and Eugene Kelly, the four archbishops—Gibbons, Wood, John Purcell of Cincinnati, Michael Hannan of Halifax, Nova Scotia—and Monsignor Quinn, the day-to-day manager of the cathedral project. After the meal, McCloskey, who had an easy platform style, rose, tapped his glass for attention, and read a congratulatory telegram from the Pope. Amid much applause, McCloskey called for a toast: "It needs no words of mine to commend to you the goodness of the Holy Father, and to call upon you to drink with one accord and hearty earnestness the health of Pope Leo XIII." The audience stood, drained their glasses, and burst into sustained cheers.

McCloskey called for quiet to remind his audience that "the cornerstone of the cathedral was laid during the pontificate of Pius IX . . . I ask you then to drink in silence the immortal memory of our late Holy Father." The drinks were refreshed, the audience rose once more, and after standing for a moment with heads bowed, drained the glasses. McCloskey then said a few words on "that great and illustrious archbishop," his predecessor, whose "true monument was the Catholic cathedral he founded," and the crowd stood once more in silence to drain a glass for John Hughes.

Turning to the head table, McCloskey—interrupted by prolonged bursts of cheering—introduced Archbishop Purcell, a venerable seventy-nine years old, who had barely managed to totter through the long procession. Purcell was "a father and brother," the Cardinal said, but "you are well aware of the misfortunes that have fallen upon him." Purcell and his brother, a priest of Cincinnati, had organized a savings bank for the diocese. But they disregarded Hughes's advice to turn the bank over to professionals, and Purcell's brother made a habit of tearing up notes for loans to Catholics on the grounds "that he did not require notes from members of his communion." The bank had just been closed by the authorities, with more than 4000 creditors and cumulative losses of some $3.5 million, wiping out the savings of many good Catholics. The archbishop's bedroom furniture, worth about $15, had been distrained, and he and his brother faced a possible indictment. The old man stood and tried to speak but could not find words. So Mc-

Closkey called for a hearty toast to Purcell's health, and announced a meeting of bishops at his house that night to discuss how to bail out the Cincinnati diocese.

The toasts flowed on. Bishop Ryan was roundly roasted for his interminable oration, and, after the audience had drunk his health, threatened to take an hour and forty minutes to reply. James Renwick's health was drunk, and he gave a brief speech. Gibbons toasted Monsignor Quinn, whose purse "grew longer and longer" whenever the cathedral's construction required. Charles O'Conor then spoke "at some length," although his speech is not preserved. Finally Gibbons remarked that it had been a long day. The time for evening Vespers service—to be celebrated by Gibbons—was drawing closer, and perhaps they should retire "for a good smoke."

For McCloskey, for the senior clergy, for the Catholic laymen like O'Conor and Eugene Kelly, the dinner was a moment of quiet triumph. After all the financial tensions of the previous twenty years, all the doubts in the lay press, all the false starts and the long hiatuses, the cathedral, if not exactly finished, was at least an accomplished fact. It was dedicated; it was the official, working seat of America's largest diocese and the grandest church in the Western Hemisphere. And there was no longer any question that one day it would be completely finished, if not quite in accord with the original plans, at least acceptably so. A chapel, if not a rosette of chapels, would eventually be built at the rear, and Gothic spires would surely one day carry Catholic prayers up to heaven.

Beneath the satisfaction, some self-doubts lingered. Ryan revealed a touch of insecurity in his sermon—there were, he said, "possibly many non-Catholics of cultured aesthetic tastes more competent to judge the beauties of such a church as St. Patrick's than most Catholics." And it is legitimate to ask, for the question was in the mind of at least some of the dinner's attendees, whether the inordinate pride in St. Patrick's as a work of public religious art was justified. The daily press, while criticizing, as the *Times* did, this or that aspect of the ceremonial or the fundraising exertions, were for the most part lavish in their praise of the cathedral itself. High-brow Protestant journals were much harsher. The brahmin *Atlantic Monthly* published a long, scathing review just before the dedication that is remarkable for its sustained vitriol. Almost half the article is an attack on Hughes, then fifteen years dead. Hughes was "a crafty and unscrupulous priest . . . playing upon the hopes and fears" of a base and corrupt city government, wrote the author, a local architectural critic named Clarence Cook, and had winkled the taxpayers out of the land for St. Patrick's "for the consideration of one dollar." Hughes, the article went on,

was not a man of educated taste, nor . . . a man of education at all. . . .
He was a politician, and one of the shrewdest and ablest of his class.
And then he was a priest . . . one of the few . . . in this country who
have been able to win, by their own character and energy, a national
reputation. . . . We are not saying it was an agreeable reputation. The
archbishop belonged to the church militant . . . always in the saddle,
never weary, and, what was more never desponding . . . so persuasive,
or at least so convincing that, when he called for money, if a widow had
but one penny, yet should he have a farthing ere he went.

The article's central charge—that Hughes had, in effect, stolen the land
for the cathedral—was false, as would have been easy to discover from the
public land registry. The city had sold the land to a private party in 1799, and
it had subsequently passed through many hands before the trustees of St.
Patrick's acquired clear title, for $59,500, in 1852. The 1799 deed included,
as was the custom, an annual "quitrent" of four bushels of wheat. When St.
Patrick's acquired title, it paid the city $83.22 to clear the quitrent, which
had not been paid for years. The story that the Church bought the land for
St. Patrick's from the Tammany machine for $83 is repeated even in modern
histories of New York. John Hassard, Hughes's biographer, pointed out the
falsity of the land-grab charge in a letter to the *Atlantic;* but Cook, hardly
abashed, insisted in a reply that any story so widely believed must contain
some truth, and there the dialogue ended.

Cook's treatment of the design and execution of the cathedral itself was,
if anything, even more savage. Renwick's work, he wrote, will "cause his professional brethren to hang their heads." The cathedral is all "clumsy repetition and copying of forms and arrangements found here, there, and
everywhere in the Gothic monuments of Europe." The "great door-way
came from nowhere unless from some confectioner's shop . . . sham and veneer are everywhere and in their most offensive forms. . . . Words cannot express the paltry character of the internal finish of this vaunted structure."
The interior stone is "the meanest of possible tints that can be found and the
sickly color of the glass makes it meaner still." Cook winds up the diatribe
with a pretense of apology: it was only because "the church never did care a
farthing for art as art, but only for the profit to be made from it, that we have
spoken so roundly."

Many of Cook's criticisms were fair. Renwick was similarly upset over
the omission of flying buttresses, and, as Cook predicted, the marble weath-
ered badly and had to be replaced about sixty years later. But the article is
too splenetic, too rabidly on the attack. The diocese had, after all, conscientiously searched out the best artisans it could find, although it was sadly true

that nineteenth-century French glazing standards and the skills of modern stone carvers were not up to those of the medieval craftsmen.

But Cook's venom was not directed at just a cathedral; the clue is his obsessive focus on Hughes—on his alleged power to cloud men's minds, his militance, his unflagging, cheerful energy—and Cook's fury at the alleged land grab, even when shown that it never really happened. Cook was perceptive enough, it seems, to understand the symbolism of St. Patrick's in exactly the same terms as Hughes did, and was sounding an alarm. The cathedral was an announcement—Hughes *intended* it as an announcement—of a great gravitational shift in the land. It enunciated a vision of Catholicism as a new power center, a major moral and political force in its own right—militant, expansionist, ethnically grounded, unapologetically separatist wherever its interests or teachings diverged from those of the rest of society. Cook was shouting, Beware! With a man of John Hughes's forcefulness at the head of the Catholic Church in the United States, anything *could* happen; even if it didn't happen in fact, the land grab *might* have been true.

The vision of the church that Hughes embodied in St. Patrick's was a sharp break from the low-profile, politically accommodating instincts of his predecessors or episcopal contemporaries. At the time of the dedication, his vision was not yet dominant, or widely understood, even within the Church. Like the cathedral, it was still a work in process, but there was little question of the direction in which the force lines lay.

CHAPTER 2

God's Own Providential Instrument

The wind in southwest Ireland blows consistently from the sea, and the ocean's fingers make an intricate tracery amid the rocks and low cliffs. The winter wind is raw, but frosts are rare, and summers are cool. Scudding clouds intersperse sudden gusts of rain with great splashes of sunshine: this is a land of rainbows, of preternaturally green fields, of mists and mystery. One can find in a cattle field, on a small promontory, a perfect little jewel of a druidic stone circle looking out to sea through a cleft in the hills; and ancient menhirs are scattered alone in the rolling landscape.

Skibbereen, a town of some 2000 souls, is tucked away in this corner of Ireland, a few miles from the sea, near the stone circle. With its imposing granite church, closely packed gray stucco houses, and narrow twisted streets, it is in all respects a typical Irish rural town, although it has spawned more than its share of radicals. Georoid O'Sullivan, who unfurled the Irish flag on the steps of the Dublin Post Office during the Easter Rising of 1916, was from Skibbereen, as was Jeremiah O'Donovan Rossa, founder of the Phoenix Society, a forerunner of the modern Irish Republican Army. One hundred and fifty years ago, Skibbereen looked much as it does today but had twice the population—a bustling, if not quite flourishing, agricultural center. Twenty thousand people lived in the immediately surrounding parishes, and the Skibbereen Poor Law district, a British local tax subdivision, had a population of more than 100,000. Like everywhere else in mid-century Ireland, the land around Skibbereen was crowded, and outside the town every available acre was given over to the potato.

Potato cultivation around Skibbereen was unusually intensive, because the area was also a center for kelp harvesting. Kelp is a tough seaweed that, chopped up, makes an excellent fertilizer. Any unsold kelp found its way into

Skibbereen's potato patches and greatly improved yields. That may have been the reason that the Great Potato Famine hit Skibbereen so hard. In the event, travelers' accounts from Skibbereen and from its twin village, Schull (pronounced "Skull"), were among the first to place before the world's conscience the true extent of the human devastation that famine was wreaking in rural Ireland. In time, "Skibbereen" became an Irish rallying cry and "Revenge for Skibbereen" the trumpet theme of countless songs and ballads, the constant goad, well into the twentieth century, whenever Irish hatred for the alien Saxon waned.

The potato blight that struck Ireland in 1845 is now known to be a fungus, *Phytophthera infestans.* First reported in Europe in 1830 and quite probably a reverse emigrant from North America, it is still the most important single cause of losses in the world potato crop, although it is kept under control by chemicals. The fungus spores are delicate, borne from plant to plant by air, and across the leaves and into the tubers by water. The smiling breezes, even temperatures, and mist-dewed fields of southern and western Ireland are perfect for *Phytophthera,* and it struck with the force of a biblical plague. One day "the crop looked splendid," the next the "air was laden with the sickly odor of decay"; almost overnight the leaves turned black, crumbling to ashes at a touch. Sometimes potatoes looked healthy when they were harvested but putrefied almost immediately when they were stored. About 30 to 40 percent of the crop was destroyed in 1845, and almost the entire crop in 1846. The next year was relatively dry and the blight retreated, but few potatoes were planted because the peasants had eaten their seed crop. Planting was hopefully resumed in 1848, but the summer was wet. *Phytophthera* wiped out the entire crop, and Ireland's peasants were left staring into the blank eye of death.

It was in the first cruel winter of total famine in Skibbereen, in early 1847, that shocked travelers found skeletal human creatures by the hundred in the peasant hovels and in the narrow town lanes where the poor were crowded, lying exhausted and listless after months of starvation, eyes glittering from emaciated skulls. As the death toll mounted—almost 10 percent of the local people died in March and April of 1847 alone—corpses lay unburied for days or were buried under only a few inches of soil. Wild dogs and giant rats unearthed bodies and gnawed at them in the thoroughfares; in one case neighbors brought a man his wife's head, which dogs had been tossing in the yard. The proliferation of corpses produced rampant pestilence; and bacillary dysentery, typhus, and cholera raged through a population debilitated by hunger and exposure. In the peasant huts, where families slept in a heap, health workers had to untangle the dead from the living, who were often found lying amid the corpses of their families, too exhausted to move or to cry out, even as the rats began their work on the bodies around them.

At the height of the Famine, the town population actually increased by several thousand, as the desperate rural folk crowded in in search of food, spreading contagion to the better-off classes. To defend itself, the town resorted to pit burials, collecting the dead in somber burial wagons. "Trap coffins" were built with hinged bottoms so they could be reused; they were suspended over the pit and the body, naked or at best wrapped in a sheet, was dropped in with a brief prayer, at least for the lucky ones. Dozens were buried this way each day in Skibbereen during the winter and spring of 1847, with the layers of bodies separated by sawdust or straw. A chipped marble plaque just outside the town still marks a large pit and its consignment of "uncoffined dead." More than once, living people were pulled from the pits in the nick of time—burial wagon workers sometimes separated the dead from the living merely by holding a lit straw in front of their faces to see if the flame moved. Tom Guerin's story is the best documented: he was dropped in a pit as a young boy but yelped when the sawdust shovel hit his legs; Guerin survived and lived in Skibbereen until 1910.

For all their suffering, the prominence of Skibbereen and Schull—the "Slain Sisters of the South"—in memories of the Famine is a quirk of historical imagination, for over the next several years the same scenes were played out through much of rural Ireland, especially in the west. Travelers told of "famished and ghastly skeletons," "demonic yells . . . such frightful spectres as no words can describe"; and of "cowering wretches almost naked to the savage

Credit: Library of Congress
Travellers' tales from the town of Skibbereen in southwestern Ireland may have been the first to bring the horrors of the Irish Famine to a broader public. In the five years after famine struck in 1845, up to 80 percent of the people in the villages around Skibbereen died from starvation or fever. Bodies were piled up in carts and hauled off to open-pit burial sites.

weather, prowling in turnip fields and endeavoring to grub up roots"; and of "little children . . . their faces bloated yet wrinkled and of a pale greenish hue . . . who would never, it was too plain, grow up to be men and women." "It was my impression," said one reporter, "that *one fourth* of those we saw were in a *dying state*"; another told how "poor people came in from the rural districts . . . literally to *die* . . . in the open streets, actually dying of starvation and fever within a stone's throw of the inn." The Irish sold their clothes to buy food and were often literally naked in the cruel winter of 1848. "Famine dropsy," the edema of the last stages of starvation, caused bodies to swell grotesquely and limbs to burst. There were many reports of cannibalism. Oddly, starvation often caused heavy growths of downy hair on children's faces as long as the hair on their heads; dying Irish children, said a traveler, "look like monkeys." Ireland's population was almost nine million on the eve of the Famine; five years later it had been reduced by two million. A million people emigrated; at least a million died. In rural areas, the impact was even worse. The death toll in Skibbereen and its immediately surrounding parishes was about a third of the population, and in some of the smaller villages, it approached 80 percent.

The Roots of Famine

Phytophthera attacked an Irish rural society already teetering on the brink of catastrophe, after centuries of bloody misrule by its English colonial masters. Queen Elizabeth subdued the Hiberno-Norman lords of Ireland and expropriated their lands, and Cromwell's exultant Protestant swordsmen imposed a sullen order by the deliberate, large-scale massacre of Irish civilians; not even Catholic babies escaped their righteous fury. The consistent objective of British policy, pursued with a devastating blend of incompetence and ingenious malevolence, was to squelch Irish initiative and keep the Catholic population poor and subjugated. Virtually all Irish lands were parceled out to the English nobility. As many Protestants as possible were imported, particularly from the Scots Lowlands. And the native Catholic Irish were burdened with "Penal Laws" as harsh as, in some ways harsher than, the Black Codes of the postbellum American South. Severe restrictions were placed on the Catholic clergy and the practice of Catholicism, and Catholics were forbidden to vote or hold office, carry a sword, own a horse or gun worth more than £5, enter specific professions, engage in certain kinds of commerce, live in a town without paying a special fee, or send their children to Catholic schools. As the passions of the seventeenth and eighteenth centuries cooled, the Penal Laws were only sporadically enforced, but arbitrary colonial officials wishing to intimidate the locals could, and did, dust them off at any time.

Colonial land policy was especially destructive. Tenure for the vast majority of Irish was by weak forms of leasehold; contracts were oral and of no certain term. In most of rural Ireland, rents could be raised or tenants expelled at any time for any reason. If a tenant improved land, say by building a house, the landlord could evict the tenant and keep the house, or raise the rent because the land had become more valuable. Policy often intentionally reinforced the worst features of Irish tradition. Irish custom, for example, called for partible inheritance—land was divided among all the sons, as opposed to the English system of primogeniture, where it was passed on intact to the eldest. Partible inheritance made rationalization of landholdings very difficult, and after many generations an individual's holdings might be scattered in a crazy quilt of tiny patches and slices throughout the village plots. The Penal Laws actually required the practice of partible inheritance unless the eldest son converted to Protestantism—adding the nasty twist that a converting eldest son could demand primogeniture, pitting him against his father and younger brothers.

English repression entrenched the static outlook of Irish-Gaelic culture. Irish village life was intensely communal: getting ahead, or acquiring more land, was frowned on as disruptive of village stability. Travelers were astounded by Irish poverty, which by many accounts was worse than that of American slaves. Peasants lived in one-room huts constructed of mud; a whole village might own but one bed or a single chair. In cold weather, livestock joined the family inside, their dung piling up at the hovel door, their lice and filth blending with the family's own. Boys and girls married very young (girls as young as thirteen or fourteen) and had very large families, and infant mortality was high. By the beginning of the nineteenth century—aside from a few islands of modernity like Belfast (flax spinning) and Dublin (government and finance)—Ireland was still mostly a primitive, preliterate society, notable for its charm, its music, and its tall tales, for the squalor of its villages, for the beauty and chastity of its young women, and for the warm hospitality and utter shiftlessness of its rural masses. The Irish peasant character that emerges from contemporary accounts is much like that of the Sambo archetype in the American South—oppressively servile (How to respect a man "who will persist in kissing your shoe strings," expostulated William Thackeray) but watchful and crafty, master of the indirect statement and the half-truth, comically lazy, and occasionally dangerous.

The potato was brought to Ireland toward the end of the eighteenth century and transformed the rural ecology. Potatoes are among the most nutritious of foods; mixed with a little milk or butter, they provide an almost perfectly balanced diet. They can be cultivated intensively—a few acres of land can easily feed a peasant family for a year—and require little work. The earth is spaded over and the seed crop sown in the spring, the ripe tubers dug out and cellared in the fall. Within a very short time, the Irish rural diet consisted almost entirely of potatoes—a healthy man ate up to twelve pounds a day. The spread of the potato coincided with the prosperity of the Napoleonic Wars, and the expansion of Irish agricultural exports, much to the benefit of Catholic "strong farmers" and merchants. For a brief time early in the nineteenth century, life may have approached the idyllic even for Irish-speaking peasants. Food was plentiful; sons and daughters were healthier and living longer. With the crop in, an Irish patriarch could look forward to a comfortable winter before the peat fire, surrounded by his neighbors, children, and animals, sipping *poitin* and smoking his pipe while biddy stirred the potato pot.

Irish prosperity touched off a frightening rural population explosion. Between 1779 and 1841, largely because of the improved, potato-based countryside diet, Ireland's population increased by an almost incredible 172 percent, and Irish peasant life came to be dominated by a desperate scrabble for plots of land to grow potatoes. Strong farmers, Catholic and Protestant alike, had tasted enough of prosperity and modernity to want to rationalize their holdings and farming methods. When farm exports fell off after the Napoleonic Wars, they switched wholesale to land-intensive grazure, producing Irish wool for the insatiable British textile industry. At the same time, English landlords, most of whom had probably never seen their Irish holdings, and who were hard-pressed at home, steadily increased cash rents. A smarmy new class of Irish middlemen allowed the more fastidious landlords to maintain a discreet distance from the brutalities of local rent collections; the middleman, who often doubled as the hated *gombeen* man, or local moneylender, leased tracts of land wholesale, then relet the individual plots to local peasants at a large profit.

Losing access to a potato patch meant starvation for Irish peasants, so they could be viciously exploited. Modernizing farmers evicted tenants as land was improved, razed their huts, and offered marginal, unimproved land at exorbitant rents. The peasants, for all their legendary laziness, performed prodigies of labor to make marginal land arable—draining fenland, or hauling buckets of earth up stony hillsides. As soon as the land was producing, they were evicted again and the process started over. Sharply rising cash rents in a largely noncash economy touched off a scramble for cash as frantic as the scramble for land. Peasants hired out as day laborers to support their rents, sold their cow, sold their pigs, eventually sold their clothes and other pitiable belongings. One of the great paradoxes of the Famine was that there was lots of food in Ireland, but it was being exported to England to raise cash for rent payments to mostly absentee British landlords. Even the strong farmers were under severe rent pressure, so they intensified their efforts to clear away peasants and make the land more profitable. At the height of the

Famine, the vicious circle grew even tighter when the Whig government, beset by its own financial problems, sharply increased landlord poor-rates, a form of welfare tax, to finance Irish relief. The landlords, of course, responded by raising rents even higher. British troops, many of them Irishmen, were always on hand, stoically enforcing the law.

By the 1830s and early 1840s, a lowering cloud of impending doom hung almost visibly over Ireland. Bands of landless peasants roamed the country byways, living in ditches and begging for food or work. The old violent Irish secret societies—the White Boys, the Steelboys, the Molly Maguires—flourished once again, committing arson and murder against strong farmers, middlemen, and rent collectors. Peasants switched to the highest-yielding strains of potato, which were often the least disease-resistant. Disastrous local crop failures were almost annual occurrences well before the arrival of *Phytophthera*. In the months before a harvest, when food supplies were shortest, the peasants ate "boners," potatoes that were only partly cooked, because the raw tubers took longer to chew and were harder to digest, making a seemingly more substantial meal. Careful estimates are that 2.5 to 3 million Irish were in a state of semistarvation most years *before* the Great Famine. Throughout the countryside, Ireland's lilting music gave way to the keening of hags.

In fairness, when near total famine finally struck in 1846, the initial English response was moderately effective. Sir Robert Peel, the Tory prime minister, was no friend of the Irish, but he was upright and competent; and as the former cabinet secretary for Ireland he was well informed on the country. His first relief measure, which split the Tory party and briefly cost him his ministry, was to repeal the protectionist Corn Laws, which prohibited the import of grain to the British Isles. A committed disciple of laissez-faire, he planned merely to keep the grain in reserve to prevent price gouging. Eventually, he set up large and reasonably effective food distribution programs in the worst-hit rural areas—although many peasants did not know how to prepare raw grain—and created a large public works program to put cash in peasant hands. The Whig government that succeeded Peel's later in 1846 was much less openhanded and even more devoted to laissez-faire; giving away food, they were convinced, would destroy initiative and disrupt grain markets. Officials also suspected, correctly, that millions of peasants would mob public works programs and food and soup centers even in the absence of famine, so destitute and malnourished had the Irish become. A British financial crisis in 1847 moved Irish relief even further down on the government's agenda. When Young Ireland, a small group of youthful romantics inspired by the nationalist risings on the Continent, staged a pathetically ineffective rebellion in 1848, even the pretense of official concern ended. From that point, for all practical purposes, Ireland was left to die on its own.

For decades after the Great Potato Famine, the Irish fueled their hatred of the English with stories of how famine was a tool of British policy and how the government sucked food and money out of Ireland as the country starved. By midcentury, in fact, there was not much any government could have done to save Ireland. The English stand indicted, not for failing to quell the Famine, but for the criminal misrule that made the ultimate catastrophe inevitable. As it was, few in England displayed regret, or even sympathy, for the calamities befalling their sister island; indeed, many were openly delighted. "In a few years more," a London *Times* editorialist ruminated happily in 1848, "a Celtic Irishman will be as rare in Connemara as is the Red Indian on the shores of Manhattan." And for sheer coldness, it is hard to match Benjamin Disraeli:

> An abused and indignant soil repudiated the ungrateful race that had exhausted and degraded its once exuberant bosom. . . . After a wild dream of famine and fever, imperial loans, rates in aid, jobbing public works, . . . the publication of the census of 1851, proved that the millions with whose evils no statesman would sincerely deal . . . had disappeared, and Nature, more powerful than politicians, had settled the "great difficulty."

The Irish Diaspora

The Great Famine triggered the immense waves of emigration that, along with starvation and fever, virtually depopulated rural Ireland, but it is far from the whole story of the Irish exodus. The stereotype of the American Irish immigrant—a Catholic rural laborer who settled unhappily in an Irish, parish-based, community in a large East Coast city—is only a partial description of a much more complicated reality.

About one out of four of the people of Ireland, in fact, were Protestants. At the very top of the social pyramid was the Ascendancy—5000 or so Anglicans of English descent or converts from the Irish upper classes who ran the government and owned the great estates. Most of the Protestants, however, were Presbyterians, the semilegendary Scotch-Irish, so named because many traced their ancestry to the Scots lowlanders enticed to Ireland by the British. Centered in northern and eastern Ireland, highly individualistic, and often harshly discriminated against by the Ascendancy, the Presbyterians were the backbone of Ireland's small entrepeneurial class—weavers and small manufacturers, smallholding farmers, and petty merchants. They were highly mobile, commercial, capitalist, and at home with legal and economic abstraction. The three quarters of the population who were Catholic also included a small and steadily growing elite of professionals and commercial farmers, but the great mass of the Catholics were peasants, most of them still Irish-speaking well into the nineteenth century, desperately attached to their village and their clan, and wary of the taxmen, bailiffs, rent collectors, middlemen, marauding soldiers, and other hostile tentacles of a modernizing society.

Up until at least the late 1830s, probably two thirds of Irish emigrants were Protestants, mostly Presbyterians, following their ambitions to England, Canada, America, and Australia. Total Irish immigration to North America during the first four decades of the nineteenth century was about a million people. A slight majority went to Canada, but most of the Canadian immigrants eventually settled in the United States, either transshipping to American ports or filtering across the border by foot. The Catholics who emigrated came primarily from the self-improving bourgeois elite. Charles O'Conor's father, Thomas, was fairly typical. He was one of Wolfe Tone's original United Irishmen, but was disgusted at the amateurishness of Tone's incoherent 1798 rising. When he shipped for America he had enough money to buy a 4,000-acre farm near Albany, New York. (He failed as a farmer and spent time in debtor's prison; young Charles rebuilt the family position from scratch.) Lower-class Catholics who emigrated often had been soldiers in the Napoleonic Wars and financed their voyage by indenturing as servants to Protestants, or by signing on as human ballast in the holds of returning timber ships.

Before the Famine emigrations, the typical Irishman in America was not a Catholic, was reasonably well situated economically, and was fairly evenly distributed throughout the country, including the West, the South, and the Southeast. Presbyterian strong farmers were particularly well represented on the Appalachian frontier and opened much of the woodlands of western Pennsylvania, Virginia, and the Carolinas. The Protestant character of the early Irish emigrants was reinforced by the tendency of Catholics to join Protestant churches in America; the Catholic servant of a Presbyterian farmer on the western Pennsylvania frontier simply had no other choice. At the end of the eighteenth century, the rolls of Trinity Episcopal Church on New York's Wall Street contained the names of a number of well-to-do Catholic Irishmen. When the city's first Catholic church, St. Peter's, opened in 1786, many, but by no means all, switched back to the old religion. William Mooney, one of the Irish Trinitarians joining St. Peter's, was the founder of the New York branch of Tammany Hall, although Tammany remained a bastion of anti-Catholicism for another thirty years. Even today, a slim majority of Irish Americans are Protestants. Almost half of America's presidents, nineteen in all starting with Andrew Jackson, have been of Irish descent, but John Kennedy is the only Catholic on the list.

For the typical Catholic Irish peasant, however, emigrating to a foreign land was like traveling to a distant planet. As a French traveler put it, "The poor Irishman . . . remains on the spot of his present misery . . . and it is a consolation for him to bear the load of life in the country where he was born, where his father and mother lived and died, and where his children will have to live and die." Mawkish ballads and poems drummed home that overseas Irish Catholics were exiles, driven from home by harsh fate and the hated Saxon. "[T]here is scarce a night when I go to Bed but it costs me Tears when I think on Ireland" was a typical sentiment of a young man abroad, although it was sometimes allayed by the more practical note: "but I look at my rich land unencumbered by rent or taxes, and ask myself, if I *were* back again, how could I command such certain *independence*." Powerful Irish family ties produced complicated emotions for emigrants, and Irish parents were often grimly manipulative—like the aging father who refused to subdivide his lands but accused his emigrating children of abandonment. The common rural practice of holding a full-dress wake for the departing emigrant, as if for a funeral, was hardly calculated to send a young man or woman away with joyfully leaping heart.

But by the 1830s, rural life was becoming intolerable. As major local failures of the potato crop followed one upon the other, fear of the ultimate famine took on an edge of religious hysteria. There were two great Irish social and political movements of the 1820s and 1830s. Daniel O'Connell, "The Liberator," a fluent Irish speaker, and the most effective politician in modern Irish history, joined with the Catholic clergy to create a mass movement to win civil liberties for Catholics; and an Irish priest, Fr. Theobald Mathew, created the antidrinking Total Abstinence Society. Both campaigns turned into mass evangelical awakenings that swept through the peasantry on waves of eschatological frenzy. Movement clerics delivered smoldering harangues to huge crowds in open fields. O'Connell and Mathew acquired the auras of messiahs, and their progress through the countryside drew throngs in the hundreds of thousands. O'Connell's visit to Skibbereen in 1843 drew a crowd estimated at between 400,000 and 750,000. Even the lowest estimates mean that virtually everyone within several days' journey somehow got to Skibbereen. It was a vast outpouring of religious fervor fueled by stark fear of the specter of death stalking the land.

As more and more poorer Catholics were forced to emigrate, traveling conditions deteriorated sharply. Earlier in the century, Protestants and Catholics alike tended to emigrate as families, in reasonable, if not luxurious, accommodations. By the late 1830s and early 1840s, single, unskilled Catholic men and women made up the majority of the passengers, crowding into uncomfortable, and often disease-ridden, steerage bunks, hoping to arrive safely in America and earn enough money to bring on their families.

The arrival of *Phytophthera* converted reluctant emigration into panicked flight. The number of Irish recorded as entering America rose from 52,000 in the 1820s, to 171,000 in the 1830s, 656,000 in the 1840s, and more than 1 million in the 1850s; in the decade of the 1850s alone, about 12 percent of the total population of Ireland were officially listed as entering an American port. The actual rate of immigration was much higher; casual statistical procedures at ports and the stream of unrecorded immigrants from Canada create a consistent downward bias in official entry statistics. Adding in the large exoduses to England and Canada, and the smaller one to Australia, one out of every four Irish citizens departed the country in the 1850s. The pace of emigration continued at a high, if somewhat moderated, rate for the rest of the century, until the population stabilized at 4 million, or about the same as in 1750.

During the peak of the Famine-inspired flight from Ireland, roughly 1846 to 1853, the sufferings of the poorest Irish emigrants were truly horrific. First of all came the psychological terror. Before the Famine, even the most conflict-ridden emigrants were still agents of their own fate, consciously gambling, however fearfully, on finding a new future abroad. But in 1846 and 1847, waves of peasants numbering in the tens of thousands—young and old, families and children, the starving and the fever-ridden, many half-naked and freezing, clutching sacks of roots—began moving like lemmings toward the ocean ports. Unscrupulous landlords discovered that paying for passage to America was cheaper than paying the Famine poor-rate and herded their tenants onto unseaworthy, badly provisioned vessels—the notorious Famine "coffin ships." Families crowded by the hundreds into dark holds without bedding or sanitary facilities, were refused access to the decks during voyages that could stretch to six or eight weeks, survived on spoiled food and fouled water, and when the ship was tossed in ocean storms, shrieked in the darkness and rolled helplessly in filth and excrement.

Lord Palmerston, a government minister, and owner of vast tracts in Sligo in northwestern Ireland, shipped virtually all of his peasants, more than 2000 altogether, off to Canada in 1847 and 1848. The shocked citizens of St. John in New Brunswick found Palmerston's ships arriving with "helpless young families, decrepit old women, and men riddled with disease." On one ship almost half of Palmerston's peasants had to be provided clothing before they could decently disembark. Virtually all the Sligo transients went immediately on public charity in St. John, prompting an angry memorial from the city council to his lordship that he "should have exposed such a numerous and distressed portion of his tenantry to the severity and privations of a New Brunswick winter . . . unprovided with the common means of support, with broken-down constitutions and almost in a state of nudity." From Palmerston's point of view, of course, the exercise was a great success; his poor-rate assessment for 1849 was only 2 percent of the 1847 assessment.

Predictably, typhus and cholera were rampant on the coffin ships. The *Larch* left from Sligo in 1847 with 440 passengers, of whom 108 died at sea and 150 arrived with fever. The *Virginius* sailed in the same year with 476 passengers, of whom 158 died en route and 106, including the master and most of the crew, arrived with the fever. During the shipboard cholera epidemics in 1853, more than 10 percent of all Irish passengers died on the ocean voyage. (The shipboard death rate for immigrants from other countries was typically about 0.5 percent.) The fear of epidemics prompted panic-stricken city officials up and down the East Coast to close their ports to Irish vessels. More than once, boats full of starving, fever-ridden peasants were turned away from New York or Boston and plied beseechingly from city to city seeking a place of entry.

The first waves of panicked flight tended to wash up in Canadian ports. The fever quarantine station on Grosse Isle, outside of Montreal in the St. Lawrence, was overwhelmed with thousands of infected patients. Dozens of fever-struck ships queued up in the harbor for days at a time, ensuring the continued spread of fever on board. When no more fever victims could be crammed onto the island, the city of Montreal, in the dead of winter, built crude sheds outside the city to house the hapless immigrants. Charitable citizens venturing into the sheds quickly caught the fever themselves, reinforcing the city's panic. A single mass grave on Grosse Isle holds the remains of 5294 Irish immigrants who never made it to the mainland. Of the roughly 100,000 Irish who arrived in Canada in 1847, according to detailed records kept by a blessedly compulsive immigration official, a third died within a year.

Many of the Famine immigrants went on to successful lives in America. William R. Grace, the South American shipping and mining magnate, a pillar of the New York business community and an antimachine mayor, shipped from Ireland as a cabin boy in 1848. Bishop John Ireland embarked with his family the following year, as did the three Cudahy brothers who dominated Chicago's meatpacking business in the 1870s. Less spectacularly, Malachi Kinney, who as a young boy lost his parents and half his family on a coffin ship, was the owner of the largest blacksmith shop in Grand Rapids, Michigan, in the 1880s. But these are exceptional stories. Most of the Famine immigrants were grossly unprepared for life in America and made pathetic attempts to re-create the Irish village in their new country. Charles Dickens, who traveled through America in the 1840s, recorded his impression of a settlement of Irish canal laborers in upstate New York: "clumsy, rough and wretched hovels . . . all were very . . . filthy. Hideously ugly old women and very buxom young ones, pigs, dogs, men, children, babies . . . all wallowing together in an inseparable heap."

Peasants who got jobs digging canals were the lucky ones. By some estimates, the life expectancy of an adult Irish peasant in America was less than six years. There is no possibility of reconstructing accurate data on immigrant death rates, but they were very high, conceivably approaching those of the hapless peasants who had stayed behind. Vast numbers of the survivors were trapped in the cities, where they took refuge in alcoholism, crime, and insanity. The well-turned-out men and women parading down the center aisle of St. Patrick's in 1879 were sons and daughters of Ireland's self-improving Catholic elite, while the drunken crones in the Five Points slums and the feral children who supplied the violent Irish gangs were the spawn of the unassimilated peasantry.

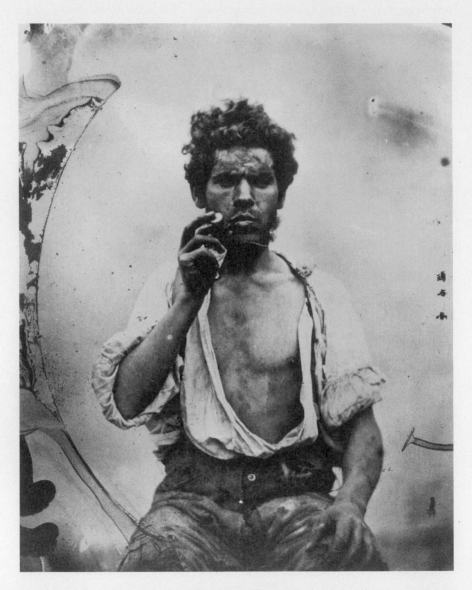

Credit: Sean Sexton

A rare photograph of an Irish peasant laborer taken in the 1850s. Contrary to legend, Irish peasants were not particularly religious. Traditional Irish culture was poorly adapted to modern society, and peasants fleeing the Famine sank into alcoholism and crime in the slums of England and North America.

The clumsy attempts of Minnesota's Bishop Ireland to convert Irish peasants into independent farmers, even long after the Famine, illustrate the great gap between the peasantry and the Catholic middle classes. John Ireland was for many years an advocate of western colonization for Irish farmers, in the hope of reducing Irish concentration in eastern cities and offsetting the prevailing plains-state Lutheranism. But he had few takers and was honest enough to admit that his handful of showcase projects were peopled by middle-class strong farmers, who, after succeeding in Pennsylvania or New York, were simply moving up to bigger, cheaper farms. Minifamines had remained regular occurrences in Ireland, however, and when the bishop learned of great suffering in the Irish countryside in 1879, he decided to take direct action and import peasants to Minnesota.

Ireland chose as the objects of his charity the peasants of Connemara in the remotest reaches of the Irish west. Connemara is a land of sparse, stark beauty—peat bogs and heather, stony hillsides and sudden gorges, solitary trees with angular, wind-gnarled branches. It was the home of the legendary "wild Irishman," and until Ireland's recent Celtic revival was one of the twentieth century's last redoubts of Irish speakers. But Ireland was convinced that Irish peasants, however backward, needed only opportunity to succeed. He arranged passage for two dozen Connemaran families, almost three hundred people in all, and mobilized the resources of his diocese to establish a farm for each family, complete with a house, livestock, tools, and supplies for a summer's crop.

The qualms started as soon as the Connemarans arrived in June 1880. The good Catholics of St. Paul were amazed at how small and emaciated they were, how furtive, shifty-eyed, uncommunicative, almost ratlike. But Ireland plunged ahead, and after putting a few of the young men and women into service in the city, he established the rest on their farms with much ceremony and then went back to his affairs in St. Paul. Trouble did not surface until fall, in the midst of an early cold snap, when the *St. Paul Press* began an exposé of the impending catastrophe on the Connemaran farms. With no idea of how to manage a farm, isolated on the lonely plains, the hapless peasants were on the brink of starvation. Some had hired out as day laborers during the summer, but they had planted no crops, built no buildings, eaten their seed, slaughtered many of their animals, and were in mortal danger from the Minnesota winter. The few peasants who talked to reporters said flatly, "The Bishop brought us here and he must care for us." Ireland finally conceded defeat, brought the Connemarans back to St. Paul on diocesan welfare, and sold off the farms. (The Connemarans argued that they should be paid for the livestock they were leaving behind.) Well into the 1950s, the Connemara Patch was a well-known St. Paul slum.

The stark fact is that the modernization of Ireland was accomplished by a savage winnowing of its redundant population. Irish peasants who could assimilate to the demands of a modern commercialized society survived, and some even prospered, if not in Ireland at least in North America. Those who couldn't died, either through starvation and fever at home or on the seas, or much less visibly, through the workings of the harsh economic systems in the lands to which they fled. The high death rates among the Irish lower classes in North America offer only a glimpse of the devastation, for the least capable emigrants never got farther than the dirt cellars of Liverpool and Glasgow, where they huddled and died by the tens of thousands. The rise of a respectable Irish Catholic middle class, in short, and of its dominant institution, the modern Irish Catholic Church, was accomplished not only by the transformation of the Irish lower classes, but in possibly equal measure, by their annihilation.

The Creation of Irish Catholicism

"Irish Catholicism" conjures up a welter of images—flickering candles in dim churches; the quick lash from the yardstick in a nun's billowing sleeve; a grimly dour view of sexuality; the cult of the mother, from the white-haired "Mother Machree" to the celebration of the Blessed Virgin; a world that is separate, strictly ordered, and submissively obedient. It is the world of James Joyce's *Dubliners,* of the narrow emotional compasses of his middle-class spinsters and bachelors, where the priest is the font of final wisdom, the flames of Hell a constant reality, and life a continuing round of devotions— the Forty Hours, the Stations of the Cross, the retreats, the temperance pledges. Joyce's Irishmen debate points of theology as readily as football scores; a little mispronounced Latin over a glass of whiskey carries the field in a late-evening argument. These are marginal people, desperately striving for respectability. The same characters, far removed from Joyce's Edwardian Dublin, people the Chicago stories of James T. Farrell and, in our own day, the novels of Mary Gordon.

The Irish Catholicism of Joyce, Farrell, and Gordon, the rigorist, militant brand of Catholicism that found its broadest field in America, is a recent phenomenon, one of the most enduring offspring of Ireland's Great Famine, with origins that can be pinpointed quite precisely to just a few decades in the mid-nineteenth century. To a striking degree, it is the creation of one man, Cardinal Paul Cullen, who between 1849 and 1878 utterly transformed the Irish Church, and through the agency of thousands of emigrant Irish priests, transformed the Church in America as well.

Paul Cullen was in the classic Medicean mold of a prince of the Roman Church—lean and ascetic, glacially cold and remote, every whisker tuned to the nuances of curial politics, a diplomat and intriguer to his fingernails.

Many people admired and feared Cullen; it is unlikely that anyone loved him. "Poor Dr. C.! . . . he makes no one his friend," lamented John Henry Newman. The human qualities that round out the character of, say, a John Hughes—the awkward warmth, the craving for personal contact, even the unmanageable temper—are missing in Cullen. By temperament and training Cullen was almost more Italian than Irish. The son of a Catholic strong farmer, he went to Rome in 1821 at the age of eighteen to begin his studies for the priesthood and did not return home, except for occasional brief visits, for twenty-nine years. After ordination, he taught at the Irish College in Rome and became its superior at the age of only twenty-nine. At the college, Cullen became the unofficial Roman representative of the Irish hierarchy, a consummate Vatican insider, and a favorite of Pius IX; for the rest of his life, he tended to slip into Italian in his informal correspondence. At the end of 1849, to everyone's surprise, for his name had not been on the official candidates' list, Cullen was appointed not only archbishop of Armagh, but also apostolic delegate, or the Vatican's official representative to Ireland. Three years later, he was appointed archbishop of Dublin, making him the primate, or senior bishop, of the country.

Cullen was taking over one of the most ragtag national churches in Europe. Catholicism in Ireland, despite some steady reforms since the 1830s, was still a lower-class religion, with a membership that was highly superstitious and mostly illiterate. There were few priests and fewer churches, and both were of poor quality. Before the Great Famine, there was only one priest for every 3000 Catholics in Ireland, and even fewer nuns. By comparison, in the 1880s the priest-to-communicant ratio in America was roughly 1:1000; in Italy, it was about 1:350. With only scattered churches in the Irish hinterlands, services were rotated among private houses, which was the source of much abuse, ranging from priests demanding excessive catering to leeringly public confessionals for young women. Clerical alcoholism, fornication, and financial extortion were apparently widespread. Not surprisingly, only about a third of the Catholic population—in many rural areas fewer than 20 percent—regularly attended Mass or received the sacraments. The famously high rate of church attendance among Irish Catholics—90 percent in both Ireland and America until relatively recently—is a post-Cullen phenomenon.

The Gaelic culture of the Irish countryside greatly influenced rural religious practice well into the nineteenth century. The peasant religion was a witches' brew of half-remembered pagan rites and fractured Catholic ritual—a jumble of hexes, fairies, banshees, saints, and Latin prayers. The Irish village enforced powerful sanctions against premarital sex and illegitimacy, even compared with other European peasant cultures, and the chastity of Irish maidens was the wonder, or frustration, of travelers. But at the same time, rural Ireland was a highly sexual society, with sexual tensions resolved by very early marriages. Nudity or seminudity were not uncommon, and visitors were surprised to see young Irish men and women bathing within sight of one another. Gaelic songs and folk dances were notoriously bawdy, while the games at the weeklong wakes, like "Mock Marriage," were full of sly double entendre. Cross-road dancing—nightlong outdoor gatherings of several villages for sexually charged dancing, raucous drinking, and usually a rousing fight—was the despair of reforming clergy. The legendary prudery of Irish Catholicism, once again, is a post-Cullen phenomenon.

Even the close identification between Catholicism and Irish nationalism, the use of religion to assert the psychological distance from the Protestant English oppressor, may be a more recent development than commonly supposed. Catholic versus Protestant was clearly a central theme of Cromwell's atrocities, as it was for the Irish noblemen, like the "Wild Geese," who supported James II and fled to France after the battle of Limerick in 1691. But gradual easing of the Penal Laws and the passage of time attenuated the link between nationalism and religion. Wolfe Tone was a Protestant, and the leaders of both his 1798 rising and that of the Young Irelanders in 1848 were Protestants and Catholics in roughly equal measure. When Daniel O'Connell mobilized the Catholic clergy behind his movement to repeal the Act of Union with England in the 1820s and 1830s, he began the reidentification of the Catholic Church with Irish nationalism. Emmet Larkin, the leading historian of the Irish Church, argues that it was not until Cullen radically increased the Church's presence in the daily life of the Irish that it came to provide a substitute national identity. "Take an average Irishman . . . the very first principle in his mind is, 'I am not an Englishman, because I am a Catholic!' " This is the statement of a Catholic preacher in 1872; a half century earlier, it would not have been so obvious.

During his long reign as Irish primate, Cullen's policies were an astute mix of ideological rigidity and political deftness. At first he appeared to make common ground with the clerical nationalists, waging all-out war against the British-supported educational system, much to the chagrin of the bishops who had worked for years to win Catholics the right to attend Trinity College. Cullen even opposed a state school for "idiots" on the ground that they might be proselytized. By dint of a long boycott he eventually won Catholic control over Irish schools, but then immediately turned on the nationalists. The issue for Cullen, in disputes like the schools controversy, was never English rule in Ireland, but *Protestant* rule. Playing one clerical faction against the other, and with the reliable backing of the Vatican, Cullen eventually succeeded over many years in reshaping the hierarchy almost entirely with men in his own image.

Cullen was remarkably unmoved by the Famine. That is hardly surprising, for his worldview was premodern: famine was simply the work of Providence, "a calamity with which God wishes to purify . . . the Irish people." While still at Rome, he urged the hierarchy to reject British aid; and on settling in at Armagh, his strongest reaction was not to the plight of his flock, but to the shoddy vestments, the wooden episcopal cross, and the uncertain ceremonial at the cathedral. The most important issue facing Ireland in 1850, as far as Cullen was concerned, was not the Famine, but the schools fight. During one of the worst of the recurring minifamines in 1859–1863, he raised tens of thousands of pounds from Catholic parishes for the Vatican's military forces. One of his correspondents, apparently reflecting Cullen's own attitude, said of a cholera epidemic, "One can hardly regret its long continuance among us" since it was "enforcing penance and weeding out the ungodly." Cullen himself suggested during an outbreak of smallpox that churchgoers were protected, since they did not lead drunk and disorderly lives; and he thought the prevalent Irish alcoholism was caused by freedom of the press. His eulogy of a priest from Waterford epitomizes the Cullen definition of a successful clergyman: the man had built several churches, greatly increased annual contributions to Rome, and closed down both the state school and the government-supported workhouse for the poor.

The powerful social forces transforming Irish society fed into Cullen's program of religious reform. If a Catholic strong farmer hoped to survive the chaos engulfing rural Ireland, he had to increase the size of his farm, keep it intact, and manage it with great thrift and discipline. He could not give his sons land, and he could not afford dowries for more than one or two daughters. In just a few decades, the average age of marriage in Ireland jumped by almost ten years, as strong farmers and striving Catholics enforced strict sexual discipline over their children. Young men and women could either emigrate or stay at home under the thumb of their parents, facing the prospect of celibacy well into adulthood. By the late nineteenth century, the maiden aunt and bachelor uncle were fixtures in Irish families, and possibly a third of Irish adults could expect never to marry. A rise in the incidence of loveless or arranged marriages is suggested by the increased age gap between brides and grooms. Prior to the Famine, fewer than 20 percent of brides were more than ten years younger than their husbands; by the turn of the century, more than half were.

In a society where feckless reproduction had just led to catastrophe, the newly rigorist doctrine of sexual purity and the Church's carefully fostered cult of the Blessed Virgin found receptive ears. Sex even among married couples was shamefaced and fleeting. Marrying so late, men often remained under the psychological control of their mothers and kept to the society of their bachelor friends after marriage—the phenomenon of the Irish "bachelor husband"—perpetuating the cycle of matriarchy in their own families. The harsh repressions within upwardly mobile Irish families produced the fierce and darkly concealed intrafamilial passions captured in the plays of Synge and O'Neill. Celibacy in Ireland, moreover, was not the monopoly of Catholics. The marriage practices of middle-class Protestants paralleled those of Catholics, and Anglican and Presbyterian ministers were as firmly censorious in their advocacy of sexual abstinence.*

In such a society, the religious life had obvious appeal. For the superfluous sons and daughters of the Catholic middle classes, a vow of celibacy came at little additional cost. Despite the thousands of clergy who emigrated after the Famine, the number of priests in Ireland rose by 25 percent between 1850 and 1870, the number of nuns doubled, and the quality and social standing of new religious candidates went up sharply. With more and better disciplined clergy, a shrinking and more bourgeois Catholic population, and newly won control over the educational system, Cullen was in a position to engineer a vast expansion of the Church's influence in Irish daily life.

Cullen's weakness for pomp and ceremony (patriots thought his head was turned by a visit from the Prince of Wales) became an important proselytizing tool. He pushed Catholic financial resources to the limit to build proper churches everywhere, as well as rectories, convents, chapter houses, retreat centers, shrines. National jubilees and days of atonement were accompanied by an almost endless stream of new devotions—processions, the Forty Hours, novenas, the *Via Crucis,* benedictions, vespers, special devotional exercises for the Sacred Heart and for the Blessed Virgin, perpetual adorations, mass rosaries—coordinated, as far as possible throughout the nation. He cajoled, ordered, embarrassed his fellow hierarchs to improve the quality of preaching and singing, to regularize ritual, to follow ceremonials to the letter. He would not brook the kind of wooden cross that greeted him in Armagh. He wanted glittering plate, candles, flowers, beautiful music, hair-raising sermons—a total sensory experience, like the ceremony in his own procathedral that, as he recounted with satisfaction, was celebrated "with great pomp and magnificence. The church is ornamented with damask . . . and what is better," he added, "crowds of people are attending." He did not exaggerate, for the Irish reaction to his reform program was stupendous. People flooded the churches, making their first confessions in years, begging to regularize their marriages, finally having their children baptized. It took all the resources of the religious communities—the Jesuits, Dominicans, Vincentians—to handle the upsurge in parish workloads.

* Irish rigorism is conventionally attributed to Jansenism imported from Europe by French-trained Irish priests. There is some truth to the story, but it is far too simple an explanation. There was a French influence at Maynooth, the most important Irish seminary, but it tended toward an anti-Vatican nationalistic stance that placed the faculty and Cullen at swords' point for much of his tenure. Cullen's rigorist party, as often as not, were recruited from the Irish College in Rome, which he controlled. The fact that Protestants preached the same rigorist sexual doctrine points to local sources for Irish attitudes.

Credit: Library of Congress
Cardinal Paul Cullen, who was more at home in Rome than in Ireland, seized
upon the Famine to create the modern, rigorist, version of Irish Catholicism that
found its broadest field in America. Cullen and his fellow bishops specifically tar-
geted America for Irish religious conquest. The picture dates from about 1865.

Ireland had been primed for religious revival by the evangelism of
O'Connell's and Fr. Mathew's movements. Then the Famine, the decades of
social unraveling, the mass flight abroad, all seemed a fearsome cosmic judgment. Devastation was compounded by a corrosive loss of national identity,
after a century of steady Anglicization, or "West Britonizing." The Irish language, Irish traditions, Irish folk practices, Irish juridical concepts were
being swept away by an English language and practice irresistibly better

adapted to the modern world. The Church itself was one of the great Anglicizing influences. It curtailed the wakes, stamped out cross-road dancing, bowdlerized the folk songs. Catholic schools taught English and European, not Irish, history. Strong farmers forbade their children to speak to peasant laborers; and as a schoolgirl put it, "The nuns say we must never miss a chance of curing people of pagan superstition." Ireland was a degraded nation, vanquished and humiliated, scorned and pitied by the world, unable to feed or defend itself, its feeble attempts at revolution a laughingstock. Now here stood the Church, mysterious, solemn, and grand, its arms open. Cullen offered explanations, direction, identity, and order, and the people flocked to his banner. Secular reformers regarded Cullen's expenditures in an impoverished country with understandable distaste. But he was offering food of a different kind, and for the vast majority of the Irish, it was obvious which they preferred.

The thoroughness and wholeheartedness with which the laity embraced religious reform was a uniquely Irish phenomenon. Superficially, Cullen's reforms were simply part of a worldwide conservative Catholic retrenchment pushed assiduously for more than thirty years by Pius IX; but everywhere else in Europe, Pius's accomplishments fell far short of his hopes. Indeed, since Pius's program was widely perceived as a Vatican-sponsored royalist/Bourbon counterrevolution, which Pius would not have denied, it helped inflame the spirit of anticlericalism. In France and Italy, Europe's leading Catholic countries, religion remained primarily a concern of women. Avoiding undue clerical influence in public affairs was advanced in the French Parliament as an important reason for denying women suffrage. Similarly, while late-nineteenth-century bourgeois marital sexual practice seems to have been very restrained throughout Europe—even fairly liberated Frenchmen did not consider it proper for a husband to see his wife unclothed—Ireland seems to have retained the constraints much longer, well into the twentieth century, and no other country came close to Irish celibacy rates.

All cultural generalizations are treacherous, but the Irish do seem to have been unusually well adapted to be the foot soldiers in Cullen's, and Pius's, militant new brand of Catholicism. Consider the Irish streak of obedient fatalism. The historian Kerby Miller points out that the Irish language abounds in passive constructions. The literal translation of the Irish for "I met him on the road" is "He was twisted on me on the road"; for "I am sad," "Sadness exists on me." Nineteenth-century observers almost uniformly comment on the passivity of Catholic Ireland. The sons and daughters of the post-Famine Irish middle classes by and large did as they were told well into adulthood. In America, during a spate of conversions of Anglican ministers, Irish-American bishops complained that the new men could not understand the virtues of obedience. A country priest in Ireland was always something of a Magus, and during his travels in Ireland at the height of O'Connell's and Fr. Mathew's movements, Alexis de Tocqueville was struck by the extraordinary unity of outlook among the clergy and laity. After Cullen's reforms, outsiders were astonished at the degree of clerical influence in every aspect of Irish life. In the early twentieth century, a sympathetic observer commented that in Ireland, "coercion, in some form or other, is the rule."

The evident Irish Catholic skill at politics and bureaucracy, sharpened during the decades of O'Connell's campaigns, is rooted in the intensely communal life of old Ireland. Decisions were made by family councils or *clachan* committees; "boldness," or independence of mind, was quickly slapped down. Catholic Ireland was a honeycomb of "societies" and unofficial organizations. In America, the Irish dominance of almost every big-city political machine by 1900 is nothing less than extraordinary; it was compounded of the genuine skill of Irish politicians and the disciplined obedience of Irish voters. In the same way, the Irish presence in highly organized skilled trades, like steam fitting, boilermaking, and plumbing, was far out of proportion to their share of the workforce. It also seemed natural for the Irish to become America's regulators. In an 1880s newspaper cartoon, a carnival booth displayed the "last non-Irish policeman in America," and to our own day, Irish Catholics dominate organizations like the FBI.

All in all, it is hard to imagine a better set of qualifications for success in the Roman Catholic Church, as the leading Irish clergy themselves were acutely aware. And it is perhaps understandable that Irish priests came to believe that they had been entrusted with a unique salvific mission: that the horrors of the Famine and the sufferings of Ireland had forged a new and purer form of Catholicism, and that God had charged them with carrying it to the very ends of the earth.

The Mission of the Irish Race

The administration of All Hallows College in Drumcondra, a north Dublin suburb, is housed in a blockish, impressively ugly Georgian mansion on a twenty-four-acre walled estate adorned by centuries-old spruce trees. The mansion was built by the Beresfords, a leading Ascendancy family, but the estate originally belonged to the ancient priory of All Hallows, expropriated for the Protestant nobility by Elizabeth. The land and the mansion fell into the possession of the city of Dublin during the lord mayorship of Daniel O'Connell, at a time when he was virtually the de facto ruler of Ireland; O'Connell in turn, in 1842, gave the estate to an enterprising young priest named John Hand. The lease to Hand was for 999 years and was subject to two stipulations: the first, a tweak at the Ascendancy, was that the estate be renamed All Hallows; the second was that the property be dedicated to the training of Irish priests for Catholic missions abroad.

Increasing the number of Irish clergy in America began to be agitated in the 1820s by John England, a native of Cork, and for many years bishop of Charleston, South Carolina. According to James Whitfield, the English archbishop of Baltimore, John England was a "warm-headed Irishman" who, Whitfield continued with evident distaste, was single-mindedly dedicated to expanding Irish influence in the American Church, an evil that the diocese of Baltimore had so far managed to resist. At the time, the primary training ground for Irish priests was, as it still is, St. Patrick's College at Maynooth, in County Kildare, an imposing granite quadrangle on the Oxford model, built by the British in 1795 in hope of inveigling Irish support against Napoleon. American bishops frequently sponsored Irish seminarians who planned to emigrate, and a number of Irish priests had already come over, but there was no formal program. Bishop England visited Maynooth in 1822, 1824, and 1832 to urge a missionary training effort, and in 1833 unsuccessfully urged an American-sponsored Irish training program on his fellow American prelates. Archbishops John Purcell of Cincinnati and Francis Kenrick of Philadelphia traveled to Ireland in 1837 in the same cause, as did the Irish bishops of Newfoundland and Trinidad.

The Irish hierarchy was interested and sympathetic, but cautious. Everyone—including several generations of historians—took at face value John England's outlandish claim that by 1836 eight million Catholics had immigrated to America, and that half of this mythical exodus had been lost to Protestantism. But in meetings in 1837 and 1838, the Irish bishops reluctantly decided against mounting a special American missionary effort. The pre-Cullen era of reform was just gaining momentum, and Ireland itself was still short of good priests, and even shorter of money. More important, as the Irish prelates must have blushed to admit, if Maynooth openly started evangelizing other English-speaking countries, the colonial government might well curtail its funding.

This was the atmosphere in which John Hand, barely thirty years old and only five years a priest, in a tour de force of spiritual zealotry and promotional flimflam, alchemized a vague expression of support from the Irish bishops and some equally vague promises of private financial contributions into papal approval of an Irish missionary college and O'Connell's gift of the Beresford estate. (Cullen, still in Rome, did yeoman work shepherding Hand's proposals through the Vatican, but he had almost certainly been misled on the extent of the backing that Hand enjoyed in Ireland.) Faced with a fait accompli, the Irish hierarchy had little choice but to endorse All Hallows—which was all the easier since no government money was involved—

and Hand and two clerical friends set up shop in Drumcondra with their first two fledgling student-missionaries.

Hand died just four years later, from consumptive pneumonia, which was probably aggravated by the difficulty of heating the cavernous reaches of the Beresford house. The college was still struggling, but the Irish attitude toward overseas proselytizing was already shifting rapidly. The very existence of All Hallows helped focus attention, and by the 1850s, there was a strong overseas demand for Irish priests. Between 1842 and 1890, All Hallows would send almost 1200 priests overseas, more than half of them to America, contributing no less than six American bishops and one cardinal, John Glennon of St. Louis. A prideful sense of an "Irish" presence in the worldwide Catholic hierarchy began to be felt in Ireland. In 1854, for example, Cullen and three Americans—Hughes, Kenrick, and Michael O'Connor of Erie, Pennsylvania—met with Jesuit theologians working on the Vatican's upcoming proclamation of the Immaculate Conception. Kenrick especially was a first-rate thinker, and he and O'Connor proceeded to poke gaping holes in the Jesuits' draft. (Hughes, wisely enough, seems to have kept quiet.) Cullen was delighted, and one observer commented on the fine performance by the "Irish" bishops. At the Vatican Council of 1869, 10 percent of the assembled bishops, seventy-three in all, were native Irishmen, although forty-nine came from overseas dioceses; if overseas prelates of Irish descent were counted, the total "Irish" share rose to 20 percent. The overseas links were cemented as the religious renascence in Ireland produced large surpluses of priests. By the 1870s, it became common practice for newly ordained Irish curates to receive their first assignment in America, postings that could last as long as ten years. Many never went back. Choosing priests for America occasionally raised issues of some delicacy. An 1890 letter from John Ireland in the Maynooth archives wonders who should break the news to a half-dozen students training for their home diocese of Tuam that their first parishes would actually be in Minnesota.

The advent of a transnational Irish Catholicism, this "unique and recent creation," was driven, at bottom, by inexorable facts of demography. In the mid-1830s, there were at most some 600,000 Catholics in America—a polyglot, and scattered, mélange of French, German, Irish, English, Portuguese, and Spanish. Although the Irish bishops may have believed John England's alarms over America's millions of underserved Catholics, they had yet to hear any real clamor from overseas Irish for priests. But the massive Catholic emigrations of the 1840s and 1850s created a completely new situation, and from that point, the relation between the American and Irish churches, while still informal, became close and continuing. The midcentury Irish emigration created the first large, sustained membership growth spurt of the American Catholic Church, and Ireland's efforts to provide for

the spiritual needs of its emigrants laid the groundwork for the long dominance of Irish Americans in the American clergy and hierarchy, as well as in
Canada and Australia.

The Irish emigrations were only the first of four great waves of Catholic
immigration to America in the nineteenth and early twentieth centuries. The
Irish made up almost half of all recorded American immigrants in the 1840s,
not counting the large numbers re-emigrating from Canada; and the Irish exodus was by this time overwhelmingly Catholic. German immigration caught
up to that of the Irish in the 1850s, at just over 1 million each, and greatly sur-
passed the Irish by the 1860s—725,000 to 425,000—peaking at 1.4 million in
the 1880s. But two-thirds of the Germans were Protestant, and for the entire
nineteenth century, Catholic immigrants from Ireland outnumbered those
from Germany by 2:1. Catholic emigration from Germany, in addition, was
more heavily concentrated in the 1870s and 1880s than in earlier periods. As
immigration continued to soar (8.2 million people entered the country from
1900 to 1909, compared with 2.8 million in the 1850s), Italians came to dominate the statistics, contributing almost 2 million people in 1900 to 1909 alone.
Finally, during the three decades from about 1900 through the 1920s, American church rolls were filled out with Poles, Czechs, Slovaks, Slovenians, and
other Catholics fleeing upheavals in Eastern and Central Europe. In the
struggle to impose an ethnic identity on the American Church, therefore—
and there was undeniably such a struggle—the Irish had the double advantage of English-language fluency and of being first on the field.

The urban settlement pattern of the Irish enhanced their advantage.
Much more so than other mainline Christian religions, the Catholic instinct
is to wrap a completely Catholic cocoon around the buzz of transactions of
daily life—not just weddings and baptisms or Sunday services, but also social clubs, schools, hospitals, charitable organizations, professional societies
for Catholic doctors and lawyers, Catholic chapters within trade unions,
Catholic veterans' organizations. The thick textures of Catholic life were easier to maintain in cities; and by the 1880s, some 80 percent of Irish lived in
cities, compared to only 20 percent for other Americans. New York City, already the de facto capital of the American Church, by the 1860s already had
more Irish Catholics than Dublin, and two decades later, Catholics were a
majority of the population. German Catholics were as strongly attached to
their Church as the Irish, but they were mostly small farmers from southern
Germany. Although there were significant German Catholic settlements in
Philadephia, Newark, St. Louis, and a few other cities, most German
Catholics gravitated to the rich soils of the Midwest, where it was harder to
sustain the same dense web of parish influences.

Italian immigrants, despite their large numbers, tended to be only nominal
Catholics and much less rooted in their new country. The first waves of immi-

grants from Italy were mostly seasonal laborers rather than true immigrants. They were overwhelmingly male, often organized as contract labor gangs by a local *padrone,* and up to 80 percent returned to Italy each year when their contracts ended. The waves of Catholics from Central Europe, on the other hand, although they were often intensely religious, arrived long after the organization and spiritual style of the American Church had been firmly established. Except in the few cities like Chicago and Pittsburgh, where Poles, Czechs, Slovaks, and their brethren achieved significant numerical concentrations, they were forced to accommodate to a church that was run mostly by Irish Americans. Consider the plight of the Czech woman who wished she had "an American name like . . . the Kellys, or O'Briens, or Sullivans."

Urban Irish Catholics were widely dispersed throughout the country. Much of America's canal and railroad systems were built by the Irish, and Irish workers gravitated to the cities springing up all along the nation's major transportation arteries. Letters in the All Hallows archives, from alumni and from bishops looking for recruits, offer snapshots of the spreading Irish presence. In 1846, for example, Dubuque was described as "wild Indians in a harsh climate"; in 1850, it was stipulated that "knowledge of French" was a prerequisite; but by 1853, Dubuque claimed 15,000 Catholics "principally Irish or of Irish descent." A writer from Kansas in 1855 tells of large numbers of Irish Catholics "coming in every day." A letter from Vincennes, Indiana, in 1846, complains that while the local clergy were still French, the "great portion" of Catholics were now Irish; the same complaint came from Sault Sainte Marie, Michigan, in 1853. A priest in Nebraska wrote that with the coming of the Union Pacific, "most" of the Catholics were Irish; a priest from California, writing in 1863, called the Irish miners "the props of the church, the support of the clergy & defenders of the faith"; and the archbishop of St. Paul, Thomas Grace, was desperate for Irish priests in 1867, because Irish were arriving in such large numbers.

By the 1860s, new generations of Irish emigrants were bringing the intense devotion to the Church, the acceptance of celibacy, and the deference to the clergy that Cullen had instilled at home. In addition, the unusually even balance of male and female Irish immigrants—Irish girls were preferred for household service—permitted Irish Catholics to marry more easily within their community than other immigrants, helping to preserve traditional marital and religious practices. Whatever the reason, Irish names account for nearly nine out of ten of the young men enrolled at the major American seminaries in the last part of the nineteenth century. American bishops drew a clear distinction between the older generation of Irish clergy—"turbulent, foolish, and ignorant old priests"—and the new post-Cullen generation, wherever they trained. Several American bishops, including Joseph Sadoc Alemany, a Spaniard who relied heavily on All

Hallows to staff his California diocese, began to send other foreign nationals, including Germans, Spaniards, and Portuguese, to All Hallows for proper indoctrination. An alternative was to request foreign-language training so Irish priests could serve non-English speakers, as Thomas Hendrickson, the bishop of Providence, did in 1874 for his large Portuguese population. Hendrickson had managed to recruit one priest from Portugal but, as he wrote to his mentor in Maynooth, "it would be better for me if I lost him where I could not find him again." Priests from Italy were particularly scorned for their ignorance and lack of discipline.

The ethnic backgrounds of American bishops consecrated between 1850 and 1910 clearly shows the rise in Irish influence. From the 1850s through the 1880s, the Irish, including native priests of Irish descent, accounted for roughly half the consecrations, rising to 60 percent in the 1890s, and to 75 percent by the early 1900s, where it remained until the 1960s. The German share, by contrast, fell from 21 percent in the 1870s to only 8 percent in the early 1900s, despite the fact that Germans by that time accounted for at least a quarter of American Catholics. Looked at more closely, the rise in Irish numbers stems almost entirely from their growing share of native-born consecrants. Throughout the entire period, the number of Germans consecrated in America stayed roughly the same from decade to decade, and immigrant German bishops continued to outnumber the native-born by more than 2:1. The predominance of foreign-born bishops is even more pronounced for the French. The consecration rolls for the Irish, however, shifted steadily away from immigrants; by the years 1900 to 1910, when almost two-thirds of all new bishops were natives, 89 percent of the native consecrants were of Irish descent. Priests of German descent later interpreted those numbers to mean that the Irish used their great weight in the hierarchy to ensure that only Irishmen made it onto the nominating lists that went to Rome.

As Irish Catholicism flourished throughout the English-speaking world, Irish churchmen and even Irish Catholic politicians began to conceive of their religious mission in something approaching world-historical terms, a mission much broader than merely serving the needs of overseas Irish. In the historian Patrick Corish's words, "Britain might have a worldwide empire, but there was an Irish world empire too, with even wider bounds, the empire of the Catholic faith." In Paul Cullen's mind, the Irish race and the Catholic faith were interchangeable, whether at home or abroad. And Cullen's great nationalist rival in the Irish hierarchy, John MacHale of Tuam, proclaimed that the Irish had a "divine mission" to "scatter . . . the blessings of the catholic religion over distant lands." Or as an All Hallows president grandly put it, England "carries to the uttermost bounds of the earth her language . . . and everywhere carries with her that damning heresy. . . . But God has coupled with the proud mistress of the seas an humble handmaid. . . . Wherever England is found, Ireland is by her side."

Leading American Irish saw it the same way. W. Bourke Cockran, a New York congressman and a major figure in Irish-American politics at the turn of the century, orated that "The rightful dominion of 'The Fighting Race' is moral primacy of the world—leadership of the forces that make for the progress of civilization throughout Christendom." The drumbeaters were not even always Irish. John Lancaster Spalding, bishop of Peoria, an indefatigable, and unremittingly purple, Catholic pamphleteer, who, except for an Irish great-grandmother, was of English descent, published *The Religious Mission of the Irish Race* in 1880. The Irish, after centuries of English depredations were "left like Christ on the Cross, abandoned seemingly of God Himself . . . [in] the sea of blood, the weary desert of starvation," wandering like "the children of Israel. . . . Nothing was left to them but faith and virtue, and yet they knelt to [the Church] with hearts of purest love nor cared to have a home or country, if she were not there." And so, "the Irish race is the providential instrument through which God has wrought this marvellous revival [of Catholicism] in England, America, and Australia."

American Protestants, of course, could not be expected to accept the new Irish crusade with equanimity, and a great many Americans had long suspected that the Irish Church was up to exactly what Cullen, MacHale, Spalding, and Cockran said it was up to.

CHAPTER 3

The Whore of Babylon Learns How to Vote

The six-hundred-foot spire of the Washington Monument is badly marred by a sharp change in color about a fourth of the way up. Even from a considerable distance, the change, from gray-white to brown-white, is jarringly visible, almost like a stripe. It can be dated, in fact, quite precisely, to March 6, 1854; and like the striations in a geologic rift valley, it is a remnant of deep strains tearing at midcentury America. Violence and the threat of more violence blocked construction of the monument in 1854, and for three decades it sat there, a jagged, 153-foot stump surrounded by building rubble, an embarrassing reminder of nativist hatreds for immigrants, "foreigners," and Catholics; of the paranoid fear that America was being delivered into the hands of Rome, the Whore of Babylon of the Book of Revelations. To understand the events at the monument, however, we must first pan the camera back twenty years to the pleasant town of Charlestown, Massachusetts.

Nuns, Sex, and the Devil

In 1834, Charlestown was a bucolic suburb of some 10,000 people, just to the north of Boston and connected to the city by a wooden bridge. The town's elite were Unitarians and included some of the leading men of Boston, but most Charlestonians made their living as craftsmen and artisans—carpenters, barrel makers, ironworkers—walking to work across the bridge to the Boston shipyards. There were also some 1200 Irish immigrants, mostly unskilled laborers, clustered together in the poorest sections. These were pre-Cullen Catholics, slovenly and raucous, and there was growing friction with the natives. In 1833, shipyard owners broke an artisans' strike by threatening to use Irish strikebreakers; and on Thanksgiving night of the same year, a noisy celebration at an Irish drinking place led to a club-wielding confrontation in which a native was killed.

Seen from the shores of the Mystic River to the north, Charlestown's profile was dominated by three hills in a line from east to west. The first two are Breed's Hill and Bunker Hill. (The battle of Bunker Hill was actually fought on Breed's Hill.) The third and smallest has long since been leveled, although the site is marked by a small stone. It was called Ploughed Hill when it was bombed by the British during the Revolutionary War, but by 1834 it had come to be known as Mt. Benedict and was entirely occupied by a finishing school for young ladies, the Catholic Ursuline Convent. The convent was ringed by an iron fence with an ornate gate at the base of the hill and boasted lovely gardens and elegantly terraced walks for the quiet enjoyment of its residents.

The convent had almost no connection with the Irish Catholics of Charlestown. It was built by Boston's Bishop Benedict Fenwick, a Maryland aristocrat of English descent, as a kind of public relations gesture to underscore Catholicism's steadily improving social status. There were about sixty students, supervised by a dozen nuns, mostly Paris-trained Irishwomen. Tuition fees were steep, and the majority of students seem to have been Unitarians, seeking to develop the tastes in music, French, and literature required of a young lady in Boston society. The Ursuline superior, Sr. Edmond St. George, called upon the best families in her carriage, received visitors with a train of servants, and ruled the convent with the hand of an autocrat. There was no effort to convert students to Catholicism; religious services, indeed, were adjusted to accommodate Protestant sensibilities. Altogether, the Ursuline convent was a most unlikely venue for the nineteenth century's first spectacular outburst of anti-Catholic violence.

The convent burst into unwonted prominence in the late spring of 1834 when a young townswoman, Rebecca Reed, claimed that after converting to Catholicism and becoming a nun, she had "escaped" from the Ursuline Convent. Her account of the adventure was made into a book, *Six Months in a Convent,* that was widely circulated in Charlestown and Boston. (It is a dull affair, obviously written by a Puritan divine, and full of elaborate ceremonials with wax tapers that would shock only a fundamentalist minister.) Sr. Edmond met the charges with disdain—Reed had been a convent serving girl discharged for dishonesty—but she intensified her calling schedule on Charlestown's leading families.

In late July, a real nun made a real escape. Edward Cutter, who owned a brickyard next to the convent, was astonished one night to open his door to a young woman with close-cropped hair and wild eyes, dressed only in a nightshift, begging to be taken to her brother in Boston. The poor woman was Elizabeth Harrison, who had suffered a nervous breakdown and had been confined to the convent infirmary. At her brother's house the next day, she changed her mind and agreed to return to the convent. Once the story was broadcast that she was back in the convent, however, rumors quickly spread that she had been dragged kicking and screaming from her brother's house, and was being confined in a "deep dungeon."

As the Boston and Charlestown papers trumpeted the case of the kidnapped nun, fiery meetings were held in Charlestown. The ringleaders were apparently Cutter, Alvah Kelley, the owner of another nearby brickyard, and the area's Congregationalist ministers. Storming the convent was on the agenda from the very start; one meeting resolved to "leave not one stone unturned of that curst Nunnery that prostitutes female virtue and liberty under the garb of holy religion." On Sunday, August 10, Lyman Beecher, the father of Harriet Beecher Stowe, and a leading Congregationalist minister, delivered a blistering harangue, "The Devil and the Pope of Rome," to a large audience, pointedly denouncing the Ursulines. A number of other Congregationalist ministers delivered violent sermons on the same day. Court records strongly imply that the ministers knew that an attack on the convent was planned for the next night and were purposely whipping up tempers.

On Monday, Charlestown's selectmen, who clearly also knew of the planned attack, made a last-ditch call on Sr. Edmond, and she reluctantly agreed to admit Cutter, whom she considered a friend. Cutter met with Harrison, who was by now calm and self-possessed, and clearly not being held against her will, and made enough of a tour to confirm there was no dungeon. He, Kelley, and the selectmen wrote a statement for the next day's papers exonerating the convent. Cutter and Kelley apparently worked the rest of the day to head off the attack, but events had already passed beyond their control.

Mobs gathered in front of the convent on Monday night, demanding the release of the imprisoned nun. Sr. Edmond, who must have been a formidable woman, met them at the gate, and sent one mob off. When a larger crowd arrived and lit bonfires, she once again went out and stunned them into silence, and for a moment at least, had them in her hand. Then she overstepped: "Disperse immediately," she said, "for if you don't, the Bishop has twenty thousand Irishmen at his command in Boston and they will whip you all into the sea." The crowd responded with an outraged roar, someone fired a musket at the nun, and she beat a retreat to the convent as the mob assaulted the gate. The nuns and girls escaped into the garden—Elizabeth Harrison was in hysterics, blaming herself for the attack—and an older nun who was ill did not survive the night. The mob stormed through the gate and charged the convent, rampaging from room to room, smashing furniture and china, and setting the rooms on fire. Drunken rowdies put on nuns' habits and danced lewdly around bonfires of books and furniture. The fire company arrived but did not intervene, because they were either complicit or frightened.

When the fire forced the mob to retreat from the buildings, platoons of armed men with torches began searching the grounds for the nuns and the girls, who were trapped in the garden against the iron fence. On the verge of panic, they were saved by Cutter and workers from his brickyard, who cut through the fence and spirited them away to Cutter's house. The mob spread through Charlestown, and a number of Irish homes were attacked and burned. Cutter had to move the girls twice more during the night as bands of men pressed their search. The bloody mood finally dissipated with the dawn. The rioters, by then exhausted and happy, many of them still in nuns' habits, twirling rosaries and singing hymns, streamed back across the bridge to Boston, as the convent smoldered up on the hill. The girls, who had been hiding nearby, and anxious to get back to their families, joined in the procession, most of them still in their nightclothes—a scene from Fellini. An eventual trial acquitted everyone but a young boy, who was pardoned because of his age.

The burning of the convent unleashed a great sordid wave of anti-nun literature, including at least three novelistic treatments of the Ursuline Convent, all of it full of a crawly, peek-through-the-curtain prurience—lubricious tales of of satanic rituals behind the granite walls, of nuns as sex slaves, as baby murderers, as torturers, with hints of darker perversions that could not be spoken. The tales follow a consistent pattern: An innocent young girl, full of love for Christ, decides to enter a convent to dedicate her life to God. Her first days at the convent and her novitiate proceed as expected. She is dutiful and prayerful, although her superiors seem stern and cold. But there are mysterious doors she may not enter, ceremonies she may not attend, unexplained footfalls in the night, until finally she becomes a nun and the full horrors of the cloister are revealed.

The paradigmatic nun's tale was Maria Monk's *Awful Disclosures*. Published in 1836, it sold at least 300,000 copies before the Civil War, and probably twice that by the end of the century, for there were many pirate versions. It has been called the *Uncle Tom's Cabin* of anti-Catholicism, or the anti-Catholic equivalent of the anti-Semitic *Protocols of the Elders of Zion*. Maria Monk claimed to have received the veil after a normal preparatory period at the Hôtel Dieu convent in Montreal. On the night of her induction, to her great shock, she discovered that her primary religious duty, as for the other young nuns, was to slake the lusts of monks and priests who came scuttling each night through a tunnel from a nearby monastery. Numerous babies, of course, were born in the convent, and the older nuns made a ceremony of baptizing and then smothering them, to ensure that they "were at once admitted into heaven," tossing the little corpses into a lime pit in the basement. Maria saw three babies murdered, and was forced to participate in the trial and execution of a nun who had protested against the murder of her baby. When the bishop pronounced the death sentence, the victim was tied to a mattress, another mattress was piled on top, and a whole crowd of nuns and priests jumped up and down on her until she died.

Credit: Library of Congress
Maria Monk's Awful Disclosures, *about sex slavery and infanticide in the convent, was the flagship of American anti-Catholic literature. First published in 1836, it was an underground best-seller well into the twentieth century. Maria, shown here in an advertisement for a lecture tour, never got any of the money from the book or her lectures.*

    The actual provenance of Maria Monk's tale was established within a relatively short time of publication. Maria, her mother confirmed, had been an unmanageable child who spent a brief time in a Catholic orphanage in Montreal, although she was not herself Catholic. She had certainly never been a nun, or ever inside the Hôtel Dieu. Maria became pregnant in Montreal and was brought to New York by William Hoyt, a former priest and a leader of the Canadian anti-Catholic movement. (According to Maria's mother, he was also the father of her child.) Hoyt introduced her to a group of nativists in New York, including several leading ministers, who financed her confinement and concocted the story. Besides the ministers, the group included Theodore Dwight, a grandson of Jonathan Edwards, a brother of the late president of Yale, and editor of the nativist *Hartford Courant*.

The Rev. J. J. Slocum, one of the group, later admitted drafting most of the manuscript, but with the close participation of the others. Slocum insisted that he wrote only at Maria's dictation, although a number of scenes—the lecheries, the prisoners in the basement, sexual abuse during confession—track closely with the staple anti-Catholic screeds that the ministers knew so well. Nor were the ministers deluded as to Maria's character; while they were composing a follow-up volume, she took off from New York to be with a lover in Philadelphia. They claimed she had been kidnapped by a band of priests.*

Compounding the disgrace, the ministers were as motivated by money as by religious bile. When the manuscript was finished, it was taken to the publisher James Harper, a friend of Dwight and later a nativist mayor of New York. Harper formed a shell company to distribute the book, since he thought it too racy for his own imprint. Advance publicity included installments of the book's juiciest episodes in a nativist journal, *The American Protestant Vindicator*, and sold-out lectures for Maria. The financial arrangements were disclosed in two separate court actions, in 1836 and 1837, in which Slocum and Maria sued unsuccessfully for their profits. The copyright, and apparently all the profits, accrued to Harper, Hoyt, and one other of the ministers. Poor Maria seems to have gotten nothing at all.

By the time of the court actions, discriminating Protestants were already embarrassed by their initial credulous acceptance of *Awful Disclosures*. The New York publisher William Stone, a fair-minded nativist, called at the convent while in Montreal on business, and persuaded the nuns to permit him to examine the premises. He toured with Maria's book in hand and confirmed that none of its physical descriptions of the convent, which were quite detailed and included a complete floor plan, bore any resemblance to the actual place; nor did a minute inspection of the basements disclose a tunnel to a monastery or a lime pit for infant corpses. Stone wrote a full report that concluded: "I most solemnly believe that the nuns and priests are innocent in this matter"—touching off a baroque intra-Protestant controversy,

---

* It is not likely that Maria herself was deluded. Another "escapee" from the Hôtel Dieu soon appeared on the scene, and she and Maria fell into each other's arms like long-lost friends when they met unexpectedly on a lecture platform. But the second woman was quickly exposed as a fraud, and it is certain that she and Maria had never before met. Maria's impromptu performance was a swindler's reflex; as much as anything else, it aroused the suspicions of previously sympathetic Protestants.

highlighted by the publication of a mock-epic poem satirizing his visit, which was answered by a full-length play.

The discrediting of Maria had little effect on book sales, which continued strong for decades. The anti-Catholic magazines that had first publicized the story, like the *Vindicator* and *The Downfall of Babylon,* became overnight successes, spawning imitators throughout the country. The low point may have been the publication of *Dreadful Scenes in the Awful Disclosures,* a hot-selling folio of "artists' conceptions" of the lurid doings at the Hôtel Dieu. None of it benefited Maria. She was cast aside by her handlers and bore another child out of wedlock in 1838, making no pretense that it had been fathered by a priest. She had a brief failed marriage, became an alcoholic, was arrested for picking pockets in a New York bordello, and died in prison in 1849.

Violence

The burning of the Ursuline Convent was the first salvo in two decades of violence against immigrants and Catholics, to the drum music of unceasing, often wildly paranoid diatribes against the scandals and corruption in the Roman Church. For at least a year after the burning of the convent, Catholics in Boston and Charlestown had to post armed guards around their churches, and Bishop Fenwick was shot in effigy in 1835. A mob burned down most of Boston's Irish quarter in 1837, and another mob attacked an Irish-American militia company. Letters in the All Hallows archives testify to church burnings throughout the country during the 1840s. Irish and native mobs clashed repeatedly in New York, Philadelphia, and Detroit, and pitched battles were a feature of almost every big-city election day. German Catholics were attacked in St. Louis, and later themselves attacked nativist speakers, while German and nativist mobs fought in Louisville and Cincinnati. The Irish, in particular, often gave as good as they got. Irish mobs beat up Protestants in upstate New York and attacked blacks in Philadelphia, and German and Irish workers fought constantly on the railroads. In 1841, in the face of repeated nativist threats, John Hughes made his famous statement that he would turn New York into "a second Moscow" if nativists attacked his churches, and for a long time armed Irishmen did nightly guard duty outside New York's Catholic institutions.

The curve of tension came to a head in Philadelphia in 1844, in what one scholar has described as nothing less than "a brutal ethnoreligious war." Philadelphia had boomed in the 1830s and had the largest concentration of Irish Catholic immigrants outside of New York. The event that precipitated the violence was specifically religious. Francis Kenrick, Philadelphia's archbishop, had quietly negotiated a series of concessions to alleviate Catholic discomfort with Protestant Bible–reading in public schools—a divisive issue in almost every big eastern city. But a garbled story spread through nativist circles that an Irish politician and school board member, Hugh Clark, had forcibly interfered with a Bible lesson in a local school. It soon became clear that Clark had behaved properly, but the local nativist party, the American Republicans, held a protest meeting anyway, and Irish hecklers disrupted the meeting.

In retaliation, the nativists, led by a pugnacious Jew named Lewis Levin, turned out some 3000 people on Monday, May 6, for an anti-Catholic rally in Kensington, just north of the city proper, and the heart of Philadelphia's Irishtown. Fighting broke out when a sudden rainstorm sent the crowd fleeing for the Nanny Goat Market, a roofed open-air bazaar that was clearly Irish territory. A nativist youth fired a pistol, striking an Irish bystander in the face. The Irish pulled their own weapons, but were quickly routed in a hail of bricks and paving stones. Irish musketmen then opened fire on the market from the surrounding houses. Gun battles raged for the next three days, with fatalities on both sides, as nativists mounted repeated assaults on Kensington. The confrontation ended only after the nativists burned out most of the area, killing a number of the Irish and chasing the rest to the woods north of the city, where at least one woman died from exposure. After burning down St. Michael's Church, the mob marched into downtown Philadelphia and burned St. Augustine's Church at Fourth and Vine, near the entrance to the present-day Benjamin Franklin Bridge. The mayor confronted the mob on the steps of St. Augustine's, but a hail of stones sent him scurrying for his life.

A few weeks later, a second round of rioting broke out on the south side of the city, when nativists attacked a church that contained a store of Irish weapons. The militia intervened, and a wild melee ensued, with upper-class cavalry officers, who were perfectly ecumenical in their disdain for the lower classes, charging up and down the dark streets stabbing and shooting at nativists. The nativists strung ropes to trip the troopers' horses and fired barrages of scrap iron from two small cannons stolen from the shipyard. When it was over, thirteen people were dead, including two soldiers, and the number of wounded ran into the scores.

The American tour of the Vatican Archbishop Gaetano Bedini in 1853 touched off another bout of violence. Bedini came as a sort of political ambassador to press the flesh of leading Catholics and bestow the papal blessing throughout the country, despite the advice of the American hierarchy that the trip was ill-advised. For most of his trip Bedini was hounded by Alessandro Gavazzi, the self-styled "Destroyer," a gaunt ex-monk and Italian nationalist, all flowing black hair and smoldering eyes, and a riveting platform presence.

Gavazzi charged Bedini with the execution of hundreds of Italian patriots, and the nativist press took up the cry. Bedini was "the Raven Butcher," "Bedini the Tiger," slayer of countless women and children, who ordered his victims to be scalped, the advance scout for a papal invasion up the Mississippi River.

The hapless priest's effigy was burned in Boston, Baltimore, Cincinnati, and New York. Shots were fired into his room in Baltimore. Armed Irishmen saved him from a lynching in Wheeling, and he was roughly handled in Pittsburgh. Desperate to get away, Bedini had to be smuggled aboard a ship in New York to avoid the angry mob awaiting him at the dock. Gavazzi went on to Canada and started riots in Quebec and Montreal, returning to New York a hero. At about the same time, John C. Orr, a Gavazzi imitator who called himself the Angel Gabriel, left a trail of violence throughout New England, upstate New York, and Brooklyn. There were church burnings throughout the country, and a resurgence of "convent" books. A priest was tarred and feathered in Maine—the experience unbalanced him for the rest of his life— and priests were beaten on their parish rounds. New York was on a knife's edge for weeks as Hughes and nativists traded threats. In Louisville in 1855, at least twenty people died on "Bloody Monday," a day of unrestrained Catholic-nativist violence, openly incited by a nativist mayor.

This was the atmosphere in which the national Know-Nothing party, or the Order of the Star-Spangled Banner, was officially organized in the summer of 1854, on a platform of straightforward nativism and anti-Catholicism, and with the full panoply of secret handshakes, finger signs, codes, alarm signals, costumes, and funny hats that nineteenth-century clubmen so loved. Even before their national convention, Know-Nothings had captured the mayoralty of Philadelphia. In November, they won 63 percent of the vote in Massachusetts, taking every state senate seat and all but two assembly seats, and they took 40 percent of the ballots in Pennsylvania and 25 percent in New York. The following year, the Know-Nothings swept local elections throughout New England and made major inroads in California and the South. One hundred and twenty-one congressmen counted themselves among the Know-Nothings in 1854. When the party nominated former president Millard Fillmore as their candidate for the 1856 election, experienced observers expected the Know-Nothings to inherit the Whig mantle. One leading historian has argued that it was only a north-south split within the Know-Nothings that prevented nativism, rather than antislavery, from becoming the organizing principle of the emerging new Republican Party.

And this was the atmosphere in which the Pope sent a 2000-year-old inscribed stone, taken from the Temple of Concord in Rome, as a gift to the people of America for their national monument to George Washington. Nativists were horrified, and rumors quickly spread that the completion of the monument would be the signal for a papal coup d'état. So in the very early hours of Monday morning, March 6, 1854, a band of men overpowered the monument's watchman, who was probably in on the plot, stole the stone, and either smashed it or dropped it in the Potomac. The next day a Know-Nothing faction took over the Monument Society, which was a private organization. With the society in turmoil, Congress declined to act on a construction appropriation; and so for almost thirty years, the stump of the unfinished monument stood by the Potomac, an ugly reminder of the limits of American tolerance, until saner times finally permitted its completion in 1882.

A Time Out of Joint

The virulence of the nativist reaction took many contemporaries by surprise. Up until the attack on the Ursuline Convent, Catholicism seemed gradually to be blending into the American landscape. In 1832, for example, a Catholic priest, the Rev. Constantine Pise, was appointed chaplain of the United States Congress—the last time a priest has served in that office.

In the 1830s and 1840s, Catholicism had begun to acquire a certain intellectual cachet. The Oxford movement in England, a romantic medieval revival, led to a spate of conversions of Anglican clergymen, most notably John Henry Newman in 1845. America had its own "little Oxford movement," and its own spate of prominent converts like James McMaster, editor of New York's *Freeman's Journal;* Isaac Hecker, founder of the American Paulists, the first native religious order of priests; and Orestes Brownson, a prominent New England writer and editor, and "an alert trend-spotter." McMaster's journal was modeled on the conservative Irish review of the same name, while Hecker's *Catholic World* (in the 1860s) was in the mode of Lord Acton's influential liberal Catholic *Rambler,* and full of learned discourses on the status of women or the inadequacies of Francis Galton's genetic theories of intelligence. A report on the miracle at Lourdes opened with the comment that "our friends may receive this with a smile of incredulity." As late as the 1840s and 1850s, stylized debates between Protestant and Catholic clergymen were almost a regular entertainment. John Hughes's, against a host of adversaries, were the most theatrical, often the most ill-tempered, and always the funniest; the bishop's humor was a fearsome platform weapon. Others were quite high-toned; a debate in Georgia had a panel of judges—three Protestant and three Catholic clergymen with a Jewish rabbi as the swing vote.

Roughly from the War of 1812 to Andrew Jackson's second term, the ideological atmosphere in America was unusually relaxed. By the standards of later decades, the stream of immigration was small. Work and land were plentiful. Europe was at peace and trade was booming. The old Federalistversus-Jeffersonian passions had ebbed. Tolerance is easy in good times; and to a Unitarian or a transcendentalist, like those citizens of Charlestown looking for a good school for their daughters, the old Bible-thumping diatribes against Catholicism looked just a bit silly.

The national unraveling about 1835 was all the more of a shock. Suddenly there were riots everywhere, to the point where they were a diplomatic embarrassment. *Niles' Weekly Register* noted only one major civil disturbance in 1832, but four in 1833, twenty in 1834, and fifty-three in 1835, and could have listed hundreds more. In the Northeast and coastal cities, violence was most often directed against immigrants and Catholics, but in the border states, there were bloody clashes between proslavers and Free-Soilers. Nat Turner's rebellion came in 1831, and there was a week of antiblack rioting in Washington, D.C., in July 1835. An angry mob chased one of Andrew Jackson's mixed-race servants into the White House and would have invaded the mansion itself had troops not intervened. Student rampages and a takeover of the administrative offices closed down Harvard University in the spring of 1834, just a few months before the attack on the Ursuline Convent. The riots in Philadelphia were preceded by many smaller incidents, involving Irish against blacks, Irish weavers against Protestant weavers, and occasionally Irish and Protestant workers against the city's establishment.

A comparison with the America of the late 1960s is altogether apt. Traditional authority structures were dissolving, and every institution was under strain. In part, it was simply that the reality of the American revolution was catching up to its rhetoric. Long-standing habits of deference were breaking down; John Adams's "natural aristocracy"—men of means, education, and civic virtue—found themselves losing control of affairs. It is probably not irrelevant that the Congregationalist church was disestablished in Massachusetts in 1833, a year before Lyman Beecher and his fellow Congregationalists began their propaganda war against the Ursulines.

Prolonged prosperity sparked a fever of speculation and debt. Jefferson's solid yeomen became deft hands at mortgage roulette, buying land on credit, making it minimally productive, without scrupling at destructive husbandry, selling out at a profit, and moving on. The antihero of James Fenimore Cooper's 1841 satire *Autobiography of a Pocket Handkerchief* is Henry Halfacre, a kind of proto–Michael Milken who became very rich speculating in New York town lots, although "Mr. Halfacre's bonds, notes, mortgages, and other liabilities [were] some drawback on this prosperity." Jackson's second-term war with the Bank of the United States removed the restraints from state-bank paper-money printing presses, and legislatures pumped out bonds for wildly impractical improvement and settlement schemes. Inflation in some western states reached Weimar Republic proportions; honest farmers went to town with wagonloads of banknotes to buy a few weeks' supplies.

America, therefore, was already slipping its psychological moorings just as it was hit by the great wave of Famine-inspired Irish immigration. The economy was veering between extremes of inflation and depression, revolutions in Europe were disrupting trade, the war with Mexico was wildly unpopular. Henry David Thoreau meditated publicly on civil disobedience, and the sectional divisions that foreshadowed the Civil War dominated national politics. A rural nation found itself confronting runaway urban growth. New York City's population quadrupled in the thirty years to 1860; Chicago's grew even faster. In 1820, there were only twelve cities with more than 10,000 people; in 1860, there were 101 such cities and eight with more than 100,000. One out of every five Americans lived in a city by 1860, up from only 6 percent in 1820.

The feeling of a world awry easily slipped into a racist reaction against the new immigrants. Here is the New York City diarist George Templeton Strong in 1848 (he was building a house): "Hibernia came to the rescue yesterday morning; twenty 'sons of toil' with prehensile paws supplied them by nature with evident reference to the handling of the spade and the wielding of the pickaxe and congenital hollows on the shoulder wonderfully adapted to make the carrying of the hod a luxury instead of a labor." Charles O'Conor—whom Strong detested while grudgingly admitting his abilities—was still working his way up the ladder of the New York bar when he lamented, "This is an English colony [with] the true Saxon contempt for everything Irish."

To be fair to the nativists, the Irish imposed immense public costs. More than 80 percent of the Irish settled in cities, so by themselves they accounted for a sizable fraction of the urbanizing trend and for much of the frightening growth in the armies of unemployed laborers. The severe shortfalls in sewage, water supply, police, and sanitary services that plagued midcentury cities could, without bigotry, be traced directly to the Irish. Poor-relief expenditures in Boston quadrupled between 1840 and 1860. The Irish accounted for three-quarters of Boston's arrestees and police detainees by the 1860s, and 55 percent of New York's. Irish pigs running loose in lower Manhattan were the despair of New York health authorities, and former mayor Philip Hone remarked that "Bishop Hughes deserves a cardinal's hat at least for what he has done in placing Irish Catholics on the necks of native New Yorkers." An *Atlantic Monthly* columnist lamented, almost with disbelief, that just a few decades before Boston could brag of but "little poverty, little gross ignorance, and little crime." Even Irish apologists like Thomas D'Arcy McGee admitted that the Irish needed time and understanding to learn the habits and disciplines required in their new country. Old-line Americans, already under siege by the Henry Halfacres of the world, found the success of Irish-based political machines especially galling—Irishmen "fresh from the bogs . . . led up to vote like dumb brutes." Anger against the Irish naturally translated into anti-Catholicism. Few bishops aside from Hughes would have accepted that the American Church was explicitly Irish, but their behavior belied their words. Archbishop Kenrick spearheaded Catholic fund drives for Daniel O'Connell in the 1830s, and the Irish could usually get legal help from the Church when they ran afoul of the law.

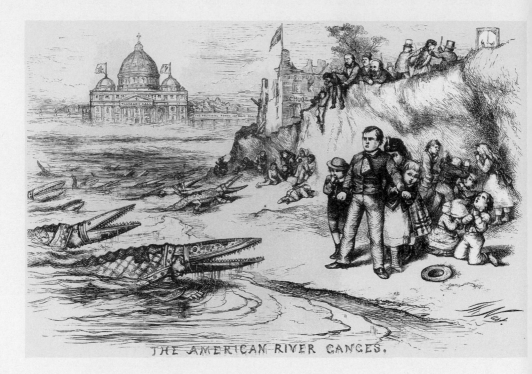

THE AMERICAN RIVER GANGES.

Credit: Library of Congress

"The American River Ganges" is perhaps the most brilliantly poisonous of Thomas Nast's popular anti-Catholic cartoons. The crocodiles' jaws are bishops' miters, and note the bishops' underslung jaws, assumed to be an Irish racial trait. On the cliff above, Miss Liberty is being led to the scaffold, the public school system is in ruins, and in the distance, the Irish and papal flags fly over the nation's capital.

The comparative smoothness of German settlement is instructive. German immigration had outstripped that of the Irish by the mid-1850s, and a significant minority of the Germans were Catholic. There was a scattering of anti-German nativist incidents, of which the worst may have been the

Louisville riot, the most poorly documented of the major outbreaks. Most German immigrants, however, regardless of their religion, were bourgeois farmers who spread themselves thinly through the Midwest, where they drew little attention. And even the large German concentrations in cities like Philadelphia and New York were rarely a charge on the public purse. On the third day of the Kensington riots, the mob marched right past a German Catholic church on its way to burn St. Augustine's.

Unsettled times breed conspiracy theories, and in midcentury there were three. The "Slaveocracy" was the nightmare of abolitionists. Andrew Jackson was haunted by the "Monster Bank," a plutocratic spiderweb enmeshing the common man in coils of debt. And the third was "Popery," a worldwide plot to install the rule of priests and princes. All were in various ways absurd, but none was necessarily crazy. The slave power was formidable, and so was the power of the Bank of the United States. And reasonable Protestants, who were neither bigots nor paranoiacs, had ample grounds for concluding that the Roman Catholic Church was not a friend of democracy.

Roman Catholicism and Democracy

The Pope headed a government as well as a Church. The Papal States were twenty provinces containing some 3 million souls in a broad swath through north central Italy. (Napoleon had taken them over in 1809, clapping the Pope in prison, but they were restored to the papacy after Waterloo.) The papal government was by common consent the worst in Europe—"inefficient and disorganized, riddled with dishonesty, self-seeking and favoritism, [run by] clerics who had little training or interest in their duties." Rebellions broke out constantly, and popes were repeatedly forced to call in Austrian or French troops, which hardly endeared them to Italians. The Pope's own armies were notoriously indisciplined; the unrestrained brutality of troops under Cardinal Albani at Cesena in 1832 and the behavior of Pius IX's Swiss troops at Perugia in 1859 were two widely publicized incidents. Even Prince Metternich, the Habsburg minister who masterminded the restoration of Europe's *anciens régimes,* found himself in the unwonted position of urging political reform as a condition of sending troops. One of Metternich's generals, after yet again retrieving a pope's military chestnuts, wrote home: "You can prop up a corpse, but to make it walk is impossible."

Pius IX (reigned 1846–1878) was hailed as a liberal reformer when he took office, but that was only by contrast to his troglodytic predecessor, Gregory XVI, who had forbidden railroads as the work of the devil. Pius was a devout priest of considerable charm and disarming humor, but the headlong political evolution of Europe was quite beyond his comprehension;

someone said that "liberal ideas filtered into his head like snow blowing in around the cracks in a closed window." When revolutions swept Europe in 1848, Pius sided with Catholic Austria against Italian nationalists. In retaliation, the nationalists marched on Rome, and Pius, in disguise, fled to the protection of Naples, where he bemoaned the inconstancy of his "ingrate" subjects until combined French and Austrian arms returned him to his see two years later.

With cardinals leading repressive armies, the papacy could hardly expect a good press in America. The monk Gavazzi's charges against Archbishop Bedini, for example, were not completely outlandish. Bedini had been governor of Bologna when Ugo Bassi, a popular priest who was one of Garibaldi's lieutenants, and fifty followers, were captured and summarily executed by pro-papal Austrian troops in 1851. Bedini had not yet been restored to his government, and it is highly unlikely that he ordered the executions or even knew of them in advance. But as Horace Greeley pointed out in a reasoned column in the *New York Tribune*, the Austrians were under papal, and in Bologna under Bedini's, jurisdiction, so a presumption of responsibility was altogether appropriate. Pius, unfortunately, saw his civil jurisdiction as the foundation stone of his papacy, and he peppered bishops with calls to "inflame more and more daily the faithful entrusted to your care so . . . they do not cease either defending the Catholic Church and the Holy See or protecting the civil dominion of the same see." Hughes, whose enthusiasm often outran his common sense, wanted to raise volunteer American troops for the Vatican, as Cullen had done in Ireland; fortunately, his proposals, which were in letters to Rome, never got into the newspapers.

As far as Rome was concerned, all the world's ills could be traced to liberalism. Nineteenth-century liberals held, with John Stuart Mill, that "the only purpose for which power can be rightfully exercised over any member of a civilized community . . . is to prevent harm to others. His own good, either physical or moral, is not a sufficient warrant." From that principle flowed all the ideological apparatus of the liberal state—freedom of the press, of religion, of speech, from search or arrest without warrant. People are to make up their own minds and within very broad limits left to behave as they choose. To a Catholic pope, as to an English puritan, both steeped in a two-millennium tradition of aboriginal human depravity, this could only be the work of Satan. What was a government for, if not to enforce morality? Who could believe that people would behave well of their own volition? And was it not self-evident that a moral government needed the firm direction of revealed religion?

Successive popes drew the appropriate conclusions in withering encyclic blasts: Pius VI—in 1775—condemned "accursed philosophers . . .

proclaiming that men are born free, subject to no one." Leo XII inveighed against "tolerance" in 1829, but urged bishops "not to lose heart. We are confident that you will have the powerful support of the secular princes." Gregory XVI in 1832 said it was "insanity to believe in liberty of conscience and worship or of the press," a doctrine that Pius IX reiterated in 1864, underscoring the word *insanity*. Almost every act of Pius's long papacy was in furtherance of his total war against liberalism. He encouraged the French journalist Louis Veuillot, who wrote that "liberty is . . . the parent of all human ills," and warmly applauded Louis-Napoleon's 1851 coup against the Second Republic. A main purpose for proclaiming the dogma of the Immaculate Conception (i.e., the Blessed Mother's freedom from original sin) in 1854 was to emphasize how depraved the *rest* of humanity was, and consequently how unfit for self-government.

Pius's most famous broadside was the "Syllabus of Errors" in the form of an appendix, or a papal allocution, attached to an 1864 encyclical. (It is reported that the cardinals of the Sacred Office suggested this form to avoid taking the heat for so pugnacious a document themselves.) The Syllabus condemned eighty separate errors, most of them fairly unremarkable. But the final grouping covered "today's liberalism" and, on a fair reading, condemned the core propositions of the American Bill of Rights, including freedom of speech, press, and religion, ending with the ringing declaration that the Pope would never "reconcile himself with progress, with liberalism, and with modern civilization." Bishops anxiously inquired whether this was sacred dogma. It made no difference, replied the Vatican's resident Jesuits, for not to adhere to the Syllabus would be "a grave sin against obedience." John McCloskey wrote dryly to Martin Spalding, the archbishop of Baltimore: "It is consoling to think and believe that our Holy Father has in all his official acts a light and guidance from on High—for according to all the rules of mere human prudence and wisdom the encyclical with its annex of condemned propositions would be considered ill-timed."

French liberals saved the day by deciding that the Pope had proposed only a "thesis"—the ideal regime in the ideal Christian state. It was up to the clergy and laity to develop a "hypothesis"—or the day-to-day compromises that worked in the real world. Parisian intellectuals had great fun with this argument: "Thesis: The Pope orders Jews to be burned at the stake; Hypothesis: M. Dupanloup [the liberal bishop of Orleans] goes to dinner with M. Rothschild." Intellectual fig leaf it may have been, but it provided some cover, and Pius mercifully refrained from condemning it. Archbishop Spalding even managed to sound aggrieved when he protested: "To stretch the words of the Pontiff . . . so as to make them include the state of things established in this country by our Constitution in regard to liberty of conscience, or worship, or of the press, were manifestly unfair and unjust."

Pius turned the screws yet again in 1869 by summoning an ecumenical council, a meeting of all the world's bishops, and the first such gathering since the great eighteen-year-long council at Trent three centuries before, when the church adopted its official hard line against Protestantism.* Pius was clearly in the same no-compromise mood and, to the great alarm of Catholic liberals, had compressed the cause of reform to a single issue—his own infallibility in matters of faith and morals—a move the Vatican had been hinting at for years. Catholics had long taken for granted that the *Church* was infallibly guided by the Holy Spirit in matters of dogma, but the details of that guarantee—that is, exactly *when* the Church was speaking under divine guidance—were vague. The broadest consensus held that the Church spoke infallibly when the Pope and the bishops of the world met in council and agreed on doctrine. A teaching that infallibility resided in the Pope himself would seem to make councils, bishops, even the principle of consultation, all quite superfluous.

To the bishops of the liberal minority (dubbed the "Gallicans" after Félix Dupanloup's party in France), this was virtually a coup d'état, a naked power play by the papal party, which included the Vatican cardinals and bishops, powerful conservatives like Paul Cullen and the English Cardinal Henry Manning, and the majority of the French who were allied with Napoleon III. (They were called "ultramontanes," because they took their cues from "over the mountains" in Rome.) The Gallicans in France deluged the Vatican with learned disquisitions on the erroneousness of the new doctrine, and a council of German bishops sent a strongly worded memorial, drafted by J. J. I. Dollinger, Germany's leading theologian, who eventually broke with the Church. Papal infallibility arguably also implied doctrinal status for the Syllabus, foreclosing bishops from adapting their religion to secular democratic regimes, as the Americans were trying to do. Peter Kenrick, Francis's brother, and longtime archbishop of St. Louis, wrote: "The Council seems to have been convoked for the special purpose of defining the doctrine of Papal Infallibility and enacting the propositions of the Syllabus as general laws of the Church. Both objects are deemed by a minority, of which I am one, inexpedient and dangerous and sure to meet with serious resistance." Embarrasingly enough, a widely used American catechism, with an eye obviously cocked at nativist critics, taught its readers:

Q: Must not Catholics believe the Pope in himself to be infallible?
A: This is a Protestant invention; it is no article of the Catholic faith.

---

* During the preparatory run-up to the Council, the Vatican asked the American bishops about the problem of Protestant servants in Catholic homes. (English and German governesses were the rage among the French nobility.) The Americans replied that they had that one under control.

War was raging throughout the Papal States in 1869, but bells were rung throughout Rome, and cannons boomed from the Pope's fortress at Castel Sant'Angelo, and the Council opened on schedule on December 8, Pius's new feast of the Immaculate Conception. Some 750 bishops attended; the Pope, who was picking up lodging expenses, said he was in a race between infallibility and insolvency. The outcome of the Council was never in doubt; the French and Italian ultramontanes—there were 200 Italian bishops, almost a solid phalanx for the Pope—could have carried the day by themselves. The issue was only whether the new doctrine would pass by unanimous acclamation, as Pius wanted. In Pius's view, if he was infallibly guided by the Holy Spirit, his conviction of infallibility must be correct, so the bishops had little choice but to see it the same way. When the Gallicans dug in their heels, Pius took personal command of the Infallibist forces: The doctrinal committees were chosen *voce,* rather than by ballot, and packed with Infallibists. Matters discussed on the floor were strictly limited to ultramontane formulations. Bishops were forbidden to discuss council affairs with outsiders, although there was much leaking and gossip. The Pope accused the liberals of the sin of pride; he called them "unworthy and heretical"; and he stormed about their "tricks, the calumnies, the sophisms." He refused to permit a Vatican Mass upon the death of a well-known French Catholic liberal, Comte Charles de Montelambert, and in a famous confrontation with a cardinal who wondered whether the new doctrine was consistent with received tradition, Pius reputedly thundered, "I am tradition!"

The Americans were a noisy but uninfluential presence. They objected mightily to the steamroller tactics of the ultramontanes. (The Americans were the most diligent in holding their own national and regional councils, and the best schooled in parliamentary procedure.) They were also frustrated by the Italian bishops' habit of speaking a kind of Italian-Latin creole. Despite months practicing their Latin, most of the Americans couldn't follow the voice votes. Peter Kenrick and Martin Spalding got high grades for reasoned presentations of the minority position—although the Italians thought Kenrick displayed "a crudity that was quite American"—and Spalding worked closely with the Gallicans in drafting a final set of alternatives. Augustin Verot of Savannah became the Council's enfant terrible, openly accusing the ultramontanes of factionalism—he was almost shouted off the platform—and speaking as often, and as bluntly, as any other bishop, to the point where Spalding was embarrassed.

In the end, the Pope did not get his unanimous vote. No one was willing to challenge him directly on the principle of infallibility—although it is not true, as sometimes claimed, that there were no "Fallibists" at the Council; they simply kept quiet. The opposition consolidated around the safer position that the declaration was merely "inopportune." The first roll-call vote listed 451 yeas, 88 nays, 62 yeas with reservations, and 76 abstentions. A third of the bishops, that is, had withheld a clear affirmative, and the Inopportunists hoped that was enough to force a compromise. But the ultramontanes would not be moved, and the Inopportunists ultimately either bowed to the pressure or left Rome to avoid casting a negative vote. The final count was 535-2, with the nays cast by an Italian and by an American, Edward Fitzgerald of Little Rock, who had said little during the debates. Twenty-five Americans voted for the final canon; twenty-two went home before the vote. Peter Kenrick may actually have considered apostasizing, although the rest of the liberals consoled themselves with the same sophistries that had helped them swallow the Syllabus. Kenrick pointedly absented himself from his diocese during the celebration of Pius's Silver Jubilee in 1871.

Pius's Council was never officially closed. During the recess following the vote on infallibility, the Franco-Prussian War ended with the French collapse at Sedan. French troops were withdrawn from Rome, and Victor Emmanuel, the constitutional monarch of a unified Italy, moved on the Pope. Victor generously offered Pius autonomy within the Roman "Patrimony," the area immediately around the Vatican. Pius stubbornly refused to treat, forcing Victor to bombard Rome. After a purely symbolic resistance—Pius was sensible enough to avoid a bloodbath, although there were casualties— the Pope retreated within the Vatican, where he remained for the rest of his life at Victor's sufferance, an old man with flowing white hair, refusing to recognize the Italian government outside his window, a worldwide symbol of resistance to everything new and disturbing.

The Political Problem in America

The humiliating end to the papacy's thousand-year tradition of civil rule was overbalanced by the complete triumph of Pius's ultramontane cause. Pius reversed the long trend toward semiautonomous national Catholic churches, and reestablished the papacy as the center of world Catholicism. Orestes Brownson once complained to Isaac Hecker that Rome would have to decide whether "we who love our country" but don't wish her "brought under the political system of Europe are to be sustained or to be discouraged." Unfortunately, Rome had decided.

In America, the Pope's attacks on liberalism focused unflattering attention on the Church at a time when it was enjoying lusty growth and acquiring considerable political and financial clout. By the 1850s, Catholicism was America's fastest-growing religion, and the only one with a well-organized national machinery. Most of the bishops, particularly the Irish bishops, had been trained in the same small number of institutions in America or Ireland, knew one another well, and stayed in close touch. There were regular councils to ensure that everyone was reading from the same playbook, and outsiders rarely saw any hint of the fierce arguments inside the Church. Catholics scoffed when Protestants worried that they were marching to a single master plan, but it could easily look that way to reasonable observers. By the standards of other denominations, it was true.

Adding to Protestant disquiet were two specifically American conflicts—over religious education in schools and over lay control of church property. Both issues flared sporadically all around the country for many years. But fate had it that both came to a head in New York, where the tone of the debate was set by John Hughes. Unlike most of his colleagues, Hughes reveled in a good fight, and once he got his teeth into an issue, he usually forced people to take sides.

The traditional American Protestant attitude toward education was as narrow-minded as the Pope's. Schools in America were of religious origin, and retained the religious impulse long after education became a public responsibility. For Protestants, raised on "covenant" religion, the Bible served as a kind of proto-Constitution and was the central text for training citizens. In most major cities, Protestant foundations—in New York, the Public School Society—supervised curricula, chose textbooks, and ensured appropriate prominence for the Bible. And in New York, as elsewhere, curricula and texts were often blatantly anti-Catholic and nativist. *The Irish Heart,* a New York textbook, for instance, wrote of its fictional hero, Phelim Maghee: "When Phelim had laid up a good stock of sins he now and then . . . got relaaf by confissing them out o' the way . . . and sealed up his soul with a wafer, and returned quite invigorated for the perpetration of new offenses."

In 1840, Hughes began documenting the long list of egregious insults to Catholics in the city curriculum and drew a sympathetic response—particularly from his friend William H. Seward, the state's Whig governor, a religious skeptic who was interested in immigrant education. Hughes took the high road in the schools debate, and when he was at his best, he could be a dazzling oratorical presence—wise, moderate, humorous, powerfully logical and persuasive. Hughes's demands were not at all outrageous: he merely asked that public schools concentrate on secular subjects and leave religion to the churches. The leadership of the Public School Society seemed to agree, and for a while it appeared that pure force of reason would carry the day. But prospects for an agreement were scuttled by a strong nativist and fundamentalist reaction, led by Henry Ketchum, a demagogic lawyer whom even the anti-Catholic George Templeton Strong called "a foolish fat bag of infragrant flatulence."

After two narrow defeats in the city's Common Council, and another in the state legislature, Hughes decided to flex a little muscle, focusing his main fire on the Democrats, who had been taking the Irish vote for granted. John Hughes on a political stump was a nativist's bad dream, and he turned the fall election into a single-issue campaign on the school bill. There stands a candidate with "a red hot iron," Hughes told his crowds,

> But suppose you ask him, what he means to do with that red hot iron? He will be sure to evade the question. He will tell you of a glorious liberty and equality . . . and all that; but press him for an answer. Tell him you want to know what he intends to do with that red hot iron [*laughter*]. "Oh," he will say. "I am a liberal man. I intend to do whatever is right. My friends, you know me . . . I belong to the party" [*great cheering and laughter*]. But press him for an answer, and make him tell you what his ideas are about the red hot iron [*laughter*].

The results were unambiguous. Democrats who lined up with Hughes won in the city; Democrats who temporized lost. Before the election, Hughes published a slate of candidates who were sound on the school issue. The "Carroll Hall Slate," named for the hall where Hughes held his rallies, was arguably the only Catholic political-party slate in American history. When the legislature reconvened in 1842, city Democrats meekly fell in line on the school bill, and it passed just in time for Hughes to withdraw another Catholic slate that had been readied for the elections in April. Having demonstrated his power, and with politicians all over the state speculating on his next move, Hughes, his theatrical sense intact, coyly withdrew from the field. When politicos and journalists flocked to hear him lecture right after the legislative session, he delivered a learned disquisition on Pius VII. In the longer run, Hughes and his fellow bishops rejected secular schools for Catholics, and created a completely separate Catholic system of education. But the display of raw political power was unnerving, the more so since it came at a time when the Catholic population was just beginning to swell.

Trusteeism was a second area where Church practice clashed with the American civil tradition. Almost all states required that religious property be held by lay trustees. The laws were not specifically directed against Catholics—the New York law dated from a time when Catholicism was still illegal—but expressed a historic suspicion of highly organized churches, whether Anglican or Roman. Lay trustees of Catholic churches, particularly in the earliest days, acted pretty much like Protestants: they managed the money and the property, and, as often as not, hired and fired pastors. As the Church began to grow in the first part of the nineteenth century, the rights of trustees were a constant sore point with bishops, the more so since trustees did not hesitate to appeal their grievances directly to Rome. Trustees in Philadelphia were especially stiff-necked, and as a young priest, Hughes witnessed several unpleasant confrontations.

Almost as soon as he arrived in New York, Hughes began circumventing the trustee laws. Since many churches were in financial difficulty, he could usually gain control as a condition of diocesan bailouts, leaving a figurehead lay board in place, but with himself clearly in charge. He allowed trustees limited oversight of funds and buildings, but they had no say in choosing priests or in other ecclesiastical matters. Parishes without financial problems could usually be brought to heel by the sheer force of Hughes's personality. And as Hughes's tenure in New York lengthened, he built hundreds of new churches, schools, convents, orphanages, and other institutions, keeping title in his own name from the outset. His methods inevitably provoked the stormy confrontations that Hughes thrived on. A trustee of old St. Patrick's, which was deeply in debt, once threatened to "horsewhip" the bishop if he showed his face at the church. Hughes promptly appeared, and according to the *New York Herald,* unleashed "a torrent of indignant scathing eloquence upon the devoted heads of the clergy and trustees" and, of course, got his way. At the height of the Know-Nothing movement, New York nativists pushed a strong trustee bill through the legislature, but Hughes simply ignored it, and it was quietly repealed in 1863. The governor, a Democrat, made Hughes a gift of the repeal bill's signing pen.

Almost all other bishops sooner or later took their cue from New York. Church administration was gradually removed from the hands of trustees, and trustee laws drifted into desuetude. The specter of central control of Catholic treasuries, along with the well-coordinated national Catholic policy machinery, could alarm even the most tolerant Protestant. A new edition of a popular anti-Catholic tract, originally written in the eighteenth century, included a special appendix detailing with reasonable accuracy the vast growth of Catholic property holdings. Little editorial comment was required. Hughes could not resist rubbing it in. In 1850, amid a flurry of Protestant worries about Catholic proselytizing, he told them that they had good cause for worry. Roman Catholicism, he said:

> will convert all Pagan nations, and all Protestant nations, even England with her proud Parliament. . . . Everybody should know that we have for our mission to convert the world—including the inhabitants of the United States—the people of the cities, and the people of the country, the Officers of the Navy and the Marines, commander of the Army, the legislatures, the Senate, the Cabinet, the President and all.

Groping Toward Accommodation

By the time of the Civil War, the great majority of American Catholics were Irish-born, and the two questions, of reaching a political accommodation with the Church, and with the Irish, had become closely intertwined. (It was not until the 1870s, when Bismarck cracked down on the German Catholic Church, that German Catholic immigrants began to arrive in large numbers.)

The Civil War reinforced two stereotypes about Irish Catholics. The first was that they were racists, which has served to justify the sometimes sneering condescension of upper-class Protestants toward Catholics ever since. The second was that they were exceptionally patriotic and loyal Americans, who suffered a disproportionate share of casualties in the fight for the Union. If there is a single event that illuminates the roots of both stereotypes, it is the New York City draft riots, the most lethal riot in American history, which stretched over five days in the summer of 1863, leaving 105 dead and thousands injured.

Irish Catholics were overwhelmingly Democratic in the 1860s. New York had the largest concentration of Irish Catholics in the country, and the largest of any city in the world, including Dublin. New York was also the stronghold of "Copperhead" Democracy, the wing of the Democratic Party that believed that the war was being fought wastefully and much too bloodily (which was certainly true); and that it could be settled quickly if only the Union would agree to leave slavery intact (which was possibly true). To a Democratic workingman, abolitionism was simply a tactic in the larger strategy of New England manufacturers to keep the South dependent. The New England interests clearly made enormous profits from the war; and the close ties among abolitionists, nativists, and anti-Catholics were all too plain. Certainly, the concern of abolitionists like the Beechers for distant black masses was not matched by corresponding sympathy for the Irish poor at home.

The conscription law of 1863 was a final straw. The war had been going badly, casualties were very high, and the law reeked of class bias—an exemption could be purchased for $300, a year's pay for a laborer. Workers bitterly compared the price the government put on their lives with the $1000 price of a slave. The frequent use of blacks as strikebreakers in New York added to the hostility, the more so since blacks were exempt from conscription and stood ready to replace white workers being hauled off to the war. It was also widely believed, and was possibly true, that conscription quotas had been juggled to punish Democratic precincts, especially in New York. Finally, there is some evidence—Hughes believed it—that Republican businessmen were using conscription to break local craft unions.

The draft riots are often treated as race riots, but they began as a fairly organized strike by craft and industrial workers, including natives, Germans, and Irish. The strike action followed a series of unrestrained speeches by Horatio Seymour, the Copperhead governor, virtually urging resistance to conscription. Violence escalated over the next two days, as the mobs first attacked the homes and businesses of prominent Republicans and abolitionists, and then attacked individual blacks. By the second and third day, the mobs were predominantly Irish, but the Irish firemen who had initially co-operated with the strikers had returned to their posts. The choice of targets was frequently odd. Brothels along the waterfront were systematically destroyed, although prostitutes were not injured. Irish industrial workers and craftsmen were more likely to attack white Republicans, while assaults by mobs of Irish laborers tended to be more overtly racial and included attacks on Chinese peddlers as well as on blacks. On the fourth and fifth day, the disturbances were put down by some 10,000 militiamen and volunteers. By modern standards, the authorities used great force, including firing cannons on crowds, but the government was extremely restrained compared with, say, the brutal crushing of the Paris Commune in 1871.

Some of the riot murders were truly horrific. There were a half-dozen lynchings of blacks, and a black man's corpse was dragged through the

Credit: Museum of the City of New York
The New York Draft Riots of 1863 were the bloodiest in American history. The riots were sparked by real inequities in Civil War draft legislation and union-busting tactics by local Republicans, but they quickly turned into race riots. The engraving shows the burning of a colored orphans' asylum by a drunken, predominantly Irish, mob.

streets by its genitals. A militia colonel (an Irish Catholic) who had fired on a mob was beaten to death over six excruciating hours by a mostly female crowd, and police who lived in Irish neighborhoods were often in great danger. On the other hand, of the 105 deaths, only twenty-one—eleven blacks and ten soldiers or police—could be traced directly to the rioters; most of the rest, presumably, were killed by the authorities. George Templeton Strong assumed that only "Celtic brutes" participated in the riots but did not mention that the police and firemen and a good number of the militia who quelled the disturbance were also Irish Catholics. The Republicans of the elite Union League, like Strong, were bloodthirsty in their demands for more force. To Strong, the only solution was "heroic doses of lead and steel. . . . For myself personally, I would like to see war made on Irish scum as in 1688."

Hughes put in a cameo appearance at the behest of the governor and other authorities, who assumed that "the Irish" would unfailingly do his bidding. The old warrior was within months of his death, physically unable to offer Mass. His voice was failing and he usually had to speak from a chair. He did his best, probably to little effect, urging crowds to protest peacefully, although he raised Republican eyebrows by agreeing that the conscription law was unfair.

Making all allowances, the Irish and their Church were racist, even by the standards of the time. New York's otherwise highbrow semiofficial Catholic journal, the *Freeman's Journal,* was often crudely so, routinely printing articles about "ugly black niggers." (It was shut down by federal authorities during the war.) More reprehensible was the fact that, despite decades of importuning by abolition societies, Rome had never unequivocally condemned slavery, mostly out of fear of offending Spanish and Portuguese royalty. Gregory XVI finally condemned the slave trade in 1839, but not slavery itself. If pressed, the Vatican fell back on the medieval argument that, while slavery was an evil, it was not an unmitigated evil, for it allowed slaves to be Christianized. Although the Vatican was officially neutral during the Civil War, Pius IX made no secret of his sympathies for the Confederacy. However deplorable its social system, the South at least was not infected with the virus of liberalism.

Union armies, Grant's in particular, did not trust Catholic bishops. Southern bishops generally supported their government but were free to travel and communicate across lines. (Ever watchful of his Democratic flank, Lincoln always intervened to ensure that bishops were tenderly handled.) Peter Kenrick in St. Louis refused to let his priests take a loyalty oath, a position eventually upheld by the Supreme Court. Charles O'Conor, who was close to Hughes, argued prominently that interfering with slavery was unconstitutional—essentially John C. Calhoun's position—and offered to defend Jefferson Davis gratis after the war.

Cincinnati's John Purcell was one of the very few out-and-out abolitionists among the American hierarchy; the rest simply hewed to the Vatican line. Francis Kenrick's moral theology textbook (1841) taught that slavery was acceptable if slaves were humanely treated and that the immorality of the slave trade did not invalidate title to slaves acquired by inheritance. Hughes was an ardent Unionist and drew much criticism from fellow bishops for his support of the government's war policies. In private he advised the government that "Catholics will fight to the death" to uphold the Union and federal law, but never for the abolition of slavery. He himself believed that slavery was legitimate. As a young man, he once worked as overseer of a slave crew and was deeply offended by the experience. But his brother-in-law, William Rodrigue, the co-architect of St. Patrick's, came from a slaveholding Santo Domingan family and seems to have converted Hughes. The Church followed the normal practice of segregating its institutions, although there were, in any case, very few black Catholics. William Elder of Natchez was one of the few bishops who actively proselytized among free blacks. Several bishops owned slaves. Peter Kenrick kept a small number, and the Baltimore archdiocese, where Martin Spalding was strongly opposed to abolition, had a number of slaves working in Catholic institutions.

But racism of all kinds was endemic in America, and the charge of Catholic racism loses much of its force when it comes from Protestants who delighted in Thomas Nast's cartoons portraying the Irish as a race of gorillas. New England Bible Societies glowed with white-hot righteousness as they sent Sharp's rifles to the likes of John Brown, who was a certifiable madman, but one could ask whether the moral equations were really that simple. Even Catholic bishops who considered slavery a terrible evil might honestly wonder whether it justified sending thousands of young men from their own flocks, and hundreds of thousands across the country, to die in such wanton slaughter, especially after Grant and Lincoln adopted their grisly strategy of attrition. The legitimacy and urgency of such questions, of course, as well as the willingness to admit to contemporary doubts, faded quickly after the North's victory.

But if Irish racism was sometimes overstated, so was their reputation for Civil War heroism. The exploits of Irish companies, like Michael Corcoran's famous "Fighting Sixty-ninth" New York regiment and Thomas Meagher's Irish Brigade; the heavy Irish casualties at Gettysburg, Fredericksburg, and Chancellorsville; and the patent unfairness of the conscription law made it seem that the Irish were carrying more than their share of the war burden. The truth is that Irish Catholics were the most *under*represented of all socioethnic groups in the Union army, with German Catholics next. Immigrants, understandably enough, had no interest in an American war, and avoided service however they could, including desertion. After the riots, conscription went smoothly in New York only because Boss Tweed's city administration created a fund to pay the exemption fee for "hardship cases," which turned out to include 98 percent of the conscripts from Irish wards not exempt under other clauses. Tweed's intervention was widely emulated by political machines throughout the country. The net effect of the conscription law was that it raised few conscripts but created a substantial war chest for recruiting volunteers.

Many Irish Catholics served in the war, but they were usually paid to join. Near the end of the war, enlistment bounties were up to $700—ten years' wages for a laborer in Ireland, and two years' in America. Local bonuses could raise the total to $1000, and bounty jumping—picking up bounties in several localities under assumed names—was common. Irish immigration actually increased sharply toward the end of the war, when the demand for troops was highest, while that from all other countries dropped just as sharply. Paying the poor to undertake risks, of course, is just class bias in another form. But the socioeconomic origins of Union soldiers track quite closely to the overall profile within the Union, with a slight underrepresentation of the lowest classes. (Confederate forces were significantly skewed toward the upper and middle classes.) The perception of outstanding Irish wartime performance was undeserved, but it was an important factor in legitimizing the Catholic presence in America.

Archbishop Hughes in New York was the first bishop to be treated as a political figure in his own right and epitomized growing Catholic political power. He was regularly consulted by both parties, was on good terms with Franklin Pierce, and was a friend of James Buchanan, a fellow Ulsterman. Both Buchanan and Lincoln treated him as the de facto spokesman for Catholics and the Irish, and they both sent him on diplomatic missions. Lincoln even lobbied the Vatican to give Hughes a cardinal's hat. By the end of the war, the political deference granted to Hughes—he died in 1864—seems to have carried over to Catholic bishops as a whole. It is striking that in 1866 President Andrew Johnson thought it advisable to attend the closing session of a bishops' council in Baltimore.

When the war ended, therefore, America was slowly acclimating to the burgeoning Catholic presence within its borders. Ideologically, however, the accommodation was still very unstable. This was, after all, the era of the Vatican Council, and there were glaring contradictions between the official teachings of the Church and the basic premises of the American system. It remained for the next generation of bishops to work out those conflicts and to create a uniquely American compromise that would prevail for most of the following century.

CHAPTER 4

The Grand American Catholic Compromise

On St. Patrick's Day in Clontarf, Minnesota, in 1879, just a few weeks before New York's Catholics gathered to dedicate their mighty cathedral, a choir of a hundred Irish Catholic schoolchildren sang traditional Irish songs in the modest but brand-new wood-frame St. Malachy's Church. The day had begun with a procession down the muddy main street, past the little cluster of buildings—a dozen frame stores and a grain elevator—jutting from flat-prairie grassland still deep in snow that stretched away in all directions to a vast, roiled sky. The break in the weather was providential, for Minnesota was plagued by blizzards and floods that entire spring. At the celebration that followed, there was no alcohol; for Bishop John Ireland, who had built Clontarf, and christened it for Brian Boru's victory over the Danes almost nine hundred years before, who had built its church and grain elevator, named its streets, and recruited its settlers, and who built neighboring Tara, Dublin, Graceville, and Kildare, was also founder and leader of the Father Mathew Society, America's Catholic temperance movement, and he did not permit alcohol in his towns.

Midwestern Catholicism was always less claustrophobic than the big-city variant of the Northeast, perhaps because Catholics were not constantly struggling against entrenched local elites, or perhaps because the frontier psyche is more attuned to possibility. Its prophet was John Ireland, a visionary and entrepreneur, who embraced America as he found it. Characteristically, he perceived that the Midwest's need for Catholics matched the railroads' need for settlers, and he had himself appointed agent for some 400,000 acres of railroad-owned land. He negotiated long-term, railroad-financed credits for his settlers, and arranged for their debts to be paid in depreciated railroad bonds, which he supplied them. If his colonies never quite lived up to his expectations—recall the disastrous 1880 experiment with the Connemaran peasants—he settled at least four thousand families, including as many Germans, Belgians, and French Canadians as Irish. Like Hughes, Ireland was impulsive, temperamental, and emotional, with the same weakness for the theatrical and the grandiose, the same stirring platform presence, the same instinct for the common man that marks the very best politicians. If he had not been a priest, Hughes could have been a power in eastern politics, perhaps a U.S. senator. Even as a priest Ireland was a major figure in midwestern Republicanism; it is easy to imagine him as governor of Minnesota and a contender for a spot on a national ticket.

Ireland was born in Kilkenny, in southern Ireland, in 1838. His family fled the Famine on a coffin ship in 1849, traversed the dreaded Grosse Isle quarantine station, and worked their way from Canada to Boston and Chicago. In 1852, eight Irelands along with six O'Gormans, another Kilkenny family, made the trek by foot, wagon, and steamer to St. Paul, a raw, polyglot frontier town—pamphlets extolled its "bracing" climate—and took up residence in a one-room riverside shack with a bedsheet between the families. St. Paul was barely a decade old but had its own bishop, Joseph Cretin, one of the last of a heroic band of Indian-speaking French missionaries, a roly-poly bourgeois whose "cathedral" church was a log chapel. He quickly identified John and the eldest O'Gorman son, Thomas, his two "dirty little Irish boys," as the most promising students in the diocese. So in 1853, when John was almost fifteen and Thomas only eleven, they were spirited away to prepare for the priesthood at the rigorist haut-bourgeois Petit Séminaire de Meximieux in southern France, under the watchful eye of Cretin's maiden sister, who lived nearby. Only four years from an Irish tenant farm, John sat in a Gothic classroom, wearing custom-made linens and trousers supplied by Mlle. Cretin, signing his name "Ireland, Jean, des Etats-Unis."

The John Ireland who returned to St. Paul eight years later was a strikingly handsome and confident young man, broadly educated for his time, and with a voice like an organ. He was ordained in a modest church that had supplanted Cretin's log chapel. O'Gorman was ordained four years later and remained Ireland's devoted follower the whole of his life. Ireland became famous as a fighting chaplain with Minnesota's Union troops—at a crucial moment at the Battle of Corinth, legend has it, he became a one-man ammunition supply line. By the time he was twenty-six, he was a national figure and became the spearhead of both the Catholic western colonization and the temperance movements. Ireland was made coadjutor bishop of St. Paul at the age of thirty-seven and became head of the diocese nine years later. His boundless energy cohabited with a genuine scholarly bent. His sermons are learned, closely argued essays, and among his per-

Credit: Minnesota Historical Society
John Ireland as a newly ordained priest in 1862. Ireland quickly became a na-
tional leader of Catholic temperance and land colonization movements, and
was the apostle of "Americanism," arguing that the American democratic spirit
was the most compatible with the Catholic tradition.

sonal papers, he left forty-nine volumes of carefully indexed multilingual clippings on history, philosophy, and theology that he had assembled throughout his life.

In the four decades between the start of the Civil War and the end of the Spanish-American War, America was transformed from an agrarian backwater to a world industrial power. Mass-production industry sprang from the "American system" of manufacturing Civil War rifles with interchangeable parts, and it gave birth to the Gilded Age industrial buccaneer. Andrew Carnegie and John D. Rockefeller created world steel and oil industries, and J. P. Morgan challenged England's venerable banking houses for leadership in global finance. As billions in capital poured into railroad construction, farms became food factories for distant urban centers, and miles-long freight-car lines of coal and iron fed the thousands of smokestacks that blackened the sky of every major city. Coal production soared twentyfold, petroleum ninetyfold, steel a hundredfold. By the 1890s, there were skyscrapers in New York and Chicago, gas lights and steam power were giving way to electricity, and people had talked on the telephone.

A mass population movement from farm to factory was matched by a huge upsurge in immigration, from 2 million in the 1860s to 5.2 million in the 1880s and 8.2 million in the first decade of the 1900s, the highest level ever, flowing into a country that had only 76 million people in 1900. The old immigrant stream from northern Europe now ran side by side with Italians and Greeks from the south, and Bohemians, Slavs, and Czechs, many of them Jews, from the collapsing Habsburg, Ottoman, and Czarist empires in the east. The country grew vastly wealthier, but the huge new armies of unskilled workers put harsh downward pressure on wages. The industrial transformation quickly outstripped the coping ability of nineteenth-century institutions. The great wealth enshrined in the glittering homes on Fifth Avenue or on grand Newport estates was overbalanced by metastasizing city slums, filthy, diseased, and violent. Corruption permeated every level of government. The country's still primitive financial system careened from one boom-and-bust cycle to another, and there were savage depressions in the 1870s and 1890s. Anarchists and Marxists churned out foreign-language pamphlets in every big city. The Haymarket Square bombing in Chicago in 1886—when police tried to break up an anarchist rally—touched off the nation's first "red" panic.

The number of American Catholics tripled between 1860 and 1890, to more than 7 million, and Catholicism became the country's largest single religious denomination, with about 12 percent of the population but more than a quarter of the churchgoers. Catholics of Irish descent were still a slim majority within the Church but were being pressed by Germans and Italians. Anti-Catholic nativism still occasionally flared, and the virulent American Protective Association (APA) enjoyed booming growth in the early 1890s. But unlike the anti-Catholic wars of the 1840s and 1850s, which were fought out in Catholic urban strongholds, APA violence was mostly restricted to the Catholic fringes, in places like Michigan and Nebraska. (The Ku Klux Klan's anti-Catholic cross burnings in the 1920s were usually in rural areas where Catholics were as scarce as Gothic cathedrals.)

The Church's ambiguous adaptation to America had sufficed for the 1850s, when it was still only a fringe sect. But by the 1880s, it had grown so big, and so politically powerful, that attitudes had to be clarified. The fundamental question was whether the Church should recommence the process of assimilating to American institutions, which had been rudely interrupted by the Irish immigrations of the 1840s and 1850s, or continue down the separatist path blazed by John Hughes. The terms of the accommodation were fought out between the hierarchy's liberal assimilationists, or "Americanists," and their conservative opponents throughout the post–Civil War period. Not for another century, in the theological disputes that followed the Second Vatican Council, would American Catholic churchmen have at one another so bitterly, or with such unrestrained vitriol. The precipitating issues were the Church's stance on unions, social reform, ethnic assimilation, and the parochial school system. It was almost inevitable that Ireland, who burned with patriotism for his adopted country, should become the natural leader of the Americanist wing.

The Americanist Controversies

John Ireland made his maiden speech before his episcopal colleagues at the Third Plenary Council of Baltimore, a kind of bishops' legislative meeting, held in the fall of 1884. It was the gathering that produced the "Baltimore Catechism," the famous series of questions and answers that every American Catholic schoolchild learned by heart for the next seventy-five years. Ireland made a good impression, although a few were put off by the plummy ripeness of his oratory. The council itself was a great success, an indicator of the growing respectability of the Church. It received courteous attention in the lay press, President Chester A. Arthur and several Cabinet members agreed to attend the opening sessions (although Arthur was a no-show after failing to be renominated), and President-elect Grover Cleveland sent his good wishes. Pope Leo XIII was lavish in his praise, and there were many requests for transcripts from other English-speaking countries.

The organizing genius of the Council was James Gibbons, the archbishop of Baltimore, who earned a cardinal's hat for his efforts. Born in America, raised in Ireland, a slender, neat little man, Gibbons was no great intellect or administrator, or even a man of strong convictions, but he had the gift of marvelous patience. He proves the principle that merely waiting on events invariably passes as good judgment, and he was rarely caught on a limb he could not safely scramble away from. During the strife-ridden period that was about to ensue, Gibbons was almost always a moderating and constructive influence. Although an ally of Ireland, he was one of the few senior prelates to stay on speaking terms with all factions.

Gibbons's close partner in preparing for the council was Michael Corrigan, coadjutor archbishop of New York and the designated successor of John McCloskey, who was on his deathbed. Corrigan was the son of a wealthy Newark grocer and liquor dealer, rich enough in his own right to bail out Seton Hall's finances when he was rector at the New Jersey college. Icily intelligent, he was the consummate bureaucrat—rigid, indefatigable, and underhanded. The extensive diaries Corrigan kept during his diocesan visitations are almost devoid of personal comment but remorselessly record every mistake in ritual and every inadequacy of decor, even to counts of missing altar candles. Corrigan was shortly to emerge as the leader of the conservatives and Ireland's most bitter enemy.

The bishops adjourned the council with two major items of unfinished business. The first was a ruling on whether Catholics could join labor organizations like the Knights of Labor; and the second was the question of chartering a national Catholic university, which required papal approval. In 1886, the archbishops agreed that John Keane, one of the younger bishops, who had been tentatively picked to head the university, and John Ireland, who was scheduled to make his *ad limina* trip to Rome (a periodic mandatory "to the steps" personal report) should be charged with presenting both questions to the Pope.

A third issue presented itself while Ireland and Keane were en route to Rome. A German-born Milwaukee priest named Peter Abbelen presented a petition to the Pope alleging mistreatment of German Catholics by America's Irish clergy, which threatened to turn into a major German-Irish ethnic blowup. All three issues—the ruling on unions, attitudes toward the university, and ethnic contentions—became hot-potato problems in the Americanist controversies.

THE KNIGHTS OF LABOR

Of all the Americanist issues, the question of the Knights of Labor bore the most profound implications, not only for American Catholics but for the entire world Church. America was arguably the only major country where Catholicism was a religion of the working classes. In Europe, where the hierarchy was dominated by royalists, and the great mass of believers were still ignorant peasants, workers' movements tended to be bitterly anticlerical, especially in France and Italy. The Knights were the largest labor organization in America, and in just a few years, membership had leaped tenfold, to more than 700,000 workers. To speak of a Knights "organization" is almost oxymoronic. It was a ramshackle confederation of many different trades, from railroad to farm workers, and its success was built on the impresario flair and political skills of Terence Powderly, general master workman for sixteen years. Powderly was a shrewd, sardonically funny Irishman of considerable self-education, and a devout Catholic. In the mid-1880s, the Knights were recruiting Irish Catholics by the hundreds of thousands.

But the Catholic Church was historically opposed to labor unions. Besides their roots in European anticlericalism, most unions, including the Knights, copied handshakes, passwords, and other symbolic paraphernalia from the Masons, who were notoriously anti-Catholic. Many Irish unions, moreover, had links to the Fenians and the Ancient Order of Hibernians, and through them, to the banned violent Irish secret societies. When labor wars broke out in the Pennsylvania coal fields in the 1870s, James Wood, the archbishop of Philadelphia, and William O'Hara, the bishop of Scranton, were "venomous" in their opposition to the Irish Molly Maguires. Powderly, who had been mayor of Scranton, ran afoul of O'Hara because his union lapel button looked like a Mason's. James Healy, the bishop of Portland, tried to bar Powderly from speaking in Maine, and in a frigid interview, Corrigan virtually accused him of complicity in a dynamite plot. The Vatican had already twice condemned the Canadian Knights of Labor, and there was no obvious reason why the condemnations should not apply to the American Knights.

The bishops had tiptoed around the question of the Knights at the Baltimore council, but such coyness would no longer serve after Haymarket Square. The Knights had helped organize the Haymarket rally, although they had no involvement with the bombing, and they were prime targets of the ensuing storm of vituperation against "socialist" and "radical" organizations of all kinds. When the archbishops met in 1886 to wind up the work of the council, they could not avoid taking a stand. Honest Catholics were confused, and the Vatican conservatives were pushing for a blanket condemnation.

The debate on the Knights was one of the few occasions when Gibbons's convictions overrode his caution and marks his greatest contribution to the Church. Gibbons was not especially pro-union, but unlike Corrigan, who had never worked in a parish, he had begun his career among working people. He understood that blue-collar families were the Church's core membership, and he feared that, with the Knights' strong Irish Catholic constituency, a condemnation would be a public relations disaster. Powderly was also anxious to avoid a condemnation and promised Gibbons that he would amend any provisions in the Knights' constitution, like the secrecy clauses, that the Church objected to. The rules of the Roman Propaganda, the arm of the Vatican that governed the American "mission," allowed the archbishops to settle an issue like the Knights by themselves upon a unanimous vote. Despite his best efforts, Gibbons could carry only six of the nine archbishops at the 1886 meeting. Two voted for outright condemnation, and Corrigan abstained, although he would almost certainly have voted with a majority to condemn. So Ireland and Keane were deputed to carry the question to the Pope, with instructions from the majority to try to win a favorable ruling.

THE CATHOLIC UNIVERSITY

Although the university question lacked the long-term significance of the Knights, it was still a major source of tension between American liberals and conservatives. It also contained one of the juicier scandals of the nineteenth-century Church and first exposed how underhanded Corrigan could be. The idea was pushed hard at the council by John Lancaster Spalding, the bishop of Peoria, and was approved only reluctantly by his fellow bishops. Spalding, clipped, precise, and aristocratic—he was once described as an "icicle" by a Roman contessa—was a descendant of an old Maryland English Catholic family and the nephew of Martin Spalding, the former archbishop of Baltimore. He was no consensus builder, and the majority of his peers probably thought that a national Catholic university was an ill-conceived extravagance. Spalding's theological liberalism, and that of his strongest supporters, like Ireland and Keane, aroused conservative suspicions, while the Vatican was wary of any permanent national Catholic apparatus in America, for fear that it would spread the infection of democratic ideas.

But Spalding was in a position to be persuasive. He had overseen the education of two young New York heiresses, Mary Gwendoline "Mamie" Caldwell and her younger sister, Mary Elizabeth, or "Lina," and was later a trustee of their estate. Their father was dead, and Mamie, who was now twenty-one, had come into her inheritance. Spalding paraded Caldwell and her young friends at the council, got them front-row seats, and announced that she would donate $300,000, a third of her fortune, for his university. With so much money in hand, the bishops had little choice but to approve the idea. There was some grumbling, however, when Caldwell insisted on keeping control of the money herself and began dictating the university's organizational details, all obviously at the direction of Spalding.

The truth seems to be that Spalding and Caldwell were having an affair, one that reeks of exploitation, although it was to last on and off for almost twenty years, well after Caldwell's marriage to a French nobleman, from whom she later separated. Spalding stayed at her house in Paris and they frequently took trips together. It is not clear whether the other bishops knew what was going on, but Patrick Ryan, the St. Patrick's dedication orator, who had been elevated to archbishop of Philadelphia, had written to Gibbons in 1885 that if Spalding were university rector, "I fear Miss C will be constantly there and attract much comment." It was therefore a great relief when Spalding unexpectedly turned down the university rectorship—he had been studying continental systems in preparation for the job—possibly because of misgivings about his own behavior, or possibly because of quiet pressure from his seniors. Both sisters left the Church when the affair finally broke up about 1900. Lina, by then the Baroness von Zedtwitz, took the story to the Vatican in 1902 in order to derail Spalding's appointment as archbishop of Chicago.

In any case, when Ireland and Keane were dispatched to Rome, they carried a detailed and favorable recommendation on the university proposal, signed by all nine archbishops, including Corrigan, who had been a member of the committee that made the recommendation. They did not know that Corrigan had just sent the Vatican a long and stinging denunciation of the same university proposal.

THE ABBELEN PETITION

Ireland and Keane learned of Fr. Abbelen's petition during a stopover in London. They secured a copy—it was a broadside attack on the "special ecclesiastical privileges" enjoyed by the Irish in America—and raised the alarm at home. Embarrassingly enough, Abbelen was armed with letters of introduction from Gibbons, whom he had met at the council, although his criticisms especially singled out Gibbons's own diocese of Baltimore.

Abbelen clearly had considerable support from the German hierarchy and clergy and from the strong German wing in the Propaganda. On their face the German complaints were unfair. It was not true, as Abbelen alleged, that the Germans had not gotten their share of bishops. Of seventy-three bishops in 1886, about half were of Irish descent and 22 percent were German, which was just about right if the goal was a bishops' quota based on Catholic ethnic origins. Complaints that the Irish opposed German national parishes were similarly overstated. Gibbons, Corrigan, and even Ireland, who became the Germans' special bête noire, consistently supported German parishes for new immigrants, but they insisted that immigrants' children should be free to choose an American parish when they came of age. As a consequence, the national parishes tended to wither away, to the consternation of older Germans, who were proud of their language and resisted cultural assimilation. Irish priests in Milwaukee complained that the archbishop, Michael Heiss, insisted on German priests if there were *any* Germans in a parish. Patriotic Irish Americans were upset by semiofficial German declarations that "America is no nation, no race, no people, like France, Italy, or Germany," and by German complaints about rule by "Irish ignoramuses" or their habit of calling all non-German clergy "Irish."

But the Germans had real grievances, although they are lost in statistical arguments. The Irish, in truth, were masters of bureaucratic maneuvering, and they were inexorably imposing an Irish Catholic style on the American church—one scholar has called it "emotional taxation without representation." After the Baltimore Council, for example, Gibbons, Corrigan, and Ryan openly debated whether to include one of the "ponderous" Germans in a delegation to Rome. Autocratic Irishmen brushed aside a rich German tradition of lay participation in church affairs, and the incessant Irish temperance drives were an insult and an inconvenience to Germans who liked their beer on Sundays. An American-born priest of German descent complained that priests just landing from Ireland treated him like a foreigner: "The Irish American looks upon the United States as a second fatherland, and as his alone; all others are only tolerated." Irish-American priests were probably right that assimilating Catholics into English-language parishes was in the long-term interest of the Church and the immigrants both, but it also was conspicuously to the career advantage of the flood of clerical emigrants from Ireland, which had become a virtual priest factory. John Ireland, in particular, developed an irritating habit of telling Germans, in effect, to go back where they came from if they didn't like it here: "He who . . . does not thank God that he is an American, should in simple consistency betake his foreign soul to foreign shores, and crouch in misery and abjection beneath tyranny's sceptre."

Whenever American ethnic laundry was washed in Rome, it heightened Vatican suspicions of the treatment of Italians. The number of Italian migrants was rising fast in the 1880s, but they were mostly male laborers who returned to their families in Italy each year, and they rarely went to church. One of Gibbons's representatives in Rome wrote, "It is a very delicate matter to tell the Sovereign Pontiff how utterly faithless" his countrymen were. Corrigan reported to the Baltimore Council that of 50,000 Italian Catholics in New York, only 1200 went to church, and of a dozen Italian priests, ten had been censured in Italy for immorality. Irish clergy were disdainful of the Italian love of "tinsel" and "brass bands." (Corrigan forbade flowers at funerals.) One priest reported that the only money he'd collected from Italians was for a "new Sanctuary *railing* to replace the one which they had thrown down in a rush for palms on Palm Sunday." Another proposed a "cheap frame or corrugated iron barn-like chapel . . . far apart from other buildings" for the Italians, because of their "filthy conditions and habits." One priest responded rhetorically to Vatican complaints with "you Machiavellian intriguers at Rome, go preach the Gospel to the Camorra of Naples and to the Mafia of Sicily." Vatican nattering, whether about Germans or Italians, clearly touched a raw nerve.

THE FORMATION OF THE AMERICANIST PARTY

Ireland and Keane, two of the most junior bishops, therefore arrived in Rome to find themselves in the vortex of all the most controversial problems swirling around the American Church. They were greatly relieved to hear that Gibbons had just been elected a cardinal and was rushing to join them. Keane was one of Gibbons's suffragan bishops, so he and Gibbons knew each other well, but this was the first chance for Gibbons to spend time with Ireland. There was also a fourth critical player, Denis O'Connell, the newly appointed rector of the North American College and their host in Rome.

O'Connell was a tradesman's son and, like Keane and Ireland, an Irish native, but ten years younger. A protégé of Gibbons, O'Connell had fallen in love with the mystique of Vatican politics while a seminary student in Rome. Diplomatic errands for Gibbons had helped polish his courtier's skills, and Gibbons had secured him the rectorship with an eye to his usefulness as a Roman agent. Bright and superficial, a lover of gossip and intrigue, O'Connell became a creature of the Roman salons, a special pet of the Pope, and, apparently, a libertine.* Working constantly together during the winter and spring of 1887, the four men bonded closely and became the heart of the Americanist party. Ireland and Keane supplied the intellectual energy and rhetorical dash for the Americanist agenda, O'Connell ran interference at the Vatican, while the cautious Gibbons lent his cardinal's prestige and his growing reputation for judiciousness and political sensitivity.

The first foray of the Americanists into Vatican politics was a signal success. They quickly disposed of Fr. Abbelen. Even before Gibbons arrived, Keane and Ireland submitted a reply under their own names and orchestrated a groundswell of denunciations from other bishops, including several moderate Germans. The archbishops of the biggest sees—Boston, Philadelphia, New York, and Baltimore—submitted a joint letter drafted by Corrigan, with the help of Bernard McQuaid, the bishop of Rochester. McQuaid was an ironhanded diocesan autocrat, in the John Hughes chief-executive-officer mold of the Irish-American bishop. (He ran a vineyard to defray the costs of his seminary.) Older than Corrigan and endlessly pugnacious, he was constantly egging Corrigan on in the war against the liberals, but this time at least he agreed with the Americanists that Abbelen's petition was a "dirty, mean, underhand business." Propaganda officials were taken aback by the strength of the American reaction and quietly shelved Fr. Abbelen's memorial. It was the last time Ireland and Corrigan agreed on anything.

The university and Knights issues did not go as smoothly, partly because, as the four Americanists soon discovered, they were up against Corrigan as well as the Vatican conservatives. More particularly, they were up against Ella Edes, Corrigan's friend and agent in Rome. Edes, "La Signora" to the liberals, was an upper-class New England spinster and convert, a for-

---

* Letters between O'Connell and Thomas O'Gorman strongly suggest that O'Connell seduced O'Gorman when the latter, a bluff and burly fifty-two, was in Rome on business for Ireland in 1894. After taking O'Gorman on a vacation trip to Avignon, O'Connell wrote him: "Poor dear little lamb that you are, lamenting your lost innocen[ce] because you came to Rome. What a sweet dear little fox you became in a few days and just as natural as if you had been born one." The letter was in response to one from O'Gorman on his loneliness since leaving O'Connell. O'Connell liked to use code names for his correspondents and somewhat cruelly dubbed O'Gorman "Avignon" thereafter. (His name for Spalding was "Achilles," perhaps suggestive of the chink in that formidable prelate's armor.) O'Gorman later strenuously represented to Ireland that O'Connell was not to be trusted.

mer Vatican secretary, and the Roman stringer for several newspapers. Possessor of a biting tongue and a talent for gossip and conspiracy, she was a Vatican insider who popped freely in and out of cardinals' offices and became a major player in the Americanist controversies. Ireland and Keane quickly discovered Corrigan's deceitfulness on the university, and found that Edes had been lobbying hard against both the university and the Knights.

To his credit, Gibbons maintained his advocacy of the Knights in the face of considerable Vatican skepticism, and he fashioned a strong memorial. (Ireland and Keane presumably did the actual drafting, for they were both fluent in French, the Vatican's diplomatic language.) The core argument was purely tactical—the Knights were already collapsing of their own weight; and a condemnation might provide a provocative organizing platform and alienate many honest Catholics. This last came with a veiled but unmistakable reference to the bad press Corrigan was receiving for opposing New York social reform movements. The memorial also waved the nativist flag, a device that John Hughes had regularly hauled out to get his way in Rome, warning that Vatican meddling in America might provoke riots. Although Gibbons and Keane had been disposed to drop the university issue in view of Corrigan's opposition, Ireland stiffened their resolve, and Gibbons argued the case during an interview with Leo, when the Pope seemed particularly friendly.

By the time they left Rome, the fledgling Americanist party had the pleasure of knowing that they had carried the field on all counts. Abbelen's petition had been buried, the university was approved—it actually opened within a year—and membership in the Knights declared acceptable. The approval of the Knights especially enhanced Gibbons's stature, and deservedly so. It contributed to a sharp reorientation of Rome's social teachings, embodied in Leo's great 1891 labor encyclical, *Rerum Novarum*. It was also a crucial step in the development of the American Church, cementing its strong links with organized labor and maintaining its position as one of the few major national Catholic churches to draw its primary strength from the blue-collar working classes. Over the longer run, the close links between the Church and blue-collar unions contributed to the social conservatism and relative lack of political radicalism of the American union movement.

The Americanists' exertions in Rome, however, left no room for disguising that they and Corrigan were now in opposite camps. McQuaid warned Corrigan that Gibbons was bent on replacing New York as the premier see, while Edes was contemptuous. "His Little Grace," as she called Gibbons, along with "his Fidus Achates O'Connell," was "an ambizioso of *the first water* for all his pretended sanctity." (O'Connell, it seems, was not all that faithful, for he supplied Edes some tidbits on Gibbons's "tricks and double-dealings" in Rome.) Corrigan pointedly refused Keane permission to raise funds for the university in New York. At the same time, Corrigan's antipathy toward the liberals was steadily hardening because of continuing confrontations with socially progressive New York priests.

Edward McGlynn and Popular Radicalism

Eighteen eighty-six was also a mayoral election year in New York City. Henry George, a progressive reformer, who advocated a "Single Tax" on land, was a third-party candidate for mayor. George had close ties to the radical Irish Land League and to the American Fenians, both of whom had been condemned by the Vatican as advocates of revolutionary violence. His candidacy greatly alarmed Tammany Hall, who feared that he would cut into their normally reliable Irish vote.

One of George's strongest supporters was Edward McGlynn, pastor of St. Stephen's parish on New York's East Side, one of the largest and poorest in the city. McGlynn was among the best and the brightest of the New York clergy, the leader of a group of reform-minded clerical intellectuals who were groping their way toward a populist Catholic social doctrine. In a day when platform oratory was a popular entertainment, McGlynn was a thrilling speaker. Even on the page, his speeches ring with Martin Luther King–like cadences. A signature bring-down-the-house line was "Our Father who art in Heaven, Thy kingdom come, Thy will be done—*on earth*—as it is in Heaven." McGlynn and his circle were openly critical of Rome's political benightedness, papal infallibility, Catholic parochialism, the hierarchy's love of pomp and splendor, and even priestly celibacy. (But McGlynn supported celibacy.) At the local level, McGlynn's favorite targets were Catholic schools—when adults "rot for want of Sacraments"—and Tammany Hall.

When McGlynn signed on as the main speaker at a George rally on October 1, complaints from Democratic Catholic stalwarts came pouring into the New York chancery. McGlynn and Corrigan went back a long way, as the Irish would have put it. Corrigan was a member of the first class at the North American College in Rome in 1859, when McGlynn was the star student at the Roman Propaganda College. McGlynn was drafted as impromptu beadle, or sort of assistant rector, for the boys at the new college. Vigorous and athletic, he disdained Corrigan as a "girlish" bookworm—in a hypermasculine age, Corrigan was notably effeminate—and Corrigan was not one to forget slights. Corrigan ordered McGlynn to cancel his speech; McGlynn offered to curtail his campaigning but went ahead with the speech. Corrigan suspended him.

The crackdown on McGlynn highlighted the awkward question of the Church's relations with Tammany, a favorite subject of Thomas Nast's poisonous anti-Catholic cartoons. The Tammany leader Richard Croker, despite his playing the twinkling Irishman for reporters, was a thug who had once been tried for murder. His baleful gaze from a splendid 1890 photograph still chills the marrow. Some Tammany underbosses, like Big Tim Sullivan on the Lower East Side, were vice czars who lived off prostitution, white slavery, and gambling. Corrigan barely knew Croker, but like McCloskey and Hughes, he was close to the city's Catholic elite—Bourke Cockran, John Crimmins, Judge Joseph Daley, Frederic Coudert (one of the few non-Irishmen), and their circle. Men of Corrigan's own class, they were all Tammany stalwarts, powers in the state Democracy, and figures of consequence in national politics. Under Tammany, the Church collected $8 per day for each Catholic school student, and Tammany smoothed the course of the Church's tireless building programs, to the benefit of Catholic realtors, bankers, and contractors. Although there seems to have been minimal direct dealings between the diocese and the Tammany bosses, the parallelism of interests was unmistakable. No one was surprised, therefore, when a number of priests preached openly against George, or when Corrigan's vicar-general, Thomas Preston, in a letter that was widely circulated by the machine, wrote that, while the Church never interfered in elections, "the great majority of the Catholic clergy . . . are opposed to the candidacy of Mr. George. They think his principles unsound and unsafe, and contrary to the teachings of the Church."

George lost the election, but he gave Tammany a good scare, despite considerable vote rigging. In mid-November, Corrigan, invoking a bishop's duty to curtail "dangerous movements," attacked George's theories in a pastoral letter. McGlynn, whose suspension had been lifted, expressed impatience in a *Tribune* interview with "ministers of the Gospel and priests of the Church [who] tell the hardworking poor to be content with their lot and hope for good times in Heaven." Based solely on the newspaper report, Corrigan suspended McGlynn again and removed him from St. Stephen's. A crowd of more than 7000 people barred McGlynn's successor from entering the church, and the new man had to be rescued by the police. Corrigan wrote to Rome that George's theories were "a civil disease bordering on madness" and began lobbying for a papal condemnation. McGlynn, with the help of his friend and fellow priest Richard Burtsell, probably America's best canon lawyer, showed that an American bishop could not suspend an alumnus of the Propaganda College. For New York's newspapers, it was a wonderful carnival.

In December, a cable arrived from the Roman Propaganda instructing McGlynn to proceed there for a hearing. (It was quite probably forged by Edes, although without Corrigan's knowledge.) In any case, McGlynn refused to go on grounds of health and finances. Stirring the pot, Edes sent Corrigan the original text of Gibbons's Knights memorial, which had implicitly criticized his handling of social reformers in New York. (The criticisms had been omitted in the published version.) Corrigan was greatly offended, and when Ireland called in New York on the way home from Rome, warned the liberals not to meddle in New York affairs. In return, Ireland was testy about Corrigan's deceptiveness on the university.

McGlynn responded to his suspension by organizing the Anti-Poverty Society, kicking it off in March 1887 with a bravura revivalist speech called "The Cross of a New Crusade": "for the proclaiming, the propagating, and the surfacing of an ancient truth . . . the fatherhood of one God and the universal brotherhood of man." Charles Dana, who was hostile to both George and McGlynn, editorialized in the *New York Sun:* "To say of the Rev. Dr. McGlynn's address . . . that it was a remarkable intellectual performance is to do it imperfect justice. The address is entitled to rank with those great orations which . . . have swayed the course of public opinion and changed the onward movement of nations." McGlynn went on a rousing national lecture tour, returning each Sunday for quasi-religious, stomping, hat-throwing meetings of his Anti-Poverty Society, turning his listeners, in the *Sun*'s words, into "a roaring, seething mass . . . as though an electric spark had touched a mine of dynamite."

With McQuaid fulminating that "half the diocese" was disloyal, Corrigan seems to have lost his moorings. He became increasingly isolated within a narrow circle of rigidly doctrinaire advisers, like McQuaid and Preston. Priests were required to sign what amounted to a loyalty oath; about 80 percent did so. McGlynn sympathizers were transferred to rural parishes and stripped of appointments to patronage posts. "The brains of the diocese," as one wag put it, were migrating up the Hudson. For the most part, their careers never recovered. Amid a major press flap, Corrigan denied burial in consecrated ground to two of Burtsell's devout parishioners because they had attended McGlynn's meetings.

The accusations against McGlynn became ever more extreme. Corrigan wrote to the Vatican that McGlynn had embezzled $37,000 from St. Stephen's—McGlynn was a sloppy administrator, but not a thief—and then prepared an extended dossier alleging sexual misconduct, much of it compiled by Tammany detectives reporting through "Catholic gentlemen." A number of women alleged that McGlynn had made them expose themselves in the confessional as penance. (Sex in the confessional was a staple of nativist screeds; to anyone who has actually been in a Catholic confessional— usually a cramped, dark little box, with priest and penitent barely visible to each other through a thick screen—it is extremely implausible.) Burtsell spent years tracking down the charges, and they almost all dissolved upon investigation. At one point, Corrigan sheltered a priest who was notorious for his sexual misconduct in Brooklyn but who was willing to retail sexual accusations against McGlynn. Corrigan's secretary, Charles McDonnell, later a long-reigning bishop of Brooklyn, accused McGlynn of living openly with a woman and their children, although the woman was an elderly house-keeper and the children were those of McGlynn's dead sister, as Corrigan and McDonnell must have known. Not all the charges could be so easily disposed of, however, and there is circumstantial evidence that McGlynn may have fathered a child by a maidservant; but Corrigan was launched on a vendetta, not a search for truth.

By this time, the Pope, who liked McGlynn, really had instructed him to come to Rome and promised that he would be fairly treated. McGlynn still refused, on the ground that he had not been informed of all the charges against him, like Corrigan's financial and sexual allegations. Even McGlynn's friends had trouble explaining his recalcitrance, but there is a later hint, if only a hint, that McGlynn may have been genuinely worried about the paternity charge from the maidservant. In any case, when McGlynn was ordered to appear in Rome under pain of excommunication, he asked his friends to stop their activities on his behalf. A torchlight parade of McGlynn supporters protested the excommunication, but it became effective in July 1887.

By the winter of 1887–1888, McGlynn's star appeal was definitely on the wane, as were Henry George's political fortunes. George and McGlynn had broken over a dispute on political tactics, and McGlynn's diatribes against the Church—he called the Pope an "old bag of bones"—were becoming offensive even to liberal Catholics. Corrigan pressed his advantage by demanding the condemnation of George. An alarmed Gibbons made a hurried trip to the Vatican in the hope of heading it off with the same arguments that had worked with the Knights—George was "politically dead," and a censure would only "resuscitate" him. He was too late; Edes had been on the case for a year. But in a classic Vatican compromise, the condemnation came with the ludicrous requirement that it be kept secret. McQuaid was disgusted: "What's the use of it, if you can't publish it!" It was an equivocal victory for Corrigan, but after their great successes of 1886, the Roman tides seemed to be swinging against the Americanists.

The Cahensly Memorial

By 1888, Corrigan was changing his position on the German question. Germans were among the most conservative of Catholics and had been the most loyal to him against McGlynn. Edes did her part in Rome. As she reported to Corrigan, in one of her meetings with her friend Cardinal Giovanni Simeoni, the head of the Propaganda, they discussed Ireland's advocacy of a liberal Belgian-born episcopal candidate: "I could not help remarking to the Cardinal the inconsistency of the 'Baltimore-Ireland clique' [in promoting a foreigner] simply because he is one of *their* clique, and will run *their* game. H[is] E[minence] answered with one of his grim smiles." The Vatican proceeded to make a series of conservative German appointments over the strong recommendations of a majority of the archbishops—although with Corrigan's and Edes's endorsement—including the appointment of Frederick Katzer, a particularly hardheaded German nationalist, as archbishop of the important see of Milwaukee. The Americanists' dismay was more ideological than ethnic, for the conservative Germans were strongly anti-assimilationist. If Corrigan and Edes could sway American episcopal appointments, the whole Americanist agenda was placed at risk.

It was at this juncture that Heaven, as it were, sent the Americanists an unexpected blessing in the person of Peter Paul Cahensly. Cahensly was a wealthy German Catholic and a founder of the St. Raphael's Society, which looked after the interests of Catholic emigrants from Europe. At a meeting in Lucerne in late 1890, the society deplored the loss of faith by "sixteen million" Catholic-American immigrants, and adopted a statement demanding same-nationality parishes and priests for all new Americans, and a national quota system for American bishops. The lost-soul count was a well-meaning fiction, of a piece with the numbers John England had flogged at All Hallows a half century before. Although fifty-one members of the society signed the statement, it inevitably became known as the "Cahensly Memorial" when Cahensly presented it to the Pope in April 1891.

In late May, Associated Press (AP) dispatches from Rome, Brussels, and Berlin hit the American papers with the sensational allegations that a German named Cahensly had concocted slanders against America with the German ambassador to the Vatican; that Berlin had secured Katzer's appointment to Milwaukee; and that the German-American Priests' Society was, in effect, the agent of a foreign power bent on Germanizing the American Church. The dispatches, in fact, had been drafted by Denis O'Connell, who smugly admitted "a modest direction" to Ireland. They were also lies, which O'Connell justified in order to "shatter this [German] movement for ten years to come. . . . I deemed a conflict of some kind inevitable, and a more favorable moment than the present I cannot imagine." Ireland merely replied that "We are in war, and we must use all our powder."

Bootstrapping on O'Connell's prevarications, Ireland released a blistering statement condemning "the impudence of the men undertaking to meddle under any pretext in the Catholic affairs of America. . . . Nor is this the most irritating fact in this movement. The inspiration of the work in Europe comes, the dispatch tells us, from a clique in America." By now, the Americanists were becoming expert in manipulating the Vatican. O'Connell wrote that the indignation of the American hierarchy at Cahensly's initiative at first "made no impression. . . . They were Irish, they were interested and their opposition and indignation was only a matter of course. But when I said the American government would settle the matter for itself, the Cardinal [Secretary of State] changed his manner."

Ireland and Gibbons could roll out heavy political guns. Ireland was immensely popular in Minnesota, and his endorsement could turn an election. There was an anti-German mood in Congress—the United States was just beginning to sense its power and was bumping elbows with Bismarck in the Pacific and in Latin America. Minnesota's Republican senator agreed to make a floor speech at the next session (in which he called Cahensly a worse threat than Chinese immigration), while Secretary of State James Blaine, who also owed political debts to Ireland, agreed to speak out if needed. President Benjamin Harrison made a personal inquiry of Gibbons. All was duly reported to the Vatican, and, within just a few weeks, the astonished cardinals disavowed the Cahensly Memorial.

Katzer, who had been quite shaken by the entire episode, proferred an olive branch by asking Gibbons to preach at his installation in Milwaukee. Gibbons delivered a strongly patriotic sermon, which included a veritable statement of what became the American Irish-Catholic creed: "We will prove to our countrymen that the ties formed by grace and faith are stronger than flesh and blood. God and our country—this our watchword. Loyalty to God's church and to our country—this our religious and political faith." The sermon drew favorable notice throughout the country and friendly editorials in the *Chicago Tribune* and *Washington Post.* At an episcopal banquet in Dubuque a few weeks later, Ireland delivered a paean to "Our Church and Our Country." The souvenir volume recorded:

> the burning words of the great Bishop of St. Paul went home to every heart, and made each aglow with love of Church and Country, patriotism and virtue. The hall resounded again and again with cheers and applause. . . . When the Archbishop sat down a perfect storm of cheering rent the air, amid which a young Priest jumped on a chair and screamed at the top of his voice: "God bless the mother that bore you and the breast that gave you suck."

Faribault and Stillwater

With the liberals' fortunes suddenly on the upswing, Ireland, pressing the advantage to the fullest, decided to challenge the Church's commitment to parochial schools. Like McGlynn, he feared that they underlined the "foreignness" of the Roman Church and delayed the integration of immigrant children into the American mainstream. The Germans expressly used their schools to fend off assimilation. Ireland was as energetic a builder and fund-raiser as any, and he owed no apologies for his educational record. But his very optimism about the growth of Catholicism in America underscored the hopelessness of the task. Working Catholics were groaning under the financial burden of their schools, yet they served fewer than a third of Catholic children. With new waves of Catholic immigrants breaking on American shores—Italians, Poles, Bohemians—Ireland saw no way the Church could keep pace.

Ireland had eagerly accepted an invitation to speak at the annual convention of the National Education Association, which was held in St. Paul in 1890. In his speech, he strongly endorsed the principle of public schools, but suggested—in language that calls to mind the century-later "values" debate—that the true struggle was not between Protestants and Catholics, but between Christians and "secularism." "I will not impose upon [secularists] my religion, which is Christianity," Ireland argued. "But let them not impose upon me and my fellow-Christians, their religion, which is secularism . . . a very loud-spoken and intolerant religion." Ireland's solution was the so-called Poughkeepsie Plan, which could be implemented by any religious denomination. The pastor in Poughkeepsie, New York, an exiled McGlynn supporter named James Nilan, had worked out a sharing arrangement with the local school board. The Catholic school was leased by the local school board during regular school hours. The nuns were paid regular salaries and taught the public school curriculum, but after hours, the school reverted to parish control and the sisters taught religion classes.

The reception to Ireland's talk was mixed at best. Protestant speakers accused him of an elaborate ruse to siphon off tax money to the Church. The Germans were appalled—Peter Abbelen "raised a dreadful clamor," and one German priest claimed that Ireland had "lost his faith." But in the fall of 1891, Ireland proceeded to implement his ideas in the Minnesota towns of Faribault and Stillwater. Both the town parishes were financially strapped, partly because of the formation of separate French and German national parishes. Shortly before the start of the school year, the parishes announced they would close their schools for financial reasons and offered the local boards the Poughkeepsie Plan. Since the public school boards were obligated to provide places for all children, they had little choice but to accept the proposals—with good grace in Faribault, and with much resentment in Stillwater.

At Gibbons's and O'Connell's urging, Ireland sent a French translation of his education speech to the Vatican along with a painstaking line-by-line defense of his arguments. Somewhat disingenuously, he insisted he was not proposing a new "system" but simply defending local expedients worked out in the face of overwhelming financial exigencies. O'Connell chipped in with another well-timed AP dispatch detailing how, in most European countries, religious schools were run by the state. The Americanists also enlisted Catholic University in the cause (Keane, the university rector, along with Gibbons, Ireland, and O'Connell, controlled almost all faculty appointments), and the liberal theologian Thomas Bouquillon produced a detailed pamphlet defending the state's role in educating citizens.

America was dotted with Protestant-Catholic compromises like those in Faribault and Stillwater, including at least eight in Katzer's archdiocese. But Ireland's allies and enemies alike understood that he was creating a test case. O'Connell lobbied hard for the Pope's endorsement, and Ireland sailed for Rome to help out, while Corrigan allied with the German bishops and the Vatican Jesuits to fight for a condemnation. The Jesuits produced a counter-pamphlet to Bouquillon's, and Salvatore Brandi, the Jesuit editor of the semiofficial Vatican paper, *La Civiltà Cattolica,* and a friend of Corrigan, called Ireland a "revolutionary." The German wing of the Propaganda reflexively opposed anything with Ireland's name on it, and Edes, Ireland wrote, "watches, and whenever she finds a number [of a journal] steeped in gall, she puts it into Propaganda."

But Ireland's timing was perfect. The Pope, if not the Propaganda, was in an unusually liberal frame of mind. *Rerum Novarum,* Leo's social encyclical, had been promulgated only a few months before, and while hardly a radical document, it moved light-years beyond the medievalism of Pius IX. Ireland and Leo had a friendly hourlong meeting. They discussed the encyclical and French politics, and Leo suggested that Ireland write another brief for his schools plan, which he promised to read himself. Ireland produced a sixteen-page document that rehearsed all the previous arguments but added the threat of American anti-Catholicism, citing Bismarck's *Kulturkampf,* the repression of German Catholics in the 1870s:

> Unfortunately . . . public opinion regards me as [the bishop] . . . in favour of the Government of the United States, and regards my opponents as those who would combine the foreigners in the United States into a danger for the republic. . . . I have reason for alarm. We are only one in eight in the United States without wealth or influence and a larger proportion than that of wealth and population did not prevent a Kulturkampf in Germany.

Ireland's memorial was secret, but Edes obtained a copy for Corrigan anyway, allegedly buying it from a Propaganda printer. Corrigan put the lie to Ireland's *Kulturkampf* threat, soliciting a statement from the conservative archbishops that there was no danger of Catholic repression in America.

The last-minute exertions of Corrigan, Brandi, and Edes only made Ireland's victory doubly sweet. The cardinals of the Propaganda approved the

Faribault-Stillwater plan in April 1892 and the Pope signed the decree the same day. But Corrigan, waving a premature cable from Edes to a cheering meeting of his loyal priests, announced that the plan had been condemned but could continue in the two towns only. Brandi ran an editorial to similar effect in *Civiltà,* interpreting the approval in the narrowest terms and calling the Minnesota program "evil." Corrigan claimed Brandi's paper spoke for the Vatican. They were wrong on all counts. When the official letter from the Propaganda was released, it interpreted the decision in the broadest terms— the Minnesota arrangement was not the Catholic ideal but was fully approved for implementation anywhere in the country. The new secretary of state, Cardinal Mariano Rampolla, in answer to a query from Ireland, expressly denied "in the most formal manner" that Brandi was a Vatican spokesman. Edes was temporarily barred from the Propaganda for purloining Ireland's memorial.

Never one to quit a lost cause, Corrigan continued to organize protest letters from other bishops challenging Ireland's representations of conditions in America, until he was sharply reprimanded by Leo himself. (Ireland seems not to have noticed the irony of Corrigan defending America's reputation for tolerance against the misrepresentations of the Americanists.) The Pope simply denied that Ireland had ever used the threat of Catholic persecution: "Since neither the said Venerable Brother nor anyone else made mention of this danger, it is clear that a mendacious public rumor gave rise to the story that led you into the wholly inane and false notion." To Ireland's infinite delight, the Pope invited him to hear the letter to Corrigan before it was sent. Corrigan still wouldn't quit, writing to two Vatican cardinals that Leo was mistaken on his facts. O'Connell leaked the letters, which he called "a direct insult" to the Pope. At that point, Corrigan feared he might be deposed and wrote the most abject apology, eliciting from the Pope: "Oh, where is the use of talking with this man[,] his head is too small?"

Ireland arrived home in triumph, although Gibbons begged him not to crow. As a practical matter, there was not much to crow about, since the school-sharing programs in Faribault and Stillwater had already been scuttled by Protestant-Catholic infighting. On his way home through New York, Ireland did not call on Corrigan but spent a lengthy period closeted with Edward McGlynn, for he was working on the final stroke, the one that would "break Corrigan's head and heart."

Francesco Satolli

A conventional view of the Americanist crisis is that a fledgling American Catholic liberal movement was stamped out by the Vatican, with the help of a conservative faction in the American hierarchy. History-minded priests still call the turn-of-the-century conservatives *"Romani."* In truth, while the Vatican loved to meddle, its American policies were mostly the thoughtless backwash of European power-jockeying and were rarely pursued with force or conviction. Lord Acton once remarked on the American bishops' habit of loudly singing Rome's praises while doing as they pleased; and it is hard to find examples of Rome making Americans do anything that a majority of bishops strongly opposed. (When the Vatican ordered public protests against Italy in 1888, for example, the archbishops responded by writing the Pope "a letter of warm and filial support and sympathy.") The controversial decisions of the Americanist era all came from one of the two sides' insisting that the Vatican choose between them.

American conservatives were by no means the most disposed to fall back on Rome. Corrigan tended to run to the Vatican with every problem, but McQuaid could be contemptuous: "We are all in a nice pickle," he wrote to Corrigan in 1892, "thanks to Leo XIII. . . . It is only a question of time when . . . we, school-children of the hierarchy, will again receive a lesson in our Catechism from another Italian sent out to enlighten us." The bishops' attitudes toward the Vatican, that is, were much like that of today's liberals and conservatives toward an "activist" judiciary: both think it's a good idea when the results are to their liking. During the Americanist battles, the Vatican was hardly more than a totem, a kind of magic club, alternatively captured by one side to use against the other. And it was John Ireland and his liberal colleagues who played the Roman card most recklessly.

Ireland got such a friendly reception from the Pope on the schools question mostly because Leo and his new secretary of state, Cardinal Rampolla, were rethinking policy toward France. They respected Ireland's contacts with French intellectuals and wanted his help. The Third Republic, which followed the fall of Louis-Napoleon in 1870, was virulently anticlerical, and the Church's privileges and property were being steadily stripped away. But the Vatican was eager to rebuild ties with France as a counterweight to Germany's new alliance with Italy, which the Vatican still considered its blood enemy. The French government, however, would not deal with Rome so long as the French Church stayed adamantly monarchist. Rampolla thought American-style republicanism might offer a path between the wistful Bourbonism of the French Catholic right and the Jacobite instincts of the left. Leo authorized the French archbishop of Algiers to say that the American Church "has developed without any conflict from the State. . . . What suits the United States has still more reason to suit Republican France."

At Leo's special request, Ireland traveled home by way of France, where he was "rapturously" received. He lectured on the virtues of republicanism to twelve hundred of Paris's Catholic elite, was widely interviewed in the lay and Catholic press, and met with senior government officials. Ireland was justifiably proud of his French—even *Le Figaro* and *Le Monde* praised its beauty—and the trip was an elixir for his spirits. He arrived in New York bursting not only with his school triumphs but with the sense of being a player in world politics, a global spokesman for republicanism, and Leo's trusted lieutenant.

As a new and true-born son of the Vatican, Ireland also returned with a fully hatched scheme to advance his and Leo's American interests, which he now assumed to be identical. For decades, the Vatican had longed for its own representative in America—recall the ill-fated tour of Archbishop Bedini in 1853—if only to find out what was going on. The American bishops, who had come to appreciate the virtues of distance, had always opposed the idea. Ireland and O'Connell, with Gibbons's acquiescence, now unfolded an elaborately engineered scheme, although even O'Connell admitted, "Some inconveniences may be involved for the future." They began by prompting a request from the United States government to the Vatican for a loan of maps to be exhibited at the 1892 Columbian celebrations. Archbishop Francesco Satolli, the Pope's choice for the post of apostolic delegate, was appointed to convey the maps to America. Once Satolli was on site, the bishops would of necessity express their gratitude for the maps and for Satolli's august presence, and the Pope would respond with the further beneficence of Satolli's permanent appointment. Which is more or less exactly what happened, amid much grinding of teeth, because all the bishops knew the fix was in. An added fillip was that Satolli reported to Rampolla and the Pope, not to the Propaganda. The new head of the Propaganda, Cardinal Mieczysław Ledochowski, was German (from the Polish district of East Prussia), so a blow was struck against the German interest as well.

Satolli's introduction to America was orchestrated with loving attention to detail. Corrigan was informed only of the date of Satolli's arrival in New York, in October 1892, and by letter, not by cable. A Coast Guard cutter with O'Gorman aboard intercepted Satolli's ship and brought him and O'Connell, who was acting as translator, ashore "down the bay" while Corrigan's representatives frantically searched the New York docks. Satolli was clearly insulted by Corrigan's failure to meet him, and the next day he was hustled on a train to Baltimore and Gibbons. Ireland joined them in Washington for a reception laid on by the secretary of state. From Washington the party entrained to Chicago, the Columbian Exposition, a few weeks' respite at Ireland's home, and round after round of receptions with the midwestern business and political elite. Ireland and O'Connell escorted Satolli back to New York for the archbishops' meeting in November, after which he took up residence at Catholic University under the watchful eyes of O'Gorman and Keane. With his vanity so pleasurably salved, Satolli sang the praises of Ireland in his letters to Rome. At one point, he breathlessly reported to Rampolla that Republican presidential aspirant William McKinley had told Ireland that someday "you and I will be governing the United States." It is highly unlikely that McKinley said any such thing, but Satolli got his political information from Ireland and his circle.

The man whom the Americanists had chosen as their instrument was a shallow and garrulous philosophy professor whose talent for diplomacy was as limited as his academic attainments. Satolli spoke only Italian and was indiscreet—meeting John Farley, a future cardinal of New York, on the ship to America, he impulsively revealed that he was coming to reinstate Edward McGlynn, confirm Ireland's schools program, and make Ireland a cardinal. But he was from Perugia, where Leo had spent almost his whole career, and he was a special favorite of the Pope. The backstairs gossip at the Vatican, which O'Connell loved to repeat, was that Satolli was Leo's son. Although there is no direct evidence for the rumor, the physical resemblance was strong, and the story became so general in Washington that O'Gorman finally felt obliged to tell Satolli about it.

More damning than possible half-century-old sins of the flesh was the persistent rumor that Satolli had been bribed by Ireland. Ireland had become wealthy from midwestern land speculation, and he had spread money around Rome in 1888 when he was lobbying, successfully, to make St. Paul an archdiocese. (Denis O'Connell marveled at "the power of 'prayer.'") When he left for his 1892 Roman trip, Ireland is reported to have drawn $79,000 from his personal bank account, which may have been intended for Satolli, who was deeply in debt. Edes called Satolli a badly educated "rogue" who was sent to America to repair his finances, while a historian of the French Church, where Satolli was subsequently posted, writes that "Satolli had come back [from America] with more money than popularity." Corrigan was duly on the case and hired Michael Walsh, a New York Catholic newspaper editor, to trace out the path of Ireland's $79,000. He failed to do so but did try to blackmail both Corrigan and Ireland. In such a sea of cynicism, who could blame him?

In any case, Satolli diligently advanced Ireland's agenda at the November archbishops' meeting. The major business was a presentation by Satolli of "Fourteen Propositions" on parochial schools. They were represented as reflecting the mind of Leo, and it was expected that the archbishops would formally endorse them. The Propositions had clearly been drafted by Ireland and O'Connell, and represented a significant climb-down from the Church's traditional insistence on Catholic education. Parents could not be refused sacraments for sending their children to public schools (as they were in Europe); teachers were required to be state-certified; cooperative arrangements with public schools, as in Faribault and Stillwater, were strongly encouraged. To Satolli's shock, the archbishops refused their endorsement, and when they began to question the Propositions sharply, he angrily stalked from the room. He had already told Rampolla that the archbishops were delighted with his schema (possibly an example of Ireland's and O'Connell's creative translations). A face-saving formula was finally concocted, but despite an agreement not to publish the Propositions, O'Gorman immediately leaked them to the press.

The Propositions received a ringing endorsement from none other than Edward McGlynn, who extolled Rome, Leo, and Satolli for their astute guidance of the American Church. In December, McGlynn, at Satolli's request, submitted a statement of his beliefs for review by a committee of Catholic University theologians, including O'Gorman and Bouquillon. The committee found nothing objectionable. On Christmas Eve, Corrigan read in the newspaper that Satolli had restored McGlynn to his priestly functions in New York. (Little ensued from the reinstatement except Corrigan's humiliation, for it made banner headlines in New York. After some jockeying, McGlynn, who was feeling old, retired with rather little fuss to the rural parish that Corrigan finally gave him.)

By now, Ireland had badly overplayed his hand. Corrigan's behavior during the McGlynn crisis had been deplorable, but McGlynn himself had become increasingly erratic, and his loyal following was much dwindled. And the liberal spin-doctoring on the Fourteen Propositions was deceitful. When O'Gorman leaked Satolli's schema to the press, and Gibbons reported to the Vatican on the archbishops' meeting, they left a clear impression that the Propositions had been approved. A number of bishops were outraged and protested directly to the Pope.

Taken aback, Leo asked all the bishops to express their views on schools to him directly. Of eighty-four bishops, only eleven were happy with Satolli's Propositions as written, and six more would accept them with reservations. Of thirteen archbishops, only two besides Gibbons and Ireland endorsed them. John Lancaster Spalding, Ireland's former comrade, wrote a blistering denunciation of the harm that Ireland had done to parochial education. McQuaid, James Healy, and other bishops complained that, with the leak of the Propositions, Catholics had already begun withdrawing their children from parish schools. Leo finally responded with a Roman masterpiece of bland obscurantism: the Fourteen Propositions would stand as written, but so could any declarations of the Baltimore Council that contradicted them. The Americans could settle their disputes themselves.

Ireland suddenly found himself almost totally isolated from his colleagues. Not even Gibbons would support the Fourteen Propositions in public. Satolli seems to have divined this, for at the conclusion of the archbishops' meeting, he advised Rampolla to defer consideration of Ireland's red hat. It was a fine irony that Ireland, the apostle of "Americanism," was now solely dependent on stage-managed ukases from Rome to advance his positions. The rest of the decade was to prove the most difficult period of his long career.

"The Opinions Which Some Comprise Under the Head of Americanism"

The defeat of the Fourteen Propositions was a turning point, and by mid-1893 Satolli was showing disquieting signs of independence. After being confirmed as apostolic delegate, he moved into his own house in Washington, D.C., and his reporting arrangements were shifted back to the Propaganda. He began to associate with Keane's enemies at Catholic University, particularly Joseph Schroeder, a narrow-minded German ultranationalist who had led the attack against Bouquillon's schools pamphlet. (Schroeder had been recruited by O'Connell, who, slothful as ever, thought he was a liberal.) Satolli traveled with Gibbons and Ireland to a Parliament of Religions in Chicago, and was shocked to see the two men sharing a platform with Protestants and Jews. He visited Nilan's school in Poughkeepsie, where Nilan made a very poor impression. McQuaid began to twit Ireland about his "Faribault plan"—would Ireland correct press reports that no such thing existed? Then Gibbons, at the Pope's request, began to build bridges between Satolli and Corrigan. In the summer of 1893, Corrigan entertained Satolli as lavishly as Ireland had. By the time Satolli's tour was up in 1896, he was passionately, even venomously, opposed to everything Ireland stood for.

In the meantime, Ireland was being overwhelmed by personal problems. For many years, he had been a close friend of James J. Hill, the railroad tycoon. Hill was a Protestant who had donated $500,000 for Ireland's seminary, advised Ireland on his settlement projects, and smoothed his path to wealth through real estate investing. Ireland's sins were ones of vanity, not sensuality, and while he lived well, he probably spent most of his income on his archdiocese. But his fortune was built on a speculative bubble that burst with rude suddenness in 1892, and for a long time raw land could not find buyers at any price. Ireland's landholdings were heavily mortgaged, and since he could not refinance his mortgages when they fell due, or sell the land, he faced the specter of bankruptcy. Ireland's financial embarrassment may also bear on his break with Satolli. Satolli had good political reasons to distance himself from Ireland, but his complete conversion to such a rabid opponent remains a puzzle—unless, perhaps, Ireland had reneged on a financial understanding.

Credit: *The Cathedral Library Association*
(Left to right) *Archbishop Francesco Satolli, the first apostolic delegate to the United States; New York's Archbishop Michael Corrigan; and Rochester's Bishop Bernard McQuaid, who formed the core of the opposition to Ireland's "Americanism." The picture is from 1896.*

Ireland naturally turned to Hill, who very cautiously, over a number of years, and after much painful groveling by Ireland, bailed him out. Hill made Ireland several substantial personal loans and eventually organized a consortium of wealthy Republicans to buy out Ireland's holdings at a price that must have been far above their market value. The names in the consortium—Rockefeller, Havemeyer, Vanderbilt, Armour, Schiff, Huntington—were a roll call of Gilded Age buccaneers. This was not an ecumenical work of charity; they were buying Ireland's services for the national Republican Party. Ireland had always been a devoted Republican, who thought Democrats were parochial, "wet," and racist. But now he was required to wink at the abuses of big business and the Republicans' coy flirtation with a reinvigorated anti-Catholic vote. Most egregiously, he traveled to New York in 1894 to campaign hard against Tammany and the Democrats in the state elections. The Republicans won handily, and their victory ensured the passage of a constitutional amendment outlawing aid to parochial schools. McQuaid was outraged and mounted his pulpit in full ecclesiastical regalia to denounce Ireland's behavior:

undignified, disgraceful to his episcopal office, and a scandal in the eyes of all right-minded Catholics of both parties. . . . But, it is well known to many that it was no love of good government that kept Archbishop Ireland so many weeks in New York City and so far from his diocese, where the law of residence obliged him to be. It was to pay a debt to the Republican party that his services were rendered.

In his subsequent correspondence with Gibbons, Ireland sounds rueful and humiliated, as he deserved to be.

With Satolli now devoted to mobilizing Ireland's enemies and punishing his friends, further humiliations were in store. In 1895, the Pope ousted O'Connell from his rectorship. O'Connell richly merited censure. He was neglectful of his duties, preferring to squire pious ladies on long trips to the Holy Land; but his downfall came, it seems, when the Pope learned of his role in spreading the Satolli bastardy stories. Gibbons rescued his protégé with a sinecure in Rome, and for the next eight years, ensconced in a fashionable apartment, O'Connell gave himself up to the life of the salons. Then Ireland suffered the embarrassment of having his recommendation of O'Gorman for a bishopric within his own archdiocese held up for months. O'Gorman finally squeaked through, but his appointment was paired with that of a German to whom Ireland was strongly opposed. Finally, Keane, whose rectorship was a papal appointment, was ousted from Catholic University. After sulking for a while in California, he accepted an archbishop's title and a bureaucrat's job at the Propaganda. McQuaid exploded with glee: "The news from Rome is astounding. . . . What collapses on every side! Gibbons, Ireland, and Keane!!! They were cock of the walk for a while and dictated to the country and thought to run our dioceses for us. They may change their policy and repent. They can never repair the harm done in the past."

Ireland was briefly heartened when the Pope and Rampolla called upon him for help in averting the Spanish-American War. Ireland's connections in the McKinley administration were excellent, since he had earned them on the campaign trail. He dutifully went to Washington and succeeded in mediating some promising contacts between the Vatican, the Spanish monarchy, and the White House. But a linguistic confusion caused a premature announcement in Rome and much embarrassment all around. Ireland's stock in Rome fell further when he lustily cheered America's victories over Catholic Spain.

The last act of official "Americanism" was played out in Europe. The Vatican's attraction to John Ireland and republicanism always had more to do with France than with America. But by the end of the decade, Rampolla's French policy was in tatters. The French monarchist right and their Jesuit allies were hauling up their intellectual drawbridges in the wake of the Dreyfus affair, and Rome was concentrating on repairing relations with imperial Germany.

It was amid these swirling crosscurrents that there appeared, in 1898, a French translation of *The Life of Father Hecker,* the American liberal Catholic convert, friend of Orestes Brownson, and founder of the Paulists. The translation was prepared by a French priest, Abbé Félix Klein, who wrote a preface calling for a less formal, more interior Catholicism, greater religious and personal independence, doctrines more in accord with modern science, and active engagement against social inequities. His preface, in short, managed to wave every red flag that could incite the French right. He buttressed his arguments with a freely translated rendition of Ireland's introduction to the English edition of the book. When Klein's book became a best-seller and cause célèbre, conservative French theologians ascribed all of the French Church's problems to America and John Ireland. A broadside attack on "Americanism," by a priest named Charles Maignen, was helped into print by the pro-German wing of the Vatican, who were outraged by America's war against the king of Spain. Satolli himself supplied a preface to the English translation of Maignen's book. A condemnation of "Americanism" as Maignen had defined it was inevitable.

When it came, it was gentle enough, much more so than a screed drafted by Satolli and the Jesuits. Leo's letter, *Testem Benevolentiae,* warmly praised the church in America but said, "We cannot approve the opinions which some comprise under the head of Americanism," listing a series of esoteric doctrines that few Americans would have recognized. Ireland responded with a public declaration that neither he nor anyone else he knew in America espoused such doctrines, and expressed resentment that his country's name had been so unfairly expropriated. Most other American bishops wrote in the same vein. But Corrigan, Katzer, and some others took exception to Ireland's letter, writing that "Americanism" indeed *had* been a danger in America, but would be no longer. Ireland tried to beard them at the next archbishops' meeting, but Gibbons would not allow it. As Ireland put it, "Baltimore cried 'peace, peace, death even for the sake of peace.' "

Leo's letter touched off a brief flap in the Catholic press, but was hardly noticed by the secular papers. Its only importance in America was as a kind of final scorecard for a fifteen-year catfight, for by 1899, the Americanist controversies were finally over. Out of the conflict, however, the contours of a Catholic accommodation with a secular state had evolved quietly, almost inadvertently. Within a very short time, they seemed so natural, were so taken for granted, that the great controversies disappeared almost without a ripple beneath the smooth surface of the American Church.

The American Catholic compromise was a peculiarly Irish-American one. Practical and politically astute, it hewed an adroit path between the extremes of the Americanist combatants. The Church that looked confidently forward to the new century was separatist, ethnically grounded, and hyperpatriotic all at the same time. Wrapping Catholics' entire lives with religion, it was yet the most formalistic, and in Protestant eyes the most unspiritual, of faiths. Committed to a sweeping program of immigrant uplift, it was yet politically conservative and fatalistic, a friend of mainstream labor unions but suspicious of grand schemes of social reform. *In* America, but decisively not *of* it, it was yet the most patriotic and nationalistic of churches.

Credit: Library of Congress
By the turn of the century, with Baltimore's politically adept Cardinal James Gibbons as its spokesman, the Church finally reached a comfortable political accommodation with America. Big-city cardinals and bishops regularly hobnobbed with governors, and even presidents. This shot of Gibbons with Theodore Roosevelt dates from 1918.

The great instrument of Catholic separatism was the parochial school, which is why Ireland's school Propositions provoked such a revolt. McQuaid expressed the separatist credo perfectly when he wrote to the Pope:

> Associations in schools . . . where all classes, Protestants, Jews, and Infidels meet promiscuously, present another danger. . . . Catholic children, in attendance at Catholic schools, frequent the sacraments regularly. . . .

When not in Catholic schools, experience has shown that only a small number, and these of pious families, can be brought to confession. Other children, not Catholic, have no such protection for morality and esteem purity, under a laxer system of intercourse between the sexes, as less sacred. These associations, ripening into friendships, lead in time to mixed marriages, the growing evil of our time and country.

The enveloping formalism of the American Church sprang from the Cullen/Hughes recipe for upgrading Irish peasants and immigrant hordes—go to Mass, receive the sacraments, send your children to Catholic schools, do as the nuns and priests say, give money, avoid drunkenness and impurity. Such mandates implied an imposing and far-flung services network, playing to the strength of Irish-American prelates, who were hardheaded businessmen and practical politicians rather than theologians.

Educated Protestants scorned the American Church's lack of mysticism, its disdain for charisma, its embrace of mundanity—how did kneeling through an hour of mumbled Latin bring a working man closer to God? Perhaps it didn't, but it created sober and, within limits, successful working men and women, reliable graduates of a petit-bourgeois boot camp, whose children had clean faces. As the Irish-American share of the hierarchy rose to 75 percent in the early 1900s, all immigrant groups, even the Germans, gradually bent their religious practice to comport with the Irish-American norm.

To the Irish American, innocent of theological nuance, there was no conflict, could be no conflict, between America and the Pope. The Catholic Church was the grandest Church in the world, and the Pope the grandest religious leader. America was at the same time the grandest country in the world, on its way to becoming the most powerful as well. Just as Catholicism came to define much of what it was to be Irish, America became Ireland's "second fatherland," very much as the Germans complained. As one writer put it, "Irish, Catholic, and American became almost identical in the Irish-American mind." The loyalty of Irish Catholics, and with the passage of time, of all Catholics, became as unquestioned as it was unquestioning. To find citizens who lived by America's stated values, who believed in their leaders, and who faithfully discharged their patriotic duties, one needed to look no further than to Catholics.

The American Catholic compromise, that is, drew from the separatism of Corrigan without his latent Bourbonism. The notion that Catholics should look to Rome for their politics made no sense in an American context. And it drew from the patriotism of Ireland and McGlynn, while rejecting their assimilationist impulses. The exemplars of the successful twentieth-century American prelate would be John Hughes and the curmudgeonly Bernard McQuaid.

The smooth success of the American Catholic compromise and the advancing age of the partisans cooled combative ardor. John Ireland traveled to Rochester and spent several days with McQuaid; the two Irishmen discovered they quite liked each other. Ireland and Corrigan at least learned to be polite.

And much to his delight, Ireland discovered that the Pope still appreciated him. He lectured in Rome amid much papal good feeling, and almost burst with pride when President McKinley chose him to present a statue of Lafayette to France. In Paris, he delivered a loving paean to America, to France, and to freedom, and was lionized by the French press. He went home to St. Paul and, like any conventional bishop, built a cathedral—indeed, after his drive to merge the Twin Cities fell short, he built two at the same time. A major St. Paul thoroughfare is named John Ireland Boulevard.

Corrigan, always the obsessive, devoted his last years to finishing St. Patrick's. He succeeded in erecting the steeples, and started a Lady Chapel in the rear to substitute for Renwick's plan for a five-chapel rosette. On a late-night inspection tour in 1902, he fell into the excavation and died a short while later. His replacement was the irenic John Farley, more genial than Gibbons, more tolerant than Corrigan, more politic than either Hughes or Ireland.

Denis O'Connell made his peace with Satolli and even with Ella Edes. All was clearly forgiven when O'Connell, his face puffy with good living, was rescued from his sybarite's exile in Rome and installed, *mirabile dictu,* as rector of Catholic University. Ireland welcomed him home with a *"Viva l'americanismo,"* but it was the last wave of a tattered banner. O'Connell ended his career as bishop of Richmond, under Gibbons's protective wing to the last. Keane survived his curial exile as well and became archbishop of Dubuque.

Cardinal Gibbons became the public face of the American Church. This small, neat man, his silver hair perfectly in place, seemed always gracious, never pompous, impeccably conservative, but instinctively fair. His caution usually passed as wisdom, and often was, and he readily lent the Church's name to all good patriotic causes.

Rome could hardly have understood what the Americans had wrought, but as anticlerical European governments hacked away at the Church's subsidies, Vatican cardinals could see that America was becoming their paymaster. Leo, at least, was satisfied. As he wrote Gibbons:

> Our daily experience obliges Us to confess that We have found your people, through your influence, endowed with a perfect docility of mind and alacrity of disposition. Therefore, while the changes and the tendencies of nearly all the nations which were Catholic for many centuries give cause for sorrow, the state of your churches, in this flourishing youthfulness, cheers Our heart and fills it with delight.

CHAPTER 5

An American Church

It was in 1850 that John Hughes boasted that the Catholic Church would conquer all of America. By 1900, that prediction looked well on the way to vindication. At the century's turn, with 12 million American Catholics, Catholicism was not only the country's largest religious denomination by a substantial margin but, with a massive new influx of Catholic immigrants and a high Catholic birth rate, was by far the fastest growing. The number of American Catholics quadrupled between 1860 and 1900, and, despite a slowdown in Catholic immigration by World War I, kept growing to almost 20 million in the 1920s. Inexorably, the Catholic share of the population was also rising rapidly, approaching 20 percent by 1930.

The canonical sixteen-team organization of major league baseball, prior to the moves west in the 1950s, is a good proxy for Catholic distribution in the first half of the twentieth century. (New York had three teams. Chicago, Boston, Philadelphia, and St. Louis each had two, while Pittsburgh, Cincinnati, Detroit, Washington, and Cleveland had one apiece. There were no teams in the South or West.) Catholicism was first of all an urban phenomenon. New York City alone, including Brooklyn, accounted for almost 16 percent of American Catholics in 1900, and about 30 percent of all Catholics lived in the dioceses of New York, Brooklyn, Chicago, Boston, and Philadelphia. Altogether, almost half of all Catholics were concentrated in the Northeast, with another 30 percent in the upper Midwest above the Ohio River. Outside of this "Catholic belt" the largest Catholic concentrations were in San Francisco—where the sizable Irish and Italian populations accounted for about two-thirds of all Catholics in the far West—and in New Orleans, where Catholicism was a legacy of the French empire. A majority of people in the sparsely settled Southwest may have espoused some version of Hispanic Catholicism, but their numbers were very small, and they were only loosely connected to the organized Church.

Runaway growth in Catholic numbers and the American Church's separatist impulse required prodigious expansion of physical facilities. Churches could be provided cheaply in rented halls or storefronts, but schools required buildings, staffs, and textbooks. The destitution of each new immigrant wave and the fear of leaving foreign innocents to the mercies of the "soulless" state impelled the construction of orphanages, "training schools" for older boys and girls, and in the larger dioceses, hospitals and sanitary clinics. The mistrust of foreign priests drove all the major dioceses to build their own seminaries to ensure a ready supply of right-thinking young curates. The requirement for a trustworthy elite of educated lay men and women to support the Church in politics, business, and in local parishes prompted the establishment of Catholic high schools, "normal" schools, and full-fledged colleges.

Rochester's Bernard McQuaid was the model of the successful American-style bishop. In thirty years, McQuaid opened twenty-six parishes and seventeen missions and built thirty parochial schools, at least seven high schools—including three for girls, one of which became Nazareth College—a number of orphanages and industrial training schools, two seminaries, a hospital, and the mandatory cathedral. By 1896, McQuaid was educating almost as many children as the public schools and was closing in on his goal of providing a free Catholic education to every Catholic child in the diocese. He was one of the first bishops to insist that all his schools meet state standards. All Catholic students had to pass the state Regents' test, and he made his teaching nuns work toward their state certification.

The first tuition-free Catholic high school for boys opened in Philadelphia in 1890, and the diocese operated 103 elementary schools in 1903. Fifty more schools were added by 1916, and school attendance doubled during the same time. In 1907, the Boston diocese counted more than 50,000 Catholic school students, from the elementary grades all the way through the university level at Boston College, and boasted the full panoply of orphans' asylums, homes for destitute children, infants' asylums, and nursing homes, as well as three hospitals. New York's Corrigan calculated that between 1890 and 1900, he had opened new buildings at the rate of one every two weeks—schools, churches, convents, rectories, seminaries, asylums, foundling homes—or more than 250 major buildings in all. Chicago's Patrick Feehan (archbishop from 1880 to 1902) still holds the parish-opening record, with 140. Nationwide, in 1900, the American church was served by 12,000 priests and 50,000 nuns, staffing more than 12,000 parishes and missions and 3300 schools. The Catholic parish-school population approached a quarter of a million students.

Outside of the booming industrial conurbations in the Northeast and around the Great Lakes and the Mississippi and Ohio Rivers, the great majority of the Church's ninety-three dioceses were still small, struggling affairs. South and west of Baltimore, Catholics were few and far between, constituting hardly 6 percent of the population. Charleston, South Carolina, for example, was one of the oldest American dioceses, founded in 1820 with the contentious Irishman John England as its first bishop. Eighty years later, the diocese reported only 8000 Catholics, or about the same number as in a good-sized New York parish, served by fifteen priests and five Catholic schools. There were fewer than 200,000 Catholics scattered through the vast Texas prairies, most of them probably Irish and German settlers, since there were still few Mexicans in the state. The Archdiocese of Santa Fe—one early incumbent said he was "bishop of all outdoors"—listed 379 parishes in 1900, but only 61 priests. While his eastern counterparts hobnobbed with governors and presidents, Archbishop Jean Baptiste Salpointe worried about the Penitente Brotherhood, bands of laymen that traveled through the tiny desert settlements performing folk-Catholic rites for funerals and weddings, seasoned with a good dollop of pre-Hispanic cults, like that of *la Muerte,* the black icon of death.

The big urban dioceses set the tone for, and defined the public image of, the American Church. Bishops of big dioceses were captains of major bricks-and-mortar-intensive business enterprises. A small number of men, all of whom became cardinals, had unusually long tenures as archbishops of the biggest dioceses—William O'Connell in Boston (1907–1944); George Mundelein in Chicago (1915–1939); Dennis Dougherty in Philadelphia (1918–1951); and in New York, John Farley (1902–1918) and Patrick Hayes (1919–1938). Stripping away the inevitable clashes of style and personality, they were extraordinarily like-minded—centralizers, standardizers, and disciplinarians. With the exception of Mundelein, the son of German immigrants, they were all Irish Americans; and Mundelein was a kind of honorary Irishman, having spent his entire early career in the very Irish diocese of Brooklyn as the special protégé of Bishop Charles McDonnell. During a quarter-century reign in Chicago, the most ethnically varied diocese in the country, he selected only Irish auxiliary bishops. A cardinal's red hat also went to all but one of Gibbons's successors in Baltimore and to All Hallows alumnus John Glennon of St. Louis, mostly by virtue of his long tenure (1903–1946). But Glennon rarely involved himself in affairs outside of his diocese, and after Gibbons's death in 1921, the Baltimore see never carried the weight of the big four.

In the established dioceses, the priesthood offered a tempting package of security and social rank to any young man with upper-middle-class aspirations. Particularly among the Irish, few, if any, occupations matched its prestige. Compared with other high-status professions, like medicine or the law, the priesthood was much more accessible to a young man without family connections or the means to finance an extended education. Seminarians paid tuition if they could afford it, but money was rarely a bar if a youth showed genuine aptitude—all of the post–World War I American cardinals were the sons of workingmen. Baltimore priests received annual salaries of $600 in 1900, the same as average family income in the diocese, and pastors received $1000; and, of course, a priest had no dependents, except perhaps his parents, and was provided with free room, board, and housekeeping services. St. Paul's priests earned $800 a year in an even poorer diocese. Bishops did much better; John Ireland's salary was $20,000, a princely sum for the day. None lived as simply as Michael Heiss had; when the cantankerous German-nationalist archbishop of Milwaukee set off for the Baltimore council in 1884, his friends took up a subscription to buy him a new suit.

Nuns were at the bottom of the religious pecking order. A nun's annual salary in Baltimore was only $200 in 1900, and it was paid to the order, not to the individual. But the number of American nuns still grew very rapidly, and nuns outnumbered priests by more than 4:1 by the turn of the century. In truth, there were few lay positions open to women that carried the prestige of a Catholic nun, and none with the authority and independence of a mother superior. Nuns ran hospitals, orphanages, schools, and colleges, jobs that in the lay world were reserved for men. Feisty mothers superior even faced down powerful cardinals like Mundelein and O'Connell with impunity. As one nun recently put it: "These were pretty independent ladies. They were the engineers who fired up the boilers in the morning. They fixed things. They managed the investments. They approved the building plans and managed the construction. We didn't know that women couldn't do all those things. On the outside, until very recently, women could only be secretaries or teachers." Nuns made many sacrifices, to be sure, but the convent clearly had its attractions, especially when compared with the plight of the working-class housewife or the younger daughter condemned to a life caring for aging relatives.

The religious celibacy requirement was a major barrier to recruitment, but much more so for, say, southern Italians, who tended to regard a priest as unmanly, than for the post-Famine Irish, who were accustomed to high rates of celibacy even among laymen. (Everyone assumed that celibacy was not an issue for women.) Discipline seems to have been quite uneven in the nineteenth-century Church. In Chicago, for example, where there was a babel of foreign priests and a succession of weak bishops—both Feehan and his successor, James Quigley (1902–1915) seem to have lost control of their clergy—clerical concubinage was apparently widespread. But by the first decades of the twentieth century, the celibacy rule seems to have been strictly enforced everywhere.

Irish Americans continued to supply a disproportionate share of the Church's nuns and priests even as their share of the Catholic population slipped below a majority after 1900, to possibly only a third by the 1920s. Just as a Tammany precinct leader like George Washington Plunkett learned to spend his days at bar mitzvahs and Italian funerals, Irish-American priests presided over parishes of Bohemians and Slovaks, while Irish-American nuns despaired at the quantities of vermin on Italian first graders. As late as the 1970s, when fewer than a fifth of American Catholics were of Irish descent, Irish Americans still accounted for more than a third of the clergy and fully half of the hierarchy.

The path to power in the Church lay through the bureaucracy, not the pastorate. Mundelein started his Brooklyn career as Bishop McDonnell's secretary and was quickly made diocesan chancellor and finally auxiliary bishop, winning a reputation for his building programs. William O'Connell spent ten years as a curate but earned his local reputation as an orator before being plucked from Boston to replace Denis O'Connell at the North American College in 1895. Dougherty never worked as a curate and went straight from a career as a theology professor to successive episcopal appointments in the Philippines and in Buffalo before returning to Philadelphia as archbishop. Farley started as John McCloskey's secretary. He spent ten years as a pastor when he was in disfavor with Corrigan during the McGlynn furor, but was brought back into the chancery as tensions began to ease in 1895. Hayes spent a year as Farley's parish assistant, then moved to the chancery with him.

A Roman education and Roman patronage were almost prerequisites for high office, and Mundelein, Dougherty, William O'Connell, and Farley had all gotten their theology training in Rome. Hayes, a Catholic University alumnus, was an exception, but the succession in New York was unusually ingrown, with contacts in the chancery counting much more heavily than in other dioceses. (Corrigan, who was from Newark, was always regarded as an outsider.) As a Roman student, O'Connell became close friends with Rafael Merry del Val, a scion of the Spanish nobility, fluent English speaker and avid tennis player; later, when Merry del Val had become the powerful papal secretary of state, he carefully watched over O'Connell's career. Dougherty had many friends in Rome and was close to Cardinal Pietro Gasparri, who was also a secretary of state. Farley was appointed with the support of Satolli, while Mundelein's patron was the papal representative to America, Cardinal Giovanni Bonzano, another friendship dating from student days.

The American Church needed tightfisted managers, politicians with a fund-raising flair, big thinkers and doers much more than saintly leaders. In the Old World, opening a new parish was a rare event; some parish boundaries existed for centuries, with churches being added or abandoned according to the slow rhythms of populations. In Europe, clergy often drew state salaries, and almost everywhere education was an affair of the state. But the Church in America was not only the fastest growing in the world—by leagues—constantly expanding into new and virtually unchurched territories but was building a complete network of Catholic institutions at the same time, and all with no assistance—indeed, often active hostility—from the state. On top of all that, the Church was absorbing wave after wave of ethnic settlers. Just when the Irish Catholic presence was stabilizing, German Catholics began arriving in large numbers, then the Italians, then the Poles, and then all the multifarious Catholic tribes from the splintering Austro-Hungarian Empire, from Ruthenians to Slovenians, each with its own language and culture, its own ideas about assimilation and separation, its own resentments and animosities, often its own versions of Catholic ritual, and its own degree of willingness to make financial sacrifices in the name of religion.

The growing wealth of the Church was both exaggerated and very real. Most bishops gradually followed Hughes's practice of putting all Church property in their own or the diocese's name. The favored technique was the "corporation sole." The archbishop of Chicago, for example, was the sole shareholder of a corporation that owned all of the diocesan assets; upon an incumbent's death or transfer, the next bishop succeeded him as shareholder. The total assets controlled by a corporation sole could be quite impressive, but physical assets were a poor proxy for wealth. Church properties were usually heavily mortgaged, and few were income producing. The bigger dioceses often had a handful of commercial holdings, like McQuaid's vineyard and some of John Ireland's real estate investments, but most were in a constant struggle to make ends meet. The market value of the land under St. Patrick's, in theory, is astronomical, but the fact that it has a cathedral sitting on it makes it almost worthless to anyone but the diocese.

But the Church was such a big player in urban real estate markets that it could be ignored only by the bravest of politicians, bankers, contractors, insurance men and lawyers. (One old joke had it that when St. Peter asked an American cardinal for his occupation, the reply was "real estate agent.") Over the years, Protestant denominations probably built more churches and charitable institutions (excluding schools) than Catholics did, but they were never as organized as Catholics. Mundelein's centralization of diocesan construction finance is a good example. Paying for a new church or school was a parish responsibility, but Mundelein established a diocesan mortgage operation, which he funded by issuing "Catholic bishop's bonds" at very favorable rates of interest. All parishes were required to use the mortgage facility to finance their buildings, with Mundelein approving both the building and the mortgage. At a stroke, Mundelein saved Catholics millions in interest costs, won control over parish building activities, and made himself one of Chicago's biggest bond issuers. Catholic bishop's bonds were an important factor in the growth of the Chicago investment banking firm of Halsey Stuart, which later challenged J. P. Morgan and Co. for control of the

Midwest's corporate finance business. If Mundelein had a problem—about anything—a lot of influential Chicagoans were delighted to sit down and listen very carefully.

Although the foreignness of Catholics was still a lightning rod for bigotry, the political power of the Church was a buffer against discrimination—in public employment or in the military, for instance. The Church's flair for organized pageantry was expensive, but it also helped underline the power and numbers of the Church's constituency. Five hundred thousand Catholics turned out to welcome John Farley when he came home to New York from Rome with his cardinal's hat in 1911, and hundreds of office buildings flew papal flags. When Farley decided to pay off St. Patrick's Cathedral's debt— Hughes had promised it would never be officially consecrated until it was debt-free—he did it in two years, all $850,000, and without a special fund drive. This was a man, as the politicians would say, with "clout."

William O'Connell's massive displays, which he could toss off at a moment's notice, may have set a new high in tastelessness, but in brahmin New England they also served to snap politicians and businessmen to attention. O'Connell became a cardinal at the same time as Farley and organized a full month of ceremonies, beginning with a military parade to welcome him at the dock. A few months later, when William Howard Taft spoke at a Boston St. Patrick's Day dinner, O'Connell, now that he was a "prince" of the Church, insisted on being seated in front of the governor and next to the president. Immigrants delighted in the fawning deference that a cardinal or a powerful archbishop received from governors, mayors, and sometimes even presidents. *Their* people and *their* Church could rise to the very top in America.

No other American institution was as autocratic as the Church. There were, of course, boundaries on episcopal authority. Certain longtime pastors were "irremovable." Religious orders, male and female alike, could be very independent. Diocesan priests had real, if limited, rights of appeal from episcopal decisions. A McGlynnite priest in Rochester almost drove McQuaid to distraction by tying up a disciplinary attempt in procedural tangles that lasted for years. But these were minimal restraints in an organization where the self-image of the senior executives was constantly puffed up with ceremony, jewelry, regalia, all the trappings of mystery and feudal authority, the persistent reminders of their role as mediators for the divine.

The corruption of power was the constant danger, one that was only increased by the terrible personal isolation of a bishop. A bishop of a big diocese had only intermittent contact with his episcopal peers and usually maintained highly formal relations with his priests. The same applied, on a smaller scale, to the archetypal tyrannical pastor. (It is easy to understand the plague of clerical alcoholism.) In his late years, John Hughes, who may have struggled with alcohol himself, reached out to his sister and her children to supply the family warmth he so painfully needed. Corrigan and Mundelein were both intensely shy men. Corrigan buried himself in the arcana of diocesan administration, while Mundelein seems to have developed intense emotional, but, it must be said in the 1990s, apparently not erotic dependence on a small number of priests. Dougherty ruled like a grizzly in a cave—his longtime, highly regarded schools director never approached him without trembling—but he built a personal life around his sisters' families, playing the benevolent uncle to his nieces and nephews. McQuaid and Ireland sublimated their personal needs in ceaseless public activity. Farley seems to have been a well-balanced man, with many friends, while Hayes was narrow, cautious, and constrained. In common, however, all of these men were at least conventionally devout, and their standards of personal discipline were high. Denis O'Connell's affinity for the salons and John Lancaster Spalding's apparent affair with Mamie Caldwell were not at all typical. Religion really did temper the seductions of power, the lapses of vanity, and the yearnings of the flesh. A dutiful bishop recited every day, in his Mass and in his Breviary, a drumbeat of admonitions to humility, forbearance, self-denial, and self-subjection.

Cardinal William O'Connell epitomized the danger of ecclesiastical power untethered by religion. In his public role, he was among the most effective of churchmen. A gifted and demanding administrator, he greatly expanded the reach and wealth of the Boston church and imposed strict standards of discipline, both financial and personal, on the clergy. Politically, he came to personify the aspirations and achievements of the disciplined, respectable, hardworking, and upwardly mobile Irish, acting as a counterweight to the raffish irresponsibility of his lifelong antagonist, James Michael Curley, the Boston Irish political boss. When the Cardinal seemed to oppose Curley on grounds of Curley's dishonesty in 1937, Irish Catholic voters duly turned out and trounced their longtime political idol.

But on a personal level, O'Connell was an irreligious hypocrite, lacking honesty or integrity, nakedly ambitious and endlessly self-aggrandizing, a kind of Gilded Age buccaneer of churchmen, who ran his diocese like a Cornelius Vanderbilt or a Jay Gould. Powerfully built, carrying 200 pounds on a five-foot-eight-inch frame, he was bald and bullet-headed, with a broad, firm mouth and square jaw. He had a fine baritone voice, some taste and talent for literature and music, gregarious self-confidence and an immensely forceful presence, whether chesting up to a potential donor or intimidating an errant pastor. O'Connell was impressive, said a hostile priest, "as an elephant is impressive." Ella Edes called him "Monsignor Pomposity." In a fine photograph that captures him waving his homburg to the crowd, his eyes narrowed against the sun, he looks for all the world like a Soviet premier on the porch of the Kremlin.

Cardinal William O'Connell, who ruled the Archdiocese of Boston from 1907 to 1944, was addicted to high-style living and sadly deficient as a spiritual leader. But he was a "Prince of the Church" in the eyes of working-class Catholics, and epitomized the heights Catholics could attain.

Much more so than his fellow bishops, O'Connell was a man of the boardroom and the country club rather than of the Church. He showed little interest in religion, rarely said daily Mass, and rushed through services at a pace that sometimes scandalized onlookers. A collection of aphorisms that he published in 1926 contains almost no religious references. Although he imposed a strict, puritanical standard of deportment and morality on his priests and on Boston's Catholics, he did not apply it to himself. When he arrived from Rome for his first episcopal assignment in Portland, Maine, he brought an Italian valet and his family, a coachman, and an Italian music master. In Boston he built a succession of ever grander houses, finally settling in a Renaissance *palazzo* in Brighton, complete with a private golf course. (His predecessor, John Williams, was content with a room in the cathedral rectory.) O'Connell had an oceanside summer estate, Villa Santa Croce, in fashionable Marblehead, and a winter home in the Bahamas, whence he sent his flock encouraging words during one of the crueler winters of the Depression. He sported a gold-headed cane, tooled around in a customized Pierce Arrow, was a connoisseur of fine wines, and spent so much time traveling to the Caribbean or to Europe that cynics called him "Gangplank Bill."

O'Connell was dishonest. When he left Portland for Boston, he took $25,000 of diocesan funds with him. (He returned the money without comment when his shocked successor called him to account.) He commingled his own and archdiocesan monies and lavished benefits upon his relatives. He appointed his nephew, James O'Connell, chancellor of the archdiocese almost as soon as the young man was ordained, and then stood by for more than a decade while James divided his time between his duties in Boston and his real estate business and wife (a divorcée) in New York. The real estate business thrived, doubtless because it was financed with perhaps three quarters of a million dollars embezzled from the archdiocese. O'Connell and his nephew lived together in Boston and were virtually inseparable, so there is little question that the Cardinal knew what was going on. Outraged Boston priests finally brought the story to the Pope; when O'Connell was confronted with it, he lied. James was finally forced out of the archdiocese, but he kept his money and his business, eventually rising to become a member of the Manhattan Board of Trade.

David Toomey was another young priest who lived with James and the Cardinal. He edited the diocesan paper and was also married, although his wife at first didn't know he was a priest, as James's did. When Toomey's wife threatened to expose him, the Cardinal hushed up the matter with money, as he had with a previous Toomey affair. According to Toomey, the Cardinal was so cooperative because he was a homosexual and was being blackmailed by James. There is no proof of the charge, although the Cardinal was a longtime friend and traveling companion of a Boston doctor and prominent Catholic layman, William Dunn, who may have been homosexual. (Dunn's sexual preferences became an issue when his relatives contested his estate, which had been left to a male friend.) At Dunn's death, the Cardinal's personal lawyer intervened to ensure that Dunn's letters to O'Connell were destroyed.

O'Connell's personal ambition was boundless. He was not on anyone's list to succeed either to the Portland or to the Boston sees but engineered the appointments through his friend, Merry del Val. When the Boston appointment was open, he did not hesitate to spread calumnies against his predecessor and the other candidates to secure the see for himself. When Farley

died, O'Connell made a rabble-rousing foray into New York, in an unsuc-
cessful attempt to enlist support for his own appointment, and peppered the
Vatican with the same calumnies against Farley as he had spread against
Williams. His letters to Merry del Val and the Pope constantly proclaimed
the dangers the Church faced in America, and how only he could save it. His
mendacity was as constant in small matters as in large. He published a collection of his letters in 1915—great men published their letters—but they
were inventions, concocted by the Cardinal for the occasion. No word of his
autobiography can be taken at face value.

O'Connell's personal behavior, however it strained the faith of the long-
suffering Boston clergy, had no apparent effect on the public success of the
Church. As much as any other prelate, O'Connell—in his public, not his
personal side—represented the new generation of American Catholicism.
John Williams, his predecessor, had been a throwback to the 1830s-style
American Church. A gentle and much loved Irishman, he was timorous, an
assimilationist who admired Yankee society, who worried about the impact
of immigration on the Church's reputation, who downplayed parochial
schools so as not to make Catholics too conspicuous and wanted his archdiocese to melt quietly into its New England surroundings. The prototypes
for Williams were the "Castle" bishops of Dublin, who worked hand in glove
with successive colonial administrations, garnering small privileges for the
Church at the price of Irish nationalism and Catholic identity. O'Connell
looked at Williams with uncomprehending scorn. For himself, chest out, jaw
thrust forward, hand raised to acknowledge the adulatory crowds, he was
leading the march into a new era of Catholic triumphalism, striding forth to
claim the Church's place as a major force in American society. A dreadful
human being and a bad priest, he was undeniably a successful cardinal.

Catholic triumphalism was especially a phenomenon of cohesively Irish
Catholic cities, like Boston and New York. In Boston, Irish Catholics controlled even the *public* school system. By 1930, half of all of Boston's school
principals were Catholics, most of them from the Jesuits' Boston College.
The head of teacher development for the public schools was the sister of the
priest in charge of teacher training at the college. In other cities, ethnic splintering was still a bar, if only a temporary one, to the Church's achieving the
same degree of self-confident militance.

The "Other" Catholics

Chicago's Kennedy Expressway links the downtown business district with
O'Hare Airport to the northwest, running parallel to Milwaukee Avenue
much of the way. Looking west toward Milwaukee Avenue, a driver on the

expressway sees the rounded steeples of monumental Catholic churches, one after the other, poking up above the trees and apartment buildings. This is the heart of Chicago's Polonia, the world's largest Polish settlement outside of Poland, and one of the most staunchly—indeed, most romantically and violently—Catholic of all American immigrant enclaves. The emotional center of Polonia is still St. Stanislaus Kostka Church, Chicago's first Polish Catholic church, rebuilt in the 1880s to the scale of a small cathedral. The rounded central arch above the rose window, with steplike scrollwork traveling up each side, is a Polish architectural motif, and together with the domed cupolas atop the steeples, gives the church a distinctly Eastern European flavor. The exterior of the church badly needs repair, and one of the cupolas was burned away by a lightning bolt thirty years ago; but the interior is beautiful, with Tiffany chandeliers, bright murals of Polish saints, and some extraordinary stained glass and carved wainscoting.

St. Stanislaus is by no means Polonia's most spectacular church. Holy Trinity, just two blocks south, and a longtime rival, was rebuilt in 1905 and is even bigger. There were thirty-five major Polish parishes in Chicago by World War I, and fifty-seven by World War II. In the early 1900s, St. Stanislaus had more than 40,000 parishioners, making it by far America's largest parish, possibly the largest in the entire world, with more Catholics than most American dioceses. (Holy Trinity, with 25,000 parishioners, was not far behind.) Like all "ethnics," Poles have been dispersing away from the city since the 1950s. The signs in the discount stores near St. Stanislaus are now in Spanish, and almost all of the parish's elementary school students are Mexican-Americans, but third- and fourth-generation Poles still come back to St. Stanislaus for weddings and baptisms. And Chicago's "little Poland" endures just a few miles farther up Milwaukee Avenue, where store signs are almost exclusively in Polish, pictures of Pope John Paul II are everywhere, and restaurants serve cabbage soup, pierogi, and Zywiec beer. Of all American immigrants, Poles have been among the most loyal to their national heritage and religion.

When Poles arrived in America, they found a Church already dominated by Irish, or in some places by German, clergy, with a hierarchy embarked on an aggressive campaign to create a centralized, highly uniform national Church, in the new American style. The fitful and awkward working out of an accommodation between Polonia and a mainstreaming Church illustrates how a series of immigrant religions was gradually being forged into a national institution.

The last remnant of an independent Polish state disappeared in 1863, after almost a century of depredations by Russia, Prussia, and Austria that Poles call their "century of sadness." Austria was Catholic, but both Prussia and Russia were in various degrees hostile to Roman Catholicism, and the

Poles came to identify Catholicism with their nationalist cause like no other immigrant group except the Irish. Unlike the Germans, Polish immigrants were predominantly peasants; and unlike the anticlerical Italians and Czechs, but again like the Irish, Poles held their priests in reverence and awe. Polish priests tended to be drawn from the bourgeoisie, and the fondest dream of every Polish family was to have a son qualify for the priesthood. Some 1.5 million Poles, at least three quarters of them Catholic, came to America before the war, almost all of them after 1880. Polish immigration data are very poor, since after the loss of independence Poles were counted in the ruling country's totals, as "Russians," for instance; but by any reasonable estimate, Polish Catholic immigration was comparable to, and may have exceeded, that of the Germans and the Italians.

The first permanent Polish-American settlement, Panna Maria, or the Village of the Virgin Mary, was in Galveston, Texas, of all places, in the early 1850s, and the settlement supplied Polish priests to the rest of the country for decades to come. Emigration came to a virtual halt during the Civil War, but picked up sharply again as soon as it ended. Postbellum mass-production manufacturing needed open spaces, access to the vast Great Lakes iron and coal reserves, and good rail transportation. Hundreds of thousands of unskilled production jobs opened up in cities like Cleveland, Buffalo, Pittsburgh, and Chicago just as Polish immigration was accelerating in the 1870s and 1880s; and Poles were often used as strikebreakers against Irish unions, as at Andrew Carnegie's Homestead steel mill in 1892. In Chicago, in addition to the settlements northwest of the city, Polish communities sprang up in the Back of the Yards area near the stockyards, and around the steel mills to the southeast stretching down to Gary. By the turn of the century, Poles were probably Chicago's most numerous ethnic group and the largest body of the Catholics.

Polish immigrant community life was thickly textured with religion, and Polish Chicago built a Catholic infrastructure that outstripped even that of the Irish—schools and high schools, parish halls, orphanages and hospitals, the massive churches, its own seminary. By the turn of the century, almost two out of every three Polish schoolchildren through high school age attended a parochial school. Daily life was organized around a liturgical rhythm derived from the calendar of saints. There were Sodalities, rosary societies, special devotions, cadet corps, theater groups, literary societies, choirs—all of them, of course, in Polish. Girls who pledged chastity until marriage were "roses," and parishes competed to build the biggest rose tree to Our Lady.

The master engineer of Polish Chicago was Vincent Barzyński, pastor of St. Stanislaus from 1874 until his death in 1899, a man with a high forehead and no-nonsense mouth who gazes out of his photographs like an eagle.

Barzyński was ordained in the Russian sector of Poland, was a gunrunner for Polish nationalists, served time in an Austrian prison, and finally emigrated to the Galveston settlement before being sent to Chicago. Like Bernard Mc-Quaid, he was no mystic but an entrepreneur, a driver, and a builder who flogged his people on to enormous exertions in the name of personal salvation and ethnic pride. Just as St. Patrick's was the ultimate Irish in-your-face to erstwhile English and Protestant overlords, the glittering infrastructure of Chicago's Polonia told the world that Catholic Poland would endure.

It was not to be expected that stiff-necked Poles would easily endure the suzerainty of Irish and German clerics. From the start, Polish immigrants viewed the American Church as "Irish," and they bristled at condescending, if well-meaning, statements from American bishops, such as, "Next to the Irish, the Poles have suffered the most for their religion." German overlordship was even harder to bear—imagine if arriving Irish immigrants had been forced to submit to Englishmen. Waeław Kruszka, the author of a monumental thirteen-volume history of Poles in America and a priest in Wisconsin, where all the bishops were German, made this bitter reflection in a 1910 speech:

> Look around you. Who is here the chief administrator of our public institutions, of our churches and schools? A German. Who educates our priests? A German. Who educates our teachers and organists? A German. Who educates our teaching nuns? A German. Who supplies the pews, altars, chalices, vestments and other decorations for our churches? A German. In a word, in our public life we are still paying rent . . . to the Germans.

German bishops, like Sebastian Messmer, a German-Swiss who had been among the most aggressive advocates of German rights, were appalled that the Poles expected their turn at the plate as well. Messmer wrote to Gibbons in 1905: "The longer I think it over the more it seems to me a dangerous experiment to give the Polish people a bishop. . . . The Polish are not yet American enough & keep aloof too much from the rest of us." Kruszka became a Polish-American hero for finally wangling an audience with Pius X and exacting a vague promise of Polish episcopal appointments; but it was years before the promise was realized, since the American hierarchy was firmly opposed to national bishops. The Poles were left to vent their frustrations on Lithuanians, who had suffered under Polish domination at home and were usually forced into Polish parishes in America, which they greatly resented.

In Chicago, however, the Irish and the Poles very quickly cut a deal. When Polish immigration accelerated after the Civil War, Chicago's Archbishop

Thomas Foley recruited priests from the Resurrectionists, a Polish missionary order, and in 1871 agreed that the order could administer Chicago's Polish parishes for ninety-nine years in return for putting all church property in the name of the diocese. In effect, the Irish hierarchy agreed to give the Poles a free hand on the local level in return for submitting to diocesan regulation and financial exactions. (Big-city Irish political machines were working out similar arrangements with Italian and Eastern European immigrant wards.)

The autocratic, business-minded Irish and Poles thought much alike when it came to religion. As Barzyński explained to his flock: "If you desire to work in the name of God, pay heed to the words of Christ . . . ; if you wish to labor for Christ, then listen to Peter . . . ; if you want to work in Peter's name, obey the Pope . . . ; if you wish to work in the Pope's name, obey the Bishop . . . ; if you wish to obey your Bishop, then you must obey your pastor, for the Bishop gave you only one pastor." Barzyński operated as if he were the Polish bishop of Chicago. A Resurrectionist himself, he assigned the other Resurrectionist priests, organized Polonia's building drives, and, since he ran a Polish bank, provided much of the financing himself. To this day, Resurrectionists operate most of Chicago's Polish parishes, including St. Stanislaus.

Barzyński's occasional frictions with the Irish and Germans were as nothing compared with those *within* the Polish community, which was sharply divided along royalist and radical-nationalist lines, reflecting political divisions at home. The imposing Holy Trinity Church down the street from St. Stanislaus was founded expressly as a radical-nationalist, non-Resurrectionist, alternative, and street fights between the two congregations flared for years. During one tense episode, a nationalist pastor was found dead in a pool of blood; the autopsy said it was apoplexy, but Trinitarians believed he had been murdered. A few years later, nationalist mobs burst into the rectory at neighboring St. Hedwig's with the declared intention of lynching Barzyński's brother, who was the pastor. When police intervened, mobs of old women threw pepper in their eyes. The same battles recurred throughout the midwestern industrial cities of the Polish belt. At one point the *Milwaukee Sentinel* commented: "There has not been an insurrection among the Polacks for two weeks. What can the matter be?"

Chicago's Poles finally got a Polish bishop after Barzyński's death—Paul Rhode, who was a great success, despite hard-liner objections to his Anglicized name—and Poles fervently hoped he would be named archbishop when James Quigley died in 1915. They were doubly disappointed at Mundelein's appointment, who, besides being German, behaved like a traditional Irish bishop. Shortly after Mundelein got to Chicago, he declared full-scale war on the national parish system in favor of "territorial" parishes, defined geographically without regard to ethnic composition. Almost all the territorial parishes, of course, were run by Irish-American pastors. Mundelein had canon law on his side, but the Polish pastors fought him to a standstill, and he had to give way. Mundelein subsequently offered a few olive branches, like highly visible fund drives for Polish war relief, but would never tolerate a Polish auxiliary. Through the 1960s at least, and still to a great extent today, Chicago's Poles have attended Polish parishes with Polish-speaking priests, and Polish priests were rarely assigned to territorial parishes. For years, the hardest-line Polish pastors forbade their young curates from associating with their non-Polish seminary classmates.

The last public eruption of Polish discontent came in 1920, when Polish-American Catholics sent the Vatican a lengthy and carefully researched remonstrance on the treatment of Poles in the American Church, with special reference to Mundelein. It was a hopeless maneuver. Mundelein was at the height of his powers, one of the most prolific builders and fund-raisers in the Church. The hierarchy submitted a blistering reply, signed by Gibbons, and drafted by Mundelein, Dougherty, and Messmer. Interestingly enough, in the course of the refutation, the bishops implied that Poles were anti-Semitic, citing cover-ups of pogroms in the Ukraine. A few years later, Mundelein got his cardinal's hat, which could hardly have made the Vatican's position clearer.

By 1920, most Polish Americans were already second generation, and were unquestionably assimilating, however slowly. Few Polish Americans had elected to go "home" when the Polish state was restored after World War I. But the most nationalistic Poles never gave up the fight. In the early 1900s, separatist Polish churches were organized in Chicago, Milwaukee, Buffalo, Scranton, and other cities. They eventually coalesced into the Polish National Catholic Church, under Bishop Francis Hodur, with headquarters in Scranton, the only successful schismatic movement in American Catholic history. It is testimony of the strength of the Polish commitment to homeland and religion that the National Catholic Church not only survived but after a fashion prospered, with 50,000 members by 1939, 130,000 in 1953, and 250,000 today.

An American Church

When even the most conscientious bishops occasionally threw up their hands at the ethnic cacophony, the good Lord was surely understanding. Italian priests refused to baptize Lithuanians, Poles detested Czechs, Germans contended with Irish. Immigrant Irish priests attacked the laxity of Irish-American priests. Ethnic pastors shamelessly competed with one another for parishioners, and territorial pastors protested bitterly when ethnic parishes siphoned off their revenues. By 1916, half the Catholic parishes used a foreign language at least some of the time. European bishops often treated America as a kind of Australia for wayward priests, a dumping ground for clergy of the lowest quality, who came to America " 'looking for a Mass' as a doctor comes looking for clients." The problem went beyond language. Many American priests had spent years in Rome and spoke fluent Italian, but immigrant Italians found American clergy, particularly Irish Americans, cold and puritanical and preferred native Italians, even when they were obviously charlatans.

Italian immigrants, in the overwhelming majority, were peasants from areas like Sicily and Calabria. In the 1880s and 1890s, they arrived almost as serfs under the control of a *padrone,* who financed their passage, provided room and board, collected their wages, and paid a risible living allowance. Over time, the *padrones* transmuted into more conventional labor contractors. Workers began to collect their wages directly, to bring their families with them, and to settle permanently. Unlike Germans and Poles, who typically built their own parishes, Italians were more likely to settle in older cities and inherit their churches from suburbanizing Irish. This was the prevailing pattern in South Philadelphia, in New York's Little Italy and Greenwich Village, in South Boston, and in Chicago. Friction between old-school Irish pastors and their new Italian flocks could be severe. In mixed parishes, Italian services were usually consigned to the church basements, and lace-curtain Irish nuns segregated Italian schoolchildren.

Italian peasants tended to see the clergy as oppressors and wore their religion lightly. The nationalist revolution in Italy had been fought partly to put an end to the Church's feudal tax impositions, so Italians were not disposed to plunk money into American collection baskets the way Irish and Poles were. When Italians ran their own parishes they typically would not pay for schooling. Only about one out of ten of Chicago's Italian parishes operated a parish school, but first-generation Italian parents often didn't make their children attend public school either. Italian parishes usually had to be subsidized by their dioceses, or sometimes by third-party fund-raising. Our Lady of Pompeii Church in Greenwich Village was the personal charity of Annie Leary, a wealthy Fifth Avenue matron who has one of the biggest crypts in the old St. Patrick's, until the pastor got irritated at having to deal with her through her maid.

Italian-American church historians still show flashes of bitterness over their early treatment in America. In fairness, the situation was clearly improving by World War I. Protestants were quick to see the opportunity in disgruntled Italians, and the evangelicals, in particular, made a number of conversions. Social reformers did not mind playing on Italian anticlericalism. Chicago priests were outraged when Hull House, the original American

Credit: Balch Institute of Ethnic Studies Library
The ethnic character of the American Church became ever more complex as
Irish immigrants were followed by German Catholics, then Italians, then Poles
and other Eastern Europeans, each bringing their own religious styles. The
photograph shows an Italian feast day procession in Philadelphia in the early
1900s.

settlement house, sponsored the Giordano Bruno Anticlerical Society—
Bruno was a contemporary of Galileo and the last heretic to be burned at the
stake. Even pastors who disliked Italians were embarrassed to be seen losing
souls to socialists and holy rollers. Most bishops did their best to recruit
qualified Italian priests, and eager young curates who were willing to help
solve "the Italian problem" found that promotions came quickly.

In the end, Italians changed more than the Church did. By the early twentieth century, all the big dioceses were running decent seminaries and were beginning to turn out homegrown Italian-American priests indoctrinated into a "correct" Catholic style. And the rigorist streak in Irish-American Catholicism was still a supremely effective technique for converting peasants into aspiring bourgeois, as upwardly mobile Italians readily perceived. A fascinating study of three generations of Italian parishioners in New York in the late 1960s shows that Italian-American religious practice tended to approach the Irish Catholic norm in the second, and even more strongly in the third, generation. In contrast to first-generation Italians, both Irish Catholics and second- and third-generation Italians had much higher rates of weekly Mass attendance and were quicker to call a priest during a dangerous illness. (First-generation Italians worried about frightening the patient.) Parochial-school attendance was very low among first-generation Italian children, but approached that of the Irish by the third generation. First-generation Italians prayed to local saints or to the Blessed Virgin; Irish Catholics and assimilated Italians prayed, austerely enough, to God. Third-generation Italians showed the same deference to the clergy as Irish Catholics did. Irish Catholics and third-generation Italians did not cry at funerals.

Almost all Catholics married Catholics, but by the third generation they were much more likely to choose partners from different ethnic groups. The New York survey shows that almost one out of four third-generation Italians married an Irish Catholic. (Al Capone's wife, Mae, was an Irish Catholic girl from Brooklyn.) Out-group marriage reached similar levels among Chicago's Poles, who married Catholic Italians, Irish, and Germans. Both assimilated Italians and Irish Catholics in New York had much smaller families than their first- and second-generation ancestors, and the size of Italian families fell even faster than among the Irish. Only 6 percent of third-generation Italian families had five or more children, compared with 16 percent for their Irish Catholic contemporaries.

The Church has long cherished its role in Americanizing successive waves of immigrants. But the less flattering reality is that most Catholic immigrants brought their churches with them and organized their own parishes, which were almost always self-supporting. It was only when they became important enough to attract a bishop's attention that they were absorbed into the dioceses—sometimes after a nasty fight—and subjected to centralized regulation and financial control. The Italians were one of the few Catholic immigrant groups who were the object of a substantial, diocesan-financed missionary effort, and the Church's response was notably slow.

This pattern of immigrant absorption also helps explain the Church's limited penetration in the black community. Irish priests, of course, were notorious for racial bigotry. The Catholic historian John Tracy Ellis was shocked in the 1940s to hear Cardinal John Glennon speak casually of a "nigger." But there were very few black Catholics, and for a long time the Church engaged in very little proselytizing of any kind. It was more than enough to keep up with the influx of people who were already Catholic. The success of Portland's Bishop James Healy, half black and half Irish, and of his two clerical brothers, is the notable counter-example to Irish Catholic bigotry. (While he was in school, Healy was emotionally adopted by a Jesuit, George Fenwick, of the College of Holy Cross, whom he called "Dad" the rest of his life.) William O'Connell could not resist remarking on Healy's "dark and swarthy complexion," and Irish were heard to exclaim at his installation in Portland, "Glurry be to God, the Bishop is a Nee-gar!" But he was widely regarded as brilliant, and he ran his parishes and diocese with an iron hand. His ancestry is otherwise almost never commented on.

It was only after World War I that the Church's immigrant-processing machinery approached the efficiency of legend. Ships arriving in Boston, Philadelphia, or New York were met by diocesan representatives holding up signs in the various languages. Same-language workers would assist Catholic immigrants through processing, help with housing and job referrals, and see that children were enrolled in parochial schools. The relatively brief period of highly organized immigrant services, before Congress shut down immigration completely, was possible only because the huge waves of Catholic immigration were finally ebbing. Immigrant numbers were dropping absolutely, and Jews and other non-Catholics were a much higher proportion of the total. The Church was now much richer, its building programs and staffing were beginning to catch up with its membership, and it was learning how to operate with polish and panache.

War helped smooth out the Church's ethnic contours, as German Catholics especially were forced to blend in with their coreligionists. Messmer was the most openly pro-German of the bishops, and he hailed the invasion of Belgium as "just punishment for its treacherous conduct." But he had the sense to keep quiet after the *Lusitania* sinking and, once America entered the war on England's side, reluctantly concluded that all Catholics "willing or unwilling" had to support their government. Woodrow Wilson was openly suspicious of German Americans. (He did not trust Catholics either and was irritated by their lobbying against Mexican anticlericalism and for Irish Home Rule.) At one point, Congress considered a bill to outlaw the teaching of German in America, so this was clearly no time to push the German agenda within the Church. The national German Catholic societies survived into the 1950s but were never again a force. (In his studies of Catholic ethnics, Andrew Greeley has shown that the German Catholic war generation suffered a sharp economic setback, from which they never fully recovered.) The Irish had also been loudly pro-German before the war—they would support any enemy of England—but either no one noticed or it was quickly forgotten in the rush of patriotic fervor that followed the declaration of hostilities.

James Gibbons was in his eighties when America entered the war. He was the most senior bishop in the world, the unchallenged unofficial head of the American Church, with just the native caution and instinctive patriotism the times called for. The bishops organized a "National Catholic War Council" but stayed out of politics, busying themselves with useful tasks like ensuring an adequate supply of chaplains and facilitating the work of Catholic service organizations like the Knights of Columbus. When Pope Benedict XV announced a peace plan in 1917 that was widely viewed as pro-Axis, Gibbons delivered it to Wilson as the Pope had directed, but he made it clear that he and his fellow bishops had no position but to support the government.

The war was a splendid opportunity to put to rest any lingering doubts about the Americanism of Catholics. Dioceses sponsored war bond drives, held victory masses, designated days of prayer for soldiers, and led celebrations of progress at the front. Army statistics used for chaplain assignments showed that Catholics accounted for more than their fair share of American soldiers. The word "Catholic" began to conjure up, not a foreign theocracy, but people like Francis Duffy. He was a much loved New York pastor, a first-rate theologian, and chaplain of the 165th Infantry (the old Irish "Fighting 69th"). Duffy's war exploits earned him the Distinguished Service Order and Medal and the Croix de Guerre, and he was a commander of the Legion of Honor. His statue stands today in Manhattan's Duffy Square.

The Church was still shadowed by American nativism, and the bishops would still trot out the nativist threat to cow the Vatican, but the fires that had burned figuratively in Lyman Beecher's breast—and sometimes literally, as at the Ursuline Convent—had been considerably banked. America was a much more secular society by 1900, and religious differences did not elicit the same passions they once had. Opposition to immigration was only incidentally anti-Catholic and in any case was shared by many Catholics. The last banners of anti-Popery were flown by the Ku Klux Klan in the 1920s, but almost always in rural areas where there were few Catholics. The condescension of Protestant and secularist elites was more exasperating than lower-class prejudice and has persisted much longer. Catholics did not feel welcome at institutions like Harvard, but those walls were falling as well.

For the first time at the war's end, the term "American Catholic Church" had real meaning. It was an immense and flourishing enterprise. Its leaders enjoyed a remarkable unanimity of purpose and direction. Its members shared an outlook on the world that was definably "American Catholic"—disciplined, rule-bound, loyal to church and country, unrebellious, but upwardly mobile and achievement-oriented. In matters of devotional practice, diocesan governance, and personal regulation, the American Church had a distinctively Irish cast, but there were too many twinings of the ethnic tapestry, too many blendings of styles and histories, to call it an "Irish" church any longer. Irish Americans still dominated the convents and the clerical ranks, but these were second- and third-generation men and women, with an expansive sense of opportunity and possibility that was uniquely American, and in no way Irish.

The American Church is sometimes called the most "Roman" of the national churches. Certainly American Catholics bowed to no one in their professed loyalty to the Pope. But the implication that the Church was minutely governed from Rome, forced against its will into conservative channels, is simply not true. Rome itself was riddled by factions that the Americans, like O'Connell, Mundelein, and Dougherty, played to their own advantage with considerable brio. The Vatican did take an ever stronger hand in the appointment of American bishops. Beginning in the early 1900s, it stopped the practice of choosing from local lists of three recommended candidates to give itself a freer hand to appoint conservatives. But as the Americanist controversies had shown, the vast majority of American bishops were quite conservative anyway, and the conservatives were by no means eager for Roman governance. Age and illness had not dulled Ella Edes's tongue in 1906, when she was still complaining loudly of the damage the Americanists had done by opening the door to an apostolic delegate in 1892. She deplored Cardinal O'Connell's courting of Rome, invoking the Irish bishop who mentally placed the names of recalcitrant priests into his chalice at Mass "& they die off like flies! . . . What a pity one could not put Pomposity [Cardinal O'Connell], Satolli, Merry del Val . . . and a few others, in that celebrated chalice and leave them at God's disposition & will."

Ever since Pius IX, Rome had been trying to increase the discipline and formalism of world Catholicism, to break down the independent national churches, to achieve uniformity and centralization. The autocratic American Church, with its deferential, loyal, and openhanded Catholics, was a Vatican showpiece. But this was a case of parallel development more than cause and effect. The knowledge that Rome shared their vision of diocesan governance was doubtless heartening for American bishops. But the style of the American Church had much more complex roots, reaching back to John Hughes and Paul Cullen, to the Irish machine instinct, the ghettoization of immigrants in large cities, and their need for powerful adaptive mechanisms in a strange and often hostile society. And in the realm of actual politics the Vatican and American bishops simply parted company. The bishops politely ignored Rome's longing for old-fashioned Catholic royalism, while Vatican cardinals scratched their heads over the Americans' tireless boosterism for religiously neutral republics.

The practical, bricks-and-mortar bent of the American hierarchy did not leave much room for intellectualism. *The New York Review,* a theological journal edited at Dunwoodie, the New York archdiocesan seminary, was one of the few bright spots—perhaps the *only* bright spot—on an otherwise fairly barren intellectual landscape. Edited by a group of young priests that included Fr. Duffy, it attempted to keep up with European theological developments and scriptural scholarship and to integrate theology with advances in modern science and philosophy. Farley was extremely proud of the *Review*—although its editors doubted that he understood it—and defended it against Vatican conservatives, until it was swept under by Pius X's broadside condemnation of "modernism" in 1907. Catholic intellectuals still lament the loss of the *Review,* suggesting that it could have pointed to entirely new directions for the American Church. But that seems extremely unlikely; it was a fragile flower in an intellectual desert—one that had spawned no imitators—and was completely dependent on Farley's patronage.

The Vatican strongly opposed the hierarchy's decision, at the end of the war, to retain the National Catholic War Council, renamed the National Catholic Welfare Council, as a kind of central administrative mechanism. To Rome, the council, like the *Review,* smacked of European modernism, a doctrine that otherwise had made hardly a ripple in the American theological backwaters. (The Vatican saw John Ireland's Americanism as a precursor of modernism. A national council sounded somehow Americanistic. QED.) But the bishops unified behind their proposal, with the notable exceptions of Dougherty and of O'Connell, who feared the council would steal his thunder as senior cardinal once Gibbons died. The Vatican eventually caved, insisting only on the word "Conference" rather than "Council."

In short, the Vatican and the American bishops worked in perfect harmony so long as their views coincided. But when the bishops had a decided view on an issue of importance, they could usually get their way. And when Vatican pronouncements conflicted with the bishops' good judgment—as in papal fulminations against free speech and religion, the repeated rallying against the Italian state, and Benedict's pro-Austrian diplomacy—the bishops, albeit with great deference and humility, simply ignored them. The accommodation with the Vatican paralleled that with the American state. There were no more patriotic Americans than Catholics, nor any Catholics more loyal to the Pope than Americans, and the American Church developed a wonderful skill at picking its own path between those loyalties.

On a crisp June morning in Chicago in 1926, 400,000 people streamed into Soldiers' Field, filling the grandstands, spilling over onto the field, packing together shoulder to shoulder in the spaces between the field seats and the grandstand wall. It was Children's Day at the Twenty-eighth International Eucharistic Congress, a weeklong celebration of Catholic faith, of prayer and meditation, and of public penance for the world's sins. A million Catholics came to Chicago for the congress, the largest Catholic gathering in America until Pope John Paul II's visit to Denver sixty-seven years later.

Credit: Archives, Archdiocese of Chicago
Chicago's 1926 Eucharistic Congress was a kind of "coming out" for the American Church. Four hundred thousand people jammed into Soldiers' Field for the Children's Mass on the first day of the Congress. Music was provided by a 62,000-voice children's choir.

A gargantuan altar had been erected at one end of the field, protected by a gilded dome, and at each corner of the dome, the flags of America and of the Pope snapped smartly in the breeze. Papal Legate Giovanni Bonzano was preceded to the altar by a processional of 12 cardinals, 57 archbishops, 257 bishops, more than 500 monsignors, and thousands of priests and nuns. The processional hymn was sung by a choir of 62,000 Chicago schoolchildren, who broke discipline and cheered wildly when their own cardinal, George Mundelein, mounted the altar. Embarrassed and delighted, Mundelein waved his arms to quiet the children as flustered nuns scurried up and down the grandstand stairs.

Securing the congress for America, and for Chicago, was a coup for Mundelein, one he contrived with his close friend Bonzano. Clerics and laypeople came from all over the world, Eskimos, Chinese, and Africans parading through Chicago in their native costumes. It was a kind of formal debut for the American Church, and the choice of Chicago as its venue, at the railroad hub of the Great Plains, signaled the expansive mood of American Catholicism, the leap from the immigrant ghetto into a wider world. Mundelein was determined to put on a show, although even he had some qualms about too strident a show of Catholic power.

The papal legate and his attendant cardinals were met in New York by a special train contributed by the Pullman Company, whose president, Edward Carry, was a knight commander of the Order of St. Gregory the Great. There were seven cars for the cardinals, painted bright cardinal's red down to the wheels and undercarriage. The interiors were finished in walnut and chrome, and each car bore Bonzano's coat of arms and a commemorative name—the Charles Carroll of Carrollton, after the Catholic signer of the Declaration of Independence; the Pope Pius XI; the Father Marquette, after the French missionary to the Indians; the Bishop William Quarter, after the first bishop of Chicago. (Mundelein invited Cardinal Dougherty to join them on the train, but Dougherty, not to be upstaged by his younger colleague, had his own train, donated by the Pennsylvania Railroad, and was bringing 10,000 Philadelphia Catholics to the congress.) The cardinals' train had right-of-way throughout its journey and was cheered on by large crowds at every station—35,000 as it rolled through Albany, 75,000 at Rochester. Several thousand Catholics, hoping for a glimpse of the legate, descended on the station in Cleveland at three in the morning, but Bonzano was sleeping. When the train finally pulled into a specially constructed terminal in Chicago, bells rang in all the Catholic churches of the city.

Politicians from throughout the country elbowed onto the platform at the congress's opening session. A greeting from President Calvin Coolidge was read by James J. Davis, the Catholic secretary of labor; Samuel Insull, the electric power magnate, welcomed the congress on behalf of non-Catholics. Children's Day at Soldier Field was followed by Women's Day, with some 250,000 women in attendance and a 12,000-voice choir of laywomen and nuns. The Men's Mass was the same evening. Church bells carilloned as dusk fell, and Chicago's Catholic workingmen, hundreds of thousands strong, filed out of factories and stockyards and streamed toward Soldiers' Field carrying candles in miles-long columns of twinkling lights.

The closing event of the congress was a Eucharistic Mass at St. Mary's of the Lake, Mundelein's new seminary, about twenty miles north of Chicago in the town of Mundelein, Illinois, renamed by its citizens in 1924 in honor of their cardinal. St. Mary's was Mundelein's joy, his legacy to the Church, the "Enchanted Forest," as his priests called it. On a 1000-acre wooded site, overlooking a pristine lake, the seminary has a dozen major buildings, arranged in a Latin cross centered on a Plaza of the Immaculate Conception, presided over by a huge statue of the Virgin. (There were never more than a few hundred students at the seminary; today there are about seventy-five, training for dioceses all around the world.) Despite his weakness for gigantism, Mundelein had a good eye, and he adopted a dark-red brick colonial motif for the buildings, an unusual choice for Catholic architecture. The "chapel," a church as grand as any in a big urban parish, is particularly attractive, modeled after a Congregationalist church in Old Lyme, Connecticut. From the central plaza, dominated by the steeple of the chapel and the Virgin's statue, a series of brick and cast-concrete walks and porticos flow down to the lakefront and an elaborate arrangement of docks.

On the morning of the St. Mary's ceremony, Thursday, June 24, all roads from Chicago to Mundelein were one-way. The Illinois Central had built a new rail line to the foot of the seminary, and trains began running in standing-room convoys starting at 4:00 A.M. Eight hundred thousand Catholics somehow got from Chicago to St. Mary's for the ceremony. The climax of the day was a Eucharistic procession around the lake, a distance of more than a mile, with Bonzano walking under a white silk papal canopy, bearing in a golden vessel a consecrated Host—the Holy Eucharist, the central mystery of Catholicism. The congress had enjoyed beautiful weather all week long, but clouds had been gathering on Thursday. As soon as the procession began, the sky turned black, and the lake was lashed by a violent thunderstorm. The papal canopy clattered in the wind, nuns' veils were whipped and torn, their habits pasted to their bodies by the driving rain; miniature flash floods curled angrily around the marchers' ankles. Most of the processants broke ranks and ran for the shelter of the woods. But Bonzano slogged on, his altar-boy canopy bearers clinging to the billowing silk. As the legate continued his march, the rest of the procession took heart and rejoined the parade.

Then, as suddenly as it began, the rain stopped, the sun came dazzling through the towers of dark clouds and painted a rainbow in a great arch across the heavens. Almost in unison, 800,000 Catholics oohed and aahed; Irish and Italians, Poles and Germans, nuns and priests, cardinals and bishops, smiled and looked up, blinking, at the sky.

PART II

TRIUMPH

CHAPTER 6

A Separate Universe

In the liturgical calendar of the Communist International, May 1, or May Day, was the official celebratory feast of the proletariat, and in 1933, the swelling ranks of radical workers' parties made the event the biggest in history. A million people jammed Moscow's Red Square to watch Comrade Stalin review a bristling display of tanks and war planes flanked by parading workers. Not to be outdone, Hitler engineered a million-plus demonstration outside Berlin's Reichstag; and in New York City, where all police leaves had been canceled because of anticipated violence between socialists and Communists, three parades—two Communist and one socialist—convened on Union Square, 50,000 people altogether, "a hot undulant sea of hats and sunbaked heads" flowing beneath a waving forest of placards and banners. And squeezing their way through the throng came a homeless, jailbird, sometime college student named Joe Bennett, wheezing with a rheumatic heart, and a tall, slender woman with luminous wide-set eyes and the calm glow of absolute self-possession. She was Dorothy Day, and the pair was hawking the first-ever edition of the *Catholic Worker,* fending off jibes from peddlers of the *Daily Worker,* the Communist newspaper they were determined to compete with.

It is an exaggeration to say that Dorothy Day was "the most significant, interesting, and influential person in the history of American Catholicism," as *Commonweal* once did, but it is a pardonable one, for her impact on the people who met her was enormous, and she transformed the social conscience of a whole generation of young clergy. Charles Owen Rice, who was a radical 1930s labor priest, and much later a civil rights and antiwar activist, says unabashedly, "She was the inspiration for everything I did. She was the most natural, relaxed, humble, self-sacrificing person I ever met."

Credit: Archives, University of Marquette
Dorothy Day, a convert from Greenwich Village Marxism, was, in the eyes of her
admirers, "the most influential" single individual in the history of the Ameri-
can Church. Almost all American Catholic social movements can trace their ori-
gins to Day. The photograph is from about 1935.

Day was born in 1897 to a working-class Protestant family, became radicalized at the University of Illinois, was active in labor and antiwar protests,
had her ribs cracked by police truncheons, spent time in jail, wrote for *The
Masses,* a socialist journal, published a novel, wrote scripts in Hollywood,
and became a rising young star on the Greenwich Village radical scene. She
was part of the circle of early Bolshevik enthusiasts like Max Eastman, John
Reed, and Mike Gold. She interviewed Trotsky, was a companion of Eugene
O'Neill, and had a series of affairs and an abortion. About the time her
daughter was born in 1927, from a common-law marriage, Day experienced
a quasi-mystical conversion to Catholicism. Her husband left her as a consequence, and, a single mother in Depression New York, she eked out a living
writing and reviewing for liberal Catholic journals.

Day's second quasi-conversion experience occurred in early 1933, when
Peter Maurin showed up on her doorstep at the suggestion of George Shus-

ter, an editor at *Commonweal.* Maurin was an aging French intellectual eccentric—whether he was brilliant or muddled is not altogether clear—preaching a purified lay Catholic mission modeled on the example of St. Francis of Assisi. By Day's own account, Maurin gave clarity and purpose to her life. He told her to start a newspaper and a communal farm and to open "hospitality houses," or shelters for the poor, and to do it without worrying about money—just *do* it.

Extraordinarily, Day followed Maurin's instructions to the letter, characteristically giving him most of the credit, although his practical contributions were negligible. She put out the first issue of the *Catholic Worker (CW),* 2500 eight-page copies, with $57 that she cobbled together from her own rent and gas money and some small contributions from friends. The first edition, which sold for a penny a copy, prompted enough donations that she could put out a second a month later. Within a year, monthly circulation was 40,000; it hit 100,000 in 1935 and was scraping 200,000 on the eve of America's entry into the war.

Day opened the first hospitality houses the same year as she started the *CW,* first next to her own 15th Street apartment, and another shortly thereafter in Harlem. By the start of the war, there were at least thirty throughout the country and one in England—Rice opened his in Pittsburgh in 1937. The hospitality houses provided soup kitchens and temporary, sometimes quasi-permanent, living arrangements for tens of thousands of people. They operated like a loose franchise tied together by their common devotion to Day and Catholic Worker principles—communal living, true charity and humility, pacifism, and at one and the same time a radical anger at the exploitation of the poor and a joyful embrace of poverty as a means of spiritual illumination. The house on 15th Street became a cynosure for Catholic intellectuals, and visitors dropped in from all over the world to participate in the nightly discussions—the French philosopher Jacques Maritain, the Jesuit theologian John La Farge, the English writer Hilaire Belloc.

A woman of exquisitely refined taste, Day lived in hospitality houses the rest of her life, wore hand-me-down clothes, and ate soup kitchen food. Despite the constant burden of managing, editing, and fund-raising for the *CW,* and doing much of the writing, she was constantly on the road, visiting her hospitality houses and inspiring and encouraging her youthful disciples. Somehow, she also found time to open a communal farm, Maryfarm, in Easton, Pennsylvania, and to be at least an adequate mother to her daughter. "She should be canonized," says Rice, "but that won't happen because of the abortion."

The glue for Day's Catholic Worker movement was the *CW,* a professional, imaginatively laid out production from the very start, with elaborate, *New York Times*-style headlines. A typical issue would contain field reports on important strikes and labor actions, perhaps an exposé of federal farm mortgage foreclosures, an essay on pacifism, or a meditation on ethics, spirituality, or poverty, and always a column by Day herself. Day wrote like an angel, in a spare, limpid, prose, with a pointillist's eye for detail. Her style was consciously emulated by almost all the young *CW* writers, just as they adopted her flatly unsentimental view of herself, of human nature, and of the motley objects of their good works, as in:

> Albert Brady is dead. Late lord of the kitchen, and hero of his own magnificent dreams, he succumbed to the abrasion of daily reality. Broken in body, a hunchback, he cherished a picture of himself as a strong, self-sufficient silent power, a man, not always a cripple, able to cope with the best. . . . [W]e can only pray for this friendly, little, queer, unhappy man. . . . He loved to get one behind a closed door, and with an air of mystery, expound upon an obvious commonplace. He lived in a world of make-believe, and cooked abominable food.

Day was strongly anti-socialist, anti-Fascist, and anti-Communist, seeing both Stalin's and Hitler's crimes with a clearer eye, and sooner, than most of her generation. She had no illusions about the murders and crimes committed by the loyalist left in the Spanish Civil War—the defining conflict for 1930s radicals—just as she had no illusions about the crimes and murders committed by Franco's right-wing rebel army, which was strongly backed by the Vatican and almost the entire body of American Catholic clergy, including leftists like Rice. "If 2,000 [Catholic clergy]," Day wrote, "have suffered martyrdom in Spain, is that suffering atoned for by the death of the 90,000 in the Civil War? Would not those martyrs themselves have cried out against the shedding of more blood?"

Even the attack on Pearl Harbor did not shake her pacifism. The first *CW* issue after the attack proclaimed, "We are still pacifists"; and after the Hiroshima and Nagasaki bombings, she wrote, "Mr. Truman was jubilant. . . . *Jubilate Deo*. We have killed 318,000 Japanese." Her resolute pacifism split the movement, and *CW* circulation dropped precipitately—although Day's testimony before Congress was an important factor in ensuring honorable treatment for conscientious objectors. After the war, the chain of hospitality houses shrank to just a handful but never completely disappeared. *CW* circulation recovered to a stable 50,000 or so, and Day soldiered on, almost to the day she died in 1980 at the age of eighty-three.

In the seedy, somewhat raffish, section of Manhattan's Lower East Side called NoHo, one can still find youthful Catholic Workers, cheerfully slicing onions for the afternoon soup line. The Workers still run their soup kitchens, and their two Manhattan hospitality houses shelter about thirty residents each. In fact, the Catholic Workers have made a substantial comeback in recent years. The war in Vietnam made pacifism respectable again; the very first young man who publicly burned his draft card was a Catholic Worker. With the upsurge of homelessness in the 1980s, hospitality houses have flourished. There are now almost a hundred throughout the country, the most ever. *CW* circulation, at 90,000, has recovered strongly, and the lead column still sounds uncannily like Dorothy Day. Contributions, the Catholic Workers advertise proudly, are *not* tax-deductible—they don't want the government looking over their shoulder. The *CW* newsstand price is still a penny, but they will be happy to give you one for free.

To secular eyes, Catholicism produced strange bedfellows. Dorothy Day was not the only voice of Catholic social teachings in the 1930s. The Rev. Charles E. Coughlin, the "radio priest," was far better known. And, although his message could not have sounded more different from Day's, he was arguing from very much the same set of Catholic premises.

An old movie reel has captured Charles Coughlin on a midsummer's afternoon in 1936, standing before an overflow shirt-sleeved crowd of perhaps 80,000 people packed into Cleveland's Municipal Stadium. The bank of microphones on the dais carried his words to tens of millions of listeners throughout the country. Coughlin was a ruddy, square-faced, solidly built man with receding black hair, rimless glasses, and the confident stride of an athlete. His voice was strong and theatrical, with rolled *r*'s and just enough of a brogue to ease a harshness in the upper registers. These were his people, working men and women with lined faces and worried eyes, and Coughlin punched out his lines like a heavyweight champion boxer.

> The Depression still waxed strong as the powers of deflation reached out to confiscate homes, to capture farms, and to keep that ever-marching army of jobless upon our streets, wondering when God in His ma-arcy would lift His hand; and I dared you, and challenged you, to *organize,* so that the people, if not the President, would drive the money-changers from the Temple. And you did it!

The crowd leaped to their feet, waving hats, cheering thunderously. Grim-faced, Coughlin turned to one side, wiped his forehead with a handkerchief, then wheeled back to the microphones, clubbing his right fist from high over his head, then hammering down the left, and then both fists on every word as he neared the climax.

> My dear friends, we . . . believe in Christ's principle of Love Your Neighbor As Yourself, and . . . I challenge every Jew in this nation to tell me he does not believe in it! . . . There is no need of communizing

all the factories and the fields, all the forests and the mines, under a new kind of God made of flesh and blood, and clay, and hatred. When men become so prideful that they believe it is their destiny to rewrite the eta-arnal law of God, it's time for their fellow citizens to rise up in their wrath, and through the agency of ballots, and not bullets, to relegate them to the pages of the past.

The crowd exploded. Coughlin stood before the microphone with his head bowed, let the tumult run its course, whispered "God bless you," and stalked from the platform.

Charles Coughlin is usually remembered only for the anti-Semitic fascism of the last years of his radio career, but the preachings that made him famous, up until roughly 1935, were much more in the American, and Catholic, mainstream. As a young Detroit priest, Coughlin was made pastor of the Shrine of the Little Flower, a new parish in suburban Royal Oak.

Credit: UPI/Bettmann Newsphotos
The "Radio Priest," Charles Coughlin began his career in the mainstream of Catholic social welfare teachings but became increasingly anti-Semitic and pro-Nazi after his break with Roosevelt in 1936. After he was silenced in 1942, he spent the next thirty years quietly ministering to his suburban Detroit parish.

There were only a few dozen Catholic families in the parish, finances were a struggle, and rural Michigan was a hotbed of anti-Catholic prejudice. When the Ku Klux Klan burned a cross on Coughlin's lawn in 1926, he received permission from his bishop, Michael Gallagher, to preach over a local radio station to respond to the Klan and to solicit donations for a church. "The Golden Hour of the Little Flower," a mixture of conventional preaching and anticommunism, was an instant success. Coughlin was by no means the only radio priest. Fr. Fulton J. Sheen's mellifluous homilies commanded a nationwide audience on NBC's Sunday evening "Catholic Hour," which debuted in 1929; and in Pittsburgh, in 1932, Fr. James Renshaw Cox, a militant pro-union priest, made his popular noontime broadcasts the command post for a citywide taxi strike.

CBS picked up Coughlin for nationwide distribution in 1930, about the time that Coughlin began shifting his message to one that was increasingly anti–Big Business and anti–Herbert Hoover, whom he dubbed "the bankers' friend, the Holy Ghost of the rich, the protective angel of Wall Street." CBS dropped Coughlin after a year, and NBC declined to pick up his contract, so Coughlin, on the advice of a parishioner, created his own radio network, scraping together enough money to lease telephone lines to twenty-six stations, mostly in the Midwest. By 1932, "Golden Hour" had the biggest radio audience in the country, arguably the largest *ever* for a regular program, and mostly non-Catholic. (Coughlin commanded up to twice the number of listeners as today's immensely popular Rush Limbaugh show, in a country half the size, without portable radios.) The network was supported by millions in contributions, and the volume of mail to Royal Oak was so heavy that the government opened a post office next to the church. Contrary to some reports, Coughlin did not live lavishly but plowed his collections back into his radio foundation. His one indulgence was a huge Great Dane that accompanied him on most of his trips, and he built a large modernistic church with a soaring radio tower, filling the pews each Sunday with busloads of pilgrims who came to hear him preach.

It is impossible to overestimate the psychological devastation of the Depression on average working men and women. In the America where every man could be a shareholder, where there was supposed to be a chicken in every pot and a car in every garage, tycoons were pleading poverty, factory steam whistles had fallen silent, farmers were slaughtering stock and burning crops, wages were in a stomach-jagging plunge, and one out of every four family heads was out of work. With no social safety net beyond the inconsistent charities of friends and neighbors, or of local churches and haphazard municipal doles, families were starving, freezing, and dying. Long lines of numbed and abject men queued up in front of employment offices, shuffled in soup lines, or, fleeing from the accusing faces of their families, huddled in

"Hoovervilles," the hobo villages that were popping up around the country like tumors.

Coughlin's remedies were a mildly left-of-center mix of banking and monetary reform, a veterans' bonus, and a federal public works program. All in all, it was a much more sensible agenda than the rigid orthodoxies preached by, say, *The New York Times*. Before 1935 or so, it takes the suspicions of hindsight to find much anti-Semitism in his broadcasts. "International banker" looks like a code word for "Jew," but in fact central banks were a big part of the problem, although they were run mostly by WASPs, not Jews. Coughlin's strongest critics were right-wing senior clerics, like Cardinal O'Connell, who deplored his attacks on the established order. Cheekily, Coughlin did not hesitate to strike back—"For more than forty years, William Cardinal O'Connell has been silent on social justice," which was all too true. O'Connell's huffing and puffing was irrelevant in any case, since Detroit's Bishop Gallagher, who had studied monetarist economics in Austria, was a staunch Coughlin ally.

Coughlin strongly backed Franklin Delano Roosevelt in the 1932 election, coining the slogan "Roosevelt or Ruin." With a radio audience of some 40 million, he had become politics' proverbial 800-pound gorilla, and he received the tenderest care and feeding from Roosevelt's political professionals. By 1934, Coughlin was disillusioned by the caution of Roosevelt's economic reforms, but the final break seems to have been prompted by vanity. The White House was genuinely frightened of a political alliance between Coughlin and Senator Huey Long, the Louisiana Kingfish, who hoped to ride his Share-the-Wealth program all the way to the presidency. Coughlin's constituency, more Catholic and more urban, was the perfect complement to Long's, and both men scouted the possibility of an alliance. But when Long was assassinated in 1935, the administration's interest in Coughlin dropped off sharply, and he suddenly found himself unable to schedule an appointment with the President. (Roosevelt had also become good friends with Cardinal Mundelein—they called each other "Frank" and "George"—and could count on Mundelein to cover his Catholic flank for anything "short of burning down a church.") It was about that time that Coughlin regretfully informed his radio audience that the campaign slogan for 1936 had to be "Roosevelt *and* Ruin."

With his national influence showing signs of slippage by late 1935, Coughlin formed a loose alliance with Dr. Francis Townsend, sponsor of a messianic plan to pay everyone over sixty $200 a month, and with Long's former lieutenant, Gerald L. K. Smith, a mesmerizing back-country preacher who became a race-baiting field general in the radical right politics of the 1960s and 1970s. A halfhearted attempt to run a third-party presidential candidate in 1936 was a miserable failure, and from about that point Coughlin's diatribes against both communism and capitalism started to become ever more shrill, and ever more blatantly anti-Semitic. His journal *Social Justice* was even worse and by 1938 was featuring excerpts from the Jew-baiting slanders of the *Protocols of the Elders of Zion* and laudatory profiles of Hitler and Mussolini. In 1942, the federal government shut down *Social Justice,* and the new Detroit bishop, Edward Mooney, ended permission for the broadcasts. Surprisingly enough, Coughlin meekly complied with the order and, for the next thirty years, quietly discharged his duties as pastor of Little Flower. He retired in 1973 and died in 1979. During the rest of his life he submitted to only a few brief interviews, in which he seemed to express oblique regrets for the excesses of his radio years.

The fact that the radically leftist Day and the Fascist-sounding Coughlin claimed to be arguing from the same fundamental principles understandably confused outsiders. Official Catholic positions on the leading social questions of the day seemed an odd mix of the left-liberal and the rigidly reactionary. Patrick Scanlan's influential *Brooklyn Tablet,* for example, was one of the most hard-line and right-wing of Catholic journals; but Scanlan was one of the earliest supporters of Dorothy Day and always gave generous publicity to her fund-raising drives.

Confronted with such apparent contradictions, secular intellectuals tended to write off Catholic thinkers as either incoherent or deliberately obscurantist. But if the Church looked anti-intellectual or confused, it was only because its conclusions were so radically at variance with those of the prevailing American secularist faith. The Catholic worldview was actually highly rational, and if anything, hyperconsistent, even though it did not fit within conventional "liberal" and "conservative" categories. It was a worldview shared to a fine-grained level of detail by almost all Church leaders and rigorously expounded down to the parish level. During the 1920s and 1930s, activist intellectuals, like John Ryan at the National Catholic Welfare Conference (NCWC), plied this unique Catholic "take" on the world as a powerful cultural weapon to fortify Catholic ramparts against American secularism and to reinforce the growing self-awareness of a burgeoning Catholic state within a state.

Catholic Social Teaching

Progressive reformers were delighted by the radical tone of Catholic economic commentary in the 1920s and 1930s: even the fairly conservative Jesuit journal *America* denounced the growing concentration of wealth in pre-

Depression America, deploring "government by a plutocracy," and the "stupid and malicious giant" of American capitalism. *Commonweal,* one of the more liberal Catholic journals, mocked businessmen's fear that socialism and communism would attack private property "when so many are owners of nothing," and concluded in 1936: "In fact, free competition long ago disappeared from large sections of American life . . . . Even under the free right of every dog to eat every other dog, there could not be such a general horror in America as all the tables indicate." The Pope himself bemoaned the immiserization of the working classes, abuse of women, exploitation of children, and "despotic economic dictatorship" that were the fruits of unregulated industrial capitalism.

But liberal intellectuals were repelled by what seemed like loopily benighted Catholic teachings on sexuality and the role of women, especially on the question of contraception within marriage. For example, *America* insisted that marital intercourse without procreative intent was just "mutual masturbation"; and in 1931 the liberal *Commonweal* likened the use of contraception in marriage to "self-mutilation or the practice of the solitary vice." The use of contraceptives, it claimed, led to "[s]terility, frequent and serious infections and even cancer, neurological and psychological disorders." Confusingly enough, a radical labor priest like Rice preached the same line on contraception as a Cardinal O'Connell; even Dorothy Day taught a strict Catholic sexual ethic. In fact there was no contradiction, for the Catholic view on sex—leaving aside the grim tonal twist characteristic of Irish Catholicism—sprang from precisely the same premises as the apparently "liberal" view of political economy.

Basic Catholic principles hold that there is an externally ordained social order that humans can understand rationally through natural law. Society is organized in a hierarchy, running from the Church through the State and through subsidiary associations like labor unions down to the family. Society is an organism; each component is bound by a complex of duties and obligations to every other. The allocation of social functions is determined by the principle of *subsidiarity*: no higher-level association, like the State, should undertake a task that a lower level one, like a union or the family, could do as well. Individuals derive their identity from a thick web of social relations—as family members, as parish members, as union members, as members of professional societies, and finally as members of a State. The modern tendency to elevate the rights of individuals, considered independently of their relational obligations, was to Catholic eyes absurdly at variance with reality and a source of endless social mischief.

The principle modern texts for Catholic social philosophy were two papal encyclicals, Leo XIII's *Rerum Novarum* of 1891 and Pius XI's 1931 *Quadragesimo Anno.* Leo's encyclical (literally, "Of New Things") specifically addressed the role of labor unions in an industrial economy, an update of Church teaching for which Catholics owed a debt of gratitude to Cardinal Gibbons's perseverance on the Knights of Labor. Pius's encyclical (literally, "In the Fortieth Year") was intended as a detailed elaboration and anniversary update of Leo's blueprint. They condemn equally the twin evils of socialism and communism on the one hand—for their materialism and coerciveness—and on the other hand, unfettered competition, or "liberalism," with its cruel burdens on the working classes.

The Catholic alternative grew out of its organic theory of society. Employers had an obligation to pay a "family wage," enough for a father "to meet ordinary family needs adequately," and, ideally, save enough to acquire a little property of his own. Wives and children should not have to work outside the home, there should be adequate free time for religious and family duties, and a worker's strength should not be overtaxed. Workers were obligated to faithfully discharge their duties to their employers; nonviolent strikes were permissible, but only as a last resort to achieve justice. The watchwords were unity and harmony based on justice and charity. Or as the economist Barbara Ward put it in 1939, Catholic thought "aims above all at balance, the balance achieved by combining planned economy with individual freedom, State control with private ownership, economic independence with political needs and social justice."

The most influential American Catholic economic thinker was Msgr. John A. Ryan, sometimes called "Right Reverend New Dealer" by critics of his unabashed support for the Roosevelt administration. A priest of the St. Paul archdiocese, assigned to Catholic University and the NCWC, Ryan was much in demand as a speaker and as a Congressional witness, and elaborated Catholic principles in books like *The Living Wage* and *Distributive Justice.* He burst to prominence in Catholic intellectual circles in 1919, when he drafted the "Bishops' Program for Social Reconstruction," banging it out in five hours when an NCWC committee decided they needed to make a public statement. The "Bishops' Program" called for a long list of basic economic reforms, including a legal minimum wage, government-sponsored health and old-age insurance, strict child labor laws, tougher anti-monopoly enforcement, and equal wages for women. The radical reformer Upton Sinclair called it a "Catholic miracle."

Although senior prelates like O'Connell grumbled about his "queer crooked views," Ryan's position as head of the NCWC Social Action Department gave him great influence. He produced hundreds of pamphlets that shaped the attitudes of a generation of priests, and as the NCWC staff became more professionalized, it was the first place that government officials or the press would turn to get an "official" Catholic view. O'Connell and a few others aside, the bishops as a group were not especially conservative on economic matters. Maurice Sheehy, the assistant rector of Catholic University and Roosevelt's political link to the Church, estimated in 1936 that three fourths of priests and most of the bishops supported the administration.

But if New Deal progressives and Ryan reached very much the same conclusions regarding economic policy, they arrived at them by entirely different routes. The New Dealers were technocrats, with an instrumentalist faith that modern theoretical and technical advances, like punch card machines, gave them the tools to manage the economy to everyone's benefit. Ryan's approach, in stark contrast, was almost entirely deductive. *The Living Wage* and *Distributive Justice,* although they were taught in Catholic economics classes, are actually works of ethics. They proceed by elaborating the teachings of the Church fathers, St. Thomas Aquinas, and the popes to establish basic natural law principles and then derive second- and third-level economic conclusions. There is scarcely a number in either book and not a single formula or graph. Ryan struggles with frameworks and permanent principles, not practical problems.

It surely would have puzzled secular economists to watch Ryan or the encyclicals take such pains, for example, to derive the right of private property from St. Thomas—why should anyone care what a thirteenth-century monk thought about forms of property holding? But to Ryan, the popes, and virtually all the writers in *Commonweal, America, Catholic World,* and even the *Catholic Worker,* it was a matter of first importance. If private property could not be grounded in natural law, the arguments against socialism and communism were considerably weakened. Ryan was also much enamored with the guild system of the Middle Ages, which was the favored social mechanism of the encyclicals. Both Leo and Pius urged the formation of "associations of industries and professions," with the encouragement, but not the control, of the State. All workers and employers would sit down together, each in their respective "syndicates," and cooperatively plan to ensure both an adequate return to capital and an adequate family wage.*

While it is not likely that anyone in the Roosevelt administration read encyclicals, ideals of planning were much in vogue in the 1930s, and there were close parallels between the papal proposals, Ryan's writings, and the creation of the National Industrial Recovery Administration (NRA) in 1933. The NRA legislation was designed "to promote the organization of industry for the purpose of cooperative action among trade groups." At least in theory, consortia

---

* The "corporativist" and "syndicalist" language used by the popes raises the question of the Church's role in Spanish and Italian fascism, which will be reserved for a later chapter. *Quadragesimo Anno,* in fact, contains a discussion of Italian fascism, and concludes that while it has attractive features, it is too much under the control of the state, and "rather serves particular political ends than leads to the reconstruction and promotion of a better social order." But there was enough ambiguity in papal words and deeds to encourage both local Fascists and the post-1935 Coughlin.

of the largest industries would sit down with government planners and trade unions to adopt a code of behavior governing wages, prices, and working conditions; code-compliant companies could sport the Blue Eagle NRA seal. The NRA consortia looked a lot like *Quadragesimo Anno*'s "associations of industries," and Catholic writers were generally lavish in their praise, although some, like Ryan's deputy, Raymond McGowan, thought the act did not go far enough. Ryan, who had been enlisted as an NRA appeals officer, felt personally devastated when the NRA was struck down by the Supreme Court in 1935, and the *Catholic World* lamented, "Now what? If we don't get reform, we shall get revolution."

When it came to sexual ethics, however, secular intellectuals who felt so comfortable with Ryan's economic writings, or who were used to engaging with him at public policy discussions, were astonished to hear him take positions that sounded medieval. It was Ryan, for example, who compared contraception to "the solitary vice." (Ryan was considered by Catholics to be a *liberal* on birth control.) But the Catholic arguments against contraception, in fact, were exactly the same as those for a minimum family wage. The family was the most fundamental of the web of relations that defined an individual, and by the rule of subsidiarity, the most elemental cog in the social machinery. Economic arrangements that left a father exhausted, that drove a mother to employment outside the home, and that pushed children into the hands of institutional caregivers threatened the integrity of the social order and were against natural law.

In the same way, contraception, by severing the link between sex and childbearing, opened the door to pre- and extramarital relations, blunted the impulse to marriage, and weakened the ties between husband and wife. Easy divorce, working mothers, the use of technology to defer marriage or to keep families small, all threatened the natural order as directly as an exploitative wage. Writers like the young Walter Lippmann (*Drift and Mastery,* 1914) rushed to confirm Catholic fears, predicting that the coming pragmatic society would dispense with traditional sexual conventions in favor of "civilized opportunities for its [the sex drive's] expression"; and that when women were freed from the bonds of family, "the care and training of infants will become specialized."

The dire Catholic forecasts for the future of families and marriage under a contraceptive regime were premised on a conviction of aboriginal human depravity, the doctrine of original sin, which has been central to Catholic teaching from the time of St. Augustine. Catholics regarded the sexual impulse as the most explosive of human instincts; Lippmann's "civilized" sexual regime was ridiculous. Experience taught that men and women routinely risked their marriages, their social standing, their children's future, their homes and fortunes, in pursuit of sex. The answer could only be discipline and control, a constant subjection of selfish impulses to Christian precepts and family duties. Slacken the grip just a little, and the slide would be fast and steep. Contraception was the first step off the precipice. The idea that sex was merely an instrument of pleasure, said *Commonweal,* was "copulationism." If the purpose of sex was pleasure, why have rules of marital fidelity at all? "Why, it must be asked, should not two people of the *same* sex . . . just give each other pleasure? Why not all the shocking excess of masturbation, sodomy, homosexuality, sadism, masochism, fetichism, etc.? The mere suggestion fills us with horror—but on what ground if sex pleasure be separated from the procreative process and made a legitimate end in itself?"

Catholic writers drummed away at the destruction of the natural order that would ensue from relaxed sexual mores—broken homes, illegitimacy, single-parent families, delinquency, runaway sexual disease. (But even Catholics rarely suggested that legal contraception would be a step toward legal abortion. In the 1930s, journals like Margaret Sanger's *Birth Control Review* still called abortion murder.) Secular reformers were just talking past Catholics when they pointed to the unhappy marriages that could be resolved by divorce. In Catholic eyes, *happiness* had nothing to do with it. The very first questions in the Baltimore Catechism taught that God made man to serve him in this world and "to be happy with Him in the *next.*" The world was "a vale of tears," not "a paradise of sensual delights." "No one is obliged to marry," said *America,* "but all who marry are obliged to fulfill the duties that marriage imposes."

The unwavering, even shrill position the Church took on contraception would, a half century later, appear even to most Catholics as grossly excessive, if not hopelessly benighted, but within a Catholic frame of reference, it was never illogical. Celibate bishops and priests may have had a narrow and prejudiced view of the role of sex in human relations, but their arguments were not based *solely* on prejudice. It would require a hypersimplistic view of social causation to trace present divorce and illegitimacy rates purely to the elevation of the recreational, as opposed to the familial and parental, role of sex; but the Catholic polemicists of the 1930s might be forgiven for insisting that the phenomena are not entirely unrelated.

Even in the 1930s, the Catholic position on family, contraception, and sexual morality was out of step with the rest of the country. (The Episcopal Church approved of artificial birth control in 1930.) Catholics had not changed, however; it was the rest of the country, or at least the country's opinion makers, that had changed. A generation before, mainstream Protestant pulpits had preached the same moral line as Catholics. But by the end of World War I, mainstream Protestantism was in full retreat, especially in the Northeast, which even more than today was the center of elite tastemakers and trendsetters. The relative stability of Protestant numbers from the 1920s through the 1960s masks a deep tidal shift in Protestant religious affiliation. The "market share" of the elite denominations—Episcopalianism, Congregationalism, Presbyterianism, northern Methodism—was being rapidly eclipsed by affective, evangelical, working class religions, and the emotional center of Protestantism was shifting to rural areas and the South.

Catholicism was the only religion that enjoyed the same strong growth as the southern evangelicals, but the Catholic growth was precisely in the big cities that were the center for America's new secular urban culture. In the space of a few decades, Catholic bishops replaced big-city Protestant ministers as the public spokesmen for traditional morality. The rigor and clarity of Catholic thought made bishops formidable polemicists, and Catholic confidence was enhanced by the fact that in the 1920s and 1930s even the best American secular intellectuals unexpectedly found themselves wandering in a desert of their own making.

Secular Intellectuals and the Crisis of Modernity

Intellectual confidence in the benign potential of purposeful science reached a high point in the decades immediately before World War I. Karl Pearson's 1892 *Grammar of Science,* which claimed "the whole life, physical and mental, of the universe . . . [as] the material of science," was a touchstone for a generation of intellectuals. In his 1899 presidential address, John Dewey assured the American Psychological Association that science "will afford us insight into the conditions which control the formation and execution of aims, and thus enable human effort to expend itself sanely, rationally, and with assurance." The historian Henry Adams devoted a whole chapter of his *Education* to Pearson's teachings and set out to find the "dynamic theory of history," the few simple scientific laws that governed public affairs. The American Sociological Society, founded in 1905, embarked on a "scientific" program to learn the rules of the "social equilibrating-apparatus" that would make possible a discipline of "social control." Lippmann's paeans to civilized sex and specialized child-rearing were produced when he was much under the influence of Dewey.

Before the war, few thinkers were aware of how uncritically they had replaced their previous theism with a faith in scientific Progress. But the old assumption of a divinely ordained order was still firmly imprinted on people's minds. The giveaway is biology. The theory of evolution was considered hardheaded science at its best, the bright line that separated moderns from outmoded religionists. But the central image in biology textbooks was almost always an evolutionary "tree" that arranged all of history's life forms as branches around a central trunk crowned at the very top by (surprise!) a white, Victorian, haut-bourgeois gentleman wearing a frock coat. This was religion, not science. Long after he declared himself an atheist, John Dewey clung to his belief in Progress with religious fervor.

But it required purblind stubbornness to persevere in the secular faith in Science and Human Progress through the twenty-five years or so after 1914. After the war came the collapse of Weimar, the Great Depression, the rise of nazism and fascism, Stalin's purge trials, and then premonitory thunder of new war. In America, the Depression persisted well into Roosevelt's third term—recovery came only with war spending—badly shaking the confidence of the more intellectually honest of New Deal technocrats.* Lippmann threw in the towel with his 1937 book, *The Good Society,* in which he argued that centrally directed economies inevitably led to dictatorship, an apostasy that even his biographer cannot quite forgive. The gossip columnist Walter Winchell announced that Lippmann was going to become a Catholic.

The seeping away of enthusiasm exposed the central vacuity of the secular intellectual construct. The impulses Freud found writhing in the mind's dark recesses mocked Dewey's hopes for a kingdom of "conscious intention." Goose-stepping storm troopers and the clamors of America's radical fringe seemed to bear out Freud. And in the 1920s, intellectuals finally began to grasp the true implications of Darwinism and Mendelian genetics. Evolution really *was* random. "Fitness" and "Progress" had nothing to do with each other. There was no quasi-divine plan ensuring the ultimate ascendancy of white men, or even of the human race. In terms of longevity, adaptability, and survival prospects, cockroaches had it all over English gentlemen.

There were other problems. Pearsonian science limited itself to measurable phenomena. In social science, the *individual* became the essential unit of analysis, and older notions of a person defined by a texture of relationships were simply swept away. Secondly, Pearson stressed the *impermanence* of hypotheses—they were valid only until something better came along. Or as William James put it more expansively in his *Pragmatism* (1907), a concept "is true because it is useful"—truth and usefulness "mean exactly the same thing."

The moral implications of all of this were unsettling, to say the least. There was no foundation for establishing permanent values, and worse, no way to escape the economist's definition of values as mere, but measurable, individual *wants.* By the same logic, within very broad limits, such as the risk of endangering others, any set of wants was as good as any other. If parents were un-

---

* Faith in a reforming technocracy enjoyed a brief fifteen-year revival bracketed roughly by the Soviet Sputnik launch in 1957 and the 1973 energy crisis, a period that also incorporated the debacle in Vietnam. The high point may have been America's moon walk.

happy in their marriage, they should divorce; their "needs" were as important as their children's, subject only to minimum legal constraints like child support. Modern social science simply didn't admit values like the primacy of the family. Combined with Freudian psychology, the secularist paradigm seemed to point to a morality of the least common denominator, the prospect of a society ruled by an ethical Gresham's law, in which socially responsible behavior would inevitably be driven out by the selfish and self-indulgent.

Dewey fought against this logic all his life, but without much success, plaintively insisting that if people were properly educated they would adopt values all could approve of. James argued, weakly enough, that people should behave as if there were a God, because God is a useful hypothesis. Reinhold Niebuhr, a longtime Dewey admirer, sank into despair: intellectuals had to face up to the "stupidity of the average man," according to Niebuhr in 1932, and provide the "myths" and "dogma" people needed to live by. The qualifications of intellectuals to offer moral guidance, however, were far from obvious. Pearson himself was an out-and-out racist, demanding, in 1915, "that all sympathy and charity shall be organized and guided into paths where they will promote racial efficiency and not lead us straight towards national shipwreck." It is unfair, of course, to judge Pearson through a post-1940s lens; but when logic and "science" were the only constraints on behavior, the path lay open to moral horrors.

The loss of moral center is perhaps best captured by Joseph Wood Krutch's *The Modern Temper* (1930), a scathing indictment of "the impasse to which the scientific spirit has conducted us." Nature "is ingenious in devising *means*," Krutch wrote, "but she has no *ends* which the human mind has been able to discover." Philosophy, "losing all confidence in its own conclusions begins to babble of 'beneficent fictions,' " like James's advice that religious ethics might be useful, what Krutch called the "feeble sanction of an 'as if.' " Men of letters—Aldous Huxley, Ernest Hemingway, T. S. Eliot—portrayed love as "an obscene joke", while Freudian psychology stripped away "such shreds of dignity as had been left." All intellectuals could offer, lamented Krutch, was Anatole France's advice that "life is an art," that everyone "seeks salvation as he may." But no society could be organized on such a principle—"The proposition that life is a science is intellectually indefensible; the proposition that life is an art is pragmatically impossible."

This was the modernist crisis,* and Krutch could see no way out, at the last retreating to the same self-mocking irony he criticized in Anatole France.

---

* Secular modernism, it should be noted, had no connection, or at most only a very distant one, with the theological "modernism" that Pius X condemned in 1907. The term "modernism" is most often applied to the literary and artistic movement of the early twentieth century that dramatized the modernist crisis a generation or so before intellectuals were able to articulate it.

Perhaps the last vestige of human greatness, he wrote, was that "we have discovered the trick which has been played upon us." Given such disarray within the fortress of secularism, it is hardly surprising that Catholics were not disposed to be intellectually humble, at least not yet.

The Triumphal Ghetto

The mood of thinking Catholics in the 1920s and 1930s was an awkward compound of swelling confidence and bitter grievance. The confidence came from Catholic unity and growth, and was reinforced by the visible confusion among non-Catholic intellectuals. Protestant leaders were often openly envious of Catholic certainty. As one minister wrote in 1927, when Catholic children were asked questions about their religion, they uniformly responded with "the clearcut, definite, and positive teachings of the Baltimore Catechism"; on the other hand, he complained, while "[o]ur Protestant grandparents had at least some definite religion as children, the present generation has none." Alexander Meiklejohn lamented in 1923 that American educators are "lost and mixed up and bewildered . . . [because] we haven't got a gospel, a philosophy, a religion" to hand on to students.

The Catholic sense of having "arrived" was confirmed by the prominence of Catholics in local politics, in the law and the courts, and the Church's highly visible institutional building boom, which hardly slowed during the Depression. Catholic papers throughout the country headlined the royal treatment that Roosevelt laid on when Mundelein visited Rome in 1938. He was met at sea by the American ambassador, brought to Naples in a fleet flagship, escorted by special train to Rome, and feted by the entire diplomatic community.

But the sense of grievance was profound. Catholics rightly considered themselves among the most loyal and patriotic of Americans. But the secular state bore down upon them from every side. Secular teachers' colleges, in the Catholic view, were completely in the grip of the moral relativism expounded by Dewey and his followers. To protect their children, Catholics willingly dug deep into their pockets to build their own schools, even while paying taxes for the secular system. And all the while, the authorities constantly raised the financial hurdles, busily proliferating regulations on required courses, physical plant, teacher training. (The 1920s were the first golden age of bureaucratic regulation, and there is evidence that in states like Pennsylvania the regulatory authorities really did target the Catholic systems.) Suspiciously enough, for a hundred and fifty years, the Constitution had managed to tolerate a fluid interpenetration between established Protestantism and the educational system. But now that Catholics were running schools, the First Amendment had suddenly acquired a new rigidity, and the fate of the republic somehow depended on denying assistance to Catholics for purposes that were clearly nonreligious, like school buses, arithmetic textbooks, and aids for the handicapped.

Secular sexual permissiveness was a direct assault on Catholic values. Catholics had a long tradition of running charity hospitals, but the proliferation of secular maternity clinics offering sterilization and contraception prompted the development of Catholic maternity clinics offering middle-class Catholics "a true alternative . . . at nominal cost." The tendency of even liberal Catholic journals to call contraception "race suicide," sounds much like the suspicions of black nationalists against abortion a half century later. All those large families reformers worried about in the 1920s and 1930s just happened to be Catholic.

Catholic frustration with secular culture was mixed with a withering scorn. With Hollywood marketing a cult of amoral sex goddesses, *America* said, "American ideals of the indissolubility of marriage are so low that it is probably impossible to bring them any lower without declaring openly for promiscuity." And Catholics mocked the hand-wringing over rising juvenile delinquency—"We have tried everything from free toothbrushes and free playgrounds to free schools and free textbooks; we have ranged from non-sectarian religion and lectures on sex-hygiene to terms in the reformatory and the penitentiary." The authorities had tried everything, that is, except teaching that "religion, morality, conscience have their place" in life.

The most bitter pill was political. The night that Al Smith was crushed by Herbert Hoover in the 1928 election, the Jesuit Leonard Feeney wrote, was a "night of sixteen million tragedies." Catholics were shocked at the outpouring of anti-Catholic hysteria that met Smith's nomination. The rumors that the Pope would move to the White House or that Protestants would lose their citizenship were, perhaps, to be expected, as were the burning crosses that lined Smith's campaign travels through the South and Midwest—these were the follies of the slope-browed and the four-fingered. The snide tone of Protestant questioning like Charles C. Marshall's "An Open Letter to the Honorable Alfred E. Smith" in the *Atlantic Monthly* was, if anything, more infuriating. Wouldn't Smith *really* have to choose the teachings of papal encyclicals on the primacy of religion over the Constitution? Marshall asked. Didn't a recent bishops' pastoral letter against the anticlerical regime in Mexico show that Smith would follow a Romish foreign policy? Wouldn't Smith be obligated to impose Catholic legislation on marriage, education, censorship?

Smith's answer was a small masterpiece. He had to seek the help of his friend Fr. Duffy to compose it, he admitted—taking the occasion to recite Duffy's string of war medals—because he could make no pretense of matching

Marshall's theological sophistication. Smith was pleased to report, however, that Marshall's Episcopal synod used almost identical language to the Catholic on the primacy of religion, but no one had called it a threat to the republic. He himself had taken an oath to uphold the Constitution nineteen times and, in four terms as governor of America's largest state, had never encountered a conflict between his religious and political duties. His record on public education was outstanding. Whatever the encyclicals might say, Duffy had assured him they were not dogma; in any case, "I, a devout Catholic since childhood, never heard of [them] until I read your letter." Smith ended with a stirring peroration: "In this spirit, I join with fellow Americans of all creeds in a fervent prayer that never again in this land will any public servant be challenged because of the faith in which he has tried to walk humbly with his God."

Later scholarship suggests that Smith really had no chance. His religion, in fact, may have helped him in the North as much as it hurt him in the South. There was simply no way a Tammany machine politician with a rasping Brooklyn accent could beat a mainstream figure like Hoover in the middle of a Republican economic boom. Richard Hofstadter has speculated that the Democrats may have let Smith make a futile run in the hope of putting the religious issue behind them. Catholics, understandably, did not see it that way. As citizens, as warriors, and as taxpayers, they had more than earned their status as Americans. Smith was the best-of-breed of Catholic public figures. But it seemed the country had declared him unfit for the presidency solely because of his religion.

The outcome of the Smith campaign greatly reinforced the Catholic separatist impulse, as did the perceived inequities of the educational system, the antireligiosity of mainstream secular culture, the commercial glorification of sin and sexual permissiveness. Without wavering in their patriotism or hypernationalism, Catholics executed a remarkable emotional withdrawal from secular America. In the decades before World War II, there was a proliferation of "parallel" Catholic organizations of every variety. Besides their Catholic newspaper and weekly radio "Catholic Hour," Catholic homes could join the Catholic Book Club or subscribe to the general-interest *Catholic Digest.* Catholic bar associations debated whether Catholic lawyers could participate in divorce cases, and Catholic medical societies formulated guidelines for Catholic obstetricians in secular hospitals. The Catholic Physicians' Guild was the largest organization of Catholic doctors in the world. The American Catholic Sociological Society set out to construct a "Catholic sociology," and the American Catholic Historical Association hoped to infuse historical studies with the Catholic "belief in God, in the purpose of creation . . . and in man's final destiny."

The National Catholic Education Association, founded in 1904, was one of the oldest Catholic professional organizations; but by the 1930s, there was a Catholic Press Association, a Catholic Writers' Guild of America, an American Catholic Philosophical Association, a Catholic Anthropological Association, a Catholic Poetry Society of America, a Catholic Economic Association, and a National Council of Catholic Nurses. The American Catholic Psychological Association was founded in 1947. The Knights of Columbus made a convenient local meeting place for Catholic businessmen; the Association of Catholic Trade Unionists was, as will be seen, a force in the rise of the CIO; and alumnae organizations of Catholic women's colleges provided much of the energy behind the Catholic Legion of Decency movie rating system.

Chicago's Bishop Bernard Shiel was the impresario of the National Catholic Youth Organization, sponsoring sports leagues, boxing tournaments, and summer camps throughout the country in competition to traditional YM- and YWCAs. Almost all big-city police and fire departments had a Holy Name Society, with monthly communion breakfasts featuring speakers on religious or political issues. Most large public school districts had Catholic Teachers' Guilds to propagate the "Catholic viewpoint" on educational matters. There was even a Catholic summer resort movement, so Catholics could vacation in spots that were explicitly or implicitly reserved for Catholics.

The professional staff at the NCWC acted as a clearinghouse, if not quite a command post, for the frenetic organizing activity. It ran an international wire service for Catholic newspapers and provided a home base for the National Council of Catholic Men (1297 paid-up associate organizations in 1935, mostly parish Holy Name Societies) and for the National Council of Catholic Women (2349 paid-up associates, mostly parish sodalities). NCWC's Catholic Action Department and the Catholic Evidence Bureau coordinated Catholic "lay apologetics," producing a stream of manuals, textbooks, and study materials to help parishes organize evening discussion groups, study programs, speaker bureaus, vacation religious schools, all to help lay Catholics understand and "defend" Catholic doctrine. In 1939, as the bishops became alarmed over the apparent inroads of communism, the NCWC announced that the Church would "mobilize its educational activities in the United States today for warfare against subversive activities." Fr. John Cronin, who later became an adviser to Richard Nixon, was brought to the NCWC to write a text on communism, and also produced two widely used texts on *Catholic Social Principles* and *Catholic Social Action*.

The distinctive Catholic worldview was carefully cultivated in almost all Catholic college textbooks. A basic introduction to psychiatry, for instance, is entitled *Psychiatry and Catholicism*. It begins, much in the manner of John Ryan's textbooks, by establishing St. Thomas's teachings on the moral law and free will, and only then considers modern teachings on psychiatry. The sections on sexual dysfunction, while they are humane enough, have a

Credit: Archives, Diocese of Rochester
Despite the defeat of Al Smith, American Catholics achieved an extraordinary
ideological self-confidence by the 1930s, much to the envy of Protestant minis-
ters. Catholic self-assurance is captured in this 1930s photograph of the future
television star Fulton J. Sheen "cheerfully" answering questions on an Ala-
bama street corner.

distinctly moral overlay. The attitude toward the therapeutic claims of the
various psychiatric schools is quite skeptical (and sensibly so, given the psy-
choanalytic enthusiasms of the times). A Catholic textbook on sociology expressly places the subject within the framework of the Catholic organic
concept of a "Mystical Body of Christ."

It is not at all paradoxical that this aggressive self-ghettoizing laid the essential foundation for the American Church's triumphal era. A later generation of Catholic intellectuals were embarrassed by the Church's carapaced

defensiveness, the ingrained habit of philosophical wagon-circling. But Catholics were withdrawing to gather their strength. The 1930s saw an upsurge of the MAC movement, short for "Make America Catholic." And a 1924 *America* article, after expressing alarm that Hollywood had discovered "the filmed sex novel," concluded matter-of-factly that it would be necessary "to Catholicize the movies."

Shoring up their own ramparts was merely preliminary to a broader Catholic program of desecularizing the rest of society. As a committee on Catholic higher education reported in 1935: "The Catholic college will not be content with presenting Catholicism as a creed, a code, or a cult. Catholicism must be seen as a culture; hence the graduates of a Catholic college of liberal arts will go forth not merely trained in Catholic doctrine . . . [but possessed of] those facts in the supernatural order which give meaning and coherence to the whole of life." The operative words here are "culture" and "go forth." The Jesuit Education Association, who accounted for the majority of Catholic colleges, consistently stressed its mission of training Catholic public leaders. And the NCWC Education Department mounted a quiet campaign to recruit more Catholic teachers for *public* schools and secular colleges. (The subjects for which a "Catholic education [of the teacher] is definitely required" included education, biology, economics, sociology, and psychology.) Even the "Catholic Hour" broadcasts carefully totted up its documented conversions at the end of each year.

The period from the 1930s to the 1950s is often thought of as the most "Romanized" era of the American Catholic Church. But this is at most half the story. American bishops were extraordinarily deferential to the Pope, and American collection baskets were quickly becoming the major source of Vatican revenue. All the forms of American Catholicism were based on Roman diktats. The insistence on Thomistic philosophy dated from an encyclical of Leo. The concept of "Catholic Action" came from Rome, as did, of course, much of the organicist social philosophy.

But the mother Church in Rome really *was* on the defensive. In the traditional Catholic countries like France, Italy, and Spain, Catholicism was being routed from popular culture, and Catholic attendance at Mass hovered in the 20 to 30 percent range, in contrast to America's 75 percent or better—90 percent in big-city Irish parishes. Reforming European governments were steadily stripping away Church lands, episcopal privileges, and clerical salaries. Birth control was widely practiced in France and Italy, causing a sharp drop in Catholic fertility. Catholic educational systems were being nationalized and secularized. Catholic Action was a right-wing political party, not a social and educational movement. In Italy in 1931, over the outraged objections of the Pope, Mussolini moved to make Catholic Action a state party, under *his* control. Working class movements were almost uniformly

anticlerical, and the antipathies built up by the centuries of feudal domination—witness the church burnings and the murders of clerics in republican
Spain—vastly eclipsed the remnants of anti-Catholic prejudices in America.
Nor were there much grounds for hoping things would get better—as the
papal nuncio to France reported: "Political action by Catholics [is] zero. Almost all the Catholic deputies belong to the nobility and are far inferior in
moral value and in their talent to their colleagues in the Chamber."

The contrast with the optimism of the Church in America could not
be greater. The Vatican did its best to stay informed on American affairs.
Eugenio Pacelli, the papal secretary of state and the future Pius XII, visited
America in 1936 to meet Roosevelt and inquire into the doings of Fr.
Coughlin. The Pope, Pius XI, appointed good conservative prelates who
would diligently curry favor with the Roman Curia. He was grateful for the
endless river of American money. He lobbied the American bishops to
nudge their government on Mexico or Spain. But on a practical level, Vatican involvement with America was very limited, even negligible. The
Roman Church was very much of a European institution, with its energies
completely absorbed in a struggle for its very life. Msgr. George Higgins
spent forty-four years at the NCWC, most of them in John Ryan's old job.
Speaking of the years before Vatican II (1962–1965)—which consciously
set up coordinating mechanisms—he says, "I can't remember a single inquiry from Rome that entire time," he says. "Never. Nothing. We always
acted completely on our own."

In the 1920s and 1930s, the Catholic Church in America was quite consciously putting the final touches on its adjustment to America. It was a
Church that insisted on its own uniqueness and rightness and on the necessity of religion's being utterly pervasive in daily public and private life. The
American State was equally insistent on maintaining a rigid separation between civic and religious life and on refusing to recognize the truth-claim of
any particular religion. At the same time, it was willy-nilly encouraging the
steady secularization of American life. The Church's solution to this conundrum was quite simply to build its own state. As it embarked on its American
triumphal era, the Catholic Church attempted nothing less than creating a
completely enveloping state-within-a-state for its own Catholic community.
The goal was to make it possible for an American Catholic to carry out almost every activity of life—education, health care, marriage and social life,
union membership, retirement and old age care—within a distinctly
Catholic environment. And no prelate pursued that goal more aggressively,
or single-mindedly, than Philadelphia's Cardinal Dennis Dougherty.

CHAPTER 7

God's Bricklayer

Cardinal Dennis Dougherty took off for a three-month European vacation in early May of 1934. Several weeks later, a declaration of war on the movie industry in the form of a pastoral letter from the Cardinal was read in all the churches of the Philadelphia Archdiocese. Hollywood's obsession with "sex and crime," said Dougherty, was a "vicious and insidious attack . . . on the very foundations of our Christian civilization, namely the sacrament of marriage, the purity of womanhood, the sanctity of the home, and obedience to lawful authority." Dougherty's archdiocese covered most of southeastern Pennsylvania, so the letter was heard by some 825,000 Catholics, almost all of whom would have been in church that Sunday, as they were every Sunday. Their marching orders were straightforward: Philadelphia Catholics were forbidden, on pain of serious sin, to go to any movies, at all, of any kind, anywhere.

Philadelphia Catholics were accustomed to doing as they were told, and movie attendance plummeted immediately, and dropped even further when prominent Protestant ministers urged their congregations to follow the Catholic lead. The total falloff in sales was about 40 percent. It was typical of the Cardinal that, with the press clamoring for a statement, he was mostly incommunicado in Europe, while chancery spokesmen were restricted to formulaic press releases that shed little light on his intentions. Dougherty was perfectly ecumenical in his aloofness, for he had not troubled to coordinate with his fellow prelates either, who were that very spring under the aegis of the NCWC, working out a far-reaching system of rating movies that was to profoundly affect Hollywood production values for a generation.

The studio owners, who at that time controlled most of the nation's theaters, joined with independent theater operators in July to issue a threat to close all of Philadelphia's movie houses. They cited the progress with the NCWC initiative to demonstrate the Cardinal's capriciousness and claimed that movie attendance had fallen off so sharply that it was uneconomic to operate theaters at all. If all 525 theaters closed, it would cost the area some 15,000 jobs in one of the hardest years of the Depression. Tracked down in Rome, Dougherty said he would be "extremely glad" if all the theaters closed, and the studios dropped their threat. But there is no question that the theaters were hit hard, and dozens were forced to close. One operator— a good Catholic with six children, aged three to thirteen, who had been "practically raised in a motion picture theater"—wrote that he was in desperate straits, having lost both his theater and his life savings of $40,000. Jack Kelly, the brick magnate, father of Princess Grace, and head of the local Democratic Party, cited the economic pain when he wrote to the chancellor, Msgr. Hugh Lamb, in August that "I am wondering if the punishment hasn't been severe enough." Besides that, he was hoping to take his children to see *Treasure Island.*

Kelly was willing to speak with the Cardinal directly, but only if Lamb thought it was a good idea. Lamb's reply is not in the record, but he almost certainly told Kelly not to waste his time. Dougherty was an absolutist, and the ban was not a negotiating ploy, which the studio owners, too, had trouble comprehending. Will H. Hays, the head of Hollywood's Production Code Office, wrote the Cardinal in October asking for a meeting. He cited the progress in the NCWC talks and pleaded that the studios had already "*capitulated to your demands.*" Dougherty was willing to meet, but not to discuss movies. Samuel Goldwyn made a quiet visit to the Cardinal's home and reportedly offered to do whatever was necessary to lift the ban. Dougherty was polite but said, "I am adamant. I will not lift it. That will be left to the moral judgment of your products." Catholics who inquired when the ban would be lifted received a form letter stating "to frequent an occasion of sin is sinful. Accordingly, to go to moving picture theaters is an occasion of sin and is sinful." And the following year, another forceful pastoral letter warned Catholics that the ban was still in effect:

> Motion picture theaters as they have hitherto been, and still are, must be shunned as occasions of sin; and the ban will remain upon them until they are transformed, even though the much-married, much-divorced actors and actresses and the Russian* producers of lascivious

---

* Almost all the studio moguls were Jewish, a fact that was frequently noted in internal Catholic appraisals of the movie problem. One imagines that Dougherty searched hard for the *mot juste* before coming up with "Russian." Catholic-Jewish tensions, as will be seen, were becoming quite sharp in the 1930s.

filth, and theater owners who purvey crime and sex films, lose some of their fabulous incomes.

In theory, for the rest of their lives, Philadelphia Catholics committed a grievous sin whenever they went to the movies, for Dougherty never removed his ban. For a former seminary professor, in fact, the Cardinal's theology was highly dubious. The Baltimore Catechism taught that to place oneself at high risk of sinning is itself a sin. (If a young couple park in a secluded place, they may have sinned by placing themselves in an occasion of sin. This could be counterproductive. As the Irish say, "as well be hung for a sheep as a goat.") In the case of movies, however, the occasion of sin would be the movie, not the theater—attending *Treasure Island* could hardly be a moral risk. All the diocesan priests, of course, knew this, as certainly did Dougherty. After exhibiting remarkable discipline during the first months of the ban, Catholics gradually drifted back to the movies. Indeed, Philadelphia's Catholic churches and schools cooperated in publicizing the NCWC's new Legion of Decency system of movie ratings. The diocese even turned a profit of $1710 selling Legion of Decency buttons to schoolchildren—which was inconsistent with the notion of a ban, and even more so with its forceful renewal in 1935. But it is highly unlikely that anyone from the Catholic community directly challenged the logic of the Cardinal's position. Dennis Dougherty was a difficult man, although undeniably a great cardinal, and while he was called many names during his long career, no one ever accused him of being reasonable.

Dennis Dougherty's Philadelphia

The symbol of Philadelphia was the statue of Billy Penn, as the natives called him, that dominated the city's skyline until it was overshadowed by the skyscrapers that accompanied a financial boom in the 1960s. The statue stands on top of the central tower of City Hall, an enormous, magnificently ugly jumble of towers, courtyards, and rococo scrollwork that sits athwart the intersection of Broad and Market Streets, at the heart of the commercial district. An unwritten but strictly enforced zoning rule specified that no building could reach the height of Penn's hat. Penn's long dominance of the landscape demonstrated three central facts about Philadelphia—it was tolerant, it was corrupt, and it was stodgy.

William Penn was a Quaker, and old Philadelphia was one of the few cities besides Baltimore where Catholics were relatively welcome. The riots in the 1840s were more anti-Irish than anti-Catholic and had no impact on the business of the banking house operated by the Catholic Drexel family.

Anthony J. Drexel, the city's premier Gilded Age financier, eventually converted to High Church Episcopalianism, but his niece, Mother Katharine Drexel, is a candidate for Catholic sainthood for her work in the Indian and black missions. Nineteenth-century Philadelphia had a far more diversified economy than either New York or Boston, and offered many more opportunities for enterprising Irish Catholics. Thomas Cahill, the coal magnate, contributed $1 million to build the nation's first central diocesan boys' Catholic high school, Roman Catholic High on Broad Street. Thomas Fitzgerald was one of Philadelphia's leading publishers; the Dolans controlled the street railways; the Keatings were banking partners of the very bluenose Biddles. James Sullivan was president of the Market Street Bank and the number-two man at Midvale Steel, while John Whalen was trustee of the Drexel estate.

The conventionally bleak picture of Irish Catholic economic progress in the nineteenth and early twentieth centuries is largely based on research in Boston, where the tightly knit Yankee commercial system offered few opportunities to outsiders. In the 1850s in Boston, for example, 20 percent of the population was Irish, but only 1 percent of the grocers. During the same period in Philadelphia, the Irish accounted for 18 percent of the population, but 22 percent of the grocers. From the 1850s through the 1880s, an entrepreneur named Bernard Rafferty organized some thirty-five parish building and loan societies; their capitalization was at least $15 million, and as far as is known, none ever went bankrupt. Philadelphia's construction trades were always controlled by the Irish, on both the labor and management sides of the table, with a healthy assist from the ceaseless building activities of the Catholic Church. Construction families like the Kellys, the McCloskeys, and the McShains were, and to an extent still are, threefold pillars of the business community, the Democratic Party, and the Church. When Catholic Italians and Poles began arriving in large numbers early in the twentieth century, Irish Catholics were already moving to the affluent suburbs to the north and west.

Unlike the Irish in Boston or New York, Philadelphia's Irish never won control of local politics and, for once, were not responsible for the corruption. The gargantuan extortion extracted from the construction of City Hall in the 1880s—it funded local politics for decades—flowed through the hands of William Stokely, a Republican boss of impeccable English descent. The Pennsylvania Republican Party during the first part of the twentieth century was controlled by Harvard-educated Boies Penrose; and the Penrose machine, in turn, controlled Philadelphia politics. The local boss was Bill Vare, one of three brothers, Protestants of English extraction, who began life as truck farmers in South Philadelphia's marshes and fought their way up the political ladder through their trash collection franchises. The Vares won the

loyalties of the Irish wards with jobs, careful organization, and petty charities—the turkey dinner left by the door at Christmas for the family whose
father was down on his luck. The Irish were well represented at the second
and third levels of the party and came close to dominating the civil service
rolls. Jack Kelly, Matt McCloskey, and the real estate magnate Albert M.
Greenfield tried to breathe life into the Democratic Party in the first days of
the New Deal, but when Kelly ran for mayor in 1934, the Irish vote split, and
the Republicans swept the elections as always. An Irish Catholic was not
elected mayor until 1964.

The real power in Philadelphia was the small WASP elite—the Potters,
the Clarks, the Drinkers, the Newhalls, the Waynes. They were not as educated or as commercial as their cousins in Boston or as rich as the vulgarians
who controlled New York, but they managed to look down their noses at
both. E. Digby Baltzell's researches on Philadelphia gentlemen shows that of
several hundred directors' seats on the leading business, cultural, and civic
institutions in the city just before World War II, well over a third were held
by only forty-two men, all of them members of one or both of two gentlemen's clubs, the Rittenhouse Club and the Philadelphia Club. These men
tolerated Philadelphia's corruption—indeed, their law firms and banks prof-
ited from it—and they gave the city its air of stodgy timelessness. They quietly enforced development controls, like the rule on building heights; they
rather favored Philadelphia's notorious blue laws that closed stores on Sundays and bars at midnight on Saturdays; and they looked relatively benignly
on Philadelphia's burgeoning Jewish and Catholic economic subcultures, although Catholics and Jews were rarely allowed into their clubs. Significantly
enough, Philadelphia's Democratic Party did not become a vehicle for reform until the 1950s, when it was taken over by WASPs.

The character of the city that greeted Dennis Dougherty as its new
archbishop in 1918 would remain remarkably unchanged for another forty
years. Philadelphia was a quiet city where blue-collar families lived in neat
brick row houses on tree-lined streets laid out in orderly rectangles. Fathers
worked in the new navy yard on the Delaware, or in the foundries and
steel mills to the northeast, or in the Sun Oil refinery spreading along the
Schuylkill River. About 20 percent of the population in the archdiocese was
Catholic, probably 25 percent within the city limits, percentages that would
steadily grow throughout Dougherty's tenure. The great majority of the
Catholics were still of Irish descent, as were virtually all of the clergy and the
prominent Catholic laymen. Catholic Philadelphia was a city of villages,
marked off by invisible parish lines, where the homes of almost all the parishioners were within easy walking distance of the rectory and parish school.
Until well into the 1950s, when Philadelphia Catholics were asked where
they were from, they would answer "St. Monica's," or "Our Lady of Ran-

som" (or just "Ransom"), precise geographic designations that were found on no official map. It was a culture that Dougherty knew and understood, and when his appointment was announced, Philadelphia's Catholics hailed him as a "native son."

There has been no full-scale biography of Dougherty. He himself left no published writings, and he destroyed most of his papers before his death. But from the correspondence preserved in the Philadelphia archives, and the recollections of the priests and laypeople who knew him, there emerges a portrait of a most anomalous man, a jumble of contradictions that in many ways mirror the still awkward but increasingly powerful position of a hierarchical, semimedieval Church in a secular, democratic America. Dougherty was the most practical of men, with a genius for real estate and the instincts of a tycoon—he loved to call himself "God's Bricklayer"—but he was also deeply religious, with a strong mystical streak. He wielded great political power within Pennsylvania, but only in private and behind the scenes. He was at once the most accessible and forbidding of prelates. He treated his priests harshly, sometimes even cruelly, but forged one of the most effective diocesan clergies. His views on sexuality were among the most conventional of his time, but alone among the hierarchy, he took the feminist position on issues affecting both laywomen and nuns. The most secure and strongly entrenched of churchmen, he was the most servile toward Rome. The Philadelphia Catholic subculture that he created was among the most carapaced and separatist in the country, but he drew his own friends from outside the Church; indeed, the men who may have been closest to him were Jews. He was shy and private and hated speaking or preaching in public, but loved the pomp and princely luxury that came with his office.

Dougherty was born in 1865 in Pennsylvania's anthracite coal region near Scranton, of the kind of lower-middle-class Irish family that produced the lion's share of America's priests. He entered Philadelphia's St. Charles Seminary in 1881, after briefly attending a Jesuit college in Montreal, and completed his studies in Rome. He was an outstanding student and an accomplished linguist—he was fluent in at least five languages and spoke as many as ten—and left Rome with the brilliant reputation and the personal contacts in the Curial bureaucracy necessary for a clerical highflier. He was friendly with Merry del Val, though not so close as O'Connell, on excellent terms with both Pius XI and Pius XII, and particularly close to Pietro Gasparri, cardinal secretary of state during much of Pius XI's reign. Like O'Connell, he was physically impressive though not tall, and carried himself like a military commander, with small, narrow eyes and a straight, stern mouth set in a broad, square-jawed face. Dougherty spent his first thirteen years as a priest teaching theology at St. Charles, where he was known as a severe taskmaster with an intimidating fluency in Latin, the language of instruction. For a substantial number of

Philadelphia's clergy, the name of Dougherty conjured up only quivering memories of their inadequacy as theology students.

The Vatican plucked Dougherty from St. Charles in 1903 to be the first American bishop in the Philippines, where a bedraggled and corrupt Church was reeling from decades of official, and much deserved, anticlericalism. He hit the islands like a thunderclap—regularizing and disciplining the local clergy, sequestering the funds of the Spanish orders and sending many of their priests packing, reenergizing the school systems, restoring diocesan finances. A local newspaper, *Renascimento,* reported in 1914 that Dougherty was fighting Protestant proselytizers by, of all things, running a movie theater where the price of admission was a Protestant Bible. A fragment of a diary Dougherty kept during a Roman trip in 1912 shows a driven and ambitious young bishop, eagerly sifting intelligence on the power jockeying for choice appointments. He cannot contain his disappointment that the Pope and the senior cardinals never directly tell him that he has done a good job, despite hearing from every side that they were pleased. He spends much time soothing the Augustinian and Jesuit superiors for his bruising treatment of their local provinces, and on his way back to the Philippines resolves "no relaxation" in the administration of his diocese. Rough edges aside, Dougherty's performance fully justified his masters' confidence, and they decided to reward him in 1915 with the see of Chicago, while the less experienced George Mundelein was scheduled to fill the vacancy in Buffalo. That plan was derailed when the British government objected to a German bishop on the border of Canada. So Mundelein got Chicago, and Dougherty settled for Buffalo, with the promise that he would have his pick of the next archiepiscopal opening, which turned out to be Philadelphia, his first choice all along.

The new archbishop took over his diocese with customary Catholic panache. On the day before his installation, Dougherty entrained from Buffalo with an escort of a hundred Philadelphia and fifty Buffalo priests. Church bells pealed throughout the city when his train pulled in. A hundred and fifty thousand Catholics cheered him on the route from the train station to the cathedral—viewing stands had been allotted to all of Philadelphia's parishes. Dougherty sat in an open limousine, ruddy and smiling, behind an entourage of roaring motorcycles, fifty brass bands, and seventy-five automobiles, holding his gloved, ringed hand outside the car. Old ladies broke through the police line all along the way to run up and kiss the ring. Four thousand of the city's civic and religious leaders, including the governor-elect, the state attorney general, the mayor, and all the important ministers and rabbis, turned out that night for a grand reception. When Dougherty entered the cathedral the next day for his installation, the hundred-strong seminary choir trumpeted *"Ecce Sacerdos Magnus"*—"Behold the Great Priest"—not a ritual to encourage humility.

Credit: Library of Congress
Philadelphia's Archbishop Dennis Dougherty personified the big-city Catholic
prelate as militant religious field-general. In this picture, probably taken at his
installation as archbishop in 1918, Dougherty, in the center-front, strides at the
head of a group of local civic leaders.

Dougherty impressed his personality on his diocese as few other bishops
have done. Msgr. George Higgins remarks that, even many years after
Dougherty was dead, when Philadelphia priests talked about "The Cardinal"
there was no mistaking who they meant. As in all of the Northeast, the
Philadelphia brand of Catholicism was ghettoized and defensive—Dougherty
refused to participate in ecumenical ceremonies commemorating the end of
World War I, for example. Northeastern Catholic culture was more sharply
defined, stood more apart from the rest of society, than in a Chicago or a St.
Paul, newer cities where Catholics did not live in the shadow of entrenched
unfriendly elites. But in 1918 almost twice as many Catholics lived in the
Northeast as in the Midwest, and northeastern Catholicism inevitably set the
Church's public tone and style. (The "other Catholics" scattered throughout
the South and West would have little impact on the politics or the public
image of the Church until the 1940s at the earliest.) And in Philadelphia, as

perhaps in few other dioceses, Dougherty succeeded in establishing the thick physical and psychological web of social, spiritual, and educational institutions that defined the ideal Catholic state-within-a-state. Whether or not Philadelphia was statistically typical of the American Church in its triumphal era, most Catholics would have agreed that it came as close as any to the design that must have existed in the mind of God.

Halcyon Days

The late Vincent Gallagher, ninety-eight years old in the summer of 1994, was Philadelphia's oldest living priest. He had all his hair and teeth, used no prescription medications, and his mind was sharp; but his body had almost totally shriveled away from his slender frame, and he sank, gaunt and weak, in an easy chair in a comfortable room at St. Joseph's Villa, a rest home for retired priests, and talked in a soft voice about the golden days of Philadelphia Catholicism. Gallagher was the son of an ice company stable worker. He went to St. Joseph's Prep in Philadelphia, spent a year at St. Joseph's College, and entered St. Charles in the fall of 1915. (He passed the stiff entrance exam after high school, with good marks in Latin and Greek—he had been trained by Jesuits—but the competition was so fierce that he was wait-listed.) His entire fifty-one years of active service, first as an assistant then as pastor, were spent at the Blessed Virgin Mary parish in Darby, where St. Joseph's Villa is located. Darby, just to the southwest of the city, was a bucolic, working-class, suburb in 1922 when Gallagher was ordained, and remained little changed until the suburban building boom that followed World War II.

"I was one of the powers-that-be," Gallagher reminisced with a broad smile, quickly adding that he did not mean to brag; it simply came with the job. He was a kind of village submayor—an institutionalized arbiter and sage—proud of his relation with Tom McClure, the Delaware County Republican boss and a Protestant, in an area that was mostly non-Catholic. One of McClure's sons told Gallagher after McClure died, "My father told me and my brother that we were to do anything for Fr. Fitzgerald [Gallagher's pastor] and Fr. Gallagher night or day." When a local nun had to make an emergency trip to the European mother house, Gallagher got her a passport in a single day. People brought him their money and family problems, and he typically ran a dozen or so trust accounts. "There was no paper or legal documents," he said. Families simply turned over their paychecks, and he'd pay their bills, supervise their savings, or dole out cash as they needed it. When he raised money to build a church to replace the two-story colonial house that had housed the parish school and church together, the parish pitched in to move the house to another site and expand it for more classrooms. An architect (who was married to a friend of Gallagher's housekeeper) reviewed Gallagher's plans, a contractor donated a foreman and supplied machinery and cement at cost, while the parish men did the actual construction on weekends and evenings. During a prolonged housing development controversy after the war, the town fathers asked Gallagher to attend their housing committee meetings and, in effect, designated him as the swing vote. For a while, developers brought their plans directly to the rectory, until Gallagher and the council president agreed on the plan that was eventually implemented.*

An alien anthropologist landing in a working-class Philadelphia parish in the 1930s or 1940s would know instantly the centrality of religion to the lives of the inhabitants. The rows of neat brick houses were invariably centered around, and dwarfed by, an imposing cluster of granite buildings—the Catholic church, always of neo-Gothic design, built to the scale of a medium-size cathedral; the parish school, sometimes even a high school; the rectory; the convent; one or more annexes for meeting rooms, overflow classes, perhaps even an auditorium. Few contemporary religions could match Catholicism's hold on the faithful. In Philadelphia parishes, particularly those comprising mostly second- and third-generation American families, attendance at Sunday Mass hovered around 90 percent, and compliance with "Easter duty"—the minimum obligation of annual reception of the sacraments—approached 99 percent. Almost all Catholic children went to parochial elementary schools, and almost two-thirds went to Catholic high schools. It was not uncommon for the majority of adults to belong to parish organizations like the Sodality and Holy Name Society. The lay turnout to annual retreats was numbered in the tens of thousands. Special devotions, like the Forty Hours' vigil for the Blessed Sacrament—people worshiped in round-the-clock shifts—were always crowded. In one parish, between eight and ten thousand people turned out for Monday-night novenas for almost twenty years.

Triumphal-era American Catholicism was a highly formal, even mechanistic creed, enshrouded in bewitching mysteries and ritual, combining to a remarkable degree theological rigor and a high degree of abstraction with a practical religion that was intensely personal and emotional. Catholicism came drenched in powerful, sometimes gory images: the pathetic figure of Jesus staggering through the Stations of the Cross; God the Father, implacable and austere, arriving in a burst of light on Judgment Day; the Blessed Mother, a refuge in adversity, the always ready intervenor, pleading mercy for undeserving sinners; and a whole litany of benign presences—St. Christo-

* See the notes to this chapter for an alternative interpretation of this episode.

pher for travelers, St. Jude for lost causes, St. Anthony for lost objects, a personal guardian angel. To outsiders, the Latin Mass was Kabuki theater—static and incomprehensible, medieval mumbo jumbo. That millions knelt unprotestingly through the Mass Sunday after Sunday confirmed secularists in their conviction that Catholics were inert hordes. But the details of the Latin hardly mattered to a lifelong Catholic. The stately cadences of the Mass were carved deep in neural pathways and had a clear dramatic structure. There was an introduction and a flurry of practical business—the readings, a short sermon, the collection—followed by the hush of growing tension approaching the Consecration; then the striking tableau, the Mass's emotional high point, as the priest, vestments flowing, held aloft the bright Host to the silver pealing of the altar boy's bell. Shuffling into line for Communion eased the solemnity, and then came a buzz of housekeeping—wiping the chalice, putting away the hosts. The tempo of the priest's prayers picked up; the rustle in the congregation increased; people in the back rows, with a quick genuflection and sign of the cross, would begin slipping out of the church; thoughts fled to the quotidian. The total experience—the dim lights, the glint of the vestments, the glow of the stained-glass windows, the mantralike murmur of the Latin—was mind-washing. It calmed the soul, opened the spirit to large, barely grasped Presences and Purposes. For a trembling moment every week, or every day if they chose, ordinary people reached out and touched the Divine.

The ethical code of Catholicism was all shining lines and sharp corners. The central text for workaday Catholics was the Baltimore Catechism. It came in three levels, each in a flat question-and-answer format. In elementary school, children memorized the whole catechism every year, moving from one level to the next as they progressed through the grades. The questions in each level were approximately the same, but the answers grew more complex, the language and ideas more complicated. The initial sequence of questions was burned into every Catholic's brain: "Q. Who made the world? A. God made the world. Q. Who is God? A. God is the Creator of Heaven and earth and of all things. Q. Why did God make you? A. God made me to know Him, to love Him, and to serve Him in this world and to be happy with Him forever *in the next*." (Emphasis added—utilitarian pragmatists threw up their hands.) Sins were listed, explicated, and graded, as were the hierarchies of the saints and angels. Sacraments had a precise ritual. Violations of form placed the passing of grace at hazard, but precise execution produced precise results. Few religions could match the gratifying closure, the guilt-resolving certainty, of the Catholic Confession. Commit any sin, sink to any level of degradation, and but kneel nameless and enshadowed in the confessional, recite the sins truthfully, and walk out to skies bright with grace. The catechism abounded in thought experiments—could

Catholic Pilot Bob continue working if his flight schedule made it impossible to attend Sunday Mass? Should Catholic Nurse Mary baptize a dying pagan if he had not requested it? Stainless-steel syllogisms clicked out correct answers. It is no surprise that Catholics excelled in rule-bound systems—the police and the FBI, civil services, large financial bureaucracies, the telephone company.

The parochial school was the centerpiece of Catholic strategy. Almost as soon as he was installed, Dougherty inquired of pastors from his own coal region why they did not operate parish schools. A pastor pointed out in reply that, as Dougherty well knew, almost all the people in the coal towns were Catholic and the public schools were staffed mostly with Catholic teachers, so why go to the expense of building another system? The reply was quintessential Dougherty:

Credit: Max Gilligan
Catholic ritual punctuated the ceremonies of growing up. This proud little girl
was photographed on the morning of her First Holy Communion in 1943.

A parochial school is a necessity, especially in this country where our children breathe in an atmosphere of heresy, unbelief and sometimes irreligion. By many, the Catholic church is here ridiculed, scoffed at, despised and persecuted; not by sword, but by hatred and opposition. Newspapers and magazines contain teachings contrary to Catholicism. On the streets, in factories, in mills, in mines—everywhere—false doctrines are propagated. . . . Priests and parents are bound to provide a religious education for children.

The schools were an unrivaled pastoral window. The rectory would know if Johnnie wasn't getting to bed at night, or if Mary was a bit "wild," or if a father was out of work and couldn't pay for a school outing. Nuns could elicit information during mandatory parent meetings, and the priest might follow up if the parents missed too many meetings. And just as today's environmental and antismoking advocates enlist children to modify their parents' behavior, Catholic schoolchildren would bring home clear instructions about the necessity for attending Mass on a holy day of obligation, and schedules for retreats or novenas or Forty Hours' devotions. Parents who slept in on a Sunday could count on a day of "S'ter said!" nagging about the state of their souls. The fact that the ranks of schoolchildren usually supplied the processants or the choir voices for major ceremonial events was a further compulsion for parents' attendance. Dougherty's tactic for drawing groups like South Philadelphia's Italians closer to the Church centered on getting more of their children to attend parish schools.

Given the high degree of adult participation in parish life, older priests are strikingly modest about their organizational accomplishments. Msgr. Joseph Dougherty, the retired pastor of St. John Bosco in northeast Philadelphia, was ordained in 1948. (He is a nephew of the Cardinal, but only rarely met him.) "Forty years ago," he says, "we would have just a couple of organizations, Holy Name or Vincent de Paul for the men, the Sodality or the Rosary Society for the women. Now we have dozens. But in those days, people didn't have the distractions they have now." "These were hardworking people," said Fr. Gallagher. "They didn't go out at night. So if I had a smoker for the men, or a Sodality meeting for the women, they would all come. They had nothing else to do." Certainly through the 1920s and 1930s and into the war years, the great majority of the men would have been manual workers, and the lot of a housewife, particularly with a large family, was very hard. Clothes were scrubbed with a washboard; there were no convenience foods or dishwashers. Putting on a hat to go to the parish hall with the other ladies, to have some light refreshments, to hear a speaker—on the movie campaign, or the work of a diocesan orphanage—to spend a half hour chatting, was a real treat. Involvement in a fund-raising drive, or perhaps an NCWC letter-writing campaign, or just hearing minutes and a treasurer's report added a sense of adult importance, of participation in activities usually closed to blue-collar people. Bigger parishes would have only a somewhat richer set of social activities, like monthly dances for young people; in an area like west Philadelphia the dances might be rotated among several contiguous parishes.

The extremely high status of the priest made organization easier. Within the sharply defined community that was Catholic Philadelphia, hardly any occupation ranked higher. "In matters of *all* importance," the priest was considered "the best-posted and ablest man" available; and, in truth, despite the narrowness of the seminary curriculum, a priest was far better educated than his parishioners. The accepted priestly image was almost wholly positive, at once wise, hypermasculine, warm, athletic, jovial—Father's jokes always brought down the house. Any fire or major disaster brought squad cars sirening up to rectories so priests could administer the last rites. (Since ministers and rabbis couldn't absolve sins, there was no point rushing them to the scene.) The mystery of the priest's calling reinforced his rank. Poems were written about the beauty of a young priest's hands—he was supposed to take particular care of them—for only he, at the altar every day, held in his hands the power of converting bread and wine into the true, the actual, Body and Blood of the Savior. The vow of celibacy, instead of making a priest an object of skepticism or derision, as it sometimes did in Latin cultures, elevated him above the common run of men, identified him as a person of unusual control and discipline, someone in touch with higher things, a man with a clear mind and a focused life.

No other high-status profession was as accessible to ambitious young men from blue-collar families. A good high school record in the right courses, a competitive mark on the entrance test, a persuasive recommendation from a pastor were all that was required. Families were supposed to pay tuition, but modest means were never an obstacle. It is hard to imagine what other career would have permitted a Dennis Dougherty from a hardscrabble coal-mining town to be so at home in European languages and culture while still in his early twenties, or even a Vincent Gallagher to become a temporary court of last resort for development decisions in Darby.

Philadelphia's priests were famous for their cohesiveness and élan, for a collective swagger that rivaled that of the Jesuits. The swagger came at a price, for Dougherty put them through a rigorous hazing. Seminarians were not allowed to smoke, even at home, and were not allowed to hold secular jobs in the summer. New priests had to promise not to take a drink for at least a year after ordination. Parish assistants were not allowed to own or drive cars; being caught driving drew a six-months' sentence to a retreat house. Priests had to wear clerical garb, including the square, three-flanged biretta hat, whenever they were in public, and priests working in the chancery were required to have frock coats and silk top hats, for formal events. (In fact, they bought a few generic sizes and kept them behind a door in case Dougherty ran a drill.) The status as an assistant stretched on for thirty years or even longer—except for a few chancery highfliers, a priest could not expect to get a church of his own until he was in his middle fifties. More than a few of the old-line pastors were tyrants, and young assistants were sometimes even bullied by the pastor's housekeeper. Philadelphia's pay scale was one of the lowest in the nation. Well into the 1940s, pastors got $1200 a year and assistants got $500, less than priests were paid in Baltimore in the 1890s. And on top of all the petty abuses, the work could be grindingly dull—the parade of elementary school confessions, pious old ladies listing their ailments over tremulously poured tea, the embarrassing need to constantly dun working-class parishioners for money.

By all reports, discipline was high. Msgr. Joseph McGlinn, Dougherty's last secretary, said there would be eight to ten disciplinary cases a year out of a population of more than a thousand priests. Two-thirds of the offenses would involve alcohol. The sexual transgressions were almost always heterosexual, although there would be the occasional priest with an eye for altar boys. Ingrained repressive mechanisms were doubtless much more powerful than they are today, popular culture was not nearly so overtly sexual, and support systems were much stronger. Most priests had trained together—indeed, most went to the same few high schools—and were rarely left on their own. A typical city parish might have three or four assistants, and parishes were close together; so priests naturally traveled and recreated in groups, usually in official clerical garb. Alcoholic priests were treated with relative lenience, so long as they admitted their problem—the typical routine was a drying-out period in a retreat house and reassignment to a less stressful parish. Dougherty was much harsher with sexual offenders; they were packed off to a monastery and often drummed out of the diocese. And if they could find a job elsewhere, McGlinn reports, Dougherty made them legally change their names, or did, until Rome finally told him that, even for a cardinal, that was overreaching. "Laicization," resigning from the priesthood with the Church's blessing, which is common now, was very rare in this period. For all practical purposes, there was no way for a priest to get out without jeopardizing his immortal soul.

The nuns were the system's faceless heroes. They tended the altars and staffed the institutions—the schools, the orphanages, the hospitals—required by a separatist Catholic state. A nun's life was highly restricted—even visits home were rare—and pay was low, only $300 a year for an elementary schoolteacher, paid to the order, not to the nun. Nuns were not entirely without psychic income: adults treated them with exaggerated respect, and they

were held in awe by schoolchildren. But they were often badly overworked.
The famed quick resort to the yardstick in schools undoubtedly reflects the
tension and strain of overcrowding, heavy class schedules, and poor training. Still, convents were turning away an onslaught of applicants, a comment, perhaps, on the power of faith, but also on the bleak prospects facing
so many working-class girls of the time. Msgr. Dougherty recalls that in the
1940s mothers superior made regular rounds of the rectories anxiously hunt-
ing out slots for their new classes of girls. The ratio of nuns to priests in the
diocese usually hovered at about 5:1.

Credit: Archives, Daughters of Charity, Evansville, Indiana
Nuns may have been America's first feminists. Although their accepted de-
meanor was shy and retiring in public, they actually financed, built, and oper-
ated most of the vast Catholic institutional infrastructure. Sr. Denise Burke of
the Daughters of Charity is shown here wielding a shovel at a 1962 hospital
groundbreaking.

Catholic Philadelphia was cool to strangers. Despite all the rhetoric about conversions, the price of such clarity, consistency, and conformity was inevitably a degree of cultural exclusiveness. By the 1930s and 1940s, Irish Americans were probably only a bare majority of Philadelphia's Catholics, but unlike Chicago, Philadelphia was not hospitable to national parishes. During the heaviest period of Italian immigration, for example, only a handful of the new parishes were Italian, and Italians and Poles often met an unfriendly reception in established parishes. (Fr. Gallagher had a smattering of Italian, so the small number of Darby Italians, who had usually traveled to South Philadelphia for religious services, began coming to Blessed Virgin Mary. When a group of Italians would approach the rectory to, say, arrange a baptism, his pastor would call out, "Here come some of your gang!") Spurred partly by aggressive Protestant proselytizing, Dougherty worked hard on the Italian problem. He introduced Italian classes at St. Charles, and mastery of the language could accelerate a clerical career path. As Italians achieved majorities in specific parishes, Dougherty moved in Italian-speaking pastors—in at least two cases prompting full-dress riots, complete with club-swinging policemen and last-stand Irish parishioners barricaded inside the church. Beyond trying to bridge the language gap, however, Dougherty would not bend the Philadelphia system; the ceremonial of an Italian parish was supposed to look exactly like that of an Irish parish. As one scholar put it, Dougherty charted "a course of religious acculturation by making immigrant churches like American (Irish) churches, upgrading the immigrant clergy, and insisting on rigid conformity of practice." His stress on elementary schools, even if they needed to be subsidized by the diocese, strove to wean children away from their parents' brand of southern Italian religion and convert them to the kind of Catholics Philadelphia could be proud of.

If the Church's attitude toward southern Italians was ambivalent, the approach to African Americans could look actually hostile. W. E. B. Du Bois accused the Church of "stand[ing] for color separation and discrimination to a degree equalled by no other Church in America." Catholic University, the only American institution chartered directly by the Pope, was officially segregated until 1950 (although there were some black students before World War I). Throughout the South, the Church followed the racist policies of the white establishment, as did Protestant churches, who, after all, *were* the establishment. In the North, the long history of Irish-black hostilities warned off prospective black converts. Dougherty, to his credit, was one of the most advanced of all American prelates in his attitudes toward African Americans. Prewar Philadelphia was about 10 percent black, the largest black population of any northern city, but there were only about 10,000 to 15,000 black Catholics. Dougherty's efforts to incorporate them into the

Church, as far as they went, were admirable, but his lack of success illustrates the inertial forces that kept Catholicism a white ethnic preserve.

There is no doubt of Dougherty's good intentions. He was chairman of the Indian and Negro Mission Board, and had a reverential admiration for Mother Katharine Drexel, the pioneer of the Catholic Indian and black mission movement. He made monthly Sunday afternoon calls on Mother Katharine for his entire tenure in Philadelphia—the fact that he paid the visits, not the other way round, was an unwonted deferential gesture. In 1923, Dougherty decreed that elementary school admissions would be parish-based and color-blind—previously, black children had been filtered to schools in two black parishes—and the edict was formally incorporated into diocesan regulatory canons in 1934. On one occasion, when it came to his attention that a nine-year-old black girl, Florence, had been rejected by a Catholic "home" for poor children because of her race, he summoned his car, picked up the bewildered Florence, and marched her through the home, assigning her place in the chapel—"This is where you will say your prayers"— and her seat in the dining hall and the classrooms. He then summoned the quaking convent of nuns and informed them that he would drum them out of the diocese if he heard of a similar incident—"I will remember this, and I will be watching you." In 1942, Dougherty wrote to Walter Annenberg, the publisher of *The Philadelphia Inquirer,* asking him not to report the race of perpetrators in crime stories. (Annenberg wrote a long reply arguing that that would be impractical.)

But to actually integrate the Philadelphia diocese, Dougherty would have had to declare war on white Catholics, and, grand gestures aside, he was not prepared to do that. In 1939, the parents of a "light-skinned" black child (his mother may have been white), who was "neat and clean," requested that he be admitted to the parish school instead of walking to the black school, twenty-five blocks away. The pastor was willing to take him but pointed out that there were at least thirty other black children in the parish with an even longer walk to the black school. If he accepted this one, the others would be sure to apply. The record does not show how the case was resolved; but the superintendent of schools, in a report to Dougherty, clearly viewed it as a dilemma. And there is a 1947 record of a black married woman convert who was denied maternity admission by Catholic hospitals because of her race. A diocesan social worker followed up the complaint and reported that, of four hospitals, only one, Misericordia, routinely admitted blacks, but on a segregated basis. The others either did not admit blacks at all or would do so only when there were sufficient numbers to make up a ward, because the other patients would refuse to be housed with them. The case was resolved by arranging an admission at Misericordia (which the woman rejected; she had a home delivery). There is no suggestion that the other hospitals should change their policies, or that Misericordia should de-segregate its wards. The clear implication is that Dougherty tolerated wide-spread evasion of his integration decree.

For all its flaws, Dougherty's Philadelphia must rank as one of the most successful of the American Catholic ministates, one that set the standard for the triumphal-era diocese. And it offers a unique lens for looking at the personal and religious strains of constructing a pervasive religious subculture in a secular country. In Europe, even in Ireland, the immense infrastructure of Catholic schools and social institutions was mostly built and maintained by the government (and the widespread withdrawal of government support in the nineteenth and twentieth centuries was a life-threatening trauma). But in America, bishops had to conceive, finance, and build the instruments of a Catholic society from scratch, entirely out of contributed resources. The best bishops were a rare combination of High Priest, entrepreneur, and corporate chieftain. The methods and style of Cardinal Dougherty, who was among the most effective bishops of all, help shed light on the costs and achievements of the Catholic system.

His Eminence, the Tycoon

A bishop was, in the first instance, an executive of a big service organization. Dougherty did not like to delegate and was a bully, but he was an extraordinarily efficient administrator. Almost all diocesan business flowed to his office, and he liked it in writing. He was at his desk early, and letters were answered immediately. Whether to open a parish, build a church, put a new roof on the school, disclose to a possibly abusive father the whereabouts of his runaway daughter—with rare exceptions, every question or request was answered, crisply, brusquely, definitively. Msgr. Joseph McCloskey, who served several years as the Cardinal's secretary, says Dougherty expected him to type the letters as they were dictated—and get them right the first time. After the mail, he was open for visitors. Anyone, lay or clerical, could see him, on any question, on a first-come, first-served basis. Possibly because of his lack of pastoral experience, Dougherty notoriously lacked people skills, and his meetings were as brusque and crisp as his letters. Msgr. McGlinn recalls a "gentle pastor" who began a meeting by asking Dougherty how he was feeling. "Why do you want to know?" Dougherty shot back. Once, when returning from a meeting where he had disciplined a group of priests, Dougherty remarked wonderingly to McGlinn on the fear they had shown; he himself had had a "reverential fear" of his first archbishop, "but why would anyone be afraid of me!" Philadelphia priests chafed under the Cardinal's tyrannical rule, but many missed the certainty and exactness when he was gone.

The schools were Dougherty's top priority, and he drove Catholics and Philadelphia religious to extraordinary accomplishments. The diocese most directly comparable to Philadelphia—in terms of size, geography, the percentage of the population that was Catholic, their ethnicity and occupations—was Brooklyn, where Catholics were as likely to use parish names as all-purpose geographic markers, and were as used to autocratic bishops. Brooklyn had slightly more than 1 million Catholics in 1930 compared with Philadelphia's 800,000-plus, but Philadelphia had almost half again as many schools. The New York Archdiocese had 50 percent more Catholics than Philadelphia, but Philadelphia still had the larger school system. Only Chicago, which was roughly the same size as New York, had more schools than Philadelphia—partly a legacy of its language-based school tradition—but the ratio of schoolchildren to Catholics was still much higher in Philadelphia. Philadelphia was also virtually unique in the 1920s and 1930s for its extensive system of regional, diocesan-run, tuition-free, central high schools, a model that was later widely copied throughout the country. A Philadelphia pastor who lagged on school building jeopardized his career. During the period of the diocese's most rapid growth, pastors built twice as many schools as churches. In the single year of 1925, construction proceeded on sixty major school buildings.

The headlong expansion of the Catholic schools inevitably meant uneven quality, haphazardly trained teachers, and makeshift, crowded, classrooms, occasionally with more than 100 children in a class. (The public system was experiencing severe growth pains of its own, but never to the same degree.) But it is remarkable how good the Catholic schools could be, especially once the runaway growth settled down about 1930. Catholic schoolchildren generally performed well on standardized tests. West Catholic won the 1924 University of Pennsylvania award for the high school whose graduates achieved the best freshman grades, and Roman Catholic got honorable mention. Girls in the top three-quarters of the college preparatory class at Hallahan High were automatically admitted to Penn, and Catholic high school students won more than their share of mayor's Scholarship Awards. (At the same time, the state educational authorities, in a campaign of petty harassment, long refused to accredit *any* Philadelphia Catholic high school and would not accept Hallahan graduates at the local state teachers' college without makeup courses. In 1930, Dougherty had to go to the legislature to overrule a move to disallow Catholic teaching experience for teacher certification.) Catholic education lacked many of the peripheral programs that were beginning to weigh down the public school curricula—a weak physical education program was a perennial sore point with the state—and per-pupil expenditure was only a fifth as high. But discipline and clarity of focus went far to compensate for shortfalls in budgets and plant.*

Msgr. John Bonner, the diocesan school superintendent for twenty years until his death in 1945, was one of the country's great Catholic administrators. Despite constant poor health, he engineered a wholesale upgrading of the Catholic teaching staff, improved the physical plant, and introduced standardized testing and tracking, demonstration schools, master teacher programs, vocational training, guidance, and over time, a greatly enriched curriculum. By the 1940s, Catholic high schools were offering aeronautics, mechanical drawing, and radio broadcasting (but not sex education), and operated a number of cooperative programs with the public system. Bonner and his staff visited all 350-odd schools every year, producing crisp, detailed, reports that the Cardinal carefully annotated with a thick red pencil. Bonner's diligence is astonishing. His staff consisted of one, and later two, priest-assistants and a handful of high school girls to help in the office. In 1929, he investigated complaints about a parish school in South Philadelphia. After inspecting the school, his report continues matter-of-factly, "I paid a visit to practically every home in the parish." Only about half of the 5:1 cost differential between public and Catholic schools is accounted for by class sizes and religious pay scales—pay in public schools was also very low, especially for female elementary teachers. Much of the remainder came from the utter lack of bureaucracy and the total commitment of people like Bonner.

Bonner is also the best example of how cruelly Dougherty could treat his best administrators. Bonner admitted that his legs trembled whenever he had to see the Cardinal. All decisions of consequence, even expanding a high school art room, had to go to Dougherty, but Bonner got the blame if anything went wrong. His poor health evoked little sympathy. At one point, after five years on the job, with a prodigious record of accomplishment, Bonner most respectfully requested another assistant—there were now 328 schools, and it was becoming physically impossible for him and his assistant to make the mandatory annual visits. Dougherty replied, "I beg to say frankly that I do not see the need of still another assistant. Time was when one man did the entire work . . . and that was not so very long ago." The letter ends with: "It seems to me a long time since I have had from either of you a report." A request for permission to receive an honorary degree in 1929 elicited a one-line: "You have my permission to receive an honorary degree . . . ," with no word of congratulation. When Bonner requested leave after an ex-

* For what it is worth, my mother graduated from West Catholic in 1929 and was immediately employed, at seventeen, as a private secretary in the general counsel's office of Sun Oil (which was known as a Protestant company) with a heavy workload of legal stenography. She had good grades in school but was by no means at the top of her class. The nuns must have been doing something right.

tended illness in 1934, the reply came from the Cardinal's secretary—a flat "I have been authorized to grant . . ." with no expression of solicitude. During another illness, he got a peevish note from Dougherty complaining that Bonner's assistants (he had finally gotten another one) seemed to be making all the visitations and, in the most patronizing tone, criticizing the writing style of their reports.

The problem, according to McGlinn, was that Bonner was one of the few priests who would stand up to the Cardinal—"With Dennis, you had to be a yes-man." McGlinn still recalls with pleasure the day that Dougherty's angry basso echoed through the chancery: "Monsignor Bonner, you are shaking your finger under my nose!" Dougherty managed to be ungenerous even when Bonner died of a heart ailment at the age of fifty-five. He was amazed at the turnout for the funeral—"bigger than Archbishop Prendergast's," he said wonderingly—and when the governor praised the splendid job Bonner had done, insisted on taking the credit himself. Only later he admitted to Cletus Benjamin, a former chancellor, "I never fully appreciated John Bonner."

The growth of Catholic institutions made the archdiocese one of the state's biggest landowners, and Dougherty's real estate skills were legendary. George Johnson, a senior executive at Albert Greenfield's real estate company, which handled most of the diocesan business, recalls that the diocese moved well ahead of the market, buying up and banking suburban land in anticipation of future Catholic expansion. In a typical transaction, Dougherty would buy land and lease it back to the previous owners until he was ready to use it—the strategy of a cash-rich, long-term player. Johnson confirms that Dougherty was "rarely leveraged" (i.e., purchasing with borrowed money) and "always stayed within his resources." Years later, when it was time to open a new parish, Dougherty would supply the land, usually at a market price, financed by a low-interest diocesan loan to the parishioners, and sell off what wasn't required. Philadelphia real estate values rose strongly throughout most of his administration, and Johnson assumes that the diocese's profits were very high. The diocese does not release financial information, but the late Msgr. Hugh Nolan, a quasi-official diocesan historian, estimated that at Dougherty's death in 1951, it was debt-free or close to it (a rare phenomenon in American Catholicism), with net assets in the "several hundred million" range. Even during the Depression, Dougherty had enough surplus cash to sustain substantial deficits in the high school program without real strain, at a time when public school programs were being cut back sharply. On his appointment to succeed Dougherty as archbishop, John O'Hara was reportedly able to make an unusually large gift to Rome.

No matter how big Dougherty's real estate profits were, however, the main source of income was the wallets of working Catholics, and Philadelphia's elaborate institutional infrastructure imposed a terrible financial burden. Paradoxically, the financial pressures themselves may have added to Catholic cohesion. Favored fund-drive devices—parish fairs, raffles, cake and candy sales, potluck dinners organized by the Holy Name Society and the Sodality—drew people together. Most of the Sunday collection funded the schools, and since almost all Catholic families had children, who mostly attended Catholic schools right through high school, they gave freely. Beyond the collections and fund drives for its own operations, each parish paid an assessment for the high schools and a tax to support the diocese, including a special tax, the "cathedraticum" for the cathedral. Then there was the annual block collection—the obligatory visit by a priest to each home to update the parish records and make a spiritual health assessment. The visits were theoretically pastoral, but the fact that they were called the "block collection" is indicative of their emphasis. Dougherty also put his full weight behind the annual "Peter's Pence" collection, the offering for the support of the Pope. Since a good Peter's Pence performance translated directly into influence at Rome, bishops in the larger dioceses competed hard to head the league tables and pushed their flocks correspondingly hard. America was by far the largest source of Vatican revenues, and Dougherty, who venerated Rome, was one of the largest producers. It is known, for example, that he made a million-dollar offering when he was appointed cardinal in 1921. (There was a minor flap when the check bounced—it was drawn on the wrong account.) The Catholic sense of embattlement, the feeling, as the Cardinal constantly drummed home, that Catholic values were under assault, impelled people to put shoulder to wheel again and again. Repeatedly, blue-collar parishes paid off huge building debts, $250,000 or more, in just a few years, and by the 1940s and 1950s, pastors in established parishes were often sitting on large cash balances.

The main collection event of the year, and a primary measure of pastoral performance, was the seminary collection. Dougherty pushed it hard from the beginning of his tenure. The annual return passed the $300,000 mark by the end of the 1920s and never dipped below that amount, even during the worst years of the Depression. (Seminary expenses did not come near $300,000; most of the money went to a diocesan surplus.) The collection was in the spring, and the priests turned out to a theater to hear the results, like a sales meeting in a big company. The chancellor would read the roll of all the parishes, with the amount each had collected. Since they produced the least money, suburban results came first, starting with the lowest parish. No one, obviously, liked to be the first name on the list. The real tension started with the roll call of the urban parishes and built as name after name was read. The room was cheering and clapping as the list dwindled to just a few parishes, breaking into a roar when the number-two parish was finally named and the

Cardinal could shake the hand of the winner. Gerald O'Hara, who was perhaps Dougherty's favorite in the chancery, followed the event even after he was appointed bishop of Savannah; a letter to Philadelphia captures the sweepstakes atmosphere: "[I see] dear Nativity in second place and very dangerously *near first.* . . . I know from experience what a task it must have been to reach $11,314.36. He kept Jimmie McMullin in third place again."

Dougherty had no close friends among his fellow prelates. His handful of cronies were men like himself, local political/corporate chieftains, like Matt McCloskey, the builder and head of the state Democratic Party (but surprisingly not Jack Kelly, probably Philadelphia's leading Irish Catholic, who thought Dougherty was a "son-of-a-bitch"). McCloskey owned a hotel in Atlantic City and gave the Cardinal an annual birthday party, with a three-piece band and a slapstick comedian. Moses Annenberg, the owner of *The Philadelphia Inquirer,* was also a good friend; when he was sentenced to federal prison for tax evasion in 1939, Dougherty wrote a character reference that "brought tears" to Annenberg's eyes. Of all Dougherty's friends, Albert M. Greenfield, the real estate mogul, may have been the closest. The two enjoyed driving together on Sunday afternoons to sniff out opportunities, and the relationship was cemented by Greenfield's substantial contributions, like the $25,000 organ at St. Charles, and by subtle family ties—the executive who handled Catholic business in the Greenfield firm was the father of the layman who managed real estate for the chancery. Greenfield's son remembers Dougherty as a frequent guest at their weekend farm—"a big jolly man" who enjoyed a cocktail—and all of the Greenfield children were highly entertained when their Catholic servants knelt to kiss Dougherty's ring. Greenfield and the Cardinal prayed together and liked to joke about switching jobs, and Greenfield was also the first Pennsylvanian, and reportedly the first Jew, to be appointed a papal chamberlain. Although he was the richest and most powerful man in Philadelphia, Greenfield was still a member of an outcaste group in the eyes of the WASP elite; perhaps that is why he and the Cardinal were so drawn to each other. The stiff-necked Dougherty ended the relationship when Greenfield was divorced, but McCloskey patched up the rift late in Dougherty's life.

This same close circle of men efficiently discharged the Cardinal's political business. (Kelly also helped, but at arm's length; Dougherty often dealt with him through Bonner.) Because the local Catholic vote was split between the Republican machine and its more natural affinity to the Democratic Party, Dougherty was never a national political power like the New York cardinals or Mundelein, and rarely spoke out on public issues. On one occasion when the Vatican sought his help on legislation affecting the Philippines, he had to ask New York's Patrick Hayes to pull the Tammany lever. Even in local politics, Dougherty moved cautiously, husbanding his resources for the handful of issues he considered important—blocking a move to tax church properties, curbing the anti-Catholic impulses of the educational bureaucracy, protecting state grants to hospitals, preventing state-subsidized contraception services. The local Republican patronage boss, Presiding Judge Charles L. Brown, a Protestant, was a friend, and seems to have reserved two or three appointments a year for the Cardinal's disposal; and at various times, both Moses Annenberg and his son, Walter, intervened for Dougherty on patronage issues. Near the end of his life, Dougherty had the signal honor of offering the invocations at both the 1948 Republican and Democratic conventions, but by then he was the senior American cardinal, aged and doddering, more of a religious icon than a political force.

Like so many steely-eyed chief executives, Dougherty was a sentimentalist in private—Irish ballads could make him cry. He clearly needed a family, and in Philadelphia he surrounded himself with the families of his two sisters, the Boylans and McCormicks, writing long chatty letters to his nephews

Credit: UPI/Corbis-Bettmann

By 1948, Cardinal Dougherty was a Philadelphia institution and had the signal honor of offering the invocation at both the Republican and Democratic (shown here) presidential nominating conventions.

in the service, and playing the role of paterfamilias at gala holiday dinners at his mansion, which he frequently ended, hypocritically enough, by showing a movie. He also treated Gerald O'Hara virtually as a son. O'Hara was part of the family clan gatherings and squired the Cardinal's sisters and nieces on European pilgrimages. When he left Philadelphia to become bishop of Savannah, he wrote to Dougherty as "my father and my friend," and Dougherty admitted in his reply that he was "lonesome." The Cardinal was a flagrant nepotist and seeded the diocese's lay positions with his relatives. (His successor, John O'Hara, almost immediately replaced the Dougherty cousin who edited the diocesan paper—it was "wretched," says McGlinn.) He nursed the priestly aspirations of a nephew, Carroll McCormick; and he made McCormick vice-chancellor of the diocese at the age of twenty-seven, when he had been a priest for only two years, and chancellor two years after that. Dougherty's strong-arming of McCormick's appointment as a bishop in 1947 prompted a strong negative reaction, and he had to call in an old debt to get New York's Cardinal Francis Spellman to preside at the ceremony.*

Dougherty thought of himself as a prince of the Church and lived that way. He drank only temperately and was never tainted with sexual scandal, but he enjoyed his table and traveled like a petty monarch. When he arrived at the airport, he expected his car to be waiting, with his secretary standing at attention. On his way back from Europe in 1934, the diocesan staff arranged special reentry procedures with the Treasury Department, New York's Mayor Fiorella La Guardia provided a boat to bring him ashore, and there was an extended debate on the landing site that would best serve his convenience. Hard-pressed functionaries were astonished when the scholarly, unpretentious John O'Hara took over the archdiocese—"When he got to the airport, he took a taxi!" McGlinn says. In his personal relations, Dougherty affected a baroque courtliness and demanded the same from his subordinates. His letters to Cardinal O'Connell began with an elaborate: "His Eminence The Most Illustrious and Most Reverend Cardinal William Cardinal O'Connell." Patronage requests to Judge Brown would start, "Once more may I venture to trespass on the goodness of your heart." His favorite, Gerald O'Hara, always ended his letters: "With sentiments of profound veneration, and kissing the sacred Purple, I remain, dear Archbishop . . ." Dougherty loved to travel and

---

* McCormick, by all accounts, was a decent, affable man who retired as bishop of Scranton. Standard procedure was that the Vatican appointed bishops from a list of worthy men maintained by the American hierarchy. McCormick never made the list, despite Dougherty's lobbying. Pius XII finally approached Gerald O'Hara in Rome and said, "We have got to do this for Cardinal Dougherty," and prevailed upon O'Hara to endorse McCormick. (It is remarkable that O'Hara had not until then.) Procedures were subsequently strengthened to prevent a repetition of the incident. Spellman's first episcopal appointment was as an auxiliary to Boston's Cardinal O'Connell. Dougherty had filled in at Spellman's urgent request when O'Connell, who detested Spellman, at the last moment reneged on an agreement to preside at his consecration.

spent months away from the diocese, with his extended family frequently in tow. (An urgent series of letters between Hayes and Dougherty on the Philippines question in 1932 was interrupted for several weeks when both men took their winter Caribbean vacations.) An embarrassed Gerald O'Hara, a few months after he had been appointed bishop of Savannah, turned down an invitation to vacation with Dougherty in Paris for fear of creating a bad impression in his new diocese.

During the depths of the Depression, Dougherty unashamedly upgraded his living quarters. Although he was already living in a grand house, in 1936 he purchased an estate called The Terraces for $115,000, which still serves as the Cardinal's residence. On magnificent grounds near the seminary, it had sixteen rooms, five baths, a pool, a stable, and a garage for six cars, but Dougherty spent another $100,000 building a new limestone front and a number of new rooms. (Dougherty's offices were in the chancery, not in the house.) Dougherty insisted that the cathedraticum, or diocesan tax for the support of the cathedral, which ran well into the six figures, was his personal income. Embarrassed by reports that Dougherty was one of the highest taxpayers in the area, the chancery priests would delicately pressure him to make large contributions to diocesan institutions. (Cardinal O'Hara, by contrast, drew a salary of $500 a month.) Much of Dougherty's money seems to have gone to his family, and he apparently set up a number of trusts. When the Cardinal's nieces were involved in a minor automobile accident in 1932, legal proceedings revealed that they used his limousine and chauffeur for beach vacations. None of this would be shocking if Dougherty were an oil baron, but he was a Catholic bishop spending blue-collar donations during a national economic crisis. There is not a hint, either in the archives or in newspaper libraries, that any Catholic in the Philadelphia archdiocese ever objected to any of it.

The Tycoon as Ecclesiastic

If the hard-driving executive, the real estate mogul, and the petty princeling were all there was to Dennis Dougherty, he would not be such an interesting character—just another worldly, power-driven prelate in the William O'Connell mold. But Dougherty, in solitude, apart from his family and cronies, was a mystic, and his religiosity is central to understanding what he thought he was about in Philadelphia.

Dougherty arose every morning between 4:30 and 5:00, said his Mass, said his rosary, and then heard his secretary's Mass. He retired each evening at about 8:00, first visiting the Blessed Sacrament in his chapel, then reading Scriptures, particularly St. Paul—he must have found the saint's masculine militance, his clarity and certainty, and perhaps his occasional intolerance, congenial. Dougherty loved relics, and he had a special veneration for St. Thérèse of Lisieux, the Little Flower, the cloistered nun who virtually charmed her way into sainthood with unassuming cheerful goodness. He made a special trip to her convent in France in 1913, interviewed locals about her life, excitedly caught a glimpse of her two sisters in the convent, and was enraptured by the sight of her "long, thick, chestnut-colored" hair preserved as a relic. Although he never advertised it, priests who knew him well credit him with engineering St. Thérèse's unusually rapid canonization in 1925, and he played a leading role both in the canonization ceremony in Rome and in the celebration at her convent. There are still a few surviving yellowed copybook pages in the Cardinal's rounded, curiously schoolboyish hand, which appear to be personal meditations rather than sermon notes—"The scene in the Garden of Olives! Oh, my God, that scene!" The same emotionalism creeps into his annual Peter's Pence appeals for the support of the Vatican. He declaims on the centuries when "the blood of Christ's followers . . . bespattered the world," the futile opposition of potentates from Napoleon to Genghis Khan, the humble submission of King Alfred the Great.

Perhaps because of his constant association with his sisters and his nieces, Dougherty, unlike so many of his fellow prelates, was happily free of misogyny. He was as kind to diocesan nuns as he could be cruel to his priests. Besides his veneration for Mother Katharine, he had a special affection for the Assumptionist sisters who had come to the Philippines at his request in 1913 to straighten out his schools. The Assumptionists ran an exclusive girls' academy, Ravenhill, that Dougherty visited almost every Friday afternoon. Liz Anne Kelly LeVine, Jack Kelly's youngest daughter, says, "I knew the Cardinal well, but not through my father. I went to Ravenhill. He came every week, and the nuns and the girls could all go talk to him." On his first day home after receiving the cardinal's hat in 1921, he piled the Boylans and McCormicks into his car and drove out to Ravenhill. At the request of a missionary order of nuns, he intervened repeatedly at the Vatican to win them the right to act as midwives, which was against canon law. At the conclusion of one frustrating audience with Pius XI, Dougherty suddenly asked the Pope who had delivered John the Baptist. "The Blessed Mother, of course!" said Pius. "Well!" said Dougherty triumphantly. "Who should be the model for women religious!" That won the argument, and soon thereafter he opened gynecological clinics in Philadelphia staffed by nuns. When feminist groups began to push an equal rights amendment in the 1940s, the NCWC and the National Council of Catholic Women led the opposition in Congress on grounds of Catholic family policy. But the St. Joan Society, a Catholic feminist group, got the Cardinal's ear, and, most uncharacteristically, he released a letter supporting the amendment, causing "a minor sensation."

There is little trace of cynicism in Dougherty's attention to ceremonial stagecraft, which in Philadelphia achieved a level of polish and consistency exceeded nowhere else. The elaborate liturgy was an expression, a validation, of who he was, as a Catholic, a priest, and a cardinal, the emissary of a two-thousand-year-old tradition, stemming directly from Christ. The massive displays were an expression of that same consciousness—the grandiose entrance into Philadelphia in 1918; the Mass for more than 300,000, the largest crowd in Philadelphia's history, in Municipal Stadium in 1926, with the main altar a precise baldachine replica of the main altar at St. Peter's in Rome; the 60,000-person procession and Mass for 200,000 on the silver anniversary of his consecration as bishop. It is remarkable, in a country founded by Puritans, how readily non-Catholics accepted such display, indeed, judging by newspaper coverage, admired its extravagance, seemed to acknowledge its appropriateness. No Protestant prelate could have commanded the turnout of *Protestants* that showed up for Dougherty's reception in Philadelphia. Non-Catholic clergymen openly lamented the hopelessness of competing for attention with a Cardinal's funeral.

Dougherty's religiosity also accounts for his veneration of Rome. Of all the American prelates, in an age when the American Church's loyalty to Rome was at a high pitch, Dougherty was *"Romanissimus,"* the most devoted of all, to the point of servility. He sent Rome rivers of money, *"con conscienza,"* as a satisfied Curial official put it, and the Vatican felt free to call upon him for the most menial of assignments. (Would he find a job for Benevento Somma, an Italian music master? Dougherty leaped to the task, setting up a long list of interviews.) Very occasionally, they asked his help on diplomatic issues—the post–World War I Italian land settlements, the Philippines—which Dougherty, on his own at least, could not much influence. But once Dougherty was ensconced in Philadelphia, Rome had little practical coin to give in return. Francis Spellman, who reigned in New York from 1939 to 1967, was the Church's supreme politician and used his Roman connections to control appointments to the American hierarchy, thereby enhancing his own power. But Dougherty was content with the lonely splendor of his own archdiocese and cared little about national episcopal politics. Aside from the boon of the McCormick appointment, the Vatican could bestow only the pettiest of patronage—papal honors for Dougherty's cronies like Greenfield and McCloskey; papal audiences for the Annenbergs, for the (non-Catholic) ladies of the Philadelphia Arts League, for the Horns of Horn & Hardart's, for a whole string of prominent Philadelphians. Indeed, a papal audience seems to have been *de rigueur* for prominent Americans traveling in Europe, like a stop at the horse guards at Buckingham Palace.*

---

* The number of audiences just for Philadelphians makes one wonder how the Pope spent his time. The papal image in America during this period was very positive, but partly as a kind of a charming Ruritania, a bit like, say, Monaco.

In the last year of Dougherty's life, Matthew H. McCloskey III, Matt McCloskey's son, recalls going to the Cardinal's house to meet a chancery priest. It was evening, there was a violent thunderstorm, and the electricity was out. As he stood in the darkened vestibule, the Cardinal's voice came out from the parlor, "Matthew, is that you? Come in." McCloskey found the old prelate—he was eighty-five—sitting alone with a single candle. "This is like the seminary in Rome," the Cardinal said. "Those were very happy days." Rome fixed Dougherty's place in the cosmos. The whole system that he had devoted his life to building—the vast pyramid of liturgy and ritual, the immense ceremonial buildings, the painfully constructed infrastructure of schools and hospitals, the thousands of religious men and women who subjected their lives to the Church's severe disciplines, the enormous sums of money that blue-collar Philadelphians somehow dredged out of threadbare purses—none of it had meaning except as an expression of a message, a mystery, a mystique, a revelatory wind blowing through the millennia from Rome, from Christ Himself.

The Imperial Creed

It was in Philadelphia in 1774, on an idle Sunday during a session of the Continental Congress, that John Adams and George Washington dropped in on a Catholic service (a service that would have been illegal in their home states). Adams found it "awfull and affecting. . . . Here is everything which can lay hold of the eye, ear, and imagination—everything to charm and bewitch the simple and ignorant. I wonder how Luther ever broke the spell." But the Church epitomized by Dennis Dougherty's Philadelphia a century and a half later was much more than the "sweet and exquisite" chants that so delighted Adams. It came freighted with a specific set of cultural norms—the emotional and sexual restraint, the deference to clerical authority, the insistence on order, the theological rigorism, all overlaid with Roman pomp and splendor. The Catholic subculture was so different from the prevailing American pragmatic secularism that it set about creating, most diligently, and expensively, its own pervasive socializing institutions. Catholics were proud of their sacrifices and bragged that their Church was not for the lukewarm or fainthearted. In 1931, *America* published a letter, presumably fictional, from a Protestant minister to a young man thinking of marrying a Catholic girl and converting. Could he really handle it? the minister asks. Does he understand the obligations of a Catholic marriage? The need for "self control versus birth control"? The requirement for subjecting his conscience to the teaching authority of the Church?

Only Catholics could judge whether the sacrifices were worth it. Beyond doubt, Philadelphia's Catholics enjoyed a comforting sense of rootedness, while the Church's constant emphasis on discipline, order, and family responsibilities ensured steady, if unspectacular, economic progress. Skeptics calculate the college educations that could have been financed with the money flowing to Rome. But to the rest of the country, the Catholic trade-off must have appeared a good one. For at least a full generation, from roughly the 1930s to the mid-1950s, the Catholic Church, in the militant, rigorist version that Philadelphia brought to its fullest flowering, was slowly becoming the dominant cultural institution in the country.

CHAPTER 8

On Top of the World

Father Chuck O'Malley faced a pastoral conundrum. Here was Carol, just eighteen years old, who'd run away from home and had no job, living in an apartment owned by a banker's son, who also happened to hold an overdue mortgage on O'Malley's church. The young people were obviously sleeping together, but O'Malley knew better than to attempt conventional moralizing. An old priest at O'Malley's church, Fr. Fitzgibbon, had tried that, but Carol had just stiffened up and walked away. Instead, O'Malley sat down at the piano and sang a song he'd written that carried a gentle message about being true to your own moral values. Carol's eyes filled with tears. When O'Malley left, her boyfriend said, "He's quite a fella," and the young couple went down to O'Malley's church and got married. It was all in a day's work for Fr. Chuck—although of course it helped to be played by Bing Crosby, with songs like "Going My Way" to help you out of tight spots.

The movies were midcentury America's dominant mass medium, and they gave Roman Catholics a spectacularly good press. In just three years, from 1943 through 1945, Catholic movies were nominated for thirty-four Oscars. *Song of Bernadette* received twelve nominations in 1943, and won four, including Best Actress for Jennifer Jones. Leo McCarey's *Going My Way*, with star turns for Crosby and Barry Fitzgerald as old Fr. Fitzgibbon, notched ten nominations in 1944, and swept seven Oscars, including Best Picture, Best Director, Best Actor, Best Supporting Actor, Best Story, and Best Song. Crosby returned as Fr. Chuck the next year playing against a bewimpled Ingrid Bergman in another McCarey vehicle, *The Bells of St. Mary's*. They got eight nominations, but only one Oscar. *The Keys of the Kingdom*, featuring Gregory Peck as a Catholic missionary priest in war-torn China, also picked up four Oscar nominations in 1945, bringing that year's

Catholic total to twelve. One newspaper commented in 1945 that even "Catholics are beginning to admit that Hollywood is overdoing attention to the church, at least to the exclusion of other religions." It was a time when the Church was vastly expanding its influence, not just in the movies, but in unions, politics, and popular culture as well.

The turning point in Hollywood's embrace of Catholicism was Spencer Tracy's Oscar-winning portrayal as the saintly, but down-to-earth, Father Flanagan in *Boys' Town,* the surprise movie hit of 1938. Tracy had already portrayed a charismatic priest in *San Francisco* (1936), but his character was overshadowed by the earthquake scenes. Up until then, the studios had used the Church only for exotic atmospherics or as a cover for sensationalistic sex. It was Claudette Colbert's nude milk bath and the lurid sadism of the martyrdom scenes, not the Christian preaching, that packed in audiences for Cecil B. De Mille's *Sign of the Cross* (1932). In gangster films like *Little Caesar* (starring Edward G. Robinson, 1930), *Public Enemy* (James Cagney, 1931), and *Scarface* (Paul Muni, 1932), the Catholic imagery is cultic and primitive, underlining how alien Cagney's Irish ghetto and Robinson and Muni's Italian ones were from the American mainstream. In *Boys' Town,* however, the central image is Spencer Tracy carrying an injured boy, a crowd of boys marching solemnly behind him—the priest as Christ the Shepherd, saving a lost lamb. *Angels with Dirty Faces,* also in 1938, with Pat O'Brien's Father Jerry Connolly playing opposite Cagney's Rocky Sullivan, clinched the stereotype of the movie priest. As kids in a tough Irish neighborhood, O'Brien outran the police and Cagney didn't, so Cagney went on to reform school, a career of crime, and the electric chair, while O'Brien became a college track star and a priest. Their lives stay intertwined, and at the very end O'Brien may save Cagney's soul, although the movie is marvelously ambiguous.

For a generation, the Hollywood priest archetype was the "superpadre," virile, athletic, compassionate, wise. O'Brien knocks out a poolroom hoodlum with one punch in *Angels.* Tracy's Father Tim Mullin whips Clark Gable's Blackie Norton in *San Francisco,* and Karl Malden's Father Barry decks the ex-fighter Terry Malloy (Marlon Brando) in *On the Waterfront* (1954). Crosby's Fr. O'Malley, who used to work out with the St. Louis Browns, inveigles a gang of dead-end kids with baseball tickets and almost overnight converts them into a cherubic, and very professional, boys' choir. Pat O'Brien rescues slum kids in *Fighting Father Dunne* (1948). The patriotic hit of 1940 was *The Fighting 69th,* with Cagney as the Irish tough guy and O'Brien as the heroic Fr. Duffy, and an all-Irish cast, driving home the patriotism of Irish Catholics. *The Fighting Sullivans* was a surprise hit in 1944; it is a true story about five brothers killed in the same World War II naval action and is drenched in warm Irish Catholic imagery. In wartime foxhole movies, the combat units were scrupulously proportioned among

Credit: Photofest
Spencer Tracy's Oscar-winning portrayal of Father Flanagan in Boys' Town,
the surprise hit of 1938, fixed the movie image of the priest as hypervirile moral
hero. This studio publicity photo self-consciously models Tracy (with Mickey
Rooney) after a famous picture of Christ the Shepherd, saving a lost lamb.

Protestants, Catholics, and Jews, but the chaplains were almost always
Catholic priests. The book that was the basis for *God Is My Co-Pilot* (1945)
was not especially religious, but the role of Fr. Mike is expanded into one of
the main characters for the screen. Even movie nuns acquire a bit of the
priestly regular-guy aura. Ingrid Bergman, in one of the best scenes in *The
Bells of St. Mary's,* teaches a weakling to box. When socialites patronizingly
invite Celeste Holm's Sister Scholastica to join a tennis game in Clare Booth
Luce's *Come to the Stable* (1949, seven Oscar nominations), she turns out to

be a former national champion and is allowed a moment of sadness when she reveals her foregone career. The hit song from the film uses a melody from Gregorian chant.

Celibacy for he-men like O'Brien and Tracy is clearly an act of massive self-discipline, but one that confers an earned righteousness that sets them apart from other men. Crosby looks appropriately wistful as he watches a former girlfriend triumph at the opera in *Going My Way*, and in *The Bells of St. Mary's* the electricity between him and Bergman is unmistakable, but the audience is sure they would never break their vows. These are talented, attractive people who have made big sacrifices for the love of God, and they are better than the rest of us for it. The extraordinary moral status accorded the Hollywood priest is still evident as late as 1967—Tracy and Katharine Hepburn are Protestant patricians whose daughter is engaged to Sidney Poitier in *Guess Who's Coming to Dinner?*, but the character they turn to for moral advice is an old friend who just happens to be a Catholic monsignor.

Credit: Photofest
*Audiences were sure that Bing Crosby's and Ingrid Bergman's priest and nun (*The Bells of St. Mary's, *1945) would never break their vows, but the electricity between them was unmistakable. The movie garnered eight Academy Award nominations.*

Since it was only in 1934 that the official Church was lambasting the Jews and "pagans" who controlled the movies, the radical transformation in Hollywood-Catholic relations is all the more remarkable. The simplest explanation is that the studios discovered that Catholic movies were good business. *The Bells of St. Mary's* and *Going My Way* were sixth and eighth on the all-time revenue list until 1950, and *The Bells of St. Mary's* still held the thirtieth spot in 1965, two decades after its release. *Come to the Stable* was 1949's seventeenth-best revenue producer, and almost all the Tracy and O'Brien priest films did well financially.

But the broad appeal of these movies suggests that they tuned into an important part of the contemporary *Zeitgeist.* The social mirror held up by the Catholic movies—close-knit communities, strong values, solid families, simple patriotism, self-sacrificing, morally impelled leaders—was one in which all Americans could find a reflection of their better selves. In a series of articles that eventually grew into the screenplay for *On the Waterfront,* Budd Schulberg wrote a paean to the Irish Catholic longshoreman: "Hard-drinking, two-fisted, high-strung, a rabid sports fan, an all-out friend, a dangerous enemy, he's also a loyal, religious, hard-working, responsible family man concerned with getting his kids through school and seeing them get a better break than their old man." That's a description that most American males would have been proud to have applied to themselves. And these rough men went to Mass every morning before the shape-up.* In the same spirit, *The New York Times*'s Bosley Crowther praised *The Fighting Sullivans,* a movie in which Church and priest guide almost every step of the boys' development, for "its simple and genuine feeling . . . for Americans as we are." Catholics were becoming Everyman.

Zeitgeist, however, was not quite the whole story. Another reason for the sudden blossoming of Catholic movies was that Hollywood and the Church, if they had not actually made a deal, had at least reached an understanding.

Martin Quigley, Joe Breen, the Legion, and the Moguls

Martin Quigley's table in the Oak Room of New York's Plaza Hotel was in the corner, on a raised platform. Movies were made in Hollywood, but in the 1940s and 1950s New York was still the center for the moneymen, the distributors and financiers. The Oak Room was where they gathered for lunch,

---

* As in the priest movies, Schulberg's natural noblemen are *Irish* Catholics. There were also numerous Italian longshoremen, but, according to Schulberg, they were mostly "ship-jumpers" who "let the wife handle church responsibilities." They were viciously exploited by Italian mobsters and "beaten like cattle" if they raised a question.

and Quigley's raised table let him keep on eye on what was going on. As a young newspaperman in Chicago in 1915, Quigley had bought a small movie industry newsletter and turned it into a publishing empire built around the *Motion Picture Daily* and his flagship weekly, *The Motion Picture Herald.* A tall, scholarly-looking man with a high-domed forehead and receding brown hair, Quigley was a graduate of Catholic University and a devout Catholic. He had a son in the Jesuits and was showered with papal honors through his long career. Above all, Quigley was a hardheaded businessman; one difference between Quigley's papers and *Variety,* his main competitor, was that he mixed industry scuttlebutt with detailed advice on improving revenues, expanding ticket sales, and exploiting foreign markets. Subtle and polished— his Bachrach portrait shows him with a cigarette in a long black holder—he was also used to getting his way. From his first days in the business, he was convinced that indecent movies were a threat to the industry's financial health, and so between 1929 and 1935 he invented the American system of regulating movies and had kept a guiding hand on it ever since.

Americans began censoring movies while Thomas Edison's patents were still warm. The young lady with the skirt whirling above her knees in *Fatima Dances,* a thirty-second nickelodeon crowd-pleaser of 1897, prompted such public outrage that thick black lines had to be drawn across the strategic areas of her torso. The NAACP cut its organizational teeth in the 1915 campaign against the portrayal of ex-slaves as sex-crazed subhumans in D. W. Griffith's *Birth of a Nation,* and in 1917 the federal government's Committee on Public Information ensured that movies toed the correct wartime propaganda line. It was filmmakers' gleeful discovery of their medium's power to titillate, however, that drew the greatest share of censorial energies. Like Philadelphia's blue laws, and Anthony Comstock's rules on obscene mailing material, the recurrent decency drives were almost always of Protestant origin. Pennsylvania was the first state to create a movie censorship board in 1913, and at least a half dozen other states and a number of major cities, including New York and Chicago, had followed suit by 1921. Cardinal O'Connell used the Curley machine to exercise a heavy regulatory hand in Boston, and Catholics dominated Chicago's film board, but the Church was relatively quiescent elsewhere. Al Smith even tried to repeal New York's law on First Amendment grounds in both 1923 and 1924.

The 1920s were the Jazz Age, the decade of the flapper, the Charleston, the roadster, and the roadhouse, when traditional mores first came under challenge from mass-production consumerism. The inevitable conservative reaction found an easy target in Hollywood, and revulsion was fueled by lurid tales like the death of starlet Virginia Rappe after kinky sex at Fatty Arbuckle's 1921 party. Quigley warned of growing public antagonism from the very first issues of the *Herald:* "The public . . . [is] increasingly demanding that pictures be made clean and wholesome to the last detail" (1915) or "audiences are rather fed up with such adjectives as 'shocking,' 'daring,' 'scandalous.' . . . You are not only fanning the spark of rebellion against oversexy pictures, but providing ammunition for the bluenoses relentlessly on the prowl for such targets" (1933). Between 1922 and 1927, at least forty-eight bills to create new censorship boards were introduced in state legislatures, and the cry for federal legislation was growing. The studios hired Will H. Hays, a gangling Republican pol who had been Postmaster General in the Harding administration, to improve their public relations, but despite his $100,000 salary he accomplished little. What was needed, Quigley was convinced, was an industry-enforced decency code, and in 1929 he set out to make it happen. It was to take him two tries, stretching over five years.

An old friend, Fr. FitzGeorge Dinneen, the leading figure on the Chicago film board, introduced Quigley to Daniel Lord, a well-known Jesuit theologian, a playwright, and an English teacher, who had been employed by De Mille as a consultant during the shooting of *The King of Kings*. (De Mille was worried about a Catholic reaction against the film and adroitly publicized photos of Lord saying his morning Mass on the set.) At Quigley's behest, Lord wrote out a comprehensive movie Production Code, a relatively compact document that was eventually to govern movie production for a generation. When Hays saw it, he was enthusiastic—"the very thing I had been looking for." With surprising alacrity, all the major studios signed on to the new code by March of 1930; in all likelihood, since adherence was voluntary, they saw it as just another public relations gimmick. Under the agreement, scripts would be submitted to a new office in Hays's shop authorized to award Production Code seals of approval. Some two-thirds of the code dealt with sexual material, the remainder with violence, crime, respect for religion, patriotism, and families. In industry jargon, nudity, homosexuality, profiting from crime, and graphic violence were "don'ts." Crime, vice, and attractive sin, like adultery, were "be carefuls"—permissible, but requiring "taste and delicacy." Wrongdoers always had to be punished; adulterers always had to meet with tragedy and heartbreak. The Catholic origins of the code were kept very quiet.

To Quigley's great chagrin, his new code was a total failure. Whatever the original intentions of the moguls, 1930 was the year that the Depression really began to bite on movie revenues, and the big studios, locked into long-term contracts with their stars, faced financial disaster. The response was to ratchet up the sex and violence. Ironically, the most famous of the so-called pre-code films, like *Public Enemy, Scarface,* and Mae West's *She Done Him Wrong* (1933—about the "finest woman who ever walked the streets") date from the early 1930s, after the code had been officially adopted. When the director Howard Hawks asked the producer Howard Hughes about obvious code violations in *Scarface,* he was told, "Screw the Hays office." By 1933, the studios were not even bothering to submit most scripts for Production Code seals; an internal memorandum at the Hays office described the situation as "hopeless."

Quigley's response was to begin a quiet campaign to back up the code with the power of the Catholic Church. He worked closely with a new ally, Joe Breen, whom Hays had hired as a public relations consultant on Quigley's advice in 1931. Breen was a product of Roman Catholic High and St. Joseph's College in Philadelphia; he had met Quigley while handling the public relations for the 1926 International Eucharistic Congress in Chicago and was working for a coal company when Quigley recommended him to Hays. He was a big man, silver-haired, red-faced, salty-tongued, a backslapping Irish politician, but shrewd and tough, and embarrassed by Hays's supineness. The Jesuit Wilfred Parsons, editor of *America,* and an old friend, helped with introductions to bishops and pushed in his editorials the case for Catholic involvement. It was surprisingly uphill work. "No member of the Hierarchy exhibited any interest," Quigley later said, "and no aid was rendered from any Catholic source." It was not until 1933 that Breen finally found a bishop with "fire in his eyes"—John Cantwell, bishop of Los Angeles, a native of Ireland, a rock-ribbed conservative, more than a little anti-Semitic, as was Breen, and completely appalled by the latter-day Sodom he saw all around him.

By the spring of 1933, the Hays office and the Church were moving on roughly parallel tracks to revive the code, with Quigley serving as communications link and backstage strategist. Breen battered Hays with get-tough memos. He was convinced that there was nothing wrong with Lord's code. The problem was simply that Hays was not enforcing it and had no power to punish studios that got out of line. Hays was listening because, as Quigley had predicted, the failure of the code had prompted a flood of new legislative proposals, especially at the federal level, which the studios feared most. These were the first days of the New Deal, and Washington was full of centralizing enthusiasts. The National Industrial Recovery Act, authorizing "industrial codes" governing wages and production conditions for all major industries, explicitly contemplated a "moral code" for the movies. At a meeting with the top movie executives in New York in March, Hays said that his staff had identified more than a hundred different proposals for censorship legislation. When he met with the West Coast production executives the next week, he said there were more than a thousand.

At the same time, Quigley, Breen, and Parsons, with the help of the president of Catholic University, orchestrated a public attack on the movie industry by the Vatican. They also stage-managed an NCWC meeting at which Cantwell fulminated against the "Jews" and "pagans" who ran Hollywood, and Lord listed the seductions, rapes, incest, fornication, adultery, sundry perversions, and graphic violence that were standard Hollywood fare. (The "sex scandals" included "a white girl falling in love with an oriental.") The bishops appointed a committee chaired by John McNicholas, archbishop of Cincinnati, and including Cantwell, to report in June 1934. Quigley stayed in close touch with McNicholas throughout the spring, and he and Breen were the only outsiders invited to the June meeting. At that meeting, Breen disclosed for the first time that Hays had reached a new understanding with the studios. Breen was to become head of a reorganized Production Code office with real teeth. Studios that released movies without the code seal of approval would be fined $25,000; much more important, all the studios, which still controlled the majority of first-run movie theaters, pledged not to exhibit a movie that lacked the seal. Quigley made an impassioned argument to the suspicious bishops that they should support the code. Cardinal Dougherty's Philadelphia boycott, still in its first weeks, was a spectacular success, but Quigley predicted that Catholics would sooner or later break ranks and drift back to the movies. Much better to force the studios to live by the code than to risk the Church's reputation by Dougherty's brand of freelancing. (Dougherty, who stayed aloof from the NCWC on principle, was not at the meeting.)

Quigley then brokered a follow-up meeting between a committee of bishops headed by Cardinal Mundelein and the studios—after first softening up the moguls with apocalyptic visions of Dougherty-style boycotts throughout the country. When Mundelein told the studio executives that the Church would not tolerate any further evasions of the code, there was a pause, and then DeMille observed that his colleagues' silence looked like acquiescence. With his usual political deftness, Mundelein immediately told his good friend Franklin Roosevelt that the bishops and the studios had reached an agreement, and in her next radio broadcast Mrs. Roosevelt praised the code as a model for the kind of industry self-regulation that the administration preferred. Pointedly, Mundelein's favorite investment bank, Halsey Stuart, which had grown rich on his "Catholic bishop's bonds" and was a major source of movie financing, let it be known that they regarded indecent movies as poor investments. At Cantwell's behest, A. H. Giannini, the president of the Bank of America, another important Hollywood funding source, made similar representations. Parsons and the editors of *America,* who had called for "Catholicized movies" a decade before, could not resist chortling that "Joseph I. Breen, a Catholic, will be virtual dictator of future film morals."

The same 1934 NCWC meeting that agreed to support the code kicked off the Legion of Decency drive to underscore the Catholic commitment. The Legion was originally conceived as a one-shot consciousness-raising campaign, involving Legion buttons, a written pledge to attend only decent movies, and mass pledge ceremonies. In contrast to many NCWC efforts, almost all dioceses signed on enthusiastically, even Philadelphia. By the end of the year, millions of Catholics had signed the pledge, as had hundreds of thousands of Protestants and Jews. The Protestant Federal Council of Churches, and the *Christian Century,* often vocal opponents of the Church, warmly praised Catholic initiative and organizing ability—"Thank God that the Catholics are at last opening up on this foul thing as it deserves! What can we do to help?"

In 1935, the Legion of Decency was organized on a permanent footing and began operating an official Catholic movie classification system out of an office in in New York,* conveniently close to Quigley. The classification scheme was the last cog in an elaborate, bicoastal regulatory apparatus. In Hollywood, Breen ran the Production Code with an iron hand. All scripts and prints were cleared through his office, no detail escaped his scrutiny, and negotiations could be excruciating—over turns of phrase, the drape of a costume, the positioning of the actors, the hidden editorial slant of a script. The Legion of Decency Office in New York got early prints of finished movies from Breen and assigned one of four classifications without editorial comment—movies classified "A-1" and "A-2" were "unobjectionable" for children and adults respectively; "B" movies were "objectionable in part for all"; and "C" movies were "condemned."

In contrast to the Breen office, the Legion executives kept a discreet distance from the studios. They would detail their objections to a movie if a studio asked but would not propose fixes, as Breen did; it was up to the studio to modify a film and try again if it wanted. The Legion classifications— "The List," as they became known—were a fixture in Catholic churches and the Catholic press and were carried in much of the Protestant and Jewish press as well, and often even in secular dailies. The joint impact of the Legion and Breen was dramatic. During the first decade of Breen's rule, some 85 to 90 percent of all movies coming out of Hollywood got one of the two Legion "A" classifications, and all the notorious pre-code movies were either modified or withdrawn. Movies for "mature" audiences—a Legion "B"— could be commercially successful, but the studios knew they would first have to sweat the details through Breen. A Legion "C," or denial of the code seal—the one almost always entailed the other—was a financial death sentence, consigning a movie to the fringe of "art houses" in big cities. There were a number of years in which the Legion did not pass out a single "C." Quigley capped off his triumph by brokering a papal encyclical, *Vigilanti Cura,* in 1936—it is widely assumed that he wrote the first draft—that recited the history of the code and the Legion and exhorted the world's bishops to "follow the example of the Catholics in the United States of America."

* Chicago had published movie ratings for years and expected its system to be adopted by the Legion. The rating office went to New York only after a nasty spat between Fr. Dinneen and Quigley. Quigley was embarrassed by Chicago's ratings; the chief rater was Dinneen's former stenographer, Sally Reilly, who condemned John Ford's classic *The Informer* because it insulted the Irish. The New York rating system was operated by a Catholic alumnae association, under the leadership of Mary Looram, that had run a film reviewing service since 1924. Although "Mrs. Looram's Ladies" were often mocked, even in the sophisticated Catholic press, they were clearly the best available solution. Reviewers received a six-month training program, reviewing standards were carefully codified, and there were multiple reviewers of each movie. Within their own terms of reference, their ratings were consistent and reliable. The priests laughing up their sleeves look merely sexist.

Breen ran the code office for two decades. His reign is remembered mostly for the comically elaborate sexual circumlocutions—the married couple's twin beds, the one-foot-on-the-floor rule when couples were horizontal, the pounding surf to suggest intercourse, closed-mouth kissing—or more harshly as a "foul-minded . . . stupid tyranny," in Tennessee Williams's words. Williams's railing is understandable, as was that of other writers and directors, but it implies that Breen was an alien imposition, which misses an essential point. At bottom, Breen was a creature of the studios; they paid his salary, and they supported the code, because they were convinced they needed it.

In the pre-Breen days, when Hays let Mae West's *She Done Him Wrong* slip past the code office, it prompted an angry letter from the president of M-G-M: "[T]hey got away with it. They promised that that story would not be made. I believe it is worse than [another risqué film] from the standpoint of the industry. . . . I cannot understand how your people on the coast could let this get by." The M-G-M executive was not worried about American morals; he was upset that a rival studio had changed the rules of competition. Sex and violence grabbed audiences and made money. Without an agreement to limit sex and violence, the studios would get trapped in a competitive spiral, a kind of sex-and-violence arms race, that could only end in government regulation, which they all agreed would be disastrous. Seen in that light, the Breen office functioned as the enforcer of a cartel, like OPEC in the oil industry, that protected the studios against their own worst instincts and made the terms of competition more predictable for everybody.

From the studios' standpoint, the Catholic Church was the ideal regulatory partner. Protestantism is inherently decentralized. A Protestant-led reform movement would inevitably mean hundreds of local film boards—being kicked to death by grasshoppers. Other than the federal government, the Catholic Church, with Breen as the focal point, was the only organization that could offer essentially one-stop shopping, with the great advantage that the Church was used to working in privacy. In addition, the Church was as opposed to federal regulation as the studios were. Despite all the anger expressed at the 1934 NCWC meeting, the bishops still voted to oppose federal movie regulation, out of fear of setting a precedent for federal control of schools. Breen, who had the politician's instinct for making his rulings stick, became the studios' point man for outside censorship bodies and greatly simplified the regulatory burden. When censorship boards in coal states vetoed *Black Fury,* a strong, if watered-down, story of coal-field union-management clashes that earned a seal in 1935, Breen went on the road and got the decisions reversed. After that, he usually lobbied the local boards in advance of a film's release, as he did for William Wyler's *Dead End* in 1937. On the few occasions when he and the Legion differed—Breen approved *A Streetcar Named Desire* (1951) after arduous negotiations, but the Legion voted to condemn it—he could be counted on to carry the studios' case to New York. In general, however, Breen-approved movies "sailed through" the local boards, and except for the Legion, most of them gradually atrophied. On the measures that counted most to the studios, the Breen office was a spectacular success. On his first full year on the job, 1935, the downward trend in movie attendance reversed, and revenues soared to one new record after another until television precipitated another crisis about 1950.

Streetcar offers an insight into the power relationships. Elia Kazan, the film's producer-director, was outraged when he heard of the negotiations with the Legion, the more so because the studio brushed him off with assurances that there was "nothing to worry about." It is a revealing scenario— Warner Bros., Breen, and the Legion working together on Kazan's picture while he stood outside, frantically pounding at the door. (*Streetcar,* with Kazan's acquiescence, eventually got its Legion "B.") In his very first year on the job, when Breen had a knock-down confrontation with Jack Warner over *Madame DuBarry,* it was the other studio owners who forced Warner to back down. By 1941, Breen had become exhausted and physically ill from the pushing and pulling between the studios on one side and the Legion and other censors on the other, and he resigned to take a production post at RKO. Code operations deteriorated almost immediately, and the studio owners lobbied to bring him back within just a few months.

Otto Preminger's *The Moon Is Blue* (1953) was the first movie to successfully defy the code office. *Moon* is a relatively sexless comedy, featuring an excruciatingly talkative ingenue, and Breen clearly made a mistake in denying the seal. Even the Legion needed convincing to condemn it—a substantial minority of a special review board voted it an "A-2." But *Moon* was not, strictly speaking, a Breen-studio confrontation. It was independently financed, and distributed by United Artists, which was not really part of the studio system. Shortly thereafter, when Howard Hughes tried to buck the code office with *The French Line,* the studios, after some initial hesitation, forced him into compliance. They still had too big a stake in the code to let an opportunist like Hughes bring it down.

By the time of the *Moon Is Blue* debacle, Breen was aging and in ill health, and the code was clearly out of date. But he gets too little credit for his first decade or so on the job. Above all, the studios valued his fairness. The highly stylized conventions governing sex and violence now look silly, but they were consistently administered and well understood by everybody. The greatest years of Hollywood's *film noir* tradition—*The Maltese Falcon; The Big Sleep; The Killers; Rope of Sand; Mildred Pierce; Double Indemnity; Sorry, Wrong Number; The Postman Always Rings Twice; The Naked City*— after all, came when the Breen office was at the height of its power. It is almost an article of faith among movie buffs that modern remakes of the *film noir* classics, like the very graphic 1981 version of *Postman,* come off poorly in comparison with the subtlety and exquisitely calibrated atmospherics of the originals. When the Motion Picture Academy awarded Breen a special Oscar in 1953 "for his conscientious, open-minded, and dignified management of the Motion Picture Production Code," they probably really meant it.

Did Breen pressure the studios to favor Catholics? Douglas Fairbanks Jr. and the screenwriter Budd Schulberg were both active in Hollywood at the time (Schulberg's father was a Paramount executive), and neither is aware of any "deal" between Breen and the studios. Fairbanks remembers only that the Irish Catholic audience was considered very important; and it never hurt to have the parish priest touting a movie like *Going My Way.* Some of the moguls were favorably disposed toward Catholics in any case. Louis B. Mayer "loved the Catholics," according to his daughter, and may even have once considered converting. Mayer kept a priest at his bedside during a long illness, was great friends with Cardinal Spellman, and displayed the Cardinal's portrait in his library. Spellman, the scourge of the movies in public, would intervene for Mayer when the New York raters got too picky. Both of the wives of Harry Cohn, the founder of Columbia, were Catholics, and his children were raised in the Church. At the same time, Breen always took pains to ensure that his Church looked good on the screen. The boxing match between Tracy and Gable in *San Francisco* was added at Breen's suggestion to offset a later scene where Gable slugs Tracy. This way the audience would know that Tracy was really the better fighter, and the clergy would not be "humiliat[ed]."

Les Keyser, coauthor of the most thorough study of the Catholic image in the movies, says that he could find no documentary evidence of an actual deal between the Church and Hollywood. But he suggests that the "gut feeling" of most scholars is that the highly favorable treatment of Catholics—which coincided precisely with the period of Breen's greatest power—was a bouquet from the studios to Breen. Breen, after all, thought and behaved like a politician. Life was a matrix, not a series of unconnected events; everything was a trade-off. There are a number of cases—*The Postman Always Rings Twice* is one—when Breen, aware that a studio had been sitting on a difficult property for some time, would take the initiative to call a meeting and work something out. He would be so well-disposed, of course, when relations with the studio were smooth, and how better to earn Breen's goodwill and fellow-feeling than to praise Catholics to the skies?

The movies were just one area where the American Church vastly extended its cultural reach around midcentury. Another is exemplified by Karl Malden's labor priest in *On the Waterfront.* Malden's great scene is his dockside exhortation of the longshoremen—"Christ is in the shape-up. . . . Christ works on a pier. . . . Christ goes to a union meeting and sees how few go." But Schulberg, who wrote the script, did not invent those lines. They are a more or less verbatim transcription of an actual sermon given, not on the docks, but in St. Francis Xavier church hall a few blocks away, and the speaker was a real-life waterfront priest, the Jesuit John Corridan.

Commies, Thugs, and the CIO

Corridan, or "Father Pete," as the longshoremen called him, was a tall, chain-smoking, prematurely bald Irishman who, along with Fr. Phil Carey, ran a Jesuit labor school near the waterfront. They were allied with a loose network called the Association of Catholic Trade Unionists, or ACTU—members called themselves "Actists"—that profoundly influenced the American union movement from the late 1930s through the early 1950s. Actists fought against union racketeers in New York, got bloodied in the AFL-versus-CIO battles in Jersey City, and were a major force in the struggles for CIO industrial unionism in Chicago, Pittsburgh, and Detroit. Carl Haessler, an assistant to Walter Reuther in the 1940s, said, "The history of the UAW [United Auto Workers] after Reuther made his alliance with the Catholics early in '39 is therefore a story of the Reuther-Catholic power caucus' march to power." Actists were the front line against Communist influence in the CIO at the end of the war and led a grim, decade-long fight against the pro-Communist leadership of the United Electrical Workers (UE), which was resolved only when the CIO expelled the UE in 1948 and set up a rival union more to the Actists' liking. Left-wing labor historians point to ACTU as the source of the much remarked upon conservatism of the American labor movement, and the historian Douglas Seaton suggests, implausibly, that ACTU masterminded the AFL-CIO merger in 1955 to curb the radical impulses of their non-Catholic CIO allies.

Industrial unionism was the glowing cause of the late 1930s, a morally transcendent movement like the civil rights crusades of the 1960s. Mass marches and torch-lit parades sang union songs of a bright someday when Americans would live in union houses and drive union cars on union roads. Pictures of burly management goons with baseball bats advancing on Reuther and a small knot of UAW officials during the Ford sit-down strike of 1937, and of the bloodied union men moments after the attack, were blazoned across the nation's front pages. Idealistic energies were focused on the CIO—the Congress of Industrial Organizations—the congeries of break-away unions that rallied around John L. Lewis, whose mine workers walked out of the American Federation of Labor (AFL) in 1935. AFL unions were organized by craft, as in the construction trades, and were poorly adapted to a new era of mass-production factories where workers were interchangeable cogs in an assembly-line machine. Lewis wanted to organize all the workers in all major industries into nationwide unions, like the United Steel Workers of America (USW) and the UAW, and he poured scorn on aging AFL leaders mired in the old ways—William Green, the AFL president, had no head, said Lewis, "his neck just grew up and haired over."

Mass-production industry was still an urban phenomenon in the 1930s and 1940s. From their base in the urban coastline of the mid-Atlantic, factory cities marched inland to the St. Lawrence River, snaked around the shores of the Great Lakes and the Midwest's great iron and coal reserves, and spread along river and rail routes to Akron, St. Louis, Pittsburgh. This was Catholic country; more than half, perhaps 60 percent, of union members were Catholics, and Catholics were heavily represented among union officers. Old-fashioned prelates like Dougherty, O'Connell, and Michael Curley of Baltimore mistrusted the leftist, antiestablishment tone of much of the union movement and were suspicious of the ties with Communists and socialists. But just as black Baptist ministers had to run to catch up with the 1960s civil rights activists who were reshaping the lives of their congregations, in the 1930s Catholic priests who cared about their working-class parishioners had to get involved with unions.

There was never an attempt to form a Catholic labor party, as in Europe, and there was no central coordinating organization, like the Legion of Decency, that could authoritatively present a "Catholic position" on trade union issues. Indeed, Catholics were often at cross-purposes. When Jersey City boss Frank Hague and the mob-ridden AFL leaders confronted the ACTU-CIO organizing drive at a showdown rally in 1938, Fr. Dennis Comey, the president of St. Peter's College and later a famed waterfront labor priest in Philadelphia, sat on the platform next to Hague. Msgr. Charles Owen Rice, the Pittsburgh labor priest and the leader of the anti-Communist fight in the UE, stuck with his old friend "Red Mike" Quill, the head of the Transit Workers' Union (TWU) and a notorious fellow traveler, when the New York branch of ACTU attacked Quill's pro-communism. Depending on the circumstances, ACTU branches, including New York, frequently allied with pro-Communist CIO slates. Corridan's antimob unionists on New York's waterfront were regularly accused of communism by Joe Ryan, boss of the corrupt International Longshoremen's Association (ILA) and a "Holy Namer" as he put it, while the waterfront's "Mr. Big," Big Bill McCormack, who controlled much of New York's shipping, trucking, and cement industries and who was the power behind Ryan, filled the ear of his friend Cardinal Spellman with stories of the damage Corridan was inflicting on the Church's reputation.

Sometimes the shared Catholicism gave protagonists on both sides of the labor battles almost a private language. John Cort, one of the founders of

ACTU, reports the following exchange during the organizing drive in Jersey City. He and George Donahue, another ACTU leader, were accosted by Hague's Irish Catholic cops and accused of littering for distributing leaflets. Cort pointed out that people throwing away leaflets might be littering, but not he and Donahue.

> FIRST COP: But you're the first cause of the littering. ["First cause" is Catholic natural law-speak, out of Aristotle through Thomas Aquinas.]
>
> CORT: If you're going to talk about first causes, then God is the real first cause because God made man.
>
> SECOND COP (*suspiciously*): Why did God make man?
>
> CORT (*firing the Baltimore Catechism with both barrels*): God made man to know Him, to love Him, and to serve Him, and to be happy with Him forever in heaven.
>
> THIRD COP: That's funny, I thought God made man to break the law so we could have a job.

Everybody laughed, and Cort and Donahue were left alone.

Cort, now an elegant, erect, octogenarian whose life has been spent in the causes of labor, civil rights, and Christian socialism, is that *avis rarissima,* someone who converted *to* Catholicism while a philosophy student at Harvard. After Harvard, he worked as a newspaperman and was active in the left-wing Newspaper Guild, until, like so many of his contemporaries, he came under the spell of Dorothy Day. Cort joined the Catholic Workers during a seaman's strike in 1936, when the Workers were helping Joe Curran in his fight to form a new CIO-affiliated National Maritime Union (NMU). The seamen's working conditions were Dickensian, and their AFL union was both corrupt and in bed with the shipowners. Cort covered a meeting of the New York AFL Central Labor Council for the *Catholic Worker*—Joe Ryan was president of the council—and watched in horror as Ryan's goons roughed up Curran's followers. Part of the problem, honest Catholic union officials told him, was the apathy of Catholic union members. Cort had the idea of forming a Catholic trade union association to stimulate Catholic union activity, a "parallel organization," as suggested in Leo's and Pius XI's labor encyclicals. As Dorothy Day put it, "Christ our Brother started with twelve men. . . . A few strong and ardent Catholic men can save the trade union movement in this country."

ACTU was formed around the kitchen table in the Catholic Worker center on Mott Street in Manhattan one night in February 1937 by Cort, George Donahue, a Manhattan College graduate who'd lost his job as a waterfront freight checker for opposing Ryan's union, and nine other men, all either

Catholic Workers or union men. Fr. John Monaghan, a fiery preacher, was signed on as chaplain. Cort drafted an ACTU Constitution, cribbing liberally from the encyclicals and John Ryan's 1919 "Bishops' Program of Social Reconstruction," and in true Catholic fashion, placing equal emphasis on worker "rights" and "duties." Within just a few months, ACTU was distributing an eight-page mimeographed weekly, *The Labor Leader,* with its signature prayer "to Jesus the Carpenter." The ACTU motto was "Straight Down the Middle," or as they put it the following year, when *The Labor Leader* was already a slick, full-size, professionally produced newspaper, to hew a path "between corrupt, frequently Irish-Catholic officials . . . [and] the wild-eyed comrade with his policy of class hatred and Strike! Strike! Strike!" With the help of priests from Fordham, ACTU opened its first labor school at Fordham's downtown center near City Hall; by 1938, 340 union workers were attending nighttime classes in labor law, Catholic social principles, the labor encyclicals, public speaking, and pamphleteering—most of it improvised by Cort and his young associates as they went along. Within just a few years, there were more than a hundred ACTU labor schools throughout the country.

Besides their enthusiasm and their idealism, the Actists' major weapon was simply their literacy. Many, probably most, employers and local union officials had only a rudimentary grasp of the National Labor Relations Act and other New Deal labor legislation. Corrupt unions and Communist locals could flout statutory requirements for union democracy because few of the rank and file understood their rights. Much like the young civil rights volunteers during the Mississippi Freedom Summer of 1964, Actists like Cort, although they had minimal labor experience of their own, were at home with the language of regulations and contracts, could knock off a pamphlet at a moment's notice, and could supply signs and slogans to rally picketers. Ed Scully, John Sheehan, and John Harold were idealistic young lawyers who virtually dropped their private law practices to devote their time to the Actist cause under the banner of the Catholic Labor Defense League. Actists often took real risks. George Donahue was beaten up by waterfront mobsters. John Acropolis, an Actist leading a drive against New York Teamster racketeers, was murdered in 1952. Union musclemen beat Richard Bergel so badly that he was blinded.

The ACTU chapters that sprang up around the country often had little in common but their name and their devotion to the principles of the labor encyclicals. Monsignor Charles Owen Rice was born in America, but he spent much of his young childhood in Ireland and still has an Irish lilt in his speech. A wiry eighty-five-year-old in mid-1994—he had just given up his long-distance running and his trampoline—he grinned self-deprecatingly at claims that he ran the Pittsburgh ACTU "out of his hat." An early radio priest, with boundless energy, Rice idolized Dorothy Day and founded his Catholic Radical Alliance on Catholic Worker principles. He opened one of the first hospitality houses outside of New York and he quickly moved from there to labor organizing and ACTU-style labor schools. Rice's constant target was the Communist leadership of the United Electrical Workers, whose stronghold was the Pittsburgh Westinghouse plant. Card-carrying Communists were never more than a small minority of American union members, but they were highly disciplined, backed by skilled organizers and publicists, and were masters of the techniques of packing meetings and bending parliamentary rules to their advantage. (The real or imagined prominence of Jews in radical leftist movements was another factor sharpening Jewish-Catholic tensions. One Catholic pamphlet spoke of the plight of "Joe Mc-Union" up against "Isador Communist." But there were also a lot of Irish ex-Catholic Communists, like Harry Bridges and Elizabeth Gurley Flynn.) Rice freely copied the Communist tactics. "We'd put some of our guys in the back and some on each side and yell 'Commie' every once in a while. [The Communists] took over by that tactic. Our group did the same thing and drove them crazy."

A natural politician, full of charm, and committed to the union cause, Rice was ubiquitous during the CIO's rise. Besides his friendship with Quill, he was close to Phil Murray, the head of the Steel Workers and president of the CIO, and to Jim Carey, the head of the UE until he was deposed by the Communists and kicked upstairs to a CIO vice-presidency. Carey and Murray were both devout Catholics—Murray was a Scotsman but insisted he was Irish—and were proud of their friendship with Rice. At the 1938 organizing convention of the CIO, Rice sat at the head table with Lewis, Murray, and Sidney Hillman, head of the Amalgamated Clothing Workers. When President Truman came to Pittsburgh on his 1948 campaign train, he was met by the governor, Murray, and Rice. When Adlai Stevenson spoke at the 1952 AFL-CIO convention, there was Charles Rice sitting right behind him at the head table. Socialists and Communists built Rice into the Svengali of the CIO, allegedly pulling the strings of the CIO Executive Council, getting his orders directly from the Pope. The fact that Pittsburgh ACTU could, out of the blue, mount lightning organizing campaigns enhanced the impression that Rice commanded a vast network ready to do battle at his bidding. The truth is much more prosaic. The vaunted network in Pittsburgh was an illusion—Charles Owen Rice with a half-dozen followers and a mimeograph machine could look like an army. As he admitted himself at the time, "We battle the UE and strike a blow for progress once in a while, but we are not the men the Commies think we are." While Rice undoubtedly influenced Carey and Murray, he was no more than an occasional adviser. Carey and Murray were cautious bargainers and broke with the CIO left wing over wartime strikes—they were patriots before they were union members. But their conservatism reflected the attitudes of their members, and they would have behaved that way if they had never met Rice.

The Detroit ACTU chapter was probably the nation's most powerful in the 1940s. In contrast to most dioceses, Detroit ACTU had the solid backing of Archbishop Edward Mooney, one of the most liberal and pro-union members of the hierarchy. Phil Weber, the head of the chapter, was an ex-newspaperman, and his paper, *The Wage Earner,* was considered one of the best labor papers in the country. There were forty-one labor schools in Detroit alone, and Weber's ACTU chapter counted tens of thousands of members, making nonsense of Douglas Seaton's claim that each member had his religious practices vetted by an ACTU priest. Along with a motley collection of Trotskyites, Schactmanites, and anti-Communist liberals, ACTU was a main base of support for Walter Reuther's rise to the UAW presidency in 1946. Reuther was a Protestant and a socialist, but he had traveled widely in the Soviet Union and worked in a Soviet automobile factory, so he had no illusions about Stalinism. His socialism also had a syndicalist twist that was music to Catholic ears. Reuther pushed hard for labor-management "industry councils" in language that could have come right from the encyclicals, and he unnecessarily prolonged a bitter 1945 strike in the hope of involving the union in automobile pricing decisions. *The Wage Earner* was, for all practical purposes, a Reuther paper by the mid-1940s, and Fr. Raymond Clancy's "Chaplain's Corner" column unabashedly endorsed the Reuther program.

Communism in CIO unions was a real threat to American interests in the 1940s. Communist CIO membership was never more than a few thousand, but they wielded power far out of proportion to their numbers. Joe Curran of the NMU, the original CIO Catholic Worker protégé, allied with the Communists against the AFL, and then read them out of the union in 1947. By that time, although he estimated that there were only 500 Communists in a 70,000-man union, they held 107 out of 150 elective offices. Almost all of Mike Quill's TWU officers were Communists, and they came close to taking over the New York City CIO Council. Based on an analysis of CIO convention votes in 1946, *The Wage Earner* estimated that thirteen CIO unions with 2.5 million members were clearly anti-Communist, another fifteen unions with 1.4 million members were Communist-dominated, while the remaining eleven unions with 1.5 million members, two thirds of them in the UAW, were waverers.

Communists were exemplary union members as long as they stuck to local issues, but their foreign policy line was slavishly subordinate to Moscow. Communist union officers were in the vanguard of the "United Front" in the 1930s, preaching the necessity of arming against the Fascist menace. But they executed an ideological backflip when the Nazi-Soviet Pact was signed in 1939 and started a wave of disruptive strikes against American war production, the most notorious of which was the 1941 wildcat strike at North American Aviation, a main supplier to the British air force, at the height of the London blitz. Then just a few months later, when Hitler attacked the Soviet Union, the Communist unions reverted overnight to their pre-1939 positions, going so far as to propose the reintroduction of piecework in UAW factories, much to Reuther's disgust. (On the eve of the 1946 UAW election fight, *The Wage Earner* pointedly published a survey of Soviet factory conditions and their wide use of piecework wages.) The Communist unions took a hard line against the Marshall Plan in 1947, at a time when the standoff in Berlin and throughout Eastern Europe was at a particularly dangerous stage and Stalin's anti-Western rhetoric was unusually bloody. Marshall aid was arguably the last hope for a Western Europe teetering on the brink of chaos, and Stalin was pulling out all the stops to block it. With only shaky Congressional support for new foreign spending, unified CIO opposition could have killed the whole program of European reconstruction. The fear of a Communist takeover of the CIO policy machinery was not hysterical.

Although John Corridan worked closely with ACTU in his waterfront wars—ACTU's Ed Scully was his legal strategist—the Jesuit labor schools were a separate network. They were founded in response to a specific 1934 directive from the head of the order that Jesuits should help combat communism in the labor movement. The New York school, the Xavier Institute, was opened at a Jesuit high school in lower Manhattan, but its archives show only minimal involvement in anticommunism. Fr. Phil Carey, Corridan's superior and director of Xavier for almost fifty years, was the son of a New York streetcar conductor who urged Carey to help "the grizzled guys" like him once he was ordained. A more retiring figure than Corridan, Carey became one of the most influential behind-the-scene figures in the New York labor movement. He was absolutely trusted by local AFL-CIO leaders like Harry Van Arsdale, played an important role in the creation of public employee unions in the late 1950s and early 1960s, and maintained an active correspondence with some 150 unions and union locals. Xavier's one important anti-Communist victory was against Quill and the TWU leadership. Unlike Rice, Carey did not involve himself in the union fight directly but trained a small cadre of activists in pro-democracy organizing tactics. When it became obvious that the dissidents had a clear majority in 1948—TWU membership was heavily Irish Catholic and anti-Communist—Quill flamboyantly tore up a copy of the Communist *Daily Worker,* fired his Communist officials, trumpeted his own Catholicism, and marched to the head of the anti-Communist cause.

Corridan's contribution to the fight against waterfront corruption was much greater than suggested by *On the Waterfront*. The Irish unionists like Joe Ryan had bullied their way to the top with the help of mobsters like John "Cockeye" Dunne, who was responsible for some thirty murders. (Dunne was eventually executed in Sing-Sing.) At the same time, Italian gangsters led by Albert Anastasia—the victim of the famous 1957 Waldorf-Astoria barber chair slaying—were taking over the Brooklyn and New Jersey piers, and the inevitable Irish–Italian clashes only escalated the violence. Corridan's was often a lonely voice of outrage. Each year, the governor, the mayor, the district attorney, the shipowners, and the leaders of the city's major unions would all dutifully turn out for the "Joseph P. Ryan Association" annual dinner—even Thomas E. Dewey, who rode to the governorship on his anticorruption record, once meekly showed up for a Ryan dinner. But the devout portion of the Irish Catholic longshoremen worshiped Corridan and took immense risks to challenge the ILA. "Long as I sure he's gonna be with me at the end to give the last rites and ease me into the hereafter, I figger I'm on velvet," one old-timer told Schulberg. (Schulberg unabashedly idolizes Corridan and even today considers him the major influence on his life. His recent stage version of *On the Waterfront*, featured an expanded role for Fr. Barry more in keeping with his view of Corridan's true contribution.) Corridan and Scully, in alliance with Joe Dwyer, a courageous longshoreman and war veteran, really did invigorate one West Side local to the point where they managed to take back control of their pier, which is the basis of the movie story.

Corridan was trained as an economist, and his private role in the waterfront corruption investigations was as important as his organizing efforts. Over the years, he built an imposing data bank on the New York waterfront, including detailed historical graphs documenting the corruption and the relations among the crime families and the shipowners, buttressed by solid statistical analyses of the system's cost. The public outrage that led to the waterfront investigations of the early 1950s was stirred in large part by a Pulitzer Prize–winning series of articles by Malcolm Johnson in the *New York Sun*, who relied on Corridan for much of his information. (When Schulberg came to Johnson looking for a guide to the docks, Johnson sent him to Corridan.) Once the investigations got under way, the staff also made extensive use of Corridan's data. Corridan once remarked that when he wanted to have some fun, "I put on my coat and hat and take the subway downtown to the District Attorney's office. All I do down there is walk through the building. I don't even go up in the elevator. I come directly back to my office, and thirty minutes later, I've had a half dozen 'phone calls from my waterfront friends. What was I doing at the D.A.'s office?"

The waterfront investigations were prompted in part by a bitter twenty-five-day strike by dissident longshoremen. At the strike's tensest moment,

Corridan came down to the docks and led the men in prayer—"God grant that our government may order us back to work in honor. God protect and preserve each and everyone of us this day." His daily presence, and the attendant publicity, may have been the picketers' only protection against violence. One longshoreman called it:

> [a] turning point. . . . We were being sold out by Joe Ryan and his council of stooges. Muscle men were roaming the waterfront. City Hall looked the other way, and most newspapers thought we were radicals. The mob called us Reds and the Reds called us Fascists. Then Father Corridan came down to the docks. It was like a sword cutting a path for us, separating us from the Commies on one hand and the mob on the other—a road for longshoremen to move ahead on.

Fr. Joseph Fitzpatrick, who had preceded Carey as director of the Xavier Institute, said that on the twenty-first day of the strike, a Sunday morning, he got a call from the Jesuit provincial that Cardinal Spellman had summoned him, Carey, and Corridan to meet him at the chancery immediately. What did Fitzpatrick think Spellman wanted? It was obviously about the strike, said Fitzpatrick, and it was obvious that Bill McCormack had gotten to the Cardinal. At the meeting, Corridan easily refuted charges that he had been working as a stevedore and using foul language; then he launched into a tirade about the threat of communism on the docks, and how Ryan and McCormack were creating conditions for a Communist takeover of the longshoremen. The charge was not implausible—Harry Bridges, who controlled the West Coast docks, was a Communist who ran an honest, exemplary union. But Corridan's own files show that he did not believe that Communists were an important factor in New York. The ploy was effective, however, and the Jesuits got Spellman's blessing for their work. Schulberg reports that later Corridan stormed into the Cardinal's office to block making McCormack a knight of the Order of St. Gregory.

In the final analysis, Corridan won many battles, but Ryan and McCormack won the war. The investigations resulted in the docks being put under the control of a Waterfront Commission that ended some of the most abusive practices, and Ryan even served a brief jail term. The AFL finally disaffiliated the ILA, and an AFL rival union ousted the ILA in most jurisdictions—but not in New York. Two bitterly fought elections ended in a narrow victory for the ILA, by a few hundred votes out of almost twenty thousand. The second election was held just weeks before *On the Waterfront* opened in New York theaters. Longshoremen thronged to see the movie, and it almost certainly would have swung the election against the ILA. In the long run, honest shipowners took their business elsewhere than New York, the wharf rats

took over the docks, and later automated loading systems virtually eliminated the longshoreman's trade.

Charles Owen Rice won only an equivocal victory in his long fight with
the UE. Although the CIO and Phil Murray secretly subsidized Rice's in-
surgents, the Communists consistently won narrow margins in honest elections. "The Communists were good, militant union members," says Rice.
He eventually resorted to denouncing the UE leadership to Martin Dies's
notorious House Un-American Activities Committee, an action he recalls
today with pained embarrassment. Carey and Murray finally read the UE out
of the CIO, and a rival union, the International Union of Electrical Workers,
eventually took over most of the UE's old representation rights. But it was a
sour triumph that left a bad taste all around. At the CIO convention of 1948,
Murray dropped his equivocation on Communist-dominated unions and
swung the convention behind the Marshall Plan. The remaining handful of
Communist unions were purged from the CIO by 1950.

ACTU was never quite so powerful a force, or so priest-ridden, as sometimes alleged. ACTU was founded by laymen, and the labor activities of
chaplains like John Monaghan and Raymond Clancy were usually part-time,
often spare-time, undertakings—"I was always trying to get *more* of Monaghan's time," says Cort, "We never had priests telling us what to do." Many
conservative priests thought that Actists were beyond-the-pale radicals, because of their frequent ad hoc alliances with Communists, as in the Newspaper Guild and the early days of the TWU and the NMU. In 1949, Cardinal
Spellman broke an ACTU-led strike of his own cemetery workers. But
extreme claims aside, the Church was an important influence in prodding
American unions away from class-based radicalism toward the kind of
stability-preserving, shared-power relations preached in the encyclicals.
Priests had immense personal and moral stature in the 1940s and 1950s; to
many Catholic working people, a priest's word was law. ("I used that all the
time," says Rice.) Clerical support, like Clancy's pro-Reuther *Wage Earner*
columns, counted heavily in organizing drives. In many working-class neighborhoods, priests bluntly told their parishioners that they had a moral obligation to join unions, and union leaders would have curbed any radical
impulses that might have endangered such endorsements.

As Catholic labor schools blanketed the industrial heartland, a sizable
fraction of American union leaders, Catholic and non-Catholic alike, and
many business managers got their training in negotiating skills with a big
dollop of Catholic social principles. Rice estimates conservatively that more
than half of all Pittsburgh union leaders attended one of his five labor
schools. The Jesuit labor school at St. Joseph's College in Philadelphia that
Dennis Comey took over in 1943 trained an entire generation of Philadelphia's personnel managers and union bargainers. Comey's curriculum, like

those at all the Catholic labor schools, drilled home that rights came freighted with equivalent duties, that workers deserved respect from management and vice versa, that fair pay required fair profits. It is fascinating to hear Jim Farrar, a former union organizer and volunteer faculty member at the Comey school, speak of organizing a Philadelphia company in the 1950s. "It was an enlightened employer," he says matter-of-factly. The personnel manager had been to the labor school "and knew *Quadragesimo Anno.*"

A priest's moral status made him a natural mediator. For almost two decades Msgr. George Higgins at the NCWC ran up to a half-dozen local industrial relations conferences each year. They were informal, but carefully prepared, union-management sit-downs stretching over several days, aimed at airing local labor-market issues, trying to anticipate points of conflict and nose out opportunities for cooperation. Phil Carey's informal mediations in New York were as important as Corridan's more publicized work. "He could drop in on management and suggest what the union might *really* be looking for," says Fr. Fitzpatrick, "and do the same with the union. Everybody trusted him, so he was a natural go-between." In Philadelphia, after a long series of damaging dock strikes, the shipowners and the longshoremen appointed Fr. Comey as the sole, and permanent, waterfront arbitrator. For most of the 1950s, Comey's word was law on the docks, and Philadelphia enjoyed a decade of unprecedented labor peace. "If Father Comey makes a mistake, at least we know it's an honest mistake," a longshoreman said. (Comey, like Corridan, was tall, bald, and sharp-tongued. *Life* magazine ran a striking Margaret Bourke-White photo of Comey addressing stevedores from atop baled cargo just before *On the Waterfront* was released. Philadelphians naturally assumed that Comey was the model for the movie.)

The image of the Church as a central player in American labor and politics was greatly enhanced by the prominence of Francis Spellman, who ruled the New York Archdiocese for almost thirty years and may have been the Church's greatest politician. No American churchman, except possibly Billy Graham, was so prominent. Spellman was close, or rumored to be close, which served as well, to Franklin Roosevelt, Joe Kennedy, John Foster Dulles, Richard Nixon, J. Edgar Hoover, and almost all important union leaders. His visits to troops abroad, both during World War II and the Korean War, were rivaled for media attention only by Bob Hope's. Politicians of all parties competed for invitations to his annual Al Smith dinners. He was by far the largest single source of worldwide Vatican revenue. New York priests, in a tone of awed pride, called the chancery on Madison Avenue "the Powerhouse." Many Americans thought that Spellman had a real shot at being the next pope.

The son of a prosperous grocer from Whitman, near Boston, Spellman graduated from Fordham and completed his studies for the priesthood in

Credit: Margaret Bourke-White, Life Magazine, © TIME, Inc.
This striking Margaret Bourke-White photo of Fr. Dennis Comey, virtual dictator of Philadelphia's waterfront labor relations, appeared in Life *magazine in 1954. The photo closely resembled Karl Malden's climactic scene in* On The Waterfront, *which was released in the same year, but the Malden role was modeled after another Jesuit, New York's John Corridan.*

Rome, where he began a long, close friendship with Eugenio Pacelli, later Pius XII. When Spellman came back to Boston, Cardinal O'Connell seems to have gone out of his way to humiliate him, perhaps fearing the young man's ambition. But Spellman parlayed an impromptu opportunity to translate for Pius XI during a Vatican visit into a job at the Curia and never looked back. When Pacelli visited America in 1936, Spellman, then a Boston auxiliary bishop, used his contact with Joe Kennedy to end-run the NCWC, which normally handled political contacts for the bishops, and personally escorted Pacelli to meet Roosevelt. New York's Cardinal Patrick Hayes died in 1938, and Pius XI apparently planned to give the appointment to Cincinnati's Archbishop John McNicholas, the longtime chair of the NCWC; but Pius himself died before signing the appointment letter, and Pacelli named Spellman, an extraordinary leap for a young auxiliary.

Although he was clearly a formidable figure in New York politics, Spellman was never quite as powerful as he sometimes seemed. In modern jargon, he was a master of the photo opportunity and the grand gesture, with the politician's talent of leveraging maximum exposure from a minimum event. Midwestern bishops, like McNicholas, Mooney, and Samuel Stritch, Mundelein's successor in Chicago, controlled the NCWC. They were more politically liberal than Spellman and chafed at his usurping the role of Church spokesman, but there was little they could do. Spellman has been savagely caricatured and was always more the public figure and corporate chieftain than spiritual leader, but he had many admirable qualities. He was open to new ideas, delegated well, and was a good judge of talent. While he dashed from one state occasion to another, he left the diocese in the hands of a succession of competent auxiliaries, some of whom, like John McGuire, are still remembered for their humanity and flexibility. Although he was not close to his priests, they seem to have liked him. As a leader of the Church at the crest of its triumphal period, it is hard to think of anyone who could have filled his shoes as well.

A Catholicizing America

The Catholic impulse was perfectly in accord with powerful forces that were transforming American society and culture in the 1940s and 1950s. Recent historians have emphasized that this was the period of the onset of the Cold War and of McCarthyism. Schoolchildren practiced huddling under their desks in case of a nuclear attack. Lynch law still reigned in parts of the South. It was not a good time to be homosexual, a Native American, a political radical, or a woman seeking challenges beyond homemaking and motherhood. But most Americans did not fit into those categories and did not spend their lives worrying about nuclear attacks. Nostalgic recollections of the 1950s as a golden era have considerable basis in fact.

All of the usual indices of social unrest dropped sharply in the 1950s. Crime rates, for example, which were very high in the 1930s, plummeted to possibly the lowest level in American history. Homicide rates did not catch up to the level of the 1930s again until the 1970s. People married young and stayed married. The growth of divorce rates decelerated quite sharply. Real wages rose steadily, particularly for men working for big companies in unionized manufacturing jobs. Average family size rose right along with wages, despite the greater availability of contraceptives. Interview data suggest that people's preferred family size did not change, but with good times, husbands and wives grew much more relaxed about family planning. Women had been entering the labor force in greater numbers for decades, but in the 1950s, they quit their jobs, stayed home, and had more children. Forced wartime savings supplied the ready cash for the purchases of new houses and cars that had been deferred since the start of the Depression. The GI Bill opened up higher education to the masses. Everything politicians had told people they had fought for in two brutal world wars seemed to be coming true. Despite worrisome rumblings in Russia, America was clearly number one, the breadbasket and manufacturer for the world, the only place where, with a little education and hard work, a family could count on having a reasonably comfortable home of their own, a car, and a measure of economic and personal security their Depression-battered parents hardly dared dream of.

Pent-up demographic forces were as powerful as the economic trends. During the hard times of the 1930s, American women had fewer children than ever before; average family size dropped to a level not seen again until the early 1980s. During most of the 1940s, the rate of childbearing stayed depressed because so many men were away from home. But from about 1948, three generations of women began having children all at the same time—the younger members of the Depression-era cohort who were still of childbearing age; the women who had come of age during the war and postponed childbearing until the fighting ended; and younger women just entering their childbearing years. The result was the famous 1950s baby boom, the "pig in a python," the enormous birth cohort that generated a frenzy of maternity hospital and school building in the 1950s, a college building binge in the 1960s, and eventually a glut of youthful workers in the 1970s.

In addition, because of low Depression-era birth rates, the number of young men entering the labor force in the 1950s was unusually small. GIs entering full-time college programs reduced the youthful labor pool that much further. With a relative scarcity of young workers, the ratio of young men's wages to older men's wages rose to its highest level ever. The demographic trends amplified one another. As high wages for young men facilitated family formation, more women left the labor market, the average age of marriage and childbearing dropped, and average family size shot upward. With the typical young man in his early twenties married, with children, earning good wages and with good job prospects, indices of social stability were unusually benign. Television shows like *Father Knows Best* and *Ozzie and Harriet* were unabashed celebrations of the joys of the nuclear family. Marriage and children became the universal formula for a happy ending in the movies, even in *The Moon Is Blue*.

Amid the general prosperity, the relations between big industry and labor evolved in a direction that was almost point-for-point consistent with the social vision of *Rerum Novarum* and *Quadragesimo Anno*. Men were getting a "family wage" and could support large families, which helped enforce marital discipline and stability. And while Reuther never managed to set up his industrial council plan, by the mid-1950s, most of the major blue-collar unions, like the Auto Workers, Steel Workers, and Rubber Workers, had negotiated stable, long-term contracts, with built-in cost-of-living increases, productivity-based wage escalators, a full platter of ancillary benefits, and substantial protection for tenure and seniority rights. The great labor crusades of the 1930s and the disruptive strikes at the end of the war became a collective mythology tended by well-fed AFL-CIO officials, a device to stir up illusions of unity at union conventions, like old alums singing school songs on Homecoming Day. On the other side of the table, big industrialists shed their buccaneering ways, or at least pretended to, joined the Council on Foreign Relations and the Committee on Economic Development, and held conferences on improving the social performance of their businesses.

Catholics benefited disproportionately from the postwar boom. For one thing, the Catholic population was growing very fast, doubling just between 1940 and 1960. During the 1950s in the Northeast, still the country's dominant media and cultural center, the Catholic share of the population increased from about a third to almost 40 percent. At the same time, the Catholic share of the nation's population increased from 19 percent to 23 percent, and its share of the Church-affiliated population from 33 percent to 37 percent. (In the glacierlike world of demographics, these are quite large changes. Changes of roughly the same order of magnitude in the youthful population in the 1960s prompted the "Youth Revolution.")

Catholic centers ruled, as much of the 1950s economic growth—leaving aside the few special cases like California and the Texas oil country—was concentrated in Catholic strongholds like New York, Philadelphia, Chicago, Detroit, and Pittsburgh. Protestant bastions in the South and Southeast lagged well behind the rest of the country. Southern Baptists, the fastest-growing Protestant denomination, were not yet an important political and social force. The massive population diaspora away from the old Catholic urban and industrial centers was still in the future.

The Catholic Church grew very rich—these were the days when Philadelphia pastors maintained six-figure checking account balances. In many of the old-line dioceses, Catholics built virtually brand-new infrastructures two separate times in a single decade—once immediately after the war, when urban Catholics made the jump from center cities to the first ring of new suburbs, and then a second time later in the 1950s, when newly affluent Catholics moved out to the second and third suburban rings. Catholics built almost 2000 new schools, and "Catholic League" and "Public League" high schools competed head-to-head for big-city football and basketball championships. Dioceses were building new seminaries to keep pace with the increase in vocations. A sign of the times was that the old Protestant estates on Philadelphia's Main Line were gradually bought up by the archdiocese to become Catholic academies, convents, and rest homes. In affluent Catholic states like Connecticut the Catholic grip on local political machinery was nearly absolute.

Anti-Catholicism was not banished from America. The *Nation* writer Paul Blanshard's best-selling *American Freedom and Catholic Power* (1949) attacked the Church as antihumanist, antisexual, a dangerous financial octopus. John Foster Dulles commented that John MacKay, the chairman of the Presbyterian General Assembly, was "so violently anti-Catholic, he probably feels a bond of sympathy with the Communists." The old saw that anti-Catholicism is "the anti-Semitism of the American intellectual" was true as perhaps never before, and fundamentalists still excoriated the Whore of Babylon, although mostly in rural areas where there were few Catholics. Will Herberg, who was probably America's leading sociologist of religion in the 1950s, commented with some wonder that Protestants, despite their 2:1 numerical majority over Catholics, "felt driven into an essentially defensive posture in which [they feel] a mere minority threatened with Catholic domination."

An eight-part series in the Protestant *Christian Century* in 1944–1945 opened with the question, "Can Catholicism Win America?" The *Century*'s editor, Harold Fey, argued that the Church was dedicated to "winning the total body of American culture to Catholicism. It has not only the right but the obligation to do precisely this if it can. But where does that leave Protestant Christianity?" Fey then proceeded to review—in a tone that was often as admiring as it was worried—the Church's movie campaign, its success in the labor movement, its impact on foreign policy, Catholic demography, wealth and political clout, and concluded: "[The Church] is mobilizing powerful forces to move this nation toward a cultural unity in which the Roman Catholic Church will be dominant. No comparable unity of effort is visible in Protestantism. . . . Until such unity appears, the answer to the question, Can Catholicism win America? is—yes."

The Protestant minister and historian Martin Marty wrote in 1959:

> Catholicism controls the urban centers with few exceptions outside the South and America is now a nation of urban dominance. . . . Protestant clergymen are usually depicted as silver-haired smilers who . . . never say anything that is not innocuous. But Roman Catholic priests . . . are real persons with authentic individuality. . . . The death of Samuel Cardinal Stritch got more Chicago newspaper lineage than did that of any political figure in memory. If an occasional Protestant, Jewish, or secularist voice complained about references in the press to Stritch as "our" Cardinal or Pius as "our" spiritual leader, the complaint was promptly rebuked . . . by other Protestants, Jews, or secularists.

Fey and Marty were too much the gentlemen to mention how fast Catholic kitsch was spreading throughout popular culture—Fr. James Keller's Christopher movement ("Light One Little Candle"), Fulton Oursler's and Jim Bishop's best-sellers on Jesus, Fr. Leonard Feeney's verse. Red Foley's "Our Lady of Fatima" was a 1950 hit single record; throughout the rest of the decade, it was recorded at least a dozen times, by Kitty Kallen, the Spinners, the Ray Charles Singers, and Andy Williams, among others. *The Foundling*, Cardinal Spellman's saccharine novel, was a 1951 best-seller.

If there was a public face of American Catholicism in the mid-1950s, it was a distinguished one, with silver hair, arresting black eyes, and a gentle smile. Bishop Fulton J. Sheen's *Life Is Worth Living* television series controlled the Tuesday night prime-time airwaves, burying Milton Berle's *Texaco Comedy Hour,* previously the most popular television show in America. (ABC made the slot available only because it was considered a commercial graveyard.) At his peak, Sheen commanded a television audience of 30 million, besides a massive radio audience, a total that far exceeded the number of American Catholics of all ages. His show won every major television award, most of them several times, and he once got 30,000 letters in a single day. When the Friar's Club did a roast of Milton Berle, Sheen was one of the major presenters. (The Sheen archive recently got a request for a series clip to use, for the sake of verisimilitude in a television production about a Jewish childhood in the fifties.)

Sheen may have been the finest popular lecturer ever to appear on television, with a style polished by twenty-three years as the star of radio's "Catholic Hour." He was elegant, elevated, relaxed, often very funny. Only Jack Benny could top Sheen's ability to hold back a punch line—for ten seconds, sometimes even longer—gazing calmly at the camera the entire time. The shows had a precise formula. Sheen, wearing his bishop's cross, crimson cape, and skullcap, would stride into a parlorlike studio, pause, tell a humorous story, and then pose the problem for the evening: Are we more neurotic today? How to deal with the rat race? with temptation? with teenagers? What is the nature of love? the meaning of intimacy? About ten minutes would be devoted to analyzing the problem, always with diagrams on a blackboard—the "rat race" lecture, for example, started with a diagram of time—and a stock joke about the off-camera angel who cleaned the board. He had a knack for flattering his audience. The lectures invariably introduced a technical term or two, usually from psychology or philosophy, which he wrote carefully on the board as if they were the key to wisdom. Every few minutes there would be another story, always on point, always seemingly impromptu. The problem analysis inevitably pointed in one direction—to humanity's need for God, for Truth, for Divine Love. Then the informal delivery would give way to a dramatic peroration, arms flung out, the cape spread wide, the voice suddenly husky with emotion, that would

Fulton Sheen's Life Is Worth Living *ruled Tuesday-night prime-time television during much of the 1950s. Sheen's performances were extraordinarily polished. He may have been the finest public lecturer in the history of the medium.*

end, with a rhetorical shake of the fine head, exactly twenty-seven minutes and thirty seconds from the moment he had first walked on stage. (The talks were live, of course. Sheen's trick was to memorize a one-minute closer, and then watch the clock and cut to the closer with one minute to go, no matter what else he was saying.) He pulled it off without a hint of sectarianism. The philosophy was very Catholic, but few people would have noticed, and Sheen never mentioned the Church or Catholic doctrine. All at the same time, he managed to be religious, undogmatic, humane, and unthreatening. Week after week, the performances were simply brilliant.

Life Is Worth Living was abruptly canceled after Sheen lost an intramural spat with Cardinal Spellman. (Spellman reportedly wanted to raid

Sheen's mission collections. Sheen complained to the Pope.) New York was not big enough for two egos on such a scale, and Sheen ended his career with a brief, unhappy stint as bishop of Rochester. But it is not likely that anyone, looking at America with a stranger's eye during Sheen's heyday, and examining much of the rest of popular culture and social mores, would have concluded that Catholicism was an alien religion, or that Catholics were an embattled minority, or that the Church was anything less than a dominant, possibly the dominant, religious and cultural influence in the country.

The Church's triumphal era in America was to be short-lived. Subtle eyes had picked out cracks in the edifice at the very threshold of Catholicism's days of glory. In *Going My Way,* when Fr. Fitzgibbon ordered Carol to go home and obey her parents, she pointedly ignored him. It took Fr. Chuck O'Malley's personal magnetism and musical heroics to return her to the narrow path. But few of America's 50,000 priests were Bing Crosbys or Spencer Tracys. A new generation was already listening to other voices, although it would not be until the end of the 1950s that the fragility of the Church's position could be appreciated.

For the most of the 1950s, however, the Church appeared preeminent. Its reach, in fact, seemed to extend well beyond the home front, to foreign affairs as well.

CHAPTER 9

Stalin, the Pope, and Joe McCarthy

When the Blessed Virgin Mary appeared to Lucia, a Portuguese shepherd girl, and her cousins, Francisco and Jacinta, in 1917 at Fatima, she told them, "I come to ask the consecration of Russia to my Immaculate Heart. . . . If [the world's Catholics] listen to my request, Russia will be converted and there will be peace. If not, she will scatter her error through the world, provoking wars and persecution of the Church." The specific request was that Catholics say the rosary every day for the conversion of Russia and receive Holy Communion on five consecutive first Saturdays of the month. Twenty years later, Lucia, by then Sister Mary of the Sorrows, wrote a recollection of the visions at the order of her bishop. In addition to her instructions on Russia, the Blessed Mother had made three prophecies, all of which had come true—that World War I would end, that Francisco and Jacinta would die as children, and that World War II would begin during the reign of Pius XI. There was a fourth prophecy, the "last secret" of Fatima, which Sister Mary gave to her bishop in a sealed envelope to be opened by the Pope in 1960. In 1948, *Life* magazine ran a full-page photograph of the good bishop, a Peter Lorre look-alike named Dom José, gazing warily at the envelope sitting before him on a table. (The letter was discreetly forgotten in the runup to Vatican II. In 1985, Cardinal Joseph Ratzinger, the Vatican's chief of doctrine, said that it was still in a Vatican safe, and that both he and Pope John Paul II had read it.)

The apparitions at Fatima, including the story that the Blessed Mother had made the sun spin at Jacinta's request to impress a gathering of 70,000 pilgrims, became more or less official Catholic lore. Pius XII strongly encouraged the Fatima devotions and sent a congratulatory telegram to pilgrims gathering for the twenty-fifth anniversary of the sun miracle in 1942.

There were many other sightings of the Virgin. When Mary Ann Van Hoof, a rawboned, bespectacled Wisconsin farmer's wife, reported visions and requests to pray for Russia in 1950, 100,000 people from all forty-eight states, along with the inevitable *Life* photographers, turned out for a scheduled apparition in August. Loudspeakers boomed the rosary out over the crowd, interspersed with pleas to stay off Mrs. Van Hoof's marigolds and zinnias, and she made a brief appearance to report that she had seen the vision on schedule. The official Church treated most such claims, including Mrs. Van Hoof's, with great suspicion, but Mariolatry was a central feature of 1950s Catholicism. Fulton Sheen made ten pilgrimages to Fatima, along with thirty to Lourdes, and he frequently mentioned them on the "Catholic Hour." The *Scapular* magazine signed up a million American Catholics for the "Blue Army of Fatima" to pray for Russia and keep the "First Saturdays." (A scapular is a brown cloth picture of Mary worn around the neck; in the 1950s, it was usually worn with a Miraculous Medal, also an icon of Mary.) Blue Army clones like the Knights of the Immaculata, the Block Rosary, and the Novena of the Sorrowful Mother, spread rapidly in the 1940s and early 1950s. In 1951, the fathers at Notre Dame University put it to their students this way: "Our Lady herself has told us at Fatima that 'we must pray the Rosary.' Will any student ignore her outright command? She promised world peace if we said the Rosary. Does any student want another world war? She promised the conversion of Russia if we said the Rosary. Will any student belittle the Russian threat?"

The intensity of Catholic Cold War anticommunism has been variously explained as an expression of status anxiety, as the hyperpatriotism of the ethnic outsider, as anti-Semitism, as a reflection of traditional political loyalties, or even as an artifact in the eye of the analyst. But these explanations typically miss the religious component of the Catholic stance. To Catholics, Stalin was the Antichrist, a satanic figure of biblical proportions. Hitler was regarded as one of history's greatest criminals, but he was still a more or less human figure, even something of a buffoon—Cardinal Mundelein called him "an Austrian paperhanger." Soviet communism and Stalin, however, were the spawn of the devil, explicitly dedicated to subverting Christianity throughout the world, to murdering the consecrated servants of God, and to rooting out religion wherever they came to power. In a confrontation of such cosmic consequence, it was not at all extraordinary that the Blessed Mother herself should come to Earth to warn her people.

In the 1930s and the 1940s, although American Catholic loyalty was no longer in question, the Vatican's foreign policy and the Church's obsessive anticommunism led to continuing friction with the Roosevelt administration, an upsurge of anti-Catholicism among secular liberals, and ugly clashes between Catholics and Jews. But by the 1950s, roughly coinciding with the peak of the Church's influence in popular culture, American mass opinion also became strongly anti-Communist—arguably, the first time that a national political consensus had come to track closely a long-held and identifiably Catholic view. It was a watershed in American Catholic history: the nagging Catholic grievance that their patriotism and Americanism had never been fully appreciated was, in Catholic eyes, finally and gloriously put to rest.

Between the Wars: Mexico, Spain, and American Catholics

The American hierarchy was usually extremely cautious about taking foreign policy positions. World War I was treated primarily as an opportunity to demonstrate the unreserved patriotism of Catholics. Cardinal James Gibbons dutifully carried Pope Benedict XV's peace proposals to the White House and passed on the Vatican position on postwar Italian land questions, but his efforts look entirely pro forma, and he was acutely aware of President Wilson's testy distaste for the Church. Nor did the Church have any involvement with the government's 1919–1920 anti-Bolshevik campaign. Catholics, in any case, were more likely to be on the radical side of the barricades, as in the 1919 Boston police strike and the strikes in the coal and steel industries. If anything, the bishops worried more about stirring up latent nativism.

Worldwide, however, the Church was obsessed with the Bolshevist threat to religion. And since the United States emerged from the war as one of the world's great powers, the American hierarchy was inevitably drawn into soliciting their government's support for foreign Catholic regimes under pressure from the left. The Church's first concerted attempt to influence policy was in support of the clerical party in Mexico. The effort was a failure, but it created frictions with every administration from Wilson's to Franklin Roosevelt's and provided a legitimate club for Protestants to use against Al Smith in the 1928 campaign. In the case of Spain in the 1930s, however, the Church's opposition to American assistance for a leftist regime was more successful and firmly fixed its image as a friend of fascism in the minds of a generation of American liberals.

Mexico's liberal party, which had taken office only after the active intervention of the Wilson administration, adopted a new constitution in 1917 that imposed severe disabilities on the Mexican Catholic Church. Episodic enforcement of the anticlerical provisions brought loud complaints from the Mexican hierarchy, protests from the Vatican, outcries in the American Catholic press, and strident demands for American intervention. The most forceful Catholic spokesman was Fr. Francis C. Kelley, the president of the Catholic Church Extension Society, and later an Oklahoma bishop. A pamphlet by Kelley, *The Book of the Red and the Yellow,* retailed stories of atrocities against the Mexican clergy and was widely circulated among Catholic organizations like the Knights of Columbus. ("Red" stood for Mexico's allegedly Bolshevik regime; "yellow" for the Wilson administration.) While there is no doubt that priests and nuns were roughly handled during the revolutionary chaos and ecclesiastical institutions were looted, Kelley's atrocity stories were simply not true.

When Mexican Catholic revolutionary firebrands precipitated a shooting war in 1926, the Coolidge administration proclaimed an arms embargo and strict nonintervention to the backdrop of a storm of protest in the Catholic press. A wealthy oilman, William F. Buckley, father of the conservative polemicist, undertook a fund-raising campaign for the rebels, and the Knights of Columbus demanded American intervention to prevent the "Russianizing" of Mexico, much to Al Smith's embarrassment. The crisis was defused when Fr. John Burke, the executive secretary of the NCWC, and Dwight Morrow, the American ambassador, with an occasional assist from Walter Lippmann, worked out a Church-State modus vivendi similar to the American system, which greatly distressed the Vatican. When fighting broke out again in 1934, a seemingly progovernment remark by Roosevelt's ambassador, Josephus Daniels, generated enough Catholic, and especially Coughlinite, protest, to create fears for the 1936 election. John O'Hara, the future Philadelphia archbishop who was then president of Notre Dame, and Cardinal Mundelein came to the rescue, if any was needed, by engineering an honorary degree for Roosevelt in 1935. Mundelein himself presented the degree with an encomium that the columnist Arthur Krock read as a campaign speech. Mexicans, sobered by the new outbreak of violence, quickly reverted to the Morrow-Burke compromise, which has been maintained ever since.

Catholics were mostly talking to themselves during the Mexican controversies. There was never any chance that the United States would intervene on the Church's side, and aside from the occasional brickbat against Al Smith, the issue drew relatively little attention from non-Catholics. The Spanish revolution of the 1930s, however, was an entirely different matter. It caught the imagination of America's literary left as few issues ever have, but in this case, it was the liberals who wanted American action and Catholics who were opposed.

Modern Spain was but a dim shadow of the naval colossus of the sixteenth century. It was a third-world nation burdened by a semifeudal nobility, poor soil, a backward peasantry, severe nationalities problems, particularly among the Catalans and the Basques, a long tradition of political and anticlerical violence, and a Church so retrograde that it embarrassed even the Vatican. After more than a century of upheaval, a bloodless revolution swept aside the monarchy in 1931 in favor of a republic headed by an unstable government of liberals from the professional classes, literary men, and assorted radicals, many with a romantic attachment to political violence. Hundreds of churches were burned, anarchist strikes popped up throughout the country, and there was an abortive military/monarchist coup in 1932.

By 1936, the economy was in free-fall, capital had taken flight, and unemployment was rising sharply. Both the right and left parties quickly radicalized. There was a wave of urban violence and hundreds of strikes; peasant risings created a reign of terror in the countryside, and political murders and assaults were rife. The conservative opposition leader, Calvin Sotelo, was taken out of his house and shot. Shortly thereafter, General Francisco Franco, the commander of Spanish forces in Morocco, accepted the leadership of a military rising to create a regime of "order." Civil war was probably inevitable. The left had been calling for a "dictatorship of the proletariat" for months, the anarchists were in full cry, and the Falangist (local Fascist) youth song, "Face to the Sun," extolled the glories of death. The race was merely whether the left or the right struck first.

Civil wars are savage, and the Spanish war was particularly so because outside powers used it as a proving ground for weapons, tactics, and propaganda. Franco's Nationalist army was quickly supplied with weapons and men by his brother dictators in Germany and Italy. With Spain already in chaos, the government, known as the Republican or Loyalist side, collapsed almost immediately. Soviet aid poured in just in time to save the Republicans. With the two sides controlling roughly equal territory, the conflict settled into the pattern of a war of attrition.

Franco, "one of the coldest-hearted" of men, was competent but quite cruel. He and the Nationalist leadership resolved from the start to employ terror to intimidate the populace. Republicans were systematically rounded up and shot, often after being tortured. Much as in latter-day Argentina during the rule of the generals, thousands of liberals who fell into the Nationalist net, like the poet Federico García Lorca, were never heard from again. Large contingents of Moroccan and Italian troops treated the Spanish population very harshly, and German troops, particularly the notorious Condor Legion, made up for smaller numbers by their utter ruthlessness. The best-known German atrocity was the carpet bombing of the civilian population of Guernica, apparently for practice. The incident was apotheosized by Picasso in perhaps the most famous antiwar painting of all time.

Republican atrocities against civilians, although less systematic, and concentrated in the first six months of the war, were almost as extensive. More than 50,000 civilians, including about 7000 clergy, were murdered by Republicans. The Republican treatment of priests was especially horrible, including eyes gouged out, crucifixions, and burnings at the stake. Republican behavior improved sharply after 1937, when they were desperately in need of support from the West. Careful calculations by the historian Hugh Thomas suggest total deaths from all causes of about 500,000, including 200,000 deaths among combatants (110,000 on the Republican side and 90,000 on the Nationalist) and 130,000 executions (55,000 by the Republicans and 75,000 by the Nationalists). In addition, another 100,000 people were executed by official Nationalist tribunals after they took power in 1939. Casualty estimates prevalent at the time were about twice as high.

The Republican government was never officially Communist, but the Communists were the only party on the left as hardheaded and ruthless as Franco. Communists were the funnel for Soviet military aid and had de facto control over the army and the police, and the Russian secret police set up a private prison system for thousands of politically incorrect radicals and Trotskyists. Perhaps 1000 anarchists and other nonconforming leftists were killed during the repression in Barcelona during the May Days of 1937, as the world's liberals averted their eyes. (George Orwell had trouble finding a publisher for his account of the incident in *Homage to Catalonia*.) The "aid" from Stalin was eventually impoverishing. For centuries, Spain had hoarded gold, and the Republic began the war with almost $800 million in bullion, the fourth largest reserve in the world. It was Stalin's idea to send it to Russia for safekeeping. At the banquet celebrating its arrival, he joked that Spain would see its gold again when one could "see one's own ears." When Stalin's interest in the Republican cause waned in 1938, it was only a matter of time before Franco's cautious tactics brought the Republicans down. The war ended when Republican officers overthrew their government and accepted Franco's harsh terms.

In the West, the propaganda war was almost as fierce as the fighting on the ground. The European nations, terrified of onrushing world war, organized a nonintervention agreement, which Germany and Italy shamelessly signed. For his part, Stalin simply denied that Russia was supporting the Republicans. In America, a resolution to embargo arms shipments to Spain carried by 81–0 in the Senate and 406–1 in the House. As the Republicans faltered in 1938, American ideological politics polarized around Lift the Spanish Embargo partisans, including almost the entire liberal establishment and a strong party in the administration, and a Keep the Spanish Embargo lobby dominated by the almost unanimous voice of the Catholic clergy and Catholic press.

Neither party occupied a moral high ground. Franco rebelled against a democratically elected state, although its constitutionality was quickly blurred by a succession of internal coups and repressions of nonconforming leftist parties. The illusions about democracy in Republican Spain at liberal journals like *The New Republic* were either naïve or mendacious. Catholics were outraged when liberals dismissed the murders of clergy as "alleged atrocities" and took a benign view of Stalin's Russia. Although Catholics exaggerated the murders of clergy, priests *were* killed by the thousands, and it was true that some priests' "heads . . . were carried through the streets." Catholics were also right that the leftists hoped to accelerate the start of World War II—by 1938, a wider war was the Spanish Republicans' last hope. But Catholics refused to recognize the improved behavior of the Republicans after 1937, when anticlerical atrocities had mostly ended and many churches were reopened. Liberals were properly insulted by the Catholic penchant for equating Franco with George Washington. They were alarmed to see foreign policy reduced to a choice between "God or anti-God," and to see the Vatican more or less demand that Catholics support the Nationalist cause. Harold Ickes, one of the strongest pro-Republicans in the Cabinet, called Catholic political pressure "the mangiest, scabiest cat ever."

Dorothy Day's *Catholic Worker* was the only Catholic paper not to endorse the Nationalists from the very start of the war. *Commonweal* broke ranks in 1937, similarly declaring a pox on both sides and lamenting that the "information available is so generally characterized by propaganda," but neither journal supported lifting the embargo. *Commonweal*'s shift of position cost it 25 percent of its subscriptions, and it was banned in some dioceses. The hierarchy seem to have been unanimous in support of Franco. A 1938 Gallup poll showed that 58 percent of Catholics supported the Nationalists, while 83 percent of Protestants favored the Republicans, a striking difference.

In the final analysis, it is not likely that Catholic pressure was the decisive factor in keeping the embargo. The issue of intervention in Spain was much like that facing the Bush and Clinton administrations in the war in Bosnia. Strong liberal sentiment for intervention was countered by a determination on the part of England and France to keep the war from spreading, regardless of who won. Emotional support for the Republicans, as for the Bosnian Muslims, did not necessarily translate into support for measures that risked widening the war. Arming the Republicans, in any case, could hardly have changed the outcome, for any intervention would have been matched by the Fascists. The Germans seem actually to have discussed the possibility of helping the *Republicans* in 1938, because the Nazi generals found the war so instructive that they wanted to keep it going.

For American Catholics, the most important consequence of the Spanish war was that it seemed to align them, as a religious body, on the side of fascism. There were good reasons to oppose the Republicans, but any Catholic with a minimal acquaintance with actual events in Spain should have been embarrassed at the alleluias in the Catholic press when a victori-

Credit: Reprinted by permission of The Tablet

The Brooklyn Tablet *was a leading organ of American Catholic anticommu-nism and had a national circulation. To the* Tablet, *the McCarthy era meant that the country was finally coming to its senses. The prominence of Jews in left-wing movements also sharpened Catholic-Jewish tensions.*

ous Franco swore his oath of office on the Gospel, in front of a crucifix, sur-rounded by priests and bishops. Pius XII's 1939 Christmas message in-cluded a special blessing for the new Spanish government. As reported in the official Vatican newspaper, the Pope praised the Franco regime for as-suming "the difficult and dangerous task of defending and restoring the

rights and honors of God and religion [but] did not omit to state frankly and
charitably that sometimes excess can come about in such defense," which
sounds smarmy. At the time, Franco was executing Republican politicians at
a rate of four hundred a day. The American bishops were much offended
when *Life* magazine editorialized in 1938 that "the Pope believes the world
is in a struggle between Communism and Fascism, and he favors Fascism."
But on a fair reading of the Vatican's behavior, it was a reasonable editorial
conclusion.

Communism, Fascism, and the Pope

The charge that the Catholic Church was allied with fascism and other
forms of right-wing totalitarianism was most often made by leftist ideologues
who were themselves hypocrites. As Orwell wrote about his experiences in
Spain, "One of the dreariest effects of this war was to teach me that the Left-
wing press is every bit as spurious and dishonest as that of the Right." Liberal magazines like *The Nation* and *The New Republic* either defended
Stalin's purges and concentration camps or studiously ignored them. The
longtime *New York Times* correspondent in Moscow, Walter Duranty, lied
about Stalin's rural terror and praised his show trials. Theodore Dreiser
warned in 1940 that England, not Russia, was the true totalitarian state. Bennett Cerf proposed repressing any book critical of the Soviet Union during
the war. When William Bullitt forecast trouble with Stalin, Max Lerner
called his article "a rotten cadaver," and the writer George Seldes said he was
"always a spy." During the violent, and anti-Semitic, purges in Eastern Europe after the war, Jean-Paul Sartre argued that it was wrong to speak out
against injustice in a Communist state. When Stalin arrested the exiled leaders of Poland, who had come to Moscow at his invitation to discuss a treaty,
the longtime liberal icon I. F. Stone assured his readers that they were really
criminals.

But regardless of the deceits and delusions of Communist fellow travelers, the Vatican's proclivity for embracing right-wing dictators and its relations with the Axis Powers before and during the war are a permanent stain
on Catholicism and especially on the reputation of Pius XII. In fairness,
many of the charges made against the Pope and the Church were false or exaggerated. But, in fairness, many were not.

Until the ecumenical council of 1962–1965, "Vatican II," no pope ever
unambiguously endorsed the concept of a liberal democratic state. Even
Msgr. John Ryan, the churchman most admired by American liberals, stubbornly insisted, in a 1940 edition of a widely used textbook on government,
that the Catholic confessional state was the political ideal. As Pius XI put it

in a 1933 encyclical, "it is a serious error to affirm that this separation [of Church and State] is licit and good in itself, especially in a nation that is almost totally Catholic . . . [and it is] impious and absurd for any people whatsoever." Ryan protested that Americans had nothing to fear, because Catholics would never win a commanding political majority, but he conceded that if they did, they would be obligated to construct a Catholic State, which did little to ease the nighttime tossings at the Protestant *Christian Century*.

In theory, the Church should have been the enemy of totalitarianism, for the Catholic principle of "subsidiarity" was designed to limit the claims of the State upon the individual and to protect the sphere of religion and family. In practice, the Church's concern to enforce what it viewed as the just claims of religion made it the natural ally of right-wing dictators. And the Catholic dictum, in Ryan's words, that "error has not the same rights as truth," made it the dogmatic opponent of the individual rights that Americans hold sacred. The Vatican confronted the same paradox as that facing dogmatic Communists or socialists—if Catholics were going to protect family and parish from the assaults of falsehood, or if Communists were going to place economic power in the hands of working people, they both needed the help of a strong State. By heritage, taste, and necessity, Vatican cardinals lined up with the decaying remnant of Europe's malodorous *anciens regimes*. Franco's Spain and Antonio Salazar's Portugal—repressive backwaters, class-ridden, sunk in poverty—were the *beaux-idéals* of the Catholic nation. As a wealthy American Catholic described Spain in the early 1960s, "[T]he churches were full. The streets were all named after saints . . . there were crosses everywhere. You breathed the Catholic thing there; it was rich and full."*

Eugenio Pacelli, who took the name Pius XII in 1939, was an upper-class Roman whose grandfather was the founder of *L'Osservatore Romano*. His brother, a Vatican lawyer, worked with Pacelli on the 1929 Lateran Treaty with Mussolini that established the legal status of Vatican City and of the Church in Italy. Cold, austere, physically frail, an odd combination of mystic and cynic, Pius had spent his entire career in the Vatican diplomatic service, including ten years as nuncio to Germany, and he spoke German like a native. It was he, as secretary of state under Pius XI, who sent the telegram to Hitler in 1933 congratulating him on his election as chancellor—the telegram was correct, rather than "warm" as sometimes reported—and he negotiated

---

* The links between Latin Catholicism and repressive dictators persisted. Charges surfaced in Argentina in 1995 that Cardinal Pio Laghi, a leading "papabile" or papal candidate, was privy to the military regime's violent repression of dissidents from 1976 to 1983. The Cardinal has denied the charge. An Argentine bishop has decried the Church's "cowardice" and "complicity" during the generals' "dirty war."

a concordat the same year to regularize the standing of the German Church. Pius XI had made it plain that Pacelli should be his successor in a time of world crisis, and the cardinals elected him pope on the first ballot. Pius XII was not a Fascist, and his relation with the Nazis was one of mutual detestation, but however much American Catholics insisted otherwise, his diplomacy and America's were constantly at cross-purposes during the war.

Pius XII's overriding objective was to preserve the Church in Europe, and he needed to ensure that reliable government structures were in place when the Axis powers fell. The Vatican was never reconciled to the Allied demand for unconditional surrender and was horrified by reports that Roosevelt contemplated "pastoralizing" Germany at the end of the war. As much as the Vatican feared the Nazis, they feared the Soviets more and desperately clung to the shreds of diplomacy with Berlin. In addition, although the Pope had little influence with Mussolini, he regarded him as the Church's only protection against either Nazi expansion southward or a Communist takeover in Italy. Pius was also certain that revolutionary violence in a Communist Italy would vastly eclipse the clerical pogroms in Spain. Those were not idle fears.

Pius always hoped to mediate a settlement between the powers and stayed grimly neutral throughout the war, even though Roosevelt had appointed a "personal representative" to the Vatican with ambassadorial rank. (The appointment went to Myron C. Taylor, an Episcopalian and former chairman of U.S. Steel. Catholic joy and Protestant outrage at the appointment were probably politically offsetting.) Only a few months after Pearl Harbor, the Vatican ostentatiously opened diplomatic relations with Japan, and the Pope gave a medal to the Japanese foreign minister. Right to the end, Pius mounted one peace initiative after another, all of which, in Allied eyes, seemed calculated to save the Axis from the just consequences of its aggressions.

Relations between the Vatican and Mussolini's Italy were never close. The 1929 Lateran Treaty was not meant as an endorsement of fascism, as many American Catholics assumed, and Pius XI strongly criticized Mussolini's statist tendencies in a 1931 encyclical. Although the Vatican opposed Mussolini's 1935 adventure in Ethiopia, the Italian clergy and hierarchy were enthusiastic, much as the American clergy had supported the 1898 takeover of Cuba and the Philippines. The Vatican also muted its criticisms of Mussolini when he became the main support of Franco in a war that the clergy regarded as almost a holy crusade. Unsavory as he was, however, Mussolini was neither a Hitler nor a Stalin. Italy did not run by internal terror. Before the Axis pact in 1938, it did not have racial laws, and there were no deportations of Jews from Italy until the Nazi occupation. In 1933, forty-three American Jewish publications selected Mussolini as one of twelve Christian leaders who had "most vigorously supported Jewish political and civil rights." One motivation for the Taylor mission was Roosevelt's hope that he and the Vatican could yet keep Mussolini out of the Nazi camp.

For most of the period of Hitler's rise, the Church in Germany had a creditable record. Whereas the largest body of Protestants enthusiastically endorsed the Nazi Reich, many Catholic dioceses refused the sacraments to Nazis, although that policy was undercut by Pacelli's 1933 concordat. Pius XI denounced the Nazis in strong terms in his 1937 encyclical, *Mit Brennender Sorge* ("With Burning Heart")—"Whoever exalts race, or the people, or the State . . . above their standard value and divinizes them to an idolatrous level, distorts and perverts an order of the world planned and created by God." The encyclical was smuggled into Germany and read from every Catholic pulpit, which was brave. It was a time when the Reich was aggressively cracking down on independent churches. State subsidies were being eliminated, confessional schools and seminaries were being closed, and priests and nuns were harassed with immorality and currency smuggling charges. In 1939, Albert Einstein praised the Church for its "courage and persistence" in standing up to Hitler. The archbishop of Münster, Clemens von Galen, was an especially outspoken critic of the Nazis for more than a decade. As late as 1941, he engineered a pastoral letter attacking the Gestapo that was signed by a substantial number of the German hierarchy. Heinrich Himmler once arrested Galen, intending to have him shot, but the reaction in Catholic Westphalia was so strong that Hitler ordered him released.

Under Pius XII, however, Vatican criticisms of the Nazis were much toned down. His first encyclical, a diplomatic *tour d'horizon* produced shortly after his accession, mentioned neither Nazi nor Fascist by name, although both Hitler and Mussolini professed irritation at implied criticisms. Pius's policy seems to have been to keep the churches open in Germany, on whatever terms Hitler would allow. By maintaining lines of communication, he doubtless convinced himself, he enhanced the possibility of a Vatican-led peace mediation, which was arguably for the greater good. (It is hard to believe that he was not also attracted by the increase of his own, and the Vatican's, stature that would follow upon a successful mediation.) The nuncio to Berlin throughout the war, Archbishop Cesare Orsenigo, was a Nazi sympathizer, and far from the only friend of the Nazis in the hierarchy. The rector of the German College in Rome, Archbishop Alois Hudal, who was useful in dealing with the Nazis during their occupation of Rome, was another, and many members of Hitler's government, like Ernst von Weizsäcker, the ambassador to the Vatican and an old acquaintance of the Pope, professed to be good Catholics. When Weizsäcker was accredited to the Vatican in 1943, the papal limousine that took him to his audience flew the papal flag and the swastika side by side, "in peaceable harmony," as Weizsäcker noted proudly.

Even under Pius XI, the condemnations of nazism and fascism were never as harsh as those of Bolshevism. *Mit Brennender Sorge* attacked Hitler's repression of the churches but held out the possibility of compromise. An encyclical against communism, issued the same week, was much more apocalyptic—"For the first time in history, we are witnessing a struggle, cold-blooded in purpose and mapped out to the least detail, between man and 'all that is called God.'" Myron Taylor's assistant in Rome concluded that the Vatican still regarded militant atheism "as more obnoxious than [Germany's] modern paganism," and Pius XII steadfastly refused to endorse Roosevelt's program of aid to the Soviets after Hitler turned on Russia in 1941. Roosevelt, on the other hand, looked foolish when he elicited a statement from Stalin on freedom of religion, in the hope of mollifying Catholics. Stalin willingly gave it, of course, and Roosevelt breezily assured the Pope that "the churches are open in Russia." In response, the Vatican frostily released a list of papal representatives in the Soviet Union who were in prison or who had disappeared. A follow-up American request that the Soviets release imprisoned clergy was ignored.

Policy toward Germany was complicated by the ancestral hatred for Russia felt by the Catholic nations of Eastern Europe, as in Poland, Hungary, Romania, and Czechoslovakia. The Soviet Union, as Poland's Marshal Piłsudski put it, was an "Asiatic monster, covered with European veneer." Russia had preyed upon her western neighbors for centuries. Even Lenin suppressed his anti-imperialist dogmas long enough to mount an invasion of Poland in 1920. Cardinal Spellman was shocked when Roosevelt told him, in 1943, that the Soviet Union would inevitably take over Eastern Europe at the war's end, and quite possibly communize Germany and Austria, and perhaps even France unless the French adopted a Popular Front government. Roosevelt's confidence that the character of the Soviets would moderate after ten or twenty years was hardly reassuring. The Soviet move into eastern Poland after the signing of the Nazi-Soviet Pact had been carried out with extreme brutality—George Kennan estimated that the Soviets deported more than a million people, about half of whom were never heard from again. The Soviets imprisoned some 200,000 Polish officers, thousands of whom were executed in the Katyń Forest massacre, and completely suppressed religion.

The collaborationist instincts of many Catholic regimes in Eastern Europe after the Nazi invasions were reinforced by a pervasive, almost medieval, brand of anti-Semitism—Jews were the race of deicides. (The worldwide Catholic Good Friday liturgy contained a prayer for "the perfidious Jews" until Pope John XXIII summarily expunged it in 1959.) The Primate of Romania, in 1941, asked the Vatican to soft-pedal its statements on behalf of the Jews (which were soft enough) because they offended the country's Catholics, who were mostly of German descent. Slovakia cheered the Nazi incursion into the Sudetenland and set up an independent collaborationist state under Josef Tiso, an anti-Semitic priest, who was disavowed by the Slovak hierarchy and the Vatican but never excommunicated. Archbishop, later Cardinal, Alojz Stepinac, a Croatian nationalist, became a Catholic hero for his resistance to the Communists after the war; but his record is clouded by his and the clergy's complicity with a collaborationist regime and its violent suppression of Orthodox Serbs. Amid all the suffering, Poland's fate may have been the cruelest. After enduring the Soviet depredations of 1939 and 1940, the savagery escalated when the Nazis turned eastward in 1941. Almost every Jew in Poland died, and whole villages, Jew and Christian alike, were executed to punish the least vestige of resistance. Then in 1945 the Russians returned in a spirit of vengeance and plunder that made even Churchill quake. More than a fifth of the Poles were killed during the war, a ratio far higher than in any other nation, including Russia.

These were extreme times, and the extreme violence that raged throughout Europe excuses much. But the questions still pose themselves, flatly and irresistibly. Why did the Pope maintain his relations with the Nazi regime until the very end? (The first strong, direct denunciation of the Nazis by Pius XII came only in June 1945.) Why did the Pope not speak out against the persecution of the Jews? Why did he not excommunicate collaborationist clergy?

First, the extenuations. All major Jewish organizations have acknowledged the many Jews saved by the Vatican—by quiet diplomacy, by strong interventions on behalf of individuals and groups, in a few cases by wholesale manufacture of baptismal certificates, and occasionally by outright ransom. Fr. Robert Graham's exhaustive researches in the Vatican archives suggests the total number of Jews saved may exceed 800,000. Moreover, in the Low Countries, when the hierarchy *did* speak out forcefully, Hitler responded by increasing the persecutions, particularly singling out Jewish converts to Catholicism like Edith Stein, the philosopher-nun, now a candidate for Catholic sainthood. Further, one of the most celebrated charges against Pius—his eagerness to stay on good terms with the Nazis during the deportation of Jews from Rome, the central incident in Rolf Hochhuth's 1960s play, *The Deputy*—is quite probably false. The charges are based on indirect quotations of the Pope in Weizsäcker's cables to Berlin. It now appears that Weizsäcker was putting words in the Pope's mouth in order to protect him from Nazi retaliation. (The SS were in Rome, and there were rumors that they would take the Pope hostage.)

Finally, the rest of the world was also silent. Even after the basic facts of the Holocaust became generally known to world leaders and foreign ministries in 1942 and 1943, it is remarkable how few people spoke out forcefully—in America, for example, not the Roosevelts, not the Protestant churches, not prominent Jews like Walter Lippmann. It was inside-page stuff at *The New York Times* and *The Washington Post*. With the notable exception of Rabbi Stephen Wise, even many Jewish religious leaders downplayed the Holocaust so as not to lose focus on Zionism.

Having said that, the fact remains that the Vatican's consistent policy of "enlightened reserve" in dealing with the Nazis, as the nuncio in Vichy France approvingly dubbed it, was shameful. Even the many rescue efforts were directed primarily at Jews who had converted or who had married Catholics. The strenuous protests in places like Germany and Slovakia against the deportation of baptized Jews carries the unpleasant connotation that rounding up *un*baptized Jews was somehow acceptable. Individual bishops may even have used the Nazi threat as an incentive to conversion. The loudest Catholic complaints about the Nazis almost always focused on the narrow interests of the Church—reduction of subsidies, burdens on confessional schools, and the like. There is a tone in Vatican correspondence that pleas to help the Jews were an annoyance, a side issue, a distraction from bigger policy issues. The secretary of state, Cardinal Luigi Maglione, tended to dismiss the stories of death camps as unverified long after he had overwhelming evidence to the contrary, as if they complicated the much more important project of dealing with atheistic communism.

John Diggins has pointed out that the Church justified its relations with Fascist dictators on pragmatic grounds. The same could be said for the circumspect dealings with Hitler. Denunciations, or a break in relations, might have made Hitler more ferocious, aided the Communists, cut off critical sources of information, caused the suppression of all religion behind the German lines. But as Diggins rightly suggests, the Catholic Church was the last organization in the world that should have been falling back on pragmatic arguments. It was one thing for socialists to cover up Stalin's crimes for the sake of the cause. But Catholicism's entire moral claim against the forces of liberalism and modernism was that it stood for the Absolute, the Good, the Constant against the relativistic, the slippery, and the merely pragmatic.

Cardinal Maglione summed up the Vatican's policy in a 1943 conversation with Weizsäcker: "The Holy See . . . has been so very prudent so as not to give to the German people the impression that it has done or wished to do the least thing against Germany during this terrible war" (Maglione's own notes). Instead of being pope, that is, Pius played the neutralist diplomat, which is not much to be proud of.

Catholics and the Anti-Communist Consensus

American Catholics' attitudes toward communism were a complex amalgam of religious and patriotic fervor, tempered by long-standing political loyalties. Even the most liberal bishops followed the straight Vatican line on communism, as did the Catholic press and the clergy. Large-circulation Catholic periodicals, like *Our Sunday Visitor, Sign* magazine, and the *Brooklyn Tablet,* which had a national circulation, were extremely conservative on almost any political test, but even the *Catholic Worker* and *Commonweal* were strongly anti-Communist. (*Commonweal* broke ranks after the war, adopting the more conventionally liberal position in favor of normalizing relations with the Soviet Union.) Although Catholic laypeople were never as unanimously anti-Communist as the hierarchy and clergy, they were still more predictably anti-Communist than other Americans, whether the issue was the Spanish Civil War, communism in the union movement, or support for Joe McCarthy. Catholic support for McCarthy waxed and waned along with that of Protestants, but it was consistently about 10 percent higher. That is considerably weaker, perhaps, than the common perception of a solid pro-McCarthy Catholic bloc, but in politics, 10 percent is the difference between a landslide and a dead heat.

For much of the 1930s, it was common for Catholic spokesmen to express a preference for fascism over communism as "the lesser of two evils," as *America* once put it. By about 1937, however, Fulton Sheen, the NCWC, and *America*'s Wilfred Parsons hit on a more politically sensitive formulation by recasting the dichotomy as not between communism and fascism, but between totalitarianism and democracy, in effect, lumping Hitler and Stalin together. As Sheen put it, "Communism is the Asiatic form of fascism and fascism is the European form of communism. There is no essential difference," an argument that was triumphantly vindicated by the 1939 Nazi-Soviet Pact. When the pact was announced, Catholics like the *Brooklyn Tablet*'s Patrick Scanlan, who had long poured scorn on the left's tolerance for Stalin and had been predicting a Nazi-Soviet alliance for some years, were entitled to a little crowing. As Fr. James Gillis of the *Catholic World,* who was as consistently anti-Fascist as he was anti-Communist, put it: "[W]hen the news came that the Swastika was actually flying over the Kremlin with the Hammer and Sickle, the Red gentry and their sympathizers here in America squirmed like Houdini in his strait-jacket. With, however, an important difference: Houdini used to get out."

Roosevelt had a strong base of support among Catholics, lay and clerical alike, and always took pains to salve Catholic sensitivity to American dealings with Russia. On the sensitive issue of recognizing the Soviet Union in 1933, Roosevelt was careful to enlist the support of Al Smith and other prominent Catholic politicians. Most of the bishops responding to an NCWC straw poll on the recognition question were opposed to the President's policy, but an even larger majority were against any public statement in opposition.

When Roosevelt began steering the country toward war, however, the bishops and the Catholic press adopted a strongly isolationist line. Even liberals like Cincinnati's McNicholas, who chaired the NCWC, were adamantly opposed to aid to Russia or American involvement in Europe, and Catholic priests were strongly isolationist. At one point, Pius XII, who was frightened at the possibility of a clear-cut Nazi victory, asked the bishops to mute their criticisms—although Roosevelt was still disappointed at Pius's equivocations. After much maneuvering, McNicholas, stressing that he was not speaking for the NCWC, produced a tepid statement of support for Russian aid, based on the distinction between helping communism and helping the Russian people. The tensions over aid to the Soviets disappeared with the Japanese attack on Pearl Harbor six months later, and from that point Catholics and the Catholic clergy were in the vanguard of American enthusiasts for the war.

But Catholics were greatly offended when the administration began a propaganda campaign to improve Stalin's American image. *Life* proclaimed in 1943 that the Russians were "a hell of a people . . . [who] look like Americans, dress like Americans, and think like Americans" and that Lenin was "perhaps the greatest man of modern times." *The New York Times* announced that "Marxian thinking in Soviet Russia is out. The capitalist system . . . is back." Joseph Davies, the sycophantic American ambassador, rhapsodized about Stalin: "A child would like to sit on his lap. A dog would sidle up to him." It appears that Roosevelt personally intervened to encourage Warner Bros. to film Davies's memoirs, *Mission to Moscow*—in the movie, Stalin's purge trials come in the nick of time to save Russia from diabolical Fascist spies. *Mission* had a command performance in the Kremlin, Stalin loved it, and it was widely shown in the Soviet Union. (Jack Warner later argued that he only shot the movie the government wanted and reportedly made *The Miracle of Our Lady at Fatima* in 1952 as a peace offering to Catholics.) Catholics could accept the necessity of fighting alongside the Russians to defeat Hitler, but the "beatification of Stalin," as *Sign* called it, was a "moral obscenity."

Most disturbing, almost unforgivable, in Catholic eyes, was the administration's acquiescence to the Soviet takeover of Eastern Europe. Realistically, there was not much Roosevelt could have done. The postwar division of the continent was implicitly settled at the Teheran Conference in 1943, but to protect his Catholic vote in the 1944 election, Roosevelt encouraged the hopes of the anti-Communist Poles, which may have prolonged a hopeless resistance. The conference at Yalta in early 1945 papered over Soviet imperialism with Stalin's promise to hold "free and unfettered elections" in Poland as soon as feasible. When it became clear that he had no intention of keeping that promise, and that the West had no intention of holding him to it, American Poles and other Slavs, the majority of whom were Catholic, felt "sold down the river," in the argot of the day. At the same time, the administration's left wing, led by Max Lerner, Henry Morgenthau Jr., and Eleanor Roosevelt, were pushing plans for radical democratization of Western Europe to root out fascism and Francoism. That these same figures were content with Stalin's expansion westward stank of hypocrisy. The Catholic Church had good on-the-ground information on the nature of the Soviet conquest and were outraged by the readiness of liberals to make apologies for Stalin. A priest attacking *Commonweal*'s editorial sympathies for Russia noted bitterly "how many who clamored for war, allegedly on moral and religious grounds, are now indifferent to the surrender of millions of non-Russian Christians."

Official American attitudes toward the Soviet Union shifted radically after Roosevelt's death. The beginnings of the Cold War, in fact, can be traced quite precisely to an extraordinary series of events in February and March of 1946—a bellicose speech by Stalin that shocked even liberals like Walter Lippmann; the imposition of a hard-line Communist government on Soviet-occupied North Korea; the exposure of a vast Soviet atomic spy ring, including the physicist Klaus Fuchs, who admitted passing on thousands of pages of detailed technical information on the atom bomb; George Kennan's famous "long telegram" describing the Soviet regime as a "malignant parasite" embarked on a worldwide effort to undermine the western powers; and finally, on March 5, Winston Churchill's historic announcement in Fulton, Missouri, in Truman's company, that "from Stettin in the Baltic, to Trieste in the Adriatic, an iron curtain has descended across the continent." Public opinion was actually ahead of the administration; the favorable view of Stalin and the Russians had dissipated well before the policy revisions at the highest levels. Events over the next three years—Soviet obstructionism over Marshall aid, the coup in Czechoslovakia, the Berlin blockade, and the Soviet explosion of its own atomic bomb—merely confirmed America's new anti-Soviet convictions.

Catholics played no role in the radical revision of the Soviet threat, and none of the architects of the new American policy toward the Soviet Union— Kennan, Charles Bohlen, Averell Harriman, George Marshall, Dean Acheson, Paul Nitze—was Catholic. But the policy volte-face was immensely satisfying for Catholics, confirming that for once they had been far in the vanguard of public opinion. Hardly less satisfying was the fact that large elements of the liberal Protestant establishment and the Jewish intelligentsia, who had long looked down their noses at Catholics, were on the wrong side of the consensus. As Daniel Patrick Moynihan put it: "To be an Irish Catholic became prima facie evidence of loyalty. Harvard men were to be checked; Fordham men would do the checking."

At the Center of Policy

Just as in so many other areas of American life, the Church's influence on foreign policy was at its peak in the immediate postwar period and the early 1950s. The Jesuit Edmund Walsh, the head of Georgetown University's foreign service program, whose anticommunism had made him non grata in the Roosevelt White House, was once again a valued consultant. The State Department viewed the Church's information network in Eastern Europe as an important intelligence source and coordinated several anti-Communist projects with the NCWC. In 1946, George Kennan and Harold Lasswell, the British political scientist, met with NCWC staff to enlist the church's help with anti-Communist propaganda behind the Iron Curtain. The Church funneled paper supplies and printing equipment, and later winter clothing and funds, to the East European underground. In 1948, the State Department and the CIA worked with the Vatican to help defeat the Communists in the Italian elections, while the NCWC coordinated a letter-writing campaign among Italian Americans to urge their relatives to vote Christian Democrat. (The Post Office reported that the volume of mail to Italy doubled.) In 1950, Dean Rusk, head of the State Department's Asian desk, sought the Church's help in soliciting support for the Catholic Bao Dai regime in Vietnam and asked the NCWC to coordinate an American visit of a Vietnamese cardinal who was a relative of Ngo Dinh Diem. (It is often assumed that Spellman helped initiate the Eisenhower administration's involvement with Catholic Vietnam and the Ngo family; the NCWC archives suggest that the State Department reached out to the Church first.) The most portentous incident, perhaps, was the night that Fr. Walsh had dinner with a midwestern Catholic Senator who was strategizing for his 1950 campaign. Joe McCarthy was thinking of focusing on housing programs. Walsh suggested that anticommunism might be a good issue.

Fr. John F. Cronin, a scholarly, cherubic-looking seminary professor from Baltimore who had been involved in anti-Communist union activities, was brought on to the NCWC staff to produce a pamphlet on communism. He had worked with the FBI in Baltimore, and the agency provided much of the material for his pamphlet. (The pamphlet itself is relatively non-alarmist. The *Christian Century*'s Harold Fey, a spokesman for liberal Protestantism, called his work "factual and objective" with "little in it that suggested the methods of the Dies committee." Almost a million copies were distributed through the U.S. Chamber of Commerce.) At some point, the FBI seems to have chosen Cronin as a preferred "leakee" for classified information on Communist penetration in America, and it was Cronin who introduced a freshman congressman named Richard Nixon to Whittaker Chambers and the Alger Hiss case. Cronin then fed a steady stream of secret FBI files to Nixon that kept the investigation alive and ultimately resulted in Hiss's perjury conviction. (It is likely both that Hiss committed espionage and that he was convicted on trumped-up evidence.) As much as any other single event, the conviction of Alger Hiss confirmed in the public mind that Communist subversion was a reality in America. It catapulted Nixon to national prominence and, coupled with the Soviet acquisition of nuclear weapons and the onset of the Korean War, created a public receptivity for McCarthyism and the great red scare of the early 1950s. Cronin went on to a long career as a pamphleteer, speaker, and Nixon adviser and speechwriter.*

But the occasional attempts of "anti-anti-Communist" writers to portray the Catholic Church, and especially Cardinal Spellman, as behind-the-scenes string-pullers for the government's security apparatus seem vastly to overrate the Church's influence. Kenneth Giniger, who was an assistant to Allen Dulles in the early days of the CIA, says that they were more often frustrated by their *in*ability to elicit any support from the Church. For all of his energy, Cronin was just one man with a very limited budget. Andrew Goodpaster was a key national security aide throughout the Eisenhower years, but his only recollection of specifically Catholic influence was in 1954 when Secretary of State John Foster Dulles reported that a conversation with Spellman had made him less pessimistic about Vietnam. Fr. Avery Dulles, Foster's son (a convert, a Jesuit priest, and one of the church's leading theologians), says that, as far he knows, his father and the Cardinal rarely met and then only on public occasions. Paul Nitze speaks of Spellman as an irritant, "always pushing and pushing," but by no means an insider. J. Edgar Hoover and Spellman were supposed to be very close, but there is little evidence of more than incidental contact between them, aside from a single instance in 1946, when two agents reportedly called on the Cardinal to propose coordinating anti-Communist efforts. Nor is a close Hoover-Spellman relationship consistent with reports that Hoover kept a file on Spellman and disparaged him to Eisenhower in 1954, although the director may have treated all his good friends that way.

The historian David Caute has suggested that Spellman masterminded a purge of Communist public school teachers in New York City in the 1950s "to promote a climate favorable to parochial schools." But the charge seems to be based entirely on hearsay and is almost certainly false. The late Albert

---

* Cronin wrote in a 1974 letter: "As to my own contribution to Mr. Nixon's career—for better or worse, it is far more substantial than generally known. The assistance was critical at two vital periods: the Hiss case, which made him a Senator and later a Vice President; the 'new Nixon,' which was a factor in winning him the 1960 presidential nomination. The second item was based on the fact that I was his sole speech writer during the years 1940–1960, excluding the 1960 campaign."

Shanker, who was head of the American Federation of Teachers, was an active union anti-Communist at the time and never heard of the Cardinal's involvement. The New York City purges, in fact, were managed almost entirely by liberal anti-Communist Jews, who were the mainstay of organizations like the Vital Center and Americans for Democratic Action. The intellectual defender of the purges was Sidney Hook, a Jewish ex-Communist philosophy professor at the City College of New York (he argued that communism was a conspiracy, not an intellectual position). The prosecutor was the New York City Corporation Counsel Saul Moskoff; and the prosecutions themselves were carried out under the state's new antisubversive Feinberg Law. A contemporaneous purge of Communists from New York City's welfare department was entirely an intra-Jewish affair.

John Cronin and the NCWC staff thought Senator McCarthy's brand of Communist witch-hunting damaged the anti-Communist cause, but the mainstream Catholic press was among McCarthy's most fervid supporters. Hardly an issue of the *Brooklyn Tablet, Our Sunday Visitor, Sign, Ave Maria,* or the *Los Angeles Tidings* passed without a major article on communism, usually painting the threat in alarmist, if not apocalyptic, terms—"the masses of Catholic electors . . . perhaps they, alone, can save the world," as the *Sunday Visitor* put it. McCarthy's Wisconsin was not a Catholic state, and he was cautious about identifying with the Church, but the support of grassroots Catholic leadership was resoundingly demonstrated by his rousing reception at a packed Chicago St. Patrick's Day dinner in 1954, in the middle of the Army-McCarthy hearings—the same fateful hearings that exposed the senator's ranting on television and effectively ended his influence. A few weeks later at a police communion breakfast in New York, Spellman himself introduced McCarthy to 6000 wildly cheering policemen and left no doubt that he was in the senator's corner. Only *Commonweal* and *America,* among the important Catholic journals, and Bernard Shiel, a liberal Chicago auxiliary bishop and erstwhile Roosevelt favorite, broke publicly with the prevailing clerical consensus on McCarthy.

Donald Crosby's careful study of Catholics and McCarthy stresses that lay Catholics were much less supportive of McCarthy than the Church leadership. But McCarthy's consistent 10 percent margin of additional support among Catholics was politically important, and Crosby seems to minimize the role of political symbolism when he writes that, after their pro-McCarthy communion breakfast, New York's policemen "went back to their beats." What else, after all, could they be expected to do? The image of 6000 lustily cheering policemen—a politically sophisticated constituency whose families voted a straight line with a near 100 percent election turnout—would give second thoughts to any politician thinking about criticizing the senator, whatever Gallup polls might say about the shallowness of McCarthy's support.

Credit: UPI/Corbis-Bettmann
New York's Cardinal Francis Spellman went out of his way to introduce Sen.
Joseph McCarthy to 6,000 cheering policemen at a New York Police Department
communion breakfast in 1954 just after the Army-McCarthy hearings, when the
senator's political star was starting to fall. The priest in the center is Msgr.
Joseph McCaffrey, the Police Department chaplain.

In the final analysis, however, the anti-Communist consensus was far too broad to be dominated by Catholics. Ninety percent of respondents in a national poll, for instance, thought a committed Communist was unfit to be a teacher, and only 35 percent of social science teachers thought Communists should be allowed to teach. Hard-line anti-Communist organizations like the American Legion and Veterans of Foreign Wars were not notably Catholic. McCarthy was a Catholic, of course, as was Senator Pat McCarran, the chairman of the Senate Internal Security Subcommittee, but Presbyterians like the Dulles brothers and Hoover did not need tutelage on antiradicalism. The leadership of the Congressional anti-Communist forces, like Karl Mundt, James Eastland, William Jenner, and Nixon in the Senate, and Martin Dies, Francis Walter, and Hamilton Fish of the House Un-American Activities Committee, were all non-Catholics. Catholics were overrepresented among FBI field agents, but the top reaches of the agency, the CIA, and all the Eisenhower foreign policy departments were manned by Protestant businessmen and financiers who had been anti-Communists all their lives. The impression of Catholic leadership, as was the case with movie decency, union radicalism, sexual mores, and family attitudes, was more a process of convergence—a prevailing national consensus finally coinciding with long and strongly held Catholic views. The Church was clearly influential, that is, but its influence was at a peak only because so many other political, economic, and demographic factors were pushing the country in the Church's direction.

Catholics and Jews

An important secondary consequence of the decades of ideological conflict was a sharp escalation of tensions between Catholics and Jews. As fellow besieged minorities, Jews and Catholics were on reasonably good terms in the 1920s, but relations had deteriorated in the 1930s over issues like movie decency and union radicalism, and by the 1950s had become quite hostile.

The American Communist Party was founded primarily by Russian Jews, and seems to have been a predominantly Jewish organization well into the Popular Front era. (Cronin estimated in 1945 that Party membership was about two-thirds Jewish.) The struggle for control over CIO unions often became an Irish Catholic versus Jewish fight—"Joe McUnion" up against "Isador Communist"—and the face-off became particularly nasty during the Spanish Civil War. When Catholics and leftists accused one another of waving away the atrocities of their own parties, they were, unfortunately, both right.

Spain, of course, was just prologue. The Church's long flirtation with fascism, and the Pope's supine attitude toward Hitler, justly infuriated liberals of all stripes, but particularly Jews. The *Brooklyn Tablet,* for example, was openly anti-Semitic. "Fr. Coughlin has fearlessly and courageously described the Jewish problem that others would pass by in cowardly silence," the *Tablet*'s Patrick Scanlan wrote in 1939. Scanlan made light of Hitler's treatment of the Jews until the very threshold of the war—"while the press and public officials bitterly denounce the attack on ten synagogues in Germany . . . the protest has not been widened to include the far worse crimes committed against Catholics in Spain" (1938). When Einstein praised the Church's anti-Hitler record in Germany, an editorial in *Ave Maria* captured the Catholic bitterness: "This is all very pretty, but if we remember correctly, Dr. Einstein did all in his power to help Spanish Loyalists who were burning churches and killing the clergy and the religious. He admires the Church in spots, where it is fighting the battle for the Jews, but he has no admiration for it when it fights to save our Christian civilization."

This photograph was confiscated during an FBI roundup of the Christian Front in 1940. The Front was a predominantly Catholic anti-Semitic organization that received shamefully sympathetic coverage in the Catholic Brooklyn Tablet.

In the Northeast, especially in Irish Catholic strongholds like Brooklyn, where Jews were visibly outperforming Catholics economically and educationally, the Catholic complaints sound much like those of Protestants about Catholics in the 1920s. Scanlan's lament in the late 1930s that Jews were better organized than Catholics is faintly comical in a city widely supposed to be in thrall to an Irish Catholic machine.* Less amusing was the brief appearance of what amounted to a Catholic Klan, the Christian Front, an openly anti-Semitic, and violent, organization centered in Brooklyn, that received shamefully sympathetic coverage in the *Tablet*. The Front was broken up in 1940 by an FBI sweep that arrested virtually the entire leadership cadre.

---

* At some level, Scanlan had a point. Much of this chapter was researched in the excellent Jewish Division of the New York Public Library, and Jewish studies is a major department of the City University—but the public library does not have even a microfilm copy of the *Tablet*, despite its immense readership in the 1950s.

Catholics regained some of the moral high ground by attacking the slavish contortions of Communists and the much larger coterie of fellow travelers who supported Popular Front militarism until the Nazi-Soviet Pact, then switched overnight to antiwar peace activism, then veered back to desperate banging of war drums in 1941. The *Tablet* ran a 1939 editorial cartoon of "Intellectuals" and "Communists," both code words for Jews, plotting to engage America in war to save Stalin. And after the war, whatever guilt Catholics may have felt for the Church's spotty anti-Axis record was assuaged by the liberal cover-up of Stalin's crimes. "In the matter of the Communist menace," *Sign* commented in 1953, "many of the liberals have a record of intellectual and moral bankruptcy, made all the blacker by their ready recognition of the evils of Fascism."

A promising opportunity for Catholic-Jewish cooperation over displaced person (DP) settlement after the war quickly dissolved into recriminations and back-biting. Jewish organizations first raised the issue and enlisted Catholic support because some 80 percent of the tens of millions of European DPs were Christian, and half of them were Catholic. But when two-thirds of the first admittees turned out to be Jewish, Catholics felt misled, and a Congressional fight broke out over national quotas and screening procedures. Catholics were opposed to admitting Communists (read "Jews"), and Jews wanted to screen out collaborators (read "Christians"). Truman signed a quota-laden special immigration bill in 1948 but blasted its alleged "anti-Semitic and anti-Catholic" provisions. Catholics endorsed Truman's message, but admitted privately that the bill wasn't anti-Catholic. Jewish groups then split badly over whether support for American immigration undercut Zionism. Catholics suspected that Jews were shifting their Congressional forces to support Jewish immigration into Israel, and Jews thought Catholics were double-dealing on quotas. Both were partly right. Overall, the immigration push must be counted a success, although it did little to foster interfaith relations. At the end, some 450,000 immigrants were admitted under the DP program; about 20 percent of them were Jewish, which was about their share of the DP population.

Zionism exacerbated tensions even further. The Vatican did not want Jews taking over Jerusalem, and a series of encyclicals in 1948 and 1949 insisted that "all rights to the Holy Places, which Catholics during many centuries have acquired and time and again defended valiantly . . . should be preserved inviolate." Even *Commonweal,* the most liberal and normally pro-Jewish of Catholic periodicals, editorialized more about Arab rights than a Jewish homeland. An Arab spokesman in the United Nations in 1953 quoted Cardinal Spellman's condemnation of "the effrontery of . . . the State of Israel" and its "overextension" into Jerusalem. The fact that the Soviet Union was the first nation to recognize Israel, and acted as Israel's special patron until the first Soviet-bloc arms sale to an Arab nation in 1955, inflamed Catholic suspicions.

The similarity between the Catholic and the liberal Jewish stance on anticommunism did little to defuse tensions. If anything, Catholic involvement probably blunted Jewish anti-Communist ardor. In Leslie Fiedler's phrase, an attack by McCarthy automatically produced "innocence by association." At bottom, there was a fundamental incompatibility between the Jewish and Catholic positions. Liberal Jews like Albert Shanker and Sidney Hook opposed communism because it suppressed free speech and thought; Catholics were anti-Communist because it was an "error."

Any prospect of a rapprochement between the official Church and liberals of the Americans for Democratic Action stripe was foreclosed by a heated disagreement over federal aid to parochial schools. For more than fifteen years, Catholics blocked federal aid bills unless they included funds for Church schools. Just as stubbornly, liberals refused to support any bill that included such aid on the alleged constitutional principle of "separation of Church and State." (Leaders of the fight against Catholic school aid, like G. Bromley Oxnam of the Protestants and Other Americans United for Separation of Church and State, also tended to take an extremely benign view of the Soviet Union. The two sides in the school aid battle, mapped closely to Cold War "left" and "right" positions.) The high, or low, point was a much publicized 1949 slanging match between Spellman and Eleanor Roosevelt, whom the Cardinal probably regarded as an honorary Jew. Spellman, this time at least, had reason to be exasperated. In its only school-aid decisions to that time, *Cochran* in 1930 and *Everson* in 1947, the Supreme Court had ruled that the provision of nonsectarian textbooks and bus transportation for parochial school students was *permissible* under the Constitution, and the logic of both decisions was readily extendible to, e.g., school health services. But no one could have guessed that from reading *The New York Times*. The *Times*'s education editor even testified in a 1949 Senate hearing in favor of a bill blocking aid to parochial schools.

Even after the demise of the Christian Front, big-city neighborhood relations between Jews and Catholics were quite tense—apparently much more between Irish Catholics and Jews than between Italian Catholics and Jews. Most Catholics did not live near, or even know, Jews. But Jews were a much smaller population, highly concentrated in a few big cities, usually in neighborhoods that were surrounded by lower-class Catholics. Jewish kids getting beaten up by Catholic kids became an urban rite of passage. (One Jewish historian of Christianity recalls that his interest was first piqued at about age twelve, as he sat on a sidewalk after being thrashed by Catholic kids. As they walked away, he noticed that their jackets said "Our Lady of Divine Mercy," which he found curious.)

Catholic-Jewish tensions appear to have eased significantly sometime in mid-decade, no doubt because of the general prosperity. People consumed with raising families and getting ahead on their jobs found better things to worry about. The 1957 Soviet Sputnik launch shifted the terms of the Cold War debate from ideology to technology and from subversion to the economy. With universities positioned to garner a big piece of the new military spending, intellectuals jumped on the Cold War bandwagon, removing both the religious and the class-based edge from American anticommunism. Just as important was the gradual secularization of the lower and middle classes. Traditional ethnic communities were breaking up—not just Catholic and Jewish urban villages, but midwestern Lutheran farm towns and southern Baptist hamlets. The postwar generation was assimilating into a broader American culture that, if not quite areligious, was at least highly latitudinarian. For the American Catholic Church, which had chosen to tie religious practice so tightly to a uniquely Catholic cultural machinery, that portended a more truly root-and-branch challenge than communism ever did.

CHAPTER 10

The End of the Catholic Culture

Walter O'Malley drove a stake through the heart of every true Brooklynite when he let it be known that 1957 would be the last year the Dodgers played in Brooklyn. O'Malley was taking his team to Los Angeles, coordinating the move with Horace Stoneham's New York Giants, who played in Manhattan. The Dodgers' stadium, the venerable Ebbets Field, was cramped and dilapidated, and the right-field wall produced caroms of such surreal angles that playing it was an art form mastered only by Carl Furillo, the longtime Dodger All-Star. The Polo Grounds, where the Giants played, was in even worse shape. Neither stadium had sufficient parking, and the streets leading to Ebbets Field were a hopeless snarl on game days. Before the war, almost all Dodger and Giant fans—probably half of them would have been Catholic—lived a short nickel subway ride away from their favorite team. A decade later the blue-collar workers who were the backbone fans for major league teams were as likely to live in the suburbs as the city. They drove to work and wanted to drive to games. More slowly, but just as inexorably, people from the northeastern and midwestern industrial centers were dispersing south and west, and professional sports dispersed with them—to California, Texas, Atlanta, Kansas City, eventually even Colorado and Washington State. O'Malley and Stoneham could read the future as well as academic demographers and were just moving with the market.

The population shift from city to suburb was one of the great social upheavals in American history, and it was made possible by the prolonged postwar prosperity. The country added more than 50 million people between 1950 and 1970, two-thirds of them in the suburbs, and per capita incomes, after inflation, increased by half. Government poured fuel on the suburban boom. The interstate highway program was the crown jewel of Dwight Eisenhower's domestic policy, while low-cost federal mortgage insurance, low interest rates, and tax incentives brought home ownership within the reach of Everyman. William B. Levitt introduced assembly-line methods to home construction. His workers dropped identical bundles of material every sixty feet along the muddy proto-roads of his Levittowns, and houses popped up in a matter of days. A Levitt house—a cramped little box to sneering intellectuals, a spacious dream come true for working families— could be purchased with a down payment of $100 and a monthly mortgage obligation that was often less than a family's rent in the city.

Just as portentous was the revolution in higher education. When Congress cobbled together a pastiche of veterans' benefits at the end of the war, the American Legion pushed hard for college tuition support, although academic authorities predicted that few veterans would exploit the opportunity. Confounding expectations, some 2.2 million veterans enrolled under the GI Bill between 1945 and 1949. Sixty thousand returning veterans applied to Harvard alone, and at one point, applications to the Massachusetts Institute of Technology ran at 4000 a month. The positive experience of the veterans—the economic returns to a college education were very high in the 1950s—presaged a fundamental shift in American education patterns. Only about 7 percent of the youthful population attended college in 1940. By 1950, the percentage was 12 percent, and it kept growing to 32 percent by 1970, all at a time when the numbers of young people were soaring. College enrollments jumped from 1.4 million in 1940 to 7.5 million in 1970. American clergy, of all faiths, had outnumbered college professors by 17:1 at the turn of the century; by 1970, there were more than four professors for every three clergymen.

Catholics accounted for 20 to 25 percent of Americans at the time of the 1960 presidential campaign, depending on whether one counted parish registries or census self-reports, and the Catholic population was growing twice as fast the rest of the country. Catholics were younger than other Americans, had larger families, and benefited disproportionately from the postwar boom. At the end of the war, the standard measures of socioeconomic ranking still showed a distinct Catholic skew toward the lower classes. (In one poll, 66 percent of Catholics were rated "lower class" and only 9 percent "upper class." By contrast, only 56 percent of the total population, and just 42 percent of Episcopalians, were "lower class," while 13 percent of the population, and 24 percent of Episcopalians, were "upper class.") But by 1970, Catholics were indistinguishable from the national average on measures of education and occupational status, and had a considerable advantage in income. In the twenty years from 1950 to 1970, the rate of Catholic socioeconomic advancement was faster than that of any other religious subgroup except the Jews.

Catholic leaders reacted to all these developments with a tangle of mixed emotions. The visible socioeconomic advance of Catholics could only be cause for rejoicing; indeed, an influential body of Catholic opinion insisted that Catholics were not advancing nearly rapidly enough, especially in intellectual pursuits. On the other hand, the American Church's bold, expensive, and extremely successful strategy of creating a virtually self-contained urban Catholic social structure was placed at risk. By every index, such as faithfulness in attending services, Catholics were more attached to their religion than any other mainstream religious community. The Church had managed the signal feat of assimilating successive immigrant groups who had arrived with quite different religious histories to a Catholic practice standard that was arguably the highest in the world. The strong religious attachments of immigrant Irish and Poles had been maintained, and even strengthened. The separatist Germans had been assimilated into the hybrid, predominantly Irish-American, brand of American Catholicism, while groups like the Italians, who had brought a decidedly casual attitude to formal religion, had been raised up to the American standard. The dispersal of Catholics away from the Church's institutional supports endangered this achievement. Church leaders were left, therefore, with the daunting alternatives of either replicating the institutional structure that had been so successful in the cities, or finding some new religious model that would be more flexible, more portable, less tied down to bricks and mortar. At bottom, it was the same problem that John Ireland and Bernard McQuaid had banged heads over seventy-five years before.

The dilemma, of course, was rarely posed so starkly in the 1950s. This was, after all, a time when the Church was marching from success to success and was at the peak of its influence in American life. Few bishops, in fact, had time to think of little else but keeping pace with their congregations' breakneck growth.

The City of Angels

The adobe walls and Spanish-mission red-tile roofs of Los Angeles's churches stake their claim as the seedbed of North American Catholicism. Franciscan padres followed the Spanish conquistadores into California more than a century before Anglo-Catholics landed in the East Coast colonies. But after the mass immigrations of the 1850s, the center of gravity of the American Church was always solidly grounded at a point somewhere between the eastern seaboard and the Great Lakes. The sole western outpost of American-style institutional Catholicism was San Francisco, dominated by highly successful Irish and Italian transplants from the East. Mexican Catholic southern California was regarded as mission territory until well into the twentieth century. Limerick-born John Cantwell (1917–1947) was the first southern Californian bishop to have a voice outside his own diocese.

Cantwell was a key figure in the Mexican crisis of Franklin Roosevelt's first term and was active in the movie decency drive, although he ceded the leading roles to Mundelein, Breen, and Quigley.

"Anglos" have always been drawn to the soft beauty of southern California's foothills, and to its splendid weather and beaches. But the region's lack of water acted as a brake on growth, leading to a continual boom-and-bust cycle of development and a literary image oscillating between expansive paradise and brutal dystopia. By the 1920s, regional development was in the tight grip of a cabal of powerful oil, water, and real estate interests led by the Otis and Chandler families of the *Los Angeles Times,* minimally counterbalanced by the fabulously wealthy Jewish movie community on the west side. The oilman Edward Doheny (who paid the famous bribe to Interior Secretary Albert Fall in the Teapot Dome scandal) was one of the few Catholics who were part of the power structure—his family foundation is still a major contributor to the archdiocese. When New Deal water projects finally permitted intensive residential development, real estate agents concentrated their recruiting efforts among older couples in the Midwest. The vast tracts of neat new bungalows came to house the highest concentration of native-born white Protestants in the country. These were the stable, sober citizens who tsk-tsked at the kooks and fringe movements flourishing in the California sunshine, who produced politicians like Richard Nixon, and who imposed punitive taxes on parochial schools.

Cardinal Spellman, who enjoyed effective control of American episcopal appointments, picked James Francis McIntyre, the New York chancellor, to be archbishop of Los Angeles in 1948. Los Angeles was the fastest-growing diocese in the country, and McIntyre helped cement a bicoastal conservative retaining wall around the liberal midwestern bishops who dominated the NCWC. In 1953, he became the first cardinal west of the Mississippi. Today, McIntyre's name is associated mostly with his sad, slightly ridiculous octogenarian flailings against the cultural and religious revolutions of the 1960s. But if he had retired at the canonical age of seventy-five in 1961, or had had the good fortune to go more seasonably to his eternal reward, he would be remembered as one of the great builders of the American Church. Lean and taciturn, with the neat gray hair and rimless glasses of a corporate chieftain, he was a gifted administrator and a rock-hard conservative, who fit perfectly with the Los Angeles Protestant establishment. As a young man, he took a job on Wall Street to support his invalid father and quickly rose to become the manager of a brokerage firm. When his father died in 1915, he entered the seminary, and was ordained at the age of thirty-five. New York had the good sense to recognize his administrative and financial talents and enlisted him to work in the chancery while he was still in the seminary. He spent most of his career in administration and was the "Mr. Inside" who ran New York while Spellman garnered headlines visiting troops and hobnobbing with world leaders.

Los Angeles's wartime boom lasted for half a century. The naval war in the Pacific made southern California a center for the shipbuilding industry, and the flat deserts and reliable weather were ideally suited to the massive American push into aerospace. Enlisted men and military workers returned with their families when the war ended, and when McIntyre took over the diocese, Catholic Anglos were arriving at the rate of 1000 a week. His first official act was to scrap plans to build a new cathedral in favor of building an infrastructure for his exploding Catholic population. By the time he finally retired, at the age of eighty-four in 1970, Los Angeles was the nation's largest diocese by far, with some 4 million members, or one out of every twelve American Catholics. He opened more than 100 parishes, built almost 200 schools, a seminary, 6 hospitals, and brought in 68 new religious orders. Like Philadelphia's Cardinal Dougherty a generation earlier, he financed a substantial portion of his construction program by speculating in a rising real estate market—picking up land in advance of new housing development, then selling off the excess to pay for schools and churches. Shy and a poor speaker, he shunned the limelight but ran a lean, spit-and-polish diocese and loved to descend on a building site with plans in hand, tartly pointing out deficiencies to the quaking pastor and contractor.

In 1950s Los Angeles, the typical Catholic family was headed by a junior aerospace engineer who'd gone to school on the GI Bill, with help from his wife, and who drove to his nonunion job on a new freeway from his tract bungalow while his wife stayed home and took care of their four kids. Angeleno Catholics were very conservative, especially if they read the *Los Angeles Tidings,* perhaps the most stunningly right-wing Catholic newspaper in America, putting even Patrick Scanlan's *Brooklyn Tablet* in the shade. During the 1950s, almost every issue was dominated by anti-Communist screeds. Douglas MacArthur was hailed as a hero in two successive issues after he was fired by Harry Truman (a "Kremlin Victory") and the editors favored using the atomic bomb in Korea. McCarthy was "the ex-Marine Captain who has taken some husky pokes—both verbal and physical—to rout out Communists in the nation's capital." The paper's militarism went hand in hand with the carapaced self-confidence so typical of the 1950s Church. An article entitled "Are Catholics Intolerant" examined the Protestant complaint of Catholic smugness, and concluded, with some relish, that it arose from "[t]he unqualified assertion that the Catholic Church is the one and only true Church founded by Christ . . . and the shocking corollary that . . . all other Churches who call themselves Christian are in error and are not entitled to the name."

Such upstanding citizens and staunch anti-Communists, led by a prelate who was such a solid businessmen, were eminently welcome to California's Protestant business elite. The parochial school taxes were eliminated in 1951, despite the strong objections of the teachers' unions. (The taxes had usually been allocated to public school budgets.) McIntyre was eagerly courted by the region's bankers, and he was a good friend of William Parker, Los Angeles's legendary *gauleiter* police chief and a Catholic. Even the *Los Angeles Times* shed its perennial anti-Catholicism. In Los Angeles, as in most other urban areas, to borrow Martin Marty's phrase, Catholics became a "virtual majority."

McIntyre's own career was to map the windstorms of change about to sweep through the Church. From the pinnacle of success in the 1950s, his rule in Los Angeles was suddenly enveloped in confusion and chaos, and he was hounded into retirement, although he remained healthy and vigorous almost until his death in 1979 at the age of ninety-three. At Vatican II, the ecumenical council that met from 1962 to 1965, he was shocked that priests and bishops leaked the proceedings to the press, despite the Pope's request for confidentiality, and he disagreed with most of its decisions. He resisted implementing the council's liturgical reforms, like the vernacular Mass, until he received a direct order from Rome. Then he badly mishandled a confrontation with the local community of the sisters of the Immaculate Heart of Mary, one of the archdiocese's most important teaching orders. In perfect accord with the council, the sisters voted to make the habit optional, to insist that all their members be properly credentialed (nuns teaching in elementary schools often had only a high school education), and to ask for minimum class sizes and supplies budgets. The Cardinal "hit the ceiling," in the words of one of the nuns, and fired them from the diocesan schools. An ugly confrontation stretched on for three years, although McIntyre always refused a personal meeting. Margaret Rose Welch, who was president of the community, and who held two doctorates in psychology, recalls crying in frustration at the absolute impenetrability of the underlings sent to deal with her. The impasse ended only when the sisters reorganized as a "noncanonical Christian community" unaffiliated with the Church.

During Los Angeles's 1960s racial upheavals, the Cardinal looked bigoted and mean—and acted the bully besides. When William DuBay, an activist civil rights priest, complained to Rome about McIntyre's racial attitudes, he was forced to kneel in front of the episcopal throne, in the presence of 200 diocesan priests, and kiss McIntyre's ring in apology. (DuBay later left the priesthood.) McIntyre transferred activist civil rights priests en masse to suburban parishes, and he thought the 1965 Watts riots—which ended the career of his friend Chief Parker—were "inhuman, almost bestial." Although the diocese had a good record subsidizing services for Los Angeles's East Side barrio districts, the official church was emphatically white-oriented. McIntyre had no sympathy with the Mexican-American La Raza movement (literally, "the Race," referring to the Spanish-Indian mestizo Mexican people), particularly since it was associated with migrant labor radicalism, although it had attracted some of his best priests and nuns.

McIntyre's career ended after radical Católicos por la Raza picketed his 1969 Christmas Eve Mass in a wealthy white residential neighborhood. As the marchers jeered outside, the old man led his white congregation in lusty rounds of carols to drown out the noise. In the space of a single decade, McIntyre had become a fossil remnant, his clergy and flock bitterly divided, his administration an acute embarrassment. He retired a month later, reportedly forced out of office by the Vatican. McIntyre, perhaps, deserves more sympathy than he often receives, for the times had passed him by, and the massive waves of Hispanic immigration were disrupting the familiar cultural assumptions on which he premised his career.

"Oxcart" Catholicism

The track and field stadium on Randall's Island, in New York City's East River, is just offshore from Spanish Harlem, and on a sweltering Sunday morning in June 1957, the stadium was a sea of brightly waving banners from New York City parishes and Puerto Rican villages. La Fiesta de San Juan Bautista, St. John the Baptist's Day, is Puerto Rico's most important saint's day, and 25,000 Hispanic Catholics jammed into the grandstand for Cardinal Spellman's Mass and procession. A dozen brass bands blasted out Spanish hymns, colorful floats representing the Mysteries of the Rosary circled around the infield, and the Cardinal's progress to the canopied altar in the center of the stadium was led by a 1000 little girls in white dresses—the Hijas de Maria, or Daughters of Mary. Another 10,000 to 20,000 people flowed around the fairgrounds outside the stadium, and when the Mass, including a sermon by the Cardinal in quite competent Spanish, ended, the stadium audience adjourned to the fairgrounds for a day of picnics, dancing, and contests. Almost all the city's leading political figures were on hand, as was "Doña Fela," Felísa Rincón de Gautier, the longtime mayoress of San Juan. New York's mayor, Robert Wagner, a Catholic, was an old friend of the Cardinal and stayed glued to Spellman's shoulder at every photo opportunity. The Manhattan Borough President, Hulan Jack, the city's ranking black politician, wielded a baseball bat to break a huge *piñata* and then leaped away from the rush of children, having been forewarned by the Cardinal, who had been almost trampled when he broke the *piñata* at the previous year's celebration at Fordham.

The postwar Puerto Rican migration to New York City was just one tentacle of a massive movement of people to the United States from Mexico, Puerto Rico, Cuba, and Central and South America, almost all of them nominally Catholic—a movement that may eventually change the face of the American Church as profoundly as the great waves of Catholic immigration in the nineteenth century did.

The central figure in the Church's adaptation to the Hispanic immigration was Robert E. Lucey, an early radio priest and social activist who had close ties to every Democratic administration from Roosevelt to Lyndon Johnson. A native of Los Angeles, he was appointed bishop of Amarillo, Texas, in 1934, and archbishop of San Antonio in 1940, where he served until his retirement in 1968. Lucey is a poignant figure. A tireless worker, he was a fighter for social justice all his life, and San Antonio was, and still is, a center for Church-supported Mexican-American activism. Lucey was arguably the first Catholic bishop to embrace the cause of migrant workers, and he was an active participant in the grape and lettuce boycott movements of the 1960s. He was also the most active Catholic bishop in the cause of desegregation in the South and he was sharply criticized by the bishop of Birmingham, Thomas Toolen, for his participation in the 1965 marches in Selma. But

Credit: Institute of Texan Cultures, The San Antonio Light *Collection*
Hispanic Catholic immigration picked up sharply after World War II, predom-
inantly comprising Mexicans moving to the American Southwest and Puerto
Ricans settling in the New York City area. The picture shows a traditional
"Blessing of the Animals" in San Antonio in the 1940s. San Antonio's Archbishop
Robert Lucey played a leadership role in adapting to the new Hispanic influx.

Lucey was also cold and remote, a man who submerged his personality in his work, and was autocratic with his priests. He was delighted when Vatican II finally seemed to vindicate his social activism but reacted angrily when his priests interpreted the same texts to support a clerical democracy movement in his diocese. After years of bitter clashes with the very priests who had been his star union and antipoverty activists, he was forced into retirement at the age of seventy-seven.

Lucey's involvement in Hispanic social welfare activities may have been prompted by a suggestion from Franklin Roosevelt when Lucey was traveling the South on the President's behalf in 1936. By the early 1940s, he had organized a "Bishops' Committee on the Spanish-Speaking," under the aegis of the NCWC's Social Action Department, which was run by Raymond McGowan, John Ryan's longtime deputy. The committee included most of the bishops from the Southwest and was nominally chaired by Cantwell, the senior bishop of the region, although the Los Angeles Archdiocese made it clear that it had no interest in Lucey's social improvement schemes. From the start, the committee was firmly under Lucey's control—its archives show him drafting almost every official letter and policy statement, planning conferences down to the last detail, and ruthlessly cracking the whip over laggard subordinates.

The programmatic initiatives generated by the committee were in the Chicago and New York settlement-house tradition. Lucey recommended a basic diocesan program, budgeted at about $150,000 a year, comprising a main physical center and a network of satellite centers, where catechetics would be entwined with an extensive program of social services—obstetrics, health education, language and literacy training, job placement, and housing cooperative development. San Antonio offered more or less the full range of services, and most other dioceses seem to have implemented some kind of program. Over time, programs expanded to include leadership training, get-out-the-vote campaigns—Lucey was almost a recruitment arm of the Democratic Party—and training conferences for clergy. Lucey constantly stressed Protestant inroads into the Hispanic population, warned of the spread of Planned Parenthood programs, excoriated the "contempt" that Hispanics received from the Anglo population, and lamented the sorry state of religious training in Mexico. The San Antonio Archdiocese also formed close links with Saul Alinsky's Industrial Area Foundation, Chicago-based specialists in civil rights and community organizing, who still work closely with many Catholic dioceses throughout the country. Most of San Antonio's service programs were eventually absorbed into the 1960s federal war on poverty; a diocesan priest was the first director of the San Antonio program.

The diffuse nature of the committee's activities makes it difficult to assess its effectiveness. In San Antonio, at least, Lucey's successors, Archbishops Francis Furey and Patricio Flores, the country's first Mexican-American bishop, have been in the same activist mold. Their continued close involvement with the local Alinsky organization has arguably made the San Antonio church more of a factor in Mexican-American community and political life than anywhere else in the Southwest.

The Puerto Rican migration to New York City, by contrast, was a much more self-contained and compact phenomenon, and was well documented from the very start. Some 80 percent of all migrating Puerto Ricans settled in New York City, and the city's Puerto Rican population ballooned from 61,000 in 1940 to 430,000 twenty years later. By 1960, the era of *West Side Story,* Puerto Ricans were the city's second-largest minority group after blacks, and by far the youngest and poorest. Because Puerto Ricans were American citizens, they often behaved more like commuters than migrants. The annual net migration for the years 1956 through 1960, for instance, was only about 40,000, but that was the result of almost a million separate trips.

The New York Archdiocese's response to the Puerto Rican influx, considering the times, and Cardinal Spellman's reputation as an exemplar of militant Irish-Catholic authoritarianism, was almost a miracle of open-armed enthusiasm. The key figure was Fordham's Fr. Joseph Fitzpatrick, who had earlier worked at the Xavier labor school. He held a Harvard doctorate in sociology and was a leading scholar of the Puerto Rican migration. By 1953, with Fitzpatrick's active assistance, Spellman had created a diocesan Hispanic affairs office, run by Fr. George Kelly, now a well-known conservative polemicist. Kelly had a degree in sociology from Catholic University and had written a prescient planning paper on the implications of the Puerto Rican migration. He was assisted by a small band of enthusiastic young priests like Ivan Illich, a much traveled immigrant, a linguist, and a dazzling intellectual.*

Since Puerto Ricans did not bring their own priests, Spellman set out to make New York's younger clergy Hispanic-friendly. Beginning in 1956, and for most of the next decade, half of each year's ordination class of thirty to forty men was sent for an eight-week immersion course in conversational Spanish. The program was first run out of the Georgetown foreign service school but was later transplanted to Puerto Rico, where the new priests could mix their schooling with weekend parish assignments on the island.

---

* In the late 1950s, Illich was sent by Spellman to the Catholic University in Puerto Rico, but when he got in trouble with the socially conservative Puerto Rican hierarchy, he moved to Cuernavaca, Mexico, where he created an intellectual entrepôt for North-South intercultural studies. Spellman gave him a free hand and absolute air cover, despite Vatican uneasiness. When the Vatican cracked down after Spellman's death, Illich gradually drifted out of the priesthood and finally married. Since the 1960s, he has become a well-known intellectual gadfly—a historian, anthropologist, linguist, and critic of modern social and intellectual systems. His writings are quirky, brilliant, and profound. Spellman's protection of Illich is quite out of keeping with the Cardinal's conservative public image.

All parishes with a significant Puerto Rican penetration were expected to have Spanish sermons and readings, Spanish confessions, Spanish religious and marital instruction, and parish organizations and social programs specially designed for Puerto Ricans. The diocese also sponsored a variety of supra-parish educational and apostolic programs and quickly found itself becoming a training resource for neighboring dioceses hit by Puerto Rican spillover from New York. The San Juan festival started as a special ethnic Mass in St. Patrick's Cathedral and, on Illich's suggestion, was eventually expanded into the elaborate citywide celebration at Randall's Island.

Bravely, the diocese determined to be tolerant of the great differences between Puerto Ricans and mainland Catholics in religious practice and social conventions. On the island, about a fourth of all stable couple relationships, and up to a third in rural areas, were consensual unions, without benefit of legal marriage or even the American protection of a common-law marriage. In addition, partly because of the shortage of priests, only about 60 percent of legal marriages among Catholics on the island were contracted in a Catholic ceremony. The rigorous practice standards that distinguished the American Church—attendance at Mass every Sunday, frequent confession, and communion—had never been the norm on the island, and islanders were not accustomed to contributing to the Church's support. It required the suppression of many years of dogmatic reflexes for a New York–trained priest to insist that the island's cultic and spontaneous brand of Catholicism was just "different" from, not "better or worse" than, the mainland religion.

The effort to adapt the New York church to the Puerto Rican influx was never more than a mixed success. On the plus side, the diocese could point to evidence that, just as with previous generations of immigrants, middle-class strivings and the adoption of middle-class religious norms went hand in hand. Although the rate of Catholic marriages on the island actually dropped during the 1950s, among Puerto Ricans in New York, it rose steadily, from only 27 percent in 1949 to 41 percent in 1959. And while Pentecostal storefront churches made significant inroads among first-generation migrants, their children returned in large numbers to more orthodox Catholicism. But relations with the established Church were never easy. Hispanic Masses were often assigned to the lower church—just as Italian Masses had been almost a century before—creating resentments over "basement-church" Catholicism, and pastors deplored the Puerto Rican refusal to stump up tuition for Catholic schools.

The 1950s successes were sharply reversed after the mid-1960s. By 1975, the rate of Catholic marriages among New York's Puerto Ricans had dipped back below the 1949 rate. Herman Badillo, for many years New York's leading Puerto Rican politician, points to several major political stumbles on the part of the diocese. The transfer of a popular priest who had created a number of

Puerto Rican antipoverty programs, Fr. Robert Fox, was widely seen as a punitive measure, and in 1966, Spellman reneged on a much publicized promise to preserve a bankrupt Catholic hospital in the South Bronx with an almost exclusively Puerto Rican patient base. Over time, attendance at the San Juan fiesta dwindled to the vanishing point as secular Puerto Rican organizations created rival celebrations, like the Puerto Rican Day Parade, just as Lucey's programs were eventually absorbed by secular anti-poverty programs. The adaptation of religious practice to Puerto Rican taste was also sharply curtailed by Spellman's successor, Terence Cooke, a notably conservative figure.

But there was more than clerical maladroitness at work. Almost all previous peasant immigrants, including the peasant Irish, came to America with religious standards that fell far short of the middle-class ideals of self-discipline and hard work preached by the priests and nuns. But their children and grandchildren came of age when the Church was enjoying a sustained period of dynamic growth and a vast expansion of its power and influence. Becoming a good Catholic both confirmed ethnic identity and signaled progress, or "getting-ahead." Second- and third-generation Puerto Ricans, by contrast, grew up at a time when the Church was suffering a severe institutional crisis and American culture was secularizing with a vengeance. A symptom of perverse assimilation is that, by about 1970, Puerto Rican single mothers outnumbered all other socioethnic groups on the New York City welfare rolls. The lesson of the Puerto Rican experience is not that the Church evidenced rigidity or insensitivity. For all of the New York program's flaws, no other immigrant group had ever been met with such an earnest attempt at accommodation. The problem was the growing weakness of the Church, and the formidable new competition from secular institutions like the welfare system.

The Hispanic influx also contributed to a marked vertical elongation of the socioeconomic profile of American Catholics. Since about the turn of the century, the Church had been solidly identified with the blue-collar working classes. But after World War II, Catholic demographics began pulling in two different directions. At the same time as the Hispanic migrations were greatly expanding the numbers of very poor and poorly educated Catholics, the Church suddenly faced the challenge of accommodating a new generation of highly educated Catholic professionals and lay intellectuals.

Why Can't Catholics Think?

"American Catholics and the Intellectual Life," a 1955 article by John Tracy Ellis, was like a match in an oxygen tent in Catholic intellectual circles. Just a few months after it appeared, *America* commented, "At every second or third

Catholic convention, someone makes a speech complaining about the lack of Catholic intellectual leadership." Ellis was a much respected historian, and his article prompted an outpouring of soul-searching lectures, articles, and books deploring Catholic backwardness. Catholics were suddenly echoing their longtime critics, like the *Atlantic Monthly,* which a few years before had mocked the "monolithic . . . mediocrity . . . of the Gallery of Living Catholic Writers." (The spectacular gallery of living *ex*-Catholic writers, like Katherine Ann Porter, Ernest Hemingway, John O'Hara, and James T. Farrell, didn't make Catholics feel any better.) Thomas O'Dea's 1958 book, *American Catholic Dilemma,* blamed the Church's "formalism," "authoritarianism," "clericalism," "moralism," and "defensiveness," and called American Catholics "neurotic" and "immature." The book was widely praised, although Catholics had vilified Paul Blanshard for making roughly the same complaints. The Jesuit theologian Gustave Weigel, in 1957, compared Catholic college administrators to Marxist doctrinaires in their anxiety to "prevent the student from meeting thought which has not been apologetically sterilized." One friendly critic wondered whether the "honorable adjective 'Roman Catholic' [is] truly merited by America's middleclass-Jansenist Catholicism, puritanized, Calvinized, and dehydrated?"

Ellis backed up his criticisms with a thudding litany of Catholic failure. Catholics were underrepresented in almost any list of American elite, except possibly in business. Catholics were even underrepresented in Congress, with only 14 percent of House seats and 10 percent in the Senate. Showings on indicia of scholarship were dreadful. A major study of the nation's colleges dismissed Catholic institutions as a "singularly unproductive sample." Catholic representation on the faculties of top colleges and universities was minuscule. With the single exception of law school, graduate school admissions from Catholic colleges were very low. (Georgetown led the nation in the rate of its graduates' law school admissions by an almost 2:1 margin over Harvard—the Jesuit brand of casuistical philosophy clearly had its uses.) No Catholic university ranked in the nation's top fifty, and Catholic representation in the sciences was almost nil. On a competitive ranking of university departments, Catholic institutions were consistently at the bottom, even in the humanities. The best American work in Thomistic philosophy, of all subjects, was being done at the University of Chicago and Princeton, instead of at Catholic institutions. Ellis blamed clerical anti-intellectualism for the malaise. American Catholic leaders, Ellis pointed out, proudly identified with the lower classes, as when Boston's Archbishop Richard Cushing bragged to the 1947 CIO convention that "[e]very one of our Bishops and Archbishops is the son of a working man and a working man's wife." Or as John Henry Newman had complained almost a century before, "The Irish bishops, not having themselves had a university education, did not properly understand what it was."

Intellectual consensus is always a lagging indicator. The desk-pounding applause that greeted Ellis's article is itself a measure of rapid change in the intellectual and social position of Catholics. (George Shuster, a *Commonweal* editor, had made the same arguments thirty years before but had encountered mostly invincible self-satisfaction.) Careful statistical researches by Andrew Greeley and his associates at the National Opinion Research Center in the 1960s and 1970s demonstrated convincingly that the notion of a "Catholic factor" retarding economic or educational progress was simply wrong. On almost all standard socioeconomic indices, Catholics were almost precisely at the national white median score by the 1960s, and substantially above average by the 1970s. Greeley, however, took the additional step of disaggregating the data by ethnic group. The vast majority of American Catholics were the descendants of four distinct waves of immigrants—the Irish, peaking in the 1850s; the Germans, peaking in the 1880s; the Italians, peaking in the early 1900s; and the Poles and other Slavs, peaking in the 1920s. When Greeley corrected for recency of immigration and education of the father, Catholics outperformed every ethnic group except Jews. In terms of education, income, and other standard measures, Irish Catholics ranked above every Protestant grouping, while all other Catholic groups were moving rapidly toward the Irish standard in rank order of their immigration cohort. (British-descended Episcopalians had lower incomes and fewer years of education than Irish Catholics but higher occupational status—the old-boy network survived.)

Stephen Steinberg's studies of the higher education performance of Catholics and Jews in the 1970s are not broken out by Catholic ethnicity, but they support Greeley's generational hypothesis. While Catholics were still substantially underrepresented on the faculties of elite universities, they were slightly overrepresented in the ranks of graduate students and teaching assistants, outperforming Protestants but still underperforming Jews. A concern frequently voiced in the 1950s that Catholic students at elite universities rarely encountered Catholic professors, in other words, was both true and well on its way to being corrected.

Greeley's work is itself a demonstration of how fast the intellectual style of Catholics was changing. In 1948, the Jesuit John Courtney Murray, the best-known Catholic thinker of his day, contributed an article on the Church to an American Academy of Political and Social Science symposium on religion. The differences between Murray's article and those by Protestants and Jews are striking. The other contributions are framed in standard socioanalytic categories, citing numbers, growth, evidence of participation, social class of members. Murray does not cite a single statistic but contents himself with a deductive exposition of the truths of Catholicism, much like John Ryan's work in economics. The formalistic bias identified by O'Dea was clearly a reality, but it was a style as alien to Greeley as it was to Murray's non-Catholic contemporaries.

Steinberg's and Greeley's data do not completely eliminate the question of a prevailing Catholic intellectual style. Even in the 1970s, Steinberg found that Catholics were more heavily oriented toward professional schools than the comparison groups, but that is plausibly still a generational phenomenon—the children of working people become teachers, doctors, and lawyers, while *their* children have the leisure to pursue pure academics. Steinberg also found a much higher weighting toward the humanities than to the hard sciences, particularly when compared with Jews. (The reasons for the off-the-charts group performance of Jews, and later Asians, on subjects requiring pure mathematics, however, is a subject of much controversy.) Finally, it is noteworthy that except for a glancing mention by Weigel, none of the critics commented on the cost of the Catholic predisposition that "smart boys should go into the priesthood." Since all of Ellis's performance data were based on lay statistics, removing 50,000 of the brightest Catholic males and an even larger number of academically inclined Catholic women out of the reproductive population had to have had an impact. (There were only 127,000 college professors in America in 1950.) Over several generations the numerical losses to a putative Catholic intellectual elite from religious celibacy must have been quite substantial.

The Catholic Campus

Worries about Catholic intellectualism inevitably came to focus on the Catholic college system, which was growing pell-mell in the 1950s. But the new emphasis on quality came freighted with philosophical dilemmas. Everyone agreed, of course, that Catholic higher education should be first-rate. The problem was that "first-rate" was defined by secular accrediting bodies who gave no weight to Catholic claims that they were educating "whole" men and women or that their students were better equipped to be competent moral agents in a confusing modern world. (Whether or not Catholic campuses actually succeeded in carrying out their moral mission is another question, but not directly relevant to the sense of its importance. A scattering of survey data suggests that Catholic college students were more religious, and considerably more conservative in sexual matters, than their secular counterparts, but one survey showed, disturbingly enough, that Catholic students were more likely to cheat on tests.)

In his 1957 article, Weigel argued that theology was *not* "the norm of valid teaching" and warned against confusing scientific truth with "credal truth"—there was no such thing, in short, as Catholic chemistry. That was a bold argument, and Weigel was departing quite far from official Catholic principles, which still espoused the deductive Thomistic intellectual style. Catholic psychology and sociology textbooks, for example, always started with Catholic

teachings on morality and the nature of man, and only then proceeded to issues specific to the subject matter. The dilemma of meeting secular standards
of quality while remaining true to Catholic philosophy was especially pointed
for the Jesuits. Jesuits educated about one-third of all American students in
Catholic colleges—in 1958, they operated twenty-eight institutions with more
than 110,000 students—and were proud of their reputation for learning and
high-quality schools. But the order's other mission was to defend changeless
Catholic principles as the main keeper of the Thomistic flame. For more than
thirty years, at meetings of the Jesuit Education Association, the umbrella organization of Jesuit colleges, the Jesuit fathers debated, with characteristic
rigor, whether a Catholic college could be true to both its secular and religious purposes. The record of the meetings offers a unique window into a
valiant attempt to reconcile contradictory objectives.

Jesuits had begun to question the quality of their colleges as early as
World War I. Secular accrediting associations, like the American Association
of Universities (AAU), had sprung into existence in response to the reluctance of European universities to accept American undergraduate degrees.
In the 1920s, Catholic University was the only Catholic institution that met
AAU standards. A list of qualifying graduate schools published in the early
1930s similarly excluded all Catholic institutions except for five departments
at Catholic University and a single one at Notre Dame. The report was
widely publicized by a scathing *New York Times* article. Robert Hutchins,
then the chancellor of the University of Chicago, and a friendly critic of
Catholic education, remarked that Catholic colleges had "imitated the worst
features of secular education and ignored most of the good ones"—Catholic
institutions, that is, replicated the athleticism and vocationalism of public
colleges, without the parallel emphasis on professional scholarship and rigorous research. If this were not enough to concentrate Jesuit minds, Maurice
Sheehy, the assistant rector of Catholic University and one of Franklin Roosevelt's favorite priests, wrote a series of letters to key Jesuits, including
America's Wilfred Parsons, arguing that "there is not the slightest probability of any Catholic university [meeting AAU standards] . . . within the next
twenty years" and recommending that Catholic University take over all
Catholic graduate departments. To say that Jesuits were insulted by
Sheehy's letter would be an understatement.*

---

* The underlying issue seems to have been control of fund-raising for Catholic higher education. Catholic University was nominally under the control of the American bishops, operating
under a Vatican charter. Bishops who took an active interest in CU and sponsored diocesan funding drives viewed the Jesuits as competition—or at least that was the Jesuit interpretation. Jesuits
needed a bishop's permission to work in a diocese but otherwise reported to their Father-General
in Rome, outside the diocesan chain of command.

Sheehy's letters coincided with a 1932 report of an internal Jesuit study group that was a devastating indictment of the state of Jesuit higher education. Compared to non-Catholic colleges, Jesuit institutions operated on a shoestring and were grossly underinvested in plant and library resources. The lack of endowments was forcing an increase in enrollments to earn tuition income, which made the plant and facilities deficit that much more acute. The administration of Jesuit colleges was under the control of the local Provincials, rather than higher education professionals, so teaching vacancies were often filled in a "haphazard" manner, without regard to academic qualifications. The state of Jesuit scholarly publication and participation in scholarly organizations, even compared with the best Catholic universities, was abysmal. Graduates of Jesuit colleges entering graduate or professional schools "often find themselves . . . completely unprepared for the advanced methods that are there taken for granted." Jesuit professors were "woefully undertrained" and were clamoring for better preparation: "In our Jesuit graduate schools, men have been appointed to teach who not only had no doctorate of any kind, and who had published no research, but who had never made any graduate studies in the subject."

The order's response was to embark on a long-term effort to move its institutions into the academic mainstream. Achieving academic excellence by secular standards became the ticket for Jesuit advancement. Promising seminarians were designated to specific fields of study and sent to earn doctorates at the best American universities. (Fr. Fitzpatrick, New York's Puerto Rican expert, earned his Harvard sociology doctorate under this program.) The order took full advantage of postwar federal support for higher education and private funding sources, like a mid-1950s Ford Foundation program to upgrade college teaching salaries. Jesuit academic entrepreneurs like Robert Gannon at Fordham and Michael Walsh at Boston College built strong alumni associations and introduced professional development and fund-raising offices. They matched the highest secular standards for faculty pay and engineered a vast expansion and upgrading of their plant and academic programs. (Walsh threw down the gauntlet to his superiors early in his career, when he refused to accept his first academic assignment until he had completed his Ph.D. in biology.) As the best Jesuit institutions, like Georgetown and St. Louis, achieved parity with the upper ranks of secular universities, control was intentionally shifted to lay-dominated boards of trustees beyond the reach of the order's command structure.

By the mid-1950s, almost all Jesuit colleges had achieved at least minimum academic respectability, although their graduate departments often still lagged badly. But success, however limited, raised nagging questions: What was so "Jesuit," or even "Catholic," about the new brand of Jesuit education? Expansion, coupled with the drive to recruit the best available faculty, meant that staffing requirements quickly outran Jesuit resources, and the ratio of Jesuit to lay faculty members shrank to the vanishing point. (Jesuits tended to control administrative positions and deanships, which fed lay faculty discontent, because it limited promotion routes.) The proponents of change, like Walsh, wanted to produce "intellectuals of national and international stature," men and women "with the spunk . . . to be intellectual adventurers." But did intellectual adventuring apply to moral questions? As one Jesuit put it at a 1962 workshop: "students find themselves in a vicious circle: the skeptical ethics teachers think that certain things cannot really be proven to be against the natural law (despite traditional statements that they can) . . . [so] reference is made to ecclesiastical pronouncements . . . (especially papal encyclicals) [which] frequently insist that the matters in question are against the natural law."

Walsh argued at a 1964 conference that to be a "*Jesuit* university," all that was required was "a few outstanding Jesuit administrators, one very competent, scholarly Jesuit in each department of Arts and Sciences, one in each professional school, and . . . a few equally well-trained Jesuits in Philosophy and Theology." Walsh was reflecting a rapidly evolving majority view of Catholic educators. Fr. Theodore Hesburgh, the president of Notre Dame, created a small stir in the early 1960s by recruiting non-Catholics for the psychology department, one of the most value-laden of academic disciplines. A nun who taught biology at a Catholic women's college, another subject once thought to be value-laden, remarked, "My knowledge of Catholic doctrine and philosophy never enters into my teaching. If it did, I shouldn't be in science." In 1967, a national gathering of Catholic educators, chaired by Hesburgh, at Land O'Lakes, Wisconsin, declared that "to perform its teaching and research functions adequately, the Catholic university must have a true autonomy and academic freedom in the face of authority of whatever kind, lay or clerical."

It is an extraordinary comment on the secularization of Jesuit colleges that Fr. Robert Harvanek, a philosophy professor who had become a spokesman for the Jesuit conservatives, felt constrained to argue before a *Jesuit* audience: "Let me state my position flatly. . . . There is such a thing as Christian philosophy. It is sometimes said that there is not, but I say . . . that there is." Harvanek contended that it was a mistake to use top secular universities as a standard for comparison, since those institutions had long since lost touch with their moral roots; and that any program that did not include a theological dimension, including a science program, was not worthy of a Jesuit university. Walsh's critics were not even always Catholic. A mid-1960s review by the president of Wesleyan University wondered whether Boston College was too slavish in its aping of its secular counterparts.

Harvanek lost the argument, but it is still an open question whether the Catholic "ambiance" on a typical Catholic campus—the handful of required philosophy and theology courses, the visible Roman collars, the lack of advertisements for gay student organizations—adds up to an independent tradition of Catholic learning and culture. Harvanek, now in retirement at Chicago's Loyola University, thinks it does not and suspects that many more Jesuits have come to agree with him. Jesuits have even lost control of their philosophy departments, he says. The problem is a deep one: high-quality university departments will always owe their primary allegiance to the professional, secular standards of their discipline, not to the keepers of a cultural flame who nominally run the school.

The Jesuit debates were a harbinger of a broader problem facing the American Church in the 1960s—the gradual unraveling of the separatist ethos that had been the source of so much Catholic organizational strength. Questioning Catholic academic standards and intellectual achievement pointed to incipient restiveness in Catholic ranks—restiveness about clerical authority, about the status of the laity, about the ambitious reach of the Church's truth-claims, about its all-enveloping cultural pretensions. There was as yet little of the confrontational edge that would mark later decades, and even the harshest self-indictments displayed the supreme confidence of midcentury American Catholicism. O'Dea's *American Catholic Dilemma,* for example, did not so much criticize Catholic incapacities as Catholic reticence, and looked forward to the time when Catholic intellectuals would be unleashed to "correct some of [modern thinking]'s most unfortunate elements."

The prominence of John Courtney Murray in the late 1950s—he made the cover of *Time* magazine in 1960—salved Catholic institutional egos. Murray taught theology at the Jesuit seminary in Woodstock, Maryland. He was a Thomist philosopher and a superb essayist, with a lucid style and a solid grounding in American history. One of the few Catholic priests ever to teach at Yale up to that time, he was a fixture on national commissions like the Rockefeller Commission on National Goals and on study groups like those organized by the Fund for the Republic, Robert Hutchins's liberal California think tank.

Murray's best-known work, like the collection of essays entitled *We Hold These Truths* (1960), showed how America's founders were steeped in the natural law tradition, and how the modern empiricist and individualistic mind-set had difficulty even talking about truths that Jefferson had found "self-evident." Murray respectfully suggested that the Vatican had consistently failed to distinguish between the French revolutionary brand of liberalism and the much more conservative American variety, an argument that got him in constant ecclesiastical hot water and drew a pointed public rebuke from a senior Vatican cardinal in 1953. But Cardinal Spellman shoe-

Credit: © 1960 TIME Inc. Reprinted by permission.
The Jesuit John Courtney Murray's decades-long project to reconcile Catholic
theology and American democracy made him America's best-known Catholic in-
tellectual, and earned him a Time *magazine cover in 1960.*

horned Murray into the Second Vatican Council as a consulting theologian,
and Murray and Spellman had the signal satisfaction, in 1965, of seeing the
fathers, for all practical purposes, jettison two millennia of pronouncements
on Church and State and more or less officially declare in favor of the American system. The canon, mostly drafted by Murray, pronounced Church and
State to be "independent of each other and autonomous in their respective
spheres."

Daniel Callahan, a youthful, and prolific, *Commonweal* editor and writer
in the late 1950s who studied philosophy with Murray at Yale, remembers
the Jesuit as an intellectual hero, proof that one could carve out a reasoned
position distinct from the prevailing orthodoxy and, by dint of conviction,
stamina, and a thick skin, pursue the assault over the very ramparts of Rome.
Even Pius XII, who is usually remembered only for his rigid anticommunism, was gently loosening traditional rules and regulations, like the four-
hundred-year-old rule against drinking water before Communion. The
scent of *aggiornamento* was in the air.

A revolution in Catholic attitudes was building steam in the 1950s, presaging a catastrophic collapse in institutional confidence. The Vatican Council, which is often credited with inaugurating the upheavals, merely baptized and advertised movements that had been under way for years. To outsiders, however, the Church still presented the smooth, ripple-free surface of old. Even so astute an observer as Martin Marty, in 1959, portrayed American Catholics striding serenely forward in harmonious unity of purpose. By all outward indices of religious success—membership, conversions, Mass attendance, collections, proliferating institutions, religious vocations—Catholicism was in burgeoning good health. As late as 1965, Cardinal John Krol of Philadelphia noted proudly that the number of new candidates for priests and nuns was up more than a third over the previous year, and his seminary enrollments were the highest in history. But already by the end of the 1950s, the intersecting intellectual and social trends undermining the premises and organizing ethos of the American Church were so many and so powerful that only a bare recital is possible.

American suburbs were one of the great experiments in social mixing. America's racial lens obscures how radically suburbs scrambled traditional ethnic and social categories. In 1950, urban Protestants, Catholics, and Jews typically socialized only with other Protestants, Catholics, and Jews. But as Herbert Gans, the Jewish chronicler of life in Levittown, reports, the neighbors who argued about lawn seed and school taxes at backyard barbecues were Italian, Polish, and Irish Catholics, European Jews, northern Methodists, and southern Baptists. The few signs of incipient anti-Semitism and anti-Catholicism were quickly squelched. The Levittown mantra was "Religious differences aren't important, as long as everyone practices what he preaches."

One of the sharpest Catholic theological debates at the end of the war was over the ancient teaching that there was no salvation outside the Church. The argument was effectively settled when Archbishop Richard Cushing, the liberal successor to Cardinal O'Connell in Boston, disciplined Leonard Feeney, the well-known Jesuit poet and essayist, for insisting on a narrow interpretation of the doctrine. At about the same time, Fr. James Gillis, the doughty editor of *Catholic World,* was politely hooted at in the pages of *America* for advocating the traditional separatist Catholic stance toward a mainstream American culture that he viewed as both bigoted and decadent. The separatist walls were crumbling.

Middle-class, workaday Catholics, with no intellectual pretensions or theological axes to grind, of necessity took a much larger role in suburban parishes. Catholic intellectuals were still inclined to refer to the laity as an "apathetic, obdurate mass," but the reality was racing ahead of the stereotype. Younger Catholic families in places like Los Angeles were as likely to be headed by accountants or engineers as blue-collar workers. They accepted Catholic doctrine without question (except for some still quiet wavering on contraception), but they could read and do sums and understood buildings and budgets. As the suburban diaspora outraced Catholic infrastructure, the laity inevitably assumed more responsibility for organizing parishes, negotiating for land, and reviewing building plans. George Ard, the bishop of the Trenton diocese, where Gans's Levittowners lived, came out of the old dictatorial tradition. But Catholic Levittowners organized a parish over his initial objections, settled on the basic designs of the new church and school, spearheaded the fund-raising drive, and rejected Ard's initial pastoral choices until he sent them a priest to their liking.

The lives of ordinary Catholics during the 1930s and 1940s had been dominated either by the struggle for existence or by exhausting wartime factory shifts. Affluence and the suburbs expanded both space and time and generated demand for organized social activities, especially for children—sports teams, scout troops, summer day camps. Catholics still instinctively looked to the parish as a social center, and priests willy-nilly became recreation directors. Buried in organizational mundanities, implicitly held to account against secular yardsticks (how did the parish eighth-grade football program compare with the local Pop Warner league?), the inexperience and incapacities of the average priest were often too painfully obvious. Parishioners who came home shaking their heads over young Fr. Smith's school planning morass would later be more disposed to question his advice on moral questions. Older Philadelphia priests uniformly point to the early 1950s as the point when they lost control of their parishioners. Andrew Greeley, in an enthusiastic 1963 book, wrote that the new breed of suburban priests were of necessity parish "team leaders" and "coordinators." But compared with, say, Vincent Gallagher in 1920s Philadelphia, who was an all-purpose village guru and even managed parishioners' bank accounts, "team leader" was a much diminished role. Priests suffered a steady erosion of their once immense prestige.

By the late 1950s, the social assimilation that Bernard McQuaid had warned so eloquently against was finally happening. Emancipated Catholics chuckled at,* were embarrassed by, or openly ridiculed the largely Irish

---

* One (Catholic) parody of a typical Catholic martyrology included: "St. Pudibunda, who on her wedding night decided that God had called her to a life of spotless virginity. The causes of her death that very night are not known. . . . St. Dragomira, the warrior nun of Bosnia. Converted from paganism . . . she spent her life fomenting religious wars, and is usually credited with Christianizing Upper Bosnia. She was clubbed to death by her pagan brother, Bogeslaw, after a long and heated argument about Christian hate. Patroness of edged weapons."

Catholic folkways that still permeated their Church. Parallel Catholic professional organizations, like Catholic medical societies and teachers' guilds, began to be abandoned by their members, or to play down their Catholic affiliation. The *American Catholic Sociological Review* changed its name to *Sociological Analysis*. Upwardly mobile parents did not scruple to choose a public school for their kids if it seemed educationally superior. Bright college-bound Catholics could figure out that Fordham or Boston College did not open the same doors as Harvard.

It is a truism that college-based intellectuals tend to be more socially liberal, less disposed to acquiesce to established authority. With the vast expansion of higher education in the 1950s, the center of gravity of enlightened opinion shifted perceptibly to the left. The stodginess of the second Eisenhower administration, the obvious excesses of McCarthyism, and the stirrings of the civil rights movement all heightened intellectual suspicions of the status quo. Books like John Kenneth Galbraith's *The Affluent Society* (on corporate giantism and mindless consumerism), Rachel Carson's *Silent Spring* (on impending environmental disaster), Peter Blake's *God's Own Junkyard* (on the despoliation of the landscape), and Michael Harrington's *The Other America* (on American poverty, mostly white and Appalachian) were best-sellers. The Babbitry of corporate boardrooms, it seemed, was not just boring; it concealed great crimes and injustices. The problem for the Church was that vehement hyperpatriotism was a key part of its long-standing political strategy—a way of masking its disdain for American secular institutions. To intellectuals, including Catholics, the simpleminded Americanism spouted by the official Church sounded like more of the corporatist Babbitry that they held in such scorn.

Cardinal Spellman's official prayers and poems—he loved to write them—embody a fascinating transformation of Catholic rhetoric. John Ireland and James Gibbons had argued only that American freedom was *compatible* with the spread of Catholicism. But in the 1950s, Spellman seemed to fuse the Church and the nation into a single shining ideal:

more precious and wondrous still is our Flag, which joyously and proudly I have seen flying aloft in all corners of the world, the flag of freedom that symbolizes justice and love of man for God and his fellowman. . . . *Red* with charity for all men and all nations of good-will— *Red* too with courage to achieve the liberties of men by personal suffering and sacrifice; *White* for the basic righteousness of our national purpose; *Blue* for our trust and confidence in God, Our Heavenly Father, and, for those who are Catholic, *Blue* too with love for the Mother of God, to whom our forebears in Faith long ago consecrated this land of loveliness."

Or:

> *America, Our America!*
> *With dignity all sublime,*
> *Thou art dedicated to Mary.*
> *Her mission is through thee;*
> *She feeds with thy hand;*
> *She soothes with thy touch; . . .*
> *To be light through thy light,*
> *To be hope through thy hope,*
> *To be love through thy love.*

Intellectuals, Catholic and non-Catholic alike, who were probing at issues like racial justice, or American implication in colonial regimes, or corporate plunder, or artistic repression, found the Cardinal's doggerel stomach-turning. Spellman persisted in tub-thumping for McCarthy-style anticommunism, became a more or less official sponsor of the Diem regime in South Vietnam, and made himself a laughingstock in a Horatio-at-the-bridge effort to forestall the collapse of the old movie decency codes. (In 1956, Hollywood *advertised* the Cardinal's condemnation of Elia Kazan's *Baby Doll*. Box office receipts boomed.)

Dorothy Day–style lay activism had become institutionalized in Chicago under the leadership of a remarkable priest named Reynold Hillenbrand, who ran the seminary in Mundelein until his labor activism went too far even for Cardinal Stritch. Hillenbrand was a disciple of Canon Cardjin, a Belgian worker-priest, who preached a Gospel-based activism with the motto "See, Judge, Act." (In the 1970s and 1980s, Latin American "liberation theology" was often explicitly Cardjinist.) To a remarkable extent, almost all the important lay-oriented movements within the American Church from the 1940s on, like the liturgical movement, Pat and Patty Crowley's Christian Family Movement, and a variety of workers' movements, were shaped by Hillenbrand, and he was the inspiration for a generation of lay-oriented, activist Chicago priests, like George Higgins, John Egan, and Andrew Greeley. (Ironically, Hillenbrand himself tended to treat his underlings and lay disciples autocratically and, rather like Lucey, spent the late years of his life estranged from many of the trends he had fostered.)

The journalistic voice for Hillenbrand-style "Chicago Catholicism"—although published in New York—was the lay-edited *Commonweal* and its stable of remarkable Catholic thinkers and writers, among them Edward Skillin, James O'Gara, John Cogley, Daniel Callahan, Dan Herr, John Cort, and William Pfaff, and later Peter and Peggy Steinfels. Although *Commonweal* occasionally conflated the Gospel message with the Democratic Party platform and could be uncharitably impatient with the level of taste and culture of the average Catholic, its intellectual level was consistently high. The magazine was immensely influential among younger clergy, for whom it was almost mandatory reading. As one establishment figure put it, *Commonweal* believed itself to be the "authentic defender of the faith against the immaturity of the official leaders of the Church, and that the field of truly enlightened thought belongs by right of appointment to [its] staff."

By the late 1950s, lay people were moving beyond social activism, and criticism of right-wing cardinals, to skeptical examinations of Catholic theology itself. In Europe, Catholic theological training took place in comprehensive university settings, as in Louvain and Tübingen, and was much more attuned to contemporary intellectual currents than in America. European intellectual fashions became an export industry in the 1950s, and American secular literati discovered French existentialism, a quasi-philosophical, quasi-literary riff on the plight of the individual in an absurd universe. (Norman Mailer wrote existentialist-inspired essays for *Esquire*.) The tide of secular European thought brought in its wake Catholic existentialists like Gabriel Marcel and adventurous theologians like Yves Congar, Edward Schillebeeckx, Hans Küng, and Karl Rahner. The new theology emphasized the individual's relation with Christ, sought the authentic meaning of the Scriptures, tried to recapture the spirit and simplicity of the liturgies of the primitive Church, and groped for an inclusiveness that made the Eucharist a shared meal, rather than a distant ritual on cold marble altars. *The Seven Storey Mountain,* the best-selling tale of Thomas Merton's conversion and entry into a Trappist monastery, introduced a highly personalized form of Catholic spirituality. The common taproot in America, as always, was Dorothy Day. Her partner, Peter Maurin, had preached French "personalist" theology in the 1930s, and she had been close to Virgil Michel, an early pioneer of American liturgical reform.

The questioning, especially from laymen, was still very respectful. A book by Callahan on the modern Catholic laity, for example, hoped that "[while] hierarchical authority would remain essential . . . the guidance of the hierarchy would be counter-balanced by the greatest possible degree of spiritual liberty. . . . [S]piritual liberty is not the opposite pole, but the correlative of the hierarchical idea"—a modest enough aspiration. Inevitably, however, the search for the primitive and the authentic exposed how much of official Catholic theology was a medieval encrustation on the Gospel teachings, the fossilized remnants of forgotten controversies with heretics and Protestants. And it illuminated as well how much the American Church was a unique cultural construct, a hybrid of Irish and other immigrant religions, a palimpsest of the insecurities and aspirations of marginal people.

In an uncertain and piecemeal fashion, American Catholic intellectuals, both clerical and lay, who were probing points of recondite theology in the late 1950s, examining the Church's political alliances, or challenging priest-laity power relations, were embarked on a fearsome exercise. It was nothing less than the dangerous and potentially catastrophic project of severing the connection between the Catholic religion and the separatist American Catholic culture that had always been the source of its dynamism, its appeal, and its power.

John F. Kennedy was awakened by an aide on the morning of November 9, 1960, to be told that he had carried California and was now president-elect of the United States. It was a razor-thin victory—Kennedy's popular vote margin was only about .02 percent, and the aide turned out to be wrong about California—but a Catholic had finally climbed the greasy pole, and the question of whether Catholics could be full participants in American society was forever laid to rest.

UPI/Corbis-Bettmann

John F. Kennedy, here fielding questions from a skeptical Houston Ministerial Association during the 1960 presidential campaign, finally put to rest the notion that a Catholic could not be elected president. Kennedy said that if there arose any conflict between his office and his religion, he would resign the presidency.

The campaign (Cardinal Cushing swore, and probably believed, that he had planned it with old Joe Kennedy in the Boston chancery office) was not without its moments of bigotry. Although Kennedy took pains to stress his independence from his Church, as at a famous meeting with Protestant ministers in Houston, and denounced aid to parochial schools as vehemently as Eleanor Roosevelt had ever done, Norman Vincent Peale still waved the old anti-Popery banner. But Peale was shouted down so vigorously by Reinhold Niebuhr and other prominent Protestant ministers that he was forced to recant. In Protestant churches throughout the country, the pre-election "Reformation Day" was changed to "Toleration Day" to underline American spiritual unity. Although Patrick Scanlan's *Brooklyn Tablet* opposed Kennedy, and the *Los Angeles Tidings* was noticeably cool, Catholics voted for him overwhelmingly, and some last-minute ballot-stuffing by the old-line ethnic Daley machine in Chicago may have swung the crucial state of Illinois. But the fact remains that Kennedy was elected by Protestants. Protestants still held a 2:1 majority over Catholics, powerful as the Church sometimes seemed, and cast more than half, perhaps two-thirds, of the votes in Kennedy's column. Kennedy, after all, hardly represented the traditional face of American Catholicism. A graduate of Choate and Harvard, skeptical, ironic, and thoroughly secular, he symbolized, rather, the social fluidity and assimilationist promise of the American experiment. His victory may have been a triumph of religious freedom, or perhaps, as the late Fr. Gillis might have complained, merely a symptom of American "indifferentism."

The foundations of American Catholicism rested on the political genius and indomitable will of men like John Hughes and Bernard McQuaid. They conceived of a Church that would be *in* America, vehemently *for* America, but never *of* America. The bishops who buried John Ireland's dreams of an Americanized religion would not have been surprised at the withering of Episcopalianism, Presbyterianism, and Methodism once they chose the assimilationist path. (Mainstream Protestantism was suffering massive losses of membership. Southern Baptists, the Pentecostals, and Catholics accounted for all of the growth in Christian churches.) The old-line bishops instinctively understood that strength lay in a prickly apartness from America's great leveling engine, a proud declaration of difference. Prelates like O'Connell, Dougherty, Mundelein, McIntyre, and Spellman, for all of their flaws and failings, wrapped their faith with the thick institutional web that underscored the clarity, certainty, and completeness of the Catholic vision and made it such a mighty cultural force.

But there could be no turning back. Kennedy's election—the moment that was hailed as the Church's greatest triumph—was an unmistakable signal that the old separatist, ethnic wellsprings of Catholic power were finally running dry. At the close of its triumphant American century, the Catholic Church would set out once more in search of its soul.

PART III

CRISIS

CHAPTER 11

Prelude: In a Dark Valley

Robert Bryan is a balding, moonfaced San Francisco criminal lawyer in his early fifties. He cut his legal teeth fighting for civil rights in his native Alabama, specializes in murder cases, and doubles as a local television commentator. A newly minted Catholic, he was born a Baptist, and when he warms to a topic, his southern accent grows a little more pronounced, his gestures become a little more florid, and his voice takes on a preacher's edge. Bryan was in full rhetorical flight on a spring night in 1995, standing in the low-ceilinged basement of the Holy Trinity Russian Orthodox Church in the city's fashionable Pacific Heights section, railing to some three dozen people gathered around on folding metal chairs about "corruption" in the San Francisco Archdiocese and the "un-Christlike men" who run the local Church.

Bryan was rallying the flagging spirits of the stalwarts of the Save St. Brigid Committee. The little group was meeting in the Orthodox church basement because they were not allowed to use archdiocesan facilities. They were the core members of the several hundred parishioners who had rallied in a futile effort to prevent the closing of their church the previous year. St. Brigid is a 134-year-old San Francisco landmark, one of the city's finest Gothic churches, a relic from the grand old days of the local Irish Catholic Ascendancy. (Unfortunately for the St. Brigid committee, the church had not yet been legally designated a landmark, although it had nearly completed the designation process when the closure order came.) There was Nellie Echavarria, an elderly Filipino, whose speeches from the floor were even more fiery than Bryan's; Chuck O'Meehan, a World War II flying ace; Lily Wong, a blind Burmese, who led the group in an almost ecstatic opening prayer; a young doctor and his wife, two engineers, a Chinese student, a couple who ran a bakery shop.

For a full year, St. Brigid parishioners wore white towels to Mass as a sign of protest, organized fund-raising drives, and hired their own engineers to challenge the archdiocese's structural studies. For one stretch, Bryan spoke after every Sunday Mass, until his microphone was cut off, and two consecutive pastor-sympathizers were transferred. Gregory Peck, a long-ago St. Brigid parishioner, wrote a letter of support. On the night of the closing, June 30, 1994, the parishioners held a candlelight vigil in the church until they were finally cleared out by the police. There was no resistance or violence, although one of their number managed to get into the bell tower and peal a last carillon. And when it was over, and the great door had been padlocked, they huddled outside and wept. Almost a year later, they were still carrying on the fight. They had hired a Vatican lawyer, and Bryan's law office file drawers were stuffed with Latin motions and briefs. The first appeal to the Vatican had been rejected, but at the basement meeting, Bryan exuded confidence about the status of their next appeal, to Cardinal José Sanchez, the prefect of the Congregation for the Clergy, the last legal recourse. He urged a letter-writing campaign to Cardinal Sanchez and to the Pope.

Credit: Siu-Mei Wong

The "Save St. Brigid's" committee marching in the 1996 San Francisco St. Patrick's Day parade. The committee, which sprang up to prevent the closing of a cherished old church, hired a Vatican lawyer to pursue its case in Rome. Similar protests have popped up throughout the country, as financial pressure has forced the Church to scale back its institutional presence.

"This has been the worst year in the history of the archdiocese," sighed a highly placed chancery official. Fights over church closings are nothing new, and Bryan's heroics are squarely in the tradition of the parish trustees who drove John Hughes to distraction. But St. Brigid was only the most adroitly publicized of a series of struggles over church closings and service curtailments. Worse, they came on top of a seemingly endless string of sexual and financial scandals that added bite to Bryan's corruption charges and, collectively, suggested a diocese in organizational *extremis*.

Overlapping the church closing controversies, it was revealed that Martin Greenlaw, a prominent pastor, known for his excellent preaching and absurd toupee, had been found beaten almost to death in his home. But most parishioners hadn't known that Greenlaw, who had just redecorated his rectory, owned a luxurious home, one with a gazebo-style hot tub and, according to police sources, an extensive collection of pornographic videotapes. A flood of revelations suggested that Greenlaw was at the center of a ring of homosexual San Francisco priests—his rectory was known as the "Pink Palace" or the "Lavender Rectory." Much more damning in sexually liberated San Francisco was that Greenlaw, for many years in two separate parishes, had been surrounded by rumors of financial irregularities—mysterious burglaries that resulted in large amounts of cash magically disappearing from the parish safe without any sign of forced entry; missing parish endowment funds; long profitable bingo evenings that suddenly began losing money; financial bequests that never made it into the parish bank accounts; a personal lifestyle marked by heavy drinking and flashy entertaining. (Greenlaw later pleaded guilty to embezzling more than $200,000.)

Then one of the city's most respected pastors, Monsignor Patrick O'Shea, a classic Spencer Tracy priest, with a square jaw and iron-gray hair, was arrested for sexual abuse of nine boys, and conceivably many more, over a stretch of twenty-two years. The charges against O'Shea portray a cold-hearted predator who routinely took altar boys for weekends of waterskiing at his lakeside trailer home with flattered parents' enthusiastic permission; and who then plied them with liquor—some of the boys were only nine—before using them sexually. Like a homosexual Humbert Humbert, he allegedly took a thirteen-year-old boy on a nightmare six-week tour of Europe, including a meeting with the Pope, abusing him in every country except Ireland, where they stayed with O'Shea's relatives.

Scandals broke one on top of the other. A civil suit by a group of former altar boys named the archdiocese, the diocese of Santa Rosa, which is part of the San Francisco province, O'Shea, and three other priests from San Francisco and Santa Rosa, charging pedophilic abuse. (The two dioceses eventually paid a $2.5 million settlement.) The papers bannered the suicide of a young man who had been sexually exploited by "Brother Sal," a Salesian teaching brother who had admitted his offenses and been sentenced to prison.

The young man's parents blamed the suicide on the archdiocese's failure to live up to its commitments to provide mental health treatment. It was revealed that the archdiocese may have paid out $1 million to Brother Sal's victims.

The *San Francisco Examiner* and a local radio station, KGO, assigned teams of reporters to ferret out clerical wrongdoing. For a time, KGO maintained a "clerical abuse hot line" to solicit Catholic complaints, and the *Examiner* ran a three-day exposé, accompanied by a series of blistering editorials—"An Archdiocese in Denial"; "Sex, the Church, and the Cops." The reporters claimed that the archdiocese had been tipped off to Greenlaw's behavior "double-digit times," in the words of Stephanie Salter, one of the *Examiner* team, and that O'Shea's behavior had persisted too long for there not to have been rumors. The stories tied the church-closing campaign to sloppy fiscal practices—several millions lost in a failed senior housing project, spending $1.7 million from a diocesan building fund to finance the Pope's 1987 visit to the city, the carelessness that allowed the anomalies in Greenlaw's accounts to be overlooked for so long. The church closings were treated as a grab for $3 million in parish bank accounts, which automatically reverted to the archdiocese. Later it was revealed that an archdiocesan study estimated that the land value of all the closed parishes was $43 million, after deducting the costs of land clearance and a sale. Salter, a recent convert—all the investigative reporters were Catholic—was a member of Greenlaw's parish and says she worried about hurting the Church, "until the little old ladies started patting me on the back. Even some old nuns! They'd say, 'Keep it up. Somebody's finally catching up to those guys.' "

That the Church establishment was rocked on its heels by the media assault is an understatement. San Francisco has always been a Catholic town, arguably the sole major western outpost of Northeast-style Catholicism. The Catholic political and business establishment rivals New York's or Chicago's. There is the same thick web of Catholic institutions and the same granite minicathedrals on every fourth or fifth street corner. The 1849 gold rush drew a steady stream of ambitious Irish immigrants like Eugene Kelly, who made his first fortune in San Francisco before returning to New York to advise John Hughes and John McCloskey on their cathedral. The journey to the Pacific was at least as daunting as that from Europe—many San Franciscan Irish, in fact, were second-stage emigrants from Australia—so a rough natural selection ensured that San Francisco's immigrants were best-of-breed. As early arrivers, they faced little discrimination and were economically and socially successful from the start. The Italian immigrants who followed a generation later were in the same mold and became successful farmers and vintners, or even tycoons like A. P. Giannini, who founded the Bank of Italy (its name was later changed to the Bank of America) in 1904 and was a pillar of the local Church. Critical media and rebellious parishes were something new in San Franciscan Catholicism.

The archdiocese argues, with some justice, that it was blindsided by events. San Francisco's longtime archbishop, John Raphael Quinn, precise, erudite, in his midsixties, was one of the hierarchy's brightest stars until he reportedly ran afoul of Rome for his outreach to San Francisco's gay community. A former president of the national bishops' conference, he is much respected by his peers. But a modern archbishop does not control his priests the way, say, Cardinal Dougherty did in Philadelphia. Clerical sexual lapses that are not illegal—Greenlaw, for example, is alleged to be a homosexual, not a pedophiliac—are treated as a matter for the confessional, not for banishment. Financial controls, such as they are, assume that priests are trustworthy—most parish income is in cash, and funds management is highly decentralized. Senior officials insist that the allegations about O'Shea were deeply shocking and that they had never heard a hint that he was a pedophiliac. The church-closing decisions were made after an elaborate review that took into account the cost of state-mandated seismic upgrading of vulnerable churches and the lamentable trends in religious practice. Mass attendance in San Francisco is less than half of what it was twenty years ago.

San Francisco chancery officials, in fact, impress one as unusually intelligent and innovative. It was the first diocese in the country, perhaps in the world, to have a woman chancellor, Sr. Mary B. Flaherty, who among her many roles has been in charge of priest evaluation and assignment. Quinn's sympathetic approach to the local gay community has been much admired. The archdiocese is engaged in an extensive and, it would appear, a reasonably participative planning effort to reconfigure the archdiocese for an era of fewer priests and shrinking resources. (In the fall of 1995, Quinn announced that he would retire in the new year, to be replaced by a more conservative bishop, William Levada, from Portland, Oregon. The Vatican has gone out of its way to emphasize that Quinn was not forced out of the archdiocese. For his part, Quinn absolutely denies that he was ever in Vatican disfavor, although he freely admits that the San Francisco media assault has been exhausting. He will—most happily, one suspects—pursue liturgical studies at Oxford at the request of the Pope.)

Still, a first-rate team has managed to appear consistently ham-handed and bumbling. In the church-closing disputes, apparently reasonable proposals* from affected parishioners were repeatedly rejected once decisions

* St. Brigid parishioners are relatively affluent, and Bryan's group promised to raise funds for a seismic upgrading. (The diocese's cost estimate seems to have been exaggerated.) When that proposal was rejected as expected, they offered to raise the money for St. Brigid and for *any other church* that the archbishop designated. Rejecting the second proposal appears merely bullheaded. Chancery officials argue that, while St. Brigid was solvent, the trends pointed ineluctably to future problems, and they did not believe that Bryan could live up to his fund-raising commitments. Perhaps it is only the wisdom of hindsight that suggests that a more politically sensitive, "messier" process, involving temporary extensions to test the committee's fund-raising prowess, might have accomplished the same result with less confrontation and adverse publicity.

were made. The history of the inquiries on Greenlaw suggests reflexive wagon-circling. Parishioners who could not "prove" an allegation were given short shrift, and the investigations themselves were cursory. Despite the long history of complaints about Greenlaw's lifestyle and financial carelessness, he was steadily moved into more responsible positions, handling large amounts of diocesan funds. One of the charges against him was that he wrote himself a check for $45,000 from the mission fund, which suggests a risible lack of financial controls. And while there is no suggestion that the archdiocese ever consciously protected pedophilia, O'Shea's high rank seems to have immunized him from suspicion. Ears and eyes were not tuned to pick up what must have been decades of clues.

A Church in Crisis?

The travails of the San Francisco archdiocese are merely one of the more striking examples of the American Church's precipitate fall from public grace. San Francisco chancery officials all began their careers at a time when the prestige and moral authority of Catholicism was at its highest peak, when priests and nuns took for granted that they would be treated with deference, sympathy, and respect, and bishops and cardinals basked in the press's unabashed tribute. It is perhaps understandable, therefore, that they should watch in paralytic disbelief as one scandal after another broke over their heads, that their reactions to media criticisms would be clumsy and defensive, that their anxiety to protect their Church's good name would exceed their zeal to ferret out wrongdoing. The three-plus decades since John Kennedy's death have not been kind to institutions of all varieties. But few have suffered so wrenching a reversal as the American Catholic Church, not only in its public image, but even more corrosively, in its own self-perception.

The steep descent of public regard for the Church can be traced in the movie and television image of Catholic priests. The Tracy/O'Brien/Crosby all-around good guy gave way in the 1970s to the semimagical shaman of *The Exorcist* and its imitators, and finally to the more recent, and utterly devastating, stereotype of priest as arrogant hypocrite. ABC's *The Thorn Birds* (1983) is one of commercial television's all-time successful miniseries. Richard Chamberlain's priest, after a dalliance that leaves his partner pregnant, returns to the fold but, it is clear, more in service of his ambition than his faith. In Fox Television's *Models, Inc.* (1994), one of the stars becomes pregnant by a priest. He excoriates her for considering an abortion but refuses to marry her or recognize his child. He returns to his rectory, and she, sadder but wiser, has the abortion. The Canadian Film Board's *The Boys of St. Vincent's* (1994), based on a true story, was shown on Canadian public television, in selected American movie theaters, and on a national American cable network. It is a harrowing portrayal of systematic sexual abuse of young boys by almost the entire staff of religious brothers in a Catholic orphanage. Watching the helplessness of the boys and the refusal of the police and diocesan authorities to intervene is almost unbearably painful. Disney/Miramax's *Priest* (1995) offers a cold and autocratic bishop, an alcoholic ex-pastor, a pastor sleeping with his housekeeper, and a homosexual curate. Ironically, although *Priest* is one of the few recent movies to draw organized Catholic protests, it is also a rare sympathetic portrait of a believing priest. The curate, who is sincerely committed to his faith and to his priestly vows, is plunged into despair after a sexual lapse and exposure, but he resolves to struggle on for the love of Christ.

A long list of dismal statistics fleshes out a Dorian Gray portrait of a Church crippled by the weight of its own sins—sins of avarice, of pomp, of

Credit: Photofest

A radically revised movie image of the priest is an index of the Church's loss of public esteem. In the 1995 movie Priest, *Linus Roache* (left) *plays a homosexual curate tormented by his breaches of celibacy, while Tom Wilkinson's pastor* (center) *is sleeping with his housekeeper, played by Cathy Tyson.*

pride, of sensuality within the very fortress of celibacy. The fight over St. Brigid in San Francisco is just a ripple in a wave of service cutbacks that has been rolling across the country—thirty-eight parishes in Chicago, thirty-three in Detroit, almost a third of all parishes in Pittsburgh. The merger of parishes to save money has been pushed so far in Seattle—the diocese has lost a third of its priests—that priests talk derisively of "Christ the King-Dome" megaparishes. Aging monuments to the American Church's imperial era—massive gilt-domed cathedrals, the Gothic sprawl of diocesan seminaries, the tattered grandeur of urban rectories and convents—loom uselessly and expensively, draining away the dwindling stream of money from the faithful.

Over the last two decades or so, a fifth of all priests have resigned their ministries. One out of every ten parishes has no resident priest. The wellspring of new candidates for the priesthood is drying up: in 1966, there were almost 9000 young men in the "theologate"—the last four years of seminary training; today there are only a third as many, although there are many more Catholics. With the exodus of younger priests, and the dearth of new recruits, the average age of American priests is now about fifty-five. Within the next decade or so, as death and retirement work their ravages, the ratio of priests to Catholics will drop to only half of what it was in the 1960s. The demographics of the convent are even worse. Only 11 percent of nuns are under forty-five, and more than a quarter are over seventy. Indeed, there are now almost as many *ex*-nuns in America as nuns. In the 1940s and 1950s, mothers superior paid sales calls on local pastors to find places for their overflowing crops of new sisters. Now, with the unfunded retirement cost of aging religious approaching $7 billion, they wonder how to care for the generation of old nuns who have been left behind.

Whispers swirl of a breakdown in clerical sexual discipline, of vows honored more often in the breach, of an immature, possibly homosexually oriented clergy, "working out their adolescent crises," in Andrew Greeley's phrase, behind a celibate masquerade. Catholic priests have been identified by some health officials as an important subpopulation at risk for AIDS. The pedophilia cases have been, perhaps, the most demoralizing. Some hundreds of priests have been identified as child sexual abusers, the worst of whom were predatory monsters who victimized dozens, even hundreds, of children—James Porter in Massachusetts and Minnesota, Thomas Adamson in Minnesota, Gilbert Gauthe in Louisiana, staff at the Franciscan seminary in California and at the Christian Brother orphanage in Toronto (the model for *The Boys of St. Vincent's*), where abuse was almost a part of the institutional routine. One ex-priest growled, "Parishioners breathe a sigh of relief when father brings his girlfriend to the parish picnic. At least their kids are safe." Legal settlements have been expensive; the diocese of Albuquerque contemplated filing for bankruptcy because of the sexual abuse claims.

The Church is ripped with theological dissensus. The rejection by rank-and-file Catholics of much of their Church's official teaching on sexual and personal morality has long been a staple of the daily press. But even more fundamental dogmas are losing their hold on the laity—fewer than half of the most faithful Catholics, those who attend Mass every Sunday, report that they believe in the Real Presence of Christ in the Eucharist, one of the Church's bedrock dogmas. Less well known is the fact that the clergy is more often aligned with the laity. Surveys from the mid-1980s found that fewer than 20 percent of the younger clergy believed that birth control is always wrong; fewer than 40 percent thought that homosexuality or premarital sex are always wrong. Older priests were more conforming to the official line, but not dramatically so. Almost a third of the younger clergy did *not* agree that the "Catholic church is the one, true church established by Christ," and almost no priest under forty-five believed that doubting one article of faith calls the whole of religion into question.

The contrast between the rigid Church teachings on divorce and the enthusiasm with which many dioceses hand out annulments reeks of hypocrisy—the American Church accounts for the vast majority of all the annulments issued in the world, on grounds as slender as "immaturity" at the time of contracting marriage. Slanging matches between theological liberals and conservatives sometimes feel like street fights between metaphysical Crips and Bloods. And they spill over from academia to eat away at the souls of loyal Catholics. Bob Smith is a devout Angeleno who runs a car-leasing business with his son. He attends an early-morning prayer meeting every Thursday with other Catholic businessmen and serves on the diocesan financial council. When their priest abruptly left the parish for a woman, Smith and his wife organized a lay management team and kept the parish going until a replacement was found. But when Smith was selected to receive the Eucharist from the Pope during John Paul II's 1987 West Coast tour, he told a shocked chancery caller, "Let me pray on that for a day." "This Pope has caused so much pain," Smith says; but he decided to participate anyway—"after all, it *is* the Blessed Sacrament."

The American Church is in serious trouble. Indeed, if its situation were as dire as sometimes portrayed in the muckraking Catholic press (notably, the *National Catholic Reporter* on the left and the *Wanderer* on the right), it would be an institution in death throes—one would avert the eyes, call for last sacraments, say pious prayers, drape cathedrals in black. But things are not quite so extreme as that.

In the remainder of the book, I will argue that despite its undeniable problems there is still much that is hopeful in the Church. Fewer Catholics go to church, but parish life is far more vibrant, far more participative, than it ever was in the Church's glory days. Laypeople no longer take their pastor's word as law, but the American laity is also far more theologically informed, far better able to uphold their end of a discussion and make informed moral decisions, than any laity in Catholic history. The bricks-and-mortar overhang from the Church's triumphal period is still a serious financial drain, but it is under much better control than just a few years ago, and religious orders are facing up to, and beginning to work off, their retirement liabilities—there are no elderly nuns eating out of garbage pails. Many priests have left, but resignations have dropped sharply from their peak. The pedophilia scandals finally appear to be winding down, and there are reasons to hope that dioceses have learned valuable lessons about honesty and about the consequences of pretending not to see catastrophes that are staring you in the face.

The truly serious issues facing the Church, however, are not about numbers, money, or even the rate of weekly church attendance. The truly hard problems are in the realm of vision, theology, and purpose. In practical terms, they come down to three issues, all of which overlap. The first is about the limits of authority and the limits of dissent, which includes, but is certainly not restricted to, questions about sexual morality and reproductive ethics. The second is about the role of women in the Church. And the third, which overlaps with both of the others, is about the future of the ministry. These are especially hard questions in America. Over the last century, by almost any measure, the American Church has been, by leagues, the most vigorous and successful of the national Catholic churches. But the American democratic tradition is much different from—some would say incompatible with—the long-standing traditions of the Vatican and of the world Church. The rigid separatism of the Church in America during its triumphal era obscured these differences, but they can be obscured no longer.

The good news is that, hard as these problems are, good leaders should be able to solve them. Setting out a coherent vision and purpose, after all, is what leaders are for. Further, although the problems can be formulated in many different ways, with many different shadings of emphasis, almost all of the many people I talked to in researching this part of the book agreed that these issues, or something very much like them, are the key ones.

The bad news is that the leadership of the Church—and I define leadership to include a much wider group of people than just the Pope and his closest advisers in the Vatican—is very far from reaching a coherent, consistent resolution of these questions, one that the vast majority of the leaders themselves can endorse, and believe, and preach with conviction. Instead of civil discourse, there is more often unrestrained mutual recrimination. And as long as its leadership remains divided, angry, and confused, the Church will continue in crisis, despite all the goodwill and high hopes of the people in the parishes.

CHAPTER 12

At the End of a Century

St. Thomas the Apostle Church, in one of the poorest parishes in Los Angeles, was packed on a soft spring night in 1994, with the crowd spilling out the front door and around the block. The faces looked mostly Indian, and the people were short and square—Nicaraguans, Salvadorans, Bolivians, Hondurans, southern Mexicans. Fr. Dennis O'Neill, the pastor, guessed that the majority were illegals. They were very young, and mostly in family groups. There were as many men as women and large numbers of teenagers. I had never been in a church as noisy. Besides the chorus of squalling babies and the low din of Spanish chatter, the whole church seemed in happy motion, with a constant milling up and down the aisles and in and out of the church. There was a choir and a six-piece orchestra—a trumpet, two guitars, an electric piano, drums, and a marimba—and the music was catchy and complicated. The Mass, offered by a guest priest from Nicaragua, was mostly sung, and the congregation's responses were loud and confident. Even my hotel Spanish could pick out the main theme of the homily—Christ is *love!* Christ is *family!* Christ is *sacrament!*—drummed repetitively home. Delightfully, the homilist got an appreciative round of applause at the sermon's end. Almost everyone plunked a dollar into both collections—St. Thomas, poor as it is, is a solvent parish—and almost everyone received the Eucharist. Almost all of the Eucharistic ministers were women, in flowing white robes. (Before Vatican II, the reform council that met from 1962 through 1965, only the priest, with his specially consecrated hands, was permitted to touch the communion host. Communion is now usually administered by lay people, who typically place the host in the communicant's hands instead of on the tongue. The crowding of lay Eucharistic ministers, especially female ministers, around the altar before Communion is one of the most symbolically fraught of the Vatican II reforms.)

Thursday night is the Charismatic service at St. Thomas. When the Mass ended, and the priest had proceeded out of the church, a handsome young man in a gray suit and dark tie strode to the front with a microphone and started a rousing chorus of a song that went on for twenty minutes, like a round, with the leader adding phrases, piling repetitions one on the other. The congregation clasped hands and swayed to the music. A preacher moved to the altar, the music dropped to a background ostinato, and, eyes closed, another man supporting him as he swayed, the preacher pealed out the same phrases as the homilist—*Cristo! Caridad! Familia! Gracias, Señor! Gracias, Señor!* More music, and more preachers followed one after the other. The congregation, people with the most tenuous grip on the lowest rung of the American economic ladder, with sunburned faces, hard bodies, and callused hands, swayed and sang, lost in ecstatic prayer. I had brought a friend for the sake of another pair of eyes, a Jewish editor for whom I write newspaper columns. After about an hour, we worked our way through the rapt singers and the twined hands. "That was wonderful," she said when we were outside. "That really *worked!*" It is hard to imagine what more could be asked from religion.

Spring Hill is in the heart of America's gerontopolis, the Medicare culture of south Florida, where clinics dot the shopping malls, grocery clerks speak sl-ow-ly and loudly, and people in a movie line exchange glucose readings. St. Frances Cabrini Church is a huge modernistic structure that swoops up from a promontory near a highway like an Eero Saarinen airport. It holds 2000 people, and the Saturday afternoon Mass, one much favored by seniors, was a sea of white hair, with hardly a seat to be had. The majority of the congregation appeared to be in their late seventies; genuflections were just a stiff bob of the head and twitch of the knee. These were classic "pre–Vatican II" Catholics, brought up to thumb their beads during Latin Masses on distant altars, but Mass at St. Frances is highly participative, and they seemed to enjoy it, declaiming the responses clearly and firmly. The music was interesting, with a good (female) cantor. It got steadily more complicated as the liturgy progressed, but most of the congregation managed their parts all the way through.

The homily, by the associate pastor, Fr. Richard Allen, a portly man with a graying full beard, was superb. As many priests now do, Allen left the altar and paced up and down the aisle as he preached—an effective bit of theater made possible in large churches by shirt-button microphones. The text was

from Luke 17—Jesus cures ten lepers, but only the Samaritan, a Judean un-
touchable, returns to thank him—and Allen expanded on the notion of out-
groups, keeping it gentle, speaking of Gypsies and Jews. But just as the
congregation seemed to relax, having gotten off lightly, he skewered them
with a comment on the O. J. Simpson trial, which had concluded that week.
"You are hearing your friends make racial comments. But you are Catholic,
and Catholics *don't do that.*" The jolt in the church was almost visible, as
embarrassed old men and women sat upright and blinked.

Later, the entire congregation joined hands during the recitation of the
Lord's Prayer. Older people are supposed to detest touchy-feely modernistic
liturgies, but the elderly lady next to me reached out and firmly took my
hand in hers. When it was time for the kiss of peace, a lean septuagenarian in
the pew ahead turned, took both my arms in her hands, fixed her bright blue
eyes on my face, and in a tone that brooked no argument, declared that "*good
health* (a liturgical concession to south Florida) and the peace of the Lord"
would always be with me. All but a dozen or so of the 2000 congregants received the Eucharist. I counted eighteen Eucharistic ministers, most of them
women, dispersed throughout the church to keep the lines manageable. The
liturgy took about an hour and fifteen minutes, a good half hour longer than
the typical pre–Vatican II Mass, but no one seemed to mind.

St. Cecilia's parish center in suburban Houston spreads over an area the size
of a couple of city blocks—parking lots, ball fields, school, community center, parish offices, a large, modern church, all well-maintained and fairly new.
Coiffed and groomed professionals and their well-dressed children crowd
the ten o'clock family Mass and turn out more than a thousand strong to volunteer for the parish's ninety-six-odd lay ministries—feeding the homeless,
running Bible classes, staffing youth trips. The pastor, Msgr. Vincent Rizzotto, who is in his early sixties, does triple duty as diocesan vicar-general
and chief liturgist. St. Cecilia's registers 9000 Catholics, and Rizzotto has
only two assistants. Houston's ratio of priests to Catholics, only about a third
of the proportion in big northeastern dioceses, is typical for the Southwest.
"I could make do with one less priest," said Rizzotto, "as long as I had some
help on weekends. We had far too many priests in the old days."

"Father Rizzotto acts like any good CEO," said Nancy Evetts, an ac-
countant who heads the parish finance council. "If you want something to
happen in the parish, it's up to you to do it. And he'll make it easy, he's a
good facilitator. But he's clearly the boss. He has a vision for the parish and
he keeps us moving in that direction." Evetts was part of a fluid group of a
dozen-plus parishioners who were gathered in the parish center after Mass

on a pleasant October Sunday morning to talk about their parish and their religion. Joan Powers, a widow who had been master of ceremonies at the Mass, said, "We have a lot of activities here, but the liturgy comes first. The Eucharist and the Mass are at the center of everything. When I first started getting involved in the parish, Father Rizzotto said to me, 'What is the most important part of the Church?' I said, 'The liturgy.' And he said, 'That's the right answer.' "

The St. Cecilia's parishioners at the meeting ranged in age from sixteen to midsixties, but most of them were in their late thirties to early fifties, baby boomers, a generation removed from the stereotype of the Catholic blue-collar worker. They were professionals or business people, and almost all were college graduates, including two Hispanic women who were spear-heading an outreach program to the parish's growing contingent of Hispanic families. I was surprised to count four converts. (They are called RCIA grad-uates, for Rite of Christian Initiation for Adults.) Jay Chaffee was raised as a Presbyterian, but he became interested in the Church because his wife is Catholic. "There is good Invitation to Inquire here," he said. "And after a while I joined an Inquiry class. It was a tremendous program, a year long. Thirty-eight of us started, and thirty-two went all the way. We joined the community in a ceremony last Easter." Lillian Wald said, "Father Rizzotto recruits a lot of lay leaders from RCIA. He comes and says, 'Well, you've spent all this time and effort to join the Church, and now how do you plan to be involved?' " Available statistics suggest that the rate of conversions in America may be at its highest level ever.

St. Cecilians enjoy the intellectual side of Catholicism. Two hundred and fifty people signed up for an eighteen-month-long program on Catholic theology and the catechism, featuring lecturers from the diocesan seminary. Eighty-five finished the entire course. Most of the people around the table had read the major texts from Vatican II, they knew about innovative theolo-gians like Karl Rahner, and they could talk about "People of God" theology espoused at Vatican II and the new importance of the laity. The *Catechism of the Catholic Church,* a new 1000-plus-page compendium of Catholic doc-trine, was originally planned as a reference work to help bishops develop local doctrinal manuals for lay people. In its first year of publication in 1994, the American edition sold 2.5 million copies. (But you couldn't find it on the best-seller lists.) By 1995, total sales were in the 4 million range, or about one for every five Catholic households.

Most of the St. Cecilians told of falling away from religion at some point in their lives, and some had been divorced. They had come back to the Church looking for spiritual stability, a reference point for ordering their lives. The weekly liturgy puts them in touch with the cosmic and eternal, shrinks their daily struggles, lends perspective. The words "community" and "family" came up frequently. "When I come to Mass on Sunday," said John Carter, "there are hundreds of people in the church, and when I look around, I know most of them. It's a good feeling."

A months-long tour of some two dozen American parishes is an antidote for too-gloomy assessments of the state of the Church. St. Monica's in Santa Monica, California, is the church that Leo McCarey used as the setting for *Going My Way*, but it is surrounded by palm trees, instead of studio-set tenement houses, and is only blocks from a surfing beach. Shucking off the Barry Fitzgerald image, St. Monica's has become a "young adult" parish, and the Sunday evening Mass looked like a *Baywatch* convention, packed with more than 1000 almost uniformly blond and tanned young adult singles and couples. ("Young adult" is clearly a term of art encompassing anyone up to the age of, say, forty-three, who chooses to be so defined.)

Msgr. Lloyd Torgerson, the pastor of St. Monica's and also a serious amateur cyclist, may be the best preacher I encountered. When I visited, the old church had been closed for earthquake repairs and Masses were celebrated in the round in the gymnasium. Torgerson, like Spring Hill's Allen, walked easily around the hall as he spoke. He led off with the day's Gospel story—Jesus allowing a glimpse of his divinity to some of his Apostles—made a brief excursus into the archaeology of the Sinai, then segued neatly into the present day, with quotes from Camus and C. S. Lewis, winding up with the moral lesson from the Gospel. The entire performance, about twenty minutes long, was reminiscent of a Bishop Sheen television lecture, without quite the crisply timed ending. At one point, Torgerson said, "I have another book for you," and the congregation laughed. But he did—Torgerson gives his young adult congregations reading lists and arranges for the books to be sold at the church. The people at the Mass were clearly regulars.

St. Monica's illustrates a new phenomenon in Catholicism—Catholics now *choose* their parishes. Torgerson's Sunday Eucharist attendances are far larger than his registrants, because he draws from all over the area. Pastors are beginning to think competitively, much as Protestant ministers have always done. The lay pastoral associates at St. Monica's, Delis Alejandro and John Simbeck, and the liturgist, Tom Franzak, had all tried up to a half-dozen other parishes before settling at the parish. When I visited, they were working on improving their "market segmentation"—a quiet liturgy for older people; better child care facilities for the nine o'clock family Mass; Bible studies geared to the young adults.

Franzak, like many lay liturgists I met, is a professional musician, and successful parishes pay a lot of attention to their liturgical music. There is a puritanical streak in American Catholicism that resists polished liturgical performances, as if they draw attention from the main point of the ceremony. But pastors like Torgerson argue that their parishioners deserve a high-quality liturgy and have a right to go elsewhere if they don't get it. The great medieval liturgical tradition would seem to be on Torgerson's side.

Old St. Patrick's in downtown Chicago is a lavishly gilded, massive old church that was once the religious headquarters of Irish Chicago. When the present pastor, Msgr. Jack Wall, arrived there fifteen years ago, there were *four* parishioners, and the church was slated for closing. Wall has turned it into a young adult church like St. Monica's. Both he and his assistant, Fr. John Cusick, are excellent preachers, and the Mass I attended was as packed, and as alive, as Torgerson's was. At a coffee after Mass, I asked a thirtysomething young man how he had found the parish. He said, "I used to go a great church in California, so when I was moving out here, I asked the pastor to recommend a parish." I said, "You used to go to St. Monica's." He asked, "How did you know?" (I affected casual omniscience.)

People drive from all over Seattle to make the sung Mass at St. James Cathedral, where the entry procession features an incense bearer and a rafter-rattling "Holy God, We Praise Thy Name," a throwback to the days before Catholics discovered folk guitars. And on the same weekend I visited Katie Doyle from the St. James parish as she set up tables at a homeless men's shelter with food prepared by the parishioners. Mexican couples with mobs of small children filled the aisles at La Placita, the barrio church near Los Angeles's downtown, for the Sunday morning mariachi Mass. The parking lot was impenetrable an hour before the liturgy, and the sprawling plaza outside, with colorful food, concession stands, and strolling players was almost as crowded as the church.

At St. Peter's school, in a gang-ridden neighborhood in San Francisco, neatly uniformed seventh graders, all of them Hispanic, stood up and greeted me with a beaming "Good morning!" before returning immediately to their algebra exercises, writing the answers in neat, Catholic-school columns. A continent away, amid the human wreckage of Brooklyn's Bedford-Stuyvesant, the halls of St. John the Baptist School are contented and quiet; there is exactly the same self-directed, studious, *happy* atmosphere as at St. Peter's. On Catholic campuses, theology courses are one of the hottest offerings. According to the campus ministry at Notre Dame, some 80 to 90 percent of the Catholic students, who account for 86 percent of the student body, go to Mass every Sunday.

The Church may be in trouble, but at least as far as the laity is concerned, the funereal gloom that one so often encounters in chancery offices or at theology conferences seems excessive. Fr. Richard John Neuhaus, one of the Church's leading conservative intellectuals, is a former Lutheran minister who converted in 1990. "I preach in a lot of different parishes," he said, "and I'm always astounded at the energy at Mass in these big thousand-person churches, all the families and their children, the intensity of the Eucharistic prayer. There's nothing like it in the mainstream Protestant churches. Then in the afternoon, I go over to the rectory to have a drink with the pastor, and he's got a long face and tells a gloomy story about how everything's falling apart, how nothing's like it used to be." Neuhaus and Fr. Andrew Greeley, who is one of the Church's most outspoken liberals, are rarely on the same side of an argument, but they are on this one. "Parishes may be stronger than ever," Greeley said. "Catholics have never been as informed and active and involved. The problem isn't the grassroots."

At the Grassroots

More Americans call themselves Roman Catholics, by far, than claim allegiance to any other religion. There are some 50 to 60 million American Catholics, depending on whether one follows parish reports (the lower figure) or census data. Overall, Catholics make up some 25 to 28 percent of the American population. Protestants of all denominations still enjoy about a 2:1 membership edge over Catholics, but Catholics outnumber the largest single Protestant denomination, the Baptists, by about 3.5:1. (There are more *lapsed* Catholics than Baptists.) Catholicism is also the only one of the so-called mainstream religions—Methodism, Lutheranism, Presbyterianism, Congregationalism, and Episcopalianism—to enjoy continued growth. The rest have all seen rapid declines in their membership as they have lost "market share" to the evangelical and Pentecostal sects, like Southern Baptists and the Assemblies of God. The Catholic share of the population is continuing to grow slowly, fueled by a high rate of Catholic, especially Hispanic, immigration. Because of the continued importance of immigrants in the Catholic population, Catholics are somewhat younger than the rest of the country. About a third of America's eighteen- to twenty-nine-year-olds call themselves Catholic.

ETHNICITY

The American Church is more multiethnic than ever. Fewer than 14 percent of American Catholics identify themselves as Irish Americans, and even fewer as Italian, German, or Polish Americans, the other traditional white Catholic ethnic groups. Hispanics of all national origins—but predominantly of Mexican and Puerto Rican descent—are now the largest single Catholic subpopulation. The actual number of Hispanic Catholics is subject to much dispute, because of the high percentage of only nominal Catholics in the immigrant Hispanic population. Arriving Hispanics, as a Church spokesman delicately put it, have typically been "sacramentalized," but not "catechized"—meaning that they may not have seen the inside of a church since their christening day.

Hispanic advocates within the Church often claim that more than half of all American Catholics will be of Hispanic origin by the year 2000. The figure seems much too high, and it appears to be derived merely by projecting the Hispanic population for 2000 at 30 to 35 million and assuming that they would all describe themselves as Catholics. Gallup poll data suggest that Hispanics account for only 16 percent of active Catholics—Hispanic advocates claim numbers almost twice as high—but Hispanics are by far the fastest-growing subgroup. The tendency of, say, third-generation Mexican Americans to stop describing themselves as Hispanic makes the numbers game even murkier. Very large numbers of Hispanics—estimates run from 10 to 25 percent—have defected to Protestant Pentecostal churches, which have mounted aggressive recruitment campaigns in all major Hispanic centers. Only some 50 to 60 percent of Hispanic high school seniors identify themselves as Catholic.

Asian immigration has brought small, but significant, populations of Catholic Filipinos, Samoans, Koreans, and Vietnamese. Filipinos are by far the largest group of Asian Catholic migrants, but their style of religion and state of religious practice have more in common with Hispanics than with the highly disciplined Koreans. Finally, black Catholics account for about 3 percent of the Catholic population, a number swelled by substantial emigration from Haiti. Brooklyn is now the American diocese with the largest number of black Catholics, most of them Haitian.

Despite the new weight of Hispanic Catholicism in the West and Southwest and the fabled mobility of Americans, the broad geographic distribution of Catholics has changed only slowly. Some 60 percent of all American Catholics still live in the Northeast or the Midwest, although most have long since left the old industrial cities for middle- and upper-class suburbs. In some New England states, like Connecticut, Rhode Island, and Massachusetts, Catholics are a majority of the population. Because of Hispanic immigration, Los Angeles is a majority-Catholic city, but in other West Coast cities, like San Francisco and San Jose, the Catholic share of the population is about a third, falling to perhaps 15 to 20 percent in the Northwest and to 10 percent or even less throughout most of the South and Southeast. Only 0.8 percent of the people within the borders of the diocese of Knoxville, Tennessee, are Catholic.

American Catholics are not nearly so diverse as their multiple ethnic origins suggest. The vast majority of white non-Hispanic Catholics are now thoroughly assimilated third- and fourth-generation Americans, making the old ethnic distinctions meaningless. Catholic professionals of Polish descent who live in the Chicago suburbs may still come back to Polonia's St. Stanislaus for family weddings, but they, and especially their children, have much more in common with their suburban neighbors than with the old ladies in black headscarves murmuring Polish prayers in the back of the church. Hispanics seem to be following the same assimilationist pattern; about 40 percent of third-generation Mexican Americans, for example, marry non-Hispanics. Of even greater significance for religious practice is the fact that about one fifth of all Catholics are married to non-Catholics, a figure that will continue to rise sharply. By the mid-1980s, about 40 percent of newly marrying Catholics were marrying outside the religion.

EDUCATION AND INCOME

The long-term trend of Catholic economic and educational advancement that showed up strongly in the 1950s and 1960s continued into the 1990s, shifting the Church's center of gravity firmly to white middle- and upper-middle-class suburbs. Catholics are wealthier than Protestants, their educational levels are at least as high, and Catholics are more likely than Protestants to be engaged in a professional occupation. Presbyterians and Episcopalians, both rapidly shrinking denominations, are the only Protestants with higher average incomes than Catholics, but even that advantage disappears if the comparison is limited to non-Hispanic Catholics. (The Protestant data, on the other hand, are dragged down by the weight of rural and small-town Baptists.) The only white ethnic/religious group that consistently outstrips Catholics in measures of income, education, and professional attainment is the Jews.

POLITICS

The stereotype of Catholics as political conservatives is reinforced by the prominence of high-profile Catholic spokesmen like New York's Cardinal John O'Connor in the antiabortion movement, the alliance of conservative Catholic politicians like Patrick Buchanan with the Christian right, and lingering memories of Catholic construction workers laying into Vietnam-era antiwar protesters. But all poll data, stretching over many years, show that the stereotype is false. Polls taken in the fall of 1995 showed that only 16 percent of the members of the right-wing Christian Coalition members were Catholics, far less than the Catholic share of the population. On virtually all political issues that divide American liberals and conservatives— welfare standards, aid to the homeless, equal rights for women, minorities, and homosexuals, gun control, defense spending, even school busing to achieve integration—Catholics are more liberal than Protestants, and in most cases more liberal than Protestants of any denomination. Although

Catholics were part of the nationwide swing toward political conservatism during the Reagan years, and again in the 1994 Congressional elections, Catholics are still more likely than Protestants to vote Democratic, particularly in local elections. The rising incomes of Catholics have moved many more Catholics into Republican voting columns, but the shift has been much less than an economic determinist would have predicted. Jews are the only large ethnic/religious group consistently more liberal than Catholics.

Credit: Catholic News Service

The Church's pro-labor policies date from the 1880s and 1890s and Cardinal Gibbons's support of the Knights of Labor. Many priests worked with Cesar Chavez, who organized migrant workers in the 1960s and 1970s, and the American bishops helped mediate the bitter grape-pickers' strike in 1970. Chavez is shown here with Bishop John Roach (left) and one of the Church's leading labor experts, Msgr. George Higgins.

The liberal bias on social issues extends even to Catholics who take the most traditionalist line on issues like contraception and papal authority. The New Deal, pro-union, pro-underdog American Catholic tradition dies hard and is buttressed by a long line of papal encyclicals and other official statements stressing human rights, decent wages, equal education, and worker living standards. Official Catholic teachings have never fit within traditional American liberal-conservative taxonomies. Conservative bishops appointed by Pope John Paul II dominate the National Conference of Catholic Bishops (NCCB)* and espouse a hard line on abortion, homosexuality, and divorce, but in 1995 they were still considerably to the left of even the Clinton administration on issues like welfare reform. The bishops' mid-1980s pastoral letters on the economy and on nuclear arms had a distinctly liberal cast and greatly irritated political conservatives of all religions. (Conservative wags call the NCCB "the Democratic Party at prayer.") Cardinal O'Connor, who is the favorite bête noire of gay activists, regularly does duty in AIDS hospices. In early 1996, during an outcry for a capital sentence for a man arrested for murdering a young policeman, the Cardinal's homily to thousands of policemen assembled for the funeral stressed the Church's opposition to capital punishment.

SEXUAL AND MARITAL BEHAVIOR

On questions of sexual morality, poll data show few discernible differences between lay Protestants and Catholics, despite all the recent efforts of the Pope and the hierarchy to reestablish stricter standards. Catholics practice birth control and regulate the size of their families more or less exactly as Protestants do, and they are somewhat more tolerant of premarital and homosexual sex than Protestants—although the Protestant data are skewed by the increasing weight of the southern evangelicals. The most recent data show that Catholics have slightly fewer children than non-Catholics, but Catholics get divorced at slightly lower rates than non-Catholics and are still slightly, but only slightly, less likely to remarry after divorce. Catholic and Protestant attitudes on abortion are indistinguishable—nine out of ten believe that abortion should be available when the health of the mother is at stake, and four out of ten find abortion acceptable to limit the size of a family.

---

* Contrary to the popular impression of the Church as a more or less totalitarian monolith, it is actually one of the most decentralized large organizations in the country. Diocesan bishops report only to the Pope, and dioceses operate quite independently of one another, except for occasional voluntary schemes like regional self-insurance pools. There are two national coordinating bodies, the United States Catholic Conference (USCC) and the NCCB, but they have little, if any, real authority. (They replace the old National Catholic Welfare Conference. As a practical matter, they work as a single organization with a shared staff.) One consequence, as will be seen, is that there is no central data repository, even on such basics as staffing, membership, and finances.

Catholic opinion data usually lump in practicing and nonpracticing Catholics, so they may overstate the gap between the hierarchy and the practicing laity on moral issues. Catholic University's William D'Antonio and his colleagues have recently analyzed the attitudes of the most committed and religious Catholics, however, and find that even these "core" Catholics exhibit substantial independence on ethical and disciplinary questions. Fifty-nine percent thought one could be a "good Catholic" without obeying the birth control teaching; and on other issues, the percentage who thought it was *not* necessary to follow the official practice were: on abortion, 30 percent; on being married in the Church, 46 percent; on weekly Mass attendance, 49 percent; and on contributing to the Vatican, 71 percent. All these figures have been rising rapidly over the past decade or so. Given the extraordinary energy the hierarchy has devoted to the abortion issue, the rate of defection among the core Church membership seems quite high. Among Catholics who are not so religious but who go to Mass at least monthly, the defection from the official teaching on abortion is 60 percent, and on birth control, 75 percent.

Catholics may still be somewhat more conservative than the rest of the country when it comes to actual sexual practices. Recent studies by Andrew Greeley show that young Catholic women have their first sexual experience somewhat later than young Protestant women do and are less likely to resort to an abortion in the event of an unwanted pregnancy. Both findings are at statistically significant levels. Rates of virginity and low levels of abortion, however, also relate strongly to churchgoing behavior. Since young Catholic women are also more likely to go to church than their Protestant peers, it may be church attendance, rather than religion, that is the explanatory variable. On all issues of sexual behavior, Jews are substantially more permissive than either Protestants or Catholics, while black Baptists are the subpopulation least accepting of abortion.

RELIGIOUS PRACTICE

Poll data turn up consistent differences in how Protestants and Catholics think about their religion. Protestants are much more likely to understand their faith and salvation in terms of a personal relation with Jesus Christ, while Catholics emphasize leading a good life and performing good works. Both attitudes follow directly from the standard self-descriptions of the two traditions. Protestants have always emphasized personal faith and the direct bestowal of grace, while Catholics emphasize the Church as a mediating structure between humanity and God—in effect, climb on the boat, follow the rules, and you'll be okay. Catholics are likely to feel their religion rather less intensely than Protestants, are more likely to envision the Devil as an impersonal evil principle than as a malevolent creature, and to feel less guilty about their sins. Protestants, after all, must expiate their sins by coming to terms with God within the deeps of their own souls, while Catholics can be absolved by a simple confession, or "reconciliation" ritual. ("But if you're a Protestant, how do you know your sins are forgiven?" we would ask in parochial school. "You don't," the nuns would reply grimly.)

The Catholic definition of Church as mediating structure necessarily assigns great weight to liturgies and sacraments, and Catholics are more likely than Protestants to attend church regularly, despite the lower intensity of Catholic religious feeling. For many years, a steady 51 to 53 percent of Catholics have reported to Gallup pollsters that they went to church within the previous week, and about two-thirds go once or twice a month. (Protestants report attendance percentages in the low forties, or about 20 percent lower than Catholics.) Actual weekly Mass attendance, however, is almost certainly lower than the traditional Gallup figures indicate. A more tightly phrased question in a 1993 Gallup poll produced a 41 percent figure, although other polls still showed 50 percent. And a recent series of studies carried out at Notre Dame by Mark Chaves and his colleagues suggest that even the 41 percent figure may be much too high. Chaves compared actual church attendance censuses in a number of dioceses with local Catholic population counts. Overall, he found that not quite 27 percent of local Catholics were actually in church on a given Sunday, although there was considerable variation among dioceses. The discrepancy between the polls and the attendance rosters is probably accounted for by fibs from people who think they *should* go to church every week, but who actually get there less often. Where Chaves had data for Protestants, he found the same gap between poll data and measured attendance—the propensity to tell white lies about going to church, at least, doesn't vary with religious preference.

When I asked pastors to estimate church attendance, most guessed that they had a third, or perhaps slightly more, of their parishioners in church each week, and that their monthly score would be in the 50 to 60 percent range, which is not egregiously higher than the Chaves figures. Parish-level estimates are necessarily imprecise because Catholics are much less likely to register in a parish than they used to be, and as in St. Monica's and Old St. Patrick's, hop from parish to parish to find a liturgical style or a homilist to their liking. By any measure, however, Catholic Mass attendance in America has always been far higher than almost anywhere else in the world except Ireland, and most especially so when compared with traditional "Catholic" countries like France and Italy, or those in Latin America.

WHY THE DECLINE IN ATTENDANCE?

The interpretation of the decline in Catholic church attendance is still controversial. The Gallup data show that the traditional weekly church attendance figure of more than 75 percent dropped to about 70 percent between 1958 to 1964, then began a very steep plunge, especially after 1968, down to the 50-percent-plus level before stabilizing about 1978. A meta-analysis by Greeley and his colleagues suggests that the initial period of decline was mostly age-related. Young people are the least likely of all age groups to go to church, and the early 1960s was the time when the first wave of the baby boomers were entering their midteens. An almost identical decline in Protestant church attendance until about 1965 supports the Greeley hypothesis. From about 1968 on, however, the decline in Catholic church attendance is much steeper than an age-based analysis would predict, and it is a purely Catholic phenomenon. Protestant church attendance stabilized in the mid-1960s and has remained roughly constant, even rising slightly, ever since.

Greeley argues that the post-1968 decline in Catholic church attendance was primarily a reaction to the Vatican's controversial anti-birth-control encyclical, *Humanae Vitae*, which was issued in that year. But Greeley may be placing too much weight on the coincidence of dates. Following Vatican II, skipping Sunday Mass was quietly, if unofficially, dropped from the Catholic catalog of mortal sins. (Whether this was justified or not is the subject of heated theological debates.) Previously, the Church taught that deliberately missing Sunday Mass was a sin punishable by a sentence to Hell for all eternity. It is hardly surprising that removing such an extraordinary sanction would result in many more Catholics sleeping in on Sunday. Rightly or wrongly, most Catholics apparently feel that once- or twice-a-month Mass attendance keeps them in sufficient touch with their religion. The fact that uncoerced Catholic liturgical attendance is still as high as it is underscores the continued centrality of the liturgy in the Catholic imagination.

CORE AND OTHER CATHOLICS

The D'Antonio surveys mentioned earlier allow a more refined view of Catholic religious behavior. Perhaps a third or so of Catholics—estimates range from 20 percent to 40 percent—qualify as highly committed, "core" Catholics, based on the faithfulness of their church attendance, their use of the sacraments, and the importance of religion in their lives. Roughly another third have almost no contact at all with the Church, while the rest fall in the middle group—the once- or twice-a-month Mass attenders, who maintain their religion, but at a lower level of commitment than core Catholics do. The core Catholics tend to be educated baby boomers with families, much like the people at the St. Cecilia's roundtable, with about a 6:4 ratio of women to men. At the other extreme, the "noninvolveds" are much more likely to be single males under thirty-five, the much maligned Generation Xers.

D'Antonio's segmentation helps explain how different analysts can draw apparently opposite conclusions from the same sets of data. If one focuses on raw numbers, like weekly Mass attendance, Catholic religious attachment has clearly fallen off very sharply over the past thirty years or so. On the other hand, the core Catholics are a very large population—at 15 to 20 million they are, by themselves, the country's biggest religious body. And *their* level of engagement with the Church, their active participation in their parishes, their taste for theology and ethical discernment, are at a very high level. On the reasonable assumption that it was mostly core Catholics who bought the new catechism, for example, it must be in almost half their homes—an extraordinary penetration rate for a twenty-dollar book that is still hard to find in bookstores.

The picture I saw during my parish tours, when I met hundreds of parishioners, volunteers, activists, parish priests, and lay ministers in all manner of settings, was very much in line with the poll data on core Catholics. (One doesn't ferret out Catholics who are *un*involved with the Church by hanging around parish halls.) Most of the parishioners I met were middle-class, educated, intelligent, liberal-minded people, with a lively, probing, interest in their religion and in living a better life. To a striking degree, they consistently spoke of the liturgy as the central focus of their religious lives. And a very large number were doing much more than just showing up for Mass.

In some parishes, a third or more of the adults were on a volunteer roster, even if their commitment amounted to only a few hours a year. A survey in the small diocese of Knoxville, Tennessee, found that fully a fifth of all the Catholics in the diocese (not just the adults) were actively involved in some sort of parish work, an extraordinary level of participation, especially when measured by the traditional passivity of American Catholics. Today's Catholics work on finance and school committees, organize youth ministries, teach in Bible studies programs, "mentor" engaged couples, put in nights at homeless shelters, and much more. In one parish, senior citizens and the homebound sign up to pray for a specific number of hours each month for parish causes. Surely, no generation of lay Catholics has ever been so theologically informed, and almost all parishes are experiencing a boom in adult religious education classes. The importance of RCIA conversion programs is striking; in some parishes, even longtime Catholics who have drifted away from the Church are funneled back through RCIA.

These are the Catholics who impress Neuhaus with the energy and intensity of their participation at Mass, and whom Greeley is talking about when he argues that the grassroots are stronger than ever. The ones I met seemed happy with their parish and happy to be Catholics. They talked freely about problems—working out marital issues, school finances, losing a trusted pastor—and they knew the Church was going through difficult times, but I detected little sense of crisis.

But pessimists can find much to worry about. If the core Catholics are more involved with their Church than ever before, the *rest* of the Catholic population display a steadily weakening attachment. The fact that large percentages of young people are not involved with the Church is by itself not surprising—many of today's core Catholics also dropped out of Church when they were young. But the newer cohorts of the "noninvolveds" may be different; for, by all accounts, they may be the least religiously informed of any Catholic generation in recent history.

One of the angriest complaints of conservative Catholic theologians like Msgrs. George Kelly and Michael Wrenn is that in the wake of Vatican II, zealous liberal reformers eliminated much of traditional Catholic doctrine from catechetic classes, shifting the emphasis to a kind of watered-down, generic "American" religion. The poll data suggest that they're right. Younger Catholics, especially those who did not go to a Catholic college, have only a weak sense of Catholic identity—they tend to speak of themselves as "Christians" rather than as "Catholics"—and often lack even the basic vocabulary about liturgy, sacraments, and saints that has always distinguished Catholicism from other religions. As one younger Catholic summed up his religious training, "We just talked about being nice to each other; it wasn't a real dogmatic approach."

If the metaphorical glass is very much half full when examining the religious involvement of core Catholics, it is decidedly half empty when one shifts the focus to the less involved. In short, the evidence on Catholic religious practice supports *both* the extremely positive and extremely pessimistic views of the state of the American Church, which is probably one reason why the internal debate on the Church's future is often so rancorous.

Dollars and Stones

The headquarters of the New York region of the Sisters of Mercy is on a rambling walled estate in Westchester County, just north of New York City. Sr. Patricia Wolfe, the regional president, is in her late fifties, a no-nonsense woman with short-cropped gray hair and a business suit. The stone central building where she has her office fit my preconceived image of a regional motherhouse of a powerful international order of nuns. A sign of the times, however, is that the house and the land are borrowed. The estate was bequeathed to the New York Archdiocese some years ago, and the order, which has sold off most of its own real estate holdings, is there as a guest until the archdiocese figures out what it wants to do with the land.

The Mercy order was founded in Ireland more than 150 years ago, by the Venerable Catherine McAuley, a wealthy woman who wanted to help girls "at risk." ("Venerable" is the first step toward official Catholic sainthood.) The order is proud of its tradition of hospitality; a visitor can always find a "comfortable cup of tea" in a Mercy convent. Mercy sisters followed the Irish emigration to America and spread through the country along the same railroad routes that the immigrants helped build. Like most religious orders, the Mercy sisters have suffered sharp losses in numbers in recent decades. Nationwide, the number of Mercy sisters is down from 18,000 a generation ago to only about 6000 now. Only about a half-dozen of the 222 nuns in Wolfe's region are under forty-five years of age, and the median age is seventy-one. About half of the nuns are able to work, and the order is still slowly losing nuns of working age at a rate of about one a month, Wolfe says.

Taking care of their aged members is the biggest issue looming over all religious orders. Srs. Janet Roesener and Laura Reicks, at the USCC in Washington, have calculated the total unfunded retirement liability for American religious orders at more than $7 billion. Priests in religious orders are typically in much better shape than nuns and brothers, because they get higher wages and could afford to buy into the Social Security system. Priests, on average, are also younger than nuns, so their orders have a much higher ratio of working members. A USCC-sponsored annual Catholic appeal for retired religious draws the best response of any national collection, but the annual proceeds, at about $30 million, are just a drop in a very big bucket of financial need.

The retirement overhang is one of those seemingly cataclysmic problems that occasionally causes the Church's well-wishers to despair. But Wolfe has proven that it can be managed. With a combination of personal sensitivity, a real love for her order, and a good dollop of financial and real estate sleight-of-hand, she has executed a "downsizing" of the Mercy sisters that would make a corporate chieftain proud. Over the past decade, she has succeeded in liquidating the order's major real estate holdings—wending her way through a minefield of collapsed deals and a local savings-and-loan crisis—consolidated her facilities, established an adequate retirement fund, and created a series of financially manageable assisted-living facilities for her oldest nuns, which will allow her to keep the community together instead of relying on outside nursing homes.

"It was really wrenching," she said, "but we're over the worst now. Some of the sisters had been at the motherhouse for thirty years, and their whole identity as nuns was bound up in that building." She sees a lot of opportunity in merging orders—the Jesuits, for example, have saved a great deal of money by consolidating most of their provincial overhead operations. Some of the larger women's orders, especially those that run hospitals, are in good financial condition and have the financial wherewithal to absorb their weaker sisters. "Most of the smaller orders are still resisting action," says Wolfe. "But that will change, and we're starting to get a lot of inquiries about how we've managed the problem."

Wolfe's experience with the Mercy sisters is a microcosm of the painful readjustments that have been going on throughout the Church. But the press headlines have focused only on the pain and the problems, not on the progress that has been made. I reviewed financial information, and interviewed either the finance directors or senior lay advisers for the dioceses of Los Angeles, San Francisco, Brooklyn, Chicago, and Detroit, skewing the sample toward older urban centers that seemed most likely to have financial difficulties. I also made a point of asking about finances in almost every parish or school I visited.

Although budgets are tight everywhere, the Church is clearly not in financial difficulty, and almost all parishes and dioceses are running in the black. Almost all dioceses have made major improvements in financial controls and reporting over the past ten years, and the best ones are quite professional.* The process almost always required opening up their books and bringing in outsiders for advice. Robert Erberu, former chairman of the Times-Mirror Company, who spearheaded the upgrading of Los Angeles's systems says, "The big hurdle was to instill the concept of budgets, that you had to spend against a plan, not just on any worthy project that came along. The Cardinal [Roger Mahony] was a real enthusiast," Erberu chuckles, "until the day I convinced him that the budgets applied to *him* too."

To my surprise, none of the dioceses I visited except Chicago had external debt, and Chicago's was small. Almost all parishes are self-supporting. In my sample, about 10 percent of the parishes were subsidized, with most of the subsidies directed toward schools in poorer areas. St. Thomas the Apostle's School in barrio Los Angeles, for example, gets about $100,000 from the diocese each year, or about 20 percent of the school budget, but the parish is otherwise self-supporting. When I visited Fr. Christopher Smith at St. Joseph's parish in Santa Ana—the congregation is in roughly equal part Hispanic, Samoan, and Anglo—he and his administrator, Ann Roth, were sweating over a $60,000 school deficit in a total parish budget of about $1 million (about an average budget for a medium-size parish). His diocese, Orange, has a no-subsidy policy but is known to be cash-rich, and Smith was hoping he could cut a deal.

Both Chicago and Detroit have recently engineered wrenching downsizings of their physical plant, especially in the inner-city areas, closing thirty-eight and thirty-three parishes respectively, or about 10 percent of

---

* It is not possible to construct a consolidated Catholic financial statement. Most dioceses voluntarily send annual reports to the USCC, but they still vary widely in coverage and content. One of my frustrations researching the Church's earlier periods was the tendency of even the more cooperative archivists to clam up when I asked for historical financials. Only later I realized that most dioceses didn't *have* financial statements until quite recently. Bishops just ran checking accounts and parked their surpluses in CDs or government bonds.

their total count. The closings brought widespread protests, especially from priests who lamented the "abandonment of the inner city." But the Church is a brick-and-mortar-intensive business, and it is financial suicide to maintain expensive infrastructures where there are relatively few Catholics. (American blacks tend to be Baptists.) Both Jack Benware, Chicago's finance director, and Detroit's Sr. Mary Virginia Korb, argue that their inner-city churches and schools are now much stronger, and that consolidation of the weaker schools has permitted a richer range of services. In a nice example of ethnic religious progression, thirty of the thirty-three churches that were closed in Detroit were snapped up by Baptist congregations moving upmarket from storefronts.

I had expected Brooklyn to have the most serious financial difficulties. It is the only completely urban diocese in the country, covering a predominantly low-income borough of New York City, and with a large recent influx of Hispanic and Haitian Catholics. But there have been no deficits in living memory, due largely, it appears, to the nearly three-decade reign of Msgr. Austin Bennett as finance director. Bennett, who is in his seventies, is a bullet-headed Irishman with the carriage of a marine colonel and a handshake that could break paving stones. He bought up all outstanding parish debt as soon as he took over the job, organized a major school consolidation in the 1970s, and moves in with both feet whenever a parish starts running in the red. The main financial worry is how much longer they can cost-effectively maintain a very old plant, one that will be hard to tear down and sell off. An entrepreneurial Catholic Charities helps considerably by renting unused church buildings for social service programs that are supported by outside funding. (But for all of Bennett's tightfistedness, his internal controls, like San Francisco's, apparently relied excessively on trust. In early 1996, a longtime lay employee—Bennett had officiated at her wedding—was charged with embezzling very large sums of money over many years. Most dioceses, I suspect, have yet to internalize the assumption of dishonesty that is basic to any good financial control system.)

Catholic higher educational and social service institutions are virtually independent from the rest of the Church. Diocesan Catholic Charities are self-supporting operations: some of their funding comes from bishops' annual appeals, but most is from state and federal grants and United Way drives, just as with any other nonprofit social service agency. Catholic colleges and Catholic hospitals are freestanding corporations, usually with lay boards. They are funded from endowments and grants, and tuition or patient revenues, just like their lay competition, and they recruit in the open market for professionals of all religions. Catholic colleges usually require a theology course or two, and Catholic hospitals do not offer abortion services, but otherwise—except for the elusive "Catholic atmosphere"—they are indistinguishable from their competitors. They pose little or no financial risk for dioceses, and their revenue streams help fund religious orders.

Schools are different. They are almost always closely integrated with their parish and are a key element of parish ministry. As of 1995, there were 2.6 million children in Catholic schools, 2 million of them at the elementary level, and enrollments had increased for three consecutive years. All Catholic schools charge tuition, usually about $2000 for elementary students, with scholarships and other adjustments for poorer children. Tuition usually covers 80 to 90 percent of total costs, with the rest coming from the parish or the diocese. San Francisco's St. Peter's relies heavily on an annual fund drive among the heavily Irish Catholic city police and fire departments. Suburban schools tend to be almost exclusively attended by Catholic children from the home parish. City schools, especially in predominantly black neighborhoods, tend to draw from wider areas and to be less exclusively Catholic—about 40 percent of the students at Bedford-Stuyvesant's John the Baptist are not Catholic, and the school draws from twenty parishes. Nationwide, black children are almost three times overrepresented in Catholic schools relative to the black Catholic population, while Hispanics are substantially underrepresented. Catholic schools everywhere are lean, orderly, very successful operations. The Church's lingering presence as an educational haven for aspiring children in poor city neighborhoods is still the crown jewel of Catholic social endeavor.

Priests everywhere complain about diocesan bureaucracies, but, in truth, they are still very small. Diocesan central educational offices, even in big cities with large parochial systems, rarely have more than about a dozen people—compare that with the thousands of bureaucrats in public boards of education—and many of the central staff do double duty in parishes. A comment by an older monsignor from Los Angeles puts the complaints in perspective. "The bureaucracy is awful," he said, "I'll bet they've added at least three people to the education office over the last ten years, and they don't do nearly the work they used to." If anything, many dioceses could stand a bit *more* centralization, especially to install tighter controls over parish financial and staffing practices.

Religious sociologists have long puzzled over the decline in Catholic giving that began in the 1960s. Catholics traditionally gave a larger share of their income to their church than Protestants did—recall Cardinal Dougherty's aggressive fund-raising in Philadelphia. Catholics do seem stingy; I was amazed to see well-dressed professional-looking people, who seemed to participate fully in the liturgy, plunk dollar bills into collection baskets, the same as immigrant Mexicans at La Placita. The polemical explanations are that Catholics won't give more until they have more control over Church policy. Or that they are angry at the birth control encyclical, or the rules on divorce, or the role of women. Or that they are angry at the *liberalization* of the Church in the wake of Vatican II. Take your pick. It also seems to be true that Catholics give to many more Catholic organizations than their parish, while Protestant giving is concentrated on the local church. And the Catholic data usually don't count school tuitions, which are a heavy burden on many families. Protestant congregations are also typically much smaller than Catholic parishes, which facilitates fund-raising.

Perhaps most important, priests don't like to ask for money. Protestants and Jews are much more professional about fund-raising than Catholics, and many dioceses are now trying to bring their own fund-raising up to speed. In just a few years, Detroit's Cardinal Adam Maida raised an endowment fund of $80 million, a huge amount for a diocese that was once broke. Chicago's Benware says, "Ted Hesburgh [the former president of Notre Dame] walks into our backyard and picks up millions of dollars every year." Pastors are present at deaths of hundreds of well-off people, but most would never dream of asking for a legacy. Priests who told me they were working harder on fund-raising could almost always point to a perceptible uptick in collections.

The Church, in short, is clearly not in financial crisis. The fabled wealth is much exaggerated and concentrated in illiquid, often unsalable, real estate. Many dioceses and parishes are straining to make ends meet, and there are far more worthy projects than cash available. But almost all dioceses and parishes are getting along, most with a reasonable margin of comfort. The structural overhang from the Church's glory days is still a problem, but it is being slowly and steadily worked down. The huge potential settlements trumpeted in the press following the pedophilia scandals (a subject to which I will return) have not materialized, and at this point they don't appear likely to. There have been painful settlements, of course, but nowhere near the bankruptcy levels once feared. Retirement funding is a difficult issue but, as Pat Wolfe has shown, is probably manageable. The traditional institutions have survived a heavy buffeting in recent years and painful readjustments are still to come, but they are in reasonable shape and the worst may well be over.

There is not the same good news, however, about the state of the Catholic ministry.

The Crisis in the Ministry

The true extent of the Church's ministerial crisis sank home when I had dinner at Colombiere House, a Jesuit residence in Los Angeles. There were nine men in the house. My host, Fr. Allan Figueroa Deck, an expert on Hispanic Catholicism, was in his early fifties; all of the other men were in their eighties, all of them working more or less full schedules in parishes. They were thoroughly delightful table company, charming and intelligent. You could tell they were Jesuits by the Latin and Greek jokes, and by some miracle of transsubstantiation, the food prepared by Juanita, the Mexican cook, had been transformed into the rectory staple of pot roast and boiled vegetables, which must be as heavy a cross as celibacy. Although I have never met a group of men who carried their age so gracefully, the demographics of Colombiere House do not paint a bright future. The sharp decline in the number of active parish priests is one of the central traumas of the post–Vatican II American Church, as is the even sharper decline in the number of women religious.

Over the twenty-year period from 1966 through 1985, almost 7000 diocesan priests, or about a fifth of the active diocesan clergy, resigned their ministries. The losses of priests in religious orders were even worse. There had always been driblets of "failed priests" leaving the clerical life, but never resignations on such a massive scale. And there were too many active, suc-

Credit: Catholic News Service

CORPUS (Corps of Reserved Priests United for Service) claims to represent more than 7000 resigned priests. The standard laicization agreement for resigning priests prohibits them from functioning as parish or liturgical assistants. In view of the shortage of qualified ministers, CORPUS has been lobbying to make better use of an ecclesiastically-trained labor pool.

cessful, apparently well-adjusted men in the ranks of the departing to write off the entire phenomenon as an epidemic of moral weakness. The blow to the Church's morale and self-image was devastating, the more so since it was so unexpected. Fr. Eugene Hemrick, the longtime director of research at the USCC, recalls that when rumors of large numbers of resignations began to mount in the late 1960s—there were no good data—he went back to his home diocese of Chicago to try to get a feel for the numbers. "When I started going through the files, I couldn't believe it," he says. "I had no idea it was that bad. There were more than fifty guys from Chicago alone. These were good guys, guys I knew, that I had gone to the seminary with. I actually sat in the record room crying."

The late Richard Schoenherr of Indiana University, himself a former priest, has constructed the most detailed analysis of the turnover in American diocesan priests, concentrating on the 1966–1985 period. Schoenherr's data show that resignations rose from 200 in 1966 to 750 in 1969, or about 2 percent of the actives, the all-time peak. The number of resignations slipped to 667 in 1971, then began a steady decline, dropping to only 181, or 0.6 percent of the actives, in 1984. Ordinations, on the other hand, averaged about 1000 a year through most of the 1960s and were still at a respectable 842 in 1970. But from that point, they fell off steadily to only 465 in 1984, although they have since recovered somewhat, to 633 in 1994. In other words, the decline in numbers was driven by resignations until about 1975, and from that point, the problem has been the low number of new ordinations. There is no immediate prospect of a large turnaround in ordinations—although bishops who emphasize recruitment can point to modest successes—since the overall number of young men studying for the priesthood has been steadily declining as well. Schoenherr forecasts, on fairly conservative grounds, that the number of active diocesan priests will continue to fall for another decade. By about 2005, the ratio of active priests to Catholics will be about half of what it was in 1966.

There is a plethora of explanations for the falloff in ordinations. The most obvious, of course, is the celibacy rule. Dean Hoge, a researcher at Catholic University, has calculated that dropping the celibacy rule would quadruple the candidate pool. (But as I hope to show later in the book, ending priestly celibacy is not quite as simple as it sometimes sounds.) Recruitment must also have been affected by turmoil in the Church and the wave of resignations in the 1960s and 1970s. Priests racked with doubts about their own vocations will be poor proselytizers. Finally, there is a straightforward demographic explanation in the cultural assimilation of Irish Americans. For the first time ever, in the mid-1980s, the inclination toward the priesthood on the part of young Irish-American men converged with that of other Catholic ethnic groups. The American Church's most reliable fountain of new priests may have dried up.

The falloff in ordinations almost automatically creates an upward skew in the average age of priests, to about fifty-five in 1996 and rising steadily. Nationwide, about one out of six diocesan priests was retired or on leave in 1985, compared with one out of thirty in 1966. The age profile of priests in religious orders is even more unfavorable. Dioceses have succeeded in masking part of the recruitment falloff by importing foreigners. But priests from countries like Poland, Nigeria, or Ireland are ill-equipped for the participative leadership style that highly educated parishioners, like those at St. Cecilia's, are used to getting from a Msgr. Rizzotto. The Church can certainly operate with fewer priests than it did in the past, but to do so will require a serious rethinking of the priestly role and of lay-clerical relationships. Individual parishes are often improvising splendidly, but there is little evidence of concerted action at the leadership level.

If the demographics of the priesthood are daunting, the future of the female religious orders is probably hopeless. Traditionally in America, there were five nuns for every priest, but the ratio is now down to about 2:1 and falling. Since nuns are "lay," or nonordained, religious, exit from the religious life was always much easier than for priests, but rare enough to make popular hits out of the book *I Leaped Over The Wall* (1958) and Audrey Hepburn's *The Nun's Story* (1959). But by the 1990s, about half of all nuns had left. The mass resignations may have related less to Vatican II reforms than to the feminist movement. Nuns filled executive positions in Catholic service institutions long before similar jobs were opened to women in secular organizations. As lay women's professional horizons broadened, the convent lost much of its comparative recruitment advantage.

The upward shift up in the age profile among nuns is even more dramatic than for priests. Each time I met a young, native-born American woman who was a nun, like Diane Steele, a graduate theology student at Notre Dame, or Laura Reicks at the USCC, it registered as a major event. An estimated population of some 85,000 nuns took in only 340 new members in 1994, compared with 2400 lost to deaths and resignations, and the median age of the new members was forty-one. More subtle is the loss of the feeling of religious community. Few working nuns now reside in convents, but instead are scattered all over the country in paying jobs in hospitals, schools, and parishes in order to earn money to support the aged sisters at the motherhouse. The experience of male religious is similar. Fr. Canice Connors, a Franciscan psychologist who is in his early sixties, says that as a young priest he was accustomed to living in communities of a hundred or more men. "I was talking to a group of young Franciscans and realized that none of them had ever lived in a house with more than four men," he says, "To me, that would have been a private party." The age structure and economic position of lay religious brothers is much the same as for nuns, but there are only about a fourth as many.

The availability of nuns has been a major factor masking the growing shortage of priests. Nuns have long since moved out of the elementary school system and into diocesan management positions, as chancellors, chief financial officers, directors of education and personnel and of various ministries, allowing bishops to rotate priests back into parish work. In addition, there are now some 20,000 lay people working in parishes at jobs that were once performed mostly by priests—liturgists, finance and administration directors, religious education directors, even "pastoral administrators," a euphemism for a lay pastor. Forty percent of them are nuns, which helps keep wages down, but their median age is about sixty, older than the priests they are displacing. The brute fact is that in about ten or fifteen years, for all practical purposes, there will be no working nuns in America. "The days when nuns were the Church's Job Corps is almost over," as Pat Wolfe put it. "Besides that, nuns have always been Prophetic Witnesses. Part of our charism includes standing up to the bishops. We don't want to get too absorbed into the institutional Church."

An Interim Report Card

John Kennedy's presidential election victory heralded the final breakdown of the separatist American Catholic subculture. A rigorous, didactic, all-encompassing brand of Catholicism—the legacy of powerful bishops and cardinals in the mold of John Hughes, Bernard McQuaid, Dennis Dougherty, and Francis Spellman—lent cohesiveness and consistency to the Catholic community; and by midcentury, the strength of the subculture had powered the Church to a near dominant, "virtual majority" status in American life. The demise of the Catholic subculture was well under way before the convening of Vatican II, but the liberalization of the Church that followed upon the Council undoubtedly accelerated the process.

The new challenge that faced the American Church in the 1960s was whether it could sustain itself as a freestanding *religion* without the support of the separatist subculture that had been its great bulwark against American secularism. Data on the Church's institutional health, the ministry, and lay religious adherence add up to a report card on its success in meeting that challenge.

At an institutional level, the Church is faring better than might be expected. The expensive old physical plant, looming retirement problems, and falling collections are all difficult issues, but none appears insoluble, and there has been considerable quiet progress in recent years. The critical challenges facing the Church are not about money and mortar.

When it comes to lay religious adherence, the picture is much more mixed. The loss of the subculture's coercive force has clearly affected every quantitative index of Catholic practice. Although Catholic young people always let their religious practice slip once they left home, in past generations the weekly family rituals of Mass and Sunday breakfasts enforced church attendance when the kids came home for visits, keeping the ties in place. But that no longer seems to be true. The falloff in parental church attendance has weakened the grip of family rituals, and parents are less able to enforce their norms on their children in any case. At the same time, the consumerization of Catholic catechetics since Vatican II has blurred the sense of Catholic distinctiveness and helped speed the erosion of the old Catholic habits.

On the bright side, however, the large numbers of very active core Catholics, whose commitment is *chosen* rather than merely inherited or imposed, have created an extraordinarily vibrant and participatory grassroots parish life, just as post–Vatican II liberals dreamed might happen. Whether smaller numbers of highly engaged Catholics are to be preferred to the larger, more passive turnouts of the 1950s is, of course, a source of endless argument. But smaller numbers in this case is a purely relative concept, for by any reasonable measure, highly commited Catholics still add up to the largest single American religious body by a good margin.

But even if one accepts a quality-versus-quantity tradeoff, core Catholics still represent a major challenge for the Church, for they are an unusually prickly and contentious lot. Far more than any previous generation of faithful Catholics, they are demanding a seat at the table in a broad range of decisions ranging from parish administration and choice of a pastor to questions of sexual ethics and policies on women's ministry—this at a time when, as we shall see, the Church has been steadily shifting the weight of decision-making authority back toward Rome. Individual pastors walk a tightrope between their parishioners' insistence on participation and Rome's impulse toward centralization, and some do so brilliantly. But it is a tough balancing act, and the two contrary impulses are generating a great deal of confusion on basic questions about conscience, authority, and the role of the laity in the Church.

The crisis in the ministry reflects the deeper confusions. Since the priesthood no longer carries the extraordinarily high status conferred by the old subculture, recruitment will require, at the very least, a clear vision of who a priest is and how he stands in relation to the laity: Is he (or, perhaps, she) primarily teacher, prophet, shaman, or team leader and counselor? These are tough issues, and priests have been mostly left to figure them out for themselves. It's not surprising that few of them are working very hard on recruitment.

The problems the Church is facing are of exquisite subtlety, and they can't be blamed on the laity. Traditionalists may yearn for the old Catholic docility, but the people filling the pews are too energetic, informed, and commited to justify a bleakly pessimistic view of the grassroots. If there has been no agreement on what to teach young people about their religion, it's not their fault. Significantly, the young people who are most informed about their religion—recent Catholic college graduates—are also among the *most* committed to the Church and among the *least* disposed to accept the rote dictates of authority.

The problems lie within the institution itself. At the risk of irreverence, if a religious stock analyst were to rate the American Catholic Church, he might say: "Dynamite product, great market, but you need to shoot some upper and middle managers." The further one penetrates into higher reaches of theology and Church administration, the more strained, the more gloomy, the nastier the atmosphere becomes. The root problem is the vision, or lack of vision—or superfluity of visions—of what the Church is and how it should carry out its mission, and who should do it. The awkward re-visioning of the Church that has been taking place over the last thirty years sweeps up questions of authority, of sexuality, of gender, of orthodoxy in matters great and small, and sets bishops and theologians at one another's throats.

In a religion with the tradition and history of Catholicism, vision and strategy start with theology. The ministerial problem can't be solved while the theological vision of priest and people is in flux and confusion. So the theological battlefields are one of the main arenas where the struggle over the future of the Church is taking place.

CHAPTER 13

Theological Visions

The 1995 annual meeting of the Catholic Theology Society of America, or the CTSA, at New York's Hyatt Regency Hotel, like most academic conventions, was an awkward amalgam of the workaday and the sublime. The usual textbook publishers' display booths, anxious job hunters, and chitter of trade gossip—"She's going *where?* To *Creighton?*"—backdropped earnest presentations on the nature of Evil or on discerning signs of the Divine in our corrupted world.

The opening ceremony, in the hotel ballroom, included a short and very pretty liturgy. A long table of candles was set up on one side of the room, the lights were dimmed, and members of the audience were invited to go to the table, pick up a candle, and bring it to the stage while the assembly and a small choir from nearby Fordham University sang a prayer-and-response litany of the saints. The music had a modern, Andrew Lloyd Webber feel, complicated and solemn, but singable enough that almost everyone joined in by the third or fourth verse. A nonsinger, I sat back, lulled by the familiar words—St. Peter and Paul. Pray for us. . . . Cosmas and Damian. Pray for us. . . . All you holy martyrs. Pray for us. . . . John Courtney Murray. Pray for us." I sat up. John Courtney Murray? The only theologian to grace the cover of *Time* to be sure, but not a saint. "John Calvin. Pray for us. . . . Martin Luther. Pray for us." I whispered to my host and guide, Fr. Robert Imbelli, a Boston College theology professor, "Bob, did they say John Calvin and Martin Luther?" "Yes," he said with a smile, "Welcome to the CTSA."

In the thirty years since the close of Vatican II, Catholic theology, and especially American Catholic theology, has clearly evolved a considerable distance and in striking directions away from the moral manuals and formulaic recitations of the 1950s. Whether it has gone too far and too fast, or whether it has not developed nearly far enough, and who, after all, is supposed to decide such things are the questions that are at the heart of the bitter controversies that are ripping apart the higher levels of the Church, not just in America but throughout the whole world.

The Contested Legacy of Vatican II

The ecumenical Council that was held in Rome over the four years from 1962 through 1965, Vatican II, is the watershed event in modern Catholic history. An ecumenical Council is a solemn assembly of all the world's bishops and the pope, the supreme legislative and doctrinal authority in the Catholic Church. The authority of councils is enhanced by their rarity. Vatican II was only the twenty-first ecumenical Council in the 2000-year history of the church and the first since Pius IX's "Vatican I," (1869–1870) which had declared the doctrine of papal infallibility. Prior to Vatican I, there had been no Council since Trent in the mid–sixteenth century. Trent sounded the tocsin for the Catholic Counter Reformation and made the definitive declarations of doctrine and theological perspective that obtained virtually unchanged through the papacy of Pius XII.

Vatican II is the most prolix of councils. Its output is almost as long as all the decrees of all the preceding twenty councils put together, a vast theological ocean that offers a wealth of quotable pearls to support the position of almost any dedicated partisan. Almost all current theological controversies can be understood, in one degree or another, as competing glosses on Vatican II—whether on the authority of Rome, on the Church's teachings on sexuality, on the role of the laity and women in the Church, on the primacy of personal conscience, or on the interpretation of Scripture. Pope John Paul II, who attended the Council as a young bishop, recently called Vatican II a "providential event . . . a proclamation of new times." But at the same time, John Paul and Cardinal Joseph Ratzinger, the Vatican's ideological chief, have used the authority of the Council to effect a substantial tightening of doctrine and recentralization of authority, much to the dismay of liberal* theologians who understood the Council as a great exercise in *de*centralization.

---

* Everyone deplores the use of simplistic terms like "liberal" and "conservative" to describe the great variety of positions espoused by theologians at the Council and subsequently, but they were often enough used by the protagonists themselves, and I haven't found any that are consistently better. In the early stages of the Council, the "Roman" and "anti-Roman" or "reformist" parties may be a bit more descriptive, and I use them in this section. Admitting all exceptions, "conservative" theologians tend to adhere to most of a cluster of positions that would include: a commitment to a broad definition of a changeless deposit of faith; a tendency to treat teachings of the Pope and the encyclicals as nondebatable; great attachment to Marian devotions; a "teleological" view of sexuality that does not admit the use of artificial birth control in marriage; a

The interpretive chaos that has followed in the wake of Vatican II has multiple roots. The preparation for the Council and its first session were dominated by a fierce struggle in which a reformist majority of bishops and theologians won a clear victory over a minority "Roman" party committed to preserving both the dominance of the Vatican and the Church's doctrinal purity. But over the course of the full council, by dint of sheer dogged committee work, many of the minority positions, which had been "so ignominiously abandoned, would surreptitiously find their way back into the various constitutions and decrees," in the words of Giuseppe Alberigo, the Council's leading contemporary historian. As a consequence, there is sufficient conflict between the majority's apparent intentions and the Council's actual texts that theological partisans can appeal at will either to "the spirit of Vatican II"—in effect, to its legislative history—or to its actual language.

The layers of interpretive controversy pile one on top of the other. Even liberals are divided over whether the Council should be understood as a onetime event—an assembly that met, deliberated, and finished its work—or, alternatively, as a catalyst for a process of continuing change within the Church. The reform of the liturgy and the adoption of vernacular languages provide a good example. The Council expressly did *not* approve the use of the vernacular for the entire Mass. But since "spirit of the Council" and "process of change" advocates were temporarily in the saddle, the use of the vernacular for the entire Mass became general throughout the Church within just a few years of the Council's close. In the same way—and even more infuriating to conservatives—elementary school catechetics almost immediately reflected the most liberal versions of doctrinal and ethical teachings, as if they had been automatically endorsed by the Council. Influential liberal theologians have occasionally demanded that the Church go "beyond Vatican II for the sake of Vatican II," although the same liberals are quick to complain that conservatives have twisted the meaning of the texts.

To further complicate matters, the history of the Council has been written primarily by theologians, not by the bishops who were actually casting votes; many of the same theologians were partisans at the Council and have

commitment to a celibate, male priesthood and to sharply distinguished male and female roles in both family and Church; and a devotion to Thomistic philosophy, "the hardware that can run any software," as one conservative puts it. "Liberals" accept a changeless deposit of faith but are more willing to reinterpret it in the light of history. They place greater emphasis on dialogue with the laity as opposed to hierarchical dictate in the the teaching mission; adopt a more intellectualized devotional model that downplays Marian and other "cultic" devotions; are more open to a non-celibate priesthood and women priests; stress the primacy of conscience in ethical matters, including sexual ethics; and are usually impatient with Thomism, or at least with its more rigid varieties. To complicate matters a bit, very conservative Americans, like Spellman, were strong advocates of democratic pluralism, which Vatican stalwarts abhorred, and Spellman would not tolerate Roman meddling with *his* theologians, no matter how liberal they were.

Credit: UPI Radiotelephoto/Corbis-Bettmann
"Vatican II" (1962–1965), the first ecumenical council of all the world's bishops
in almost a century, and only the twenty-first in the entire history of the Church,
was an ideological watershed in Catholic history. This scene, from the Council's
opening day, shows the bishops arrayed on either side of St. Peter's, while Pope
John XXIII is carried down the center aisle to the altar.

used their histories to continue their polemics. Some of the more liberal theological partisans, moreover, like Hans Küng, are able popularizers, and their books have been influential best-sellers. Further, even the Council's leading reform theologians have been deeply divided on the meaning of the Council. Ratzinger, Henri deLubac, and Jean Daniélou, for example, are known to have been seriously disappointed by the changes in the Church following the Council; others, like Karl Rahner and Yves Congar, were heartened; and a few, like Küng and Edward Schillebeeckx, have argued that the true council has been subverted by the defeated minority. On the opposite flank, Michael Novak, an influential Catholic lay writer, who was a warm supporter of the Council in the 1960s, has argued that the theological chaos that followed the Council threatens "the very meaning of Catholicism" and has "squandered the inheritance of the church."

The Council was also the first ever to be conducted under the glare of the mass media, and that fact itself may have forever changed the balance of power between hierarchy and laity. The ebb and flow of the debates were laid before the world in excruciating, irreverent detail by "Xavier Rynne," the pseudonymous correspondent of *The New Yorker,* whose "Letters from Rome" were later turned into several best-selling books. Rynne's witty dissection of backstairs Vatican politics, and of the relentless stage-managing by the Roman minority, or his cameo of an angry cardinal stomping from the hall after losing a parliamentary maneuver, were a signal contribution to the modern demystification of the Church. With so many council fathers in violent disagreement over fundamental issues, all the Church's hard, bright doctrinal lines suddenly appeared rather arbitrary. The almost out-of-hand rejection of Pope Paul VI's 1968 anti-birth-control encyclical by the vast majority of the Catholic laity would have been inconceivable before the Council. The "event" of the Council, that is, may have had as much impact as its texts.

Xavier Rynne is actually Fr. Francis X. Murphy, a priest of the Redemptorist order, now in his early eighties and semiretired in Annapolis, Maryland, a ruddy-faced polymath and linguist with a snow-white Vandyke beard. "I owned up to Rynne only a few years ago," he said. "If I hadn't, the Jesuits would have claimed him after I died, and the Redemptorists wouldn't have argued with them." Murphy was teaching medieval history at the Gregorian Institute in Rome when the Council opened, and he had planned to write some essays, probably for *Commonweal.* But a literary agent introduced him to Robert Giroux, of Farrar, Straus & Giroux, who arranged a meeting with William Shawn at *The New Yorker.* Shawn jumped at the project, and Giroux suggested a pseudonym to keep Murphy out of trouble. "The name popped right out," said Murphy, "and it really shouldn't have been hard to guess who I was. Xavier is my middle name, and Rynne is my mother's maiden name. A lot of people suspected me, of course, but as long as I didn't admit it I couldn't be fired from my job, although a couple of close friends lost their chance to be bishops." Murphy's letters themselves influenced the council debates. Advance sheets of his *New Yorker* letters were eagerly scanned by the participants to find out what was going on, and they irrevocably fixed the image of the Council as a titanic "white hat/black hat" struggle between majority liberals and a minority of conservative troglodytes. "That's the way it was," he said. "And it wasn't a slim majority, it was at least 80 percent. The minority still hasn't given up."

Pope John's New Pentecost

Vatican insiders expected Angelo Roncalli to be a caretaker pope when he was chosen to succeed Pius XII in the fall of 1958 and took the name John XXIII. Roncalli was almost seventy-seven at his election and was known primarily as a pastor, not as a diplomat or theologian. Born a peasant, the third of thirteen children, he was beguilingly ugly and seemed amused at the pomp that came with his new job, as when he gave a raise to the papal chair bearers because he weighed so much more than his ascetic predecessor. It was a shock, therefore, when, hardly three months after his election, he announced to a group of senior Roman cardinals that he planned to hold a general council of the Church. The cardinals could not have been pleased. They greeted the decision only with "devout and impressive silence," as John himself recalled, and when he asked them for suggestions in carrying out the plan, there were few replies, and those were in "cold and formal language." John said that the inspiration for the Council came to him "like a flash of heavenly light," although he wonderfully confused the record with several quite different versions of the inspiration. A careful reconstruction by Peter Hebblethwaite suggests that he may have thought of a council as early as the day of his election.

By the time of John's accession, the highly centralized Roman system created by Pius IX had become an airless, self-referential bureaucracy, one that for sheer hermetic impenetrability could be matched, ironically enough, only by the monolithic state apparatuses of the Communist regimes. As deLubac described the Vatican mandarins:

> They know their craft, but little else. You sense in them a certain indifference to Scripture, the Fathers . . . ; a lack of interest in and uneasiness with regard to contemporary doctrines and intellectual currents. . . . They are, it seems, too certain of their own superiority; their practice of judging does not incline them to work. . . . The result is a little academic system, ultra-intellectualistic, but without much intellectual quality. The Gospel is folded into this system, which is the constant *a priori*.

John made only a few general statements of his hopes for the Council, but they were enough to strike panic into the heart of a Roman apparatchik. He spoke of the need to "come to grips, in a clear and well-defined way, with the spiritual needs of the present time." He spoke of "ages of renewal" and the necessity to "distinguish between what is sacred principle and eternal gospel and what belongs rather to the changing times," and he later stressed "the recommendation of Jesus that one should know how to distinguish 'the signs of the times.' " And he spoke of a "strengthening of religious unity," which seemed to suggest an open-armed approach to Protestants and to the Orthodox East.

The world response to John's initiative was almost universally enthusiastic, especially among liberal, reformist bishops and theologians concentrated in France, Germany, Austria, and Holland. Official Protestantism and Judaism warmly greeted the opportunity for renewed dialogue. In America, the announcement of the Council came just as John Kennedy was kicking off his New Frontier presidential campaign, and the "Two Johns," in Garry Wills's phrase, became swept up together as symbols of the American spirit of optimism. Even quite conservative American Catholic organs, like *Sign*, jubilantly hailed the Council as a once-in-a-lifetime world-historical event.

Having announced his council, however, John inexplicably withdrew from the fray and allowed the Vatican insiders, led by Cardinal Alfredo Ottaviani, the half-blind head of the Holy Office and chief custodian of doctrine, to seize control of the preparatory process, which they shrouded in a deep cloak of secrecy. The apparatchiks set about drafting decrees that raised the walls of the fortress Church ever higher, strengthened the authority of the Pope, and declared war on a host of deadly errors, including "naturalism, atheistic humanism, evolutionism, relativism, indifferentism, Marxism, [and] laicism." They called on all civil governments to acknowledge God, and identified the practices and ceremonials of the Church with divine revelation. Ecumenical enthusiasms were dampened by reminding Catholics that they were not even *allowed* to attend meetings of bodies like the World Council of Churches. Ottaviani claimed that the conclusions of his own commission on theology were nondebatable. The insiders hoped for a short, noncontroversial council and seriously discussed whether bishops should be allowed to speak on the floor. It also appears that they dragged out the preparatory process to inordinate length in the hope that John's ill health and "Providence" might intervene before any lasting damage was done.

By 1962 at least, a growing sense of alarm at the direction of the preparatory work was spreading in liberal circles. Theologians like deLubac, Congar, and Rahner, who sat on the preparatory commissions, and reformist cardinals, like Leo Suenens of Belgium, Augustin Bea of Germany, Franz König of Austria, and Paul Léger of Canada, all of whom had the ear of the

Pope, became the center of a quiet counterreaction. (The Americans were only peripherally involved. The attitudes of the American hierarchy ran the gamut from mild reformism to Cardinal McIntyre's brand of rock-hard conservatism. As a group, they probably tilted slightly toward the Romanists, except for their commitment to pluralist democracy.) The reformers were heartened by occasional statements by the Pope reconfirming his original goals for the Council, which were grossly at variance with the great body of preparatory work. Finally in early 1962, John suddenly announced that the Council would open in October, although the preparatory work was not nearly completed. Preliminary drafts of the Council's decrees, mostly reflecting the output of the mandarins, were circulated to the world's bishops only in late summer. By the time the bishops began gathering in Rome, the outline of a still amorphous, but sizable, reformist majority was already becoming visible.

In retrospect, the first great battle of the Council was over when John made a powerful introductory speech, excoriating the pessimists and "prophets of doom" who feared change and growth, and inviting all to join "in mystic exultation" as the Council "rises in the church like the daybreak" to meet the "modern expectations and needs of the various peoples of the world." The very first proposal considered by the Council, the draft schema on revelation, was voted down by the assembly and sent back for redrafting. The extent of the reformist victory became clear when Ottaviani himself took the platform to present the critical constitution on the governance and structure of the Church. For almost a whole week, bishop after bishop rose to attack the schema for its rigidity and defensiveness, for its preoccupation with the power of the the Vatican, for its disregard of local churches and bishops, for its exclusion of the laity, for its lack of any sense of mystery or redemptive vision. Finally, Suenens rose to suggest that the schema needed to be completely rewritten. When Giovanni Battista Montini, the powerful cardinal of Milan, rose to back Suenens, it was clear that John had decided to scuttle the preparatory work. It was a decisive psychological moment. The following week John ordered that *all* the preliminary drafts should be withdrawn and reconsidered. All bets, that is, were off. Commentators were already talking of a "revolution" in the Church.

The final output of the Council is contained in sixteen major documents. Many of them, like those on Christian education, on the missions, and on the mass media, deal primarily with internal or administrative matters of limited long-term consequence. But several were of major significance. The document on religious liberty, which was a personal triumph for John Courtney Murray, reversed a long-standing Catholic position; and in the new spirit of ecumenism, the Council substantially modified the traditional teaching on the impossibility of salvation outside the Church. The document on liturgy introduced the use of vernacular languages in the Mass and initiated the still ongoing process of liturgical reform, while the document on revelation reasserted the primacy of sacred Scripture in Catholic theology. (Suspicion of Scripture-based Protestantism had greatly damaged Catholic biblical studies.)

The two most cited and most contentious documents, however, are the one on the internal workings and structure of the Church—usually known by its Latin name, *Lumen Gentium* ("Light of Nations")—and the one on the Church's relation to modern society, *Gaudium et Spes* ("Joy and Hope"). Much of the dualistic tension that pervades the decrees of the Council can be traced to the apparent oppositions between the precise language of *Lumen Gentium* and the much more open-ended "pastoral" spirit of *Gaudium et Spes*.

Text and Spirit

Of the two constitutions, *Lumen Gentium* was by far the more carefully debated. Compared with any other document, it consumed more time and emotional energy, led to more angry recriminations, and touched more of the hot-button issues dividing the Church today—papal infallibility, the relationship of pope and bishops, and of bishops and priests, and the role of laypeople in the Church. And it best illustrates, in Alberigo's words, how the majority became "contented by the euphoria generated by its unexpected success when it confronted the mythical power of the curia" and subsequently allowed much of the insiders' preparatory work to filter into the final decrees.

Pope John died in June 1963, to be succeeded by Montini, who was John's own first choice for the job. Montini, who took the name Paul VI, was a lean ascetic in the mold of Pius XII, a longtime Vatican insider and consummate diplomat, but with a reputation for occasional indecisiveness. He almost immediately weighted the drafting committees and commissions with prelates of progressive views and set up procedures to ensure that theologians like Rahner and Congar could get a full hearing. The revised machinery produced a new draft constitution on the internal life of the Church that, in the liberal view, was vastly improved. The legalistic recitation of the Church's "rights" against the rest of the world was mostly gone. The draft opened with a chapter on the "Mystery" of the Church, emphasizing Christ, Scripture and the teachings of the early Church fathers. The importance of the laity was confirmed by an entirely new chapter devoted to the "People of God," preceding even the section on bishops. The chapter's very existence was as important as its contents. "People of God" theology stresses the universal priesthood of Christians, laity and clergy alike, and suggests a more horizontal approach to decision making.

But the dramatic confrontations came with the chapter on the hierarchy. The "empiricists" in the Vatican could tolerate grand declarations of "Mystery" and "People of God," but when it came to the crucial relation between pope and bishops, the issue was *power*. The battle was masked in a fog of technicalities: Did bishops receive a special sacramental grace at their consecration? When Scripture spoke of "Peter and the Apostles," did it mean "Peter and the *other* Apostles" or did it imply that Peter had a separate status? Did the world episcopacy constitute a "college," in the "juridical" sense of a distinct entity with its own rights and duties? For a week, the hall glittered and clanged with scriptural rapier-thrust-and-parry. The Council majority could not challenge the ultimate infallibility of the Pope, but they insisted that the Pope was one of their own ("Peter and the *other* Apostles") and that the college of bishops was also infallible. The bolder among them went so far as to suggest a permanent senate or parliament of bishops drawn from throughout the world to share power with the Pope. In the face of deadly assault, the Roman party fought a desperate holding action, resorting to every parliamentary maneuver. Progressives began to fear that the Council might stumble on forever, and a number of bishops threw up their hands and went home.

Once again, Suenens made the decisive intervention by proposing test votes to determine the mind of the fathers. After two weeks of frantic backstage maneuvering, Suenens finally got his vote, in the form of five propositions. The first four stated that the episcopacy was a sacramental order; that the bishops formed a college; that together with the Pope they enjoyed "a plenary and supreme authority over the universal church"; and that they held their authority by "divine right." All passed by margins ranging from 60:1 to 4:1. A final proposition, restoring the active ministry of the diaconate and opening it to married men, passed by 3:1. The mind of the Council, presumably, was clear, if tempers were badly frayed. At one point, Cardinal Josef Frings of Cologne charged that Ottaviani's doctrinal office was "a cause of scandal to the world," and Ottaviani replied in "a voice shaking with rage." Outsiders, at least those who could follow Latin, could only stare in incredulity at the spectacle of such senior figures having at each other, although it was widely reported that the Pope called Frings and thanked him for his speech.

Lumen Gentium was finally approved in the third session (1964), but not without more fireworks. In informal remarks at the start of the session, Paul explicitly repudiated a conservative faction, the self-styled "remnant of Israel," who considered collegiality to be the rankest heresy. On the contrary, Paul said, episcopal collegiality would be the doctrine that "distinguishes this solemn and historic synod in the memory of future ages." The Council moved quickly to a vote on collegiality, and all the key propositions carried overwhelmingly. Out of a total of some 2500 bishops, the hard-core minority disposed of only about 300 votes.

Amazingly, at this point Paul intervened on behalf of the minority, apparently because he feared a damaging split in the Church. When the final text on collegiality was released to the Council after the floor vote, it was prefaced with a "Preliminary Explanatory Note" that read in part: "at the command of higher authority. . . . The doctrine set forth in this . . . chapter must be understood and explained in accordance with the mind and statement of this note." The "higher authority" was never named, but it was clearly the Pope. Scholars still dispute the meaning of the addendum, but if there are critical concessions in the main text, they are severely hemmed in by the note. It states that the word "college" is not to be interpreted in the Roman legal sense as a group of equals, but just means "a stable group." The relationship between Peter and the Apostles does not imply that bishops stand in the same relationship to the Pope, for the Pope is much more than a first among equals. Episcopal consecration confers the *ability* to perform the functions of office but specifies that they are to be exercised only at the direction of the Pope, at his discretion. The note stipulates that the college of bishops can never act independently of the Pope, but only in union with him, with his consent and according to rules that he lays down. The Pope, on the other hand, can always act either on his own or in union with the bishops as he chooses. The "collegiality" that had been so painfully fought over on the floor was turning out to be thin gruel.

The majority, perhaps because they were exhausted, perhaps because they trusted Paul, perhaps because they had no stomach for further confrontations, approved the final text, including the note, with hardly a murmur. Almost all of the minority faction voted for the text as well. When Paul, in his address closing the third session, praised the Council for confirming "the monarchical and hierarchical" character of the Church, liberals assumed that "hierarchical" was merely a slip of the tongue for "collegial."

The Council wound up its work in the fourth (1965) session. The assembly approved the very controversial text on religious liberty that repudiated centuries of dogmatic opposition to secular states and more or less endorsed the American system of pluralist democracy. But the session is most remembered for approving the "pastoral constitution," *Gaudium et Spes,* which stands today as one of the major pillars of the Council. Archbishop Mark McGrath of Panama, who was on the drafting committee, recalls that the constitution was almost an afterthought, sailing through with little controversy. The conservatives regarded *Lumen Gentium* as "the heart and soul" of the Council and viewed *Gaudium et Spes* as "of not too much importance." With issues of power and authority safely disposed of, they were willing, perhaps, to let the liberals indulge in a little rhetoric

In form, *Gaudium et Spes* is an extended meditation on the role of the Church in the world. It is addressed to "people everywhere," rather than just

Catholics. Its tone and language are radically different from those of the other decrees. It extols the advance of "biological, psychological, and social sciences" and the capacity of humanity for "forecasting and controlling its own demographic growth." It recognizes that a "more critical judgment is purifying [religion] of a magical approach to the world and of still widespread superstitions. . . . [F]aith which shows everything in a new light and clarifies God's purpose . . . point[s] the mind toward solutions which are fully human." It extols human freedom and individual conscience, "the most intimate centre and sanctuary of a person." The Church of *Gaudium et Spes* "is sensitive to the gravity of the questions which atheism raises" and concedes that it "does not always have a ready answer to particular questions." It agrees that religion should not encroach on "the autonomy of earthly realities" and acknowledges "the help the church receives from the modern world" in adapting its message to the "concepts and languages of various peoples . . . through the wisdom of philosophers," stimulating "a fruitful interchange . . . between the church and various cultures."

The contrast between *Gaudium et Spes* and *Lumen Gentium,* and even between the hierarchical and the "People of God" chapters of *Lumen Gentium,* is sometimes so sharp that it raises the question of whether the Council is self-contradictory. The detailed language of *Lumen Gentium* on the personal infallibility of the Pope and the "religious assent" owed even to his noninfallible teachings clearly preserves the centralized, authoritarian system of Pius IX. Can that be consistent with the new importance assigned to the laity, the stress on the doctrinal role of bishops, the acknowledged interplay of doctrine and local cultural conditions, and the modest tone of *Gaudium et Spes*?

Most theologians reconciled the tension by assuming that, while the Pope technically reserved his old powers, the Council had ended the era of papal absolutism, of "an exaggerated fascination with infallibility," as one put it. Collegiality would be the new order of the Church. The old powers remained, that is, but pastoral considerations, respect for local conditions, and a more "horizontal" conception of ecclesial authority would modulate their use. Typical glosses were: "[T]he episcopal college has full and supreme power in the universal Church, no less than the pope," and "Vatican II . . . made it clear that the infallibility of the pope and bishops must always be related to the faith of the whole Church, that there must always be close, collegial cooperation between the pope and the bishops in the process of definition [of doctrine]."

The aggressive recentralization of authority under John Paul II in recent years has upset these confident expectations. Reportedly, only the strenuous intervention of Cardinal Ratzinger prevented the Pope from declaring that two of his 1990s encyclicals, *The Splendor of Truth* and *The Gospel of Life,*

were infallible teachings. To make matters more confusing, John Paul's encyclicals make a special point of drawing equally from *both* of the rhetorical
threads of Vatican II. More so than any of his recent predecessors, the Pope
is a charismatic figure, a philosopher, and a mystic. His encyclicals are extended meditations on Scripture, on the Mystery of the Church, on the
yearnings of the People of God, in very much the tone, often the same language, as *Gaudium et Spes.* But at the same time, he has a penchant for un-
leashing doctrinal thunderbolts not seen since the days of Pius XII. More
than any other Pope, for example, he has ringingly proclaimed the equality
of women and the importance of women to the Church, but his doctrinal office has ruled that the impossibility of women's ordination is an infallible
truth of the faith. An extended meditation on the primacy of individual conscience is followed by an equally emphatic statement on the "intrinsic evil"
of contraception, which is "always wrong." While he is devoted to pluralism,
he has moved aggressively against theological dissent and sharply reined in
national episcopal conferences. Praise for "inculturation," or the adaptation
of the Church to local conditions, is matched by the appointment of bishops
devoted to a Romanocentric, top-down vision of the Church.

Supporters of the Pope argue that none of these positions is inconsistent, and that John Paul has perceived a deep unity in the decrees of Vatican
II that escapes his critics. The Pope at least has the advantage of arguing his
position from the actual language of the Council, rather than from a poorly
defined "spirit." Even more important, his positions are clear, regardless of
one's view of their substance. And it is a fair question whether the great body
of liberal critics have offered a convincing theological vision of their own.

When Is Theology Catholic?

Few college campuses are as beautiful as Notre Dame's, especially on a crisp
fall day with touch football games on the lawns, the trees a riot of color, and
the famous golden dome, all freshly gilded, gleaming against a blue sky. On
the day I visited Fr. Richard McBrien's doctoral-level theology seminar, an
unexpected bonus was that Archbishop McGrath had dropped by to give his
insider's account of the Council (including vignettes like Ottaviani's telling
McGrath's committee that they would draft whatever he told them to draft).
There were nine seminar students, all of them bright and engaging, and all in
their late twenties and early thirties. Six of the nine were women. My guess is
that about 40 percent of the members at the CTSA convention were also
women, and the current CTSA president was a woman, Elizabeth Johnson
from Fordham. As we went through the text of *Gaudium et Spes,* using the

Austin Flannery translation, I felt more than a twinge of embarrassment at the thudding repetition of the generic "man." Susie Babka, a second-year student, finally couldn't hold back a comment about the guys "not getting it."

Diane Steele was the only nun in the class. With the vigorous good looks of a backpacker, Lands' End clothes, and her own apartment off-campus, she was a far cry from the bewimpled movie stereotype. One of the men, Steve Wilson, was studying for the Methodist ministry. All except Wilson were Catholic, and all had been deeply involved with their churches as volunteers and lay ministers; but except for Wilson and Steele, none is planning a career in the clerical or religious life, mostly because of the celibacy rule. Karen Vlahutin seemed to speak for the group when she said she had chosen theology to "integrate her spirituality with an academic career." Like graduate students anywhere, they were nervous about the availability of teaching jobs when they completed their degrees. Only Steele had a guarantee—she would teach theology in one of her order's colleges—but theology is a growth area on liberal arts campuses, and McBrien said that Notre Dame usually places all of its people.

The laicization of American Catholic theology is one of the portentous developments of the post–Vatican II era. At the CTSA convention, there was a display of photographs from the founding meeting in 1945. The gathering is all male, all are priests, all are wearing Roman collars, and almost all were seminary theology professors. Until the 1940s, Jesuit colleges didn't even *offer* theology courses to laypeople; the required "Catholic" courses were in Thomistic philosophy. The first graduate-level theology courses outside of seminaries came only in the 1960s. Now almost all Catholic campuses have theology requirements, and laypeople were probably a majority at the convention. (I finally learned to spot priests from their standard uniform of knit golf shirts and sport coats.)

As McBrien put it, being a Catholic theologian in the old days was "like being the press secretary to the president. Your job was to present organizational policy as effectively as possible and defend it as necessary." And since theology was taught almost exclusively in seminaries, the challenge was merely to cover all the material that had to be crammed into a four-year program. The emphasis was on clarity and completeness, not on creativity—when parishioners asked what the rules were, priests were supposed to have them at their fingertips. Students who wanted to specialize went to Europe, and, in any case, the standard chancery career path was through canon law, not theology. In Europe, by contrast, theological training had been integrated into comprehensive universities, as at Louvain and Tübingen, for centuries, and Europe was the source of almost all the theological ferment leading up to Vatican II.

Credit: CTSA Archives, Catholic University of America
*Until Vatican II brought theological issues to a wide public, Catholic theology
was deemed to be virtually the exclusive province of priest-theologians training
priest-candidates in seminaries. This shot is from the founding meeting of the
Catholic Theological Society of America in 1945.*

A theologically informed laity has obvious foundation-rattling potential.
Diktats from on high are not accepted nearly as readily as in the past; and effective pastors in highly educated parishes, like St. Cecilia's Msgr. Rizzotto,
have long since switched to reasoning *with* their parishioners, instead of for
them. In the same way, the gradual feminization of the theological establishment and of the professional lay ministry pressures the sharp distinctions
between male and female ecclesial roles so treasured by the official Church.

Even more important, with the laicization of theology, the most important academic work has moved from the safe confines of seminary walls into
the much more freewheeling environment of secular universities. As an inevitable consequence Catholic academic theology has gradually absorbed
the university intellectual style and standards of achievement. Job promotions are based on publications and the approval of one's peers, not on fidelity to the latest encyclical from Rome. Imagination and creativity count
for more than the good opinion of Cardinal Ratzinger. The scope for origi-
nality expands at the expense of the space occupied by received Truth.

The worldviews of the modern academy and of the Church diverge
sharply around the question of whether humans *construct* reality or *discover*
it. For the Greeks, as for medieval thinkers, reality was "out there." Human
beings are players on a stage where all the apparatus is in place before they arrive. When Aristotle constructed his science of ethics, which St. Thomas

Aquinas catholicized in the thirteenth century, he proceeded by trying to tease out the "natural laws" that govern human affairs. Neither Aristotle, nor even Thomas, it should be said, thought of ethical laws as the immutable universals they sometimes became in later centuries. Aristotle considered ethics to be a "practical" science like medicine or navigation: "[W]e must be satisfied with . . . arguing about what is for the most part so from premises which are for the most part true . . . for it is a mark of the trained mind never to expect more precision in the treatment of any subject than the nature of that subject permits." Thomas's version of natural law also left considerable room for uncertainty, although divine revelation often cleared up doubtful cases.

For all their reservations, however, both Aristotle and Thomas treated moral standards as things that you *find.* They are part of an objective reality that exists quite apart from humanity. But at least since Kant, Western thought has taken a radically different tack. The problem posed by moderns like Harvard's John Rawls, perhaps the best known contemporary moral philosopher, is how to *design* a system of ethical rules from scratch. In effect, we wake up each morning to a moral stage that is quite empty; it's up to us to build the furniture from whatever we can find at hand.* Rules development is a constant *process;* nothing is fixed in stone. Lawyers, philosophers, psychologists constantly reexamine ethical, moral, and legal assumptions to see whether they still make sense.

No Catholic theologian would go so far. But the stress in so many of the texts of Vatican II, especially *Gaudium et Spes,* on the interaction between the Church and the world and the Church and cultures, marks a critical shift of perspective. Instead of merely polishing and displaying a trove of timeless truths, like so many family heirlooms, doctrinal discernment becomes a "process firmly located in history," as one priest-theologian put it. Moral questions, and sometimes even basic dogmas, like the Trinity or the nature of the Eucharist, are constantly examined for reinterpretation or active reconstruction, to meet the needs of the era. While a modern Catholic theologian's moral stage will never be as depopulated as Rawls's, the old rules are always subject to challenge and possible revision. It is the apparent acceptance of a much greater scope for the reinterpretation and redevelopment of

---

* I confess that I find Rawls's work rather sterile and legalistic. Like most contemporaries, he uses the *individual* as the unit of analysis and applies tools from microeconomics and rational choice theory to construct a quasi-legal regime designed to maximize self-interest, minimize damage to others, and incorporate a mild egalitarian bias. It is all very clever, and it feeds into the current, and depressing, tendency to see society as a collection of atomized individuals with absolute rights that are enforced in courts. A parent's reflex response to a selfish five-year-old, "*Share* your toys. She's your *sister!*" (true "family values") makes no sense in a Rawlsian world. Alasdair MacIntyre, I think, is also right to deplore the modern vision of morality as an endless series of new dilemmas. The older notion of *character* implies that the well-formed person usually knows what is right without much analysis.

basic doctrine in light of current conditions—in effect, making Catholic theology much more of a continuing, constructivist enterprise—that constitutes the essential modernity of Vatican II.

Creative theologians have a whole panoply of tools at their disposal for reexamining the traditional teachings—scriptural analysis, history, archaeology, patristics (the study of the ancient church fathers), philosophy, all collectively sometimes called the "historical-critical method." The problem is that historical criticism usually plays havoc with comfortable assumptions handed down through the ages. Onan's sin, it seems, was not spilling his seed but refusing to impregnate his dead brother's wife, as Jewish law required. The sin of Sodom was not homosexuality but inhospitality. When Jesus said, "What God has joined together let no man put asunder," he may have been referring to the Jewish/Roman practice of putting away a wife without benefit of legal procedure—and, anyway, Matthew's Gospel has a loophole for unchastity (19:9), and Paul made a waiver of his own (1 Cor. 7:15). And so on. Around the turn of the century, Protestant theologians expected that a disciplined examination of the biblical era could clear up most of the questions that divided Christians. But the deeper they probed, the more the received teachings became enmisted with uncertainty. Who compiled the original Gospel texts? How many versions were there? Who made the final choices? How to cut through the layers of translations, redactions, and oral traditions, the overlay of Palestinian localisms, to an ultimate scriptural bedrock? Rudolf Bultmann famously remarked in 1926, "In my opinion, we can sum up what can be known of the life and personality of Jesus as simply nothing."

Critical theology, moreover, is coming of age in an academic environment in which all variety of established norms have been under attack for years. If all meaning is merely an intellectual construct, the path to wisdom is to "deconstruct" the layers of imposed meanings carried by a literary text, a historical document, or even a law, before deciding what it means for *you*. One's own agenda—be it antipatriarchal, antiracist, or whatever—naturally helps define the layers of imposed meanings to be deconstructed. The emphasis is on the uniqueness of each interpretive event, not on perduring standards of analysis. In the more extreme cases, entire fields of academic inquiry have collapsed into mere subjectivity, including absurdities like "critical legal studies" that insists on subjective interpretations of case law and statutes. "Postmodernists," "poststructuralists," and "post-Marxists" gleefully attack the foundations of meaning, while traditionalists bewail the loss of standards and the decline of content.

Not surprisingly, there is a simmering debate among Catholic theologians on how to set boundaries for their subject—what sort of tethers make theology "Catholic"? The discussion maps closely to the very hot academic

Credit: *By permission, Catholic Theological Society of America*
The Board of Directors' table at the 1995 annual meeting of the Catholic Theological Society of America. About a third of CTSA members are now women, and most members teach in secular colleges and universities, where orthodoxy is not a key issue in career advancement. Only six of the eleven directors are priests, and the membership is primarily lay.

controversy on whether there is a literary canon—and if there is, who decides what's in and what's out? In theology, much as in literature, feminist scholars have tended to chart a course of their own; elsewhere, "liberation theology" has acquired a quasi-Marxist cast, concentrating on attacking oppressive social structures—often, of course, with good reason. (Liberation theology is mostly indigenous to Latin America, although with genetic links to Canon Cardjin and Dorothy Day through American and European missionaries. The lines reconverged in the United States in the antiwar protests led by nuns and priests like the Berrigan brothers in the 1960s and 1970s.)

Even liberals concede that there have been excesses. One commentator notes that theology in France, for example, has been "devastated" by deconstruction and postmodernism "until it almost ceased significantly to exist." In a CTSA seminar exchange, Fr. Gerald Fogarty, a historian of the American Church and its theology, and Monika Hellwig, a Georgetown professor and former CTSA president, lamented that their students expect to start with their *own* experiences, not with doctrine. Hellwig said, "Less and less information gets through. . . . Religion is becoming just a funny way of saying what philosophy is about." A friendly Protestant theologian, who worries about *Protestant* identity if Catholicism gets too flexible—what would they "protest" against?—has remarked that Catholics seem determined "in four decades to commit every major mistake that it took Protestant theology fully four centuries to make."

For me at least, Fr. David Tracy's keynote address at the 1995 CTSA meeting, "Evil and Hope," illustrated the pitfalls of the academy. Tracy is a modest, soft-spoken, formidably well-read theologian at the University of Chicago who for some years has been consciously adapting the tools of literary criticism to theology—in his words, reinterpreting Christian symbols around some "focal meaning" or "contested concept" to transform the symbols into some new meaning. (Not without fruitful results: at Old St. Patrick's in Chicago, for example, they have revived the delightful ceremony of the "May crowning" of the Blessed Mother, partly inspired by Tracy's emphasis on "recovering the symbols.") His CTSA talk was a dazzling riff on Western literature—from Aeschylus to Mircea Eliade—exploring the transformative power of suffering, with the help of occasional detours into the Gospels. The problem is that the whole scene—mostly middle-aged, mostly tenured, mostly white people sitting in an upscale hotel ballroom seeking prophetic insights from slave narratives—could just as easily have been at a Modern Language Association convention, the English lit department's version of the CTSA. In fact, the MLA has been doing it longer, and probably better (although their recent tendency has been to be *very* weird).* Tracy's official responder immediately invoked Toni Morrison, the just then very in vogue novelist, which clinched the comparison.

A century ago, Matthew Arnold warned the English literary establishment about the decline of standards and the turn toward subjectivity. Arnold's mantle in American Catholic theology is being assumed by Fr. Avery Dulles. Dulles, who is tall, gaunt, and patrician—very much of an Arnold figure—commands immense respect from all sides of the theological spectrum. Although he has insisted in recent years that Catholic theologians have to abide by "the official teachings of the Church," as he put it in an interview, it is hard to classify him as a conservative. He defended Richard McBrien when the orthodoxy of one of McBrien's books was challenged by the American bishops, and he has been among the most original and creative, and probably the most cited, of recent American theologians. At the CTSA convention, there was a large turnout for Dulles's workshop "Criteria in Catholic Theology," in which he proposed that "Catholic" theology had to be, among other things, subordinate to Catholic faith and pursued in communion with Rome. It was Dulles's researches, as much as anyone's,

* The American Association of Religion, however, can hold its own with the MLA. The AAR is not a Catholic organization, although the one convention I visited seemed to have a heavily Catholic attendance. I sat in on a presentation on the symbolic linkages between the vulva and the Trinity.

that revived the ancient concept of a "parallel magisterium," or an independent teaching authority of theologians alongside that of bishops, but he argued that the theologians' authority applied only so long as they were working within Church structures, and not in open opposition. His plea was for a "hermeneutic [an interpretive approach] of trust" rather than a "hermeneutic of suspicion." In the hallway gossip afterward, the ratings of Dulles's talk ranged from "wonderful" to "platitudinous."

In any case, the controversy on what is, and what is not, Catholic theology continues to boil. Theology professors from the more conservative seminaries have recently boycotted the CTSA and founded a conservative counterorganization, the Fellowship of Catholic Scholars, although its membership is still very small. Middle-of-the-road conservatives like Dulles stress that allegiance to the magisterium, or the Church's official teaching authority, is the final test. McBrien snorts, "But what is the magisterium? It takes theologians to define it." For McBrien, and perhaps for the majority of academics, the discipline itself, the criticism of other scholars, and the received methodology for interpreting Scriptures and reading the ancient fathers are enough to keep the enterprise within bounds. In practice, "Catholic" theology has splintered into an often bewildering array of schools ranging from feminist, environmental, and liberation theologies on the far left to the "sedevacantists" on the far right who argue that Vatican II was an outlaw Council. (Sedevacantist, or "vacant chair," suggests that the Pope has abdicated.)

Polemics have grown very sharp. McBrien said in exasperation, "I'm being positioned as some kind of left-wing radical. I'm *mainstream,* for heaven's sake. I'm a priest! I believe in *Chalcedon* [the ancient Council that defined the basic teachings on the nature of Christ]! That doesn't mean I have to agree with everything the Vatican says on in vitro fertilization." A conservative priest mirrored McBrien's complaint. "If you want to call me an ultraconservative, go ahead, I guess. But I'm just *orthodox*! I don't think of that as conservative." Fr. Joseph Fessio is a Jesuit theologian at the University of San Francisco, a founding member of the Fellowship of Catholic Scholars, and publisher of the conservative Ignatius Press. In conversation, Fessio is relaxed, humorous, and open-minded, but when I asked him about Richard McBrien, he said, "I'm *opposed* to McBrien. I think he's done real damage to the Church! I couldn't appear on a platform with him" McBrien retorts, "How can these people say they know just what Christ wants? That's almost idolatrous!" In an especially nasty twist, as tensions have heightened, both liberals and conservatives have taken to blaming the other's ideology for the sexual lapses in the Church. Andrew Greeley throws up his hands at the tone of some recent exchanges: "They're *academics.* What do you expect?"

The theological controversies could hardly have been expected to pass unnoticed by Rome. A liberal historian of the post–Vatican II Church wrote,

"[B]y 1970 'new theology' meant a very different thing" from what it meant at Vatican II. For Ratzinger, in particular, who was considered a progressive at the Council, the "road back to traditionalism could appear the only way to escape a theological disintegration." Whatever the motivation, the Vatican's reactions have steadily escalated from expressions of concern to increasingly heavy-handed interventions and, most recently, to what could reasonably be construed as a declaration of all-out war.

Rome Cracks Down

A gradually hardening Vatican line on theological heterodoxy was evident by the mid-1970s. Policy toughened further when John Paul II assumed the papacy in 1978, and even more so after Cardinal Ratzinger took over the Congregation for the Doctrine of the Faith, the Vatican's ideological bureau, in 1982. Pope Paul had decentralized Curial operations after the Council, but in the new regime, there was a steady recentralization, and by 1989 Ratzinger had regained more or less all the power that Ottaviani had enjoyed. Edward Schillebeeckx's Christology was subjected to detailed, hostile examinations in the late 1970s, and Hans Küng was forbidden to represent himself as a Catholic theologian, mostly because of his challenge to the doctrine of papal infallibility. The Vatican silenced Fr. Leonardo Boff, a leading Latin American exponent of "liberation theology," in 1984; but the discipline was lifted several months later, and Ratzinger issued an instruction that was considered quite friendly to liberation theologians, although warning against extremism and violence. There was also a crackdown on the ultraright French archbishop, Marcel Lefebvre, who eventually led a traditionalist schismatic movement.

In America, controversies tended to center around matters of sex and gender. The most celebrated case is that of Fr. Charles Curran, a former tenured theology professor at Catholic University. Curran, whose personal life is widely attested to be exemplary, questioned the Church's traditional teachings governing sexuality, including homosexuality, premarital sex, and remarriage after divorce. Curran's challenge was a nuanced one: he did not argue that the traditional teachings were wrong, but only that they were not "exceptionless norms"—in other words, while homosexual acts might normally be sinful, they were not necessarily so in every case. (I will return to the Church's teachings on sexuality in the next chapter.) The Vatican withdrew Curran's authority to teach theology at Catholic University in 1986, and he was effectively fired by Washington's Archbishop (now Cardinal) James Hickey, who is the university's chancellor. Hickey's action was upheld in court, on the ground that Catholic University's special status as a pontifical theological institute limited Curran's contractual right to academic freedom.

The Curran controversy sent a collective shiver through the theological establishment because of the far-reaching character of the Vatican's argument. Even the CTSA had always accepted that in seminaries, and presumably now also in the pontifical departments of Catholic University, the claims of academic freedom could be limited by the requirement of orthodoxy. But the Vatican signaled that it would enforce a provision of canon law that placed *all* Catholic theology teachers, regardless of where they taught, under the jurisdiction of the local bishop. At the same time, Archbishop (now Cardinal) Pio Laghi, the Vatican's representative in America, said that a 1968 instruction by the American bishops approving "lawful freedom of thought" and "norms of licit dissent" for theologians was "simply unworkable." The CTSA reported several instances of theological appointments at presumably lay-controlled Catholic colleges being vetoed by local bishops on grounds of orthodoxy. Shortly thereafter, the Vatican announced that all Catholic theologians would have to take a detailed oath designed to ensure their orthodoxy. A tense confrontation was finally defused in 1990 with the issuance of a set of rules that, while not waiving any of the Vatican's claims, endorsed local resolutions of orthodoxy issues—in effect, allowing bishops, who normally detest public controversies, to leave sleeping dogs alone.

Whether the Vatican's actions represent a "vicious assault" on academic freedom, as one scholar put it, or "gentle" handling, as Dulles suggests, depends on one's perspective. But by the standards of the past, at least, Dulles has a point. Curran—who is now a tenured professor at Southern Methodist University—Küng, and Schillebeeckx are all still priests, and, in Dulles's words, "They have all their sacramental faculties, they can preach, they can write whatever they please, their books are best-sellers. They simply can't represent their teachings as Catholic theology." He goes on, "American citizens can say whatever they want, but if you're an ambassador working for the State Department, you have to represent the official line."

The Vatican's clampdown on Seattle's Archbishop Raymond Hunthausen, which hit the headlines at the same time as the Curran controversy, was more complicated. Hunthausen was a very popular bishop and an excellent administrator, but he was reputedly "soft" on sexual issues, especially in his sympathetic approach to homosexual Catholics. It was his antinuclear stance that got him in trouble, however. In 1982, he began withholding half his income taxes to protest high levels of military spending, which may have prompted a complaint from the Reagan administration. (At the time the administration and the Pope were working quietly together to support Eastern European democracy movements.) The Vatican's imposition of an auxiliary in Seattle drew sharp public protests, and the arrangement broke down when the auxiliary, Bishop Donald Wuerl, tried to overrule Hunthausen's support of a local gay antidiscrimination ordinance. After a long standoff, the National Conference of Catholic Bishops (NCCB) finally mediated a solution, which was, arguably, even harsher than the Vatican's, since Wuerl was replaced by a coadjutor, Thomas Murphy from Montana, with full authority and the right of succession. But Murphy was a better politician than Wuerl, and he and Hunthausen, who by that time had suffered a bout with cancer, worked together amicably enough until Hunthausen retired in 1992.

Meanwhile, the Vatican has been steadily appointing more and more conservative bishops. In an interview, San Francisco's Archbishop John Quinn spoke of "an emphasis on what is called orthodoxy without an appropriate balancing emphasis on other qualities that are desirable." Orthodoxy on birth control is by all reports now a "litmus test," and the NCCB has been polarizing between a shrinking band of liberals and the majority conservatives. Bishop Raymond Lucker of Minnesota complained in a CTSA seminar about the growing lack of collegiality, and Quinn said, "You can't have real collegiality unless we're friends, and we can't be friends unless we trust each other. And there's not much trust." In June 1995, a dozen bishops published an extraordinary protest at the deterioration in the NCCB's functioning. They guessed another forty bishops supported the statement but had chosen not to sign it. The letter set out:

> current issues in the church that we seem not to address openly. These would include: the priest shortage, priest morale, ecumenical issues, school funding, women and equality in the church, better preaching, better liturgy . . . the relationship of the conference with Rome, the public face of the church on abortion, the annulment process . . . contraception, sexual ethics, the kind of candidates being attracted to the priesthood, the ordination of married men, and rumors of a high percentage of homosexual men in seminaries and the priesthood. In particular, the issue of pedophilia among priests. . . .

The bishop-signators complained that Rome had been "systematically reinterpreting" Vatican II to centralize authority in the Vatican and that "loyalty" had come to mean "a strict and undifferentiated application of all Roman norms . . . and the notion of the church as a multinational corporation with headquarters in Rome and branch offices (dioceses) around the world." They cited repeated instances when NCCB documents had been sent to Rome for approval before being debated at the conference, or when Rome had unilaterally changed documents that the conference had approved. The bishops particularly singled out the 1994 apostolic letter, *Ordinatio Sacerdotalis* ("Priestly Ordination"), which "definitively" declared that the Church had "no authority whatever" to ordain women to the priesthood:

"[The letter] was issued without any prior discussion or consultation with our conference. In an environment of serious questions about a teaching that many Catholic people believe needs further study . . . this new apostolic letter present[s] an immense pastoral problem that might have been prevented had there been more regular and open communication from us to Rome.

If the minority bishops expected Rome to apologize for jumping the gun on *Ordinatio Sacerdotalis,* they were to be sadly disappointed. The following November, the Vatican massively upped the ante by declaring the ban on the ordination of women to be an *infallible* teaching, a fundamental doctrine of the faith, a Truth guaranteed by divine revelation and the workings of the Holy Spirit. The announcement drew relatively little attention in the American lay press, because it was signed by Cardinal Ratzinger rather than by the Pope, although the release makes clear that the Pope expressly approved it and ordered its publication. But it is a declaration of what is effectively an extraordinary new papal power that opens the possibility of shifting a whole list of traditional Church teachings into the realm of infallible Truths, with critical implications for long-term relations between the American Church and Rome. The source of the problem is, once again, the ambiguity inherent in the documents of Vatican II—the conflict between an interpretation based on legislative history and a strict reading of the text, between the "spirit of the Council" and what it actually says. The trail of the argument is labyrinthine, but it is worth following in detail.

The Ordinary Universal Magisterium

One of the central aims of the majority at Vatican II was to restore the balance of power between the Pope and the world's bishops. Although the Vatican had actually exercised its power of infallibility only once since 1870, when Pius XII defined the doctrine of the Assumption in 1950, successive popes had bootstrapped the duty of obedience into something like the functional equivalent of infallibility. The high point was Pius XII's 1950 encyclical *Humani Generis,* written to stamp out "error" in Catholic theology—"error" included the teachings of a number of theologians who later played key roles at Vatican II. Once a Pope had officially expressed himself on an issue, according to the encyclical, it was no longer "a matter of free debate among theologians."

The final text of *Lumen Gentium* mandated obedience to the Pope in language similar to that of *Humani Generis* but, in an important victory for the liberals, implicitly permitted continued theological debate about noninfallible papal teachings. Then, after reconfirming the Pope's power of infallibility, *Lumen Gentium* adds a declaration of the teaching infallibility of bishops: "[Bishops] maintaining the bond of communion among themselves and with the successors of Peter, when teaching authentically matters concerning faith and morals, they agree about a judgment as one that has to be definitively held, they infallibly proclaim the teaching of Christ." This was not novel doctrine. In the controversy over papal infallibility at Vatican I, for instance, no one doubted that if the bishops of the world declared a doctrine in unison with the Pope, the Holy Spirit would protect them from error. Dissidents like St. Louis's Peter Kenrick complained only about the Pope's arrogating the power to himself acting alone.

When Paul VI forbade the practice of artificial contraception in the encyclical *Humanae Vitae* ("Of Human Life") in 1968, the press and lay Catholics immediately asked whether it was an infallible teaching and were assured that it was not. Certainly, it did not meet any of the obvious tests in *Lumen Gentium.* The Pope did not declare it infallibly—at the initial press conference, the papal spokesman twice stated that it was never intended as an infallible teaching. And he did not act collegially. In fact, the majority of the bishops Paul consulted disagreed with him. The reception by national episcopal conferences was at best sullen, and the laity almost universally ignored the doctrine. Although *Humanae Vitae* required "religious assent," under *Lumen Gentium,* it was not beyond the possibility of error and was open to continued debate by theologians; priests were therefore presumably on solid ground when they told parishioners to follow their consciences on the issue.

One of the Pope's key advisers in the drafting of *Humanae Vitae,* an American Jesuit, John Ford, had argued that the Pope had no right at all to overturn the traditional teaching. In a memorandum to Paul, he wrote: "The Church cannot change this answer [that birth control is inadmissible] *since this answer is true. . . .* It is true because the Catholic Church, instituted by Christ to show men the sure road to eternal life[,] could not err so atrociously through all the centuries of its history." Paul himself once said that changing the traditional rule "would have the effect of . . . showing the fallibility of the Church which then, like the Jewish synagogue, would have imposed too heavy a yoke on the people."

Ford resurrected and greatly elaborated this argument in a 1978 *Theological Studies* article, written with a Maryland seminary professor, Germain Grisez, which has become a rallying point for theological conservatives. Ford and Grisez argue that the birth control proscription is infallible teaching, not because *Humanae Vitae* is infallible, but because the college of *bishops* had

always taught it unanimously, and therefore infallibly. It is indeed undis-
puted, even by liberals, that the Church consistently taught the sinfulness of
contraception at least since the fourth century. According to Ford and
Grisez, such unanimity, over such an extended period, clearly meets the test
for episcopal infallibility in *Lumen Gentium,* called "the ordinary universal
magisterium" in theological jargon. The fact that many 1960s bishops did
not agree with the teaching was irrelevant, they argued, since the doctrine
had been infallibly declared long ago. There is no opting out of a divinely revealed, infallibly declared, Truth.

The insistence that moral teachings are of universal application, it might
be noted, naturally predisposes toward an expansive position on infallibility.
Even the most conservative theologians concede, on the same grounds as
Aristotle, that it is very difficult to derive "exceptionless" norms of behavior
purely from natural law arguments. Resort must therefore be made to divine
revelation, and definitive declarations of divine revelation inevitably rely on
the Church's infallible teaching authority. It is no accident, therefore, that
conservative interest in infallibility has heightened at a time when the Vatican
has been making uniform sexual norms a central axis of its doctrinal strategy.

In any case, mainstream theologians mostly regarded the Ford-Grisez
argument as a curiosity. One of the few to take it seriously, ironically, was
Hans Küng, who wrote in his 1981 book *Infallible?*:

> the moral inadmissibility of contraception has been taught as a matter
> of course and even emphatically by all bishops everywhere in the
> world, in moral unity, unanimously, for centuries. . . . [I]t is therefore
> to be understood in the light of the ordinary magisterium of pope and
> bishops as a factually *infallible* truth of morals, even though it has not
> been *defined* as such.

Küng was actually writing to express his doubts about the whole concept of
infallibility. In his view the birth control teaching is obviously wrong, yet
Ford and Grisez seemed to be reading the text of Vatican II correctly, so,
Küng argues, the doctrine itself must be at fault.

The doctrinal bombshell that the Vatican dropped in November 1995
was that they had applied what is essentially the Ford-Grisez argument to the
question of the ordination of women and concluded that the prohibition had
long since been infallibly declared by the world's bishops.

In form, the Vatican's statement is a response to a *"dubium,"* or a
"doubt," a question that some hypothetical troubled soul had posed to
Rome. (The procedure dates from the days of the Roman Empire, when
provincial governors wrote to Rome for clarifications of law.) The *dubium* is:

Whether the [teaching in the Pope's letter *Ordinatio Sacerdotalis*] is to be understood as belonging to the deposit of the faith.

And the "*responsum*" is:

In the affirmative. This teaching requires definitive assent, since . . . it has been set forth infallibly by the ordinary and universal magisterium [citing the language from *Lumen Gentium* on episcopal infallibility].

To doubting bishops, the Vatican says, in effect, "*You* have already declared this doctrine infallibly, so it is therefore beyond discussion."

The transmission also carries a "Reflection" that notes, in somewhat Orwellian style, that since the publication of the Pope's letter, "Many consciences which in good faith had been disturbed . . . found serenity once again thanks to the teaching of the Holy Father." But doubts persisted among those "distant from the Catholic faith" and among those to whom "the exclusion of women from the priestly ministry represents a form of injustice or discrimination against them." But according to the "Reflection," the Church has always taught "as an absolutely fundamental truth of Christian anthropology, the equal personal dignity of men and women, and the necessity of overcoming and doing away with 'every type of discrimination regarding fundamental rights.' " But the ban against women's ordination does not contradict this principle because "the ministerial priesthood . . . is a service and not a position of privilege or human power over others. Whoever, man or woman, conceives of the priesthood in terms of personal affirmation, as a goal or point of departure in a career of human success, is profoundly mistaken."

Although the ban is therefore logical and reasonable, the "Reflection" continues, such demonstrations are merely "a matter of convenience," for the question is determined by divine revelation, not by logical proofs. The ban on ordaining women:

derives from the truth of the doctrine itself since, founded on the written word of God and constantly held and applied in the tradition of the church, it has been set forth by the ordinary universal magisterium (cf. *Lumen Gentium,* 25). Thus the reply specifies that this doctrine belongs to the deposit of faith of the church. It should be emphasized that the definitive and infallible nature of this teaching did not arise with the publication of the [Pope's] letter *Ordinatio Sacerdotalis.* . . . In this case, an act of the ordinary papal magisterium, in itself not infallible, witnesses to the infallibility of the teaching of a doctrine already possessed by the church.

Ordinatio Sacerdotalis, in other words, was not an infallible teaching, just as *Humanae Vitae* was not; but as Ford and Grisez argued in the case of *Humanae Vitae*, it didn't *have* to be infallible, for it was merely witnessing to a doctrine that had *already* been infallibly declared by the universal Church.

To say that liberal theologians were alarmed would be an understatement. In the first place, the Vatican's statement contains no standard whatsoever for *which* traditional teachings might be declared infallible. Liberals argue that the record of episcopal teachings on the ordination of women is actually very sparse, for the simple reason that the question rarely came up in traditional societies; and when it did, the negative answer was usually based on the assumed natural inferiority of women, which is no longer an acceptable premise. There are equally clear episcopal teaching records on the acceptability of slavery, or of judicial torture, or on the historicity of Adam and Eve, or the hand of the devil and the saints in the random occurrences of everyday life. The record on birth control is incomparably richer; *a fortiori,* it would seem, Ford and Grisez must be right. For many centuries, in fact, bishops taught that "error has no rights" and that freedom of religion is an abomination. Why was that not infallible?

The casualness of the process is equally unsettling. No council ever gave the Curia the authority to decide which teachings are infallible. And the process would seem to open the door to almost unlimited papal and Curial doctrinal freelancing. Conciliar language that most people understood to shift power *away* from the Vatican to the bishops has been twisted into an incomparably flexible weapon for increasing centralized control.

The most soothing interpretation from Vatican watchers was that the *responsum* was seized on as a convenient way to cut off an increasingly embarrassing debate. Several million northern European Catholics had signed a petition calling for the ordination of women, and there are reports that the expectations of ecumenically inclined Protestants who ordain women in their own denominations had been unrealistically raised. But cutting off debate hardly seems consistent with the "spirit of Vatican II," however narrowly it is defined.*

---

* A somewhat Machiavellian and entirely speculative construction on the Vatican action is that it was Ratzinger's way of keeping the issue of women's ordination *open*. Hans Küng has recently pointed to Ratzinger's role in restraining the Pope's instincts for wielding the infallibility weapon freely. Küng has had much publicized differences with Ratzinger, so he is not likely to praise Ratzinger lightly; he is also known for his good Vatican connections and is probably a reliable informant. Ratzinger is an expert theologian and certainly knows that his doctrinal office can't make infallible declarations. From Ratzinger's point of view, however, such an anomalous action might have the multiple virtues of sending a clear signal to Protestants and other interested parties that the Vatican is strongly committed to its position, of simultaneously satisfying a papal urge for closure, but at the same time, of leaving the doctrine in a sufficiently unsettled state that a subsequent pope could change it with only minor embarrassment.

Bishop Kenneth Untener, who is among the more liberal members of the episcopacy, was scathing: "It's theologically incomprehensible—bishops can't make infallible declarations without being conscious of it. And it's painful and offensive to bishops. These are cherished words! *Infallible. The deposit of faith.* Are we supposed to pray now, 'I believe in God the Father Almighty. . . . I believe in the Holy Spirit. . . . I believe in the prohibition of the ordination of women'?"

Avery Dulles is one of the relatively few leading theologians to vigorously defend the substance of the ruling. (I summarize his arguments in the notes to this chapter.) But even Dulles has said, in a paper delivered to the American bishops:

> In any case, it is not the kind of truth that belongs to the basic profession of Christian faith, as found, for example, in the creeds. If it is a revealed truth, it stands relatively low in the hierarchy of truths. Because of these considerations, I do not think it necessary to treat those who doubt or deny the doctrine as heretics. But if they show obstinacy, such dissenters are subject to just canonical penalties.

Untener, at least, insists on looking at the bright side: "It wonderfully points up the need for defining some *process* around infallibility. Vatican II specifies all these powers but ducks the question of how they're to be exercised. This kind of a statement makes it hard to avoid that issue."

It is depressing, but inevitable, that all complicated debates become defined by their extreme positions, more especially so when they draw the attention of the mass media, as the dissensus within Catholic theology has assuredly done. Few theologians seem to be able to resist climbing on a soapbox when the reporters call, and elements of the Catholic media shovel coal onto the flames. "The Vatican reads the *Wanderer* and the *National Catholic Reporter* and thinks we're some kind of loony bin over here," one priest said.

Sorting out responsibilities is probably a fruitless exercise. Catholicism does assume that a core Truth lies beneath all the theological accretions and that the Pope has the key role in sorting it out; so it is perfectly reasonable to insist that the Catholic brand name be attached only to specific theologies. On the other hand, the zanier experiments in theology or liturgy—few of which have probably had much impact anyway—have been used to justify the reestablishment of a highly vertical approach to decision making, which has only sharpened partisan divisions. Intermediate authorities, like bishops and religious superiors, perhaps should have done a better job in moderating their internal mavericks. But the Vatican, presumably jealous of its own powers, has been hamstringing national and local ecclesiastic authority, instead of patiently building them up. All the language in Vatican II about "inculturation," and "the autonomy of earthly realities," and "fruitful interchange" between Church and local culture must mean more than just using the vernacular in the Mass. And even if the Vatican is "right," in some cosmic sense, when it rules on, say, the ordination of women, the unilateral nature of the process and the lack of restraint in multiplying edicts seem gratuitously insulting, in this case not only to women, but to all the rest of the "People of God" who don't happen to be members of the Curia.

In any case, the ruling on women's ordination serves notice, especially on American Catholics, that Rome intends no quarter on sexual and gender issues, which, more than any other, are at the root of the tensions in the Church.

CHAPTER 14

The Struggle with Sexuality

Fr. Tom Hayes, the AIDS minister for the San Francisco Archdiocese, works out of Most Holy Redeemer parish, in the city's famous Haight-Ashbury district, the very fountain and source of the outré in American culture. Most Holy Redeemer is San Francisco's "gay" parish. On paper, it is a parish like any other, but for more than a decade, it has consciously directed its outreach and counseling programs toward San Francisco's large population of gay Catholic men and women. Over the years, gay people from all around the city have gravitated to Most Holy Redeemer and, save for a shrinking remnant of old people from the neighborhood, its congregation is now predominantly gay. The parish ministry includes an on-site AIDS hospice with about seventeen residents, housed in the former elementary school building across the street from the church.

Hayes is a slender, balding, unprepossessing man in his early sixties. He is soft-spoken and almost shy, but he was recently singled out by *Commonweal* as an example of an outstanding preacher—not for his charisma or delivery, but for his thoughtfulness, sincerity, and preparation. He did graduate work in microbiology before entering the seminary; was ordained into a missionary order, the Oblates of Mary Immaculate; and switched to diocesan work when his order cut back because of shrinking membership.

Most of Hayes's time is spent ministering to dying young men and the rest to providing pastoral care to a Catholic population whose position within the Church is ambiguous, to say the least. First meetings are often at the deathbed, when a gay man who has been estranged from the Church decides to make a last-minute reconciliation. "His partner and friends will usually be there when I come into the apartment," Hayes said, "You often feel a great coldness. There is a lot of anger toward the Church on the part of the gay community." "Sometimes," he admitted, "it can be a terrific strain."

Each fall, Most Holy Redeemer has a Forty Hours' devotion for AIDS victims. The church keeps a scroll with the names of parishioners who died during the previous year. At the closing ceremony, members of the congregation read off the list of new names. "Each reader does ten names," Hayes said, "one reader after the other. The list goes on and on. It's very wrenching." Archbishop Quinn always made a point of attending the closing liturgy, a gesture that was much appreciated in the parish. The one year he had to be in Rome, the ceremony was rescheduled so he could attend.

Hayes has a dry humor and a store of Felliniesque tales of life at the parish. But except for the rate of funerals, he insists that Most Holy Redeemer is for the most part a normal parish. "We're very participative," he said. "There are a number of former priests and nuns who know a lot about their religion and the liturgy. Most parishes have trouble recruiting lectors or choir members, but we have a yearlong waiting list. And I do think gays often have a more highly developed affective and intuitive side. We have a lot of artists and designers." He smiled. "When we decorate, we *decorate*. Wonderful asymmetric stuff that you'd never see in the average church."

I asked how he measured success. "When people begin to center their lives on the reality of their love by Jesus Christ and know that they're accepted and loved by this parish community and that they're part of a worldwide community of love and faith." It is an answer that could easily sound trite and practiced, but Hayes said it with real conviction.

How did he handle his parishioners' sexuality? "I stress an informed conscience. I tell them, 'You know the difference between a life-giving and a death-dealing relationship.' We can't marry people, obviously, but we want them to distinguish between promiscuity and a bonded relationship. There's no point deluding ourselves and telling people never to have sex. We try to apply Catholic morality in a pastoral way. The important point is that God loves all of us, and calls all of us to goodness and to holiness. But we have to allow the individual to make the last practical decision. Everything we do here is scripturally and historically accurate, but inclusive."

The Tuesday 5:30 P.M. Mass at Most Holy Redeemer is usually well attended, and the evening I was there the Church was about three-quarters full. The congregation was young, and mostly male, although with a scattering of women. In one attractive liturgical twist, after the priest finished the prayers for ill or deceased parishioners, congregation members took turns announcing prayers of their own from the pews.

After Mass, there was a soup-and-crackers supper in the parish hall, and the conversation was pretty much the same as at all the other after-Mass coffees I've visited. We talked about the parish, the lay ministries, the opportunities for serving others. People told of having been estranged from the Church and of the emotional tugs that drew them back. When I asked about the Church's teaching on sexuality, I got the same answers as when I asked people in family parishes about birth control. The Catholic parishioners at Most Holy Redeemer believe in Jesus Christ. They believe that the Catholic Church is the true path to salvation. They believe in the sacraments, especially the Eucharist. They think that the worldwide identity of the Church through Rome and the Pope is very important. And they think that the Vatican and John Paul II are simply wrong when they stipulate what kind of sexual practices are necessary to get to heaven.

The visit to Most Holy Redeemer dredged up almost all the divisive issues that the Church keeps grinding its teeth over: the pertinency, the correctness, or, in some versions, the infallibility of the official teachings on sexual ethics; the yawning gap between what the Vatican prescribes in ever more ringing tones, what the bishops pay lip service to, and what priests are actually telling people out in the parishes; the relation between sexuality and sin, and whether unapproved sexual practices place one at risk of eternal damnation. And bound up with the Church's attitude toward sexuality is the question of whether to maintain a celibate priesthood, the attendant problem of recruiting "normal, healthy" young men into the priestly ministry, and, ultimately, the issue of women in the Church.

The arguments over sex and gender are really about fundamental definitions of Catholicism: What is the Catholic Church? What is the essence of being a Catholic? Does the core reduce only to Christ, the sacraments, and the community of the faithful? Are Catholic ethical norms inseparable from the core, an intrinsic part of an eternal plan that God has revealed to the faithful? Do those norms reduce to an apparatus of rules and procedures detailed enough to encompass individual sexual behavior? And who decides what those rules and procedures are?

The Unraveling of the Traditional Teaching

Mario Cuomo, the former New York governor, tells a story: "Jimmy Breslin was coming over to dinner one Saturday. I wasn't home when he got there, and Matilda told him that I'd gone to confession. He said, 'You'd better watch him, Matilda, he must be playing around. You know that the only sins Catholics can commit are about sex.' Boy, did I pay for that," says Cuomo. "It took me a couple of years to convince her that everything was okay. But sometimes it does look as if sex is all the Church cares about. But that's not what Catholicism should be about. Catholicism is so strong, and people want to know about love and family and the soul and the heart of Christ, and moral guidance. It's not just about sex."

The Catholic suspicion of sex is summed up in a once widely used manual on moral theology:

God's intention is that [sexual] pleasure should be experienced in, and should attract to, that mutual act between man and wife, designed by nature for the propagation of the race. . . . No other purpose . . . can be rationally assigned, and therefore no use of it outside wedlock can be rational. Even the smallest degree of incomplete venereal pleasure has reference by its very nature to legitimate sexual intercourse and to that alone. No other purpose can be rationally assigned to it. If, then, such pleasure be procured or accepted with no reference to its only purpose, a serious perversion of nature has taken place. It is grievously sinful in the unmarried deliberately to procure or to accept even the smallest degree of true venereal pleasure; secondly, it is equally sinful to think, say, or do anything with intention of arousing even the smallest degree of this pleasure.

Even in the sexually restrained 1950s, few other religions went so far. For Catholics, *any* indulgence in sexual pleasure outside of marriage was a mortal sin—a sin so grave, that is, that if you died before confessing it, you could count on spending all eternity in Hell. If a dating couple became sexually stimulated by a good-night kiss and did not immediately break off the contact, they were, in theory at least, each guilty of a mortal sin. Taking pleasure in a sexual, or "impure," thought, an impure picture, or an indecent movie were all mortal sins. Masturbation was not only mortally sinful, it was listed among the "unnatural" vices, along with bestiality and homosexuality. Premarital sex, even when the couple were engaged to be married, was always seriously sinful. The use of contraception within marriage was a particularly reprehensible form of masturbation. Normal sexual exploration by young people was a constant flirtation with damnation that could provoke terrors of conscience in the scrupulous.*

---

* Conservative theologians occasionally deny that their teachings were, or are, so severe. At a 1984 bishops' seminar on moral theology, the following exchange took place:

BISHOP: To many of us it seemed strange that in all the other commandments, even in the ones pertaining directly to God, there is parvity [smallness] of matter, but in this one commandment . . . there is no parvity of matter.

THEOLOGIAN: If you actually look precisely at what the classical moralists said, they said . . . [sexual sins] could be venial [not serious].

BISHOP (*possibly irritated*): But . . . [w]hy is it that moral theologians never use that expression, no parvity of matter, in relation to any of the other commandments, only to the sixth?

THEOLOGIAN: . . . The reason may be the fear that in the area of sexuality, if you give people an inch, they'll take a mile!

The implication that Hell could be threatened merely for policy reasons is as striking as the fact that a bishop appears confused about the actual teaching.

The pre–Vatican II Church could be strikingly casual in invoking the sanction of mortal sin. Eating meat on Friday, missing Mass on Sunday, receiving communion without absolutely fasting, including water, from the previous midnight were all capital offenses. Cardinal Dennis Dougherty didn't hesitate to use the threat of eternal fire to enforce his Philadelphia movie ban. The stringency of the rules was mitigated only by the availability of Saturday confession; you had to be extra careful not to be hit by a truck for a week at most. With a God so quick to lethal anger, the sexual disciplines were perfectly plausible, whatever the difficulties of compliance. If eating meat on Friday was such a dangerous disruption of cosmic harmonies, masturbation surely must have been as well.

My conversations with pre–Vatican II Catholics suggest that the rules may have weighed more heavily on some Catholic subgroups, like Irish Americans, than on, say, Italian Americans—witness also the persistence of guilt and sin as themes in Irish-American fiction. Luigi Barzini has pointed to the Italian penchant for constructing and then ignoring baroque systems of rules. The notorious noncompliance with the Italian tax code, compared with the relatively good record in the United States, suggests that America is still a much more rule-bound society. But when there are two parties, one of which is accustomed to passing many rules, and treating them lightly, and the other to making fewer rules, but taking them seriously, the possibility of miscommunication in matters of religious doctrine must be very high. A Jesuit quoted a senior Italian cardinal as saying disgustedly, "You Americans! You keep dragging the ideal down into the mud of reality." After Vatican II, notions of Hell, damnation, and mortal sin, almost overnight, virtually disappeared from the American Church—another example of the "spirit of the council" prevailing over the texts. The Church has been struggling to restore a sense of sin, although with mixed success—the consequence, perhaps, of using the weapon so casually in the past.

The very strict view of sexuality has a long Christian tradition but owes more to Greek Stoics than to Scripture. St. Paul indulges in some fierce strictures against nonmarital sex, but even conservative biblical scholars concede that Paul's directives were aimed at specific local pastoral problems and may not have been intended as exceptionless universal norms.* Stoic philosophy

---

* This is not an uncontroversial question. But the 1984 bishops' conference cited in the previous footnote provides some insight into the state of the issue. The conference was sponsored by the Pope John Center, a conservative ethical research organization, Cardinal Ratzinger was in attendance, and the program was devoted to shoring up the traditional teachings. But no one challenged the biblical expert who, after reviewing Paul's teachings in some detail, said: "[W]hat relevance [do] Paul's suppositions have to a modern discussion of 'absolute' norms[?] The short answer to this is, I think, that they have *no* immediate relevance. The fact that Paul considered his injunctions to be 'absolute' does not necessarily mean that they are 'absolute' in our sense. . . . [They] need imply no

was influential early in the Christian era: in reaction against the extreme licentiousness of a dying Greek culture, Stoics promoted an ideal of disciplined rational control of all the faculties. Since they regarded intercourse as an extreme case of losing control, Stoics recommended engaging in sexual relations only for the express purpose of producing children. In the theology manual quoted above, the emphasis on rational purpose marks its Stoic pedigree; neither St. Paul nor Jesus talked that way.

A strong aversion to sexuality extended for almost the whole of Christian history. St. Jerome (d. 419) taught that a man who was "too ardent a lover of his wife" was guilty of adultery. St. Augustine (d. 430), who was famously shamefaced about his own youthful libertinism, decided that even marital intercourse to sate concupiscence was a venial sin. A millennium later, priestly warnings against enjoying sex drew the moan "Allas! That evere love was synne" from Chaucer's Wife of Bath. Medieval manuals are full of doubts on the legitimacy of sex between aged couples or with a pregnant or sterile wife, and chew over the refinements of *amplex reservatus,* or intercourse without male orgasm. For all the aspersions cast on the "rigid scholasticism" of the thirteenth century, it was actually St. Thomas who defended sexual pleasure in marriage, since he saw it as part of the natural end of the generative apparatus and proportional to its purpose.

The suspicion of sex was reinforced by European monasticism. Nothing so disrupted orderly monastic life as a breakdown of sexual restraint. St. Basil had warned that in the monastery, "even when rigorous self-restraint is exercised, the glowing complexion of youth can be a source of desire to those around them. If, therefore, anyone is youthful and physically beautiful, let him keep his attractiveness hidden until his appearance reaches a suitable state." St. Thomas worried about cataloging sexual sins, but he decided it was safe so long as his speculations were "accompanied by . . . abhorrence." Christian skepticism about sex survived the Reformation. Some of the early Lutherans and Calvinists were so censorious in sexual matters that Catholics actually lightened their teachings a bit to underline their differences. The Catholic practice of aural confession, however, imposed a necessity for detailed manuals for the guidance of priests that Protestants did not have to trouble with. Since sexual transgressions made up the great percentage of or-

more than that, in his judgment, and given the presuppositions of his time and culture, they were valid proclamations of what was right and wrong for those who shared these presuppositions." In the transcript of the discussion that followed, the expert remained unchallenged when he made the point even more strongly: "[W]e have to admit soberly that we cannot find from the pages of scripture a criterion to assess the permanent validity or otherwise of its moral teaching," citing other forceful commands of Paul, like those on the subordination of women, that are no longer considered binding. (The theologian did not question the existence of universal norms but argued that discovering them was the task of the moral theologian, not the scriptural scholar.)

dinary people's confessional material, Catholic theologians spun out vast oceans of exquisitely detailed discriminations, weighing and rating the various modes and styles of sexual sins and creating the pettifogging tone of so much of Catholic moral theology.

So long as the world was primarily agrarian, there was minimal conflict between Church teachings and lay predilections. Sex outside of marriage was severely disruptive of traditional society and was treated with commensurate severity. When Thomas Hardy's Tess has a brief dalliance with a young nobleman, she becomes pregnant, wanders homeless in search of her lover, kills her newborn in a fit of temporary insanity, and is duly hanged before the now shattered young man (who gets off with only a bad case of remorse). Rural young people experimented with sex, of course, but they were hastily married. Single, potentially sexually active adults were a threat to village stability, so widows and widowers were pushed into quick remarriages. A husband who allowed his wife to stray sexually was roughly handled by the French *charivari*. Peasants, moreover, had a stake in large families. Sons and daughters meant extra hands, and frequent pregnancies offset high rates of child mortality. But even among the peasantry, withdrawal was widely used as a contraceptive technique. Curates instructed wives to remain passive during coitus interruptus, for then only the husband would sin. Peasant husbands had little time for curates anyway.

The gradual emergence of an urban bourgeoisie inevitably challenged the traditional ethic. For the commercial classes, the expenses of education and households, the need to preserve capital for inheritances and dowries, the greater refinement and social status of the mistress of the house, all conduced to the regulation of family size. The same social developments brought a rethinking of Church doctrine against lending at interest—John Noonan, a historian of dogma, suggests that the Church's commercial interests were an added incentive to revise the usury rule; but there was no similar incentive in the sexual arena. In the modern era, for Catholics and Protestants alike, family size became an inverse indicator of social status—the Roncallis had thirteen children, but the upper-class Montinis had only three. And it was those most top-drawer of Protestants, Great Britain's Anglican bishops, who first officially, if still grudgingly, approved the practice of marital birth control in 1930. The Vatican, however, held firm. Pius XI's 1930 encyclical, *Casti Conubii* ("Of the Chaste Marriage"), was a direct response to the Anglican defection and set out the Catholic teaching in terms that seemed to brook no dissent: "Since . . . the conjugal act is destined primarily by nature for the begetting of children, those who . . . deliberately frustrate its natural power . . . sin against nature and commit a deed which is . . . intrinsically vicious."

The first real breach in the firewall was made by Pius XII. Medical researchers had identified the female ovulatory cycle in the 1930s and gradually defined markers like body temperature that roughly indicated fertile and infertile periods. In a 1951 address to Italian midwives, Pius approved the use of the "rhythm," or calendar, method of birth control and suggested that "serious motives," which might include both economic and health reasons, could legitimize the use of rhythm for extended periods. Shortly thereafter, the Pope said, "We have affirmed the legitimacy . . . of a regulation of offspring . . . which, unlike so-called birth control, is compatible with the law of God." Simply put, married people were permitted to enjoy sex even while trying to avoid conception. St. Jerome and St. Augustine would have been appalled.

The discovery of the progesterone birth control pill in 1953 greatly complicated matters, for it could also be prescribed to stabilize irregular menstrual cycles. In 1958, Pius, who liked speaking to technical gatherings, told a conference of doctors that medical use of the pill was permissible; any consequent birth control effect would be "indirect" and therefore not objectionable. The principle of "double effect" was descended from St. Thomas: it was wrong to *try* to kill an assailant, but there was no sin if the assailant's death followed from a reasonable self-defense. The same logic permits "indirect" abortion—e.g., excising a fallopian tube to end an ectopic pregnancy. John Rock, a Catholic doctor who was a codeveloper of the progesterone pill, went a step further and touted the pill as an extension of the rhythm method, eliminating the necessity for thermometers and other apparatus. Some prominent theologians agreed with Rock.

By the late 1950s, there was considerable confusion at the parish level. Some priests would permit the use of rhythm for only a few months between pregnancies, some left it to a couple's conscience, some endorsed the pill. Some doctors routinely wrote "irregularity" on birth control pill prescriptions for their Catholic patients. For the first time, Catholics discovered the possibilities of moral forum–shopping. After the Dutch bishops dropped their opposition to the birth control pill in 1963, John XXIII, at Cardinal Suenens's suggestion, quietly convened a papal commission to review the traditional teaching.

Cracks in glaciers turn into avalanches. Pius XII changed the rule on fasting before communion, and then Paul VI dropped the prohibition against eating meat on Fridays. These had been hanging offenses. Before Vatican II, it was sacrilegious to touch the host, but after the Council the priest simply handed it to you. The Church said that Mass was the same without Latin, and with folk guitars instead of organs and hymns, but it didn't look that way to laypeople. Catholics had been trained to think of the Church as an imperishable rock, eternal in every detail, but granite was turning to moss. Priests were forced to argue that although God no longer cared what Catholics ate on Fridays, he *still* cared about the kind of birth control they used, or at least would until further notice.

Expectations for a rules change quickened when the existence of the birth control commission was revealed in 1964. Paul clearly seems to have been prodding the commission. It had been John's idea, and Paul was under no obligation even to retain it. When the early meetings, despite signs of wavering, supported the traditional teaching, Paul brought in additional theologians known for their liberal views, and finally introduced a number of lay experts on fertility and population studies, and even married couples. One of the couples, Pat and Patty Crowley of Chicago, the cofounders of the Christian Family Movement, conducted a survey that turned up real anger among their movement's women. These faithful daughters of the Church, worn out by childbearing, with swollen legs and distended veins, were tired of placing their lives at risk by too frequent pregnancies and multiple miscarriages. The tombstones in old cemeteries attested to how many women died in their youth, and male celibates told them it was their lot and their glory. One woman wrote that priests should be forced to take their rectal temperatures for a few weeks before giving advice on rhythm. Patty Crowley herself had almost died during the birth of her fourth child.

Colette Potvin of Canada, another commission member, who had had five children, three miscarriages, and a hysterectomy, explained that women,

Credit: By permission of Patricia Crowley

Chicago's Pat and Patty Crowley (center), the cofounders of the Christian Family Movement, and among the small number of laypeople invited to attend Pope Paul VI's Birth Control Commission, are shown here after a Commission meeting. (No photographs were allowed of the sessions.) A Crowley survey showed what severe hardships the traditional teaching worked on women and contributed to the Commission's vote in favor of a change.

too, had sexual urges, and that they were often strongest during ovulation. With a good sex life, a woman was calmer with her children and kinder toward her husband; marriages were stronger and richer. Theologians who only a few years before had been cautious about accepting the pill were finding it harder to explain why *any* method of birth control, excluding abortion, should not be permissible in a Christian marriage. One holdout theologian asked, "What then with the millions we have sent to Hell if these norms were not valid?" Patty Crowley interjected, "Father, . . . do you really believe that God has carried out all your orders?"

At its final meeting, in 1966, the full commission voted 52–4 to drop the ban on artificial birth control in marriage. The recommendation was reviewed by a committee of sixteen cardinals and bishops, who held the real voting power; only one member, Archbishop Karol Wojtyła of Kraków, the future Pope John Paul II, did not attend. After a painstaking review of the commission's findings, the prelates finally called the question. They were polled three times. On the question of whether contraception was intrinsically evil, they voted 9–3, with 3 abstentions, that it was not. On the question of whether permitting contraception would violate the continuity of the Church's teaching tradition, they voted 9–5, with 1 abstention, that it would not. On the question of whether the Church should declare its position as soon as possible, they voted 14–1 that it should. The results of the voting and the commission report were quickly leaked to the world press.

It was therefore a profound shock when Paul, after a two-year delay, strongly reconfirmed the traditional doctrine in his 1968 encyclical *Humanae Vitae* ("Of Human Life"). Paul reached his decision only after much agonizing—hence the long delay—and after he had been subjected to unremitting lobbying by Ottaviani and other conservatives. The encyclical itself seems to reflect his indecision. In the opening paragraphs, Paul reviews the problem of increasing population, the difficulty of supporting large families in a commercial society, the desirability of subjecting nature to rational will and intelligence, and writes:

This new state of things gives rise to new questions. Granted the conditions of life today and taking into account the relevance of married love to the harmony and mutual fidelity of husband and wife, would it not be right to review the moral norms in force till now . . . ? Moreover, if one were to apply here the so-called principle of totality, could it not be accepted that the intention to have a less prolific but more rationally planned family might not transform an action which renders natural processes infertile into a licit and provident control of birth? Could it not be admitted, in other words, that procreative finality applies to the totality of married life rather than to each single act?

The encyclical continues with a paean to married love and the married state, draped in the "personalist" language of Vatican II. After stressing the obligation of "responsible parenthood" for married couples, Paul writes:

> those are considered to exercise responsible parenthood who prudently and generously decide to have a large family, or who, for serious reasons and due respect for the moral law, choose to have no more children for the time being or even for an indeterminate period.

And *then* Paul concludes that:

> the natural law, which [the Church] interprets by its constant doctrine, teaches as absolutely required that *in any use whatever of marriage* there must be no impairment of its natural capacity to procreate human life.

And goes on:

> to force the use of marriage on one's partner without regard to his or her condition or personal and reasonable wishes in that matter, is no true act of love, and therefore offends the moral order. . . . In the same way, if they reflect, [a couple] must also recognize that an act of mutual love which impairs the capacity to transmit life, which God the Creator, through specific laws, has built into it, frustrates his design . . . and contradicts the will of the Author of life. Hence, to use this divine gift while depriving it . . . of its meaning and purpose, is equally repugnant to the nature of man and woman, strikes at the heart of their relationship and is consequently in opposition to the plan of God and his holy will.

All the personalist buildup notwithstanding, artificial birth control violates the natural law and God's law and is as repugnant as marital rape. Paul expects married couples to see it the same way.

Vatican II and the birth control encyclical stand as the twin peaks of Paul's papacy—the first letting loose the sometimes unbridled "spirit of Vatican II," and the second, coming so shortly after, beating such a visible retreat to the old verities. If the laity was shocked by the sudden hard line after expectations had been raised so high, Paul was equally distressed by the open rejection that greeted his encyclical, even by priests. Among lay Catholics, disregard of the teaching quickly approached unanimity. Catholic acceptance of the morality of contraception actually *rose* in the wake of *Humanae Vitae,* as if the Pope's intransigence merely confirmed the Church's fallibility. Paul was Pope for ten more years, but *Humanae Vitae* was his last encyclical.

Digging In

The long delay in promulgating *Humanae Vitae* fed the rebelliousness that marked its reception. Because almost everybody expected that the traditional teaching would be revised, theologians had worked intensively to develop new approaches to moral theology. The Vatican's admission that *Humanae Vitae* did not represent infallible teaching, moreover, seemed to invite continued debate, so dissenting theologians only redoubled their efforts. The loose consensus that emerged is usually called "proportionalism," prominently associated in America with Fr. Charles Curran, and it was his embrace of proportionalism while at Catholic University that led to his problems with the Vatican.

Proportionalism is reluctant to designate any act as "intrinsically evil." The evil of killing depends on whether you are robbing a bank or fighting a war. Proportionalists are inclined to assume that most sexual acts, considered in the abstract, are "premoral"; judgments of morality must take into account all the circumstances and intentions of the parties. Marriage does not by itself make exploitative sexual relations moral; and the lack of a marriage license does not by itself make a loving, responsible, relationship sinful. Hayes's distinction between "life-giving and death-dealing" relationships is a proportionalist position.

At one point during his confrontation with Church authorities, Curran summarized his position on sexual issues as follows:

> On the question of contraception and sterilization, I have maintained that these actions . . . can be good or evil insofar as they are governed by the principles of responsible parenthood and stewardship. However, I have also pointed out the danger of abuse. . . . Masturbatory acts are ordinarily not very important or significant and usually do not involve grave matter. . . . However, masturbation falls short of the full meaning of sexuality and should not generally be seen as entirely good or praiseworthy. . . . I propose that for an irreversible, constitutional or genuine homosexual, homosexual acts in the context of a loving relationship striving for permanency can in a certain sense be objectively morally acceptable . . . [but] homosexual relationships fall short of the full meaning of human sexuality. This position obviously does not accept or condone homosexual acts without personal commitment. . . . I insist that the full meaning of human sexuality involves a permanent commitment of love between a woman and a man. . . . Only in very rare and comparatively few situations would I justify premarital sexuality on the basis of a theology of compromise.

I spoke to dozens of priests in the course of preparing this book—I make no claim that the sample is scientific—and almost always asked about their positions on sexual issues. In the light of all the controversy over a perceived loosening of Catholic sexual teachings, I was struck by how very *conservative* priests are, including priests who are well known as "liberals." And even in academic theology, as Boston College's Lisa Sowle Cahill, a former CTSA president, put it, "[T]he arguments between so-called liberals and conservatives are really over a few degrees on the very conservative end of the spectrum. Most of us are working in a neo-Thomist natural law tradition. We believe in the existence of right and wrong, and in universal laws. The question is really about how specific a universal law can be."

Despite their overall conservatism, I found only a handful of parish priests who regarded contraception in marriage as seriously sinful. The exception was Lincoln, Nebraska, which is known as one of the two or three most conservative dioceses in the country. Fr. Robert Barnhill is the director of Lincoln's Family Life office, which coordinates diocesan marital counseling and education programs. Even in Lincoln, Barnhill said, although "this is one of the few dioceses where 99.9 percent of the priests support *Humanae Vitae,* I would guess that 80 percent of our married couples contracept. Maybe it's 85 percent everywhere else. I like to think that we've moved the rate down a little." As a practical matter, *Humanae Vitae* is a dead letter in American parishes.

On the other hand, parish priests are virtually unanimous in opposing abortion. Almost every parish has a Life Ministry, including outreach programs offering alternatives for women considering an abortion and a "Rachel" ministry to reconcile those who have already had one. Most priests seem to have adopted the "seamless web of life" argument prominently associated with Chicago's late Cardinal Joseph Bernardin. By linking abortion and capital punishment, Bernardin smoothed over apparent inconsistencies in the Catholic attitude toward different varieties of killing.

But the priests' "seamless web" position is more conservative than that of the academy, for it accepts the Vatican principle that human life must be protected from "the moment of conception." Academics tend to be less sure. Fertility research shows that the majority of fertilized human ova are not successfully implanted in the womb and are simply passed during menstruation. Implantation itself takes a week or longer, twinning can occur within the first two weeks or so after fertilization, and genetic material is sometimes significantly modified during the same time. Curran, therefore, and many other Catholic theologians suggest that ending a pregnancy in the first few weeks, before a fully individuated human person is present, is a much less serious matter than a later-stage abortion. Similarly, medieval canonists taught that an abortion before "ensoulment," which was assumed to occur sometime between the second and third month of pregnancy, was sinful but not a homicide.* Measured by secular standards, however, even academic Catholic theologians are quite conservative on the abortion issue. Cahill said: "I don't think an abortion, especially an early-stage abortion, is the same as murdering your two-year-old, but that doesn't make me pro-choice."

The question on sexual ethics I tried out most often went like this: The traditional teaching on premarital sexuality presumed that young people abstained from intercourse until the late teens and then married. The modern economy, however, imposes such an extended period of education and training that marriage is often not practical until people are in their late twenties or early thirties. Is it reasonable to insist on abstinence over such an extended period? Shouldn't the Church be developing a practical sexual ethic for young people that recognizes that delayed marriages are now the norm?†

Almost all the priests I talked to, even very liberal ones, answered no. Msgr. Lloyd Torgerson of St. Monica's, whose pews are packed with unmarried thirtysomething couples, said he sticks with the traditional teaching. "We're not as hard in the confessional as we used to be," he said, "but I hold to the view that premarital sex is wrong." (Torgerson's youthful lay ministers, however, were more liberal.) Fr. Thomas Reese, a Georgetown Jesuit who often writes on the liberal side of theological issues and works in a young adult parish, said, "I'm very conservative on sexual issues. Talk all you want about a 'responsible sexual ethic,' but as far as I can see from my pastoral work, women are being terribly exploited. The guys move from relationship to relationship and leave a trail of shattered lives." Andrew Greeley echoed Reese: "I think the old system worked better," he said. "The so-called new rules are really hard on young women." When I asked Reese what he said when couples sought advice on premarital sex, he reflected for a minute and said, "They don't ask us."

---

* The Church fathers unanimously condemned abortion from the very earliest period. Traditionally, however, early-stage abortions, while viewed as gravely sinful, were not considered as serious as later-stage ones, and medieval casuists developed a number of exceptions in the interest of protecting the health of the mother and dealing with special circumstances like rape. The casuists' exceptions came under attack by Rome beginning in the eighteenth century. Medical science also cast doubt on the Aristotelian concept of a definite "ensoulment," while the emerging dogma of the Immaculate Conception taught that Mary was free from sin from "the instant of conception." John Noonan has pointed out that the Roman legislative impulse usually produces less nuanced guidelines than the distinction-oriented enterprise of theologians, an important observation that extends across the whole of moral theology. The teaching against abortion hardened rapidly in the late nineteenth century, culminating in Pius XI's 1930 encyclical, *Casti Conubii*, which arguably allows *no* exception, even to save the life of the mother.

† The conservative editor Fr. Richard John Neuhaus pointed out that my question had an upper-class bias, which is probably right. His formative experience was as a (Lutheran) pastor in Bedford-Stuyvesant, a very poor, predominantly African-American section of Brooklyn. Higher-income and highly educated people may be able to manage under a system of less structured sexual rules, he said, but in poor neighborhoods the effects of a relaxed sexual regime has been "catastrophic."

But conservative as all these priests are, their positions are still far to the left of the Vatican's. After the rough reception accorded the birth control encyclical, the Vatican began pounding home that the traditional teachings not only still applied but were a crucial element of Catholicism. The campaign escalated steadily through the 1970s and 1980s, and has been marked by a striking reversion to the more rigid versions of natural law theology. The purpose of any faculty, the Vatican argues, can be divined from its design, therefore the "finality," or final end, of the sexual act can only be procreation, and therefore permissible sexual acts are "limited to unimpeded spilling of semen into the vagina," as one dissenting theologian put it.

The heroic string of "therefores" is typical of medieval natural law thinkers, but it sometimes conceals circular reasoning. For example, Thomas Aquinas writes, "[M]oney, according to the Philosopher [Aristotle], was invented chiefly for the purpose of exchange: and consequently the proper and principal use of money is its consumption or alienation. . . . Hence it is by its very nature unlawful to take payment for the use of money lent, which payment is known as usury." Thomas's conclusion is embedded in his premise: if money is inherently a medium of exchange and not a form of capital, treating it as a form of capital must be opposed to natural law. Bishops pointed out the pitfalls of natural law reasoning as early as the Council of Trent, when Thomas's version of natural law was anointed as more or less official Catholic theology. That council also had a Xavier Rynne: he was Paolo Sarpi, writing from archives about fifty years after the event. Sarpi was a priest, later excommunicated, a prodigiously learned polymath and a friend of Galileo. In his history of Trent, a dissident asks plaintively as the Council moved to adopt yet another natural law formula, "[P]erhaps if Aristotle had not made this speculation, we would not have known it until now, and yet there is made of it an Article of Faith, necessary to salvation."

The "Declaration on Certain Problems of Sexual Ethics," issued by the Vatican in 1975, virtually identifies divine revelation with the Thomistic natural law:

> Since revelation and, in its own sphere, philosophy have to do with the deepest needs of mankind, they inevitably at the same time reveal the unchangeable laws inscribed in man's nature and which are identical in all rational beings. . . . Throughout its history the Church has always held a certain number of precepts of the natural law to be absolute and unchangeable.

The declaration then proceeds to condemn nonprocreative sex within marriage and necessarily, therefore, all other nonprocreative sexual acts. Masturbation is "an intrinsically and gravely disordered action" (an extraordinary amount of theological ink has been spilled over masturbation), and premarital or homosexual sex is absolutely forbidden. The declaration repudiates proportionalism and reiterates that all violations of sexual morality are "objectively grave" and, saving only the possibility of diminished responsibility, are normally mortal sins.

Drawing such hard, bright, hyperrational lines in an area as protean as human sexuality has inevitably tangled the teaching Church in a host of awkward conundrums. For one thing, it permits almost no gradation of sins. A narrow but bottomless abyss separates all mortal sins—calling for eternal damnation—from all others, leading to some oddly disproportionate groupings. In his encyclical *The Splendor of Truth,* John Paul II writes that there are acts "which by their very nature are 'incapable of being ordered to God,' " which are always and through themselves, regardless of motive and circumstances, "intrinsically evil." And he proceeds to list them: "genocide, abortion, euthanasia, and voluntary suicide . . . mutilation, physical and mental torture and attempts to coerce the spirit, subhuman living conditions . . . arbitrary imprisonment, prostitution and trafficking in women and children" And then, citing Paul VI, the Pope adds "contraceptive practices" to the list. The vast majority of Catholic married couples, that is, stand on the wrong side of the abyss with Hitler and Pol Pot.

The effort to wean Catholics away from contraception has led conservative moralists to an enthusiastic embrace of "natural family planning" (NFP), an updated form of the rhythm method. Advocates claim that NFP is almost foolproof and greatly enhances the quality of married love. There are international NFP journals, replete with drug company advertising for vaginal thermometers, and there is a simmering ideological war between adherents of the temperature method and the mucus method. The tone of advocacy is captured in a statement by Gerard Brunelle, a Canadian NFP leader: "In our family, when our daughters had their first menstruation, the best gift we could think of for them was an ovulation chart along with an explanation of how to use it." Brunelle also recommends that teenage sex education programs in Catholic schools should include "charting instructions for young women . . . leading to precise ovulation detection. The sooner positive knowledge is acquired . . . the sooner they will be able to impart this reality to their male peers," which seems like strange advice. I also found it mildly incongruous to listen to an earnest young priest, an advocate of the mucus method, explain how a woman should take a vaginal wipe and stretch the mucus between her thumb and fingers; when it was "stringy and opaque," she could be sure that she was infertile, and when it was "clear and watery," she would be approaching ovulation.

Perversely for a family-centered religion, the Vatican's hermetic logic greatly limits the use of modern fertility technology for Catholic couples seeking to conceive. Artificial insemination with sperm from a third-party donor is impermissible because it violates the marital relation, involves masturbation, and could possibly be a form of adultery. Further, the Vatican suggests, it "deprives [the child] of his filial relationship with his parental origins and can hinder the maturing of his personal identity," which may surprise adoptive parents. The use of a *husband's* sperm is permissible, but only if it is recovered from intercourse. Using a condom with holes apparently passes the "open to transmission" test, and the sperm can then be injected into the woman, although presumably right away so it "merely facilitates the conjugal act" instead of substituting for it. In vitro techniques are disallowed because they are "deprived of the meanings and the values which are expressed in the language of the body and in the union of human persons." Fertilized ova, moreover, are "human beings," so it is obviously criminal to store them, freeze them, or allow excess ova to die, all of which are normal accompaniments of in vitro procedures. (But no one suggests baptizing fertilized ova, although there are lingering doubts, especially among conservatives, as to whether unbaptized infants are saved. The new *Catechism* merely surrenders them "to the mercy of God.")

Despite the "suffering of spouses" who cannot have children, the Vatican insists that "marriage does not confer upon the spouses the right to have a child, but only the right to perform those natural acts which are per se ordered to procreation." Brunelle dismisses the whole question with: "Contraception takes life away from love while in vitro techniques take love away from life. They are the two sides of the same anti-life coin." One hopes that God judges epigrammatic smugness more harshly than an adolescent's masturbation.

Few people would dispute that present-day sexual ethics are in considerable disarray, whether the issue is date rape or unwed motherhood. Amid secular confusion, the clarity and consistency of the Church's position on issues like abortion, coupled with the great personal charisma of John Paul II, have undoubtedly shifted the terms of the debate. Even pro-choice advocates, to a degree that was not true only a few years ago, now frequently concede that abortion is fundamentally a moral issue (see chapter 16). Attitudes toward casual divorce and unwed pregnancies may be undergoing similar shifts.

Paradoxically, even as the Church's public influence may be on the upswing, the Vatican's positions on issues like marital contraception and in vitro fertilization seem ever more remote from the moral perceptions of the great majority of thinking, believing Catholics. It is simply snide to dismiss the good people I met on parish visits as "cafeteria Catholics," because they find so many of the Church's positions morally and intellectually unconvincing. My own impression is that, far from juggling ethics to fit hedonistic impulses, they were sincerely commited to Catholic values and were attempting to construct moral responses to real-life problems with precious little help from their Church. The plight of the priest caught between the latest thunderbolt from Rome and the reality of his parishioners' lives can be especially poignant. Ivor Shapiro's fine study of the ethical struggles of a single Catholic congregation over the course of a year, *What God Allows,* illustrates the daily dilemmas beautifully.

The rigidity of the Vatican's rhetoric, moreover, is not completely supported by its own theology. John Paul's *Splendor of Truth* is among the more emphatic recent pronouncements on acts that are "intrinsically evil" and "always wrong"; but it also contains a section stressing the primacy of individual conscience in making moral decisions, which has always been the Catholic teaching, although one not often emphasized: "The judgment of conscience is a *practical judgment,* a judgment which makes known what man [*sic*] must do or not do, or which assesses an act already performed by him. It is a judgment which applies to a concrete situation the rational conviction that one must love and do good and avoid evil." And further: "The judgment of conscience states 'in an ultimate way' whether a certain particular kind of behavior is in conformity with the law; it formulates the proximate norm of the morality of a voluntary act, 'applying the objective law to a particular case.' " Which is more or less what most pastors tell their parishioners about birth control and Fr. Hayes tells his about homosexuality. Although the Pope places great stress on the requirement of a good conscience to be formed in accord with Church teachings, and the whole weight of the encyclical greatly narrows the compass for individual decisions; even in *Splendor of Truth,* in the final analysis, the primacy of conscience still stands.

In a similar fashion, the teaching on abortion is more subtle than most Catholics may appreciate. Despite the use of terms like "human being" in discussions of embryos, the Church does *not* teach that an early-stage fetus is a "person," only that it is a "human life." For most non-Catholics, however, the critical ethical question is when a fetus attains the moral status of a *person,* which non-Catholic ethicists typically place at about the time the brain and nervous system develop, in the third or fourth month of pregnancy. (There is an imprecise, but suggestive, analogy to the brain-dead hospital patient.) The Vatican, however, treats the issue of personhood as a merely "philosophical" question and premises the abortion prohibition on an absolute ban against killing *any* "human life."

Moreover, the Church itself frequently bends its principles to accommodate reality. Conservative moralists, from Cardinal Ottaviani at Vatican II down to the present day, have always sought to condemn American nuclear policy, since a city-targeting strategy deliberately contemplates the destruction of innocent human lives, and on an inconceivable scale. A clearer violation of the ban against taking human life would be hard to imagine. But the Vatican has never accepted the argument, purely, it seems, because it would be politically inexpedient to do so. Cardinal Spellman's clout prevented Ottaviani from pushing a condemnation of American nuclear policy at the Council; and in 1984, when the American bishops followed an essentially proportionalist argument in deciding that deterrent effects of the American policy outweighed its evils, the Vatican, which was working closely with the Reagan administration at the time, approved the bishops' statement. This despite the fact that John Paul II has expressly condemned proportionalism in *The Splendor of Truth* and said that actions that were intrinsically evil could never be justified by their effects. The very wobbly teaching against capital punishment fits into the same category.

The Church's pragmatic streak also seems to place great weight on rhetorical self-consistency, sometimes at the expense of its moral positions. The current policy toward marital annulments is the most egregious example. Rather than acknowledge divorce, the Church accedes to a pretense that long-standing marriages, celebrated in church, ones that produced children, *never happened.* Honesty would seem to call for a "Catholic divorce," with much tougher standards for the emotional and financial support of children than are imposed by civil courts—retrieve the Catholic *value,* that is, rather than save the rhetoric. Consistency with past rhetoric, as we have seen, may also have been the decisive argument in the birth control decision. Better, presumably, to create painful moral dilemmas for millions of faithful Catholics than admit that the Church could have been wrong. It is hardly surprising that so many good Catholics decided that the moral dilemmas were, at the end of the day, not all that painful.

John Paul II, in his *Gospel of Life* and especially in his 1995 *Letter to Women,* may be recasting the Vatican's traditional natural law–based deductions into a more mystical, scripturally based approach that sees sexual "complementarity" as an intrinsic part of God's plan for the world. The masculinity of Christ, the femininity of Mary, the procreative purpose of sexuality, the sacredness of motherhood, all become part of a deep underlying universal reality. The detailed conclusions, however, are unchanged—the "iconic" nature of the masculine priesthood makes it impossible for women to be priests, and artificial birth control is still forbidden. The Pope is a most impressive thinker, writer, and personality, but he opens himself to the charge that he is spinning a theological argument around preconceived positions, just as feminist or liberation theologians are often accused of doing.

The primacy the Pope assigns to issues of sexuality leads directly to the question of the sexuality of priests. When I visited Bishop Joseph Sullivan, the respected head of Brooklyn's Catholic Charities, once a professional baseball prospect, and a noted liberal, he expressed his doubts on the teaching on homosexuality. If it is true that homosexuals are *born* that way—a point that Andrew Sullivan, the staunchly Catholic, and gay, former editor of *The New Republic* has poignantly argued, and that the Vatican has accepted in principle—Bishop Sullivan wondered, can it also be true that all homosexual acts are "unnatural"? "And who are *we*," he said, waving his hand to include all the clergy, "to be so certain, on *this* issue?"

Under a Glass: Management, Morale, and Priestly Sexuality

St. Luke's Institute is in suburban Maryland, a short drive from downtown Washington, housed in a rambling white building that was once a nuns' retreat house. St. Luke's is one of two or three main treatment centers for pedophiliac priests. The normal treatment period is six months, involving mostly intensive group therapy, and costs $60,000, which is usually paid by the sending diocese. At the time I visited, in the fall of 1995, there were about forty-five men in residence. After St. Luke's they will typically be funneled into specialized halfway houses. A few will get priestly jobs again, in settings like nursing homes, far away from young people. Most will be retired or simply drummed out of their dioceses and left to fend for themselves. The director of the Institute is Fr. Canice Connors, a Franciscan priest with a doctorate in clinical psychology. Connors is tall, trim, and professorially tweedy, and his voice is soft, clipped, and cultured. Besides running St. Luke's, he conducts priestly development workshops around the country and consults with dioceses on abuse issues and on the screening of candidates for the priesthood.

Connors is very worried about the state of the American priesthood, but he does not think that pedophilia is the major problem. There seem to have been a relatively small number of priests who were genuine predatory monsters, serial victimizers of very young boys. "But most of the people we get here," Connors said, "are just pathetic little men fixated at an early-adolescent stage of development," not systematic predators. A recent comprehensive review of the data by Philip Jenkins, a Protestant professor at Pennsylvania State University, bears out Connors's contention. Probably the majority of the priests swept up in the pedophilia scandal were actually homosexuals having relations with teenagers, rather than true pedophiliacs. Connors has sat on a number of pedophilia investigative panels and reports a wide gamut of fact situations, from instances of coldhearted priest-victimizers to cases where the priest was arguably the seducee.

If Jenkins's data are correct, the incidence of pedophilia among Catholic priests is about the same as among clergymen from other denominations, a conclusion also reached by Andrew Greeley. According to Mark Chopko, general counsel of the USCC, the huge tort settlements that some feared would push dioceses into bankruptcy have not materialized. (Diocesan financial officers confirmed Chopko's impression; the biggest expense relating to clerical abuse in Chicago is the permanent review apparatus created to speed complaint handling.) Most of the cases outstanding are very old, and Chopko's impression is that quality of the evidence, which is usually of the "recovered memory" variety, has been declining. Conceivably, the publicity itself began to generate new and less reliable recovered memories. The high point of the "pedophilia panic," as Jenkins calls it, was the accusation by a former seminarian against Cardinal Bernardin in 1993. When that accusation was retracted, the panic receded with an almost audible sigh, as if air was suddenly released from a dirigible balloon.

Credit: New World-Chicago/Catholic News Service
The Church's pedophilia scandal came to a head when a young man accused Chicago's late Cardinal Joseph Bernardin of sexually abusing him decades before. The charge, from a "recovered memory," was later retracted. Cardinal Bernardin meets with the press after his ordeal had ended.

But saying that the vast majority of priests are not pedophiliacs is not a proud claim. The pedophilia scandals have shed a pitiless light on management and disciplinary structures within the Church; on the problems of recruiting and training "healthy" men willing to live by the rule of celibacy; on the stresses and isolation of the priestly life; and, finally, of an institution stuck awkwardly in midtransition from one vision of Church and ministry to another, frightened of going forward, but not quite able to go back.

THE MANAGEMENT VACUUM

In the 1950s, the American Catholic Church was frequently praised as one of the best-managed large institutions in the country. The truth is the Church worked with marvelous smoothness without any management at all. Pastors, chancery officials, nuns in the parochial schools, bishops, all had more or less exactly the same vision of the Church and how they fit into the enterprise. Bishops wrote the checks, gave troop-rallying speeches, and offered their rings to be kissed as they made stately progress from ceremony to ceremony. Pastors worried about mortgages and plumbing and lorded it over their curates. The curates said three or four Masses on Sundays, heard hours of confessions on Saturdays, joked with the schoolkids, made the endless rounds of parish visits, played golf with other priests on Tuesdays, and waited for the distant day when they would get a church of their own. Laypeople stumped up the money and followed the rules. There wasn't much to talk about. Linked-arm uncommunicativeness was the usual attitude toward the outside world; inside, everyone knew what to do without being told.

The burst of theological creativity that followed Vatican II was purchased at the cost of coherence. The binding vision broke into puddles of quicksilver and slipped away. The stresses of the past thirty years have pitilessly exposed the lack of any real policy apparatus or management structure outside of the Vatican. An organization premised on timelessness is ill-equipped to manage change.

When the first wave of priestly resignations hit in the wake of the Council, the Church's instinctive response was to deny that anything was happening. There was no attempt even to collect data until well after the phenomenon had passed its peak. When Richard Schoenherr began to publish his detailed analyses projecting serious shortfalls in priestly manpower, Los Angeles's Cardinal Roger Mahony blamed the messenger:

> I reject [the study's] pessimistic assessment and feel that the Catholic Church in our country has been done a great disservice by the . . . report. . . . The study presumes that the only factors at work are sociology and statistical research. That is nonsense. We are disciples of Jesus Christ, we live by God's grace, and our future is shaped by God's design for his church—not by sociologists. . . . Had sociologists studied the life of Jesus up through his crucifixion and death, I can just imagine the projections that would have resulted. But the resurrection and God's grace are not the product of research and surveys.

The irony of Mahony's statement is that Los Angeles has one of the lowest priest-to-Catholic ratios in the country and has responded with an aggressive laicization of parish ministries. The laicization program is partly coordinated at the diocesan level and is partly an unplanned consequence of entrepreneurial marketing of ministry extension courses by local Catholic colleges. Catholic University's Dean Hoge points out that the new Los Angeles model is a radical shift from the traditional priest-centered style of the American Church. Diocesan Family Life offices, for example, typically spearhead the local programs on Catholic sexual ethics, but the great majority of directors are now laywomen or nuns, usually with degrees from theological schools like Creighton or Notre Dame, who are likely to be far more liberal than their bishops. The point is not whether Los Angeles's model is right or wrong, but that it is a substantially new pastoral strategy with implications far beyond the organization chart—even though the chief executive denies that any change is afoot.

Management-by-denial has produced a grab bag of strategies and stopgaps to cope with the priest shortage, most of them unarticulated. Seattle, Saginaw, and Houston, for example, seem to be following a Los Angeles–style laicization model. (Under Archbishop Hunthausen, Seattle was one of the few dioceses to establish an explicit and forthright pastoral planning process; it was under way by 1978, long before other dioceses began to think about the problem.) Elsewhere, bishops are scouring the world to fill up their priestly ranks with Filipinos, Sri Lankans, Indians, Poles, Irish, and Nigerians. There are extremes of laxity and restrictiveness in recruitment standards. "Jesus Christ couldn't qualify in Chicago," says Connors, but being "eighteen years old with a 98.6 degree body temperature" will get you in elsewhere. I was told of older recruits with histories of financial and other problems, and of one man with an annulled marriage and child support issues. Because of worries about homosexuality and pedophilia, most dioceses and religious orders now require extensive personality and psychological testing for their recruits, and some have even resorted to penile response tests.

I originally sought out Saginaw's Bishop Untener because of his reputation as a pastoral manager. (I hadn't known that he was also a controversial liberal.) Shortly after he was appointed, Untener sold the bishop's house and now rotates his residence among rectories—he figures he's moved fifty-five times in fifteen years. Perhaps uniquely among bishops, he requires his priests, in rotating groups of six priests at a time, to submit advance drafts of their sermons. Untener submits one of his own, and he and the group then work over the sermons together and do second drafts. The system has recently been extended to include videotapes of Masses—at one legendary session, a tape from a "participative" parish showed that the congregation prayed aloud for fifty-eight seconds during a fifty-nine-minute service. Untener said, "The point isn't to put anyone on the spot. The tapes show up all kinds of things, like acoustics and sight lines. You find yourself saying, 'Joe, nobody can *hear* anything. We have to do something about your church.' Let's face it, preaching and Mass are the primary contacts that most people have with us, so we should do it well. And for us, these small sessions often turn into real occasions for spiritual development."

If Untener worked anywhere else, his behavior would be entirely unremarkable. In any good service organization, *all* middle-level line executives spend a significant part of their time in supervisory and development activities. But there are no standards for the performance of a bishop. He reports only to the Pope and within very broad limits can do as he pleases, doctrinally, pastorally, setting recruitment standards, whatever—just as long as, unlike Hunthausen, he doesn't challenge a party line too publicly. Pastors, unless they have financial problems, are almost as independent. Barry Sullivan, former head of the First Chicago Bank and chairman of Cardinal Bernardin's financial restructuring task force, said, "I had never realized that this is a *presbyterian* church. The pastors are like barons. Nobody tells them what to do." Fr. Joseph Fessio said, "Aside from running a marriage tribunal and recruiting, there's not much a diocese can do for you." When I asked pastors for a definition of a good bishop, they almost always answered, "One who leaves you alone."

The price of independence can be isolation. Timothy Ragan is a Catholic layman who has been running regional leadership conferences for upper- and middle-level Church officials—pastors, chancery officials, heads of local religious orders and colleges. "The most striking thing," he said, "is that most of them have never *met* each other before." By all reports, few priests feel they have much input into major diocesan decisions or get much guidance back. A California pastor said to me, "I'm not sure if I'm responsible for my curate's spiritual development or discipline. Perhaps I shouldn't be, but no one's ever raised the issue." Despite the obvious strains of Fr. Hayes's job at Most Holy Redeemer, no one is looking over his shoulder to note that he hasn't taken a day off in three years. The most telling conservative complaint about the bishops' statements on the economy and nuclear war is that their time would have been better spent attending to their real jobs and finding out what was going on with their priests and in their dioceses. Discontent sometimes bubbles to the surface, as in Andrew Greeley's recent newspaper column attack on American bishops as "semi-literate incompetents" and "proud, arrogant time-servers and careerists, men who couldn't care less about anything save their position in the Vatican poltical game."

A hierarchy that can't deal straightforwardly with an issue like pastoral staffing is bound to fumble hot potatoes like pedophilia. Some dioceses still do not report cases to the NCCB, and the hush-hush, keep-it-within-the-walls instinct frustrates the development of measures like registries of priests with histories of professional misconduct. Without the initial cover-ups, the ultimate press reaction might have been much less savage than it turned out to be. Dioceses have greatly improved their handling of misconduct complaints but only after ten years of headlines; and as the painful recent history in San Francisco suggests (see chapter 11), performance is still spotty.

MORALE

The self-image of priests has been taking a battering ever since the first wave of resignations in the late 1960s. The pedophilia scandals felt like a final blow. "It was very unvalidating," said Tom Hayes. "People looked at you differently." Connors says that his workshops uncover "a lot of repressed anger among priests, especially at all the men who resigned—that they walked away and left their brothers in arms holding the bag." The self-perception of a ministry in crisis is undoubtedly a major factor in the falloff in vocations. Thirty years ago, every priest was constantly on the lookout for young men who were likely candidates for the seminary, but now it appears that few priests actively recruit, seeming to confirm, as a layman put it to me at an after-Mass coffee, "It's a terrible job. Who would want to be a priest?"

Fr. Bill Justice, who runs an ethnically mixed parish in South San Francisco, said, "My parents came to see me sometime in the early 1970s to tell me that if I felt I should leave the priesthood, they would understand and be supportive. I really appreciated the gesture, but it was a sign of how times had changed." The declining prestige of the priesthood coincides with a shift in the public perception of celibacy. In the days when all priests were Spencer Tracy, celibacy confirmed their virility—they were simply stronger and more self-controlled than other men. Now people are more likely to assume that celibates are "unhealthy" or, as Greeley fumes, that they are homosexual, which he calls "a moral if not a legal defamation."

Morale starts at the top. From a purely process perspective, the Vatican's fateful decision, right or wrong, to pick so controversial an issue as birth control as the test of orthodoxy, and to insist that the world Church publicly toe the line, is a major problem. With no room for official dissent, almost everybody lies. San Francisco's Archbishop Quinn was "brutally slapped down" by Rome when he suggested at a 1980 synod of bishops on family policy that the Church develop its position on sexual issues in dialogue with the laity. The next day he said he was misquoted. During the formulation of a bishops' statement that referred to the "compelling" logic of the birth control doctrine, Untener asked the floor, "I wonder how we can claim credibility when we make a statement like that," and went on to compare the bishops "to a dysfunctional family that is unable to talk openly about a problem everyone knows is there." Untener later recalled, "A lot of men thanked me privately for making the statement, but none of them would say a word on the floor." The combination of loose management with jealously guarded, rigidly centralized rhetoric produces a wide divergence between word and deed. A culture of hypocrisy—of winks, of code words and little pretenses up and down the line—takes hold. A fairly conservative bishop, one who does not sign protests, said, "We get treated like children. We were all in Washington when [the 1995 statement on women's ordination] was issued. The delegate spoke to us and never mentioned it. I get home and it's on my fax! So we had a regional meeting and we all ranted and raved and finally decided that they were just trying to cut off discussion for a while." And so they agreed not to say anything. When I asked him about birth control, he looked a bit embarrassed and said it was "a high ideal."

The thinning of priestly ranks has dissolved traditional informal support systems. The glory days of a Philadelphia, with four or five men to a rectory and dozens more priests within a ten-minute trolley ride, are long in the past. Two-thirds of all the parishes in the country have only one priest. The life can be very lonely, and priests now must seek their friends from among laypeople. All data show that priests work long hours and that their jobs are stressful. Morale problems are typically most serious among younger priests—they have the least control over their assignments and only limited recourse against a tyrannical or an uncommunicative pastor. Professional stratification and the dispersal of religious communities further weaken group identity. "Hyphenated" priests, the priest-professors and the priest-psychologists, have a much better deal than the grunts in the parishes—better pay, a professional and social network of lay colleagues, and as much priestly work as they please on weekends.

On the other hand, the morale problem among priests is often exaggerated. The flip side of the Church's weak management structure is that an entrepreneurial, energetic priest has a lot of autonomy. If he is doing a good job, his parishioners know it, and a successful pastor, like a Torgerson or a Rizzotto, gets a good deal of satisfied feedback. Almost all the priests I met said they enjoyed their work and thought they were good at it. (I believed them; many of the conversations were quite unguarded.) Untener suggested that the quality of priestly work is also much better. "A funeral used to be a minimum time commitment," he said, "But now it's at least a full day's work. You have to preach, you're involved in all the services, and it brings you much closer to the families in your parish. You have to know them."

There is a good deal of consistent research data that show that priests are happy in their work. For decades, researchers have measured a clear stratification of Americans' happiness by gender and marital status. Single women rank at the top, followed by married men, then married women, then far down the list, single men, who tend to be a fairly miserable lot, particularly as they get older. (The list says volumes about the differential benefits of marriage for men and women.) Priests, however, rank with married men, not single men. They tend to live longer than other men and be better adjusted, physically healthier, and less anxious than their lay peers. Priests like being priests, and by and large they think they do their jobs well. Possibly because the resignation crisis is over and the postconciliar disruptions in the Church have settled down—to the level of a migraine headache rather than a massive heart attack—morale is probably rising. In addition, priests' democracy movements have slowly effected change in internal procedures, often after bitter fights. Priests now have more input into their assignments and there are at least some priest-to-bishop feedback mechanisms in place everywhere. In some dioceses, as in Orange, California, the priests themselves have organized continuing education and career development programs outside of the diocesan structure.

One persistent complaint from older priests is that new recruits are too "conservative and monastic," as one pastor put it, or "more into their own personal holiness," as another said. The limited data that are available suggest that the impression is true, although possibly overstated. In the 1950s and 1960s, the prestige and psychic returns from the priesthood were quite high. Older priests reminisce fondly about their high-profile roles in dealing with disasters, social action breakthroughs, the camaraderie of the labor movement. Most of that is gone, so it is likely that new recruits have more purely religious motivations than older generations did. A fairly high proportion of seminarians have backgrounds in faith-based communities, charismatic prayer groups, or similarly intense forms of religious expression. The consequence is a reversal of traditional ideological patterns—it is now the older priests, whose formative experiences were in the 1960s and 1970s, who are the liberals on theological and doctrinal issues.

The ideological distance between older and younger priests possibly flavors the persistent worry about whether the new men are "healthy," a comment I heard again and again. An article by a pseudonymous seminarian in *Crisis,* a conservative Catholic journal, put it this way: "It is too late to deny that there are numerous seminarians and priests who are sexually active, both with women and with men. An even more widespread problem—effeminacy and lack of masculinity among priests—has become an open secret, widely discussed in private, even as it is never brought up in public."

A Jesuit, who was talking about the percentage of gay men among new recruits, stopped himself and said, "I shouldn't say that, because I'm really talking about sexual *ambiguity*—guys that like dressing up in cassocks and doing liturgy." Connors said, "After one of my workshops, I had dinner with a group of young priests, all of them ordained six years or less. I would not have thought it possible to sustain an entire dinner's conversation on *incense,* but we did it." Even priests who are proud of their young curates spontaneously bring up the effeminacy issue. As Msgr. Rizzotto put it in the course of praising Houston's seminarians: "These are healthy young guys. They don't spend their time ironing surplices." The worry about effeminacy is wrapped up with the fear—in some quarters, approaching panic—about whether the priesthood is slowly becoming a homosexual enclave.

THE SEXUALITY OF PRIESTS

Clerical sexuality is an area where rumors far outweigh data. The liberal bishops who publicly complained about the operations of the bishops' conference in June 1995 flagged "rumors of a high percentage of homosexual men in seminaries and the priesthood" as one of the key issues facing the Church. The data that do exist are based largely on self-selected samples, so there is no way of knowing how representative they are. One survey of 101 gay priests, mostly from the Midwest, showed that the majority were sexually active, often with other priests. Many were going to therapists and had rationalized their homosexual activity as not sinful. One man claimed that homosexuals made better priests—they were more sensitive counselors, more affectively attuned; they did not get into trouble with women and, since they could keep their liaisons within the walls, were less likely to give scandal. The younger priests in this sample gave extremely high estimates of the incidence of homosexuality among their peers and in the seminaries, but they might be expected to overestimate.

A. W. Richard Sipe, a psychologist and former priest, has developed a database on 1500 priests, a third from records of therapy, a third from volunteer interviews, and a third from priests' sexual partners. It is a large sample but clearly not random. For what it is worth, Sipe estimates that about half of priests are celibate at any one time—celibacy is defined to exclude masturbation—but that there is much turnover in the celibate group. Sipe also estimates that at any one time about 20 percent of all priests are sexually involved with a woman, and that about 20 percent of priests are "homosexually oriented," with about half of them sexually active. Sipe also suggests that the percentage of homosexually oriented priests may be rising.

Most Holy Redeemer's Hayes said, "There's always been a percentage of gay priests, including many very effective men, and quiet support groups for gay priests have been around for a long time. It's becoming more open now, and the percentage is probably going up. We get calls from around the country from priests who want to work here. We turn them down. We can't have people trying to work out their own sexuality here—'I'm gay, but I don't play, but I may.' " Connors suggested that the number of homosexuals joining seminaries has probably not increased, but, he says, "the number of heterosexuals has gone down, so the proportions are higher." Even Greeley, who bristles at the homosexuality charges, conceded that Connors may be right.

Eugene Kennedy, another psychologist and former priest, suggested that the "hypervirile, controlling, all-wise" traditional image of the priest was a kind of "symbolic sexuality that concealed the fact they didn't know much about human relations." An extensive mid-1970s study by Kennedy showed a high degree of "psychosexual immaturity" among priests, but the study lacked controls. (Ask any single woman how many "psychosexually" *mature* men she meets on the dating scene.)

Male-only esprit-based groups have a long history—Marines, Jesuits, athletic training camps, and, until relatively recently, Cambridge and Oxford dons. They doubtless fostered social immaturity and, as in the English universities, have often harbored homosexual subcultures. But all the evidence suggests that the old esprit-based American priesthood enforced a high degree of sexual discipline. The camaraderie and security of an intensely group-oriented culture supplied an unspoken set of rules and expectations policed by multiple well-disposed, but watchful, eyes. Connors says, "There was always a man or two that you just didn't assign to work with young boys. It would never be mentioned, but everybody would quietly take care of him. But now the support and control systems are gone, and all that's left is the secrecy and silence."

The "spirit of Vatican II" intersected with the cultural upheavals of the 1960s and 1970s, a time of rudderless yawing for almost all established institutions. Since the Vatican had recommended that seminary training "be supplemented by the latest principles of sound psychology," some seminaries, amid worries about the "psychosexual immaturity" of priests, removed disciplinary restraints, encouraged dating, and introduced professionals to help seminarians explore sexual issues. As Connors said, "The emphasis turned to *my* sexuality, *my* personal development." That some such experiments went seriously awry is hardly surprising. In the wake of *Humanae Vitae,* thousands of priests challenged the old Catholic sexual ethic. That many should thereupon question the value of their own celibacy was inevitable. At the same time, many priests stopped wearing clerical garb and moved into their own houses and apartments, so it became much easier to stray. A priest who was a virgin into his thirties, and who has since had a number of affairs with women, told me that other priests had chaffed him for his lack of experience.

Sexual innuendos have added a nasty edge to the ideological struggles within the Church. I found it striking that the most partisan liberals *and* the most partisan conservatives both tend to make the highest estimates of homosexuality or pedophilia, and both blame the other side for the problem. According to liberals, the insistence on celibacy and the search for sufficiently orthodox candidates has so narrowed the pool that only "unhealthy" men would consider the priesthood. Conservatives counter that liberal sexual permissiveness has caused a breakdown in discipline and fostered "lavender" seminaries and rectories.

There may be some truth in both arguments, but the lack of restraint in tossing around toxic accusations is astonishing. An article in the *Wanderer* claimed that "the homosexual priests" who allegedly control the Pittsburgh chancery jury-rigged pedophilia charges against a conservative priest to force him out of his parish. And in Winona, Minnesota, where there had been a serious pedophilia problem, a spit-and-polish reformist chancellor, according to the *National Catholic Reporter,* was accused by liberal priests of sending dissidents to sex-abuse treatment centers; then, to complete the circle, the chancellor himself was accused of sex abuse by two former seminarians. In the case of the charges against Cardinal Bernardin, the young man who brought the charges was advised by a priest with a long history of antagonism to the Cardinal. Who would recruit for such a fetid soap opera? No wonder lay people throw up their hands and say, "Let them get married! Please!"

The concerns over clerical sexuality throws the question of priestly celibacy into sharp relief. Is it true that in the modern era a celibate order will draw only men "who haven't worked out their own sexual identities," as Fr. McBrien put it? When I was at Notre Dame, McBrien told me, "You should visit Lincoln" (the very conservative Nebraska diocese, which manages to recruit large numbers of priests), "then you'll see what's really going on." When I visited Fr. Fessio a few weeks later, he said, "You should visit Lincoln. Then you'll see a Church that really works."

So I visited Lincoln.

CHAPTER 15

Styles, Themes, Dilemmas

Conservatism Ascendant: Lincoln, Nebraska

Nebraska in winter is painted with a palette of gray and white. The sky is gray, presaging snow. In the fields that stretch off on every side, gray patches of soil peek through the snow, and the winter's corn stubble is a bleached-out gray and white and dun. It is very cold. Lincoln is the state capital, a prosperous university town in the southeastern corner of the state, with one of the lowest unemployment rates in the country. It is festooned with the red and white of its football team, the University of Nebraska Cornhuskers, a perennial national champion and an avatar of a straight-ahead, powerhouse football style. Nebraska occasionally elects liberal politicians, like Bob Kerrey, the present Senator and former governor, but like most of the agrarian Midwest, it is a natural home of bedrock conservatism. Geographically, the state is an irregular rectangle about 350 miles long, divided roughly in half in the long direction, east to west, by the Platte River. All of Nebraska south of the Platte is assigned to the diocese of Lincoln, so the diocese is shaped like an eel with its head in the east and an attenuating tail of little farm towns, many with only a few hundred souls, stretching all the way to Wyoming in the west. About 15 percent of the people in southern Nebraska are Catholic, rising to about 25 percent in Lincoln.

The Lincoln chancery office is a modest one-story building in the shadow of a surprisingly modernistic cathedral in one of the city's better residential neighborhoods. On an evening in December 1995, twenty-one of Lincoln's theology-level seminarians had assembled to get their religious teaching assignments for the Christmas vacation period. Altogether Lincoln had thirty-nine men in advanced stages of seminary training, a remarkable number for a small diocese. Too small to operate its own seminary, Lincoln farms its students out, mostly to Dunwoodie in New York, St. Charles in Philadelphia, and St. Mary's in Emmitsburg, Maryland, the big three of conservative theology. The session at the chancery took about an hour—mostly details about transportation, curricula, and dress code (black suits and ties or Roman collars) interrupted by chaffing about who was likely to oversleep or get lost. I was a fly on the wall, somewhat awkwardly introduced as a visiting writer. After the session almost all of us repaired to the Newman Center at the university for pizza and beer.

Altogether, I spent about four hours with the group. I didn't interview each one, but I was able to watch them interact with each other, I had some lengthy roundtable discussions with shifting groups of four or five at a time, and I talked with a few individuals in some depth. They were, frankly, an impressive group of young men. They were not effeminate. They did not seem to be "unhealthy" or immature, or to have rigidly dependent personalities. The ones I talked to did not come from broken homes or problem families. Their theology was very orthodox, as all of Lincoln's theology is, but no one sounded fanatical. As in any group of twentysomethings, some were more gregarious and self-confident than others. Raymond Jansen could pass for an Ivy League swim team captain, but his shoulder span came from hauling bricks on construction sites, not from swimming. The presence and professional directness of Chris Kubat, the oldest at thirty-eight, was striking; but he is a board-certified urologist who jettisoned a thriving practice, an active social life, and a contemplated marriage because "the call became too strong." In my mind's eye, I put the whole group in suits and ties and envisioned them in a training program for Wall Street junior executives. They did fine. If a daughter brought one of them home, a father would be perfectly content. Any bishop would kill to get them.

The ratio of active priests to Catholics in Lincoln is about 1:700, more than half again higher than in the rest of the country, and about three times the ratio in Los Angeles. From the diocesan directory, I calculated the median age of active priests to be about forty-three, an astonishing twelve or thirteen years younger than the national median. About a third of the priests are under thirty-five. The diocesan chancellor, Msgr. Timothy Thorburn, was forty-one. After meeting so many older priests in other dioceses, the succession of recruitment-poster priests in their midthirties was almost disorienting. Lincoln's recruiting secrets offer real insights into the choices faced by the American Church.

Fr. Joseph Nemec (a Czech name, pronounced "Nemetz") is slender, with a boyish face, and at thirty-nine, is young to be a pastor even in Lincoln. His church, St. Teresa's, is in a strongly Catholic, middle-class section of the capital. Like many of Lincoln's priests, Nemec was raised on a farm, one of

Credit: Adrian Bartek

Lincoln, Nebraska, a small and very conservative diocese, has had extraordinary success in attracting young men to the priesthood and enjoys a priest:laity ratio reminiscent of big urban dioceses in the 1950s. The 1995 ordination class (four new priests, seven new deacons) is shown here with Lincoln Bishop Fabian Bruskewitz.

nine children in a staunchly Catholic family. Elementary school was in a one-room country schoolhouse, but all of the children attended a tuitioned Catholic high school. Nemec is a musician, like his father, and he went to the University of Nebraska as a music major. "I had never thought of being a priest," he said. "I wanted to get married, have a large family, and teach music." But he became involved with the Newman Center at the university and was recruited for the seminary from there.

Nemec insisted that he is *orthodox,* not conservative. "In Lincoln," he said, "we follow the Pope. A whole string of Popes have said that artificial birth control is seriously sinful, so that's what we tell people. We don't preach on it every week, because that could get counterproductive, but we do preach it consistently. Missing Mass is sinful, so that's what we tell people. The Church teaches that there are mortal sins, and you go to Hell for them, so that's what we teach. It's all in the *Catechism.* Lincoln isn't inventing anything. We just teach the official doctrines." St. Teresa's has three

Masses a day, and the children in parochial school go every morning. There are confessions six days a week, with a full schedule on Saturdays. The tuition in the school is only $100 a year, and almost all Catholic children are enrolled.

We talked about recruitment, and about problems in the seminaries, and I was struck that he and the much more liberal Fr. Canice Connors had many of the same views. "If you don't know what you're about, if it's simply 'Come one, come all,' then you're naturally going to have problems," Nemec said. But Lincoln has a clear idea of the men it is looking for—"Men who love the church, who are submissive and obedient, who are true servants of the Lord, who want to bring people to Jesus, who have a sense of the sacred." He continued, "The Holy Sacrifice of the Mass is the greatest prayer on earth, it is the reenactment of Calvary. And, yes, we expose and adore the Blessed Sacrament here." (Blessed Sacrament devotions have fallen into desuetude in many parishes.)

The "submissive and obedient" in the list of priestly virtues caught my attention, for Nemec is a very self-confident young man with not a trace of eyes-cast-down monkishness. I asked about the lay role in the parish and, in light of his very youthful appearance, about his relationship with his parishioners. "I'm their father," he said. I said, "You're thirty-nine and look even younger and you're their *father*?" He was not at all abashed. "Yes, I'm their father. That's what a pastor is." And he went on, "We're very participative here, but as in any good Catholic family, parents love their children and still control them. They need to be told what's right and wrong with the love and care of a father." Nemec's "submissive and obedient" attitude, that is, flowed in a clear, straight line. Children honor and obey their parents. Parents honor and obey their pastor. Pastors honor and obey their bishop. And bishops honor and obey the Pope, who speaks for Jesus Christ.

Obedience is not a virtue that is much prized in America. Among religious liberals, "orthodox" occasionally sounds like a code word for "neurotic." I met some Catholic conservatives who struck me as unusually rigid people, but the best ones—like Nemec, Joseph Fessio, or Ralph Martin, a Charismatic leader—are anything but lobotomized robots. They are conservative by intellectual conviction, not psychological compulsion. Fessio says, "Christ handed on his teaching authority to St. Peter, and it descended through Peter to the popes. Vatican II confirmed very clearly that Catholics, and especially priests, owe religious assent to what the Pope teaches."

The commitment to strict orthodoxy and to obedience comes bundled with a very exalted view of the priesthood. In Lincoln, priests are *fathers*, not parish coordinators, team leaders, or therapy directors. There are subtle touches in the liturgy that reinforce the priest's apartness. The solemnly paced consecration, the use of a bell, the priest's genuflection before the host and chalice, all underline the magical quality of the Mass. More than just father, the priest is also shaman and sacral figure. If he is submissive and obedient to his superiors, he expects the same from his flock, not because he is thirty-nine-year-old Joseph Nemec, but because he is the local spokesman of a vast salvific enterprise—of the one true Church, the chosen vessel for an eternal deposit of faith bequeathed directly from the hand of Christ. Being a priest in Lincoln, in short, is a *good job,* and if only a fraction of 1 percent of well-balanced, college-capable, eligible-age-group Catholic males decide that the spiritual, emotional, and personal payoffs are worth the price of celibacy, Lincoln will continue to turn out plenty of trophy priests.

Lincoln is also one of the few dioceses that is successfully recruiting nuns. The diocese has its own two orders of teaching nuns; they are small, with just a couple of dozen women each, but are big enough to make an impact on the parochial school system. I drove out to one motherhouse on a Sunday afternoon and visited with Mother Joan Paul, who is about thirty-five—the order's median age is about thirty-two—and three of the other sisters. Their convent life is the traditional mix of prayer, study, and teaching, and they wear a full habit. If you're going to be a nun, they said, be a nun! Why join an order if you're going to look and act just like everybody else? They'd all been to secular universities before joining the order, they all held master's degrees from the University of Nebraska, and they were bright and funny young women—effectively, the female counterparts of the Lincoln seminarians and priests.

The orthodox character of the Lincoln diocese, and its single-minded commitment to vocational recruitment, are the legacy of Glennon Flavin, a strong-willed bishop who ruled Lincoln for twenty-five years until his retirement in 1992. His replacement, Fabian Bruskewitz, an archconservative with an extensive Roman background, is clearly not tampering with a successful formula. Bruskewitz made national headlines in early 1996 by threatening to excommunicate Catholics who joined a long list of proscribed organizations, like Planned Parenthood or "Call to Action," a Catholic liberal organization.

But the real secret to Lincoln's recruiting success is Msgr. Leonard Kalin, who doubles as vocations director and director of the University of Nebraska Newman Center, the social and religious center for Catholic students on the Lincoln campus. Kalin is in his midsixties, with a gray crew cut, one of three priest-brothers from a large Nebraska farm family. His strong presence and personality still showed clearly through a serious case of Parkinson's disease that has left him unsteady on his feet and able to speak only in a whisper. Kalin was assigned to the Newman Center in 1968. Flavin, who was a new bishop, was convinced that the center was a hotbed of liturgical experimentation and heterodoxy, so he ordered Kalin in to create an orthodox operation. Kalin carried out the mission, doubled the student

membership, and has reigned ever since as a combination guru, social director, and aggressive recruiter of priests and nuns. Over the years, he has directed 435 University of Nebraska students into the convent or the seminary.
Almost all the priests I met in Lincoln, almost all the teaching nuns, and the
great majority of the seminarians were Kalinites, as Fr. Robert Barnhill, the
diocesan Family Life director, put it with a grin.

It is hard to overstate the advantages of the Kalin/Newman Center
pipeline. The average Lincoln seminarian has spent two or three years at the
University of Nebraska before entering the seminary. The Lincoln campus is
at the top of the state system, so they are prima facie academically qualified.
Since Kalin does nothing by halves, the center's social agenda is very active,
and all the Kalinites have at least some dating experience. When I asked
Kalin about homosexuality, he said, "I get to know a candidate pretty well
before I recommend him to the seminary, and if I think someone is an active
homosexual, I'll take him aside and we'll agree that the priesthood isn't for
him. On the other hand, Bishop Flavin always said that he didn't care what
someone's inclinations were, as long he was sincerely committed to a chaste
life." On pedophilia, he said there had been one case where parishioners
complained about a priest's suspicious behavior; the man was reassigned
and kept under observation. "But he was from New York."

Kalin's system reinforces itself in a virtuous feedback cycle. Kalin himself
serves as a kind of personal glue to weld the priests and seminarians from the
Newman Center into a cohesive, high-morale, mutually supportive body. The
esprit facilitates recruitment, and the relatively large numbers prevent isolation, even in rural areas. "Notice the way we use titles," Kalin told me. "I've
known Joe Nemec for twenty years, but I call him 'Father,' not 'Joe,' and he
calls me 'Monsignor.' Bishop Flavin always insisted on that. You go around
the rest of the country, and you see parishioners calling pastors by their first
names. But if the priesthood isn't an elevated position, if you're just a spiritual
coordinator and social director, why would you give up marriage, family, and
all the rest?"

By any institutional measure, the Lincoln system is a smashing success—
Fr. Fessio was clearly right. But I doubt that it is widely replicable. In the first
place, Lincoln itself is a very small diocese in a very conservative setting.
Mostly conservative Protestant pressure had prevented the opening of abortion clinics until just a few months before my visit. The parishioners I met at
St. Teresa's stressed how conservative they were. "This is a middle-class conservative parish," one of them told me. "It's a kind of Catholic ghetto, but we
like it that way." One of the teaching nuns mentioned that it was harder to
maintain St. Teresa's level of cohesiveness in more affluent neighborhoods.
Most of the priests and nuns I talked to came from small-town farm families
and were natural social conservatives. When I asked Barnhill what his career

goal was—Barnhill is a diocesan officer; he studied in Rome and is much traveled—he said, "I want to be a country parish priest in the kind of town I grew up in. That's all, just a country parish priest." The Kalin recruiting pipeline is unique, and Kalin's powerful personality is clearly a factor in its success. Whether it can survive his retirement is questionable.

More important, Lincoln has maintained the high status of its priests partly by excluding women from the ministry. Flavin insisted that lectors and acolytes be formally "installed" according to canonical procedures that limit the eligible pool to men. St. Teresa's was the first parish I'd been to where the liturgy was an all-male affair—the entry procession, ushers, readers, the acolyte, altar boys, communion ministers. Flavin justified the policy, I was told, on recruiting grounds; many lectors and acolytes go on to the seminary. Bruskewitz has recently authorized women lectors and acolytes in cases of necessity, and, since the Vatican has now officially approved altar girls, some Lincoln parishes have begun using them. When I asked parishioners about the exclusion of women, they seemed a bit embarrassed but assured me that it "was not a problem" in Lincoln. Mother Joan Paul told me women went along with Lincoln's male-oriented policies because they had been "properly educated." Nemec said, just as the Vatican says, that women and men simply have different roles in the Church, and that in any event there is no higher status than motherhood. It would have been interesting to see him explain that to, say, the young women in Richard McBrien's theology seminar. Even very conservative Catholic women in another diocese run on the Lincoln model, Arlington, Virginia, were infuriated when their daughters were told they couldn't serve on the altar.

The Lincoln system is precisely in line with the model of the Church that many conservatives—and possibly the Vatican—appear to insist is the only permissible one. To place the conservative and liberal models of the Church in sharper relief, I visited another parish, in another midwestern, fairly conservative city, but in Bishop Kenneth Untener's very liberal diocese of Saginaw.

Liberalism Ascendant: Saginaw, Michigan

Saginaw is in central Michigan, roughly at the cusp of the state's gradual metamorphosis from its industrial Rust Bowl southern half into the pristine wilderness to the north. With an economy partly based on small-farm agriculture and partly on heavy industry, it has a tatterdemalion, down-at-the-heels, redbrick look. The Catholic share of the population, at about a third, is higher than the national average but typical for a Rust Belt diocese. Saginaw's total Catholic population is about three times that of Lincoln's.

Sr. Honora Remes (also Czech, pronounced "Remesh") is the "pastoral administrator"—the term of art for a nonordained person functioning as a parish pastor—of the cathedral parish of St. Mary's in Saginaw. She is a tall, graceful woman in her late fifties, with short brown hair and an arc-light smile, whose working uniforms are dark mid-calf-length business suits. About 2000 American parishes, or about 10 percent of the total, are without priests, but most are small, and are served by priests from neighboring parishes. About 300 parishes are run by pastoral administrators. Most of the pastoral administrators are women, and most of the women are nuns. The diocese of Seattle, for instance, has ten pastoral administrators, while Saginaw has eight. All of them are women, and nine of the ten in Seattle, and seven out of the eight in Saginaw, are nuns.

A pastoral administrator does everything a pastor does, except say Mass and administer the sacraments. She hires the staff, manages the finances and budget, provides counseling and advice to parishioners, oversees the liturgies and supervises the religious, social, and educational programs. A few of the pastoral administrators in Seattle have resident curates on their staffs, but more frequently, the Mass and sacraments are provided by visiting priests, known as "sacramental ministers." Canon law requires every parish to have a "canonical pastor" who is a priest; in Saginaw, Bishop Untener serves as the canonical pastor for the parishes run by administrators.

In the Masses I attended at St. Mary's, the sacramental minister was Fr. Bert Groh, a chancery priest in his forties. Remes preceded Groh in the entry processional, and during the first part of the Mass, the two stood side by side in front of the altar and took turns leading the prayers. After Remes read the Gospel and preached the homily, she stepped down from the altar until it was time for communion. She was the lead lay communion minister, then returned to the altar for the final prayers and the exit procession. It all looked smooth and natural. At one Mass, I was sitting near some elderly ladies, and I leaned over and whispered, "I'm just visiting, who is she?" One of them answered, "She's the pastor—well, I'm not sure what she's called—but she's in charge of everything, except that Fr. Groh comes in to say Mass." Another lady looked at me narrowly, as if I might be from the testosterone police, and said, "And she's *wonderful!*" They all nodded their heads defiantly.

They were right. Remes's empathy, warmth, and energy lit up the church. When she came out and circulated among the congregation before the Mass, it was obvious that she knew everybody personally, and they returned her greetings with an affection and regard that was patent. A former college-level English teacher, she is a fine reader and homilist. She read the Gospel, a fairly long text, without looking at the book, and her preaching showed a nice flair for the dramatic. When she quoted the Gospel words "not a hair of your head," she pulled out one her own hairs with an almost audible *ping*—just corny enough to keep people's attention.

Fr. Philip Murnion of the National Pastoral Life Center speaks of the gradual "feminization" of pastoral ministries. There are about 20,000 paid

About ten percent of all American parishes are without a resident priest, and some dioceses have begun to appoint lay "pastoral administrators," most of whom are nuns. Sr. Honora Remes, the pastoral administrator of the cathedral parish in Saginaw, Michigan, assisting at Mass, with Fr. Bert Groh, a circuit-riding "sacramental minister."

lay ministers throughout the American Church, an average of one per parish, and about 80 percent of them are women. Murnion speculates that the emergence of women as pastoral leaders is related to the changing role of the Church in parishioners' lives. Old-line pastors were a combination of political leader, immigrant spokesman, and master builder. But modern Catholics are more likely to use their parish for small-group faith support activities—marriage encounter, religious education, parenting support groups, social involvement activities—of a kind that in the secular world have long been the province of professional women. When I asked parishioners at St. Cecilia's in Houston about women priests, Joan Powers, who was that Sunday's lector and is the mother of a priest, said simply, "We already run the Church."

As one would expect, Remes operates a very participatory parish. One of her objectives, which she pushes hard from the altar, is to get *every* parishioner involved in some form of volunteer activity—even the elderly and homebound are asked to commit to a certain number of hours of prayer for parish causes. "Participatory" is not quite the same as democratic. A group discussion with lay volunteers and parish staff is perfectly open and Remes is a good listener, but her personality is so strong that she dominates almost without being aware of it. Other effective pastors I met operate the same way; strong and self-confident personalities exercise natural leadership without insisting on the trappings of office.

I asked Remes about the relationship with the sacramental minister. "Bert is wonderful to work with," she said, "but the arrangement is hard on both of us. It's hard on the pastoral administrator, and it's hard on the sacramental minister." Watching Remes and Groh together, however, my impression was that the priest is in the more anomalous position. Remes is so obviously the parish leader, and St. Mary's is so obviously her territory, that Groh is inevitably cast as a special guest star, a visiting shaman who does his routine and is gone. Fr. Jim Picton, who is responsible for pastoral planning in Seattle, said that only mature, well-established priests adapt easily to the sacramental minister role. The other side of the coin is that pastoral administrators must grow accustomed to tiny slights (like being left off the list for pastoral meetings), although both Saginaw and Seattle work hard to prevent them. Diocesan priests in good standing are also guaranteed a job and a salary; when Remes's six-year term is up, she has to find another job on her own, possibly even in another diocese.

The fact that women grace Saginaw's altars, however, is merely a surface suggestion of the profound differences between a Saginaw and a Lincoln. The soul of the Church, says Vatican II, is its liturgies. The form and text of a Saginaw liturgy, of course, are exactly the same as in Lincoln; but in the subtle whispers of body language, in the intonations and attitudes that are not captured in manuals, the liturgies are quite different. The interior of Remes's cathedral, for one thing, has been redecorated in a way that quite consciously reduces its awesomeness. A photograph of the old church shows a spangled ceiling of gilt and empyrean blue, while the rest is an Italianate riot of statuary and strong colors. The new interior is spare and uncluttered, with a carpeted floor. The top half of the church is a quiet cream, while the carpet and the accent color on the walls are a Williamsburg blue. Instead of pews, there are individual cushioned chairs and kneelers, arranged in a semicircle around the altar, which has been moved out toward the center of the church, with a minimal elevation. It is very attractive but has a secular feel, like Mt. Vernon or the renovated Washington, D.C., train station.

The differences were most marked in the liturgies surrounding the Eucharist. In Lincoln, the liturgical strategy is designed to *distance* the priest from the congregation and stresses the sacral, rather than the communal, element of the consecration. Lincoln places great emphasis on the traditional Catholic ceremony of the exposition and adoration of the Blessed Sacrament. The consecrated host is exhibited in a sacred vessel called the monstrance, which is made of gold and contains the host in a round glass case surrounded by a circle of radiating golden spears, like the rays of the sun. Since the consecrated host *is* the Body of Jesus Christ (the doctrine of the Real Presence), the ceremony expressly calls for praying to and worshiping the consecrated host.

In Saginaw, by contrast, Remes and Groh lead the Mass in a friendly, almost conversational, tone, and the music is modern and attractive, with the Andrew Lloyd Webber/Stephen Sondheim sound that characterizes much of the newer Catholic church music. At the consecration, Groh elevates the bread and wine only about eye-high and pronounces the "This is my body . . . This is my blood," formula in the same conversational tone as the rest of the Mass. There is no bell and no genuflection. Instead of using the traditional round, white, paper-tasting host, St. Mary's uses a kind of Syrian flatbread, an unusual touch but canonically correct; indeed, it is much like the bread Jesus probably used at the Last Supper. The communion ministers break stacks of the consecrated bread into little pieces for the communion, which are carried on plates rather than in ciboria, the more usual chalicelike containers for the communion hosts.

The whole effect, which is quite intentional, is to *reduce* the distance between priest and people, to downplay the magical, sacral elements of the Mass, to create the feeling of a community celebration by a priesthood of the "People of God." The use of workaday bread emphasizes the communal "meal" aspect of the Eucharist, but it also seems to exclude Blessed Sacrament services. The traditional round white host is so unlike normal bread that Catholics associate it only with the Eucharist. Although Saginaw teaches the same Real Presence doctrine that Lincoln does, it would still seem a little silly to worship a chunk of Syrian flatbread.

The Saginaw liturgy is quite in keeping with Vatican II's liturgical instructions on the Eucharist:

> [The Eucharist] is a . . . sign of unity, a bond of divine love, a special Easter meal. . . . And so the church devotes careful efforts to prevent Christian believers from attending this mystery of faith as though they were outsiders or silent onlookers: rather . . . they should learn to offer themselves as they offer the immaculate victim—not just through the hands of the priest, but also they themselves making the offer together with him.

The liturgy at St. Mary's, however, had a bit of the feel of a Congregationalist communion service I attended a few weeks later. The minister repeated virtually the same Gospel words and used the same chunks of bread, but when the congregation came forward for their symbolic communal meal, it was clearly a meal of bread and wine, not of the body and blood of Christ. One of the primary worries of conservative theologians like Fessio is that thirty years of post–Vatican II progressive "communal meal" liturgies have undermined the Catholic belief in the Real Presence. Survey data suggest that they may be right. The majority of Catholic weekly church-attenders, the most faithful Catholics of all, believe that the consecrated host is only a symbolic representation of Christ, rather than Christ himself.* (Avery Dulles, however, points out that the survey questions raise such a blur of complicated theological issues that the answers may be meaningless. In most Catholic parishes, including St. Mary's, parishioners receive communion quite reverentially.)

In the same vein, just as Lincoln underscores the hierarchical structure of the Church by emphasizing titles, Saginaw demystifies by virtually eliminating them. Remes was on a first name basis with most of her parishioners, and the prayer at Mass for the bishop is for "Bishop Ken." An important consequence of a leveling, nonauthoritarian approach to religion, however, is that priests and pastors have to *earn* their leadership. They can't fall back, as a Joseph Nemec can, on the claim that they have been appointed by Christ as their parishioners' father, like it or not. (Although Nemec, I think, would be effective in almost any setting.) Remes can carry this off, as can the other effective pastors I met, but it is a Protestant approach to pastorship. Catholics don't yet elect their pastors as Protestants do, but the spread of Saginaw-style priest-laity relations, coupled with the recent Catholic trend toward parish-shopping, represents an important shift of power away from the institutional Church.

---

* It would be hard to overstate the centrality of the Real Presence in Catholic doctrine, but progressive theologians are not comfortable with its current form. The theology of the Real Presence, or "transsubstantiation," was codified at Trent and has strong overlays of Thomist/Aristotelian physics. Aristotle taught that substance comprised an indefinite "matter" that was infused with a particular "form." The "accidents"—taste, color, smell—inhered in the substance and distinguished individual objects. In his *Summa,* Thomas adapted Aristotle to argue that in the miracle of the Eucharist the substances of the bread and the wine were each transformed into the substance of Christ but retained their old accidents. Trent adopted Thomas's version of the miracle almost word for word, despite warnings by Franciscans against tying the doctrine so tightly to a specific natural philosophy. (The science of the time was just beginning a broad-scale movement away from Aristotle.) Breaking the link between doctrine and Aristotelianism was a key element in the "modernist" movement in theology that was condemned by Pius X in 1907. Both Paul VI and John Paul II have strongly reconfirmed the traditional formulas, in terms that Richard McBrien has called "closer in orientation to the Council of Trent than to Vatican II." Dulles suggests that the Popes were merely imposing a justifiable "language discipline"—that the miracle of the Eucharist is best connoted by the approved term "transsubstantiation," with or without its medieval overtones.

Saginaw and Lincoln, however, merely exemplify alternative *parish*-based visions of Catholicism. Over the last thirty years, developments outside of the traditional parish have been just as important.

Charismatics and Healers

Ralph Martin was onstage in early 1996 at the parish hall at St. Joseph's Church in Babylon, Long Island, about an hour's train ride east of New York City. Martin is a leader of the Catholic Charismatic Renewal movement, and he and a younger associate, John Herbeck, were giving a full-day retreat for about 200 people from throughout the area, sponsored by a consortium of local charismatics and Marian devotional societies. At the opening session, Martin spoke for about an hour and a half. He has a fine platform style, managing to be intense and humorous at the same time. After a bleak review of the state of the Church—sex scandals, corruption, the falloff in Mass attendance, the confusion in theology—he brought his message of salvation: "Jesus *died* for us. He didn't wait for us to complete our CCD [religion] classes. He *loves* us, so he died to save us. Don't be afraid of that word 'save.' It's not a Protestant invention. It's biblical. It's *Catholic.* You just have to accept the message of the Spirit!"

Following the talk there was a prayer liturgy, and Martin and Herbeck invited people who felt touched by the Spirit to come to the stage. About half the audience did so, filing up to the front where Martin and Herbeck laid on their hands and prayed with them. One older man visibly staggered when Herbeck touched him, and a few minutes later, a young woman in the line screamed, keeled over backward, and lay on the floor shaking violently and shouting nonsense syllables. Martin came over and held her hand until she quieted down, while Herbeck took the microphone and told people not to worry—when the Spirit enters your heart, the effects can be powerful. The phenomenon—being "slain by the Spirit"—is common enough in Pentecostal churches, but it is a fairly recent import into Catholicism. After a few moments, the woman slipped into a deep sleep that lasted for about ten minutes, then she woke up and looked fine. But when Martin started to pray aloud again, she keeled right back over. The people in the line moved past her as if nothing had happened.

THE CATHOLIC CHARISMATIC RENEWAL

The Catholic Charismatic Renewal originated in a campus retreat at Duquesne University in 1967. The retreatants meditated on the Acts of the Apostles, in which the Apostles and their disciples, inspired by the Holy Spirit, speak in all the known tongues of the world, prophesy, heal the sick, and cast out demons. Some of the retreat participants experienced an intense spiritual awakening and began themselves to speak in tongues and prophesy. The Duquesne contingent reported these remarkable events to friends from Notre Dame, including Martin, a Notre Dame graduate who was working in the campus ministry at Michigan State University. Both groups were also involved in the *cursillo* movement, a spiritual import from Spain, featuring emotionally intense, "encounter"-style weekend retreats, and were primed for a charismatic awakening. The leadership of the fledgling movement quickly shifted to Notre Dame, and the first conference of the "International Catholic Charismatic Renewal Movement" was held just a couple of months after the first experience at Duquesne. "We used 'charismatic' to distinguish ourselves from Protestant Pentecostals," Martin said when I met him at his office in Ann Arbor, and added with a grin, "and since there was a nun from Canada there, we decided we were 'international.' " Martin is a thoroughly charming man in his early fifties. He has an air of unaffected sincerity, but he is obviously very smart and theologically sophisticated.

The movement's development has been anything but smooth. The most active charismatics typically form covenanted communities—Martin is a leader of the People of God in Ann Arbor, one of the largest. Communities normally comprise mostly married couples, who hold lay jobs. Life revolves around intense prayer and worship activities, often a parent-run school for the children, and local social service missions. Covenanted communities, however, have shown a depressing tendency to be taken over by patriarchal, highly controlling leaders. Fr. Paul Bernardicou is a Jesuit who served as chaplain to a San Francisco community that had followed its leader, Kerry Koller, from Notre Dame. The community grew rapidly, he said, but split when Koller became increasingly "authoritarian and apocalyptic." Koller led about 140 families back to South Bend, while the remnant in San Francisco was dispersed to parishes.

Martin freely acknowledges past excesses. He led his own group out of the international federation of charismatic communities, the Sword of the Spirit, in 1990 because "too much authority was being exercised in people's lives." The departure was "supposed to be a peaceful, friendly thing," he said ruefully, "but it got pretty bloody." In addition, many bishops were suspicious of the movement because it developed under lay leadership outside of established Church structures, and Paul VI made some highly skeptical observations in a 1975 exhortation.

A signal event in charismatic history was the visit of an elderly Belgian priest, who called himself Fr. Michel DuBois, to Martin's community in the early 1970s. After several days at the community, DuBois revealed that he was Cardinal Suenens, the liberal catalyst of Vatican II, searching for a true expression of the Council's evangelizing message. Suenens adopted the movement as his own and brokered its recognition by Paul VI—cynics speculate that Paul was delighted that Suenens, a leading dissenter on *Humanae Vitae*, had found something else to occupy his energies. Paul himself welcomed world charismatic leaders for a tenth anniversary celebration at St. Peter's in 1977 and heard the basilica echo for the first time with the ululation of tongues. Martin and his family joined Suenens in Belgium in 1980 and spent four years developing the international movement, which is now active in more than sixty countries. Charismatic Renewal is a special favorite of John Paul II, and Martin has visited with the Pope more than a dozen times. Almost every diocese I visited has an official charismatic liaison office.

In a movement as loosely structured as Charismatic Renewal, numbers are impressionistic at best. There are plausible estimates that, worldwide, some 60 or 70 million Catholics have been involved in the movement at one

Credit: *L'Osservatore Romano*
The Catholic Charismatic Renewal has brought an emotional, pentecostal-type faith style to the Church and has been warmly endorsed by Pope John Paul II. Ralph Martin, one of the founders of the charismatic movement, is shown here in a 1995 meeting with the Pope.

time or another. In America, membership has been declining in recent years, but perhaps 5 to 10 percent of Catholics have some consistent contact with the movement; adding in the "postcharismatics," people who spent at least some time as members, produces quite substantial numbers. American charismatics are typically in their forties, with higher than average educations and lower than average incomes. The vast majority are white, although the movement has been spreading among Hispanics and Filipinos. Raw numbers understate the movement's influence, for among lay ministers and seminarians, the proportion of charismatics and postcharismatics is much higher than in the general Catholic population. Including the *cursillistas,* it is probable that the majority of the newer generations of church leaders have some attachment to a highly personal, "affective," faith style in the charismatic mode, which may be an important factor in their pronounced conservatism.

THE CHARISMATIC "GIFTS"

As an outsider, I wanted to know about the charismatic "gifts." Most priests I asked adopted a position somewhere between dismissiveness and skepticism. Even Bernardicou seemed to maintain an emotional distance—after all, he is a Jesuit—and spoke of it as "folk religion." When I asked Martin, he said simply, "You don't have Christianity without the supernatural. Christ and the disciples healed people, cast out demons, and prophesied. That's what happened. Christianity is about God breaking in." He went on, "When the Church is uncomfortable with the supernatural, it's impoverishing. There are unbalanced people, unsound people roaming around. But as Paul said, don't despise prophecy, test it. Don't quench the Spirit, test it."

Fr. John Hampsch, a Claretian priest based in Los Angeles, operates a traveling charismatic ministry through the western states, and I arranged to meet him at an evening Mass in a white working-class neighborhood in West Los Angeles. Hampsch is a small, bubbling seventy-year-old with a weakness for bad puns. ("Posi-lutely, abso-tively," he said when I asked about charismatic orthodoxy.) He was accompanied by Fr. Desmond McMahon, an Irish Benedictine from Seattle who is a noted healer. Hampsch said that occasionally there is a triple miracle at his Masses. "Someone speaks in tongues, without understanding the language he is speaking in. A second person, who *also* doesn't understand the language, interprets it. And it turns out to be a prophecy." The church was about half full, mostly white couples in their fifties, but with a scattering of younger Filipinos and Hispanics. No one looked well-to-do.

Almost everybody in the congregation spoke in tongues, which they could summon up at will. All of the congregation's parts of the Mass were prayed in tongues, usually standing with the arms raised above the head, the signature charismatic praying position. Hampsch led the Lord's Prayer in tongues, although he prayed the rest of the Mass in English. Hampsch's dialect sounded like Arabic, while the congregation's was more like a sibilant Polish. People did not repeat nonsense phrases but produced a mix of syllables, with the tonal rise and fall and varied sequences of consonants and vowels of a real language. (Hampsch, however, occasionally coaches his congregations in tongues, which seems like cheating.) After the communion, when Hampsch asked if anyone was inspired to prophesy, a tall, heavyset man with a biblical beard and a bass voice, rose to forecast a coming judgment. When the Mass was over, Hampsch and McMahon blessed salt and oil that most of the congregation had brought with them. The blessed salt would protect a house from burglary, Hampsch said, and recommended "sprinkling some around your cars." The oil would expedite healing and was good for colds.

HEALING AND EXORCISMS

The leading Catholic healer is Francis MacNutt, whose books, like *Healing, The Power to Heal,* and *Deliverance from Evil Spirits,* a "practical manual" for exorcism, sell in the millions. MacNutt's Christian Healing Ministry in Jacksonville, Florida, operates out of a modest complex of buildings that once served as an Episcopal church and rectory. The Episcopal minister, now deceased, was a well-known local healer, and the buildings were donated by the local Episcopal diocese after he died. The minister's son is now a local judge whose wife, Norma Dearing, is one of MacNutt's senior staff members.

MacNutt is a tall, rangy, WASPish septuagenarian with shaggy eyebrows and an arresting presence who was ordained a Dominican priest in 1956. Before entering the seminary, he served as a medical corpsman in World War II, majored in English at Harvard, and earned a master's degree in theater from Catholic University. His specialty in his order was preaching, and he ran preaching conferences and workshops around the country, along the way making many friends among Protestant ministers. "One day, about 1960," he said, "I went to a lecture at a Presbyterian seminary by an Episcopalian priest on healing. I thought it was bizarre and assumed everyone else did too. Afterward, there was a reception, and I realized that everyone was talking shoptalk! One minister asked whether anyone else's hands got hot and swollen during healing. And another one said that he kept a bucket of ice water next to him during healing sessions."

MacNutt's own charismatic conversion came in 1967, when a renowned healer named Agnes Sanford laid on her hands and he experienced a "flooding with grace," cried, and spoke in tongues. He first tested his healing prowess on a severely depressed nun he had been counseling. He said, "I remember thinking how silly I was going to feel if nothing happened, but I had her kneel down and prayed over her—just whatever popped into my head that seemed appropriate—and laid on my hands. And when I opened my eyes, she was crying. It was her first expression of emotion in years." The nun, he reports, seems to have made a permanent recovery.

It was MacNutt who introduced the Duquesne/Notre Dame charismatics to healing, and he formed close ties to the charismatics and to the Franciscan University of Steubenville, Ohio, an ultraconservative Catholic college. The college president, Fr. Michael Scanlan, is a regular on Martin's television show, and Martin's eldest daughter is a Steubenville graduate. In the 1970s, MacNutt and Scanlan collaborated on healing conferences and workshops that drew more than 1000 priests at a time. MacNutt, however, left the priesthood in 1979 to marry (his wife, Judith, is also a therapist and healer). Since the marriage was irregular—John Paul II had stopped granting laicization requests—MacNutt was summarily cut off by the Catholic charismatic movement. His laicization and marriage have now been regularized, and when I met him, he had just begun to develop some new projects with Scanlan, although his ministry has become quite ecumenical.

MacNutt claims a long list of healing successes, especially with depression, with the psychic effects of sexual abuse, and with arthritis, endometriosis, and some cancers. When I observed that all of those diseases could have a high psychosomatic component, he replied, "Sure, but I've been able to do some bone straightenings too. There was a woman who had two quite different sized feet. It wasn't a disease, but it was embarrassing. One foot was 7½ and the other was only 5. After I prayed over her, the small foot grew to match the big one in about ten minutes." He also says he can "cure" homosexuals. Success is not uniform and is not always predictable. He and his wife prayed over their daughter's asthma for two years without success, but a visiting healer-couple cured her in a matter of hours. He does not have a Christian Scientist–style aversion to physical medicine and has a mutual referral arrangement with several psychiatrists. MacNutt's results are not documented in a rigorous way, but foot growing aside, I would wager that he helps a great many patients.

While we were talking, Dearing and another staff member came in for a whispered conference. When MacNutt said he had to excuse himself for a few minutes, I asked what was up. He said, "I have to do an exorcism. A woman came in last night, a black woman who had driven all the way from Texas. She had serious problems with her family, and there seems to be a history of sexual abuse. They've put a hex on her, and it's more than the staff can handle by themselves." I asked if I could watch. MacNutt hesitated, then said, "Normally, I wouldn't have any problem, but it looks like voodoo and black magic is involved, and it just might not be a good idea."

He came back about fifteen minutes later and said everything had gone smoothly. He had prayed, and the woman said she felt pain in her neck and shoulders and that her head was being compressed in a box—Dearing suspected an intrauterine experience—then the box opened up, the pain stopped, and the woman fell into a relaxed sleep. "She's not *healed,*" MacNutt said, "She has a lot of psychic damage, but the demons are gone. We'll find her a place to live nearby and she should be completely recovered in a few months or so." I asked if he ever felt threatened during an exorcism and he said not, although his book recounts several incidents that sound at least mildly frightening. (In one of his first exorcisms, the demons spoke through the victim's mouth and told him he wasn't experienced enough.)

I mentioned that many progressive theologians preferred to speak of the devil as a negative principle rather than as a real creature. "I know," he said with a half-snort and half-laugh, spreading his palms in a gesture expressive of the idiocies of progressive theologians. MacNutt says that genuine possessions are rare, but "infestations" are common, and an interest in exorcism seems to be spreading in the Church. New York's Cardinal O'Connor was criticized in 1994 for authorizing a diocesan priest to perform exorcisms at the rate of about two a week. In his Babylon talk, Martin recounted a number of signs of Satan's infiltration of the Church in recent years.

A DIRECT LINE TO GOD

Catholic charismatics are quite orthodox doctrinally, which is a main source of the movement's attraction for the Pope, and for conservative theologians like Scanlan and Fessio, who is Martin's publisher, and recently even Avery Dulles. Martin said, "You can't have people making up their own religion. After Vatican II, a lot of seminaries and theologians were going off into some kind of happy-happy land." He said that adherence to *Humanae Vitae* was not a "litmus test" for belonging to a charismatic community, but most members "come to it themselves." He conceded that there was no intrinsic connection between charismatic religion and orthodoxy but said that perhaps "by providential design, the original leaders were orthodox and were able to lead people to that outcome."

But Martin's preaching and ministerial activities have a very Protestant flavor. His television show, *The Choices We Face,* is a top draw on the Catholic cable Eternal Word Network. (Eternal Word originates in Alabama, and is run by Mother Angelica, an elderly but very feisty nun—picture Yoda in a full habit—whose own call-in cable show has a loyal nationwide audience. She keeps a gimlet eye even on the Vatican's orthodoxy and has engineered nationwide letter-writing campaigns at a hint that a curial cardinal is veering from the straight and narrow.) Martin's shows rarely mention charismatic gifts, since he is trying to broaden the movement's appeal; instead, they push a simple message of opening one's heart and soul to the love of Jesus. They are in a talk-show format, usually with a guest like Scanlan or Ann Shields,

Martin's longtime collaborator, buttressed by tape clips of born-again witnesses and guest preachers like Charles Colson, the Protestant evangelist and veteran of the Watergate scandal. Despite Martin's orthodoxy, the implicit message is often quite anti-institutional. Some representative sound bites from recent shows:

MARTIN: Jesus makes clear that the relationship he wants is personal. Come to Me! . . . He didn't say, "Go to the Church. Go to an institution." The Church isn't God.

COLSON: We've got to fight for justice . . . but only as it flows out of our being a holy community . . . until we *are* the people of God, we cannot make a difference. . . . If we try to change the world without doing this, we fail and discredit the Gospel.

SCANLAN: We have to get the Good News so far out front that it doesn't get muddled and caught up with a lot of doctrinal concerns and moral questions.

Luther couldn't have said it better.

In all the shows I saw, Martin made explicit sales pitches for orthodoxy, but they had the ring of afterthoughts, like safe-driving commercials during the Indianapolis 500. A testifier on a Martin show spoke of God personally "wooing" her with a "passionate love." The "wooing" included little favors like finding baseball tickets that had blown out of her hand on a windy day. Some of the great Catholic mystics spoke this way, but the direct channel to God through faith is a Protestant concept. The conventional Catholic position is that the *Church* is the divinely ordained mediating structure that links people to Christ, which is what makes the Pope and his teaching authority so important. Ironically, the conservative theologian Germain Grisez, who is close to both Scanlan and Fessio, has recently complained that *liberal* theologians have been developing a new understanding of Revelation, in which "there is immediate contact of the human spirit with God, which does not have anything to do with propositions of Faith." But the centrifugal forces within the American Church come from the right as well as from the left, from the grassroots as well as from the academy.

Hispanics

The acceptance of charismatic Catholics has been eased by the increased weight of Hispanic Catholics, who have been importing the more affective

Latin style of worship and also reinvigorating the American Church's old high-profile social action agenda. But the new waves of immigration are yet another centrifugal factor in the American Church. Fr. Greg Boyle, a Los Angeles Jesuit, is a vigorous, ruddy-faced bear of a man with a luxuriant black beard who runs the diocesan gang ministry and operates a job development program for Hispanic youth. Boyle's formative experience was as a missionary in Bolivia, where he worked in a "basic ecclesial community," one of the central concepts of Latin American liberation theology.

Basic ecclesial communities, or BECs, are small local social-activist cells loosely based on the Cardjinist "See, Judge, Act" principles.* Boyle has organized BECs in local public housing projects that have undertaken a variety of self-help programs in violence prevention, women's shelters, mentoring for teenagers, and a cooperative bakery. Most of the programs are centered around the Mission Dolores church near Boyle's office, one of the poorest in the city. Boyle told of going to the church on a summer evening: "About a hundred homeless men sleep in the church at night," he said, "and were assembling for the evening meal. The bakery had a sales booth going, several women's groups were meeting, and a lot of teenagers were just hanging around. I spoke to an older man outside who'd been watching all the activity, and he shook his head and said, 'This used to be a church.' And I said, 'No. Now it's *finally* a church.' " Although there is a long, deeply Catholic tradition of BEC-style social activism, it carries anti-institutional overtones. Much like Martin's direct-pipeline style of religion, while it is *compatible* with doctrinal orthodoxy, it is not likely to grant orthodoxy pride of place among religious values.

The centrifugal pull of the Hispanic ministry is evident even when the style is not so action-oriented. Dennis O'Neill, the pastor of St. Thomas the Apostle in East Los Angeles, has a congregation that comprises a half-dozen different Spanish-language immigrant groups, most of them recent arrivals. O'Neill is in his midfifties, and spent a major portion of his career in Alaska. Although he is competent in Spanish, he has no illusions that he could act as the personal spiritual leader, in the Boyle mode, for so diverse a population. Instead, he has pulled off a virtuoso feat of identifying, and in most cases per-

---

* The development of BECs had more North American influence than is generally acknowledged. San Antonio's Archbishop Robert Lucey absorbed Cardjinist principles from Reynold Hillenbrand and adopted them for his Bishops' Committee on the Spanish-speaking. (See chapter 10.) Lucey organized hundreds of Cardjinist workshops run by American priests throughout Latin America in the 1960s. In the first heady years after Vatican II, the movement was officially endorsed by Latin American bishops at a 1968 conference in Medellín, Colombia. More recently, its Marxist overtones have brought it under close scrutiny by the Vatican, and John Paul II has been appointing much more conservative Latin American bishops, less friendly to liberation theology concepts.

sonally training, a cadre of lay ministers from each ethnic group to do the main work of evangelization. Although the services get highly emotional, O'Neill says, everything is "sound," and he tries to stay away from "weird stuff."

The moral message at St. Thomas's is a highly simplified repetition of "Christ," "love," and "family." Although the church is packed with ardent young families, relatively few of them are married. So Moral Imperative Number One is to love and take care of your family and children. And Moral Imperative Number Two is to *get married.* The moral refinements that engage a Charles Curran and a Cardinal Ratzinger almost never come up. Christ, sacraments, the Eucharist, and family are the "intrinsic" elements of Catholicism, says O'Neill. Formulism, Thomism, and the detailed sexual rules are "extrinsic." When I mentioned O'Neill's moral imperatives to Lincoln's Fr. Barnhill, he said, "Gee. 'Get married!' Sometimes we can forget how different things are in other places." If Barnhill were in O'Neill's shoes, I got the impression, he would be preaching the same line. In a provocative paper, Fr. Allan Deck, a Jesuit who is one of the leading figures in training for the Hispanic ministry, has declared "a pox on both your houses," arguing that the penchants of theological liberals to relativize moral questions and of conservatives to insist on logically crisp dogma are both irrelevant to the Hispanic situation. While Catholic liberals and conservatives have indulged themselves in their "culture wars," as many as a fifth of American Hispanic Catholics have already defected to Protestant evangelical churches.

Themes and Counterthemes

Monolithism has never been the central genius of Catholicism. Over the centuries, it has found room for an enormous variety of religious expressions and doctrinal positions. Split-ups over doctrine, like those with Protestants and with the Eastern churches, are rare. No other religion has managed to maintain such a blend of rarefied intellectualism and cultic devotional practices. Great towers of systematic theology, with liberal borrowings from Plato through Augustine, and Aristotle through Thomas, sit atop a daily religious experience enriched by a panoply of concrete images and symbols—protective saints and lurking devils, sacraments of forgiveness and commitment, funerals and baptisms, weddings and confirmations, liturgies evoking centuries-long pasts and hopeful futures, a transgenerational connectedness with communities of love and faith, and families and decency.

John Paul II himself embodies many of the polarities. On the one hand, he has emphasized doctrinal centralization and a rigorist, legalistic approach to questions of authority and morality; but he has also strongly endorsed local, affective religious expressions, like the charismatics and the worldwide proliferation of Marian apparitions—in Japan, Syria, Argentina, Venezuela, New Jersey, South Korea, Poland, Egypt, and, most famously, in Medjugorje, Yugoslavia, where a shrine has drawn some 20 million Catholic pilgrims since 1981. As the most globe-trotting pope in history, John Paul surely understands the incompatibility of a narrowly defined, rule-based religion with the Church's claim of 800 million Catholics throughout the world.

Institutions are more brittle than in the past. Contradictions are sharpened and pushed more quickly to the snapping point. Theologians have *always* fought without quarter—they are, after all, academics, and theological disputes, like literary ones, can't be settled in this world. Struggles between Franciscans and Dominicans, and the centuries-long slanging matches between theological "nominalists" and "realists," were at least as vicious as anything going on today. But with modern communications and a newly sophisticated, theologically attuned laity, especially in America, the doctrinal battles reverberate right through to the grassroots in a way that is entirely new.

The liturgical reforms initiated by the Council are a good example. Once the switch was turned, they swept through the Church with shocking speed, badly rattling the faith and loyalties of millions of traditional Catholics. Theologians blithely assumed that if people didn't *understand* the Latin liturgies, they couldn't be attached to them, missing the ritualistic significance that the liturgies had acquired. The liturgies now seem to have settled down, despite lingering spats over the male-centered language, and they are probably a marked improvement on the old ones. But it has taken a generation and was much more disruptive than anyone anticipated. A century or so ago, the process would never have been so abrupt. The Council's bright ideas would have been filtered through myriad intermediate structures for years, cushioning the change. Even after Trent, except for the primary liturgies that could be readily managed from the top, Catholic Europe never achieved the uniformity and consistency of practice and behavior of the American Church in its triumphal era.

Humanae Vitae's ruling against marital contraception, to take another example, was announced at a Vatican press conference and instantly became an evening news item. (When Napoleon clapped Pius VII in prison, by contrast, almost no one noticed except the diplomats.) Instantaneous worldwide dissemination of the encyclical made it a dramatic test of papal authority in a way it never would have been previously. When the laity revolted, the papacy, apparently unable to back off such a crisply declared position, dug in, and battle lines between "liberal" and "conservative" Catholics have been drawn ever since. Priests and bishops are torn between their loyalties to the laity and to the Pope and fall back on equivocations and hypocrisy.

The reach of television, the Pope's charisma and appetite for travel, the access of theologians to the mass media are all temptations to win arguments, to clinch a single "right" vision of what Christ intended for his Church. But the Vatican's authority, the cohesiveness of the Church, and the faith of the people may be better preserved if the bonds are not tested so frequently. Any but the Catholic Church would long ago have splintered into multiple "conservative," "reformed," "evangelical," and countless other versions, just as Protestant sects do. Over the centuries, however, the Church has always managed to contain its multiplicity within unity. Popes were frequently moved to curb the multiplicity but rarely had the tools to do so. Modern communications technology provides the tools, and they can destroy the Church if they are not used with restraint.

A Church that can accommodate a Martin and a Remes, an Untener and a Fessio will be a much richer institution, which is a good reason for lowering voices. The visits to Lincoln and Saginaw suggest some others.

EXAGGERATING DIFFERENCES?

When I mentioned to a nun in the Saginaw chancery office that Lincoln was the next stop on my itinerary, she said, "You're going to *Lincoln*!?"—and her body language suggested second thoughts about even talking to me. But when I was in Lincoln, I found myself lecturing several of the seminarians about their exaggerated impressions of Saginaw—they seem to have expected altar-top bacchanals. And the Lincoln seminarians had a right to feel bruised by liberals' cruel assumption that they are "unhealthy," a code word for homosexual or sexually ambiguous. The styles of the dioceses are, in fact, quite different, but the differences tend to be caricatured—a caricature admittedly reinforced by Bishop Bruskewitz's recent threats against Catholics joining Call to Action.

How important are the differences? One test would be whether the two dioceses' religious approaches, and the much richer staffing levels in Lincoln, make a visible difference in lay practice. Surprisingly enough, it seems not. When Fr. Fessio directed me to Lincoln, he predicted I would see a Church that "worked." With respect to the *internal* workings of the Church, he was clearly right. The Lincoln diocese has high morale, a coherent vision of what it's about, and a remarkable corps of young priests and nuns. But Fessio also implied that Mass attendance would be much higher in Lincoln than elsewhere, and that does not appear to be the case.

The only weekly Mass attendance figures collected on a diocesan basis are the Notre Dame studies by Mark Chaves and his colleagues. (These were the data that showed that actual weekly Mass attendance may be much lower than appears from the Gallup polls.) Chaves studied forty-eight dioceses; Lincoln, unfortunately, is not among them, but Saginaw is. Despite all its "liberalism," and Bishop Untener's distaste for threatening hellfire to enforce Mass attendance, Saginaw ranks in the top third in weekly Mass attendance, with a 31.5 percent weekly average, compared with a median of 26.7 percent. Although there are no comparable statistics for Lincoln, the envelope and collection count from St. Teresa's allows a rough estimate. St. Teresa's is a cohesive and family-oriented parish even by Lincoln standards, and one would expect high Mass attendance; but the collection suggests a weekly attendance of about a third, or about the same as in Saginaw.

Where Chaves's data do allow the pairing of "liberal" and "conservative" dioceses, there is no consistent relationship between theological outlook and lay Church attachment. Milwaukee, for example, is arguably the most liberal urban diocese in the country, and the controversial tenure of Archbishop Rembert Weakland has long prompted strenuous complaints from conservative Catholics hoping for Vatican intervention. But Milwaukee ranks eighth out of forty-eight dioceses in Mass attendance and, along with Cincinnati, is the top-ranking big-city diocese in the sample. On the other hand, four theologically conservative dioceses—Newark, Denver, New York, and Portland, Oregon—all rank in the bottom third; but so does San Francisco, and the very liberal Seattle is close to the bottom of the list. The only semiconsistent result from Chaves's data is that rural dioceses have higher rates of Mass attendance, probably because rural parishes are smaller than average and generate a greater sense of family feeling.

Fr. Ron Lewinski, a Chicago priest who has been studying effective parishes around the country, suggests that the lack of correlations simply demonstrates the limited influence a bishop has over the day-to-day workings of his parishes. But that would not seem to apply to Saginaw and Lincoln. Bishop Flavin in Lincoln was, and Bishop Untener in Saginaw still is, a model of the highly focused, unusually hands-on leader; over an extended period of time both of them forged a pastorate very much in their own images. But it doesn't seem to make a lot of difference. Lincoln's Fr. Barnhill concedes that, although virtually all the diocesan priests have preached the sinfulness of contraception for years, Lincoln's Catholics use birth control at almost the same rate as everybody else. And despite the fact that Saginaw's Catholics are not being forced to go to the sacraments, their Mass attendance turns out to be higher than average.

One is driven to Greeley's conclusion: Catholics stay Catholic because they like being Catholic. They go to the sacraments because they want to. The Church adds meaning and connectedness to their lives, and they see it as the surest path to Heaven, but they tune out the clamor of arms on the theological battlefields. As well they should—and that alone might conduce to a humbler, less partisan, theological establishment.

The biggest cost of the Lincoln system has been the delay in integrating women into its ministries. Now that the door is slightly ajar, that may change very rapidly. But Saginaw has problems of its own. The post–Vatican II, nonauthoritarian model of the priesthood—of being "one with his people, not 'set apart' or 'above,' but united with, immersed in, a servant of his people"—has turned out to be a poor recruiting slogan. People with the skills to be effective pastors in the Rizzotto, Torgerson, or Remes mode have many other career alternatives that pay better, have a clearer path to the top, and don't require celibacy. Although Saginaw is a much bigger diocese than Lincoln, it has fewer active priests, a low priest-to-Catholic ratio, and very few men in the pipeline—the 1995 *Catholic Directory* listed a total of forty-two seminarians in Lincoln, at all levels, and only five in Saginaw. But the favored liberal solution to the problem—dropping the celibacy rule—may minimize the consequences of a rule change, much as happened with the liturgical reforms of a generation ago.

MINIMIZING CONSEQUENCES?

The arguments for dropping the celibacy rule are probably overwhelming. In such a family-centered religion, the risk of gradually evolving a homosexually oriented priestly caste seems unacceptable. The great majority of lay people strongly favor married priests (and women priests), partly because of the cloud of sexual scandal that has hung over the Church in recent years. When given a choice, Protestant congregations almost always choose married ministers because they are deemed steadier, more reliable, and less prone to scandal. Simple arithmetic clinches the argument, and in the case of Hispanics, with their very low ratio of ethnic priests, clinches it threefold. With the sharp decline in vocations, as Dean Hoge argues, the choice is not between a married or unmarried priesthood but between parishes run by priests or by lay people. Insisting on the celibacy rule is an implicit vote for an ever more laicized Church, which is just Protestantizing by another route.

But changing the celibacy rule is much more complicated than advocates usually let on. Perhaps only for reasons of historical accident, the celibate priesthood is deeply tied to a "high-tension" version of Catholicism, to something like the Lincoln model of the Church—the priest as a man apart and above, the consecrated, sacred minister, the shamanistic mystic and worker of daily miracles; not the married priest who fights with his wife and has a credit card balance at the department store, who regulates the size of his family, gets divorced and remarried, and manages the sexuality of his teenage children about as well, or as badly, as lay people do. With a married priesthood, spiritual leadership will be a process of sharing dilemmas and trying to work out solutions within generalized Catholic norms. The Church is arguably moving in that direction anyway, but advocates of dropping celibacy are arguing for a specific new model of the Church, not just an incidental change in discipline.

The American Catholic priesthood has never been a conventional profession. Unlike ministers, priests do not pass on their careers to their sons. Each generation of priests is newly recruited, usually from the newest rising generation of the Catholic working classes, and has therefore always been psychologically and emotionally close to its mainstream parish constituency. The historians Rodney Finke and Roger Stark have documented how mainstream Protestant congregations fled to the upstart Pentecostal sects in droves when sons of ministers came home from Ivy League divinity schools to take over the family enterprise.

There are already straws in the wind of a professionalizing priesthood. Again and again, I bumped into seminars called "Twelve-step Approaches to Spirituality" and the like—the clergy co-opting the jargon of the therapeutic and social work professions in a bid for professional credibility. A married priesthood can only accelerate that process. Priests will become counselors, therapists, and social workers. Pressures of earning a living will multiply the numbers of "hyphenated" priests working in lay social service bureaucracies or moonlighting as school counselors. Chancery career ladders will proliferate, at least until the money runs out. Professionalism is already a looming problem in the lay ministry. People with a master's degree in divinity (an "Em-Div" in the jargon) from a Creighton or a Marquette are elbowing aside experienced, but undegreed, lay ministers and pushing up salary scales. It's bound to be worse when the priesthood finally becomes an ordinary career. The model is clearly workable, as Protestants have long demonstrated, but people should be braced for a much more radical change than is commonly supposed.

The arguments for moving slowly are as strong as the ones for change. While a ministerial staffing crunch is clearly in the offing, the Church is still getting by and presumably can continue to do so for some time. And the low level of recruitment is in some degree caused by the disarray within the Church, not just by the celibacy rule. In a few cases where bishops have focused hard on recruitment, the numbers have visibly ticked up. Bishop Anthony O'Connell of Knoxville, Tennessee, a stocky Irishman with a musical brogue, hews a centrist, "pastoral" path on the more divisive theological issues and welcomes female liturgical participation. At the outset of his tenure, he offered the job of vocational director to any priest who had personally tried to enlist young men the previous year, but there were no qualifiers. So O'Connell took on the job himself and has been almost as successful in recruiting priests as Lincoln is. New York's Cardinal O'Connor has also generated increased vocational activity just by personally interviewing young men interested in the seminary.

A sensible first step might be to lift the celibacy rule on a special-exception basis in countries that are suffering severe shortages of priests, as in Africa and Latin America. There was strong interest in such a step at Vatican II, and circumstances surely have not altered for the better in the intervening thirty years. The Church could thereby gain experience with the new discipline outside of the glare of publicity that would be likely in the industrial countries. It will not be possible to maintain a dual system for long, and a dual system within a single country or region of the world is probably unfeasible. But some phasing would seem to be required to work out questions of spousal participation in assignment decisions, attitude toward priests whose marriages break up, the informal ministerial role of wives, and many others. None of these is an issue of first impression for Christian religions, but the Church will need time to get them right.

In the meantime, there are thousands of married former priests who would be happy to serve as nonsacramental ministers. A standard provision in laicization approvals prohibits them from serving in any formal Church role, which seems mean-spirited. It is possible, of course, that there could be frictions between ex-priests acting as lay ministers and priests who have chosen to stick with the discipline and stay through hard times. But experiments could be conducted on a diocesan basis that could offer insights into how to manage an eventual transition to a noncelibate ministry.

WOMEN MINISTERS

Most advocates for a married priesthood, like Hoge and the late Richard Schoenherr, avoid the issue of ordaining women. Archbishop Quinn favors lifting the celibacy rule, but when I asked about women priests, he said, "The question just isn't theologically mature. Right now it would be terribly divisive. Perhaps some day, but not now." As a purely practical matter, given the present theological tensions within the Church, he is probably right.

None of the senior nuns I interviewed expected any change in the male-only ordination rule. (All the interviews, including Quinn's, predated the Vatican's fall 1995 announcement on the putative infallibility of male-only ordination.) Sr. Patricia Wolfe, a Sisters of Mercy regional president, said simply, "I'd be a better pastor than most of the priests I know, but that's not my charism. I'm happy doing what I do now." Sr. Mary Flaherty, the San Francisco chancellor, said she had no interest in the priesthood. Then she added in a wistful tone, "When our community gathers for spiritual retreats, we like to close with a Mass. We've tried communion services, but it's not the same. It would be so nice if one of our own could celebrate the Mass, just on those occasions, instead of bringing in an outsider"—poignant comment from a loyal churchwoman. Sr. Remes had no expectation of a rule change in her lifetime.

By insisting on the impossibility of ordaining women, however, the Vatican has, sadly enough, only sharpened the partisan tone of the debate. Avery Dulles, who supports the Vatican's reasoning on women priests, has suggested that the persuasiveness of the ruling depends on the degree of trust one places in the Vatican's teaching authority. Its initial reception, at least, suggests that trust has been badly frayed in recent years. (The consensus of a large gathering to hear a Dulles lecture on the question, as far as I could divine, was simply to wait, relying on a comment attributed to John XXIII—"What a pope can do, a pope can undo." The Church has immense casuistic resources and has executed doctrinal reversals of similar dimensions many times in the past.)

Dulles, however, has been among those who have suggested an immediate exploration of the possibility of ordaining women as deacons and expanding women's ministry in a proactive way. For example, while women are currently allowed to offer "Reflections" in church, they are not allowed to read the Gospel or deliver a homily—although Sr. Remes and other pastoral administrators do so. None of the objections against ordaining women priests listed by the Vatican seem to apply to nonsacramental ministries, and Church history includes a long tradition of women preachers and prophets, and possibly of women deacons. Evidence from the early Church is always ambiguous, but there seems to be no justification for not interpreting it in the way most favorable to the expansion of women's ministries. Indeed, in the absence of genuine theological obstacles to elevating women within the Church, it would seem to be the Pope's duty to do so. Anything less would call into question the good faith of his statements in favor of women's equal rights and equal dignity. The Church is short enough of good ministers, and there is no excuse for not utilizing half, or more, of the talent base.

For that matter, there is no canonical requirement that *cardinals* be priests. Current practice restricts the College of Cardinals to consecrated bishops, but there have been lay cardinals in the past. Appointing women to the cardinalate—perhaps drawn from the ranks of the most senior of the women deacons—would leave little doubt of the Vatican's good faith; such women, of course, would also have the right to vote for the next pope.

In general, however, it is hard to imagine any solutions to the difficult questions facing the Church, whether the ministry problem, or the question of women, without some mutual backing off from the ideological barricades. In some months of conversations with theological partisans of various hues, I have heard the opposition variously called unhealthy, self-interested, anti-Catholic, rigid, doing the work of Satan, power-driven, and much else besides. Liberals did not seem noticeably more restrained than conservatives, or vice versa.

One of the very few recent hopeful straws in the wind was that Chicago's Cardinal Bernardin, a moderate and a bridge builder, had organized a "Catholic Common Ground" project in the hopes of dispelling some of the acrimony and polarization in the Church. The steering committee included Los Angeles's Cardinal Mahony, who is usually associated with conservatives on doctrinal issues, and Milwaukee's very liberal Archbishop Weakland. Whether Bernardin's death from cancer spells the end of the initiative remains to be seen.

DILEMMAS

Both the Saginaw and Lincoln models of the Church—or the charismatic or Hispanic models—are fraught with pitfalls. The risk of the "liberal" vision of the Church is that Catholicism will go the way of mainstream Protestantism. Finke and Stark have suggested that only "high-tension" religions prosper in America. Once a religion assimilates to the culture, it almost invariably diminishes into a social center or low-cost group therapy program. There are now fewer Episcopalians in America than there are Catholics in Los Angeles. (I asked an Episcopalian friend if Episcopalians have sins. He replied, "Of course," but had to think a bit. Then his face brightened. "Littering," he said proudly. "Smoking in restaurants.")

Perhaps the Catholic Church, with its longer history and hardier theological tradition, is different—or so I have heard liberals claim. Richard John Neuhaus speaks of "ecclesial fundamentalists" who think that nothing can go wrong with the Church. "I came from Lutheranism," he says, "and I lived through the collapse of mainstream Protestantism. It could happen here too."

But the conservative taste for papal absolutism—the penchant for parsing every nuance of the flood of new encyclicals, and the cult of personality that seems to be forming around John Paul II—fits uncomfortably with the American tradition. Conservatives say all the right things about participatory structures, just as the Pope has said all the right things about the equality and dignity of women, but the content seems to fall short of the rhetoric. The traditionalists also underestimate the importance of America in world Catholicism. None of the so-called Catholic countries of Europe and Latin America can match the activism, wealth, and dynamism of the American Church, with all its recent problems. The risk of the conservative vision is that the Church will dwindle to a narrow sect of true believers, too small to sustain the world symbolism of the Church—the papal tours, the global missionary reach, the doctrinal councils and synods, the traditional infrastructure.

The challenge, in short, is the same one that American bishops faced in the nineteenth century—how to create a Church that is both *American* and

Catholic, drawing from the best in both traditions. The initial solution, which worked splendidly through the first half of the twentieth century, was the creation of a separate Catholic subculture with a religion-based ministate of its own. But now that the subculture has broken down, the Church has been left groping for a new accommodation. The process has been painful, public, and not very pretty; and it is still far from assured of success.

CHAPTER 16

The Church and America

In October 1995, in the bleak dawn of a raw, drizzly morning, 150,000 people tramped through New York City's Central Park to the Great Lawn, where for some three hours they stood in intermittent rain or huddled under blankets and trees awaiting the celebration of an outdoor Mass by Pope John Paul II. The crowd—I guessed it was about one-third Hispanic, with the rest largely white—was surprisingly young. Teenagers and twentysomethings may even have been a slight majority, and despite the rain and the chill, everyone was in a festive mood. The tedium of the waiting was eased by an all-star warmup cast—Roberta Flack, Natalie Cole, a marine chorus, the Harlem Boys' Choir, with Placido Domingo on hand for the communion hymn. At one end of the lawn a pharaonic altar and stage, hung with billowing draperies of Cleopatran purple, dwarfed the performers and the small band of clerics preparing the altar for the Mass. Giant video screens, like those used at rock concerts, loomed on either side of the altar, and sound towers blasted music and crowd notices at a volume audible for miles.

At about 8:45, to a loud cheer, the video screens flashed "The Pope Is 20 Mins. from the Park Entrance," and the loudspeaker announcer asked everyone to return to their designated areas, which, to a remarkable degree for a New York crowd, they did. Every three or four minutes the screens flashed news of the Pope's progress, feeding a low roar of anticipation punctuated by rhythmic bursts of "John Paul Two, We Love You!" Finally, there was a shout from one end of the lawn, and the Pope was in the park, perched in his "Popemobile," a chunky, white Jeeplike vehicle with a bulletproof-glass-enclosed platform, his hand raised in blessing, his facial expression projected in close-up on the huge video screens as he made a slow progress toward the altar.

Remarkably enough, the Pope *scowled*. He didn't appear angry, but he looked as if he was skeptically sizing up the crowd, appraising the sincerity and quality of its Catholicism. When he finally got to the stage, limping slightly from the aftereffects of a hip injury, he took the microphone and said, "Goot mornink," to an ecstatic response. He made a comment about the rain and said that he knew he was in "great, great New York" and not in Denver— a pointed reference to the youth of the crowd and his smash-hit visit to some 400,000 well-behaved young people at the 1993 Denver Youth Congress— and said they'd get the Mass under way in just a few minutes. Deftly, John Paul made himself the host, not the guest, of the gathering on the lawn.

No American politician could have pulled it off. At the sight of so rapturous a crowd, a Bill Clinton, a Bob Dole, a Newt Gingrich, an Al Gore would have been flushed with quivering gratitude, visibly savoring each drop of affirmation. John Paul managed to look both stern and genial, rather like a strict grandfather. He acknowledged the adulation cheerfully enough, as if it came with the job, but he wasn't there to bask in applause; he was there to tell people how to *act*, which he proceeded to do in a lengthy sermon:

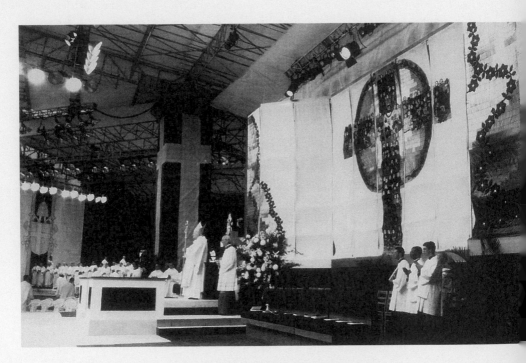

Credit: Michael Okoniewski/Catholic News Service
Pope John Paul II celebrating Mass from a gigantic stage in New York's Central Park in 1995. The Pope's message of moral discipline received an extraordinarily positive reception from the usually cynical New York press.

You . . . are called to "visit" the needs of the poor, the hungry, the homeless, those who are alone or ill; for example, those suffering from AIDS. You are called upon to stand up for life. You are called to respect and defend the mystery of life always and everywhere, including the lives of unborn babies, giving real help and encouragement to mothers in difficult situations. You . . . are called to work and pray against abortion, against violence of all kinds, including violence done against women's and children's dignity through pornography.

Stand up for the life of the aged and the handicapped, against attempts to promote assisted suicide and euthanasia! Stand up for marriage and family life! Stand up for purity! Resist the pressures and temptation of a world that too often tries to ignore a most fundamental truth: that every life is a gift from God our Creator, and that we must give an account to God of how we use it either for good or evil.

After the sermon, I repaired to a nearby apartment to watch the rest of the Mass on television. In aerial view, the communion service, which stretched on for thirty or forty minutes, was awesome—150,000 people patiently lining up in the rain to receive the Eucharist. Even more amazing was the gushing of the New York television reporters. Their medium is hardly a stronghold of traditional morality, and it is quite unlikely that any of them agreed with the Pope's position on abortion or on the definition of "purity," or even on assisted suicide. But, as a print reporter wrote, "Watching the city's notoriously brutal press corps the last two days has been a little like seeing Nicely-Nicely and his fellow thugs sing hymns at the mission in Times Square." During the communion service, a young woman reporter said reverently, "We all feel the need to have someone finally stand up for morality." In one television newsroom, the reporters were caught *in flagrante* singing "Let there be peace on earth" along with a televised children's chorus. The conservative editor Fr. Richard John Neuhaus, who served as a television commentator on the Pope's trip, heard a feminist pro-choice reporter sum up the trip with "You look at the world today and you have to ask yourself the question, Who else is there?"

Several weeks after the Pope's visit, I spent most of a day at St. John the Baptist School in the heart of Bedford-Stuyvesant in Brooklyn. The yellowing marble lining the halls testifies to the Church's faded grandeur, for the building once housed St. John's Prep, where Brooklyn's Irish Catholic elite sent their sons. But the very best of the American Catholic tradition still rules at St. John's, in the person of Sr. Mary Jane Raeilhe. In her sixties, in a dark suit, a nun's half-veil, and sensible shoes, Raeilhe walks with a flat-footed, straight-ahead, plow-through-mountains stride and looks on the world through practical, unsurprised Irish blue eyes. In a half day of touring the halls and visiting classrooms, at least a dozen children came to her with personal and family questions.

I had spent enough time in New York City public schools to feel something seriously out of kilter in a St. John's seventh-grade math class—a kind of cognitive dissonance that took a few minutes to sort out. There were thirty kids in the classroom. The teacher, a young white man, came to the door and we talked for about five minutes. He had his back to the classroom all the time. There were two separate groups of four or five kids each working at the blackboard on algebra problems. Another group of half-dozen kids worked in a circle of chairs in one corner of the room, and the rest were working by themselves. These were poor kids of color, possibly most of them from non-Catholic, single-parent, female-headed families, in a neighborhood that was desperately poor and frighteningly violent. *And they all kept working quietly at their math problems.* Public school teachers in New York inner-city neighborhoods do not turn their backs on classrooms and converse with strangers while their charges work busily on. Only slowly did it dawn on me that the entire school was marvelously quiet, with a pervasive air of contented concentration.

The kids do fine academically. "I'll show you the test scores," said Raeilhe, pulling out files that showed standardized marks well above the norms. "We slip back in the sixth and seventh grades," she went on, "because we usually take in a lot of kids from the public schools then. They haven't been taught anything. It's really sad. I can go down score sheets without any names and pick out the public school kids nine out of ten times. But if we have them for a year or so, we can get them up to par." Edina Lawson is a St. John's alumna, a young African-American woman who has returned as an elementary grade teacher. "When I went here," she told me, "it was called Bedford Middle School [an unusual name for a Catholic school]. People would stop us on class trips and ask what school we went to. When we told them, they would always say, 'Oh, we thought you went to a Catholic school because you're so well behaved.' " She laughs. "The city bus drivers all knew us too. If we were fooling around on the back of a bus going home, they'd turn around and say, 'Cut it out back there, or I'll tell Sister Mary Jane.' "

When I was waiting for Raeilhe outside of her office, there were two very unhappy-looking girls, both about thirteen, sitting there too. They were still sitting at the end of the afternoon and I asked why. "They're being punished," Raeilhe said, "and I have a meeting with them after school. They've had something going on between them outside of school, and they cursed at each other in the hall. They know we don't do that here." The matter-of-fact "*we don't do that here*" is central to what was going on at St. John's. In theo-

Credit: Rick Cronin
The success of Catholic schools in poor urban neighborhoods is now widely recognized by secular scholars. The picture shows the eighth-grade graduating class of St. John the Baptist School in Brooklyn's Bedford-Stuyvesant. Sr. Mary Jane Raeilhe is at the extreme left in the half-veil.

logical jargon, not cursing in the halls was an "exceptionless moral norm." It wasn't arrived at by voting or by debate, and there were no extenuating circumstances that opened the door to occasional cursing. Raeilhe didn't plan any further punishment for the girls; their own awareness that they had broken a basic norm of civil society at St. John's, she thought, would be quite sufficient.

I asked Raeilhe what made education at St. John's "Catholic." "We take religion seriously," she said. "Everybody has to go to Mass and chapel and pray, whether they're Catholics or not. If they're not Catholic, they can just sit and pray quietly or meditate, but they go. And we teach what it is to live in a community where you're supposed to love each other and treat each other that way." I got almost the same answer from Vicki Butler, the principal of St. Peter's School, a splendid oasis of sanity and learning in a gang-ravaged poor Hispanic neighborhood in San Francisco. "We teach traditional Catholic values," she said. "Love and respect each other, and respect yourself. We teach the kids to look at you directly in the eye when they speak. And everybody prays."

Catholic schools clearly start with some advantages over public schools. No child goes to St. John's or St. Peter's unless some adult takes an interest in him or her. Raeilhe and Butler also have the power to expel the most unruly students, although they rarely do. The staffs at St. John's and St. Peter's are paid considerably less than public school teachers, but they are very dedicated, carry bigger class loads, work longer hours, and stay on for years. Inner-city public schools are sometimes staffed almost entirely by substitutes. But the core advantage, which public schools may have lost forever, is that St. Peter's and St. John's exercise moral authority over their kids—that's why teachers return year after year. And the kids seem to love it, just as the New York press corps fell into a swoon over the moral authority of John Paul II.

The week of the Pope's visit, Naomi Wolf, a pro-choice secular feminist writer, in a featured article in *The New Republic,* applied the language of morality to the pro-choice movement, worrying that advocates of abortion rights had abandoned their movement's "ethical core":

> *The Well Baby Book,* the kind of whole-grain, holistic guide to pregnancy and childbirth that would find its audience among the very demographic that is solidly pro-choice reminds us that: "Increasing knowledge is increasing the awe and respect we have for the unborn baby and is causing us to regard the unborn baby as a real person long before birth."
>
> So what will it be? Wanted fetuses are charming, complex, REM-dreaming little beings whose profile on the sonogram looks just like Daddy, but unwanted ones are mere "uterine material"?
>
> It was when I was four months pregnant, sick as a dog, and in the middle of an argument, that I realized I could no longer tolerate the fetus-is-nothing paradigm of the pro-choice movement. . . . [A conservative said,] "You're four months pregnant . . . Are you going to tell me that's not a baby you're carrying?" The accepted pro-choice position at such a moment in the conversation is to evade: To move as swiftly as possible to a discussion of "privacy" and "difficult personal decisions," and "choice." Had I not been so nauseated and so cranky and so weighed down with the physical gravity of what was going on inside me, I might not have told what is the truth for me. "Of course, it's a baby," I snapped. And went rashly on: "And if I found myself in circumstances in which I had to make the terrible decision to end this life, then that would be between myself and God."
>
> Startlingly to me, two things happened: the conservative was quiet; I had said something that actually made sense to him. And I felt the great relief that is the grace of long-delayed honesty.
>
> Now, the G-word is certainly a problematic element to introduce into the debate. And yet "God" or "soul"—or, if you are secular and pre-

fer it, "conscience"—is precisely what is missing from the pro-choice discourse. . . . We on the left tend to twitch with discomfort at that word "sin." . . . [But] it may mean that [the woman choosing an abortion] must face the realization that she has fallen short of who she should be; and that she needs to ask forgiveness for that, and atone for it.

Several weeks later, Jane Mayer wrote in a similar vein in *The New Yorker,* usually a bastion of slick hipness. Making the case for legal abortion, she wrote, "requires a willingness to draw subtle moral distinctions. . . . The advocates of choice, by refusing to entertain the idea that some abortions under some circumstances might in fact be wrong, are preventing themselves from arguing convincingly for those that are right. By locking themselves out of the moral arena, they have created a vacuum in[to] which zealots [can rush]."

Clearly, there is a large gap between Wolf's or Mayer's position on abortion and that of the Pope, or even of the more liberal academic Catholic theologians. But they have in common the assumption, as the Pope put it, that our "life is a gift . . . and that we must give an account to God of how we use it either for good or evil." Wolf and Mayer would not have phrased it quite that way, but their insistence that abortion decisions have moral content implies an external standard of right and wrong, or in the more emotive language that makes secularists "twitch with discomfort," of good and evil and sin and redemption.

Mary Ann Glendon, a Harvard law professor, argues that while abortion and divorce are readily available in all Western democracies, it is only in America that the laws have been stripped of moral content. Only in America are abortions treated, as *Roe v. Wade* put it, as purely "medical" decisions; and only in America is it considered reasonable to speak of "no-fault" divorce. Laws, Glendon argues, are not just rules of behavior. They are "constitutive"—they express, and help define, who people *are.* Almost everywhere else, abortions and divorce are treated as small tragedies, as civic failures, as tiny rents in the social fabric, unavoidable at times, to be sure, but no less to be regretted. In Japan, where abortion laws are very permissive, it is common to hold a memorial service for the soul of the departed fetus, underlining that this was not an outcome that anyone preferred. To the degree that Glendon is right, and that laws are "constitutive," the American laws bespeak a society that denies the existence of external standards, one where people are free to define "right and wrong" pretty much as they please. But as Wolf points out, few people, even educated, liberal, pro-choice people, really feel that way.

The idea of America as a country that has more or less officially repudiated moral values would have seemed absurd not too many decades ago. And the rise of the Christian right, of neoconservatism, and of New Age spirituality suggests stirrings of discomfort that the nation could have arrived at such a place. During the early days of the 1996 presidential race, Bill Clinton, who possesses political antennae of preternatural sensitivity, bragged of praying over difficult decisions. As Wolf's article, the reaction to the Pope's visit, and the success of books like Stephen L. Carter's *The Culture of Disbelief* all attest, even liberals are uncomfortable with the notion that morality must be reinvented with each morning's first cup of coffee.

America, the Vatican, and the Church

John Courtney Murray and, more recently, Richard John Neuhaus have pointed to the Vatican's failure to distinguish between the American and the French revolutions. It was Danton and Robespierre who attempted to banish God and morality from public life, not Jefferson and Adams. The "self-evident truths" of the Declaration of Independence are rooted in the natural law tradition. "State a moral case to a ploughman and a professor," said Jefferson, and "the former will decide it as well, and often better than the latter." A common "moral intuition" was the glue that made republicanism possible.

But all revolutionists are in some degree cultural relativists, and Jefferson and Adams also knew their Montesquieu. Montesquieu's *Spirit of the Laws* showed how much of morality was socially constructed—behavior that was shocking in one country was considered normal in another. Tom Paine embodied the distrust of organized religion that was threaded through the revolutionary period, and his hopes for liberal "infidelity" were sorely disappointed by the religious revival that swept the country right after the war for independence.

Much of American history is marked by the tensions between the two traditions. A shared "moral intuition" implies a community of values, a web of reciprocal obligation that is the glue of citizenship. But those same communities have frequently suppressed the most basic of individual rights, as in the case of racial minorities or homosexuals. A commitment to individual equality and freedom, on the other hand, inevitably pushes to maximize self-expression and fulfillment of desires. But desires are not quite the same as values and, the human clay being what it is, self-expression often enough degenerates into dysfunctional self-indulgence.

America's periodic swings between liberalism and conservatism partly reflect the alternating dominance of the individualist and the communitarian traditions. Conceivably, over the past generation, America's wealth may have tipped the balance permanently toward the individualist side. Although there are plenty of poor in America, it is still a country where even the less-well-off live in houses, drive cars, and have multiple television sets and

VCRs. Even as wealth eases the consequences of irresponsibility, aggressive marketers have made the "consumer society" a paean to the collective id—the morality of daytime television would shame a barnyard.

There seems to be growing agreement that the country could better balance its commitment to individualism and self-expression with some shared standard of what is substantively, not just procedurally, decent and good and just, some external criterion of right behavior compelling enough, for example, to quell pornography and violence, to keep families together even during hard times, and to prevent parents from deserting their children. As Tocqueville noted, "Religion is more necessary . . . in democratic republics. . . . How is it possible that society should escape destruction if the moral tie is relaxed?" If America does not need the Catholic Church, it may need something very much like it, a confident and constant source for the kind of norms of responsibility and mutual respect that Sr. Mary Jane drills into the kids at St. John's.

But the Catholic Church is almost a mirror image of America. If America has made an idol of choice, and enthroned process over substance, the Church devalues process, limits participation, and is suspicious of pluralism. Cutting off discussion of the ordination of women by declaring the male-only rule to be infallibly correct is the classic example, but there are many more. Vatican II reformers, apparently including the then-Father Ratzinger, had hoped to decentralize decision making through the use of national episcopal conferences, but the experiment has apparently been dropped, and the episcopal ranks are being stacked with centralizing loyalists. Despite the fact that the great majority of most married Catholics the world over, most priests and theologians, and probably most bishops, are convinced in conscience that the Church's rules on birth control within marriage are simply wrong, the Vatican has dug in its heels harder and harder.

John Paul II, for all his virtues, seems more willing than his recent predecessors to settle argument by resort to authority. Although he is reportedly anxious to understand American values, the Polish Church is notoriously command-oriented, and he has little personal experience with democratic institutions and structures. He was recently reported in the press as claiming that Catholics must "obey the church on all matters, not just on issues of strong papal statements." That is not the understanding of the vast majority of American Catholics, even *on* issues of strong papal statements. Nothing erodes authority faster than its overuse.

And the Catholic Church also badly needs America. Several conservatives stressed in interviews that America inflates its importance in the scheme of world Catholicism. "Americans make up only about 7 or 8 percent of the world's Catholics," one of them told me, implying that even if *all* American Catholics chose to desert the Pope over issues like birth control, or divorce, or abortion, it would make little difference in the larger picture. I think that is quite wrong. Indeed, with only slight exaggeration, there is a good case that America, and perhaps Australia and Canada, which derive from the same tradition, may be the *only* places where the Church really works.

In the traditional Catholic countries of Europe—Italy, France, Spain, and Portugal—the Church is just a gilded shell. The percentage of Italian Catholics who go to Sunday Mass barely makes it into double digits (the numbers are based on the same polling processes that produce a 50 percent turnout in America) while in France the Church has almost ceased to exist. Only 10 percent of French people between the ages of forty and fifty describe themselves as practicing Catholics, and only 2.5 percent of those under twenty-five. Only about half of the babies born in France are even baptized, and the situation in Italy is only marginally better. The fortunes of the Church are in free-fall even in Poland. Long one of the most devoutly Catholic countries of Europe, Poland has a native-born pope, and the Church was a symbol of national resistance during the dark years of communism. But less than a decade after the liberation, Mass attendance may already be lower than in America and falling fast, while the Church's ham-handed attempts to intervene in national politics appear to be costing it the allegiance of the middle classes.

More than a third of the world's Catholics live in Latin America, where for centuries the local Church not only has failed to evangelize the great mass of the populace, but also has covered some of the world's more repulsive dictators with clouds of Catholic incense. American dioceses in the Southwest take it for granted that Hispanic immigrants will arrive uncatechized, just as the Pope's own Italian immigrants did in the nineteenth century. The Vatican's claims of great progress in Africa must be taken skeptically. Uganda is one of the most Catholic countries on the continent, but after generations of unspeakable rulers and internecine wars, and with perhaps a fifth of its adult population infected with the AIDS virus, it is sunk in social chaos. Benin is theoretically almost all Catholic, but it somehow manages also to be the world center of voodoo, and priests were involved in the atrocities in Rwanda. The number of African seminarians has risen sharply, but from very low levels, and one must wonder how many are in search only of a decent meal. The ratio of priests to nominal Catholics, at about 1:20,000 is far too low to staff a functioning Church, and there are many reports of native priests with wives, or sometimes several wives, and large numbers of children.

In the wake of the nineteenth-century European diaspora, American Catholics created their own strong, blue-collar-based Church, one that paid its own way, built its own infrastructure, and picked up much of the tab for the Vatican and the world missions besides. At about the same time, a series of cataclysmic papal misjudgments—by the same popes who insisted on a strong definition of infallibility—irretrievably alienated European workers. While European prelates languished in the tawdry palaces of a deracinated nobility and extracted money and spirit from ignorant peasants, the American blend of patriotism, unionism, social moderation, and religiosity produced one of the world's most vibrant popular churches. Absent the money and energy from America, the course of the world Church from about 1850 on would have been thorn-strewn indeed. More recently, the Banco Ambrosiano scandals have done nothing to burnish the Vatican's reputation for good judgment and straight dealing.

Almost all priests I met greatly admire the Pope's energy, his intellect, and his powerful personality, and conservatives quote his sayings like mantras. (One Lincoln priest said, "If we can stay true to the teachings of John Paul II"—then caught himself—"I mean of the Church, of course.") But much of the old deference for everything Roman is gone. "These are the same people," said the Jesuit Thomas Reese bitterly, "who lost the working classes in Europe, and now they're trying to alienate women, who are the heart of the Church, the ones who really make it work." He went on scornfully, "And what does *Eastern Europe* have to teach America about living peacefully in a pluralist society?"

Pluralism, Values, and Morals

Philosophers and theologians have been debating the role of religion and morals in a secular, democratic society for at least three hundred years. Judging by the outpourings from academia, interest in America may be at an all-time peak. There are two polar positions. The utilitarian, or "consequentialist," measures an act by the good it produces, and the utilitarian standard of "the greatest good for the greatest number" is deeply embedded in the American tradition. At the other pole, the natural law moralist starts with first principles and decides if acts are *permissible* before passing on their desirability. When the utilitarian Lenin asks, "What is to be done?," the natural law moralist replies, "But first, what is *not* to be done?" Utilitarian arrogance has often enough led to moral horrors, but the natural law tradition also has a bad habit of confusing current injustices with the Divine order, especially those that have worked to the moralist's advantage, like the privileges of the nobility or the subordination of women.

As a practical matter, most people make decisions by picking and choosing from one position or the other, as seems sensible or convenient. Liberal secularists invoke exceptionless, natural law–like standards as readily as the Pope—with regard, for instance, to racial or sexual discrimination, to the extinction of species, to capital punishment, or to military policies that endanger noncombatants. In all of these cases, it is the conservatives who tend to be the utilitarians—balancing the interests of loggers and endangered species, for instance. Any institution that has played the game of European realpolitik for as many centuries as the Vatican has is also bound to have its utilitarian moments, as the current policy on marital annulments suggests.

The balance is apt to be particularly precarious in a pluralist society like America. Not only will there be a multiplicity of utilitarian positions, but there also exists considerable disagreement on what the bedrock natural law–like values are. For the most part, contending claims are resolved in private—one's sexual habits, for example, are usually nobody else's business. But disagreements become acute when they acquire a civic dimension. The great drama of the civil rights revolution of the 1960s was that the whole nation, through a process that a theologian would call a collective act of "moral discernment," came to the conclusion that racial discrimination was fundamentally, and always, wrong. And judging by the behavior of some members of the southern Catholic hierarchy, lay people reached their consensus even before the Church did.

The struggles over American abortion policy has, in many respects, involved a similar process of discernment. As far as Catholics are concerned, it came to a head in the 1984 confrontation between Church officials and New York's then-governor Mario Cuomo over Cuomo's refusal to veto a bill permitting the use of state funds for abortions.

There can hardly be an American politician who takes his religion more seriously than Cuomo, a self-described "Catholic, a lay person baptized and raised in the pre–Vatican II church, attached to the church first by birth, then by choice, and now by love. An old-fashioned Catholic who sins, regrets, struggles, worries, gets confused and most of the time feels better after confession." Some conservatives suspect he was merely playing politics on the abortion issue. I don't find that credible—unlike many politicians, when Cuomo says that he is personally opposed to abortion, you believe him. When I interviewed him more than ten years after the event, his run-in with the New York hierarchy was still in the forefront of his mind. He raised it as soon as we sat down, and we talked about it for more than an hour.

When Cuomo signed the abortion legislation, he was sharply criticized by then-Archbishop O'Connor. Later, Cuomo told me, he was at home with his wife and one of his children, watching a television interview with the archbishop. "Somebody asked him whether I should be excommunicated. I thought the question was offensive, and I expected him to brush it off, the way you do with questions like that. But he *didn't.* He actually *considered* it! And gave some kind of answer that implied that maybe I should be. You can't imagine how devastating that is. To be sitting there with your wife and one of your children and have that said about you. My son—he was thir-teen—said, 'Dad, is that true? Could you be *excommunicated*?' I said, 'No. And even if he is the archbishop, he's wrong.' But I was so upset—can you imagine someone saying you could be *excommunicated*?—I couldn't sleep and I said to Matilda, 'I have to answer that.' And she said 'Mario, don't. Nothing's happened. Just leave it alone.' "

As Cuomo tells it, he worked for five weeks on a response, to the exclu-sion of almost all his other activities, consulting with a number of theolo-

Credit: Chris Sheridan/Catholic New York

Former New York governor Mario Cuomo is a devout Catholic who clashed sharply with New York's Cardinal John O'Connor over state funding for abor-tion. The Governor and the Cardinal are shown here in a more companionable moment.

gians. At the time he had a long-standing invitation to address Richard McBrien's theology seminar at Notre Dame. "I called Father McBrien and canceled my talk," Cuomo said. "There had been a lot of publicity about my abortion position and I didn't want to embarrass them." McBrien at first agreed, but later called to say that he and Fr. Theodore Hesburgh, the university president, thought Cuomo should come anyway in the interest of the free exchange of ideas. "By then I'd finished this long and complicated paper," Cuomo said, "and it dawned on me that Notre Dame was the only forum I had. I couldn't call a press conference to read an hour-long paper. And all the time Matilda—who is always right about these things—is saying, 'Mario, drop it. Better that you be wrong than the Church.' But I decided to do it." On the way out to Indiana, the state plane was struck by lightning and went into a heart-stopping plunge—"Matilda is in the back, her face is white, she's looking at me, and I know what she's thinking." Getting off the plane, Cuomo fell on the stairs and got a nasty rap on the head; at the hotel, he spilled a pitcher of orange juice on his only shirt; and as he walked to the stage—with all the publicity, the seminar had expanded to fill an auditorium—a former seminarian on his staff pressed a rosary into his hand, "and that got me really rattled."

Especially by the standard of American politics, the speech is a small masterpiece:

[T]he Catholic who holds political office in a pluralistic democracy . . . bears special responsibility . . . to help create conditions . . . where everyone who chooses may hold beliefs different from specifically Catholic ones—sometimes even contradictory to them; where the laws protect people's right to divorce, their right to use birth control devices and even to choose abortion. . . .

And they do so gladly . . . because they realize that in guaranteeing freedom for all, they guarantee our right to be Catholic. . . . We know that the price of seeking to force our belief on others is that they might some day force their belief on us. . . .

Now, as a Catholic, I have accepted certain answers as the right ones for myself and for my family, and because I have, they have influenced me in special ways, as Matilda's husband, as a father of five children. . . . As Catholics, my wife and I were enjoined never to use abortion to destroy the life we created, and we never have. We thought church doctrine was clear on this, and more than that, both of us felt it in full agreement with what our own hearts and our own consciences told us. . . .

But not everyone in our society agrees with me and Matilda. And those who don't—those who endorse legalized abortions—aren't a ruthless, callous alliance of anti-Christians. . . . In many cases . . . [they] are the very people who have worked with Catholics to realize the goals of social justice set out by popes in encyclicals. [He then cites a long list of religious bodies endorsing legal abortion.]

The hard truth is that abortion is not a failure of government. No agency . . . forces women to have abortions, but abortions go on. Catholics, the statistics show, support the right to abortion in equal proportion to the rest of the population. Despite the teaching we've tried in our homes and our schools and our pulpits, despite the sermons and pleadings of parents and priests and prelates, despite all the efforts we've so far made at defining our opposition to what we call the sin of abortion, collectively we Catholics apparently believe—and perhaps act—little differently from those who don't share our commitment.

Are we asking government to make criminal what we believe to be sinful because we ourselves can't stop committing the sin? The failure here is not Caesar's. This failure is our failure, the failure of the entire people of God. . . .

We can remember where we come from, the journey of two millennia. We can cling to our personal faith, to its insistence on constancy and service and example and hope. We can live and practice the morality that Christ gave us, maintaining his truth in this world, struggling to embody his love, practicing especially where that love is most needed, among the poor and the weak and the dispossessed—not just by trying to make laws for other people, but by living the laws already written for us by God, in our minds and in our hearts.

Cuomo argued, in effect, that the first stage of the process of discernment was over, that it had been engaged in seriously by ethically and religiously motivated people—the long citation of non-Catholic religious authorities is crucial to his case—and that, for non-Catholics at least, the Church's position had not carried. Cuomo still could have vetoed the legislation, but it would have passed anyway. Rightly or wrongly, he decided that by maintaining relations with the pro-choice groups, he could more effectively implement policies that would reduce the overall abortion level in the state, as the record confirms he conscientiously attempted to do. The Naomi Wolf article suggests that the discernment process on abortion still continues. The evolving consensus, including among Catholics, is clearly in favor of maintaining legal abortions, but with many more moral qualms, especially about later-term abortions, than may have been the case a decade or so ago. The Church's consistent line in opposition to abortion has almost certainly contributed to the shift in American attitudes. (Stephen Carter has pointed out that *neither* political party, at least in their official 1996 election platforms, reflects the prevailing American view on abortion—that it should be generally legal and safe, but is immoral and should be actively discouraged.)

While the Church has absolutized the abortion issue, secular liberals have tended to absolutize the question of capital punishment, and the Pope has been edging in their direction, in part, no doubt, for the sake of consistency. In his *Gospel of Life,* John Paul II says that the death penalty can be justified where it is necessary to protect society, but argues that "such cases are very rare, if not actually non-existent." The Pope then cites the teaching of the *Catechism,* "If bloodless means are sufficient to defend human lives against an aggressor . . . public authority *must* limit itself to such means" (my italics). The *Gospel of Life,* like *Humanae Vitae* on birth control, is not an infallible teaching, but it has been reported that John Paul did consider declaring it infallibly.

When Cardinal O'Connor spoke against the death penalty at a policeman's funeral in 1996, however, he specifically allowed for the possibility of Catholic dissent on the issue. He did so even though New York can impose life sentences without the possibility of parole, which would seem to call the Pope's mandate into operation. Police and prison guards, however, are at risk from *other* aggressors, and tend to favor capital punishment for its possible deterrent effects. That is a broader ground than the one allowed by the Pope but not obviously unreasonable, and the Cardinal's deference to their view is sensible, although seemingly inconsistent with the tendency of Catholic conservatives—including, on most issues, Cardinal O'Connor—to insist on absolute deference to papal encyclicals.

Both the abortion and capital punishment issues illustrate the reality of accommodating to a pluralist society. Presumably, if there were a religious sect in New York that killed girl babies at birth, all major ethical traditions would condemn the behavior with one voice, just as they would condemn a proposal to execute welfare cheaters or shoplifters. But first trimester abortions, "morning-after" pills, and executions for cop killers are closer calls, and responsible ethical traditions reach different conclusions. Catholics can demonstrate their devotion to their Church by their teaching and their example, but not by imposing their rules on their fellows. That is a messy resolution, perhaps, but pluralist societies are inherently messy.

The Church and America

During his 1995 visit, the Pope asked, "Is there room for the mystery of God in American society?" The great mysteries of the Catholic faith dissolve much of the bleak current reality of the Church—the "culture wars" among theologians, the sexual scandals, the financial problems, the politics of the episcopal conference, the crumbling inner-city infrastructure, the retirement overhang. The Catholic vision that keeps tens of millions of people actively working and praying and worshiping in their parishes encompasses Christ and salvation, and the Holy Spirit, and a path to God through Mass and the sacraments, and a bedrock sense of the importance of family and children, and living up to obligations, and treating other people decently. The Pope and Rome are part of that vision, because they confirm its antiquity and stability, add resonances of ancient desert fathers, towering cathedrals, kings standing barefoot before popes, and a grand disputatious tradition of chewing over moral dilemmas and teasing out rules of right behavior.

The vision has its practical side. Mario Cuomo has a favorite speech that "always gets raves from Jewish groups." There are three great problems in America, Cuomo tells his audiences: economic inequality; social dysfunction, like drugs and family breakup; and values. "Well, my Church has something to say about those problems," Cuomo says. "On economic equality, read the great social encyclicals. We've been speaking to that for a long time. And on social problems, we preach individual responsibility. But we also teach that we're all connected—your failure is my loss. We don't just cut people off, just as we wouldn't reject our own child who was a drug user. We keep trying to recover them because we're all a family. And finally, on values—do we have *values*? Take all the values you need, we'll still have more left over."

America needs a constant defender of traditional sexual ethics—only look at the plague of illegitimate pregnancies, divorce, sexually transmitted disease, the violent behavior of fatherless children, and the disintegration of families. Even secular intellectuals now recognize the enormous social capital represented by well-functioning families and how difficult it is for other institutions to supply their deficiencies.

Mary Ann Glendon was a persuasive advocate for the Catholic tradition as the Pope's representative to the 1995 Beijing Conference on Women. The original conference drafts almost invariably linked women's rights solely with abortion, and marriage with victimization and exploitation. Glendon became the spokesperson for the right to education, and self-improvement, assistance with children, a decent living, the freedom from coercion *not* to have children, and of the privacy and the primacy of the family. These are all Catholic values that get short shrift in the modern world, and the Church is sometimes their lonely defender.

But if the Church has much to teach America, its leaders are thrown off balance when confronted with American pluralism—the insistence on participation, the conviction that the *way* you get an answer can be as important as the answer itself, the commitment to persuasion over diktat. The pluralist ethic, in one form or another, is spreading throughout the world, but the

Church has yet to make a deep accommodation to that reality, preferring the old fortresses of ancient doctrine and submerging the Catholic vision in a forest of rules about in vitro fertilization and spacing children. Even John Paul II, who, of all recent popes, has the breadth of vision and intellect to define a new dialectic between Catholicism and pluralism, is resorting more and more to command solutions, actively cutting off the discernment processes that are constantly working throughout the Church. Cardinal Ratzinger, of all people, has recently warned that the drive for consistency in theology could become "an ideology whose sole interest is the acquisition and preservation of power"—precisely what so many people worry that Ratzinger and the Pope are doing.

Catholics who love their Church and draw strength from its traditions are learning to ignore it when it doesn't make sense—pretending not to notice the "crazy aunt of Catholic dogma," in Ivor Shapiro's phrase. That is not a healthy development for the Church or for Catholics. One justification offered for the summary ruling on the ordination of women is that the Vatican was convinced of the rightness of its position—engaging in dialogue would merely have raised false expectations, as happened with the birth control encyclical. But that is precisely wrong. Doctrine will have to evolve *out of* dialogue with Catholics, not separately from them, especially on the issues that matter most to them, like the pastorate and family ethics.

The violent swings of academic theology must inflate the perception of the risk of a more participatory development of Catholic positions. But the people in the parishes are, in the main, more sensible than extremists in the professoriate. They are not radical feminists, cultic "earth goddess" worshipers, Marxist poststructuralists, or feckless hedonists who seek an end to all rules. They are just ordinary Catholic Americans trying to navigate a confusing world and guide their children, using their conscience, their own best judgment, and the Church's teachings as their compass, and they deserve more respect for their efforts.

The great strength of the American Church is the 20 million or so active Catholics in the parishes—not its bishops or cardinals, or the hospitals and universities with Catholic names, or the public policy apparatus of its bishops' conference. If the Church is ever to recover the "noninvolveds" and the lukewarm, it must first retain its active members.

Like no other generation in the history of the Church, active American Catholics are educated, literate, informed, and *interested* in their religion. And they are participants in it. Theological niceties aside, the message from Vatican II has been taken to heart: *they,* the people in the parishes, along with clergy and nuns and bishops and Pope, *are* the Church. To a remarkable degree, they run the parishes, plan liturgies, carry out works of mercy, supervise the budget. They treat their priests with respect as sacramental ministers but don't hesitate to pass judgment on them as leaders and teachers.

They still look to their Church for moral guidance, but they are searching for principles, not for rules. The traditional Catholic codebook of behavior was perfect for peasants fighting their way out of the bogs, and it worked well enough for second-generation immigrants on the first rungs of middle-class respectability. But except for the newest waves of Hispanic immigrants, American Catholics have long since made it in America. As much as any other religious body, they are middle-class, suburban, educated, affluent. They exercise control over their own lives in ways that their grandparents never did. When they turn out by the hundreds of thousands to listen to and pray with the Pope, it is because they see him as a symbol of the authority and continuity of their religion, and proof of the workings of the Spirit and the power of changeless principles in an unsettled moral era. But *not* because they are prepared to obey him "on all matters," as he occasionally demands.

The rhythms of Church history are measured in centuries-long pulses. But how the standoff between the tradition of Rome and the tradition of America is resolved is of central importance for the future of the Church, not just in America but everywhere. Pope John called the fathers together at Vatican II to read the "signs of the times," and the encounter between the Church and the modern world was the Council's main theme. The crucial question for the American Church is whether, after all the turmoil of the past thirty years, the era of Vatican II is ending or is just beginning.

Notes

PART I. RISE

1. *"We Laugh to Scorn"*

Except as specifically noted below, the details on the building of St. Patrick's and the dedication ceremonial are drawn from: John Cardinal Farley, *St. Patrick's Cathedral* (New York: Society for the Propagation of the Faith, 1908), which is itself primarily a redaction of two commemorative volumes, *The Solemn Blessing and Opening of the New Cathedral of Saint Patrick, New York* (New York: Catholic Publication Society, 1879), and William J. Quinn, *St. Patrick's Cathedral of New York: A Full Description of the Exterior and Interior of the New Cathedral, the Altar, and the Windows* (Westchester, N.Y.: The Catholic Protectory, 1879); also see John Cardinal Farley, *The Life of Cardinal McCloskey* (New York: Longmans, Green, 1918) (actually written by Peter Guilday of Catholic University); *Souvenir of the Centennial Celebration of St. Patrick's (Old Cathedral)* (New York: Catholic Publication Society, 1915); and the extensive coverage in *The New York Times, Herald,* and *Tribune.* Tom Young, the volunteer archivist of St. Patrick's, has assembled an extensive file on the design and construction of the cathedral and was an invaluable source of information, particularly on personal and political nuance. And see also Margaret Carthy, *A Cathedral of Suitable Magnificence: St. Patrick's Cathedral of New York* (Wilmington, Del.: Michael Glazier, 1984). For its predecessor cathedral, see Mary Peter Carthy, "Old St. Patrick's: New York's First Cathedral" (master's thesis, Catholic University of America, 1948).

For John Hughes, see Richard Shaw, *Dagger John: The Unquiet Life and Times of Archbishop John Hughes of New York* (New York: Paulist Press, 1977); John R. G. Hassard, *Life of the Most Reverend J. H. Hughes, D.D., First Archbishop of New York with Extracts from His Private Correspondence* (New York: Appleton, 1866); and *Biographical Sketch of the Most Rev. John Hughes, D.D., Archbishop of New York* (New York: Metropolitan Record, 1864). There is also a fine fictional evocation of Hughes—but with some presumably intentional historical inventions—in Peter Quinn, *Banished Children of Eve* (New York: Viking, 1994). Hughes's quotes at the cornerstone ceremony and the editorial comment are from the *Times,* August 16, 1858; the full address is in Lawrence Kehoe, ed., *Complete Works of the Most Reverend John Hughes, D.D., Archbishop of New York* (New York: Lawrence Kehoe, 1865), 2:263–70. The "lazy, dreamy" quote is from the *Bergen County Democrat,* February 3, 1871.

The description of Fifth Avenue and the Irish tenements are from James McCabe, *Lights and Shadows of New York Life* (Philadelphia: National, 1872); and Eric Homberger, *Scenes from the Life of a City: Corruption and Conscience in Old New York* (New Haven, Conn.: Yale University Press, 1994). See also Matthew Josephson, *The Robber Barons* (New York: Harcourt, Brace, 1962) pp. 315–46. For Madame Restell, see Homberger, pp. 86–140. Flower Mission quote is in the *Times,* May 23, 1879. "Cleanliness" quote is in McCabe, *Lights,* p. 694. Bricklayers' pay is in Irwin Yellowitz, "Eight Hours and the Bricklayers' Strike of 1868," in Irwin Yellowitz, ed., *Essays in the History of New York City* (Port Washington, N.Y.: Kennikat Press, 1978), p. 87. Protestant reaction to Irish giving: e.g., *Times,* May 7, 1875. Dress details are drawn from newspapers and contemporary issues of the *American Cutter and Tailor. Times* "ticket" editorial: May 27, 1879. Eugene Kelly's background: *Times,* December 20, 1881. Emigrant's founding details are in William H. Bennett, "A Chronological History of the Emigrant Industrial Savings Bank," in the files of the bank. For O'Conor, see *Times,* May 14, 1884; for his role in Tweed's fall, see Jerome Mushkat, *The Reconstruction of the New York Democracy, 1861–1874* (East Brunswick, N.J.: Associated University Presses, 1981), pp. 182–83.

For John Kelly, see M. R. Werner, *Tammany Hall* (New York: Greenwood Press, 1968); "political army" quote is on p. 276. Also see Alfred Connable and Edward Silberfarb, *Tigers of Tammany* (New York: Holt, Rinehart and Winston, 1967), pp. 173–96; Croker's "theory" quote is on p. 197; see also Thomas H. Henderson, *Tammany Hall and the New Immigrants: The Progressive Years* (New York: Arno, 1976). On the Healys, see Stephen J. Ochs, *Desegregating the Altar: The Josephites and the Struggle for Black Priests: 1871–1960* (Baton Rouge, La.: Louisiana State University Press, 1990), pp. 26–29. For Heeney, see William Harper Bennett, "Cornelius Heeney," *The Journal of the American Irish Historical Society,* 1918, pp. 215–23. Hecker's meeting with McCloskey is in Farley, *Life,* p. 154.

Rodrigue background is in Shaw, *Dagger John,* p. 321. Hughes's quotes on cathedral and financing plan are in letter to "Bd. of Trustees of St. Patrick's Concerning New Cathedral," May 29, 1858, in the Archives of the Archdiocese of New York, Dunwoodie, New York. "Bled" and "taxed" quotes are in Clarence Cook, "The New Catholic Cathedral in New York," *Atlantic Monthly,* February 1879, pp. 173–77. For the marble controversy, see Gordon R. Urquhart, "St. Patrick's Cathedral and the Westchester Marble Scandal," *The Westchester Historian,* Spring 1988, pp. 44–52. Hughes's thoughts on quarry are in letter of May 29, 1858. The Pleasantville specification (contract dated March 5, 1859, between Hughes and Joyce and Hall) is in the St. Patrick's Cathedral Archives, as is the *Sun* article (April 1873—precise date illegible). The McCloskey-Joyce quarrel is in Nelson Callahan, ed., *The Diary of Richard L. Burtsell, Priest of New York: The Early Years, 1865–1868* (New York: Arno, 1978), p. 50; Burtsell got the story from a priest who dined with McCloskey.

The pew auction in the *Times,* May 30, 1879. The dinner at the orphanage is covered in detail in both the *Times* and the *Tribune.* Purcell's troubles are in the *Times,* May 24, 1879. See Cook, "New Catholic Cathedral," for his attack on the cathedral. The exchanges between Hassard and Cook are in the *Atlantic*'s April and May 1879 issues, pp. 415–16, 552. For the persistence of the charge that Hughes hoodwinked the city of the land, see, e.g., Connable and Silberfarb, *Tigers,* p. 127.

2.   *God's Own Providential Instrument*

The basic argument in this chapter regarding the impact of social and demographic changes in nineteenth-century Ireland on Irish emigration follows in broad outline Kerby A. Miller's splendid, encyclopedic *Emigrants and Exiles: Ireland and the Irish Exodus to North America* (New York: Oxford University Press, 1985). I benefited greatly from the advice of Patrick Corish and William Smyth at St. Patrick's College in Maynooth and was generously assisted by Rachel O'Brien, the archivist at All Hallow's College in Dublin.

The local details of the Famine in Skibbereen are from materials provided me by Patrick Cleary of the Skibbereen Famine Commemoration Society, and from his own local researches. Printed materials include: Skibbereen Committee of Gratuitous Relief, *Statement of the Present Condition of the Skibbereen Poor Law District Union* (February 1, 1847); Lord Dufferin and the Hon. G. F. Boyle, *Narrative of a Journey from Oxford to Skibbereen During the Year of the Irish Famine* (Oxford: Parker, 1847); Joseph Sturge, *Three Days at Skibbereen and Its Vicinity* (Birmingham: n.p., 1847); numerous selections from the correspondence of Sir Randolph Routh, the conscientious chairman of the Relief Commission for Ireland, to his superiors in the British colonial office and the Cabinet; and a wealth of statistical material, most of it in the form of Treasury Minutes. Impressions of the Famine in the rest of Ireland and the effects of *Phytophthera* are from Miller, *Emigrants,* pp. 260–86; and Cecil Woodham-Smith, *The Great Hunger: Ireland, 1845–1849* (New York: Penguin, 1991).

The social and economic sketch of pre-Famine Ireland follows Miller, *Emigrants*; see also Patrick J. Corish, *The Irish Catholic Experience: A Historical Survey* (Wilmington, Del.: Michael Glazier, 1985). Peasant poverty in Ireland, while shocking to travelers from England and America, was actually fairly typical of European peasant—as opposed to independent farmer—societies. See, for example, Eugen Weber, *Peasants into Frenchmen: The Modernization of Rural France, 1870–1914* (Palo Alto, Cal.: Stanford University Press, 1976). Nor is it surprising that peasants were often worse off than slaves, since slaves were valuable capital assets. The Thackeray quote is in Miller, *Emigrants,* p. 43; the "Sambo" typology is from Stanley M. Elkins, *Slavery: A Problem in American Institutional and Intellectual Life* (New York: Universal Library, 1963). Population increase is from Woodham-Smith, *Great Hunger,* p. 29.

G. Poulett Scrope, M.P., *The Irish Relief Measures: Past and Future* (London: James Ridgway, 1848), is a trenchant contemporary criticism of the British response to the Famine. *The Times* of London quote on "Red Indians" is in Miller, *Emigrants,* p. 307. The Disraeli quote is from Benjamin Disraeli, *Lord George Bentinck: A Political Biography* (London: Colbourne & Co., 1852), p. 124. Bentinck was the leader of the anti-Peel Tories and Disraeli's mentor; the quoted words are Disraeli's commentary. William Bullock Webster, Esq., *Ireland Considered as a Field for Investment or Residence* (Dublin: Hodges & Smith, 1852), written almost at the famine's height, is a paean to the attractiveness of Irish real estate with the peasants cleared away.

The class- and religion-based Irish emigration patterns follows Miller, *Emigrants.* For Canada-to-U.S. flow, see Cecil J. Houston and William J. Smyth, *Irish Emigration and Canadian Settlement: Patterns, Links, and Letters* (Toronto: University of Toronto

Press, 1990), pp. 25–26. O'Conor background is from Charles Owen O'Conor Don, *The O'Conors of Connaught: An Historical Memoir* (Dublin: Hodges, Figgis, 1891), pp. 309–15. For Irish Catholics on Trinity Church rolls, see Michael J. O'Brien, *In Old New York: The Irish Dead in Trinity and St. Paul's Churchyards* (New York: American Irish Historical Society, 1928), pp. 27–31. The calculation of presidents of Irish descent was made by James A. Michener, letter to *The New York Times,* December 12, 1993.

The quotes on Catholic reluctance to emigrate are from Miller, *Emigrants,* pp. 237 and 266. Immigration statistics for the Irish and below for other national groups are from the U.S. Bureau of the Census, *International Migration and Naturalization,* Series C 89-119, "Immigrants by Country: 1820 to 1970." Nineteenth-century overall immigrant death rates are in Maldwyn A. Jones, *American Immigration* (Chicago: University of Chicago Press, 1992), p. 90. For details on "coffin ships," Palmerston's clearing of his peasants, and Grosse Isle, see Woodham-Smith, *Great Hunger,* pp. 217–38; the 10 percent 1853 cholera death rate is in Miller *Emigrants,* p. 316.

Canadian and Irish historians have done careful work on the Irish immigration to Canada, and particularly through the major port at St. John, New Brunswick. In addition to Houston and Smyth, *Irish Emigration,* see P. M. Toner, ed., *New Ireland Remembered* (New Brunswick: New Ireland Press, 1988). The death rate for the 1847 Canadian immigrants is in Houston and Smyth, p. 3. The quote from Dickens is in Dennis Clark, *Hibernia America: The Irish and Regional Cultures* (Westport, Conn.: Greenwood Press, 1986), p. 25. Immigrant death rate estimates are in Miller, *Emigrants,* p. 319. An extended discussion of Ireland's Connemaran venture is in James P. Shannon, *Catholic Colonization on the Western Frontier* (New Haven, Conn.: Yale University Press, 1957), pp. 154–71; additional detail, including the persistence of St. Paul's "Connemara Patch" is from "The American Response to the Second Irish Famine of 1879–1882," an April 13, 1992, lecture at the American Irish Historical Society by Dr. Gerard Moran.

For the reformation of Irish Catholicism, the basic sources are Emmet J. Larkin, *The Making of the Roman Catholic Church in Ireland: 1850–1860* (Chapel Hill, N.C.: University of North Carolina Press, 1980), and *The Consolidation of the Roman Catholic Church in Ireland: 1860–1870* (Chapel Hill, N.C.: University of North Carolina Press, 1987), part of a projected nine-volume series on the Irish Church. I benefited from a helpful conversation with Dr. Larkin. Corish, *Irish Catholic Experience,* pp. 151–225, is also excellent. In addition to these works, the portrait of Cullen draws on Desmond Bowen, *Paul Cardinal Cullen and the Shaping of Modern Irish Catholicism* (Dublin: Gill & MacMillan, 1983). Bowen is a Protestant, and both Larkin and Corish (interview) consider his work unremittingly and unfairly hostile. Cullen, to the modern eye, is not an attractive character, but a judgment of his influence in Ireland will turn crucially on the presuppositions of the evaluator. To a meliorist, humanist reformer—Bowen's viewpoint—Cullen's lack of consideration for the plight of the lower classes appears abhorrent; but for a churchman steeped in the Tridentine, premodern Catholic tradition, the absolute priority he granted to the souls of his flock and the health of his church was altogether appropriate. Aside from his correspondence, large samples of which are in Bowen, Cullen did not leave a large body of writings. A collection of sermons, *Ireland and the Holy See, a Retrospect, 1866–1883: Illegal and Seditious Movements in Ireland Contrasted with the Principles of the Catholic Church as Shown in the Writings of Cardinal Cullen* (Rome: Propaganda Press, 1886), shows his deep social conservatism.

Sean J. Connolly, *Priests and People in Pre-Famine Ireland, 1780–1845* (Dublin: Gill & MacMillan, 1982), is the best-documented source I found on, e.g., prereform Irish village superstition, illegitimacy rates, and sexual practices. Emmet J. Larkin's "The Devotional Revolution in Ireland," *American Historical Review* 77 (June 1972): 625–52, is also essential. The Newman quote is from Corish, *Irish Catholic Experience*, p. 218. The Catholic preacher quote is in Larkin, "Devotional Revolution," p. 649. Cullen's "purify" quote is in Miller, *Emigrants*, p. 301. The cholera epidemic quote is in Bowen, *Paul Cardinal Cullen*, p. 282. Irish marriage data are in Miller, *Emigrants*, pp. 403–7. For matriarchal families, see also Marjorie Fallows, *Irish-Americans: Identity and Assimilation* (Englewood Cliffs, N.J.: Prentice-Hall, 1979), pp. 96–111; and Hasia Diner, *Erin's Daughters in America: Irish Immigrant Women in the Nineteenth Century* (Baltimore: Johns Hopkins University Press, 1983). Middle-class attitude toward lower classes and nuns' instructions are in Miller, *Emigrants*, pp. 419–20. The "pomp" quote is in Larkin, "Devotional Revolution," p. 646. For French anticlericalism retarding women suffrage and for bourgeois sexual practices, see Eugen Weber, *France, Fin de Siècle* (Cambridge, Mass.: Harvard University Press, 1986), pp. 92, 257. For Jansenius, see Corish, *Irish Catholic Experience* pp. 117–18, 131, 162; Miller, *Emigrants*, p. 421. For Jansenius himself, see the entry in *The Catholic Encyclopedia* or the discussion in Louis Dupré, *Passage to Modernity* (New Haven, Conn.: Yale University Press, 1993), pp. 216–20.

Miller, *Emigrants*, pp. 114–30, presents a trenchant argument for an Irish Catholic worldview. Historians like David N. Doyle, in *Irish Americans: Native Rights and National Empire* (New York: Arno, 1976), dispute such stereotyping. I believe they succeed in demonstrating both that stereotypes are applied too broadly and that they linger too long, but not that they are basically false. For Irish-American bishops on obedience, see, e.g., Samuel J. Miller, "Peter Richard Kenrick, Bishop and Archbishop of St. Louis, 1806–1896," *Records of the American Catholic Historical Society of Philadelphia* 84 (1973): 51. The "coercion" quote is from Miller, *Emigrants*, p. 129.

All Hallows background and early American-Irish missionary contacts are in Kevin Condon, *The Missionary College of All Hallows: 1842–1891* (Dublin: All Hallows College, 1986); and Patrick F. Murray, "Calendar of the Overseas Missionary Correspondence of All Hallows College, Dublin, 1842–1877" (master's thesis, Department of History, University College, Dublin, 1956). Both the Maynooth and All Hallows archives are well indexed, with much more material at All Hallows because of its missionary focus. Large selections of All Hallows correspondence are also published in the college's annual *Annals of All Hallows College* (Dublin: various years) starting in 1851. The Whitfield quote is in James H. Moynihan, *The Life of Archbishop John Ireland* (New York: Harper, 1953), p. 54. For England's claims on Catholic numbers, see Richard J. Purcell, "Missionaries from All Hallows (Dublin) to the United States, 1842–1865," *Records of the American Catholic Historical Society*, December 1942, p. 206. Wildly erroneous claims of Catholic numbers persisted until Gerald Shaughnessy, later bishop of Seattle, published *Has the Immigrant Kept the Faith? A Study of Immigration and Catholic Growth in the United States, 1790–1920* (New York: Macmillan, 1925), still a basic source. The Jesuit incident is in Larkin, *Making*, pp. 256–59. The tabulation of Irish bishops at the Vatican Council is in Corish, *Irish Catholic Experience*, p. 215, and Bowen, *Paul Cardinal Cullen*, p. 205. The "unique and recent" quote is in Larkin, *Consolidation*, p. 693. For the mid-1830s numerical estimate, see Shaughnessy, *Has the Im-*

migrant, pp. 125–26. Shaughnessy's data stand up very well under analysis by Roger Finke and Rodney Stark, *The Churching of America, 1776–1990: Winners and Losers in Our Religious Economy* (New Brunswick, N.J.: Rutgers University Press, 1992), pp. 110–15.

For German emigration, see Colman J. Barry, *The Catholic Church and German Americans* (Milwaukee: Bruce, 1953), especially the useful statistical reconstructions on pp. 4–6. Italian religious practices are in Silvano Tomasi and M. Engles, eds., *The Italian Experience in the United States* (New York: Center for Migration Studies, 1970); and Silvano M. Tomasi, *Piety and Power: The Role of Italian Parishes in the New York Metropolitan Area, 1880–1930* (New York: Center for Migration Studies, 1975). A useful collection of essays on diverse Catholic immigrants is in George E. Pozzetta, ed., *The Immigrant Religious Experience* (New York: Garland, 1991). Jones, *American Immigration* offers a concise overview of national patterns. The Czech woman's quote is in Fallows, *Irish-Americans,* p. 59. For Irish Catholic urban and regional distribution, see Doyle, *Irish Americans;* Clark, *Hibernia America;* and Lawrence J. McCaffrey, *The Irish Diaspora in America* (Bloomington, Ind.: Indiana University Press, 1976).

The seminary figures are from my inspection of enrollment records at the two of the largest seminaries of the time, St. Charles in Philadelphia and St. Mary at Emmitsburg, Md. St. Charles's alumni names are published in James F. Connelly, *St. Charles Seminary, Philadelphia* (Philadelphia: St. Charles Seminary, 1979); St. Mary's are in the college archives. The earliest American seminary was St. Mary's in Baltimore. Class rosters from the 1830s show no such Irish concentration; see *Memorial Volume of the Centenary of St. Mary's Seminary of St. Sulpice* (Baltimore: Murphy, 1891).

I made a tabulation of the ethnicity of American bishops from the entries in the *Dictionary of the American Hierarchy* (New York: Longmans, Green, 1940). I necessarily made some assumptions—e.g., if a native American with native-born parents had an ambiguous surname like "Moore," but the mother's name was clearly Irish, like "Kelly," I assumed the individual was of Irish descent.

For Corish quote and Cullen's identification of Ireland and Catholicism, see Corish, *Irish Catholic Experience,* p. 215. The MacHale quote is in Miller, *Emigrants,* p. 302. The All Hallows quote is in *The Annals* for 1860, pp. 7–8. The Cockran speech is in the collection of the American Irish Historical Society. The Spalding quotes are from John Lancaster Spalding, *The Religious Mission of the Irish Race and Catholic Colonization* (New York: Catholic Publication Society, 1880), pp. 41, 53, 61–63.

3. *The Whore of Babylon Learns How to Vote*

I am indebted to Senator Daniel Patrick Moynihan for many helpful suggestions that helped shape this chapter. The incident at the Washington Monument is in Fred L. Harvey, *History of the Washington National Monument and of the Washington National Monument Society* (Washington, D.C.: Elliott, 1902), pp. 52–71. A detailed recent study of the events at the Ursuline Convent is Wilfred J. Bisson, *Countdown to Violence: The Charlestown Convent Riot of 1834* (New York: Garland, 1989). Additional details are in Louise G. Whitney, *The Burning of the Convent* (Boston: Osgood, 1877). Whitney's is the only published eyewitness account—she was a student at the school—but was written forty years after the event. The "not one stone" quote is in Bisson, p. 110. Rebecca T.

Reed, *Six Months in a Convent* (Boston: Russell, Odiorne, and Metcalf, 1835), is the first "escapee's" story. I appreciate the help of Fr. Mahoney of St. Francis deSales Church in Charlestown in locating the site of the convent.

For Maria Monk, see her *Awful Disclosures of the Hôtel Dieu Nunnery in Montreal* (1836; reprint, Hamden, Conn.: Archon, 1962); also Ray A. Billington, "Maria Monk and Her Influence," *Catholic Historical Review* 22 (1936): 283–95; and Carleton P. Beals, *Brass-Knuckle Crusade: The Great Know-Nothing Conspiracy, 1820–1860* (New York: Hastings House, 1960), pp. 42–49. The infanticide quote is in Monk, *Awful Disclosures,* p. 58, the actual killings on p. 175, and the nun's execution on pp. 114–17. Other contemporary well-known anti-Catholic books included Mary Sherwood's *The Nun* (Princeton, N.J.: Moore Baker, 1834); and Anthony Gavin, *A History of Popery* (Hartford, Conn.: Case, Tiffany, & Burnham, 1846), and *Master Key to Popery* (n.p., 1812). *The Nun* has no sex scenes—which would have hardly befit the author of *The Little Girl's Keepsake* and *The Little Woodman and His Dog Caesar*—but there were prisoners, a trial scene, and sadistic, if not lustful, priests; Gavin's books date from the eighteenth century and include convent lechery and sexual abuse of the confessional. (When Leopold Bloom visits a pornographic bookstore in *Ulysses, Awful Disclosures* is one of the books he is offered, some seventy years after publication.)

For nativist violence, see Charles E. Schrader, "The Organizer of the Church in New England: Benedict Joseph Fenwick (1782–1846)," *Catholic Historical Review* (1936), pp. 172–84; Ray A. Billington, *The Protestant Crusade, 1800–1860* (New York: Quadrangle, 1962), pp. 295–319; James Hennesey, *American Catholics: A History of the Roman Catholic Community in the United States* (New York: Oxford University Press, 1981), pp. 116–27; and Michael Feldburg, *The Philadelphia Riots of 1844: A Study of Ethnic Conflict* (Westport, Conn.: Greenwood Press, 1975). Beals, *Brass-Knuckle,* and Billington, *Protestant Crusade,* detail the rise of the Know-Nothings. Although originally published in 1938 and superseded in many details, Billington's is still the basic source. For Bedini, see James F. Connelly, *The Visit of Archbishop Gaetano Bedini to the United States of America (June, 1853–February, 1854)* (Rome: Pontificiae Universitatis Gregorianae, 1960). The Know-Nothing political gains are in David Potter, *The Impending Crisis, 1848–1861* (New York: Harper & Row, 1976), pp. 248–52. Potter argued the potential of Know-Nothingism absent the split over slavery.

For Newman's conversion and the English Catholic revival, see John Henry Newman, *Apologia pro Vita Sua* (New York: Doubleday/Image, 1956). And for America, see Edwin Ryan, "The Oxford Movement in the United States," *Catholic Historical Review* 19 (April 1933): 33–49. The Brownson "trend spotter" quote is from Leonard Gilhooley, *Contradiction and Dilemma: Orestes Brownson and the American Idea* (New York: Fordham University Press, 1972), p. 3. The *Catholic World* articles are from the issues of November 1867, p. 209, and September 1870, pp. 712 and 752 (quote). Richard Shaw's *Dagger John: The Unquiet Life and Times of Archbishop John Hughes of New York* (New York: Paulist Press, 1977) details Hughes's many debates; the Georgia debate panel is in Billington, *Protestant Crusade,* pp. 248–49.

The *locus classicus* for American ideology in 1820s and 1830s is Marvin Meyers, *The Jacksonian Persuasion: Politics and Belief* (Stanford, Cal.: Stanford University Press, 1960). The summary from *Niles' Register* is in Bisson, *Countdown to Violence,* p. 4. The Washington riot is in Robert Remini, *Andrew Jackson,* vol. 3, *The Course of American Democracy* (New York: Harper & Row, 1984), pp. 268–69. The Harvard riot is in Bisson, pp. 95–100. For the breakdown of traditional authority patterns, see Gordon S. Wood, *The Radicalism of the American Revolution* (New York: Knopf, 1992), especially pp. 347–69; and also J. G. A. Pocock, *The Machiavellian Moment: Florentine Political Thought and the Atlantic Republican Tradition* (Princeton, N.J.: Princeton University Press, 1975), pp. 506–52. The Cooper quote is in James Fenimore Cooper, *Autobiography of a Pocket Handkerchief* (Evanston, Ill.: Golden Booke Presse, 1897), pp. 126–27. For Jackson's bank war, see Remini, *Andrew Jackson,* pp. 142–78, and, for its consequences, Bray Hammond, *Banks and Politics in America* (Princeton, N.J.: Princeton University Press, 1957), pp. 405–50.

Urban population data are in Marvin Meyers, *Jacksonian Persuasion,* pp. 111–12. The Strong quote is in Allan Nevins and Milton H. Thomas, eds.; Thomas J. Pressley, abridgment, *The Diary of George Templeton Strong* (Seattle: University of Washington Press, 1952), p. 52. For the O'Conor quote, see Kerby A. Miller, *Emigrants and Exiles: Ireland and the Irish Exodus to North America* (New York: Oxford University Press, 1985), p. 276, and see Strong's *Diary,* p. 144, for attitude toward O'Conor. Irish crime rates are in Oscar Handlin, *Boston's Immigrants: A Study in Acculturation* (Cambridge, Mass.: Harvard University Press, 1991), pp. 240–57; for New York's arrests, see Maldwyn A. Jones, *American Immigration* (Chicago: University of Chicago Press, 1992), p. 114. The Hone quote is in Bernard A. Weisberger, *The American Heritage History of the American People* (New York: American Heritage, 1971), p. 171. The *Atlantic Monthly* quote is in the issue of May 1879, p. 602. For McGee, see Thomas D'Arcy McGee, *A History of the Irish Settlers in North America* (1851; reprint, Bowie, Md.: Heritage Press, 1989), pp. 194–96. The "bogs" quote is in Beals, *Brass-Knuckle,* p. 99. For the Louisville riots, see Thomas W. Spalding, *Martin John Spalding: American Churchman* (Washington, D.C.: Catholic University Press, 1973), pp. 70–71, and Billington, *Protestant Crusade,* p. 421.

Owen Chadwick, *The Secularization of the European Mind in the Nineteenth Century* (Cambridge: Cambridge University Press, 1975), is an excellent introduction to the papacy's ideological problems. For Napoleon and Pius VII, see Margaret M. O'Dwyer, *The Papacy in the Age of Napoleon and the Restoration* (Lanham, Md.: University Presses, 1985), pp. 83–124. For Metternich and the Papal States, see Alan J. Reinerman, *Austria and the Papacy in the Age of Metternich,* vol. 2, *Revolution and Reaction, 1830–1838* (Washington, D.C.: Catholic University Press, 1989); the "inefficient" quote is on p. 187, the "corpse" quote and the Cesena incident on p. 103. The Perugia incident is in Frank J. Coppa, *Pope Pius IX: Crusader in a Secular Age* (Boston: Twayne, 1979), p. 132. The "liberal ideas" quote is in Priscilla Robertson, *Revolutions of 1848: A Social History* (Princeton, N.J.: Princeton University Press, 1967), p. 327; "ingrate" is from Coppa, p. 75.

The Mill quote is from John Stuart Mill, *On Liberty* (New York: Penguin, 1985), p. 68. Encyclical quotes are from Claudia Carlen, *The Papal Encyclicals, 1740–1978,* (Raleigh, N.C.: McGrath, 1981) 2:173, 202, 256. (The "insanity" quote does not appear in quite that form in Gregory's 1832 encyclical but is the form in which Pius IX *quotes* Gregory in 1864.) The Veuillot quote is in C. S. Phillips, *The Church in France: 1848–1907* (New York: Russell & Russell, 1967), p. 13; see pp. 49–50 for Pius and Louis-Napoleon's coup. For the political implications of the Immaculate Conception, see James Hennesey, "The Baltimore Council of 1866: An American Syllabus," *Records of the American Catholic Historical Society of Philadelphia* 76 (1965): 158–59. For the Sacred Office and the Syllabus, see Coppa, *Pius IX,* p. 146. The text of the Syllabus is in Colman J. Barry, ed., *Readings in Church History* (Westminster, Md.: Christian Classics, 1965), 3:70–74. For the "grave sin" quote: Damian McElrath, *The Syllabus of Pius IX: Some Reactions in England* (Louvain, Belgium: Publications Universitaire de Louvain, 1964), p. 144. For the impact of the Syllabus, besides McElrath, see Chadwick, *Secularization,* pp. 111–13. McCloskey's comment is in Hennesey, *American Catholics,* p. 165. The Spalding quote is in Hennesey, "Baltimore Council," p. 164.

The history of the Council is in Coppa, *Pius IX,* pp. 169–80, and Phillips, *The Church in France,* pp. 148–71. A survey of councils with special emphasis on Trent is in Charles R. Morris, "The Three Ages of the Catholic Church," *Atlantic Monthly,* July 1991, pp. 105–12. For the American role, in addition to the Hennesey works already cited, see James Hennesey, "James A. Corcoran's Mission to Rome, 1868–1869," *Catholic Historical Review* 48 (1962): 157–81, "Nunc Venio de America: The American Church and Vatican I," *Annuarium Historiae Conciliorum* 1 (1969): 348–73, and "Papacy and Episcopacy in Nineteenth-Century American Catholic Thought," *Records of the American Catholic Historical Society of Philadephia* 77 (1966): 175–89; also Raymond J. Clancy, "American Prelates in the Vatican Council," *Historical Records and Studies* 28 (1937): 7–135; Thomas W. Spalding, *Martin John Spalding,* pp. 313–14; and James H. Smylie, "American Protestants Interpret Vatican I," *Church History* 38 (1969): 459–74. For the presence of Fallibists, see Margaret O' Gain, *Triumph in Defeat: Infallibility, Vatican I, and the French Minority Bishops* (Washington, D.C.: Catholic University Press, 1988), pp. 68–85. For Newman, see J. Derek Holmes, "Cardinal Newman and the First Vatican Council," *Annuarium Historiae Conciliorum* 1 (1969): 374–98. The Kenrick quote is in Coppa, p. 163. The American catechism quote is in Hennesey, "Papacy and Episcopacy," p. 185. Pius's quotes are in Coppa, p. 168, and Phillips, p. 154. The *"La Tradizione son' Io"* story was never officially confirmed by the Cardinal who was its alleged target. Dupanloup had the Pope speaking French, which he often did: *"Des témoins de la tradition? Il n'y a qu'un. C'est moi."* The "crudity" quote is in Hennesey, "Nunc Venio," p. 359.

The Brownson quote is from Joseph F. Gower and Richard M. Leliaert, eds., *The Brownson-Hecker Correspondence* (South Bend, Ind.: University of Notre Dame Press, 1979), p. 200. Hughes on the Constitution is from Shaw, *Dagger John,* pp. 192–93. For the school and trustee issues in America, see Hennesey, *American Catholics,* pp. 107–10, 76–77, 94–99, and Patrick Carey, *People, Priests, and Prelates: Ecclesiastical Democracy and the Tensions of Trusteeism* (Notre Dame Ind.: University of Notre Dame Press, 1987). In New York, see Shaw, pp. 139–75, 181–82, and 292–95. Quotes are from pp. 142, 155, 166, 227. The church property holdings are in the 1846 edition of Gavin's *History of Popery,* pp. 416–19. Hughes's lecture is quoted in Beals, *Brass-Knuckle,* p. 116.

The account of the New York draft riots follows that in Iver Bernstein, *The New York City Draft Riots: Their Significance for American Society and Politics in the Age of the Civil War* (New York: Oxford University Press, 1990). The quotes from Strong are in *Diary,* pp. 243, 245. The *Freeman's Journal* quote is from September 7, 1862; it is a reprint of an article about runaway blacks terrorizing white women. James McMaster, the editor, was once interned by the federal government on suspicion of sedition. For the Church on slavery, see O'Dwyer, *The Papacy,* pp. 189–94, and especially John T. Noonan, "Development in Moral Doctrine," *Theological Studies* 54 (1993): 662–77. Peter Kenrick's Supreme Court case is *Cummings v. State of Missouri,* 4 Wallace 1866,

278–332 (Dissent in *Ex Parte Garland*, ibid., 381–399). Cummings was a priest imprisoned for obeying Kenrick. Kenrick's lawyer, David Dudley Field, was one of the most famous in America. The Hughes quote is in Shaw, *Dagger John*, p. 344. Elder's proselytization is in an 1864 letter from Elder to the faculty at All Hallows, in the All Hallows archives. For Peter Kenrick and slavery, see Samuel J. Miller, "Peter Richard Kenrick"; for Spalding and slavery, see Hennesey, *American Catholics*, p. 152. For Francis Kenrick, see Noonan, "Development," p. 666. The data on socioethnic participation in the war, and the impact of conscription, is in James M. McPherson, *Battle Cry of Freedom: The Civil War Era* (New York: Oxford University Press, 1988), pp. 600–611. The attractiveness of the bounty in Ireland is in Miller, *Emigrants*, p. 361.

4.   *The Grand American Catholic Compromise*

The celebration in Clontarf is reconstructed from John G. Cooney, *Clontarf Centennial: 1878–1978*, in the records of the Minnesota Historical Society (hereafter MHS), and from the *Northwestern Chronicle*, March 15 and March 22, 1879. John Ireland's career follows, in addition to the John Ireland Papers at MHS, primarily Marvin R. O'Connell's excellent and detailed *John Ireland and the American Catholic Church* (St. Paul: Minnesota Historical Society Press, 1988), supplemented by James H. Moynihan, *The Life of Archbishop John Ireland* (New York: Harper, 1953). The definitive discussion of the Catholic western settlement movement, including the details of Ireland's financial arrangements, is in James P. Shannon, *Catholic Colonization on the Western Frontier* (New Haven, Conn.: Yale University Press, 1957). For an overview of the Gilded Age, see Sean Dennis Cashman, *America in the Gilded Age: From the Death of Lincoln to the Rise of Theodore Roosevelt* (New York: New York University Press, 1993). Catholic growth is from Roger Finke and Rodney Stark, *The Churching of America, 1776–1990: Winners and Losers in Our Religious Economy* (New Brunswick, N.J.: Rutgers University Press, 1992), pp. 113–14.

The "Americanist" ideological struggles within the Church have been extremely well documented over the course of many years. In addition to O'Connell's *John Ireland*, the major sources used in this chapter were: Robert Emmett Curran, *Michael Augustine Corrigan and the Shaping of Conservative Catholicism in America, 1878–1902* (New York: Arno, 1978); Gerald P. Fogarty, *The Vatican and the Americanist Crisis: Denis J. O'Connell, American Agent in Rome, 1885–1903* (Rome: Gregorian University Press, 1974); John Tracy Ellis, *The Life of James Cardinal Gibbons, Archbishop of Baltimore, 1834–1921*, 2 vols. (1952; reprints Westminster, Md.: Christian Classics, 1987); and Frederick J. Zwierlein, *The Life and Letters of Bishop McQuaid*, 3 vols. (Rochester, N.Y.: The Art Print Shop, 1925–1927). The O'Connell, Curran, and Fogarty books follow the current, welcome trend in Catholic historiography of presenting an unvarnished account of the actors' behavior and motives as disclosed in the records. The Ellis book, while less frank, contains an extremely detailed account of the daily comings and goings of the participants, while the Zwierlein volumes are valuable for their extensive reprints of primary documents. An early account, John J. Meng, "Growing Pains in the American Catholic Church," *Historical Records and Studies* 36 (1947):17–67, contains generous excerpts from the sometimes blistering correspondence of Ireland, Corrigan, and Gibbons. Thomas T. McAvoy's *The Great Crisis in American Catholic History, 1895–*

1900 (Chicago: Henry Regnery, 1957), is an important early survey. In the notes that follow, I make specific citations to the works listed above only for direct quotations or for the more controversial matters, and not for uncontroverted chronological details. Corrigan's diary is Joseph F. Mahoney and Peter J. Wosh, eds., *The Diocesan Journal of Michael Augustine Corrigan, Bishop of Newark, 1872–1880* (Newark: New Jersey Historical Society, 1987).

The public reception of the Baltimore Council is in Ellis, *Gibbons,* 1:245. For the background of labor unrest: Bruce C. Nelson, *Beyond the Martyrs: A Social History of Chicago's Anarchists, 1870–1900* (New Brunswick, N.J.: Rutgers University Press, 1988); Wayne G. Broche, *The Molly Maguires* (Cambridge, Mass.: Harvard University Press, 1964) (the "venomous" quote is on p. 175); Jonathan Garlock, "A Structural Analysis of the Knights of Labor" (Ph.D. dissertation, University of Rochester, 1974); and Terence V. Powderly, *The Path I Trod: The Autobiography of Terence V. Powderly* (New York: Columbia University Press, 1940). Powderly, pp. 317–82, recounts his dealings with the Church. He concluded that priestly enthusiasm for the Knights probably did more public relations damage than censorious bishops.

For Spalding and Caldwell, see David F. Sweeney, *The Life of John Lancaster Spalding* (New York: Herder & Herder, 1965), pp. 166–70, 272–76, 308–12, 342–52; O'Connell, *John Ireland,* pp. 373, 468–69, 511–12, 589; C. Joseph Nuesse, *The Catholic University of America: A Centennial History* (Washington, D.C.: Catholic University Press, 1990), pp. 25–50; and C. Walker Gollar, "The Double Doctrine of the Caldwell Sisters," *Catholic Historical Review* 81 (July 1995): 372–97. The Ryan "Miss C" quote is in O'Connell, p. 214. The evidence on whether other bishops knew of the affair is ambiguous. Patrick Riordan, who was close to Spalding, was incredulous when Lina first made her charges, but he was convinced after visiting a London priest, a former head of a religious order whom he trusted completely and who knew the sisters well, who confirmed the charges. Riordan himself recommended that Spalding be passed over for the Chicago appointment. Corrigan once visited Spalding and discussed Church politics with "him and her," an apparent traveling companion, in New York; if the "her" was Miss Caldwell, it would suggest that they openly behaved virtually as husband and wife. And when the Chicago appointment was bruited, a Georgetown Jesuit told the apostolic delegate that Spalding was known for "his public association with his lady friend" (Nuesse, *Catholic University,* p. 28). Caldwell later told an anti-Catholic writer that Spalding was a "whited sepulchre," a "very atheist and infidel," and a "sensual hypocite" whom she used to know *intimately*" (her emphasis). Gollar, "Double Doctrine," pp. 393–94). Gollar's article contains the most complete review of the evidence and argues that the charge against Spalding was never definitively proven, which is true, and that Riordan later regretted his advice to Rome, although it is not clear why he changed his mind. The evidence, if one chooses to disregard Lina's testimony, is only circumstantial but is such that if Spalding were anyone but a bishop the case would be regarded as proven.

Colman J. Barry, *The Catholic Church and German Americans* (Milwaukee: Bruce, 1953), is the most complete account of the German-Irish contentions, and generally sympathetic to the Germans. See also Philip Gleason, *The Conservative Reformers, German American Catholics and the Social Order* (South Bend, Ind.: University of Notre Dame Press, 1968). The "no nation" quote is in Silvano M. Tomasi, *Piety and Power: The Role of Italian Parishes in the New York Metropolitan Area, 1880–1930* (New York:

Center for Migration Studies, 1975). p. 146. For "ignoramuses," see Barry, *German Americans*, p. 105; all non-Germans "Irish," ibid., p. 121. The "emotional taxation" quote is in George E. Pozzetta, ed., *The Immigrant Religious Experience* (New York: Garland, 1991), p. 226. The Ryan "ponderous" quote is in Ellis, *Gibbons*, 1:262. The "second fatherland" quote is in Colman J. Barry, ed., "Tour of His Eminence Cardinal Francesco Satolli, Pro-Apostolic Delegate to the United States," *Historical Records and Studies* 43 (1954): 92.; and Ireland's "foreign shores" quote is in Barry, *German Americans*, p. 118. The "delicate matter" quote is in Henry J. Browne, "The Italian Problem in the Catholic Church of the United States, 1880–1900," *Historical Records and Studies* 35 (1946): 59. Priest quotes on Italians are in Tomasi, *Piety and Power*, pp. 81, 123–24; and Silvano Tomasi and M. Engles, eds. *The Italian Experience in the United States* (New York: Center for Migration Studies, 1975), p. 178, for "*railing.*" Denis O'Connell to O'Gorman quote and code name is in O'Connell, *John Ireland*, pp. 393, 579. The McQuaid "dirty, mean" quote is in Barry, *German Americans*, p. 71. Edes's "Little Grace" quote is in Ellis, *Gibbons*, 1:219; "tricks" is in Curran, *Corrigan*, p. 272.

Curran's *Corrigan* contains an extremely detailed account of the McGlynn affair with much careful detective work. Msgr. Florence D. Cohalan, whose *A Popular History of the Archdiocese of New York* (Yonkers, N.Y.: U.S. Catholic Historical Society, 1983) is a quasi-official history, provided helpful details on the early McGlynn-Corrigan relationship in an interview. For McGlynn generally, see Stephen Bell, *Rebel, Priest, and Prophet* (Westport, Conn.: Hyperion, 1975), and Sylvester Malone, *Dr. Edward McGlynn* (New York: n.p., 1918), a memorial collection. The "Our Father" quote is in Bell, p. 37; "rot" and "girlish" are in Curran, pp. 176, 34. For Tammany, see the sources cited in chapter 1 and, in addition for Croker, Mark D. Hirsch, "Richard Croker: An Interim Report on the Early Career of a 'Boss' of Tammany Hall," in Irwin Yellowitz, ed., *Essays in the History of New York City* (Port Washington, N.Y.: Kennikat Press, 1978), pp. 101–31.

An interesting light on the easy acceptance of Irish Catholics in New York is shed by a speech by, of all people, Henry Ward Beecher, Lyman's son and a prominent New York Protestant minister, at the American Irish Historical Society in 1884. It is full of easy banter and lots of laugh lines on the Irish political control of New York, mixed with considerable praise for Irish loyalty and patriotism; see John D. Crimmins, *An Irish-American Historical Miscellany* (New York: American Irish Historical Society, 1905), pp. 306–14. Crimmins was typical of the Irish Catholic elite. He was a Tammany sachem, past president of the historical society, a wealthy contractor, city parks commissioner, and a political conservative. He was outraged when Satolli reinstated McGlynn, and Beecher's speech had several applause lines attacking the Fenians. The Preston quote is in Zwierlein, *McQuaid*, 3:6–7. McGlynn on "ministers of the Gospel" is in Bell, *Rebel*, p. 43. For Corrigan "civil disease" quote and the possible forgery of the cable, see Curran, *Corrigan*, pp. 214, 215–216.

McGlynn's "Cross for a New Crusade" speech is in Patrick Carey, ed., *American Catholic Religious Thought: The Shaping of a Theological and Social Tradition* (New York: Paulist Press, 1987), pp. 220–41, and the Dana quotes are in Bell, *Rebel*, pp. 81, 108; "seething" and "brains" quotes are in Curran, *Corrigan*, p. 252. The "old bag" quote is in Curran, p. 290. McGlynn's "The Old Know-Nothingism and the New," *North American Review*, August 1887, pp. 193–205, attacks the Church's separatist tendencies, particularly as expressed in parochial schools. Gibbons quotes on George are from Gibbons to Ireland, March 19, 1888, John Ireland Papers (MHS); McQuaid quote is in Ellis, *Gibbons,* 1:584–85.

Edes's Simeoni conversation is in Barry, *German Americans,* p. 165; Denis O'Connell "modest" and "shatter," and Ireland "war" and "impudence" quotes are in O'Connell, *John Ireland,* pp. 311–12; Ireland to Gibbons, Gibbons sermon, and toast reaction are in O'Connell, pp. 314–16.

Ireland's claims about his school building performance may have been exaggerated. See O'Connell, *John Ireland,* p. 584. The title of his NEA talk was "The State School and the Parish School: Is Union Between Them Impossible?" (NEA program in John Ireland Papers at MHS); the excerpt quoted is in O'Connell, p. 297. Ireland's papers contain several descriptions of Nilan's Poughkeepsie Plan and endorsements from a local minister and Protestant business leader. Brandi quote, Ireland on Edes, Ireland on public view of himself, and "evil" quote are in O'Connell, pp. 335, 341–42, 344. Quote "in most formal manner" is in Rampolla to Ireland, May 23, 1892, John Ireland Papers (MHS); Leo response is in Zwierlein, *McQuaid,* 3:172; "direct insult" is in Denis O'Connell to Ireland, June 23, 1892, John Ireland Papers (MHS); "head is too small" quote is in Curran, *Corrigan,* p. 364; and "head and heart" is in O'Connell, p. 361.

For the archbishops' "filial" response to Leo, see Gibbons to Ireland, November 24, 1888, John Ireland Papers (MHS); McQuaid on Leo is in Zwierlein, *McQuaid,* 3:187. The Algiers quote is in E. E. Y. Hales, *The Catholic Church in the Modern World* (Garden City, N.Y.: Hanover, 1953), p. 231. Ireland's "rapturous" reception is in C. S. Phillips, *The Church in France: 1848–1907* (New York: Russell & Russell, 1967), p. 246. For praise of Ireland's French speeches, see Moynihan, *John Ireland,* pp. 137–45. The background to the Satolli 1892 trip follows primarily O'Connell, *John Ireland,* pp. 348–59; Denis O'Connell's "inconvenience" quote is on p. 368; for the bastardy story, see p. 390; for "power of prayer" quote, p. 246. Bribery and Walsh story suspicions are in Curran, *Corrigan,* pp. 397–415 and 441–43. Edes's "rogue" quote is at p. 412; Satolli in France quote is in Phillips, *The Church in France,* p. 8. The Fourteen Propositions are reprinted with minor elisions in Zwierlein, *McQuaid,* 3:182–86. Fogarty, *Vatican and Americanist Crisis,* pp. 214–15, suggests that O'Connell wrote the Fourteen Propositions in Rome. Ireland, O'Connell, and Satolli were together for several weeks prior to the archbishops' meeting, however, and the Propositions must have been one of the major topics of discussion.

Ireland's financial problems follow the account in O'Connell, *John Ireland,* pp. 380–85, 395–97. McQuaid's irritation at Ireland's intervention in New York politics was compounded by Ireland's just previous, and very high-handed, intervention with his Republican friends to block McQuaid's appointment to the State Board of Regents (the state school authority) and engineer the appointment of Sylvester Malone, a Brooklyn priest who was one of McGlynn's closest friends and allies. The texts of McQuaid's sermon and of a subsequent McQuaid philippic to Rome that fully discharged his mind upon the subject of Ireland are substantially reprinted in Zwierlein, *McQuaid,* 3:207–10, 216–25. For Satolli gossip bearing on Denis O'Connell's dismissal, see O'Connell, p. 410. McQuaid on "collapses" is in Zwierlein, 3:241. And see William E. Akin, "The War of the Bishops," *The New-York Historical Society Quarterly,* January 1966, pp. 41–61. To the modern eye, it is surprising how closely ecclesiastical infighting was followed in the lay press. For example, *The Washington Post,* October 28, 1896, had an extended, informed commentary on Satolli's conversion to anti-Americanism, including details of his relations with Schroeder.

See Phillips, *The Church in France,* pp. 250–58, for Dreyfus background. Dreyfus was a Jewish military officer accused unjustly of espionage; when his case became a cause célèbre, the Catholic right and the Jesuits, including Brandi's *La Civiltà Cattolica,* were among the strongest anti-Dreyfusards, a position with more than a tinge of anti-Semitism. The background to Leo's *Testem Benevolentiae* letter is laid out in some detail in Ellis, *Gibbons,* 2:64–80; Ireland's "peace" quote is at p. 74. Gerald P. Fogarty's *The Vatican and the American Hierarchy* (Stuttgart: Hiersemann, 1982), pp. 143–94, is an excellent, detailed history with much material on the Roman politics of the issue. Fogarty suggests (pp. 143–46) that Ireland had proselytized among the French liberals rather more than he later admitted. McQuaid's quote on mixed schools is in Zwierlein, *McQuaid,* 3:192. The quote on Irish Catholic patriotism is from Will Herberg, *Protestant-Catholic-Jew: An Essay in American Religious Sociology* (Garden City, N.Y.: Doubleday, 1955), p. 163. Ireland's "viva" is in O'Connell, *John Ireland,* p. 494. Leo's letter to Gibbons is in Ellis, *Gibbons,* 2:80.

5. *An American Church*

For statistical and demographic information on American Catholics, I relied primarily on Roger Finke and Rodney Stark, *The Churching of America, 1776–1990: Winners and Losers in Our Religious Economy* (New Brunswick, N.J.: Rutgers University Press, 1992), pp. 109–44, from the most recent and authoritative study. The Finke and Stark Catholic population estimates are generally lower than in other studies. The basic source for earlier periods is still Gerald Shaughnessy's 1925 study, *Has the Immigrant Kept the Faith? A Study of Immigration and Catholic Growth in the United States, 1790–1920* (New York: Macmillan, 1925), which stood up well under the Finke and Stark scrutiny. A recent very useful study is Jay P. Dolan, ed., *The American Catholic Parish: A History from 1850 to the Present,* 2 vols. (Mahwah, N.J.: Paulist Press, 1987), which is organized by six major geographic regions and includes historical tables on every American diocese. Both Shaughnessy's and Dolan's contributors appear to rely primarily on the annual *Catholic Directory,* compendia of statistical data that began to be collected in 1840. (My summations of the tables in Dolan agree closely with Shaughnessy's uncorrected totals.) The *Directory* data are diocesan self-reports, with many lacunae and inconsistent reporting standards, particularly in the earlier years. The *Directory* data give much lower numbers for nuns than Finke and Stark, probably because they omit some religious orders not under diocesan jurisdiction. Finke and Stark suggest that even their numbers for nuns may be too low.

In addition to the regional studies in the Dolan volumes, and works cited in the previous chapters, local detail and the biographies of the major prelates are drawn from Thomas W. Spalding, *The Premier See: A History of the Archdiocese of Baltimore: 1789–1989* (Baltimore: Johns Hopkins University Press, 1989); Charles Shanabruch, *Chicago's Catholics: The Evolution of an American Identity* (Notre Dame, Ind.: Notre Dame Press, 1981); Edward R. Kantowicz, *Corporation Sole: Cardinal Mundelein and Chicago Catholicism* (Notre Dame, Ind.: Notre Dame Press, 1983); Florence D. Cohalan, *A Popular History of the Archdiocese of New York* (Yonkers, N.Y.: U.S. Catholic

Historical Society, 1983); Mileta Ludwig, *Right Hand Glove Uplifted: A Biography of Archbishop Michael Heiss* (New York: Pageant, 1968); Robert F. McNamara, *The Diocese of Rochester, 1868–1968* (Rochester, N.Y.: Diocese of Rochester, 1968); James F. Connelly, ed., *History of the Archdiocese of Philadelphia* (Philadelphia: Archdiocese of Philadelphia, 1976); and James M. O'Toole, *Militant and Triumphant: William Henry O'Connell and the Catholic Church in Boston, 1859–1944* (Notre Dame, Ind.: Notre Dame Press, 1992).

The Irish Catholic share of clergy in 1900 is from David N. Doyle, "The Irish and the Christian Churches in America," in David N. Doyle and Owen Dudley Edwards, eds., *Americans and Ireland, 1776–1976: The American Identity and the Irish Connection* (Westport, Conn.: Greenwood Press, 1980), pp. 177–91. The 1970s data on Irish-descent clergy are from Andrew M. Greeley, *The Catholic Priest in the United States: A Sociological Investigation* (Washington, D.C.: United States Catholic Conference, 1972), p. 28. Doyle estimates that Irish-descent Catholics account for one fifth to one fourth of American Catholics today. Greeley reports one sixth, based on self-reports—that is, Irish Americans who call themselves Catholic—so would presumably not include nonpracticing Catholics, which may account for the difference. I used one fifth as a median number.

The personal sketch of O'Connell is from O'Toole, *Militant,* especially pp. 173–205; and see William H. O'Connell, *Recollections of Seventy Years* (Boston: Houghton Mifflin, 1934); Donna Merwick, *Boston Priests, 1848–1910: A Study of Social and Intellectual Change* (Cambridge, Mass.: Harvard University Press, 1973), for the difference between Williams and O'Connell; and Jack Beatty, *The Rascal King: The Life and Times of James Michael Curley (1874–1958)* (Reading, Mass.: Addison-Wesley, 1992), especially pp. 103–7. O'Toole, it should be said, casts doubt even on O'Connell's abilities as an administrator.

My thanks to Fr. Joseph Glab, C.R., the pastor of St. Stanislaus Kostka Church for his courtesy during a visit. John Joseph Parot, *Polish Catholics in Chicago, 1850–1920* (DeKalb, Ill.: Northern Illinois University Press, 1981), is a first-rate history. The story here follows Parot, supplemented by Anthony J. Kuzniewski, *Faith and Fatherland: The Polish Church War in Wisconsin, 1896–1918* (Notre Dame, Ind.: Notre Dame University Press, 1980), particularly for Wacław Kruszka, as well as Kantowicz, *Corporation Sole* and Shanabruch, *Chicago's Catholics.* The Kruszka (on Germans) and Messmer quotes are in Kuzniewski, pp. 59 and 81; the Barzyński quote is in Parot, p. 124; the *Sentinel* quote is in Kuzniewski, p. 26. For Poles and Mundelein, see Kantowicz, pp. 65–83. For the anti-Semitism imputation, see Parot, pp. 211–12. For the Polish National Catholic Church, see William Galush, "The Polish National Catholic Church: A Survey of Its Origins, Development, and Missions," *Records of the American Catholic Historical Society* 83 (1972): 131–149. The estimates of present-day membership is Parot's, the earlier estimates are Galush's.

James J. Olson, *Catholic Immigrants in America* (Chicago: Nelson-Hall, 1987), is a comprehensive survey. See pp. 65–82 for Eastern Europeans and pp. 83–88 for Italians. Henry J. Browne, "The Italian Problem in the Catholic Church of the United States, 1880–1900," *Historical Records and Studies* 35 (1946): 46–72, is still useful. For Italian Catholics generally I used Silvano Tomasi and Madeline Engles, eds., *The Italian Experience in the United States* (New York: Center for Migration Studies, 1970); Silvano M. Tomasi, *Piety and Power: The Role of Italian Parishes in the New York Metropolitan*

Area, 1880–1930 (New York: Center for Migration Studies, 1975); Humbert S. Nelli, *The Italians in Chicago, 1880–1930* (New York: Oxford University Press, 1970), especially pp. 181–200; Mary Elizabeth Brown, *From Italian Villages to Greenwich Village* (New York: Center for Migration Studies, 1992); Sr. Mary Consuela, "The Changing of Philadelphia, 1884–1918," in James F. Connelly, *Archdiocese of Philadelphia,* pp. 271–338; and Luciano J. Iorizzo, *Italian Immigrants and the Impact of the Padrone System* (New York: Arno, 1980). The "looking for a Mass" quote is in Tomasi, *Piety and Power,* p. 181. The New York survey is in Nicholas John Russo, "Three Generations of Italians in New York City: Their Religious Acculturation," in Tomasi and Engles, *Italian Experience,* pp. 195–213; see also Francis X. Feminella, "The Impact of Italian Immigration and American Catholicism," *American Catholic Sociological Review* 22 (Fall 1961): 233–41, suggesting that Italians either apostatized or adopted American Catholic practices. Andrew Greeley has also suggested that Italian Catholics become "Hibernicized" with successive generations.

Richard M. Linkh, *American Catholicism and European Immigrants, 1900–1924* (New York: Center for Migration Studies, 1975), parses the myth and reality of the Church's response to immigration. For black Catholics, see Cyprian Davis, *The History of Black Catholics in the United States* (New York: Crossroad, 1990). The Glennon quote is in John Tracy Ellis, *Catholic Bishops: A Memoir* (Wilmington, Del.: Glazier, 1984), p. 113. According to Davis, on pp. 146–52, at their father's death, one of the Healy brothers, although at considerable personal risk, "passed" well enough to return to Georgia and close his estate, which included selling off fifty-seven slaves. Messmer on the war is in Kuzniewski, *Faith and Fatherland,* pp. 117–18. For Gibbons, the war, and the National Catholic War Council, see John Tracy Ellis, *The Life of James Cardinal Gibbons, Archbishop of Baltimore: 1834–1921* (1952; reprint, Westminster, Md.: Christian Classics, 1987), 2:204–59; his caution on Benedict's peace plan is in ibid., pp. 245–46. Catholic army chaplains were 37.8 percent of the total, a figure that was supposed to represent the percentage of Catholic soldiers (Cohalan, *Archdiocese of New York,* p. 218). Other scholars—e.g., James Hennesey, *American Catholics: A History of the Roman Catholic Community in the United States* (New York: Oxford University Press, 1981), pp. 225–26—consider this figure too high. Patrick Hayes was bishop of the military ordinariate, i.e., the Catholic chaplaincy service. The characterization of later American nativism follows John Higham, *Strangers in the Land: Patterns of American Nativism, 1860–1925* (Westport, Conn.: Greenwood Press, 1980). And for condescension, see Andrew M. Greeley, *An Ugly Little Secret: Anti-Catholicism in North America* (Kansas City: Sheed, Andrews, McMeel, 1977).

Relations between the hierarchy and Rome follows Gerald P. Fogarty, *The Vatican and the American Hierarchy* (Stuttgart: Hiersemann, 1982), pp. 195–236. The Edes quotes are on p. 203. If she is to believed, O'Connell paid well for his Boston appointment. For *The New York Review,* see R. Scott Appleby, *"Church and Age, Unite!": The Modernist Impulse in American Catholicism* (Notre Dame, Ind.: Notre Dame University Press, 1992), pp. 91–167; and Michael DeVito. *The New York Review, 1905–1908* (New York: U.S. Catholic Historical Society, 1977). The condemnation of modernism came in 1907, and the *Review* folded the following year. The official story was that it closed for financial reasons, and Farley denied pressure from Rome. But there was certainly such pressure, although the journal was also struggling financially. For the modernist episode, see Marvin O'Connell, *Critics on Trial: An Introduction to the Catholic Modernist Crisis* (Washington, D.C.: Catholic University Press, 1994). Ireland, Gibbons, et al. warrant barely a mention in this book, even though Marvin O'Connell is Ireland's biographer; the intellectual crisis, that is, was entirely a European affair.

Details on the Eucharistic Congress (including the rainbow) are drawn primarily from C. F. Donovan, *The Story of the Twenty-eighth International Eucharistic Congress* (Chicago: Eucharistic Congress Committee, 1927), a 500-plus-page compilation and narrative. The event was also extensively reported in the lay press, e.g., *The New York Times,* June 19–27. Philadelphia papers reported the 10,000 figure for Dougherty's contingent, but only about 1000 actually accompanied him on his train.

PART II. TRIUMPH

6. *A Separate Universe*

The definitive biography of Dorothy Day is William D. Miller, *Dorothy Day: A Biography* (San Francisco: Harper & Row, 1982); see the same author's *A Harsh and Dreadful Love: Dorothy Day and the Catholic Worker Movement* (New York: Boni & Liveright, 1973). Robert Coles, *Dorothy Day: A Radical Devotion* (Reading, Mass.: Addison-Wesley, 1987), is a warm personal portrait, and see Mel Piehl, *Breaking Bread: The Catholic Worker and the Origin of Radical Catholicism in America* (Philadelphia: Temple University Press, 1979). Day tells of her conversion in Dorothy Day, *From Union Square to Rome* (New York: Arno, 1978), originally published in 1933, and of the CW movement in *Loaves and Fishes* (San Francisco: Harper & Row, 1983), originally published in 1963. A generous selection of her writings is in Robert Ellsberg, ed., *By Little and by Little: The Selected Writings of Dorothy Day* (New York: Knopf, 1983). The *Commonweal* quote is in ibid., p. vii (it was by David O'Brien), and the Rice quotes are from an interview. The Albert Brady quote is from Miller, *Harsh and Dreadful,* pp. 116–17—although it is a perfect mimic of Day, it was written at the Cleveland hospitality house by Bill Gauchat, one of the workers.

The Coughlin speech in Cleveland is from a newsreel clip on "The Radio Priest," Tape #111, *The American Experience,* WGBH, Boston. My thanks to WGBH for the loan of this videotape, which also contains brief clips of Gerald L. K. Smith. The portrait of Coughlin presented on the tape, however, is of a jackbooted proto-Nazi from the start, as well as of a swindling proto–Jimmy Swaggart–style televangelist, both of which are simply ahistorical. (The tape intercuts Coughlin speeches with clips from American Nazi conventions.) Arthur M. Schlesinger Jr., *The Age of Roosevelt,* vol. 3, *The Politics of Upheaval* (Boston: Houghton Mifflin, 1960), pp. 553–61, emphasizes Coughlin's proto-fascism, while Robert S. McElvaine, *The Great Depression* (New York: Times Books, 1984), pp. 237–41, more correctly places Coughlin as a man of the populist left. For biographical details and generous selections from Coughlin's broadcasts, see Charles J. Tull, *Father Coughlin and the New Deal* (Syracuse: Syracuse University Press, 1965); also Sheldon Marcus, *Father Coughlin: The Tumultuous Life of the Priest of the Little Flower* (Boston: Little, Brown, 1973); and also Philip A. Grant, "The Priest in Politics: Father Charles E. Coughlin and the Presidential Election of 1936," *Records of the American Catholic Historical Society,* Spring 1990, pp. 35–47. Limbaugh (*New York Times,* July 27, 1994) has a radio audience of about 20 million; recognizing that audience counting is much more scientific now, Coughlin's audience was variously estimated to range between 30 and 50 million at its peak. For the *Times*'s economic orthodoxy, see, for example, almost any issue in the spring of 1933, when various monetary and gold bills were being debated in Congress. The quote on O'Connell is from Tull, *Father Coughlin,* p. 70. Regarding Gallagher's economic studies, David O'Brien notes that the Austrian school was known for its anti-Semitism. See his *American Catholicism and Social Reform: The New Deal Years* (New York: Oxford University Press, 1968), pp. 12–13. For Mundelein and Roosevelt, see Edward R. Kantowicz, *Corporation Sole: Cardinal Mundelein and Chicago Catholicism* (Notre Dame, Ind.: Notre Dame University Press, 1983), pp. 217–36; the "burning" quote is at 219.

The economic quotes from Catholic journals are from *America,* April 18, 1924, and April 11, 1931; also *Commonweal,* June 3, 1931, and May 8, 1936. One could find similar quotes in almost any issue. And see Lawrence B. deSaulniers, *The Response in American Catholic Periodicals to the Crises of the Great Depression* (Lanham, Md.: University Presses, 1984), a useful survey. For the texts of the encyclicals, I used Claudia Carlen, *The Papal Encyclicals: 1740–1978,* 6 vols. (Raleigh, N.C.: McGrath, 1981). And see Richard L. Camp, *The Papal Ideology of Social Reform: A Study in Historical Development, 1878–1967* (Leiden: Brill, 1969). Among many elaborations of the papal themes, see John P. Delaney, "Fifty Years Ago, Leo Charted the Economic Seas," *America,* May 10, 1941; John La Farge, "Ten Years Ago, Pius Lit New Beacon of Safety," *America,* May 10, 1941; and George G. Higgins, "Toward A New Society," *Catholic Mind,* November 1936, pp. 629–35. The quote on "mutual masturbation" is from *America,* April 11, 1931. The "solitary vice" quote is John Ryan's, cited by Edward Roberts Moore, "The Malice of Contraception," *Commonweal,* May 20, 1931. The vehemence of Moore's article is not exceptional. I read and browsed through almost twenty years of *America* and *Commonweal* articles and the same sentiments are expressed in almost every other issue; and, of course, *Commonweal* and even *America* were much more liberal than, say, *Our Sunday Visitor* or the *Brooklyn Tablet.*

The Barbara Ward quote is from her "Planned Economy in Catholic Social Thought," *Dublin Review,* January 1939, pp. 85–99. For the life of John Ryan, see Francis L. Broderick, *Right Reverend New Dealer, John A. Ryan* (New York: Macmillan, 1963). The text of the Bishops' Program is in John Tracy Ellis, *Documents of American Catholic History,* rev. ed. (Wilmington, Del.: Michael Glazier, 1987), 2:589–607; the document was actually issued under the auspices of the old National Catholic War Council, before approval was received for the new NCWC. Ryan's major writings include *A Living Wage* (New York: Macmillan, 1920); *Distributive Justice: The Right and Wrong of Our Present Distribution System,* 3d ed. (New York: Macmillan, 1942); his autobiography, *Social Doctrine in Action: A Personal History* (New York: Harper, 1941); and hundreds of pamphlets, which are available in the archives of the United States Catholic Conference, the successor to the National Catholic Welfare Conference, in Washington, D.C. The negative O'Connell quote is in Broderick, *John A. Ryan,* p. 158. For the NRA, see Arthur M. Schlesinger Jr., *The Age of Roosevelt,* vol. 2, *The Coming of the New Deal* (Boston: Houghton Mifflin, 1959), pp. 87–102, pp. 97–98 for quote. *Catholic World* quote is in deSaulniers, *Response,* p. 158.

For Ryan's comparative liberalism on birth control, see John T. Noonan Jr., *Contraception: A History of Its Treatment by the Catholic Theologians and Canonists* (Cambridge, Mass.: Harvard University Press, 1965), pp. 422–23. The Lippmann quotes are from his *Drift and Mastery: An Attempt to Diagnose the Current Unrest* (Englewood

Cliffs, N.J.: Prentice-Hall, 1961), pp. 131, 143. "Copulationism" is in Moore, "Malice of Contraception." David J. Garrow, *Liberty and Sexuality: The Right to Privacy and the Making of Roe v. Wade* (New York: Macmillan, 1994), suggests, pp. 42–43, that Catholic women were already departing from the Church's position on birth control in the 1930s, which may explain some of the official vehemence, and see p. 274 for the Sanger position on abortion. The discussion of the decline of mainstream Protestantism follows Roger Finke and Rodney Stark, *The Churching of America, 1776–1990: Winners and Losers in Our Religious Economy* (New Brunswick, N.J.: Rutgers University Press, 1992).

For the modernist crisis, see Dorothy Ross, ed., *Modernist Impulses in the Human Sciences, 1870–1930* (Baltimore: John Hopkins University Press, 1994). The Pearson quote is from Karl Pearson, *The Grammar of Science,* 3d ed. (London: Black, 1911), p. 15. Dewey's presidential quote is in James T. Kloppenberg, "Democracy and Disestablishment: From Weber and Dewey to Habermas and Rorty," in Ross, *Modernist Impulses,* pp. 68–90. For Henry Adams, see *The Education of Henry Adams* (New York: Modern Library, 1931), especially pp. 449–61 on the immense impact of Pearson. For the American Sociological Society, see Dorothy Ross, *The Origins of American Social Science* (New York: Cambridge University Press, 1991), pp. 219–56. The two-volume Joseph Ratner, ed., *Characters and Events* (New York: Henry Holt, 1929), includes generous selections of Dewey's vast body of writing on public issues. For Lippmann's defection and biographer's disapproval, see Ronald Steel, *Walter Lippmann and the American Century* (Boston: Little, Brown, 1980), pp. 323–26.

James's quote on truth is in his *Pragmatism* (Cambridge, Mass.: Harvard University Press, 1975), p. 98. For Dewey's struggles to avoid moral relativism, see Robert B. Westbrook, *John Dewey and American Democracy* (Ithaca, N.Y.: Cornell University Press, 1991), e.g., pp. 429–62; it is an accessible if somewhat hagiographical biography. (I should confess that I find Dewey's writings on public affairs to combine naïveté and self-importance to a remarkable degree.) For Niebuhr, see Richard Fox, *Reinhold Niebuhr* (New York: Pantheon, 1985), pp. 136ff.; Pearson's racial quote is from his "Scope and Importance to the State of the Science of National Eugenics," *Eugenics Labor Lecture Series* (Cambridge, 1915), p. 25. The quotes from Krutch are in Joseph Wood Krutch, *The Modern Temper* (London: Jonathan Cape, 1930), pp. 200, 39, 235, 224, 103, 194, 184, 170, and 249.

The 1927 minister quote is from Herbert Parrish, "The Breakup of Protestantism," *Atlantic Monthly,* March 1927, pp. 295–305. The Meiklejohn quote is in Philip Gleason, *Keeping the Faith: American Catholicism, Past and Present* (Notre Dame, Ind.: University of Notre Dame Press, 1987), p. 142. For regulatory pressures in Pennsylvania, see Thomas J. Donaghy, *Philadelphia's Finest: A History of Education in the Catholic Archdiocese, 1692–1970* (Philadelphia: American Catholic Historical Society, 1972), pp. 182–83. A few states, led by Oregon, tried to outlaw religious schools altogether in the 1920s; the issue was resolved by the Supreme Court only in 1925 (*Pierce v. Society of Sisters*). In Pennsylvania, a typical ploy was to disallow Catholic school experience in teacher certification. There was an unpleasant Catholic-Jewish undertone to all of this. In the East, at least, the educational bureaucracies were dominated by liberal Jews, who were offended by the Catholic systems. Catholics, on the other hand, had a tendency to regard almost any regulatory initiatives as evidence of bigotry and needed little encouragement to ascribe antireligious motives to Jews. Unfortunately, both sides were probably half right most of the time.

The quotes on maternity clinics, permissiveness, and delinquency are from *America,* April, 11, 1931, May 23, 1931, May 3, 1924, and April 26, 1924. The Feeney quote is in William M. Halsey, *The Survival of American Innocence: Catholicism in an Era of Disillusionment, 1920–1940* (Notre Dame, Ind.: University of Notre Dame Press, 1980), p. 70. For Marshall and Smith, see Charles C. Marshall, "An Open Letter to the Honorable Alfred E. Smith," *Atlantic Monthly,* April 1927, pp. 540–49; and Smith's reply, Alfred E. Smith, "Catholic and Patriot: Governor Smith Replies," *Atlantic Monthly,* May 1927, pp. 721–28 (quotes at 724 and 728). The *Atlantic*'s editors seem to call Smith the winner, proclaiming that he had answered the challenge "straightforwardly, bravely, and with the clear ring of candor." Marshall did not retire gracefully; he found a widely used elementary school text, *The Manual of Christian Doctrine,* that seemed to insist on papal authority over the secular state—which, of course, it clearly did. The fact that everyone ignored such teachings made them no less embarrassing. For Hofstadter, see Richard Hofstadter, *The Paranoid Style in American Politics and Other Essays* (New York: Knopf, 1965).

For the American Catholic withdrawal, Halsey, *Survival of American Innocence,* is excellent and, I believe, correctly divines the underlying optimism and cultural imperialism in the Catholic attitude. Gleason, *Keeping the Faith,* also contains several excellent essays on the same topic, although he takes issue with Halsey on some minor points. Halsey, p. 57, gives the founding dates of a number of Catholic organizations. Except as indicated, the detail on organizational activity is from the *Annual Reports* of the National Catholic Welfare Conference, various years, in the archives of the U.S. Catholic Conference in Washington, D.C. The quotes from the sociological and historical societies are from Gleason, pp. 68, 140. For summer resorts, see *America,* April 4, 1925, and correspondence in subsequent issues. The "mobilize" quote is from the *Philadelphia Bulletin,* November 25, 1939. For Teachers' Guilds and the need for Catholic public school teachers, see the correspondence of the NCWC Education Department in the Catholic University Archives. The two cited texts are James H. Vanderveldt and Robert P. Odenwald, *Psychiatry and Catholicism* (New York: McGraw-Hill, 1957); and Paul H. Furfey, *Fire on the Earth* (New York: Macmillan, 1932). A hostile review of Catholic texts is Harold R. Rafton, *What Do Catholic Colleges Teach?* (Boston: Beacon, 1953). For movies, see *America,* July 5, 1924. The higher education quote is in Gleason, p. 145. Richard M. Freeland kindly provided me with extensive materials from the archives of Boston College on the Jesuit Education Association. For the decrepit state of religion in "Catholic" Europe, see, e.g., William Bosworth, *Catholicism and the Crisis in Modern France* (Princeton, N.J.: Princeton University Press, 1962), pp. 321–42; and for Spain, Hugh Thomas, *The Spanish Civil War* (New York: Touchstone, 1986), pp. 49–56. For French birth rate, see Noonan, *Contraception,* pp. 389–90. For Mussolini and Catholic Action, see "Caesar Challenges Peter," *Commonweal,* June 10, 1931. Higgins quote is from an interview.

7. *God's Bricklayer*

The only substantial published account of Dougherty's career is Hugh J. Nolan, "Native Son," in James F. Connelly, ed., *History of the Archdiocese of Philadelphia* (Philadelphia: Archdiocese of Philadelphia, 1976), pp. 339–418. The account here is based primarily on the Dougherty archive at the Catholic Historical Research Center of the Archdiocese of Philadelphia (hereafter HRCAP) and the Urban Archive at Temple University, particularly its well-indexed clipping archive of the *Philadelphia Evening Ledger* and the *Philadelphia Evening Bulletin,* supplemented by interviews and the secondary sources noted below.

Dougherty died in 1951, and there are only a small number of priests or others still living who were senior enough at his death to be firsthand informants. I interviewed Msgrs. Joseph McGlinn, Hugh Nolan, Joseph Dougherty, and Joseph McCloskey, and Fr. Vincent Gallagher, all of whom were priests during Dougherty's tenure. (I located a few others who were either ill or did not wish to be interviewed.) Nolan, now deceased, and McGlinn are the primary sources for anecdotal material. McGlinn was the Cardinal's secretary during the last eight years of his life and helped him destroy most of his papers. Nolan, an accomplished historian in his own right, was close to Cletus Benjamin, a longtime chancery official, who was his main informant. Nolan also gave me access to a substantial amount of archival material for a projected biography of the Cardinal, including a detailed chronological card file, extensive transcriptions of primary material, and several boxes of unindexed primary material. Nolan's archive (referred to hereafter as NA) is now at the HRCAP. Nolan is an admirer of the Cardinal in almost all respects, while McGlinn did not hesitate to be critical. (I did not find him at all hostile, and his criticisms seemed quite reasonable, whereas Nolan occasionally strained to justify some of the least admirable aspects of Dougherty's character.) I also interviewed Albert M. Greenfield Jr. and Matthew H. McCloskey III, both of whose fathers were close to the Cardinal, as well as George E. Johnson of the Greenfield firm, and Liz Anne Kelly LeVine, Jack Kelly's surviving child. Chris McCullough at HRCAP and Margaret Reher, a Catholic historian at Immaculata College, were helpful guides to sources, as was Andrew Harrison of Temple University, who is preparing a biography of Greenfield.

On Dougherty and the movies, there is an extensive collection of materials and clippings at HRCAP. Dougherty's pastoral letters and public statements and the public response of the theater owners are from the coverage in the *Bulletin.* The "practically raised" quote is James Dick to Dougherty, from letter of September 7, 1934. Kelly wrote Lamb on August 23, 1934. Will Hays wrote Dougherty on October 5, 1934. Goldwyn visit is from Nolan interview; Dougherty's quote was repeated by Benjamin, who was present. Example of form letter is Dougherty to Edna de la Corza, December 4, 1934. Dougherty's statement reinforcing the ban came on March 1, 1935. The Jewish issue was raised repeatedly in the NCWC material, much of which is at HRCAP; see, e.g., *Report of the Episcopal Committee on Motion Pictures* (Washington, D.C.: National Catholic Welfare Conference, 1935) (a bound and printed but unpublished volume), statement of Bishop John Cantwell (Los Angeles), and see James M. Skinner, *The Cross and the Cinema: The Legion of Decency and the National Catholic Office for Motion Pictures, 1933–1970* (Westport, Conn.: Praeger, 1993), pp. 43–44. HRCAP, in the movie file, has a report on the button sale; it is undated, but from its placement in an otherwise chronological sequence it appears to be from the 1934–1935 school year.

For Philadelphia political and economic background, I used: Dennis Clark, *The Irish in Philadelphia: Ten Generations of Urban Experience* (Philadelphia: Temple University Press, 1973), pp. 38–87, an important counterweight to the conclusions drawn from the Boston Irish experience; Sr. Mary Consuela, "The Changing of Philadelphia, 1884–1918," in Connelly, *Archdiocese of Philadelphia,* pp. 271–338; Sam Bass Warner,

The Private City: Philadelphia in Three Periods of Its Growth (Philadelphia: University of Pennsylvania Press, 1987); Peter McCafferey, *When Bosses Ruled Philadelphia: The Emergence of the Republican Machine, 1867–1933* (University Park, Pa.: Pennsylvania. State University Press, 1993)—a careful and detailed study of ethnic and machine politics; John T. Salter, *The People's Choice: Philadelphia's William S. Vare* (New York: Exposition, 1971), primarily anecdotal, rather than analytical; and E. Digby Baltzell's classic *Philadelphia Gentlemen: The Making of a National Upper Class* (New Brunswick, N.J.: Transaction, 1989), and his *Puritan Boston and Quaker Philadelphia: Two Protestant Ethics and the Spirit of Class Authority and Leadership* (New York: Free Press, 1979). The John B. Kelly Jr. transcript in the Walter Phillips Oral History at the Temple University Urban Archive tells of his father's attempt to revive the local Democratic Party. When my own father was young, he lived in Bill Vare's neighborhood and was a minor functionary in the party. Until I began research for this chapter, I had always assumed that Vare was an Irish Catholic, like almost everybody else in the neighborhood and almost all other contemporary urban bosses. My father, though a blue-collar, devout Irish Catholic, was a lifelong Republican, who would not cross party lines even for John Kennedy in 1960. (His sole defection was for Roosevelt in 1936, which he regretted.)

The *Renascimento* story, February 14, 1914, is transcribed in NA. The diary fragment is "Memorandum (private) of D. J. Dougherty: Jaro, Ilcila, Philippine Islands, 1912–1913" in NA, I assume typed by Nolan. For Philadelphia parish life, in addition to interviews, I used Kathleen Gavigan, "The Rise and Fall of Parish Cohesiveness in Philadelphia," *Records of the American Catholic Historical Society*, March–December 1975, pp. 107–31; Nolan's "Native Son"; and Joseph J. Casino, "From Sanctuary to Involvement: A History of the Catholic Parish in the Northeast," in Jay P. Dolan, ed., *The American Catholic Parish: A History from 1850 to the Present*, 2 vols. (Mahwah, N.J.: Paulist Press, 1987), pp. 7–116. (Casino is the Philadelphia archdiocese archivist and includes a substantial amount of Philadelphia material.)

The details of Gallagher's account of the housing project are vague. But it appears that the site was originally selected by federal authorities for low-income housing targeted at a black population, which was the only way it could be approved, given wartime construction limitations. Gallagher was asked to sit in on the presentation. He objected to the program on the ground that the increase in population would cause a large local tax increase. A sequence of events then ensued, which took several years, whereby he and the council president selected a project they liked. (It was almost all white, and to Gallagher's surprise and consternation, almost all Catholic, increasing his parish size by a factor of almost 8.) It is conceivable, in short, that Gallagher was used as a front man by the local politicians to block a black housing project. In deference to his age, I did not press him on the point. (Gallagher died in 1996 at age 100.)

Reproductions of the Baltimore Catechism are available from Tan Publishing Co., Rockford, Ill. There are several editions, all with slightly variant language. It was later replaced in Philadelphia, in the 1940s, by Michael A. McGuire, *Fr. McGuire's The New Baltimore Catechism and Mass* (New York: Benziger Brothers, 1941); McGuire's language is slightly different from that of the original Baltimore Catechism. The "best-posted" quote is in Robert Cross, "The Changing Image of the City," *Catholic Historical Review* 48, no. 1 (April 1962): 50. The "religious acculturation" quote is from Gavigan, "Parish Cohesiveness," p. 126. The Du Bois quote is in Paul Czuchlewski,

"Liberal Catholicism and American Racism," *Records of the American Catholic Historical Society*, September–December 1974, p. 144. The Florence story is from Nolan interview. Letter to Annenberg is December 11, 1942, filed with Annenberg reply. For "light-skinned," see John Bonner to Dougherty, August 11, 1939. Obstetric case file begins with a complaint to Dougherty dated January 22, 1947.

For Philadelphia's Catholic schools, see Thomas J. Donaghy, *Philadelphia's Finest: A History of Education in the Catholic Archdiocese, 1692–1970* (Philadelphia: American Catholic Historical Society, 1972); and Francis J. Ryan, "Monsignor John Bonner and Progressive Education in the Archdiocese of Philadelphia: 1925–1945," *Records of the American Catholic Historical Society*, Spring 1991, pp. 17–44. The diocesan comparisons are from the statistical tables in the Dolan compilation of parish histories, which rely primarily on the *Catholic Directory*. The data for Philadelphia for these reports show a smaller number of schools than the archdiocese's internal records, thus possibly understating the Philadelphia performance advantage. (Since the *Directory* data, however, were based on self-reports, the discrepancy is odd.) The Bonner file at HRCAP contains his reports for most years. The 1929 investigation is in Bonner to Dougherty May 28, 1929. The analysis of the reasons for the cost differential is mine. I assumed that salaries in public schools were double those in the Catholic system, which is aggressive (female teachers in the public lower grades got $450 per year, only 50 percent more than the nuns), that class sizes were 50 percent larger in the Catholic system, and that the ratio of public to Catholic students was 2:1. Catholic students also typically supplied more of their consumables than public school students did and often bought their textbooks.

For Bonner standing up to Dougherty, see letters of May 28, 1930, April 3, 1929, December 17, 1934, and July 2, 1938. Bonner wrote a very sharp reply on September 21, 1936, when Dougherty passed on a complaint questioning his honesty: "If I have not given enough evidence in these past ten years that I possess common sense . . . and personal integrity . . . no words of mine, to that effect, will be of any good." The letter includes none of the groveling characteristic of other clerical letters to the Cardinal, confirming McGlinn's assessment of Bonner. (McGlinn and Bonner were distant cousins and knew each other well.) Dougherty's initial reactions to Bonner's death are from McGlinn; his comment to Benjamin is from Nolan interview.

The bounced check story is from Nolan interview. Some of the seminary collection atmospherics are in Gavigan, "Parish Cohesiveness." Letter on collection from O'Hara is to Dougherty, April 9, 1936. The full quote from Kelly, per McGlinn, was made when Bonner was sent to ask his intervention in Harrisburg—"I'll do it for you, monsignor, but not for that son-of-a-bitch on Race Street [the chancery]." For Annenberg, see Dougherty to Attorney General Frank Murphy, October 5, 1939, and Annenberg response. Walter Annenberg (private communication) confirmed that his father and Dougherty were close friends who enjoyed discussing politics. Walter intervened with the mayor (letter of December 28, 1949) to move up one Bernard Murphy on the police sergeant's list—which seems an oddly trivial matter for the Cardinal, the mayor, and Philadelphia's most powerful publisher all to be working on. There is an extensive correspondence with Judge Brown; on at least one occasion, Dougherty's patronage was on behalf of a relative, Helen McCarthy, February 25, 1932.

O'Hara and Dougherty fatherly exchange is in NA, O'Hara, January 22, 1936, and Dougherty reply of January 24. Report by O'Hara on trip to Rome with Carroll

McCormick and Boylans, August 9, 1933, HRCAP. The seminary librarian and choir director were both Boylans. The McCormick story, including the quote from the Pope, came separately from McGlinn and Nolan, but the O'Hara endorsement is from McGlinn, who got the story from O'Hara. Nolan, who was teaching in Minnesota on temporary assignment at the time, said he was deluged with demands for explanations for McCormick's advancement by the local priests. The Cardinal's other priestly nephew, Joseph Dougherty, however, was apparently not from a favored side of the family and the Cardinal had almost nothing to do with him. According to McGlinn, he turned down an invitation to Dougherty's ordination "lest I be accused of nepotism." For report on travel arrangements, O'Hara to Dougherty, July 1, 1934. For John O'Hara, see Thomas T. McAvoy, *Father O'Hara of Notre Dame, the Cardinal-Archbishop of Philadelphia* (South Bend, Ind.: Notre Dame University Press, 1967). Cardinal O'Hara demonstrates the possibility of being an effective bishop without acting like a medieval monarch. For O'Connell salutation, see letter of December 15, 1922; for Brown language, May 29, 1929. O'Hara closing is the same in all his letters. Hiatus in Hayes-Dougherty correspondence was from January 4 to February 9, 1932. On Paris trip, O'Hara to Dougherty, see February 17, 1936, NA, in which he also praises "your beautiful new house." Details of The Terraces and chauffeur incident are from the *Bulletin*. The cathedraticum and pressure to make donations are from McGlinn, who also prepared letters on family trusts. Nolan loyally apologizes for Dougherty's spending as "a quirk," a lower-class Irishman's desire to show that he "had made it." (Dougherty's father was the local tax collector; he was not *that* lower class.) There is also a feeling from both McGlinn and Nolan that Dougherty thought a "prince of the Church" needed a certain lifestyle to keep up appearances.

Both Nolan and McGlinn agree in detail on Dougherty's religious practices. Few people outside of his immediate circle seem to have known how religious he was. The visit to Lisieux is from the "Memorandum," in NA, which also has the handwritten meditations. Peter's Pence quote is in HRCAP, May 26, 1938. For nuns as midwives, see Margaret Mary Reher, "Dennis J. Dougherty and Anna J. Dengel: The Missionary Alliance," *Records of the American Catholic Historical Society,* Spring 1990, pp. 21–33—but the story here came from Nolan—and for the 1940s equal rights amendment, see James J. Kenneally, "Women Divided: The Catholic Struggle for an Equal Rights Amendment: 1923–1945," *Catholic Historical Review* 75 (April 1989): 249–68. "*Con conscienza*" is quoted by O'Hara in report from Rome on July 27, 1935. Adams quote is in James Hennessey *American Catholics: A History of the Roman Catholic Community in the United States* (New York: Oxford University Press, 1981), p. 62. *America* quote is from issue of August 1, 1931, p. 394.

8. *On Top of the World*

Almost all of the movies mentioned in this chapter are available on tape. I viewed all of them except *San Francisco, Fighting Father Dunne, The Fighting 69th,* and *God Is My Co-Pilot*. I also could not find tapes of *Come to the Stable* and *The Fighting Sullivans* but saw them years ago. Detailed plot synopses, cast notes, and commercial data are in Jay Robert Nash and Stanley Ralph Ross, *Motion Picture Guide: 1927–1983* (Chicago: Cinebooks, 1987). The most thorough study of Hollywood's portrayal of Catholics is Les and Barbara Keyser, *Hollywood and the Catholic Church: The Image of Roman Catholicism in American Movies* (Chicago: Loyola University Press, 1984). Academy Award nominations are from Richard Shale, *The Academy Award Index: The Complete Categorical and Chronological Record* (Westport, Conn.: Greenwood Press, 1993). The newspaper quote is from *The Dallas Morning News,* December 18, 1945. The article comments that the studios had tried "Protestant" movies, but they did poorly at the box office. "Superpadre" is the Keysers' coinage. Financial comparisons are from the clipping files at the New York Public Library. The Schulberg quotes are from his "Joe Docks, Forgotten Man of the Waterfront," *New York Times Magazine,* December 28, 1952, p. 30.

The story of Quigley and Breen is drawn primarily from Gregory D. Black, *Hollywood Censored: Morality Codes, Catholics, and the Movies* (New York: Cambridge University Press, 1994); Leonard J. Leff and Jerold L. Simmons, *The Dame in the Kimono: Hollywood Censorship and the Production Code from the 1920s to the 1960s* (New York: Grove Weidenfeld, 1990); and James M. Skinner, *The Cross and the Cinema: The Legion of Decency and the National Catholic Office for Motion Pictures, 1933–1970* (Westport, Conn.: Praeger, 1970). Black's is by far the most meticulously researched of the three, with large amounts of fascinating original material. Black, however, writes from the position of an outraged opponent of censorship, insisting on treating Breen as an outside imposition. I believe this interpretation is against the weight of his own evidence, for it is clear from his book that the studio owners, despite some initial resistance, came to regard Breen as a savior, whatever the screenwriters and directors might have thought. The real split was between the artists and the businessmen. Black also attempts to portray Hays as the regulatory mastermind, but again, on his own evidence, that seems implausible. Leff and Simmons, although indulging in the usual, and justified, ridicule of Breen, take greater pains to show the commonality of interest between Breen and the studios. The "OPEC" analogy is my own. Skinner is also excellent, but he concentrates on the intra-Catholic side of the story.

Paul W. Facey, *The Legion of Decency: A Sociological Analysis of the Emergence and Development of a Social Pressure Group* (New York: Arno, 1974), is also useful. It is a reprint of a 1945 Ph.D. dissertation, written with the cooperation of the principals, and contains considerable detail on the Catholic background, but it underplays the intra-Catholic controversies and is superseded in most respects by Skinner. A special issue of the *Motion Picture Herald* dated September 25, 1948, contains extensive material on Quigley; see especially Terry Ramsaye, "Martin Quigley: This Third of a Century." Once the system was established, Quigley and Breen constantly feuded over control of the code; Quigley also thought that Breen was too accommodating to Hollywood.

For censorship history, I used primarily Edward De Grazia and Roger K. Newman, *Banned Films: Movies, Censors and the First Amendment* (New York: Bowker, 1982). The quoted *Herald* warnings are from August 21, 1915, and September 2, 1933. I found many more browsing through the intervening years, and the 1948 special issue on Quigley includes a selection of his pro-decency editorials. The quotes from Hughes on *Scarface* is from Black, p. 130; "hopeless" and "No member" are both from Leff and Simmons, *Dame,* pp. 40, 31. The "fire in his eyes" quote is from Skinner, *Cross,* p. 34. The NCWC's *Report of the Episcopal Committee on Motion Pictures* (Washington, D.C.: National Catholic Welfare Conference, 1935) demonstrates the great depth of feeling among virtually all bishops against the movies; Cantwell's quotes are on pp. 38–39.

Lord's NCWC presentation was written up as a pamphlet, and is in HRCAP; the pamphlet is the source of the "white girl" quote. The two *America* quotes are from the issues of July 5, 1924, p. 280, and July 7, 1934, p. 292. The calculation of Catholics signing Legion pledges is from Facey, *Legion of Decency;* the *Christian Century* quote is in ibid., p. 61. The Legion's reviewing organization was the International Federation of Catholic Alumnae. Its annual reports for the early 1930s are in HRCAP and confirm the overall impression of professionalism. I used the text of *Vigilanti Cura* in Claudia Carlen, *The Papal Encyclicals: 1740–1978* (Raleigh, N.C.: McGrath, 1981), 3:517–23; the quote is on p. 521. The Williams quote is in Rudy Behlmer, *Inside Warner Brothers (1935–1951)* (New York: Viking, 1985), p. 322. The book is a collection of letters from the Warner files, including a number of back-and-forths with the Breen office. The M-G-M quote is from Leff and Simmons, *Dame,* p. 31. For Kazan and *Streetcar,* see Behlmer, pp. 323–33; the quote is on 332. The Breen Oscar citation is in Shale, *Academy,* p. 293. Fairbanks's views are from personal communication with the author; Schulberg from an interview. On Mayer and Cohn, see Neal Gabler, *An Empire of Their Own: How the Jews Invented Hollywood* (New York: Crown, 1988), pp. 285–87. The account of the *San Francisco* script changes is from Nash and Ross, *Motion Picture Guide;* "humiliated" quote is in Keyser, *Hollywood,* p. 67. Keyser "gut feeling" quote is from an interview. I am grateful to John C. Cort, who knew Corridan well, for pointing out that the Malden speech was virtually a transcript, and I confirmed the point with Budd Schulberg in an interview.

My primary sources for the Catholic labor movement were interviews with John Cort, Msgr. Charles Owen Rice, Msgr. George Higgins, Fr. Joseph Fitzpatrick, S. J., and, at the Denis J. Comey School of Industrial Relations at St. Joseph's College, Nate Spizeman and Jim Farrar. My thanks to Bob Moore, the director of the Comey School for setting up the interviews and for providing curricular material from the early years. I also used the Philip Carey and the John Corridan Papers at the Fordham University Archives. My thanks to Fr. Jerry Connelly, S.J., the archivist, for his courtesies, and for an unusually well indexed collection. John Cort also provided me with extensive selections from his unpublished autobiography and much additional material from his personal files, as did Fr. Fitzpatrick. I also reviewed issues of *The Labor Leader* and the Detroit *Wage Earner* (formerly *The Michigan Labor Leader*) for most of the late 1930s and 1940s. George H. Hildebrand, *American Unionism: An Historical and Analytic Survey* (Reading, Mass.: Addison Wesley, 1979), is a succinct history of American unions.

The most complete history of ACTU is Douglas P. Seaton, *Catholics and Radicals: The Association of Catholic Trade Unions and the American Labor Movement, from Depression to Cold War* (Lanham, Md.: University Presses, 1985); however, it contains a number of major errors of fact and interpretation and must be read in conjunction with John C. Cort, "Review of *Catholics and Radicals*," *Commonweal*, August 12, 1983, p. 438; and see also Neil Betten, *Catholic Activism and the Industrial Worker* (Gainesville, Fla.: University Presses of Florida, 1976). Michael A. Harrington, "Catholics in the Labor Movement: A Case History," *Labor History,* Fall 1960, pp. 231–63, demonstrates the diversity of the Catholic labor movement. Patrick J. McGeever, *Reverend Charles Owen Rice: Apostle of Contradiction* (Pittsburgh: Duquesne University Press, 1989), is a detailed biography of Rice, written with Rice's cooperation, but is an oddly peevish and nitpicking book. Anyone would tremble to be sentenced to such a biographer. The

Haessler quote is from Roger Keeran, *The Communist Party and the Auto Workers Union* (Bloomington, Ind.: Indiana University Press, 1980), p. 255. For ACTU in New York and Jersey City, I rely primarily on Cort, his autobiography, and the coverage in *The Labor Leader,* which was mostly written by Cort. Lewis's remarks about Green are from Cort. The "Straight Down the Middle" and "between corrupt" quotes are from *The Labor Leader,* January 1, 1938, and June 1, 1938. The "out of his hat" quote is in Harrington, "Catholics," p. 259; the "Joe McUnion" is from Seaton, *Catholics and Radicals,* p. 146; "yell 'Commie' " quote is from Rice interview; and "We battle" from Harrington, pp. 260–61.

Catholic involvement in the UAW is well documented in Keeran, *Communist Party,* pp. 254ff.; John Barnard, *Walter Reuther and the Rise of the Auto Workers* (Boston: Little, Brown, 1983), pp. 103–11; John Cort, "ACTU and the Automobile Workers," *U.S. Catholic Historian,* Fall 1990, pp. 335–51; and see Jack Skeels, "The Background of UAW Factionalism," *Labor History,* Spring 1961, pp. 158–81. It is worth noting that, while Rice strongly supported Reuther, his friend Murray quietly supported Reuther's Communist-backed opponent, R. J. Thomas, another example of the lack of monolithism in Catholic labor circles. (Murray feared that Reuther would challenge him for the CIO presidency if he won in the UAW.) The count of Communist officers in the National Maritime Union is from a memorandum in the Corridan Papers, dated May 1947. The CIO union count is in Cort, "ACTU," p. 336.

Keeran argues that the wartime Communist-led strikes were mostly legitimate strikes, and not as anti-American or as pro-Nazi/Soviet as they are conventionally interpreted. His case may be weakest in the North American Aviation strike, which is generally considered the most egregious example of a pro-Axis strike—although wages were low—and I follow the conventional interpretation. My interpretation of the importance of the Marshall Plan, which is related to the perceived dangers of Stalin's contemporaneous putsch in Czechoslovakia, the formation of the Cominform, and the pressure on Berlin is in my *Iron Destinies, Lost Opportunities: The Postwar Arms Race* (New York: Harper & Row, 1988), pp. 34–41, and see the sources cited therein. The definitive "neo-revisionist" assessment of American postwar foreign policy is in Melvyn P. Leffler, *A Preponderance of Power: National Security, the Truman Administration, and the Cold War* (Stanford, Cal.: Stanford University Press, 1992). For Truman's European policy in 1947–1948, see pp. 182–219. Although he is highly critical of American Cold War policies after 1949, Leffler gives Truman, Marshall, Kennan, and company high marks for policy during the creation and implementation of the Marshall Plan, and he leaves no doubt of the reality and seriousness of the Communist threat to Western Europe absent American firmness. Defeating European aid through union pressures in Congress would have been a major victory for Stalin, with possibly catastrophic consequences.

Fr. Fitzpatrick's homily at Philip Carey's funeral (mimeograph), May 31, 1989, sketches Carey's life. New York newspapers carried extensive notices of his death, including, e.g., Murray Kempton, "The Priest Whose Parish Was the Docks," *Newsday,* May 31, 1989. For Carey and Quill, see Jules Weinberg, "Priests, Workers, and Communists," *Reader's Digest,* January 1949, pp. 2–6 (condensed from *Harper's Magazine,* November 1948). When Quill died in 1966, he was buried from St. Patrick's with full Catholic honors, despite a divorce and a remarriage; Rice preached the homily. The story of Corridan and the New York waterfront is in Malcolm Johnson, *Crime on the*

Labor Front (New York: McGraw-Hill, 1950), especially pp. 214–26 on "Priests on the Waterfront"; Allen Raymond, *Waterfront Priest* (New York: Henry Holt, 1955); Schulberg, "Joe Docks"; Budd Schulberg, "How One Pier Got Rid of the Mob," *New York Times Magazine,* September 27, 1953, p. 17, and "Waterfront Priest," *Commonweal,* April 3, 1953, pp. 643–46. Corridan also received wide publicity in *Collier's, Fortune,* and *Argosy,* to name a few, and was frequently mentioned in the daily papers. Corridan's files contain extensive researches on waterfront crime. There is also a letter from Schulberg's mother saying that Corridan had changed her son's life. "As long as" is from Schulberg, "Waterfront," p. 646. Johnson's articles in the *Sun* and later in *The New York Times* provide extensive waterfront coverage. "I put on my coat" is from Johnson, *Crime,* p. 226; the "God grant" prayer is in Corridan's papers. Cort noted the timing of the *Waterfront* movie, just after the election.

McGeever, who strongly criticizes Rice for "Red-baiting," concedes, however, that his charges were always well documented and factual. James J. Matles and James Higgins, *Them and Us: Struggles of a Rank-and-File Union* (Englewood Cliffs, N.J.: Prentice-Hall, 1974), is the story of the UE battle from the other side of the ramparts. Matles was the pro-Communist, Stalinist UE leader who battled Rice over the years. His treatment of Rice is of course quite hostile. The book is difficult to find; Msgr. Rice, who accepts his critics in good spirit, gave me a copy. Comey tells of his years as an arbitrator in his *The Waterfront Peacemaker* (Philadelphia: St. Joseph's University Press, 1983); the "honest mistake" quote is on p. 200.

Richard A. Easterlin's *Birth and Fortune: The Impact of Numbers on Personal Welfare* (New York: Basic Books, 1980) is a compelling analysis of the demographic basis of the 1950s phenomenon and includes a detailed statistical appendix. Church membership data are from the "Religious Bodies" tables of the U.S. Bureau of the Census, for various years. See also James Hennesey, *American Catholics: A History of the Roman Catholic Community in the United States* (New York: Oxford University Press, 1981), pp. 283–84. Paul Blanshard's *American Freedom and Catholic Power* was published by Beacon Press. The Dulles quote is in Donald J. Crosby, *God, Church, and Flag: Senator Joseph McCarthy and the Catholic Church, 1950–1957* (Chapel Hill, N.C.: University of North Carolina Press, 1978), p. 136. The Will Herberg quote is from his *Protestant-Catholic-Jew: An Essay in American Religious Sociology* (Garden City, N.Y.: Doubleday, 1955), p. 251. Harold A. Fey, "Can Catholicism Win America?" (eight-part series), *Christian Century,* November 29, 1944–January 17, 1945, is, like Fr. John Cronin's writings on communism, a calm, largely accurate survey that errs by assuming much more Catholic forethought and coordination than really existed—master plans are always obvious in retrospect. Fey tends to treat paper organizations as reality. He writes of the military chaplaincy under Spellman, for instance, as if it were a well-oiled conversion machine; but see Donald J. Crosby, *Battlefield Chaplains* (Lawrence, Kans.: University of Kansas Press, 1993), for the uncoordinated, catch-as-catch-can nature of the enterprise. The quotes are from the first and last articles in the series. The Martin Marty quote is from his *The New Shape of American Religion* (New York: Harper, 1959), pp. 74–75. Tapes of Bishop Sheen's telecasts are available from the Sheen Institute in Victor, N.Y. My appreciation to Fr. Sebastian Falcone, director of the St. Bernard Institute in Rochester, where the Sheen archive is maintained, for providing me with background information on the telecasts. Statistics on audiences are also in an appendix to Sheen's autobiography, *Treasure in Clay* (Garden City, N.Y.: Doubleday, 1980). A version of the

Spellman/Sheen falling out is in D. P. Noonan, *The Passion of Fulton Sheen* (New York: Dodd, Mead, 1972), pp. 66–86.

9. *Stalin, the Pope, and Joe McCarthy*

In preparing this chapter, I benefited from the researches of Lisa Moreno and Patrick McNamara, Ph.D. candidates at the University of Maryland and Catholic University, respectively. Overviews of the interactions of the Church and American foreign policy include: Wilson D. Miscamble, "Catholics and American Foreign Policy from McKinley to McCarthy," *Diplomatic History,* Summer 1980, pp. 223–40; Robert L. Frank, "Prelude to Cold War: American Catholics and Communism," *Journal of Church and State,* Winter 1992, pp. 39–56; Philip Gleason, "Pluralism, Democracy, and Catholicism in the Era of World War II," *Review of Politics* 49 (Spring 1987): 208–30; George Q. Flynn, *American Catholics and the Roosevelt Presidency: 1932–1936* (Lexington, Ky.: University of Kentucky Press, 1968), and *Roosevelt and Romanism: Catholics and American Diplomacy, 1937–1945* (Westport, Conn.: Greenwood Press, 1976); and David O'Brien, *American Catholicism and Social Reform: The New Deal Years* (New York: Oxford University Press, 1968).

Thomas A. Kselman and Steven Avella, "Marian Piety and the Cold War in the United States," *Catholic Historical Review,* July 1986, 403–24, is one of the few explorations of the religious impulse behind the Catholic view of the Cold War, and is the source for the "Blue Army" and related aspects of Marian devotion in America. The story of Fatima is in William T. Walsh, *Our Lady of Fatima* (New York: Macmillan, 1947), a pious account, but based on interviews with Lucia and access to her memoir. Mary's quote is on p. 83. The *Life* photo essay on Fatima is in the December 20, 1948, issue. For Van Hoof, see Kselman and Avella; also *Life,* August 28, 1950, and Margaret Frakes, "Setting for a Miracle," *Christian Century,* August 30, 1950, pp. 1019–21 (there are various renderings of Mrs. Van Hoof's name). The Church's unease was compounded by the local Chamber of Commerce's boosterism and the likelihood that Mrs. Van Hoof herself was profiting from the offerings. She was estranged from the Church when she died in 1984; her funeral service was officiated by a non-Catholic minister and she was buried at the shrine to her apparitions. The Notre Dame quote is from Kselman and Avella, pp. 412–13. Mundelein's Hitler quote is Edward R. Kantowicz, *Corporation Sole: Cardinal Mundelein and Chicago Catholicism* (Notre Dame, Ind.: Notre Dame University Press, 1983), p. 225. It created a major diplomatic flap, and Hitler temporarily withdrew his ambassador to the Vatican in protest.

For the "red scare" of 1919–1920, see M. J. Heale, *American Anticommunism: Combating the Enemy Within, 1830–1870* (Baltimore: Johns Hopkins University Press, 1990), pp. 60–78. The account of the Mexican revolution is based primarily on Robert E. Quirk, *The Mexican Revolution and the Catholic Church, 1910–1929* (Bloomington, Ind.: Indiana University Press, 1973); supplemented by Arthur S. Link, *Wilson: The Search for Neutrality, 1914–1915* (Princeton, N.J.: Princeton University Press, 1960), pp. 456–94, and *Wilson: Campaigns for Progress and Peace, 1916–1917* (Princeton, N.J.: Princeton University Press, 1965), pp. 124–64; and Flynn, *American Catholics and Roosevelt,* pp. 150–94. Randall Pond, "Mexico Sees Red," *Sign,* March 1936, pp. 462–63, is a characteristic Catholic commentary. For Lippmann involvement, see Ronald Steel,

Walter Lippmann and the American Century (Boston: Little, Brown, 1980), pp. 235–43, which seems to inflate Lippmann's role. Morrow's compromise essentially required the government to ignore the hostile intent of its anticlerical legislation. For example, the law required that all clergy register with the government. The intent, it seems clear, was to limit the number of Mexican clergy, but the government agreed to treat it merely as a statistical provision. From the government's perspective, in a country that was secularizing anyway, the continual conflicts with the Church were an expensive distraction from economic reform.

For the chronology of the Spanish Civil War, I rely primarily on Hugh Thomas, *The Spanish Civil War* (New York: Touchstone, 1986), the definitive English-language history. I also used: Flynn, *Roosevelt and Romanism,* pp. 29–62; Allen Guttmann, *The Wound in the Heart: American Interpretations of and Reactions to the Spanish Civil War* (Glencoe, N.Y.: Free Press, 1962); and J. David Valaik, "Catholics, Neutrality, and the Spanish Embargo, 1937–1939," *Journal of American History,* June 1967, pp. 73–85. Guttmann's *American Neutrality and the Spanish Civil War* (Boston: D. C. Heath, 1963) is a collection of contemporary polemics on the war; and Anonymous, "The Martyrdom of Spain," *Dublin Review,* October 1936, pp. 201–16, is a contemporary Catholic estimate of atrocities. Paul Johnson, *Modern Times: The World from the Twenties to the Eighties* (New York: Harper & Row, 1983), pp. 321–40, is a rare modern defense of Franco. The figures for casualties and outside assistance to the two sides are still controversial; I have used Thomas's—see pp. 926–27 and 974–85. Franco's postwar tribunals condemned almost 200,000 people to death, but about half the sentences were commuted to long terms of imprisonment, usually thirty years. For Soviet-run purges in Spain and the assertion of control over the police apparatus, see Robert Conquest, *The Great Terror: A Reassessment* (New York: Oxford University Press, 1990), pp. 409–12. George Orwell's *Homage to Catalonia,* vol. 6 of *Works* (London: Secker and Warburg, 1968), originally published in 1938, is a splendid evocation of a war fought mostly by frightened amateurs. He was in Barcelona recuperating from a wound during the Communist suppression of the non-Stalinist parties and narrowly escaped with his life because he had fought with a "Trotskyist" company; some of his friends did not get out. His commentaries on the Communists' actions, which are harsh and realistic, are published as appendices in the 1968 edition, pp. 189–244. He later took pains to make clear that he still supported the Republicans; see his essay "Reflections on the Spanish Civil War," in *My Country, Right or Left,* vol. 2 of Sonia Orwell and Ian Angus, eds., *The Collected Essays, Journalism, and Letters of George Orwell* (New York: Harcourt, Brace, 1968), pp. 47–73, originally published in 1942. For a review of recent evidence on Soviet control of the Republicans, and particularly the Brigades, see Ronald Radosh, "Spanish Illusions," *The New Republic,* January 30, 1995, pp. 40–45.

The "coldest-hearted" quote is in Thomas, *Spanish Civil War,* p. 514; Stalin's "ears" quote, p. 450; "alleged atrocities" quote is from a statement by 150 Protestant ministers in Guttmann, *American Neutrality,* p. 59. The "heads" quote is from G. M. Gaddis, "Communist Operations in Spain, 1931–1936," *Dublin Review,* October 1936, p. 232. The "God or anti-God" quote is from Archbishop John McNicholas, chairman of the NCWC Executive Board, among the most liberal of the American bishops: Flynn, *Roosevelt and Romanism,* p. 37. *L'Osservatore Romano,* the official Vatican paper, denied that Catholics could be neutral in the war, quoted in the *Brooklyn Tablet,* January 21, 1939. Flynn, *Roosevelt and Romanism,* p. 43, for Ickes quote. See "Civil War in Spain and in the United States," *Commonweal*, June 24, 1936, pp. 229–30, for the magazine's change in editorial policy. The Gallup poll is in James Hennesey, *American Catholics: A History of the Roman Catholic Community in the United States* (New York: Oxford University Press, 1981), p. 272. After-the-fact comments by Roosevelt suggest that he regretted the embargo, which historians like Valaik have taken as a measure of Catholic obstructive power. But Roosevelt was prone to such off-the-cuff comments, and the reasons *not* to get involved seem overwhelming. The war was already lost when the Lift the Spanish Embargo lobby reached a fever pitch; the isolationist mood in Congress was strong (see the overwhelming 1937 vote); and the countries Roosevelt was steering toward an alliance with were strongly opposed. Ickes and Eleanor Roosevelt stressed the weight of Catholic opposition, but Roosevelt did not, mentioning instead the objections of the allies, which by themselves would seem decisive. See the discussion in Flynn, *Roosevelt and Romanism*. For Franco's swearing in, see, e.g., the *Brooklyn Tablet*, August 19, 1939, and *Ave Maria*, August 26, 1939. The Pope's message is quoted in the *Tablet*, January 21, 1940. The *Life* editorial, dated January 3, 1938, and the hierarchy's reaction are in the NCWC Archives at Catholic University (hereafter NCWC).

For leftist fellow traveling, see David Caute, *The Fellow-Travellers: Intellectual Friends of Communism* (New Haven, Conn.: Yale University Press, 1988); Tony Judt, *Past Imperfect: French Intellectuals, 1944–1956* (Berkeley, Cal.: University of California Press, 1992); and William L. O'Neill, *A Better World: The Great Schism: Stalinism and the American Intellectuals* (New York: Simon & Schuster, 1982). The quotes on Bullitt are in O'Neill, pp. 88–89. For Ryan quote, see Francis A. Broderick, *Right Reverend New Dealer, John A. Ryan* (New York: Macmillan, 1963), p. 248. The quote on Spain is in Patrick Allitt, *Catholic Intellectuals and Conservative Politics in America, 1950–1985* (Ithaca, N.Y.: Cornell University Press, 1993), p. 144. The speaker is William F. Buckley Jr.'s sister, Patricia Bozell. Footnote on Laghi is from *Catholic New York*, April 20, 1995; quote is from Argentine bishop from *New York Times*, April 29, 1995. Pius XI on Church and State is from *Dilectissima Nobis*, June 3, 1933, in Claudia Carlen, *The Papal Encyclicals: 1740–1978* (Raleigh, N.C.: McGrath, 1981), 4:492.

For Catholics and fascism, see John P. Diggins, *Mussolini and Fascism: The View from America* (Princeton, N.J.: Princeton University Press, 1972), especially pp. 182–203; and Anthony J. Joes, *Mussolini* (New York: Watts, 1982), pp. 215–35. Denis Gwynn, "Italy and the Vatican," *Sign*, January 1936, pp. 332–34, and "Italy's Triumph and the Future," *Sign*, June 1936, pp. 668–70, are clear statements of the papacy's dependence on Mussolini for protection against Nazis and Communists, as is Owen Chadwick, "Weizsäcker, the Vatican, and the Jews of Rome," *Journal of Ecclesiastical History*, April 1977, pp. 179–99. Pius XI encyclical attacking Mussolini is *Non Abbiamo Bisogno*, June 29, 1931, in Carlen, *Encyclicals*, 4:445–58. The precipitating issue was Mussolini's insistence that the Catholic Action movement was a political party and should come under state control; the subtext was that the Catholic Action leaders were anti-Fascists. Pius denied both charges, which seems disingenuous. See also "Caesar Challenges Peter," *Commonweal*, June 10, 1931. The quote on Mussolini and Jews is in Diggins, p. 202. For the Taylor mission, see Flynn, *Roosevelt and Romanism*. It has long been rumored that Pius XI had started the preparation of an antiracist encyclical before he died, but the draft was apparently buried by the Jesuits and Pius XII. A purported draft, in French, surfaced in 1995; it was written by three Jesuits, including the American John La Farge, who was a strong anti-anti-Semite. The draft deplores anti-Semitism, but, awkwardly enough, contains hostile animadversions on the Jews that would today be considered anti-Semitic. While it is unlikely that such sentiments could have come from La Farge, they might well have from his French and German collaborators. (The French Jesuits had been tainted with anti-Semitism in the Dreyfus affair.) The tale of the "lost encyclical" may take years to clear up. See Frederick Brown, "The Hidden Encyclical," *The New Republic,* April 15, 1996, pp. 27–32.

For the repression of religion under Hitler, see J. S. Conway, *The Nazi Persecution of the Churches, 1933–1945* (New York: Basic Books, 1968); and Heinrich Waellermann, "Crucifixion on the Swastika," *Commonweal,* May 8, 1936, pp. 35–37. *Mit Brennender Sorge,* March 14, 1937, is in Carlen, *Encyclicals,* 4:525–35. The encyclical is quite strong, but still hopeful—"We have no greater desire than to see in Germany the restoration of a true peace between Church and State" (534)—but, to be fair, it predated events like *Kristallnacht.* The quote in the text is on p. 527. Einstein's comment is quoted in an *Ave Maria* editorial, September 9, 1939. For Archbishop Galen, besides Conway, *Nazi Persecution,* see Most Rev. Clemens Augustinus Count von Galen, "German Bishop Warns That Gestapo Menaces Reich," *Catholic Mind,* December 8, 1941, pp. 1–11, a reprint with commentary of Galen's pastoral letter with a list of signators, which appears to be a majority of the bishops. The Himmler incident is in Jean Lacouture, *Jesuits: A Multibiography* (Washington, D.C.: Counterpoint, 1995), p. 399, which is quite good on this period. Pius XII's inaugural encyclical is *Summi Pontificatus,* in Carlen, 5:5–22. For Orsenigo, see John Morley, *Vatican Diplomacy and the Jews During the Holocaust* (New York: Ktav, 1980), pp. 102–28, which makes him an almost pathetic figure. The Pope regularly bypassed Orsenigo to deal directly with the local bishops, and he had no influence with the Nazi regime. Morley's is an important book based on detailed examination of Vatican records and a country-by-country examination of the records of the various nuncios. Orsenigo is a character in Rolf Hochhuth's controversial *The Deputy* (New York: Grove, 1964), which portrays him consistently with Morley's researches. The "peacable harmony" quote is in Chadwick, "Weizsäcker," pp. 181–82. The encyclical against communism is *Divini Redemptoris,* March 19, 1937, Carlen, 4:537–53; the quote in the text is on p. 541. Taylor's assistant's (Harold Tittman) quote is in Flynn, p. 162, and Roosevelt quote on churches, p. 164.

The Piłsudski quote is from Hugh Thomas, *Armed Truce: The Beginnings of the Cold War: 1945–1946* (New York: Atheneum, 1987), p. 240. Spellman kept a detailed aide-mémoire on his 1943 meeting with Roosevelt that is reproduced in Robert I. Gannon, *The Cardinal Spellman Story* (Garden City, N.Y.: Doubleday, 1962), pp. 221–224. He recorded his reactions in his diary, which has, unfortunately, been closed to researchers—see Flynn, pp. 217–18. For the 1939 Russian invasion of Poland, see George F. Kennan, *Memoirs, 1925–1950* (Boston: Atlantic/Little, Brown, 1967), pp. 200–203. Morley, *Vatican Diplomacy,* devotes a chapter to the record of the Church in each of the major European countries. In addition, for the Slovak regime, see Yeshayahu Jelinek, "The Vatican, the Catholic Church, the Catholics, and the Persecution of the Jews During World War II: The Case of Slovakia," in Bela Vago and George L. Moss, eds., *Jews and Non-Jews in Eastern Europe, 1918–1945* (New York: Wiley, 1974); and Livia Rotkirchen, "Vatican Policy and the 'Jewish Problem' in 'Independent' Slovakia (1939–1945)," in *Yad Vashem Studies,* vol. 6 (Jerusalem: Yad Vashem Remembrance Authority, 1967), pp. 27–53. For clouds on Stepinac's record, see *The Economist,* October 26, 1946 (NCWC clipping), and Morley chapter on Croatia. For the Russian "liberation" of Poland, from British Foreign Office notes, see Thomas, *Armed Truce,* pp. 240–42.

For the Vatican's record in the Holocaust, I basically follow the analysis in Morley, *Vatican Diplomacy;* see especially pp. 195–207, which carefully recount all reasonable extenuating circumstances. It is much harder to fault the Vatican on specific cases than on a general accommodationist attitude in the early years of Hitler's rise, one that created an environment in which later protests were useless. For the Pope's reactions to the deportation of Jews from Rome, see Chadwick, "Weizsäcker," a careful side-by-side analysis by a non-Catholic scholar of Nazi records, Vatican records, and Weizsäcker's private papers; it concludes that the most accommodationist comments by the Pope were manufactured by Weizsäcker. Vatican diplomacy, with Weizsäcker's connivance, did halt the German roundup, but an initial trainload containing more than 1000 Jews destined for Auschwitz went out, and the Vatican did not try to stop it, presumably on the calculation that further protests would only incite further deportations (which was arguably correct). All but fourteen of the deported Jews died. Several thousand Jews were hidden in Roman convents and monasteries, and the Vatican was desperately trying to head off a search of those institutions. The search was announced but called off.

For the neglect of the Holocaust by almost all Americans of every religious and ethnic stripe, see David S. Wyman, *The Abandonment of the Jews: America and the Holocaust, 1941–1945* (New York: Pantheon, 1984), especially pp. 311–30, and Andre Kuczewski, "From Political Expediency to Moral Neglect: The United States and the Religio-Ethnic Experience," *American Jewish Archives* 37, no. 2 (1985): 309–21. Helen Iwolsky, "Rebuilding in France," *Commonweal,* July 11, 1941, pp. 6–8, a paean to the recovery of religion in Vichy France, is an embarrassing example of softness on nazism in a generally enlightened Catholic journal. See also Alexander Ramati, *While the Pope Kept Silent: Assisi and the Nazi Occupation* (London: Allen & Unwin, 1978), an "as told to" autobiography of an Italian priest who saved a considerable number of Jews, which is just a sample of a vast literature. The "enlightened" quote and the Maglione quote are in Morley, p. 185 and p. 208.

For what are, in effect, lawyers' briefs defending the Pope and Vatican policy, see J. Derek Holmes, *Pius XII, Hitler, and the Jews* (London: Catholic Truth Society, 1982); Michael O'Carroll, *Pius XII: Greatness Dishonored, A Documentary Study* (Dublin: Laetare Press, 1980), which is very strongly argued; and *Pius XII and the Holocaust: a Reader* (Milwaukee, WI: Catholic League for Religious and Civil Rights, 1988). The last includes the pamphlet, *Pius XII's Defense of Jews and Others* by Fr. Robert A. Graham, who was the editor of the Vatican's diplomatic correspondence during World War II. It also includes editorials from the *New York Times,* expressly praising the Pope's statements in 1941 and 1942. Additional details are in Robert G. Weisbrod and Wallace P. Sillanpoa, *The Chief Rabbi, The Pope, And The Holocaust: An Era in Vatican-Jewish Relations* (New Brunswick, NJ: Transaction Publishers, 1992). They cast cold water on the story that the erstwhile Chief Rabbi of Rome converted because of Pius's stance against the Nazis. Suffice it to say that the issue is not a black-and-white one, and that a historical consensus is unlikely.

Commonweal (see, e.g., Waldemar Gurian, "The Soviet Union—Apocalyptic Nightmare or Political Reality," June 29, 1945, and editorials on October 26 and November 9, 1945, urging concessions to Stalin aimed at "drawing Russia into a policy of wholehearted international collaboration") was one of the very few Catholic journals to follow a conventionally liberal line on the Soviet Union. William Henry Chamberlin, "The Treason of Some Intellectuals," *Sign,* March 1948, pp. 17–19, is more typical Catholic commentary. Frank, "Prelude to Cold War," is a useful review. For the interplay between the Catholic hierarchy, the Vatican, and the Roosevelt administration, see Flynn, *Roosevelt and Romanism,* and especially Gerald P. Fogarty, *The Vatican and the American Hierarchy* (Stuttgart: Heirsemann, 1982), pp. 271–345, for a detailed discussion. For postwar Soviet-American relations, see, e.g., John Lewis Gaddis, *The United States and the Origins of the Cold War: 1941–1947* (New York: Columbia University Press, 1972), especially pp. 52–56 for Catholic role; Thomas, *Armed Truce,* especially pp. 239–54 on Poland (Roosevelt was quite open with Stalin and Churchill about his Polish vote problem); and Melvyn P. Leffler, *A Preponderance of Power: National Security, the Truman Administration, and the Cold War* (Stanford, Cal.: Stanford University Press, 1992). The Cold War chronology here follows that in my *Iron Destinies, Lost Opportunities: The Postwar Arms Race* (New York: Harper & Row, 1988), pp. 23–31; and see extensive sources cited therein. The *Mission to Moscow* story is in the introduction to the published movie script, David Culbert, ed., *Mission to Moscow* (Madison, Wis.: University of Wisconsin Press, 1980). The once prevailing American academic view that tended to exonerate Stalin for responsibility for the Cold War, at least in its extreme versions, has been discredited, even in the Soviet Union (perhaps more thoroughly in the Soviet Union).

For quotes in this section: "lesser of" and Sheen's "Communism is," Gaddis, *Origins of Cold War,* p. 53; Gillis's "[W]hen the," *Brooklyn Tablet,* September 16, 1939; pro-Soviet quotes: "a hell of," "perhaps the," "Marxian," "A child," Gaddis, pp. 33–38; "beatification" is from Flynn, *Roosevelt and Romanism,* p. 169; "free and unfettered" Gaddis, p. 163; "how many" letter of Florence Cohalan, a well-known New York priest-historian, in *Commonweal,* August 10, 1945; "long telegram" quotes are from the text in Thomas H. Etzold and John Lewis Gaddis, *Containment: Documents in American Policy and Strategy, 1945–1950* (New York: Columbia University Press, 1978), pp. 50–63, and Churchill's Fulton quote is in Gaddis, p. 308. Moynihan's "To be" is from Nathan Glazer and Daniel P. Moynihan, *Beyond the Melting Pot,* 2d ed. (Cambridge, Mass.: MIT Press, 1970), p. 271.

Except as noted, all of the details for Catholic-government anti-Communist efforts are from the NCWC archives. Both the friendly attitude toward the Church and most of the specific incidents, such as the assistance with paper and printing presses, were confirmed in an interview with Paul Nitze. Nitze briefed Myron Taylor for Truman and had a number of meetings with Vatican officials, primarily on Eastern European questions. See also James E. Miller, "Taking Off the Gloves: The United States and the Italian Elections of 1948," *Diplomatic History,* Winter 1983, pp. 35–55. The American Church also paid an annual stipend to the State Department for many years for the support of Cardinal Josef Mindszenty in the American embassy in Budapest. For the claim that the Church initiated American involvement with Vietnam, see, e.g., George McT. Kahin, *Intervention: How America Became Involved in Vietnam* (New York: Knopf, 1986), p. 79, considered a definitive history; the NCWC incident happened several years earlier than those pinpointed by Kahin. For Walsh and McCarthy, see Donald J. Crosby, *God, Church and Flag: Senator Joseph McCarthy and the Catholic Church, 1950–1957* (Chapel Hill, N.C.: University of North Carolina Press, 1978), pp. 47–52. For Cronin background, see Joshua B. Freeman and Steve Rosswurn, "The Education of an Anticom-

munist: Father John F. Cronin and the Baltimore Labor Movement," *Labor History,*
Spring 1992, pp. 217–47. Various versions of Cronin's pamphlets are at NCWC—the
U.S. Chamber of Commerce sales included multiple versions—and the Fey quote is
from the January 3, 1945, installment, "Catholicism Fights Communism" in Harold A.
Fey, "Can Catholicism Win America?," *Christian Century* (eight-part series), November 29, 1944–January 17, 1945.

For Cronin and Nixon, there is a detailed account in Roger Morris, *Richard Milhous Nixon: The Rise of an American Politician* (New York: Henry Holt, 1990), pp.
350–53, 391–93. Morris makes Cronin almost a Nixon Svengali, which seems overdone,
and reports that Cronin allowed the FBI to bug his mediation efforts with Communist
union officials in Baltimore. Morris is disgusted with the Hiss case, which clearly colors
his rhetoric. Garry Wills, *Nixon Agonistes: The Crisis of the Self-Made Man* (New York:
New American Library, 1970), pp. 25–30, has an interview with Cronin on his role in the
Hiss case. Allen Weinstein, *Perjury: The Hiss-Chambers Case* (New York: Knopf, 1978),
highly unfavorable to Hiss, is usually taken as the last word on the Hiss case. Morris
shows additional evidential problems in the perjury trial that go more to the procedural
adequacy of the trial than to the question of what Hiss actually did. Curt Gentry,
J. Edgar Hoover: The Man and His Secrets (New York: Norton, 1991), p. 471, suggests
that Cronin may have fed Nixon FBI reports on Kennedy's personal life during the 1960
campaign, which seems inconsistent with letter (April 19, 1960, NCWC) from Cronin to
his superiors that he had decided not to participate in the 1960 campaign because he
feared Nixon would use him to mask a subtle anti-Catholic attack on Kennedy—"one
can hardly be associated with a man for thirteen years without getting some intuitive
sense of his method of working." The letter quoted in the footnote is from Cronin to
William Reuben, a scholarly researcher, June 24, 1974 (Cronin Papers, Notre Dame
Archives). The letter says that the bishops wouldn't permit his participation in the 1960
campaign. His 1960 letter, however, suggests only that they were uncomfortable and that
he made the decision himself. Cronin also says in the Reuben letter that Nixon went into
"a major depression" in early 1960. "I am convinced that in fact he was afraid of the presidency in 1960 and probably subconsciously threw it away."

Giniger comment is from an interview; Goodpaster from a personal communication; Avery Dulles and Nitze "pushing" from interviews. Two recent biographies of
Hoover, Richard Gid Powers, *Secrecy and Power: The Life of J. Edgar Hoover* (New
York: Free Press, 1987), and Gentry, *J. Edgar Hoover,* both mention that Hoover and
Spellman were friends, but otherwise hardly mention Spellman again. Hoover's Spellman file (on the Cardinal's alleged homosexuality) and Eisenhower report are from
Gentry, p. 436. The FBI meeting is in John Cooney, *The American Pope: The Life
and Times of Francis Cardinal Spellman* (New York: Times Books, 1984), pp. 136–38, a
gossipy and probably unreliable source. See David Caute, *The Great Fear: The Anti-
Communist Purge Under Truman and Eisenhower* (New York: Simon & Schuster,
1978), pp. 434, 443, for alleged Spellman role in school purges; however, the allegations
are speculations by discharged teachers. Caute's book is fairly hostile to Catholics,
whom he describes as "not so much poets, scholars, scientists, and artists as security officers, immigration officers, policemen, customs officers and prison wardens"; see especially pp. 108–10. Shanker comment is from an interview, and he stressed that he
considers himself well informed on the question. Neither of the two standard sources on
the school purges—Robert W. Iverson, *The Communists and the Schools* (New York:

Harcourt, Brace, 1959); or Diane Ravitch, *The Troubled Crusade: American Education, 1945–1980* (New York: Basic Books, 1983)—mentions a Catholic role. For the welfare purges: I was the successor to the New York welfare director who ran the purge, and I was often regaled with purge stories, a cherished topic among the old-timers. Even the most elaborately conspiratorial versions never mentioned a Catholic role, although Caute, *Great Fear,* suggests otherwise at pp. 342–44. "The masses" quote is from Crosby, *God, Church, and Flag,* p. 74.

The literature on McCarthy is immense. I find Richard M. Fried, *Nightmare in Red: The McCarthy Era in Perspective* (New York: Oxford University Press, 1990), an unusually well balanced account. The basic McCarthy defense, William F. Buckley Jr. and L. Brent Bozell, *McCarthy and His Enemies: The Record and Its Meaning* (Chicago: Henry Regnery, 1954), freely admits that the senator was rarely inhibited by the truth. Crosby, *God, Church, and Flag,* is fundamental for Catholic involvement. Both Fried and Crosby have good accounts of the great variety of sociological and other explanations for McCarthyism.

Esther Yolles Feldblum, *The American Catholic Press and the Jewish State: 1917–1959* (New York: Ktav, 1977), is an excellent—and surprisingly sympathetic to Catholics—account of Catholic-Jewish relations. Her comment that Scanlan viewed himself as a "one-man Anti-Defamation League" (p. 139) for Irish Catholics seems exactly right. See also Gershon Greenberg, "American Catholics During the Holocaust," *Journal of American Jewish History,* September 1983, pp. 175–201. Patrick J. McNamara, "A Study of the Editorial Policy of the *Brooklyn Tablet* Under Patrick F. Scanlan" (master's thesis, St. John's University, 1994), is a thoroughly researched account of an important Catholic polemicist; see especially pp. 74–84 for Scanlan's anti-Semitism and the Christian Front. Also see Alden V. Brown, *The Tablet: the First Seventy-five Years,* (Brooklyn: Tablet Publishing, 1983), a commemorative book. The DP account follows Haim Genizi, *America's Fair Share: The Admission and Resettlement of Displaced Persons, 1945–1952* (Detroit: Wayne State University Press, 1993), pp. 66–111, which is based primarily on Jewish sources. An editorial, "What Price Israel?," in *Sign,* February 1954, accuses Zionists of scuttling DP legislation.

The anti-Zionist encyclicals are *Auspicia Quaedam* (May 1, 1948); *In Multiplicibus Curis* (October 24, 1948); and *Redemptoris Nostri Cruciatus* (April 15, 1949), all in Carlen, *Encyclicals,* 5:157–65. The American apostolic delegate, Amleto Cicognani, also made strong anti-Zionist representations to Myron Taylor—"Catholics the world over would be aroused" (Feldblum, *American Catholic Press,* p. 62). *Sign,* a large-circulation magazine, was so strongly anti-Zionist that it probably looked anti-Semitic as well. See, e.g., editorial "Israel and the Arabs," January 1956. The school aid dispute is in Ravitch, *Troubled Crusade,* pp. 29–41. The exchanges between Spellman and Mrs. Roosevelt are quoted extensively in Gannon, *Cardinal Spellman,* pp. 314–20. For the state of the constitutional issues at the time, see Robert F. Drinan, *Religion, the Courts, and Public Policy* (New York: McGraw-Hill, 1963), pp. 170–79.

For the quotes in this section: "Fr. Coughlin" and "while the press," Feldblum, *American Catholic Press,* pp. 46, 45; "This is all," *Ave Maria,* September 9, 1939; the *Tablet* cartoon is from issue of January 14, 1939; "In the matter," editorial, "The Missing Liberals," *Sign,* March 1953; Truman's "anti-Semitic" is from *The New York Times,* July 22, 1948; "all rights" is from *Redemptoris,* Carlen, 5:164; and "innocence" is in O'Neill, *Better World,* p. 313. Spellman's "effrontery" and "overextension" are in Gannon, *Car-*

dinal Spellman, p. 357. The beating-up story came secondhand through David Tracy from one of his University of Chicago colleagues.

10. *The Breakdown of the Catholic Culture*

Details of the Dodgers and Giants moves are from *The New York Times.* For the postwar exodus to the suburbs, see Kenneth T. Jackson, *Crabgrass Frontier: The Suburbanization of the United States* (New York: Oxford University Press, 1985); Anthony Downs, *Opening Up the Suburbs: An Urban Strategy for America* (New Haven, Conn.: Yale University Press, 1973); and Andrew M. Greeley, *The Church and the Suburbs,* rev. ed. (New York: Paulist Press, 1963). John Keats, *The Crack in the Picture Window* (Boston: Houghton Mifflin, 1956), is a prototype of intellectual screeds against the suburbs. For the postwar higher education boom, see Richard M. Freeland, *Academia's Golden Age: Universities in Massachusetts, 1945–1970* (New York: Oxford University Press, 1992), pp. 70–119, supplemented by the Bureau of the Census, *Statistical Abstract of the United States* for the appropriate years. The professor-to-clergy ratios are from Lewis Perry, *Intellectual Life in America: A History* (Chicago: University of Chicago Press, 1989), p. 435. The range of possible calculations for Catholics is in Theodore H. White, *The Making of the President, 1960* (New York: Atheneum, 1961), pp. 237–43. The 1945 socioeconomic status of Catholics is from Liston Pope, "Religion and Class Structure," *Annals of the American Academy of Political and Social Science,* March 1948, pp. 84–91. These estimates are widely quoted—David Caute used them in his anti-McCarthyite strictures on Catholics, for instance. An earlier study by the same organization had placed Catholics rather higher on the scale; see Pope. For the data on Catholic improvement, see Andrew M. Greeley, William C. McReady, and Kathleen C. Court, *Catholic Schools in a Declining Church* (Kansas City, Kan.: Sheed & Ward, 1976), a fundamental contribution to religious and ethnic demography.

For the development of the Church in postwar Los Angeles, I am indebted to Msgr. Francis J. Weber, the archdiocesan archivist. Msgr. Weber knew Cardinal McIntyre well and was the prime source on his personality and style. Msgr. Weber's *Century of Fulfillment: The Roman Catholic Church in Southern California, 1840–1947* (Mission Hills, Cal.: The Archival Center, 1990) is the most complete history of the local church, and his *Past Is Prologue: Some Historical Reflections, 1961–1991* (Mission Hills, Cal.: St. Francis Historical Society, 1992) contains sketches of Cantwell, McIntyre, and diocesan statistical growth, pp. 100–109, 110–12, 717–20. Mike Davis, *City of Quartz: Excavating the Future in Los Angeles* (New York: Verso, 1990), is a lively local history, from a decidedly left-wing perspective, with a chapter on the recent development of the Church. The prologue to Roger Morris's *Richard Milhous Nixon: The Rise of an American Politician* (New York: Henry Holt, 1990) also contains a superb short history of the region. My appreciation to Fr. Gregory Coiro and the *Los Angeles Tidings* staff for giving me access to bound volumes of back issues. Statistical growth of the diocese under McIntyre is from the issue of January 23, 1970. The quoted *Tidings* articles are "Kremlin Victory," April 20, 1951; "ex-Marine Captain," January 5, 1951; and "unqualified assertion," January 19, 1951. The Immaculate Heart story is from a taped lecture by Pat Reif and Margaret Rose Welch entitled "The IHM and IHCC Story" (private recording), supplemented by an interview with Reif, who lent me the tape. For DuBay, see John Leo, "The DuBay Case"

Commonweal, July 10, 1964, pp. 477–82. The "inhuman" quote is in Davis, *City of Quartz,* p. 333.

The accounts of the Randall's Island festival are from *The New York Times* and the diocesan *Catholic News.* For Robert E. Lucey, see Saul E. Bronder, *Social Justice and Church Authority: The Public Life of Archbishop Robert E. Lucey* (Philadelphia: Temple University Press, 1982); and Stephen A. Privett, *The U.S. Catholic Church and Its Hispanic Members: The Pastoral Vision of Archbishop Robert E. Lucey* (San Antonio: Trinity University Press, 1988). The activities of the Bishops' Committee on the Spanish-Speaking are based primarily on the extensive committee archive in the Robert E. Lucey Papers at the Notre Dame University Archives. And see Peter Skerry, *Mexican Americans: The Ambivalent Minority* (Cambridge, Mass.: Harvard University Press, 1993), pp. 33–58 and 191–215, for San Antonio, Alinsky-style organizing among Mexican Americans, and the different attitudes of Church officials in San Antonio and Los Angeles.

The narrative of New York's response to Puerto Rican immigration relies primarily on an interview with Msgr. Robert Stern, who headed the diocese's Hispanic affairs office from 1969 to 1973 and who was active in the Puerto Rican ministry from its earliest days, and on his "Evolution of the Hispanic Ministry in the New York Archdiocese," in Ruth Doyle and Olga Scarpetta, eds., *Hispanics in New York: Religious, Cultural, and Social Experiences* (New York: Archdiocese of New York, Office of Pastoral Research and Planning, 1982, 1989), 2:305–38. Fr. Joseph Fitzpatrick was also a source for this book, on Jesuit labor schools, but he died before we began in-depth discussion of Puerto Rican issues. He wrote dozens of scholarly articles on New York's Puerto Ricans, the findings of which are collected in his *Puerto Rican Americans: The Meaning of the Migration to the Mainland* (Englewood Cliffs, N.J.: Prentice-Hall, 1971). Msgr. George Kelly provided me with a copy of his 1953 paper from his personal files—George A. Kelly, "Catholic Survey of the Puerto Rican Population in the Archdiocese of New York" (New York, 1953). The statistical data are drawn from Fitzpatrick and from Dorothy Dohen, "Marriage, Family, and Fertility Patterns Among Puerto Ricans," in Doyle and Scarpetta, *Hispanics in New York,* 2:187–212.

Ana Maria Diaz-Stevens, *Oxcart Catholicism on Fifth Avenue: The Impact of the Puerto Rican Migration upon the Archdiocese of New York* (Notre Dame, Ind.: Notre Dame University Press, 1992), is highly critical of the diocese's efforts along the lines suggested in the chapter. However, Diaz-Stevens, who worked in the diocesan office, has kind words for Fitzpatrick, Fox, and Stern. Her book suffers from an excess of theoretical sociological apparatus. And see Orlando O. Espin, "Popular Catholicism Among Latinos," in Jay P. Dolan and Allan Figueroa Deck, *Hispanic Catholic Culture in the U.S.: Issues and Concerns* (Notre Dame, Ind.: University of Notre Dame Press, 1994), pp. 308–59. Espin argues that Latino popular Catholicism is rooted in a pre-Tridentine "Iberian" matrix of practices brought to the Americas by Spanish explorers. The argument would be more convincing if he distinguished Latino popular religion from the virtually identical forms of peasant Catholicism in Italy, France, and many other countries that were never conquered by Spain. The argument seems to be generally accepted, however, among commentators on American Hispanic Catholicism. The "different" quote is Stern's (interview). Herman Badillo's criticisms are from an interview. The Cardinal's hospital problems are from *The New York Times* and the diocesan *Catholic News.*

For Catholic intellectualism, see John Tracy Ellis, "American Catholics and the Intellectual Life," *Thought,* Autumn 1955, pp. 353–86; Gustave Weigel, "American Catholic Intellectualism—A Theologian's Reflections," *Review of Politics,* July 1957, pp. 275–307; Thomas F. O'Dea, *American Catholic Dilemma: An Inquiry into Intellectual Life* (New York: Sheed & Ward, 1958); Louis G. Martin, "Intellectual Life at the Parish Level," *America,* August 27, 1955, pp. 507–9; Thomas Molnar, "The Plight of the Intellectual," *Commonweal,* August 19, 1955, pp. 487–89; and William A. Osborne, "Catholic Education for What?," *Commonweal,* September 23, 1955, among many others. The "every second" quote is from Joseph A. Breig, "Preparing Youth for Intellectual Leadership," *America,* September 3, 1955, p. 530. The *Atlantic* quote is from Harry Sylvester, "Problems of the Catholic Writer," *Atlantic Monthly,* January 1948, p. 109. O'Dea's summary is from pp. 155–60, 39; "prevent the student," Weigel, p. 304; for "honorable," "singularly," "feel compunction," "[e]very one," and "The Irish," Ellis, "American Catholics," pp. 381, 372, 377, 368, and 369. Ellis's data on Catholic underrepresentation in Congress is at first surprising, given the Irish prominence in politics. Italians and Germans, however, were much less oriented toward political careers than the Irish, although the Poles—e.g., in Chicago—were well represented. The data may also reflect the rural skew of Congressional district apportionment in the 1950s and the long tenure of many congressmen.

For earlier debate, see George N. Shuster, "Have We Any Scholars?," *America,* August 15, 1925, pp. 418–19; for responses, see W. O. West, "And Have We No Scholars?," *America,* September 12, 1925, pp. 511–12, and R. R. MacGregor, "The Catholic Lay Professor," *America,* September 12, 1925, p. 513. For Greeley study, see Greeley, McReady, and Court, *Catholic Schools,* which builds on an earlier study by Greeley and Peter H. Rossi, *The Education of Catholic Americans* (Chicago: Aldine, 1966); also Stephen Steinberg, *The Academic Melting Pot: Catholics and Jews in American Higher Education* (New York: McGraw-Hill, 1974). The Murray article is John Courtney Murray, "The Roman Catholic Church," *Annals of the American Academy of Political and Social Science,* March 1948, pp. 36–42. For "smart," see Weigel, "American Catholic Intellectualism," p. 299. For the number of professors, see Perry, *Intellectual Life,* p. 435.

For Jesuit higher education, see Freeland, *Academia's Golden Age,* and Paul A. Fitzgerald, *The Governance of Jesuit Colleges in the United States, 1920–1970* (Notre Dame, Ind.: Notre Dame University Press, 1984), which is a useful chronology, although preoccupied with organizational details. Through the courtesy of Freeland, I had access to extensive archival material, maintained at Boston College, of the Jesuit Education Association, the coordinating body for American Jesuit colleges and universities (hereafter JEA), as well as transcripts of his extensive interviews with Fr. Michael Walsh, one of the leading figures in the postwar expansion and upgrading of Jesuit colleges. I also interviewed Fr. Robert Harvanek, a spokesman for the antiexpansion view. The caliber of the internal Jesuit debates is very high, combining intelligence, frankness, and civility to a remarkable degree. Although the Jesuit debates have a peculiarly Jesuit slant, the larger issues all track closely to debates in the larger Catholic community; see, for example, Andrew M. Greeley, *Religion and Career* (New York: Sheed & Ward, 1963), which is primarily a study of differences between Catholics and non-Catholics on campus; Theodore M. Hesburgh, "The Work of Mediation," *Commonweal,* October 6, 1961, pp. 34–35; and the summary of research findings on student attitudes on Catholic and non-Catholic campuses in Edward Wakins and Joseph F. Scheuer, *The De-Romanization of the American Catholic Church* (New York: Macmillan, 1966), pp. 76–93. JEA, "The Society of Jesus and Higher Education in America: Proceedings of the Woodstock Institute" (October 1964), pp. 37–59, also contains a good summary of current research.

There are suggestions in the JEA material that the Ford Foundation program for improving faculty pay was extremely helpful. The grants were administered on a non-sectarian basis, but Jesuit and other religious institutions may have done somewhat better than their lay counterparts, since the value of religious faculty's "contributed services" was counted in the base formula. And since religious faculty were not actually paid their share of the salary increase, it could be used for other faculty-related purposes. Gannon was on the Ford Foundation advisory committee overseeing the grants. The religious advantage diminished to the degree that lay faculty made up an increasing share of the teaching staffs. See Ford Foundation, *The Pay of Professors: A Report on the Ford Foundation Grants for College-Teacher Salaries* (New York, February 1962). My appreciation to Jonathan Green, a Ford Foundation archivist, for pulling together material on this program.

Weigel quotes are in Weigel, "American Catholic Intellectualism," p. 286. Jesuit numbers are from JEA, "A Study of Jesuit Education" (August 1958). Sheehy letter to Parsons is dated June 18, 1932, and is included along with several others as an appendix to JEA, "Report of the Commission on Higher Education of the American Assistancy of the Society of Jesus" (1931–1932) (this report actually was the impetus for creating the JEA to replace a much weaker existing coordinating body). The quotes "haphazard," "often find" "woefully undertrained," and "In our" are all from this 1931–1932 report, pp. 37, 59, 65, 67–68. Walsh gauntlet story is from interview. Walsh's "intellectuals" and "with the spunk" quotes and Jesuit "students find" quote are from JEA, "Final Report of the Workshop on the Role of Philosophy and Theology as Academic Disciplines and Their Integration with the Moral, Religious, and Spiritual Life of the Jesuit College Student" (August 1962), vol. 5, pp. 110, 112–13, 439. Walsh and Harvanek 1964 quotes are from JEA, "Society of Jesus and Higher Education," pp. 28, 61. The nun's quote is in Wakins and Scheuer, *De-Romanization,* p. 83. The Land O'Lakes quote is in Jay P. Dolan, *The American Catholic Experience: A History from Colonial Times to the Present* (New York: Doubleday, 1985). Wesleyan review of Boston College is in Freeland, *Academia's Golden Age,* p. 259.

Robert Hassenger, "The Structure of Catholic Higher Education," in Philip Gleason, ed., *Contemporary Catholicism in the United States* (Notre Dame, Ind.: Notre Dame Press, 1969), pp. 295–323 is a careful summary of the current research, and further confirms the generational change among Catholics. (For example, the dogmatism and authoritarianism sometimes found on Catholic campuses appears to relate fairly precisely to the recency of family immigration and the home environment. More assimilated and less dogmatic Catholic students were less likely to be on the Catholic campus.) The "correct some" quote is from O'Dea, *American Catholic Dilemma,* pp. 79–80. There is as yet no good Murray biography. The quote "independent of" is from Vatican II's "Pastoral constitution on the church in the world of today," p. 1124, vol. 2, of Norman B. Tanner, ed., *Decrees of the Ecumenical Councils* (London and Washington: Sheed & Ward/Georgetown University Press, 1990). For the relevant debates, see Francis X. Murphy [Xavier Rynne, pseud.], *Vatican Council II* (New York: Farrar, Straus & Giroux, 1968), pp. 454–66. Callahan is from an interview.

Philip Gleason's "The Crisis of Americanization," in Gleason, *Contemporary Catholicism*, pp. 3–31, is an excellent discussion of the revived "Americanization" impulse. John Ireland's reputation was substantially refurbished during this period; see Robert D. Cross, *The Emergence of Liberal Catholicism in America* (Chicago: Quadrangle, 1968). Daniel J. Callahan, ed., *Generation of the Third Eye* (New York: Sheed & Ward, 1965), is a collection of personal histories of young intellectual Catholics worried about the Church's relevance to modern America. For Martin Marty, see his *The New Shape of American Religion* (New York: Harper, 1959), and the discussion on pp. 73–75. Krol's comment on vocations is from the *Philadelphia Evening Bulletin,* January 2, 1965. The Levittown quote is in Herbert J. Gans, *The Levittowners: Ways of Life and Politics in a New Suburban Community* (New York: Pantheon, 1967), p. 84, and see pp. 166–69 for social heterogeneity. A discussion of the crumbling of the Church's semiofficial separatism after the war is in Cross, *Emergence,* pp. 207–24, with extensive citations to contemporary Catholic periodicals, and includes the Feeney and Gillis-versus-*America* incidents; and see Joseph C. Fenton, "Extra Ecclesiam Nulla Salus," *American Ecclesiastical Review,* April 1944, pp. 300–306, for the traditional view. The "apathetic" quote in Cross, p. 214. For Catholic Levittowners, see Gans, pp. 68–85. Greeley's book is *The Church and the Suburbs.* The parody is in Wakins and Scheuer, *De-Romanization,* p. 270.

The Spellman quotes and the rhetorical transformation are from Dorothy Dohen, *Nationalism and American Catholicism* (New York: Oxford University Press, 1968), pp. 121–27. John Cogley, ed., *Catholicism in America: A Series from Commonweal* (New York: Harcourt, Brace, 1954), is a conveniently available collection. I was a bit put off by an occasional "poor white trash" view of ordinary Catholics; there was also a tendency to identify correct religion with the Adlai Stevenson wing of the Democratic Party. Callahan remembers the political spin, but not the haughtiness. William Pfaff, who was the foreign affairs specialist, also provided an extended letter on his experiences. The "authentic defender" quote is from William L. Doty, *Trends and Counter-Trends Among American Catholics* (St. Louis: Herder, 1962), p. 234. Doty was not a mossback but a progressive priest who had been active in the labor movement. Daniel J. Callahan, Heiko A. Oberman, and Daniel J. O'Hanlon, eds., *Christianity Divided: Protestant and Roman Catholic Theological Issues* (New York: Sheed & Ward, 1961), contains essays from both Protestant and Catholic theologians, including the Europeans mentioned in the text. The gap between the theological sensibilities and issues in the Callahan collection and that of, say, the Fenton article cited above is measured in centuries.

For Hillenbrand, I used the Hillenbrand papers in the Notre Dame Archives. Patty Crowley's oral history of the Christian Family Movement (CFM) also has extensive comments on Hillenbrand. He was clearly a seminal figure in their movement, but "the Monsignor" clearly comes across as a dictatorial figure who disapproved of some of the directions she and her husband charted for the movement. See Patricia Crowley interviewed by Robert Burns, "Oral History of American Catholicism" in CFM Archive, University of Notre Dame. For CFM itself, see John R. Maiola, William V. D'Antonio, and William T. Liu, *The Christian Family Movement: A Profile,* 4 vols. (Notre Dame, Ind.: Department of Sociology and Anthropology, University of Notre Dame, 1968–1970), a cooperative study contracted by CFM to the Notre Dame sociology department, in the CFM archives at Notre Dame. Hillenbrand's favorite project may have been the Young Christian Workers' Movement, directly modeled after Cardjin, but it was a failure. See Robert Carroll, John Hill, Laurence Kelly, and Peter Rodriguez, "City Chaplains" (First Through Third Progress Reports on the Young Christian Workers' Movement) (Archdiocese of Chicago, 1960–1963). For a concise summary of Hillenbrand's career and influence, see Stephen M. Avella, *This Confident Church: Catholic Leadership and Life in Chicago, 1940–1965* (Notre Dame, Ind.: Notre Dame University Press, 1992), pp. 151–86.

Thomas Merton, *The Hidden Ground of Love: Letters,* ed. William H. Shannon (New York: Farrar, Straus & Giroux, 1985), is an excellent introduction to the range of Merton's thought and contacts. For the links between Dorothy Day and other progressive Catholic movements, including a discussion of Merton, see James Terence Fisher, *The Catholic Counterculture in America: 1933–1962* (Chapel Hill, N.C.: University of North Carolina Press, 1989). For the history of the American liturgical movement, see Paul B. Marx, *Virgil Michel and the Liturgical Movement* (Collegeville, Minn.: The Liturgical Press, 1957). See Doty, *Trends,* pp. 94–101, for skepticism about liturgical enthusiasts. The Callahan quote is from his *The Mind of the Catholic Layman* (New York: Scribner's, 1963), p. 188. For Kennedy's election, see White, *Making of the President;* and for Peale and Niebuhr, see Francis J. Lally, *The Catholic Church in a Changing America* (Boston: Little, Brown, 1962), pp. 62–64.

PART III. CRISIS

11. *Prelude: In the Dark Valley*

The events in San Francisco were extensively covered in the *San Francisco Examiner,* the *San Francisco Weekly,* and the *National Catholic Reporter.* I interviewed Robert S. Bryan and a number of the members of his parish committee, attended the meeting described in the chapter, and reviewed legal materials and videotapes of the church closing and related events provided by Bryan. I also interviewed Elizabeth Fernandez and Stephanie Salter of the *Examiner* team, and for the chancery, Deacons Bill Mitchell and Leon Kortenkamp, Sr. Mary B. Flaherty, Fr. Harry Schlitt, and later Archbishop John R. Quinn. (The Quinn interview focused on broader questions of Church policy and discussed the events described only in terms of media pressures on the Church.) The archdiocese provided its planning materials, "A Pastoral Plan for the Archdiocese of San Francisco" (November 1993) and "A Journey of Hope Toward the Third Millennium (December 1994). For the history of the Church in San Francisco, see R. A. Burchell, *The San Francisco Irish: 1848–1880* (Berkeley, Cal.: University of California Press, 1980); and Dennis Clark, *Hibernia America: The Irish and Regional Cultures* (Westport, Conn.: Greenwood Press, 1986). For Quinn's success as a National Conference of Catholic Bishops chairman, see Thomas J. Reese, *A Flock of Shepherds: The National Conference of Catholic Bishops* (Kansas City, Mo.: Sheed & Ward, 1992), pp. 51–54.

The Church's problems have been amply covered in both the religious and lay press. On parish closings and finances, see, among many others, *National Catholic Reporter,* January 8 and February 12, 1993; *Business Week,* June 10, 1991; *The Economist,* October 8, 1988; and *America,* May 27, 1995. The problem of sexual abuse by American priests has received worldwide coverage; a database search turned up hundreds of articles. Useful roundups are by Peter Steinfels, *New York Times,* June 27, 1993; and Howard Chua-Roan, *Time,* May 16, 1995. Jason Berry first broke the story in the *National Catholic Reporter* in the late 1980s; *NCR* has provided the most extensive coverage since then; and see Berry's *Lead Us Not into Temptation: Catholic Priests and the Sexual Abuse of Children* (New York: Doubleday, 1992), which includes a detailed investigation of a Louisiana case. The most credible recent review is Philip Jenkins, *Pedophiles and Priests: Anatomy of a Contemporary Crisis* (New York: Oxford University Press, 1995), which begins the process, which I expect to continue, of deflating the crisis and putting the problem into better perspective. See chapter 14, below. For reviews by a lawyer specializing in sex abuse cases and by the general counsel of the National Conference of Catholic Bishops, see Jeffrey R. Anderson, "Visiting the Sins of the Fathers upon the Church—A View from the Victim's Lawyer," and Mark E. Chopko, "Liability for Sexual Misconduct of the Clergy: An Institutional Overview," both in *Tort Liability for Charitable, Religious and Nonprofit Institutions* (American Bar Association, 1992) Tab H.

For statistical data summarized in this section, see the references in the next chapter. The "adolescent crisis" quote is from Andrew Greeley and William C. McReady, "The End of American Catholicism?," *America,* October 28, 1972, p. 334. Priests as an AIDS at-risk subpopulation is in Katie Leishman, "Heterosexuals and AIDS," *Atlantic Monthly,* February 1987, pp. 39–48. The data on priests' theological attitudes are from Dean R. Hoge, Joseph J. Shields, and Mary Jeanne Verdieck, "Changing Age Distribution and Theological Attitudes of Catholic Priests, 1970–1985," *Sociological Analysis* 49, no. 3 (1988) 3: 264–80. The Smith quote is from an interview.

12. *At the End of a Century*

The parish summaries are based on visits and interviews through the spring and fall of 1995. My thanks to Fr. Ron Lewinski of Chicago and Fr. Greg Coiro of Los Angeles for suggesting some of the sites. My thanks also to Mary Greeley Durkin, Eileen Durkin, and Julie Durkin Montague for introductions and background for Old St. Pat's. The Neuhaus and Greeley quotes are from interviews.

The most recent data on the Catholic laity is in William V. D'Antonio, James D. Davidson. Dean R. Hoge, and Ruth A. Wallace, *Laity: American and Catholic, Transforming the Church* (Kansas City, Mo.: Sheed & Ward, 1996), which is the primary source for this section, supplemented by: George Gallup Jr. and Jim Castelli, *The American Catholic People* (Garden City, N.Y.: Doubleday, 1987), and *The People's Religion: American Faith in the 90's* (New York: Macmillan, 1989); Andrew M. Greeley, *Religious Change in America* (Cambridge, Mass.: Harvard University Press, 1989); Mark Chaves and James C. Cavendish, "More Evidence on U.S. Catholic Church Attendance," *Journal for the Scientific Study of Religion,* Fall 1994, pp. 376–81. Useful summaries of recent research are in: "The CARA Report: Research on American Catholics and the U.S. Catholic Church," a monthly newsletter of the Center for Applied Research on the Apostolate (CARA), at Georgetown University. The reports of David C. Leege and Joseph Gremillion, eds., "The Notre Dame Study of Parish Life," Reports No. 1–14 (Notre Dame University, 1983–1989), are very useful; most of the research is summarized in Jim Castelli and Joseph Gremillion, *The Emerging Parish: The Notre Dame Study of*

Catholic Life Since Vatican II (San Francisco: Harper & Row, 1987). I also benefited from conversations with Fr. Andrew Greeley, Dean Hoge, Jim Castelli, and Mark Chaves on the interpretation of their research. Gerald Early and Brian Froehle at CARA were generous with their research files.

For Hispanic Catholicism, see, e.g., Allan Figueroa Deck, *The Second Wave: Hispanic Ministries and the Evangelization of Cultures* (New York: Paulist Press, 1989), which I supplemented by several interviews with Deck. For Hispanics and other ethnic groups, see Ruth Doyle and Olga Scarpetta, eds., *Hispanics in New York: Religious, Cultural, and Social Experiences,* 2 vols. (New York: Archdiocese of New York, Office of Pastoral Research and Planning, 1982, 1989); and Suzanne Hall, Ruth Doyle, and Peter Tran, *A Catholic Response to the Asian Presence* (Washington, D.C.: National Catholic Educational Association, 1990). For Mexican-American assimilation, see Linda Chavez, *Out of the Barrio: Towards a Politics of Hispanic Assimilation* (New York: Basic Books, 1991), p. 81. The Greeley study of young women's sexual mores is in his "The Abortion Debate and the Catholic Subculture," *America,* July 11, 1992, pp. 13–16. For Greeley and the reasons for decline in church attendance, see *Religious Change,* pp. 48–52.

Wolfe quotes from an interview. My thanks to Srs. Janet Roesener and Laura Reicks at the USCC for basic retirement information and the introduction to Sr. Wolfe. Sources for diocesan financial information were: Los Angeles, income statements published annually in the *Los Angeles Tidings,* supplemented by interviews with Chancery Analyst Kathleen Ryan and Robert Erberu and Robert Smith of the Cardinal's finance council; San Francisco, review of diocesan and parish income statements provided by Senior Development Consultant Michael DeNunzio, supplemented by an interview with DeNunzio; Chicago, review of balance sheet and income statements and interviews with Finance Director Jack Benware and Development Director Ray Coughlin, and with Barry Sullivan, a lay executive who chaired the Cardinal's finance council; Brooklyn, review of balance sheet and income statements and interview with Finance Director Msgr. Austin Bennett; Detroit, review of balance sheet and income statements, and interview with Sr. Mary Virginia Korb. I also had a useful discussion of my initial impressions with Frank Doyle, chief administrative and finance officer of the USCC. Benware summarized the Chicago experience in his paper, "Dioceses and Parishes: Mutual Expectations in Financial Matters" (June 22, 1995), prepared for a presentation at the priests' council.

Chicago, Brooklyn, and Los Angeles consolidate parish and central results, a practice that appears to be spreading. Although many dioceses don't yet keep balance sheets because of the difficulty of assigning values to plant, the practice, again, seems to be spreading. Chicago uses an appraised disposal value for its old inner-city plant, which seems conservative enough. Almost no dioceses use centralized payrolls, which might help avoid problems like those in San Francisco with Martin Greenlaw. Parish job descriptions, pay, and tenure terms still tend to be rather informal, although the better-run dioceses have begun to standardize employment conditions. On the other hand, there are already unhappy signs of a credentialing trend, like divinity degrees as employment prerequisites. Lay employees are slowly developing enough clout to take better care of themselves, as happened a generation ago in Catholic schools.

Spending appears to vary considerably from diocese to diocese, although the data are too sparse for definitive conclusions. Los Angeles seems to spend about half as much per Catholic as San Francisco and has a much lower priest/Catholic ratio. But Los Angeles's large Hispanic presence balloons the Catholic count, and its physical plant is much newer—churches are modern, low-rise, and easy to maintain, in contrast to Gothic extravaganzas like St. Brigid. (My sample suggests a nationwide average of perhaps a hundred diocesan staff per million Catholics, with half that in Los Angeles.) The newer dioceses, in terms of membership growth, like Los Angeles, typically have a much cheaper physical plant than those that peaked before World War II. The figures for Catholic school enrollment are collected by the National Catholic Educational Association and are reported in the summer 1995 CARA Report.

The basic source tracking the decline of parish priests is Richard A. Schoenherr and Lawrence A. Young, *Full Pews and Empty Altars: Demographics of the Priest Shortage in United States Catholic Dioceses* (Madison, Wis.: University of Wisconsin Press, 1993). And see Lawrence A. Young and Richard A. Schoenherr, "Changing Age Distribution and Theological Attitudes of Catholic Priests Revisited," *Sociological Analysis* 53, no. 1 (1992) 73–87 (the same issue contains Dean R. Hoge, Joseph J. Shields, and Mary Jeanne Verdieck, "Response to Young and Schoenherr," 89–90, which reviews both the Schoenherr/Young findings and the Hoge, Shields, Verdieck data on theological attitudes cited above); Eugene F. Hemrick and Dean R. Hoge, *Seminarians in Theology: A National Profile* (Washington, D.C.: United States Catholic Conference, 1986); and Dean R. Hoge, *The Future of Catholic Leadership: Responses to the Priest Shortage* (Kansas City, Mo.: Sheed & Ward, 1987). The Hemrick quote is from an interview.

A table from Schoenherr clearly shows the changing importance of resignations versus ordinations; note the growing percentage of inactive priests over the analytic period:

	Active	Total	Ordinations	Resignations
1966	35,087	36,330	994	200
1967	35,107	36,558	1,062	338
1968	34,915	36,750	1,034	579
1969	34,402	36,684	847	750
1970	33,555	36,169	842	634
1971	32,914	35,894	692	667
1972	32,182	35,408	647	609
1973	31,518	35,006	831	499
1974	31,163	34,860	732	380
1975	30,808	34,732	768	296
1976	30,595	34,763	700	258
1977	30,501	34,699	667	295
1978	30,126	34,626	574	238
1979	29,773	34,473	647	223
1980	29,667	34,455	544	231
1981	29,472	34,267	544	176
1982	29,354	34,102	511	190
1983	28,925	33,912	530	194
1984	28,618	33,756	465	181

The data on nuns and brothers is from United States Catholic Conference "Retirement Needs Analysis" (Washington, D.C., 1995), supplemented by interviews with Roesener and Reicks. About 76 percent of the orders on the USCC census list responded to a detailed survey. My estimates of new entrants, retirements, and deaths of nuns project the survey results across the entire population. See also Elizabeth Durkin and Julie Durkin Montague, "Surveying U.S. Nuns," *America,* February 11, 1995, pp. 8–12, which lists a slightly larger number of nuns than the USCC. The Connors quote is from an interview. For nuns as lay parish ministers, see Philip J. Murnion, *New Parish Ministers: Laity and Religious on Parish Staffs* (New York: National Pastoral Life Center, 1992), a study that has also been widely reported in the lay press.

13. *Theological Visions*

The theologians I interviewed specifically for this chapter include Fr. Avery Dulles, Fr. Joseph Fessio, Fr. Robert Imbelli, Fr. Joseph Komonchak, Fr. Thomas Reese (technically a political scientist, but one who writes on theological issues), Fr. Richard McBrien, Prof. Monika Hellwig, Msgr. George Kelly, and Msgr. Michael Wrenn. I also interviewed Fr. David Tracy when the book was in very early stages, but not specifically on the issues covered in this chapter. In addition, I learned a great deal merely by associating with a large number of priests during the preparation of this book, since theology is their favorite shoptalk.

The section on Vatican II was greatly improved by a detailed critique by Komonchak. The definitive history of the Council is now in preparation, in what will be a six-volume account under the general editorship of Giuseppe Alberigo and, for the English language edition, Komonchak. I had available the first volume of the project: Giuseppe Alberigo and Joseph A. Komonchak, eds. *History of Vatican II,* vol. 1, *Announcing and Preparing Vatican Council II* (Maryknoll, N.Y.: Orbis Press, 1995). Otherwise, I used primarily: Francis X. Murphy [Xavier Rynne, pseud.], *Vatican Council II* (New York: Farrar, Straus & Giroux, 1968), supplemented by an interview with Murphy; Adrian Hastings, ed., *Modern Catholicism: Vatican II and After* (New York: Oxford University Press, 1991); Peter Hebblethwaite, *Pope John: Shepherd of the Modern World* (New York: Doubleday, 1985), and *Paul VI: The First Modern Pope* (New York: Paulist Press, 1993); Giuseppe Alberigo, Jean-Pierre Jossua, and Joseph A. Komonchak, eds., *The Reception of Vatican II* (Washington, D.C.: Catholic University Press, 1987); Joseph A. Komonchak, "Interpreting the Council," in Mary Jo Weaver and R. Scott Appleby, eds., *Being Right: Conservative Catholicism in America* (Bloomington, Ind.: Indiana University Press, 1995), pp. 17–36; and Bonaventure Kloppenberg, *The Ecclesiology of Vatican II* (Chicago: Franciscan Herald Press, 1974). Hans Küng's *The Council in Action: Theological Reflections on the Second Vatican Council* (New York: Sheed & Ward, 1963), which had been published in German before the Council was convened, was an important contributor to liberal expectations for the Council. For John Paul II on the Council, see his *Toward the Third Millennium (Tertio Millennio Adveniente)* (St. Paul: Pauline Books, 1994). The "beyond" and Novak quotes are from Komonchak, "Interpreting," pp. 22, 23. For a conservative view on the changes in catechetics, Michael J. Wrenn, *Catechisms and Controversies: Religious Education in the Postconciliar Years* (San Francisco: Ignatius Press, 1991). For a sense of how far the Church has come in recent generations, see the story of the persecution of Pierre Teilhard de Chardin, the great Jesuit paleontologist and philosopher, in Jean Lacouture, *Jesuits: A Multibiography* (Washington, D.C.: Counterpoint, 1995). pp. 406–39. The Murphy quotes are from my interview.

Quotes "impressive," "cold," and "flash" are in Giuseppe Alberigo, "The Announcement of the Council," in Alberigo and Komonchak, *History,* pp. 2, 6. "They know . . ." is in Komonchak, "The Preparation of Vatican II," in ibid., pp. 245–46; For John's quotes on goals, see Alberigo in ibid., pp. 4–5; "naturalism" is in Komonchak, ibid., p. 228. John's opening speech is as reported in *The New York Times,* October 12, 1962.

Quote "contented" is from Giuseppe Alberigo, "Preparing for What Kind of Council?," in Alberigo and Komonchak, *History,* p. 507. The Ottaviani-Frings exchange, "remnant" and "distinguishes" are in Murphy, *Vatican Council II,* pp. 221–23, 287, 313. For conciliar texts, I used Norman P. Tanner, ed., *Decrees of the Ecumenical Council,* vol. 2 (London and Washington: Sheed & Ward/Georgetown University Press, 1990). The "Preliminary Explanatory Note" is at p. 899. (The dispute over the meaning of the note revolves around whether or not there were any concessions in the main text. A fair reading of the main text suggests that the conservatives in fact had carried all important substantive points; the note would then have merely squelched any "spirit of the council"–based excessive expectations.) Paul's "monarchical" is from Murphy, *Vatican Council II,* p. 426. The "heart and soul" and "of not too much" quotes are from Archbishop Mark McGrath (my notes from a Notre Dame seminar). The *Gaudium et Spes* quotes are from the Tanner text, pp. 1069, 1071, 1072, 1075, 1077, 1080, 1089, 1090, 1093, and 1098. Quote "exaggerated fascination" is from Joseph A. Komonchak, "*Humanae Vitae* and Its Reception: Ecclesiological Reflections," *Theological Studies,* June 1978, p. 247. "[T]he episcopal" is from Ladislas Örsy, "The Revision of Canon Law," in Hastings, *Modern Catholicism,* p. 212; "Vatican II," from Richard P. McBrien, *Catholicism* (San Francisco: HarperSanFrancisco, 1994), p. 765.

McBrien "like being" from interview. For the intellectual shift comprising modernity, see Charles Taylor's splendid *Sources of the Self: The Making of the Modern Identity* (Cambridge, Mass.: Harvard University Press, 1989); also see Albert R. Jonsen and Stephen Toulmin, *The Abuse of Casuistry: A History of Moral Reasoning* (Berkeley, Cal.: University of California Press, 1988); and Alasdair MacIntyre, *After Virtue: A Study in Moral Theory* (Notre Dame, Ind.: Notre Dame University Press, 1984). The Aristotle quote is from his *Nicomachean Ethics,* Book One, III; I used the Penguin edition (New York: Penguin, 1976), p. 65. For Aquinas on the element of contingency in good and evil, see, for example, *Summa Theologica,* Part I–II, Questions 7 and 18 (esp. arts. 3, 10, and 11), pp. 622–25, 664–65, and 670–71 in the Westminster edition. For Rawls, see John Rawls, *A Theory of Justice* (New York: Oxford University Press, 1971), and for a critique, Michael Sandel, *Liberalism and the Limits of Justice* (New York: Cambridge University Press, 1982).

Multiple examples of historical-critical method are in Philip S. Kaufman, *Why You Can Disagree and Remain a Faithful Catholic* (New York: Crossroad, 1995). The Matthew "unchastity" loophole is in ibid., p. 111; some Catholic versions, like the *New American Bible* have "unless the marriage was unlawful"; the Greek word was *porneia,* which apparently had a range of meanings from adultery to marriages within forbidden degrees. Paul's exception, known as the "Pauline privilege," applies to divorced non-Christians, one of whom subsequently converts, but there is a long, subtle casuistical history of its application in practice. For a discussion, see Thomas J. Deidun, "Exceptionless Norms in New Testament Morality: A Biblical Theological Approach," in Donald G. McCarthy, ed., *Moral Theology Today: Certitudes and Doubts* (St. Louis: Pope John Center, 1984), pp. 165–81, especially the notes. Bultmann is quoted in Craig A.

Evans, "Life of Jesus Research and the Eclipse of Mythology," *Theological Studies,* March 1993, p. 9.

For representative works in feminist and liberation theology, see Rosemary Radford Ruether, *Sexism and God-Talk: Toward a Feminist Theology* (Boston: Beacon, 1983); and Leonardo Boff, *When Theology Listens to the Poor* (San Francisco: Harper & Row, 1970). Also see Christian Smith, *The Emergence of Liberation Theology: Radical Religion and the Social Movement Theory* (Chicago: University of Chicago Press, 1991). Quote "devastated" is from Adrian Hastings, "Catholic History from Vatican II to John Paul II," in Hastings, *Modern Catholicism,* p. 11. Hellwig quote was confirmed in an interview. Quote "in four decades" is from Thomas Oden, *Agenda for Theology* (San Francisco: Harper & Row, 1979), p. 66. For Catholic liberal excesses, from a conservative vantage point, see George A. Kelly, *The Battle for the American Church Revisited* (San Francisco: Ignatius Press, 1995); and less pugnaciously, William McSweeney, *Roman Catholicism: The Search for Relevance* (New York: St. Martin's, 1980); and Robert P. Imbelli, "Vatican II—Twenty Years Later," *Commonweal,* October 8, 1982, pp. 522–26, and "Catholic Identity After Vatican II," *Commonweal,* March 11, 1994, pp. 12–16. The central figure in defining the "liberal" Catholic consciousness—the sense of a communal dialogue in and with history—is unquestionably Karl Rahner. Geffrey Kelly, ed., *Karl Rahner: Theologian of the Graced Search for Meaning* (Minneapolis: Fortress Press, 1992), is a selection of Rahner's writings.

Quotes from David Tracy are from his *The Analogical Imagination: Christian Theology and the Culture of Pluralism* (New York: Crossroad, 1981), pp. 422–23. (The May crowning example is from interview with Mary and Eileen Durkin and Julie Montague, Andrew Greeley's sister and nieces. The idea was suggested by Greeley but inspired by Tracy.) The AAR paper was Serene Jones, " 'Two Lips' and the Trinity: Irigaray and Barth," 1988 Annual Meeting, American Association of Religion/Society of Biblical Literature. For Matthew Arnold, see his *Culture and Anarchy* (New Haven, Conn.: Yale University Press, 1994). Dulles's talk followed closely his *The Craft of Theology: From Symbol to System,* rev. ed. (New York: Crossroad, 1995). McBrien quote is from an interview. McBrien expands his point in "Conflict in the Church: Redefining the Center," *America,* August 22, 1992, pp. 78–81. The conservative priest is Fr. Joseph Nemec (see chapter 15) and Fessio quote is from an interview. Greeley quote is from an interview. Quote "by 1970" is Hastings in Hastings, *Modern Catholicism,* p. 11. A key Ratzinger statement is his (with Vittorio Messori) *The Ratzinger Report: An Exclusive Interview on the State of the Church* (San Francisco: Ignatius Press, 1985), a wide-ranging analysis of the state of the Church.

For centralization, see Peter Hebblethwaite, "The Curia" and "Pope John Paul II," in Hastings, *Modern Catholicism,* pp. 175–81 and 447–56. For crackdowns, see John McDade, "Catholic Theology in the Post-Conciliar Period," in ibid., pp. 422–43. For Curran and Hunthausen, I used the chronology in Kenneth Briggs, *Holy Siege: The Year That Shook Catholic America* (San Francisco: HarperSanFrancisco, 1992), supplemented, for Hunthausen, by an interview with Fr. Michael Ryan, Hunthausen's chancellor. Laghi on standards of dissent is in ibid., p. 12. Quote "vicious assault" is from Fr. Thomas Reese interview, and Dulles is from interview. Quinn on appointments and trust is from an interview. I interviewed two of the protesting bishops, Joseph Sullivan of Brooklyn and Kenneth Untener of Saginaw. The quotations are from the text given in *The National Catholic Reporter,* June 30, 1995.

Episcopal infallibility is from *Lumen Gentium* 25, 2, in Tanner, *Decrees,* p. 869. The Ford memo to Paul is quoted in John C. Ford and Germain Grisez, "Contraception and the Infallibility of the Ordinary Magisterium," *Theological Studies,* June 1978, p. 302; the Paul VI quote is from Hebblethwaite, *Paul VI,* p. 476. The Küng quote is from his *Infallible? An Enquiry* (Garden City, N.Y.: Doubleday, 1971), p. 58. For the difficulty of extracting universal norms from natural law, by one of the leading advocates of a broad application of natural law thinking, see German Grisez, "Are There Exceptionless Moral Norms?," in Russell Smith, ed., *The Twenty-fifth Anniversary of Vatican II: A Look Back and a Look Ahead* (Braintree, Mass.: Pope John Center, 1990), pp. 117–35. The quotes from the Vatican statement follow the text in *Origins,* November 30, 1995, pp. 403–9. The Untener quotes are from an interview. The Dulles quote is from a paper delivered at meeting of NCCB in Portland, Ore., June 22, 1996, "The Pastoral Response to the *Responsum,*" p. 2.

For commentary on the Vatican statement regarding the infallibility of the prohibition against ordaining women, see the series of articles in the London *Tablet:* Nicholas Lash, "On Not Inventing Doctrine," December 2, 1995; Avery Dulles, "Women's Ordination and Infallibility: Tradition Says No," December 9, 1995 (Dulles is the only one of the four who seems to support the decision, which he finds based "on good grounds" and "a keener sense of the tradition" than its critics', but Dulles does not discuss the process that was involved); Hans Küng, "Waiting For Vatican III," December 16, 1995; and Francis Sullivan, "Room for Doubt," December 23, 1995. There is also a symposium of theologians on the question in the January 26, 1996, issue of *Commonweal.*

In a lecture at Fordham University in April 1996, Dulles identified four "converging" rationales for the doctrine:

1. *Biblical,* including (a) Christ ordained only men; and (b) the Apostles in turn created only male bishops and priests.
2. *Tradition:* Bishops always followed this norm, and all sects that ordained women were declared heretical; the issue was considered settled by the Middle Ages.
3. *Theological:* The priestly minister serves an "iconic" role—Christ is the "bridegroom" of the Church, and only a male can fill that role.
4. *Magisterial authority.* The doctrine has been the constant teaching of Pope and bishops and has been particularly explicit for the last twenty years.

Dulles then recognized, and attempted to refute, ten objections to the ruling:

1. (a) *Christ didn't ordain anyone.* Not so, says Dulles. The Last Supper has long been recognized as an ordination ceremony. (b) *If Christ did ordain, accidental elements are not binding.* But sacramental forms *are* binding, as in bread and wine, and water for baptism, so the male ordinand.
2. *Weak evidence in the apostolic era.* Not so. The New Testament may not be dispositive, but the continuous masculine character of the early leadership is clear.
3. *Question is recent and needs debate.* Not so. It was raised repeatedly in patristic period and by sects of Middle Ages, like Cathari. Even when woman theologians, like Edith Stein, raised the question they concluded it was settled.

4. *Issue is socially conditioned.* Not so. There were many priestesses in Greco-Roman world; in fact, most religions of Jesus' time probably had them.
5. *The rule was predicated on biological inferiority.* Not so. Thomas, for one, mentions that point but does not use it as a premise, admitting that women are often more able than men.
6. *Iconic argument is fanciful.* Not so. Not sufficient for proof, perhaps, but Christ's decision not arbitrary.
7. *Injustice to a class.* No discrimination, and many roles open. Mary ranks above all the saints and angels. Christ in any case not bound by American political correctness.
8. *Unecumenical.* Cuts both ways. Eastern churches and conservative Protestants would have objected to women priests.
9. *Still open, for magisterium has not truly settled.* Pope decides that.
10. *Bishops don't agree and weren't consulted.* No procedure spelled out, and Pope is free to consult across time, not just the current bishops.

My impression was that no minds were changed one way or the other. Counter-refutations that I particularly noted include:

1. The "iconic" argument, Christ as bridegroom, is asymmetrical; by the same reasoning only women could be laity (bride).
2. The central sacramental element at the Last Supper was the love between Christ and the disciples, not his gender.
3. Dulles himself had written that recourse to revelation and infallibility should concern only the most central issues. Isn't this merely disciplinary?
4. The *ex parte* character of the process was wounding.

The entire proceeding was extremely civil, with an appealingly anachronistic aura, conjuring up images of, say, the University of Paris in the fourteenth century, with the exception, perhaps, of the civility. The "loony bin" quote is from an interview with Fr. Philip Murnion.

14. *The Struggle with Sexuality*

Fr. Hayes's quotes are from an interview. The Cuomo story is from an interview. The theology manual is quoted in Anthony Kosnik, ed., *Human Sexuality: New Directions in American Catholic Thought* (New York: Paulist Press, 1977), p. 159. The exchange between the bishop and the theologian is in Donald G. McCarthy, ed., *Moral Theology Today: Certitudes and Doubts* (St. Louis: Pope John Center, 1984) pp. 96–97. For Italians, see Luigi Barzini, *The Italians* (New York: Atheneum, 1964). The history of Catholic teachings on sex follows for the most part John T. Noonan Jr., *Contraception: A History of Its Treatment by the Catholic Theologians and Canonists* (Cambridge, Mass.: Harvard University Press, 1965). For the analysis of Paul's teachings, see Thomas J. Deidun, "Exceptionless Norms In New Testament Morality: A Biblical Theological Approach," in McCarthy, *Moral Theology Today,* pp. 165–81. The quote is from p. 178, and the quote from the following discussion is on p. 203. The "too ardent" quote is in

Noonan, p. 80; and also see James A. Brundage, "Allas, That Evere Love Was Synne: Sex and Medieval Canon Law," *Catholic Historical Review,* January 1986, pp. 1–13. The St. Basil quote is in John Boswell, *Christianity, Social Tolerance, and Homosexuality: Gay People in Western Europe from the Beginning of the Christian Era to the Fourteenth Century* (Chicago: University of Chicago Press, 1980), p. 159. Thomas's "abhorrence" is from *Summa Theologica* Part II-II, Q. 154, Art. 5 (p. 1814 in the 1981 Westminster edition). For peasant sexuality, see Eugen Weber, *Peasants into Frenchmen: The Modernization of Rural France, 1870–1914* (Palo Alto, Cal.: Stanford University Press, 1976), especially pp. 399–406.

The history of the birth control encyclical follows Robert J. McClory, *Turning Point* (New York: Crossroads, 1995), supplemented by Patricia Crowley interviewed by Robert Burns, "Oral History of America Catholicism" in CFM Archive, University of Notre Dame. Peter Hebblethwaite's *Paul VI: The First Modern Pope* (New York: Paulist Press, 1993) also has extensive material on the encyclical. The *Casti Conubii* quote is from Claudia Carlen, *The Papal Encyclicals: 1740–1978* (Raleigh, N.C.: McGrath, 1981), 3:399. The quotes from Pius XII are in McClory, *Turning Point,* pp. 23–34. The Crowley/theologian exchange is in ibid., p. 122. The *Humanae Vitae* quotes are from Austin Flannery, ed., *Vatican Council II: Conciliar and Post-Conciliar Documents* (Collegeville, Minn.: The Litugical Press, 1982), 2:397–416.

A clear summary of proportionalism is in Lisa Sowle Cahill, "Contemporary Challenges to Exceptionless Moral Norms," in McCarthy, *Moral Theology Today,* pp. 121–35, and the notes thereto, which I supplemented with an interview. The Cahill quotes in this section are from the interview. For a critique of proportionalism, including the nuclear deterrence argument, see Germain Grisez and Russell Shaw, *Fulfillment in Christ: A Summary of Christian Moral Principles* (Notre Dame, Ind.: University of Notre Dame Press, 1991), pp. 60–74. The Curran statement is from *Origins,* March 27, 1986, p. 669. For wavering among academic theologians on abortion, see Lisa Sowle Cahill, "The Embryo and the Fetus: New Moral Contexts," *Theological Studies,* March 1993, pp. 124–36. The Barnhill, Torgerson, Reese, and Greeley quotes are from interviews. A perception that theologians may be much more liberal on sexual issues than priests was fueled by Kosnik, *Human Sexuality,* which was sponsored by the CTSA and which was singled out for especial criticism by the Vatican. By secular standards, the book is actually quite conservative; but in the eyes of Catholic conservatives, it went off the reservation by its reluctance to label *any* sexual act as intrinsically evil. For example, while the authors couldn't imagine that wife-swapping would be permissible—this was the mid-1970s, when some lay therapists were recommending the practice—they would not say that it was impossible that such situations could arise.

For Catholic teaching on abortion over the centuries, see John T. Noonan Jr.'s admirable survey, "An Almost Absolute Value in History" in John T. Noonan Jr., ed., *The Morality of Abortion: Legal and Historical Perspectives* (Cambridge, Mass.: Harvard University Press, 1970), pp. 1–59, well summarized by the essay's title. While Noonan's researches have been extremely influential in the revolt against the official teaching on contraception, he supports the traditional teaching on abortion. James M. Gustafson, "A Protestant Ethical Approach," in the same volume, pp. 101–22, contrasts the Catholic search for juridical, rational, unvarying rules maintained by an external judge with the Protestant tendency to frame the issue as a conflict of values to be weighed by the personal conscience in each particular fact situation.

The "limited to" quote is from Joseph A. Komanchak, "*Humanae Vitae* and Its Reception: Ecclesiological Reflections," *Theological Studies,* June 1978, p. 255. Thomas on usury is from *Summa Theologica* Part II-II, Q. 78, Art. 1 (p. 1513 in the 1981 Westminster edition). The Sarpi quote is from Paolo Sarpi, *History of the Council of Trent* (London: J Macock, 1676), p. 377. The 1975 Vatican declaration is in Flannery, *Vatican Council II,* 2:486–99. John Paul II's quote is from *The Splendor of Truth (Veritatis Splendor)* (St. Paul: Pauline Books, 1993), pp. 101–2. The NFP quotes are from Gerard Brunelle, "Part II: The Bishops and Natural Family Planning: Theological and Pastoral Implications," in McCarthy, *Moral Theology Today,* p. 306, and the discussion transcript on p. 331. The Vatican on fertility is from "Instruction on Respect for Human Life in Its Origin and on the Dignity of Procreation," *Origins,* March 19, 1987, pp. 698–710. For baptism, see *Catechism of the Catholic Church* (San Francisco: Ignatius Press, 1994), pp. 319 and 321 (paras. 1250 and 1261). The "Contraception takes" quote is from Brunelle, "Bishops and Natural," p. 329. And see Ivor Shapiro, *What God Allows: The Crisis of Faith and Conscience in One Catholic Church* (New York: Doubleday, 1996). The Pope on conscience is from *Splendor,* pp. 76–77. For abortion and "person" question, see his *The Gospel of Life (Evangelium Vitae)* (New York: Times Books, 1995); he says "mere probability" of person status is enough (pp. 107–8). For bishops' pro-deterrence argument, see "Nuclear Deterrence: Are the Conditions Being Met?," *Origins,* November 21, 1985. Andrew Sullivan's argument (for granting gay people no special status or protection, but allowing them to marry) is in his *Virtually Normal: An Argument About Homosexuality* (New York: Knopf, 1995). Bishop Sullivan's quote is from an interview.

Except as noted, the quotes in "Under a Glass" from Connors, Hayes, Justice, Kennedy, Greeley, Untener, Rizzotto, and Fessio are from interviews. (There are a few quotes in this section where I decided not to identify the speaker. No one requested anonymity, but I saw no necessity to embarrass anyone for his frankness.) On pedophilia, see Philip Jenkins, *Pedophiles and Priests: Anatomy of a Contemporary Crisis* (New York: Oxford University Press, 1995); Thomas C. Fox, *Sexuality and Catholicism* (New York: Braziller, 1995), pp. 184–97; and Jason Berry, *Lead Us Not into Temptation: Catholic Priests and the Sexual Abuse of Children* (New York: Doubleday, 1992). For adversarial statements of the sexual abuse issue, see Mark E. Chopko, "Liability for Sexual Misconduct of the Clergy: An Institutional Overview," and Jeffrey R. Anderson, "Visiting the Sins of the Fathers upon the Church—A View from the Victim's Lawyer," both in *Tort Liability for Charitable, Religious and Nonprofit Institutions* (American Bar Association, 1992), Tab H. Anderson is known as the leading plaintiff's lawyer in the abuse cases. He did not return my calls requesting an interview. For what it's worth, Chopko, the councel for the USCC, believes that his caseload is drying up (interview).

The Mahony quote is in Richard A. Schoenherr, and Lawrence A. Young, *Full Pews and Empty Altars: Demographics of the Priest Shortage in United States Catholic Dioceses* (Madison, Wis.: University of Wisconsin Press, 1993), p. 351. My observation on the laicization of Los Angeles is based on two visits and interviews with Monica Hughes, who coordinates lay minister training for the archdiocese, and with Fr. Allan Deck, who runs Hispanic-oriented ministry training for Loyola Marymount University. The diocesan Family Life director data are from a survey that Fr. Robert Barnhill, the director of the office for the diocese of Lincoln, Nebraska, shared with me. The observation on Seattle's professionalism is based on interviews with Colleen Branigan and Fr. Jim Picton of the chancery office and review of diocesan planning materials. Picton stressed that they began their planning years before other dioceses. The Sullivan quote is from an interview. Ragan quote is from an interview. And see National Center for Pastoral Leadership, "Ministry in the Church of the 21st Century" (preliminary draft report) (Annapolis, Md.: September 1995). The California pastor is Fr. Christopher Smith. The Greeley 'semi-literate' quote is from his "Confusing the Laity," *The Daily Southtown*, April 28, 1996.

Greeley "moral" quote is from his "In Defense of Celibacy," *America*, September 10, 1994, p. 11. For priestly job satisfaction, see Andrew M. Greeley, *The Catholic Priest in the United States: A Sociological Investigation* (Washington, D.C.: United States Catholic Conference, 1972), updated in "A Sea of Paradoxes: Two Surveys of Priests," *America*, July 16, 1994, pp. 6–10. A review of the literature is in National Federation of Priests' Councils, "Consultation on Priests' Morale: A Review of Research" (Chicago, 1991). The "brutally slapped" quote is from Greeley, "Sea of Paradoxes," p. 10. The "conservative and monastic" quote is cited in Priests' Councils, "Consultation," p. 9. The "personal holiness" quote is from Smith interview. See Eugene F. Hemrick and Dean R. Hoge, *Seminarians in Theology: A National Profile* (Washington, D.C.: The United States Catholic Conference, 1986), for religious background of recent recruits.

For priests' coping strategies, see James Walsh, John Mayer, James Castelli, Eugene Hemrick, Melvin Blanquette, and Paul Theroux, *Grace Under Pressure: What Gives Life to American Priests* (Washington, D.C.: National Catholic Education Association, 1995), based on detailed, focus-group-based interviews with thirty-six "effective" priests, selected by peer votes. The fight for a more effective voice for priests in Chicago is detailed in Charles W. Dahm, *Power and Authority in the Catholic Church: Cardinal Cody in Chicago* (Notre Dame, Ind.: Notre Dame University Press, 1981). Cody responded to a "democracy" movement with harsh repression, and resignations in Chicago were among the highest in the country. I also reviewed the Association of Chicago Priests Archive in the Notre Dame University Archives. (I greatly regret not developing this story further, but space considerations made it impractical.) Archbishop Jean Jadot, who was apostolic delegate from 1973 to 1980, is widely credited with trying to redirect episcopal appointments to more pastoral, innovative men. Both liberals and conservatives speak of "Jadot bishops," the liberals fondly, the conservatives much less so. Thomas Reese, a careful scholar of the hierarchy, argues that the distinction between "Jadot" men and the more orthodox "post-Jadot" men is often overdrawn. See his *A Flock of Shepherds: The National Conference of Catholic Bishops* (Kansas City, Mo.: Sheed & Ward, 1992). (Untener was the last Jadot appointment—the "reductio ad absurdum," he laughs.)

The *Crisis* article is Francis Sullivan (pseud.), "Meet Father Freud: An Eyewitness Account of Seminary Life," *Crisis*, July–August 1988, p. 11. For the survey of homosexual priests, James G. Wolf, ed., *Gay Priests* (San Francisco: Harper & Row, 1989). The priests in the survey estimated that 48.5 percent of priests and 55.1 percent of seminarians were gay. Those ordained in or before 1960 had the lowest estimates—44.5 percent for priests and 50.9 percent for seminarians. Those most recently ordained (1981–1984) estimated 54 percent of priests and 70.5 percent of seminarians. For Sipe, see A. W. Richard Sipe, *A Secret World: Sexuality and the Search for Celibacy* (New York: Brunner-Mazel, 1990). Also see Jeannine Gramick and Pat Furey, eds., *The Vatican and Homosexuality: Reactions to the "Letter to the Bishops of the Catholic Church on the Pastoral Care of Homosexual Persons"* (New York: Crossroad, 1988); and

Jeannine Gramick, ed., *Homosexuality in the Priesthood and Religious Life* (New York: Crossroad, 1989). Kennedy's study is Eugene M. Kennedy and Victor J. Heckler, *The Catholic Priest in the United States: Psychological Investigations* (Washington, D.C.: United States Catholic Conference, 1972). The *Wanderer* article is in the issue of October 14, 1995, and the *National Catholic Reporter* article is in the issue of April 21, 1995. Jenkins, *Pedophiles,* draws particular attention to the "socially constructed" character of the pedophilia panic—that is, how the story was amplified and manipulated to partisan advantage by theological ideologues of both conservative and liberal stripe, which is shameful. I had come to the same conclusion, on impressionistic data, but Jenkins documents the case strongly.

15. *Styles, Themes, Dilemmas*

The account of Lincoln is based on interviews with Msgrs. Timothy Thorburn and Leonard Kalin, Frs. Joseph Nemec, Robert Barnhill, and Jim Walsh; seminarians, among others, Deacon Laras Grell, Jamie Hottovy, Raymond Jansen, Jeremy Hazuka, and Christopher Kubat; for the School Sisters of Christ the King, Mother Joan Paul and Srs. Anne Joelle, Mary Joseph, and Maura Therese. I also visited Lincoln's Sisters of the Perpetual Adoration, a cloistered order, Srs. Mary Catherine, Mary Inez, and Mary Henrita; and among the St. Teresa's parishioners (whose names I got), John Kapetzky, Jennie Powell, and Jill Ullman. Fessio's comments in this chapter are from an interview. A history and description of the diocese is in Loretta Gosen, *History of the Catholic Church in the Diocese of Lincoln, Nebraska, 1887–1987* (Lincoln, Neb.: Catholic Bishop of Lincoln, 1986).

The account of Saginaw is based on interviews with Bishop Kenneth Untener; Srs. Honora Remes and Janet Fulgencia; and St. Mary's staff and parishioners, including Kevin Bourassa, Dan and Annie Hull, Bill Quinnan, and Beverly Corso. Murnion on lay ministers is from Philip J. Murnion, *New Parish Ministers: Laity and Religious on Parish Staffs* (New York: National Pastoral Life Center, 1992); and see his "The Laity and the Shape of Things to Come," *Commonweal,* September 11, 1992, pp. 23–29, and "The Potential and the Anomaly of the 'Priestless Parish,' " *America,* January 29, 1994, pp. 12–14; also the *National Catholic Reporter,* June 2, 1995. I also had an extended interview with Fr. Murnion. The data on Seattle are from Picton interview. The Vatican II quote is from Norman P. Tanner, ed., *Decrees of the Ecumenical Councils* (London and Georgetown: Sheed & Ward/Georgetown University Press, 1990), 2:830 (Constitution on Sacred Liturgy). For Catholic doctrine on the Real Presence, see ibid., 1:695, chap. 4 (Council of Trent), which adapts Thomas's formula from *Summa,* Part III, Q. 75, Art. 4 (pp. 2443–44 in the 1981 Westminster edition). The McBrien quote is from his *Catholicism* (San Francisco: HarperSanFrancisco, 1994), p. 826. For a good statement of the traditional Catholic view and the impact of "modernizing" liturgies by a friendly critic, see Eamon Duffy, "Discerning the Body," *Priests and People,* June 1994, pp. 226–30.

The quotes from Martin's Babylon talk are from my notes. The account of the charismatic movement relies primarily on interviews with Ralph Martin, Leon Kortenkamp (a member of the original Notre Dame contingent), Fr. Paul Bernardicou, and Fr. John Hampsch. Dorothy Ranaghan of the South Bend People of Praise community provided me with additional historical accounts by her husband, Kevin, culled primarily from movement newsletters, but the Ranaghans declined an interview. The San Francisco story is from Bernardicou and Kortenkamp, who accompanied Koller to San Francisco and ended up on the other side of the split. Recent surveys of the movement are Ken Metz, "Twenty-five Years of Growth," International Catholic Charismatic Renewal Services (Rome, 1996); and Jim Manney, "The People's Movement at Age Twenty-five," *New Covenant,* February 1992, pp. 7–13. Also see Ralph Martin, *The Catholic Church at the End of an Age: What Is the Spirit Saying?* (San Francisco: Ignatius Press, 1994). For seminarian background, see Eugene F. Hemrick and Dean R. Hoge, *Seminarians in Theology: A National Profile* (Washington, D.C.: United States Catholic Conference, 1986), pp. 15–20; and for lay ministers, Murnion, *New Parish Ministers,* p. 28. Paul VI's skeptical comments are in his exhortation, *Evangelii Nuntiandi,* in Austin Flannery, ed., *Vatican Council II: Conciliar and Post-Conciliar Documents* (Collegeville, Minn.: The Liturgical Press, 1982), 2:738–39. The official "papal preacher to the pontifical household" since 1980 has been Fr. Raniero Cantalamessa, a well-known charismatic. For Hampsch teaching tongues, see his audiotape, "The Gift of Tongues," Claretian Tape Ministry, Los Angeles.

The MacNutt account is from an interview. Two of his representative books are *Healing* (Notre Dame, Ind.: Ave Maria Press, 1974) and *Deliverance from Evil Spirits: A Practical Manual* (Grand Rapids, Mich.: Chosen Books, 1995). The Martin television shows are available on tape. Quotes are from "The Choices We Face, 1995," Renewal Ministries, Inc., Ann Arbor, Mich.; and "A Place Called Home, with Ralph Martin," Servant Films, Inc., Ann Arbor, Mich. I make a point of watching Mother Angelica when I travel. (She is not shown in New York City.) The Grisez comment is in *Catholic World Report,* July 1993, p. 36.

It is probably worth noting that I found no sign that any of the charismatics I met were financially exploiting their adherents, in the Jim and Tammy Bakker style. Hampsch, whose ministry I thought was the most contrived, is clearly poor, while Martin and MacNutt live very modestly. Martin *gives away* his books on his television show. The entire movement reportedly receives substantial financial underwriting from Thomas Monaghan, the primary owner of Domino's Pizza. He declined an interview.

For Hispanic Catholicism in this section, I conducted interviews with Frs. Dennis O'Neill, Greg Boyle, and Allan Deck. Also see Allan Figueroa Deck, *The Second Wave: Hispanic Ministries and the Evangelization of Cultures* (New York: Paulist Press, 1989), and his "A Pox on Both Your Houses: A View of Catholic Conservative-Liberal Polarities from the Hispanic Margin" (ms., 1995). Peter Skerry, *Mexican Americans: The Ambivalent Minority* (Cambridge, Mass.: Harvard University Press, 1993), pp. 187–216, is a good account of Hispanics' sometimes very attenuated relationship with the official Church in Texas and Los Angeles. The footnote comment on the American origins of BECs is based on my review of the Lucey Papers at the Notre Dame archives, which have extensive materials on his Latin American activities. There was local resentment at the presumed takeover by American priests.

For Marian devotions, see C. J. Maunder, "Marian Apparitions," in Adrian Hastings, ed., *Modern Catholicism: Vatican II and After* (New York: Oxford University Press, 1991), pp. 280–82. Mass attendance data are from Mark Chaves and James C. Cavendish, "More Evidence on U.S. Catholic Church Attendance," *Journal for the Scientific Study of Religion,* Fall 1994, pp. 376–81. For the decline in vocations and the arguments for dropping celibacy, see Dean R. Hoge, *The Future of Catholic Leadership:*

Responses to the Priest Shortage (Kansas City, Mo.: Sheed & Ward, 1987), supplemented by an interview, and Richard A. Schoenherr and Lawrence A. Young, *Full Pews and Empty Altars: Demographics of the Priest Shortage in United States Catholic Dioceses* (Madison, Wis.: University of Wisconsin Press, 1993). The "one with his" quote is from a former president of the Canon Law Society of America, quoted in Roger Finke and Rodney Stark, *The Churching of America, 1776–1990: Winners and Losers in Our Religious Economy* (New Brunswick, N.J.: Rutgers University Press, 1992), p. 269. For Knoxville, interviews with Bishop Anthony O'Connell, and parishioners Rick and Ann Donovan, and Patrick Donovan, diocesan youth minister. The Quinn, Wolfe, and Flaherty quotes are from interviews. The Bernardin initiative was widely reported in the lay press—see, e.g., *The New York Times,* August 13, 1996. The Cardinal's initiative was accompanied by the distribution of a statement by the National Pastoral Life Center, "Called to Be Catholic: Church in a Time of Peril" (New York, August 1996). The statement forthrightly sets out many of the same issues listed by the dissident NCCB bishops (see chapter 13), on the role of women, the gap between official teachings and lay moral perceptions in matters of family life and sexuality, declining vocations, and the morale of priests.

The pitfalls of liberalism are laid out in Finke and Stark, *Churching.* Most American Protestant denominations show a consistent life-cycle pattern. There is a burst of upstart, high-tension growth, followed by stabilization and secularization, ending in precipitate decline. Methodism started as a revivalist New England alternative to the established Presbyterianism and Congregationalism and siphoned off their most motivated members. But during the nineteenth century, erstwhile backwoods circuit-riding ministers gradually became ensconced in permanent churches. Salaries rose, wives and daughters shopped from catalogs, and sons went off to university to train to succeed their fathers. A prominent twentieth-century Methodist leader extolled the new generation of "cool-headed leadership." With "an educated minister in the pulpit," he enthused, "there is little chance that an extreme emotional revivalism will arise" (pp. 157–58). He was right—the cycle had come full circle, and his people left in droves for a new generation of upstart sects. The Northern Baptist convention followed the same route as Methodism, scorning the anti-intellectualism of the Southern Baptists, who stuck to their fundamentalist roots. But it is the Northern Baptists who are on the brink of extinction. Also see William V. D'Antonio, "Autonomy and Democracy in an Autocratic Organization: The Case of the Roman Catholic Church," *Sociology of Religion* 55, no. 4 (Fall 1994): 379–96; and Helen Rose Ebaugh, "The Revitalization Movement in the Catholic Church: The Institutional Dilemma of Power," *Sociological Analysis* 52, no. 1 (1991): 1–12. The Neuhaus comment is from an interview.

16. *The Church and America*

The details of the Pope's visit are reported in *The New York Times* for October 4–8, 1995; I also used the United States Catholic Conference's "Pope John Paul II Papal Visit, October 4–8, 1995, Media Guide" (Washington, D.C.: 1995). The "Nicely-Nicely" quote and the newsroom reporters sing-along are from the *Times,* October 6, 1995. I did not get the name of the television reporter quoted on "We all feel," but wrote it down contemporaneously. The Neuhaus reporter quote is from *First Things,* January 1996, p.

69. The Raeilhe, Lawson, and Butler quotes are from interviews. The Wolf quotes are from Naomi Wolf, "Our Bodies, Our Souls," *The New Republic,* October 16, 1995, pp. 26–35; the *New Yorker* article is Jane Mayer, "A Harder Choice," *The New Yorker,* December 4, 1995, pp. 5–6. And see Mary Ann Glendon, *Abortion and Divorce in Western Law* (Cambridge, Mass.: Harvard University Press, 1987). See notes to chapter 14 for a historical sketch of the Church's teaching on abortion.

For Neuhaus, see Richard John Neuhaus, *The Catholic Moment: The Paradox of the Church in the Postmodern World* (New York: Harper & Row, 1987), supplemented by an interview. The Jefferson and Paine quotes are from Gordon S. Wood, *The Radicalism of the American Revolution* (New York: Knopf, 1992), pp. 240, 331. For the influence of Montesquieu, see Peter Gay, *The Enlightenment,* vol. 2, *The Science of Freedom* (New York: Norton, 1969), pp. 319–36. Tocqueville is quoted in Benjamin R. Barber, "Liberal Democracy and the Cost of Consent," in Nancy L. Rosenblum, ed., *Liberalism and the Moral Life* (Cambridge, Mass.: Harvard University Press, 1989), pp. 54–68, n.2 (p. 261). The "obey the church" quote was reported in *The New York Times,* November 25, 1995. "Americans make up only" quote was from Fessio interview. A good review of the state of the world Church is in Ralph Martin, *The Catholic Church at the End of an Age: What Is the Spirit Saying?* (San Francisco: Ignatius Press, 1994), pp. 35–83. See also Jean-Marie Guenois, "The Mass Is Ended," *Thirty Days in the Church and the World,* October 1989, pp. 22–23; and Gianni Cardinale, "Poland, Back to Square One," *Thirty Days in the Church and the World,* September 1991, pp. 60–65. For Benin and voodoo, see *New York Times,* March 10, 1996.

In the Banco Ambrosiano scandal, which included the suicide, or possible murder, of a prominent Italian financier, Roberto Calvi, in London, foolish investments ultimately cost the Vatican about a quarter of a billion dollars, or more than half its liquid assets, forcing massive resort to the papal begging bowl. Dark rumors to the contrary, it appears that the Vatican did not itself engage in any wrongdoing but was hoodwinked by its traditional friends from the Italian upper classes. By 1989, all the worldwide Peter's Pence collection, which is supposed to fund worldwide missions and papal charities, was being absorbed by the Vatican's cash flow deficit. Since then, through a combination of spending cuts and fund-raising, the budget has been balanced and finances are under the sharp eye of an American cardinal, Edmund Szoka, who previously put Detroit on the financial straight-and-narrow. (Americans shouldn't crow over the Vatican's financial missteps: the fateful investments were overseen by an American, Archbishop Paul Marcinkus, who was later temporarily under an arrest warrant in Italy.) See Shawn Tully, "The Vatican's Finances," *Fortune,* December 21, 1987, pp. 28–40; Robert J. Hutchison, "A Cardinal for the Money," *Thirty Days in the Church and the World,* March 1990, pp. 24–28; and for Calvi, Patrick Barnes, "God and Mammon," *Catholic World Report,* January 1993, pp. 15–16; and Margaret Scifi, "Was He Murdered?," *Catholic World Report,* January 1993, pp. 16–17. Calvi was found hanged from a London bridge. The coroner's verdict was that it was suicide; but a jury later rendered an "open verdict" of either suicide or murder. According to the British press, recent laser analysis of Calvi's shoes do not show the metal flecks that should have been present had he climbed the metal ladder leading to his hanging place, raising suspicion that he was carried there and hanged to look like suicide.

The "if we can" is from interview with Fr. Robert Barnhill in Lincoln, and the Reese quote is from an interview. I consistently find Charles Taylor to be the clearest thinker on issues of democracy and values. In addition to his *Sources of the Self: The Making of the Modern Identity* (Cambridge, Mass.: Harvard University Press, 1989), see his *The Ethics of Authenticity* (Cambridge, Mass.: Harvard University Press, 1992); "Cross-Purposes: The Liberal-Communitarian Debate" in Rosenblum, *Liberalism* pp. 159–82; and "Religion in a Free Society," in James Davison Hunter and Os Guinness, eds., *Articles of Faith, Articles of Peace: The Religious Liberty Clauses and the American Public Philosophy* (Washington, D.C.: Brookings, 1990), pp. 93–113. A good taxonomy of ethical positions is Steven Lukes, "Making Sense of Moral Conflict," in Rosenblum, *Liberalism,* pp. 127–42, from which I borrowed the Lenin example. Lukes also identifies a third, or "particularist," position that opposes the claim of family or tribe to the other two—do I turn in my brother the Unabomber? The Cuomo story is from an interview. The quotes from the speech are from the version in the *Times,* September 14, 1984. For a discussion of Cuomo's speech, see Ronald F. Thiemann, *Religion in Public Life: A Dilemma for Democracy* (Washington, D.C.: Georgetown University Press, 1996), pp. 9–16. For a highly critical review of the speech, see Garry Wills, "Mario Cuomo's Trouble with Abortion," *New York Review of Books,* June 28, 1990, pp. 9–13. And see Stephen L. Carter, "A Curse on Both Tents," *New York Times,* August 13, 1996.

The death penalty quotes from John Paul II's *The Gospel of Life (Evangelium Vitae)* (New York: Times Books, 1995) are on p. 100. If I heard correctly, on the Sunday after Cardinal O'Connor's statement, the priest at Mass, on instructions from the Cardinal, said that Catholics were "completely free to make up their own minds on the death penalty," which seems inconsistent with the injunction to obey the Church "in all matters." Since O'Connor is one of the foremost papal loyalists, the episode once again raises the issue of why the Church places such heavy emphasis on sexual matters and takes such a latitudinarian view on a question that many people would see as of much greater moment.

The Ratzinger quote on "preservation of power" is cited in Robert Imbelli, "Theological Education in the Catholic Tradition: Theologians and Bishops," *Dunwoodie Review* (forthcoming). Archbishop John R. Quinn proposed a more participatory internal management process for the upper reaches of the Church in his 1996 Campion Lectures at Oxford, reprinted in *Commonweal* as "The Exercise of Primacy: Facing the Cost of Christian Unity," July 12, 1996, pp. 11–20. In time-honored fashion, Quinn blames Rome's current taste for command-style management on the Curia, not the Pope. He revives a proposal—which was once adopted, although never implemented, by the medieval Church, at the Council of Constance—that ecumenical councils should be regular events scheduled, say, every ten years. Regular councils would, in all likelihood, effect a decisive power shift away from Rome to the world's bishops.

Index

ABOUT THE AUTHOR

CHARLES R. MORRIS is the author of many books and articles on a wide range of topics. His books include *The Cost of Good Intentions: New York City and the Liberal Experiment, 1960–1975,* chosen by *The New York Times Book Review* as one of the Best Books of the Year; and *Computer Wars: The Fall of IBM and the Future of Global Technology,* selected by *BusinessWeek* as one of the Ten Best Business Books of the Year. Mr. Morris is a regular contributor to *The Atlantic,* including his articles on Catholicism: "The Price of Orthodoxy" and "The Three Ages of the Catholic Church." His profile of the theologian Avery Dulles recently appeared in *The New Yorker.* He lives in New York City.